HANDBOOK ON THE ECONOMICS OF THE
INTERNET

Handbook on the Economics of the Internet

Edited by

Johannes M. Bauer

Michigan State University, USA

Michael Latzer

University of Zurich, Switzerland

EE Edward Elgar
PUBLISHING

Cheltenham, UK • Northampton, MA, USA

Published by
Edward Elgar Publishing Limited
The Lypiatts
15 Lansdown Road
Cheltenham
Glos GL50 2JA
UK

Edward Elgar Publishing, Inc.
William Pratt House
9 Dewey Court
Northampton
Massachusetts 01060
USA

Paperback edition 2017

A catalogue record for this book
is available from the British Library

Library of Congress Control Number: 2015957876

This book is available electronically in the **Elgar**online
Economics subject collection
DOI 10.4337/9780857939852

ISBN 978 0 85793 984 5 (cased)
ISBN 978 0 85793 985 2 (eBook)
ISBN 978 1 78811 677 0 (paperback)

Typeset by Servis Filmsetting Ltd, Stockport, Cheshire
Printed and bound by CPI Group (UK) Ltd, Croydon, CR0 4YY

Contents

v

Contributors

Shivom Aggarwal, Adjunct Professor, IE Business School, Spain.

Cristiano Antonelli, Professor, University of Torino and Fellow, Bureau of Research on Innovation, Complexity and Knowledge (BRICK), Collegio Carlo Alberto, Italy.

Bart van Ark, Executive Vice President, Chief Economist and Chief Strategy Officer, The Conference Board, New York, USA and Professor, University of Groningen, the Netherlands.

Hadi Asghari, Assistant Professor and Researcher, Delft University of Technology, the Netherlands.

Johannes M. Bauer, Professor, Michigan State University, USA.

Steven Bauer, Research Affiliate, Massachusetts Institute of Technology, USA.

Yochai Benkler, Professor, Harvard University, USA.

Stanley M. Besen, Senior Consultant, Charles River Associates, Inc., USA.

Ian Brown, Associate Director, Oxford University's Cyber Security Centre and Senior Research Fellow and Associate Professor, Oxford University, UK.

Edward Castronova, Professor, Indiana University, USA.

David D. Clark, Senior Research Scientist, Massachusetts Institute of Technology, USA.

Carol Corrado, Senior Advisor and Research Director, The Conference Board, New York; Senior Policy Scholar, Georgetown University Center for Business and Public Policy, USA.

Michel van Eeten, Professor, Delft University of Technology, the Netherlands.

Claudio Feijóo, Professor, CeDInt-Universidad Politécnica de Madrid, Spain.

D. Linda Garcia, Associate Professor, Georgetown University, USA.

José-Luis Gómez-Barroso, Associate Professor, Universidad Nacional de Educación a Distancia (UNED), Spain.

Christian Handke, Assistant Professor, Erasmus University, the Netherlands.

Justus Haucap, Professor, University of Düsseldorf, Germany.

Katharina Hollnbuchner, Doctoral student, University of Zurich, Switzerland.

Natascha Just, Senior Research and Teaching Associate, University of Zurich, Switzerland.

Günter Knieps, Professor, University of Freiburg, Germany.

Isaac Knowles, PhD student, Indiana University, USA.

Johann J. Kranz, Assistant Professor, University of Göttingen, Germany.

Lucy Küng, Professor, University of Oslo, Norway and Senior Visiting Research Fellow, Oxford University, UK.

Michael Latzer, Professor, University of Zurich, Switzerland.

William H. Lehr, Research Associate, Massachusetts Institute of Technology, USA.

Yu-li Liu, Professor, National Chengchi University, Taiwan.

Wenjuan Ma, PhD student, Michigan State University, USA.

Patricia Mazepa, Associate Professor, York University, Canada.

Vincent Mosco, Professor Emeritus, Queen's University, Canada.

Nic Newman, Research Associate, Oxford University, UK.

Eli M. Noam, Professor, Columbia University, USA.

Pier Paolo Patrucco, Associate Professor, University of Torino and Research Fellow, Bureau of Research on Innovation, Complexity and Knowledge (BRICK), Collegio Carlo Alberto, Italy.

Robert G. Picard, Professor, Oxford University, UK.

Arnold Picot, Formerly Professor Emeritus, Ludwig-Maximilians-Universität, Munich, Germany (1945–2017).

George Sadowsky, Member of the Board of Directors of the Internet Corporation for Assigned Names and Numbers (ICANN), USA.

Florian Saurwein, Research Associate, University of Zurich, Switzerland.

Barbara van Schewick, Professor, Stanford University, USA.

Volker Schneider, Professor, University of Konstanz, Germany.

Stephen J. Schultze, Associate Director, Princeton Center for Information Technology Policy, Princeton University, USA.

Ryland Sherman, PhD student, Indiana University, USA.

Paul Stepan, Chairman, Austrian Society for Cultural Economics and Policy Studies (FOKUS), Austria.

Torben Stühmeier, Assistant Professor, Westfälische Wilhelms-Universität Münster, Germany.

Ruth Towse, Professor, Bournemouth University, UK and CREATe Fellow in Cultural Economics, University of Glasgow, Scotland, UK.

Hal R. Varian, Chief Economist, Google, Inc. and Professor Emeritus, University of California, Berkeley, USA.

David Waterman, Chief Economist, Federal Communications Commission and Professor Emeritus, Indiana University, USA.

Richard S. Whitt, Corporate Director for Strategic Initiatives, Google Access, Alphabet Inc., USA.

Steven S. Wildman, Professor Emeritus, Michigan State University, USA.

Sacha Wunsch-Vincent, Senior Economist, World Intellectual Property Organization (WIPO), Switzerland.

Preface

This book project started with an inquiry from Alexandra O'Connell, Senior Supervising Editor at Edward Elgar Publishing, as to whether we had any interest in putting together a *Handbook on the Economics of the Internet*. Both of us had researched advanced communications and the Internet for some time and both of us had taught courses in which the economics of the Internet figured prominently. It had often been difficult to find readings that were both up-to-date and comprehensive yet could be used in advanced undergraduate and graduate courses. We had worked together in Vienna, Austria during the late 1980s, intense days and long nights of writing – often concluded in the Café Alt Wien – which we both remember as some of the most energizing work experiences. After one of us moved to the United States and the other to Switzerland, our collaboration became more sporadic. A visiting professorship for Johannes at the University of Zurich, made possible by a generous invitation to teach and research at the Institute for Mass Communication and Media Research (IPMZ), offered a perfect opportunity to revive our collaboration.

Nearly three years later the book project has taken shape. It was by orders of magnitude more time-consuming than anticipated. Coordinating and synchronizing 49 authors was sometimes challenging, often took longer than hoped, but ultimately was always rewarding. Our sincere gratitude goes to all contributors who have volunteered their time and effort to write original chapters. We highly appreciate everybody's willingness to respond to multiple requests for revisions, often with a short timeline. Moreover, we are humbled by the patience of authors who delivered early in the process but then had to wait until contributions with a longer gestation were finalized (sometimes necessitating updates to earlier versions of chapters). As is to be expected in a large project like this, some envisioned contributions did not materialize, but we trust that the 27 chapters in the *Handbook* provide an original map of the current state of research in the field of Internet Economics that will provide a durable resource to students, researchers, and practitioners seeking a comprehensive understanding of the many economic and management challenges related to the Internet.

In addition to the authors, our work was facilitated by numerous people and organizations, and we would like to acknowledge a few who have been particularly supportive. Able editorial assistance was provided by Seven Bryant and Jessica McLeod at Michigan State University as well as David Westacott at the University of Zurich. Charles Felker at Michigan State University helped improve figures. At the University of Zurich, Katharina Hollnbuchner and Noemi Festic contributed logistical support to the project. Alexandra O'Connell and Matthew Pitman at Edward Elgar Publishing provided unwavering assistance on overarching editorial issues and advice on strategic decisions that had to be made along the way. Meticulous copy-editing by Dee Compson and Chloe Mitchell greatly improved the quality of the *Handbook*.

Big thanks also go to our families and friends. Johannes could not have dedicated the amount of time and intellectual energy needed to the book project without the boundless patience and understanding of his soulmate Susan W. Woods. Tatia and Max Bauer generously put up with requests for solitary periods of writing, especially during family vacations and holidays. Several times over the past years Johannes's parents Herbert and Adelinde Bauer (1927–2015) have kindly offered their home in the foothills of the Austrian Alps as a refuge to focus on writing and editorial tasks. He would like to dedicate the book to all of them. Michael promises neglected family members and friends that work–life balance will be immediately restored after the publication of this book and would like to thank them for always smilingly pretending to believe him.

Johannes M. Bauer
Michael Latzer
East Lansing, Michigan, USA
Zurich, Switzerland
August 2015

PART I

PROLOG

1. The economics of the Internet: an overview
Johannes M. Bauer and Michael Latzer

1.1 INTRODUCTION

In the Internet economy many of the theoretical assumptions and historical observations upon which economics rests need to be reexamined. Economics built a very successful research program by focusing on the choices and behavior of rational individual decision-makers under conditions of scarcity. In this highly stylized framework, eventually increasing incremental costs, decreasing marginal utility and resource constraints result in negative feedback that moves economic processes toward equilibrium states. The rigorous analysis of these equilibria at the micro and macro level is a major achievement of economics. In an economy built around digital technology some of these conditions change fundamentally. Scale economies, interdependencies, and abundance are pervasive and call for analytical concepts that augment the traditional approaches.

Technological progress has yielded exponential performance improvements of components and networking during the past decades that have resulted in rapidly declining unit costs for information processing. In addition, economic activities in the digital economy are increasingly interrelated due to complementarities between networks, applications and services, as well as increasingly dense networks of communication between economic agents. Both characteristics contribute to direct and indirect network effects and externalities. Network effects and the ubiquity of high upfront and low incremental costs in many production processes result in significant economies of scale on the supply side and demand side of the market. In the Internet economy positive feedback effects often amplify dynamic processes of change, rendering the central concept of market equilibrium, which has proven such a powerful tool of economic analysis, less germane, perhaps best seen as a special case of a more general theory of a continuously changing economy.

These new conditions have stimulated a plethora of innovative research in economics and related social and engineering sciences. Initial work on the Internet economy applied concepts of industrial organization to examine infrastructure market segments (e.g., backbone markets, access markets, domain names), interconnection, pricing, auctions, non-linear dynamics such as bandwagon effects, and shed first light on multi-sided markets (e.g., McKnight and Bailey, 1997; Madden, 2003; Majumdar et al., 2005).[1] Expanding these topics with concepts from information economics, Shapiro and Varian (1999) expertly synthesized the knowledge on information industries, much of it foundational to the Internet. In a similar vein, the economics of network industries (e.g., Shy, 2001) succeeded in generalizing concepts of traditional industrial organization to the specific conditions of the Internet. The discussion has also spawned new fields of inquiry, such as Internet Studies (Dutton, 2013) and the highly interdisciplinary fields of web science, network science, and Internet science (Börner et al., 2008; Hall and Tiropanis, 2012; Tiropanis et al., 2015). Bridging computer science, sociology and economics, some of this research has developed sophisticated concepts and rigorous models of highly connected economic processes in networks (e.g., Jackson, 2008; Easley and Kleinberg, 2010; Jackson and Zenou, 2013). This literature is complemented by contributions from statistical physics and network science (Pastor-Satorras and Vespignani, 2004; Newman et al., 2006). Innovative and important contributions were also made by scholars adopting a political economy lens (e.g., Mansell, 2012).

These changing technical and economic conditions also pose significant challenges for managers and policy-makers. In parallel to the emergence of the Internet as a major platform for commerce, an increasing number of publications have been dedicated to business and managerial aspects of the digital economy. While some of this research aims at understanding sector-wide phenomena, much of it also examines the characteristics of optimal choices and the conditions under which agents – organizations and individuals – are able to realize them (Illing and Peitz, 2006; Peitz and Waldfogel, 2012). Brandenberger and Nalebuff (1996) recognized that the increasingly complex value networks of modern production places firms in ambiguous positions, often having to compete and to cooperate with other organizations. The interrelatedness of markets has led to a burgeoning literature on two- and multi-sided markets (Rochet and Tirole, 2003, 2006; Armstrong, 2006), which is particularly relevant for many digital economy market segments. A vast volume of contributions in the business economics and management literature adds to these analyses (Coyle, 1997; Cortada, 2001).

Many of these topics are also addressed in this *Handbook* but they are approached differently and with a broader audience in mind. We deliberately adopt an inclusive view of the economic discipline, bringing together, in Part II of the *Handbook*, mainstream, institutional and evolutionary theory, thinking rooted in the theory of complex adaptive systems, as well as approaches from critical political economy. All of these frameworks, although not equally developed at a formal and empirical level, have important bearings on the dynamic Internet sector that often elude the equilibrium-oriented models of mainstream economics. The chapters in Part III are dedicated to the institutional arrangements and technical architecture affecting the Internet. Part IV is dedicated to exploring the business and managerial economic dimensions of the pervasive utilization of the Internet. Although the chapters are authored by experts from different geographic regions, they mostly adopt the perspective of countries in which the Internet is widely available and used. Two integrative chapters in Part V address the past trajectories and possible future development of the Internet.

The remainder of the chapter gives a brief synopsis of the global adoption of the Internet before it introduces the overarching themes of the next four parts of the book and the respective chapters.

1.2   TECHNOLOGY, ADOPTION AND USES

Since its inception during the 1960s the Internet has developed into an indispensable communications infrastructure. Within a few decades, it evolved from a multi-purpose to a general purpose network that can serve a broad range of uses (Bresnahan and Trajtenberg, 1995). During this expansion, and especially during the past two decades of accelerated growth into a mass market technology – sparked by several critical innovations, including the World Wide Web, user-friendly browsers, and increasing connectivity since the early 1990s – the Internet has been transformed by the co-evolution of technological, political, social and economic forces interacting in mutually reinforcing ways (Greenstein, 2015).

The development of the Internet from a network connecting a few computing centers to a global network carrying massive amounts of data was facilitated by continuous technological change in component technologies, including semiconductors, fixed and wireless networking technologies, and computing. Jointly these developments have resulted in a rapid decline of the costs of transporting, processing and storing digitized information and the ability to pack increasing computing power into smaller and mobile devices. Digitization of information flows has contributed to two waves of convergence, first between computing and telecommunications ('telematics'; see Nora and Minc, 1978) and subsequently between telematics and media ('mediamatics'; see Latzer, 1998, 2013). In parallel to the resulting integration or fusion of formerly separate communications activities, the sector has differentiated and diversified, even if information increasingly flows over an integrated network infrastructure. As traffic migrates to next-generation networks (NGNs) the legacy specialized voice, data, audio, and video networks are gradually being replaced and retired.[2]

The type and quality of Internet access and use show strong differentiations. National Internet patterns reveal considerable access (first-level) and usage (second-level) divides related to differences in socio-demographic factors like age, income, education level, race and ethnicity, as well as urban–rural inequalities (Büchi et al., 2015; Ragnedda and Muschert, 2015; Robinson et al., 2015). Because these dimensions interact with public policy decisions and other factors, considerable variations exist within and across nations. Consequently, any comparison of national performance metrics needs to take the specific contexts into account, especially when drawing lessons for policy and management.

Fixed and wireless access networks have been continuously upgraded throughout their history but performance has increased exponentially since the 1980s, supporting ever higher download and upload speeds. Figure 1.1 shows (using a log scale) that the maximum capacity of access networks using the telephone network grew steadily from 9.6 Kbps in a typical dial-up link in 1988 to 1 Gbps in 2015 using advanced technologies such as G.fast. Similarly, mobile access networks could support 14.4 Kbps in the late 1980s but by 2015 maximum download speeds of up to 1 Gbps using LTE-A (long-term evolution–advanced) were achievable. Cable networks were initially designed for one-way delivery of video signals and therefore have historically provided broadband capacity. They continue to have a distinct lead over upgraded legacy telephone networks and mobile wireless networks, with download capacities that increased from the widespread 42.88 Mbps in 1996 to 10 Gbps by 2013. Even higher bandwidths can be provided by active and passive fiber optical networks (PONs), although they require considerable new investment. While the maximum download capacity of different platforms has become comparable, important differences between these technologies remain. For example, mobile access networks and cable networks are shared, dividing the available capacity among multiple users. Optimal, cost-minimizing network configurations will most likely include multiple technologies, for example, wireless at the edges and fiber for high-volume

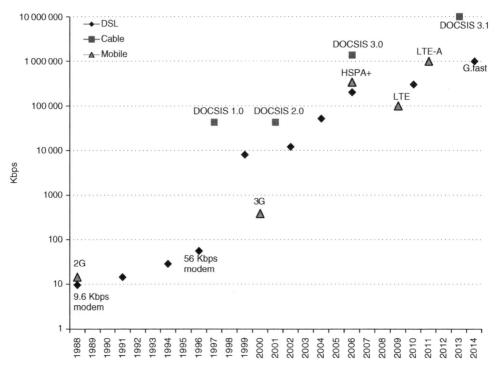

Note: ADSL = asymmetric digital subscriber line; DOCSIS = data over cable service interface specification; DSL = digital subscriber loop/line; HSPA = high-speed packet access; LTE-A = long-term evolution–advanced; VDSL = very high bit rate digital subscriber line.

Source: Own research.

Figure 1.1   Download capacity for DSL, cable, and mobile access platforms, 1988–2014

routes. With the continued migration to all-IP technology, specific network transportation services will increasingly be software-defined so that they can be configured flexibly.

These performance increases and the associated price decreases have accelerated the diffusion of Internet access since the 1990s although considerable regional differences remain (Figure 1.2). The introduction of smartphones, essentially mobile computing devices, has boosted wireless and mobile broadband[3] Internet use on a global scale. By 2015, there were 47.2 mobile broadband subscriptions compared to 10.8 fixed subscriptions per 100 inhabitants worldwide (ITU, 2015). A growing body of research takes advantage of this variation to better understand the drivers and impediments of Internet adoption and use. Although several factors, such as the intensity of competition, income and Internet literacy, are frequently identified as key drivers of Internet adoption, there is considerable variation between countries even within comparable income groups (Cambini and Jiang, 2009; Gruber and Koutroumpis, 2013; Bauer et al., 2014; Briglauer, 2014). Figures 1.3 and 1.4 show the variation in fixed and mobile broadband adoption in the OECD member states. At the end of 2014, fixed broadband adoption rates varied

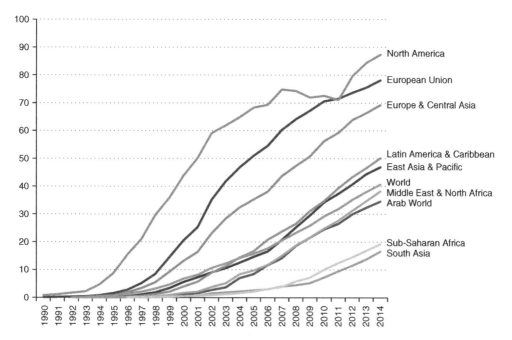

Source: The World Bank, World Development Indicators, accessed 18 August 2015 at http://data. worldbank.org/indicator/IT.NET.USER.P2.

Figure 1.2   Internet users per 100 inhabitants, 1990–2014

from 10.7 percent in Mexico to 48.9 percent in Switzerland. Mobile subscriptions, which in contrast to fixed are typically bought on an individual and not household basis, varied from 34.4 percent in Hungary to 138 percent in Finland. More recent research has generated evidence that technological, economic, socio-demographic and policy factors work as constellations and that several combinations exist that may result in similar outcomes if they are appropriate to the specific national context (Groenewegen et al., 2009; Künneke et al., 2010).

This diversity of network access platforms is also visible in the quality of the Internet infrastructure. Applications and services are becoming more differentiated with heterogeneous bandwidth and quality needs. At the same time, network access platforms are increasingly capable of supporting high bandwidth and different service qualities, which can be software defined and software configured. One important attribute of network quality is download speed, but other characteristics such as jitter and latency also matter for certain types of applications. Figure 1.5 provides a snapshot of actually measured download speeds in OECD countries. As measurements can be taken at multiple points in the network and using different metrics, numbers generated by different providers vary. Download speeds measured by Ookla are higher than data from Google M-Labs and Akamai. The latter two are fairly consistent, as is the pattern across countries.

Enabled by more bandwidth and more widely available connectivity, the range of network uses has changed significantly over time. During recent years, real-time

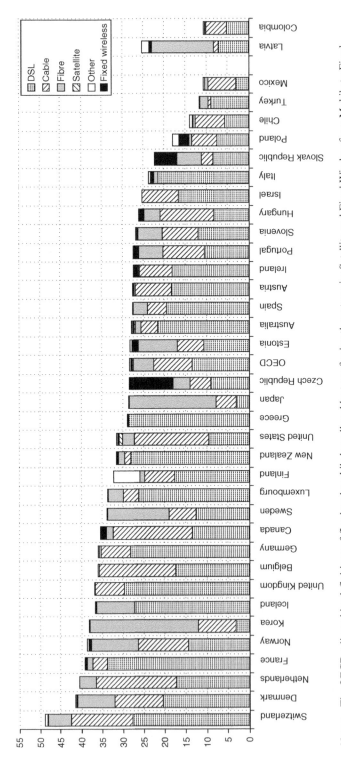

Notes: The OECD adjusted its definitions of fixed and mobile broadband by transferring the categories Satellite and Fixed Wireless from Mobile to Fixed Broadband. Fiber subscriptions data includes FTTH, FTTP and FTTB and excludes FTTC. Germany: DSL includes VDSL (FTTC); Cable excludes cable infrastructure based on FTTB/FTTH; FTTB/FTTH includes fibre lines provided by cable operators. Mexico: Data for 2014 are preliminary. Mexico is currently reviewing the Fixed broadband data in relation to the implementation of the methodology. Israel, Switzerland and United States: Data for 2014 are estimates; United Kingdom: DSL includes FTTH, FTTP, FTTB and FTTC as the breakdown between these technologies is not available yet; Colombia and Latvia are in the process of accession to the OECD.

Sources: OECD, Broadband Portal, accessed 18 August 2015 at www.oecd.org/sti/broadband/oecdbroadbandportal.htm. Information on data for Israel: http://oe.cd/israel-disclaimer.

Figure 1.3 Fixed broadband subscriptions per 100 inhabitants in the OECD, by technology (December 2014)

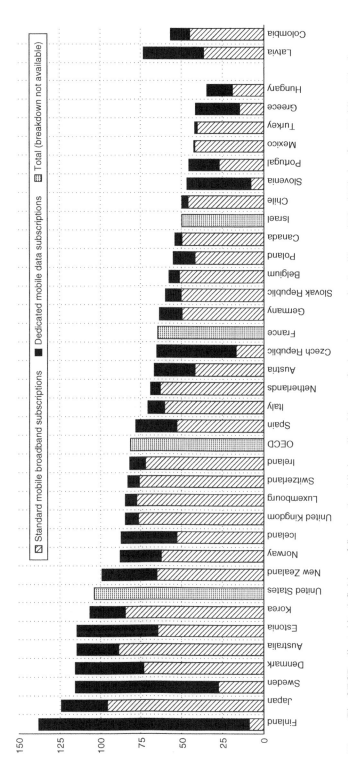

Note: The OECD adjusted its definitions of fixed and mobile broadband by transferring the categories Satellite and Fixed Wireless from Mobile to Fixed Broadband. Mexico: Data for 2014 are preliminary; Israel, Switzerland and United States: Data for 2014 are estimates; Colombia and Latvia are in the process of accession to the OECD.

Sources: OECD, Broadband Portal, accessed 18 August 2015 at www.oecd.org/sti/broadband/oecdbroadbandportal.htm. Information on data for Israel: http://oe.cd/israel-disclaimer.

Figure 1.4   Mobile broadband subscriptions per 100 inhabitants in the OECD, by technology (December 2014)

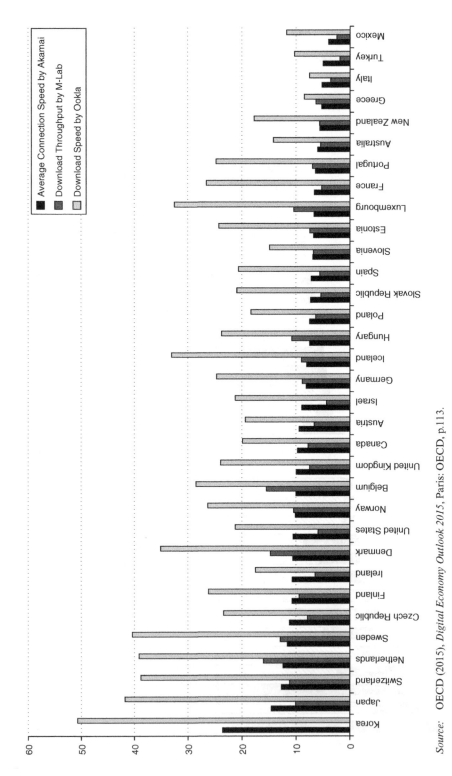

Source: OECD (2015), *Digital Economy Outlook 2015*, Paris: OECD, p.113.

Figure 1.5   Alternative measures of actual download speeds (Mbit/s, 1Q2014)

entertainment (e.g., video streaming, online gaming) has been growing rapidly. In North America, its share on fixed networks during peak periods expanded from 29.5 percent of total traffic in 2009 to 64.5 percent in 2015 (Sandvine, 2011, 2015). During the same period, peer-to-peer (P2P) traffic, which had been the third largest traffic category in 2009, declined from 15.1 percent to 5.4 percent, falling out of the top five uses. Web browsing experienced an even more dramatic decline from 38.7 percent to 7.2 percent of total traffic. On the other hand, social networking, which made up only a miniscule share of total network traffic in 2009, grew to 4.6 percent of total traffic by 2015. On mobile networks the share of real-time entertainment increased from 30.8 percent in 2011 to 41.9 percent in 2015. In the same time period, social networking traffic increased from 20 percent to 22.5 percent but web browsing declined from 27.3 percent to 13.7 percent (Sandvine, 2011, 2015).

Near ubiquitous Internet access in many parts of the world has allowed migrating processing and storage of information from local machines to servers on the network (the 'cloud') and made it possible to develop innovative new information architectures. The Internet's unique characteristics, including flexibility, plasticity, and scalability, have not only changed the technological basis of communications but have also had wide repercussions on all work and private activities relying on it. These features, combined with the ease of imitation in some areas (e.g., apps), have greatly intensified the competitive pressure in the digital economy. As many Internet-based innovations are software based or have a strong software component, the technology of innovating in the digital economy has also changed, allowing continuous experimentation via the combination and recombination of features, real-time feedback, and the rapid upscaling of successful solutions (Brynjolfsson and McAfee, 2014). Many of these effects seem to be contingent on a threshold level of adoption. Röller and Waverman (2001) found evidence that the productivity and growth effects of telecommunication networks were particularly strong in countries where a critical mass of connectivity had been reached. Koutroumpis (2009) found similar critical mass effects for broadband, although these were achieved at a much lower adoption rate.

These technological transformations have changed the economics of the Internet and have had far-reaching economic consequences for private and public sector users. Through the mid-1990s, the Internet was largely funded by the public sector. This allowed investments and technological decisions to be made with a broader public interest perspective in mind. Once infrastructure investment decisions were predominantly made by commercial investors, this societal calculus was superseded by private profitability considerations. An overarching assumption of stakeholders was that in the competitive Internet market coordination would assure that these decisions were aligned with the public interest. There is considerable evidence in support of this premise but, like other information and communication technologies (ICTs), the Internet has a unique cost structure that interacts with the dynamics of decentralized decision-making and influences the outcomes of unfettered market coordination.

With the exception of dedicated local access links, the costs of networks are shared. High upfront investment costs go hand in hand with very low incremental costs of transporting, processing and storing information. To recoup investment costs, network operators need to find ways to significantly mark up incremental costs. Pursuing such a strategy is complicated by the fact that the implementation of Internet technology has contributed to a commodification of network services. At the same time, value generation moved to the higher layers of the stack where applications and services are configured. Among the possible responses of private companies to these economic structures are horizontal and vertical integration as well as attempts to introduce differentiated network services, all major trends visible in the Internet today. The chapters in this *Handbook* address these challenges in more detail.

1.3   THEORETICAL FOUNDATIONS

The seven chapters in Part II develop theoretical frameworks to analyze the Internet economy. Some of the contributions offer complementary perspectives but others are alternative takes on the economics of the Internet. Günter Knieps and Johannes M. Bauer outline elements of an industrial organization perspective on the Internet in Chapter 2. Using a framework grounded in the dynamic analysis of markets they develop basic economic concepts relevant for the Internet with an emphasis on all-IP networks. The authors examine the Internet from micro and macro perspectives with a particular emphasis on innovation in complementary technologies. Stephen J. Schultze and Richard S. Whitt in Chapter 3 offer a complementary perspective by conceptualizing the Internet as a dynamic, layered socio-technical system. Approaching the topic from evolutionary and complexity economics vantage points, this chapter develops a framework for understanding dynamic economic change and innovation in the Internet economy. Models based in the theory of complex adaptive systems hold considerable promise for future research. Volker Schneider and Johannes M. Bauer in Chapter 4 broaden these lenses in a different direction with an overview of approaches emerging from network science. This innovative body of research is particularly powerful in examining, theoretically and empirically, the highly interwoven economic and social processes unfolding on the Internet.

The Internet has unleashed fundamental transformations of the organization of production in the commercial sector and also in the not-for-profit and gift economies. Three chapters address different aspects of these impacts. Yochai Benkler in Chapter 5 provides a comprehensive discussion of the role of peer production as an emerging new mode of production that exists in parallel and in competition with traditional forms of market production. He examines the constitutive features of peer production, its economic importance as well as the diversity of motivation of participants and the governance of peer production systems. In Chapter 6 Carol Corrado and Bart van Ark examine the effects of the Internet on productivity and economic growth. In contrast to computers, whose effects on productivity did not show in statistics for a long time, the positive contribution of communications technology and especially broadband Internet is less contested and substantiated by empirical evidence. However, as the differentiated discussion shows, the effects of the Internet are not evenly spread across economic activities and some negative impacts can also be observed.

Information goods and services form a core piece of the Internet. Their production, dissemination and consumption change compared to the offline world. Insights from cultural economics can help to understand these changes in creative industries, as Christian Handke, Paul Stepan and Ruth Towse explain in Chapter 7. Taste formation and supplier-induced demand, intrinsic motivation, decision-making under extensive uncertainty, and new forms of user–producer and user–user interaction are, for example, topics where cultural economics can contribute to a better comprehension of the Internet ecosystem. Nevertheless, there are also gaps and unfulfilled potentials for research on technological change in cultural economics, as the authors indicate in their contribution.

The final chapter in this section, Chapter 8, co-authored by Patricia Mazepa and Vincent Mosco, develops a critical, political economy perspective on the Internet. This brings otherwise largely ignored aspects into view, such as the emergence of a global poorly paid digital workforce and the power structures of information and communication markets. The implications of the Internet on labor markets, the organization of information production, and the role of political economy in academic research are all addressed.

Taken together, these chapters span a broad spectrum of theoretical and methodological approaches, ranging from mainstream economics to radical political economy. Each chapter reflects on the state of research, important contributions and open questions so that readers can develop their independent assessment of the uses and limitations of each of the frameworks.

1.4   INSTITUTIONAL ARRANGEMENTS AND INTERNET ARCHITECTURE

Market and non-market production are embedded in multiple layers of formal and non-formal institutional arrangements. Moreover, the technical architecture and protocols of the Internet influence information flows and outcomes like other types of institutional arrangements (Reidenberg, 1998; Lessig, 1999). Some institutional arrangements, such as regulations and voluntary governance agreements, adapt more frequently to changing technological and economic circumstances but others such as norms and broader cultural conventions may evolve rather slowly (Williamson, 2000). Important institutional arrangements affecting the Internet include competition and antitrust policies, intellectual property rights, legal protections of privacy, and provisions governing cybersecurity. Of similar importance are standards and protocols, the overall network architecture, and provisions governing interconnection. These are the topics addressed in Part III.

Internet-based markets show remarkable concentration tendencies, fueled by the unique economic characteristics of the online world (Noam, 2009). The effects of high supplier concentration in technology industries, including the Internet, are highly controversial. While there is some evidence that high concentration is an outcome of Schumpeterian competition, and hence superior efficiency, there are also increasing concerns about its detrimental effects. Consequently, competition concerns (e.g., regarding Microsoft, Google and Apple) and related antitrust cases are gaining prominence in the public and academic debate. Starting with an economic analysis of competition in the Internet, Justus Haucap and Torben Stühmeier discuss major competition concerns and recent European and US antitrust cases in Chapter 9. The authors also analyze the net neutrality debate driven by concerns about incentives of network operators to discriminate against competing application and content providers.

Standards, and the occasional 'wars' surrounding them, are an important topic of competition policy in the Internet era. Internet standards influence the degree of compatibility of services and products from different vendors and thus affect the relevance and impact of network effects and switching costs. Given this high economic importance the best institutional model for promulgating standards (e.g., markets, voluntary committees, government) of standardization processes is disputed. Stanley M. Besen and George Sadowsky explain in Chapter 10 the basics of the economics of standards, and provide a case study of the Internet standardization process, mainly under the auspices of the Internet Engineering Task Force (IETF). The conflict between nations supporting stronger leadership for the International Telecommunication Union (ITU) and supporters of the existing decentralized, private sector–driven approach highlights the importance of institutional arrangements for the future development of the Internet.

Although challenged on multiple grounds, copyright has long been considered an essential intellectual property right and a precondition for deriving sustainable income streams in creative industries. Fast-growing Internet applications change business models for creative works, not only value propositions and production conditions, but also revenue models for creators and the copyright-based industries. In Chapter 11, Sacha Wunsch-Vincent reassesses the economics of copyright in light of these changes. He explains and transposes the baseline model of copyright economics to the online world. The absence of data for empirical research, new online intermediaries, and complex financial and legal linkages between the various agents involved are identified by Wunsch-Vincent as obstacles to progress in the copyright debates.

Fast-growing social online networks and the mass customization of Internet products and services contribute to the rising importance of personal data, often called the 'new oil' of the information economy. Awareness of the risks of privacy violations and surveillance grew considerably in the wake of the American National Security Administration (NSA) scandal of 2013, which revealed that the agency had collected data on millions of Americans' electronic communications. The economic analysis of privacy data protection and surveillance, presented in Chapter 12 by Ian Brown, looks at the cost, benefits and incentives of all parties involved, and at the aggregate social welfare impacts. It seeks to explain the voluntary disclosure and commercial use of personal data with the help of behavioral and industrial economic approaches. Differences and problems of corporate and public privacy policies in the US and Europe, and of companies like Facebook, Google and Apple, are also explored.

Chapter 13 by Hadi Asghari, Michel van Eeten and Johannes M. Bauer focuses on the economic research on cybercrime. Protecting cyberspace from relentless attacks by criminals and hostile state actors faces daunting challenges. Recent research has made great strides in understanding the patterns of criminally motivated cyber attacks through the lens of security economics. Integrating engineering and economic perspectives to examine the incentives of interrelated players in the Internet ecosystem to invest in security has proven a particularly fruitful approach to understanding patterns of success and failure in securing the Internet economy.

By also emphasizing the importance of the technical architecture of the Internet, the cybersecurity chapter is a bridge to the theme addressed by Barbara van Schewick in Chapter 14. Her detailed examination of the effects of architectural choices on innovation in the Internet summarizes and expands her pioneering work in this area. Starting with a review of the basic design principles upon which the Internet is built, van Schewick proceeds to discuss the architecture of the Internet and examines in detail its effects on the amount and quality of application innovation.

Chapter 15 by Cristiano Antonelli and Pier Paolo Patrucco is also dedicated to an analysis of innovation, but the authors focus on the users and uses of ICT. The Internet is seen as an enabler of platforms, organizational innovations that are enabled by and instrumental for the further generation of technological knowledge. Platforms facilitate the generation and exploitation of knowledge and innovation, seen as a recombinant process of existing yet often distributed knowledge. They allow their members to internalize externalities and hence help overcome some of the public good problems associated with knowledge, including partial appropriability and divisibility, non-excludability, non-exhaustibility and intrinsic tacitness. Building on a thorough and original theoretical framework, the chapter also discusses cases that illustrate the variety and dynamics of Internet-enabled platforms.

David D. Clark, William H. Lehr and Steven Bauer in Chapter 16 focus on interconnection in the Internet. Historically, and different from other telecommunications networks, two principal models have been used by Internet service providers (ISPs) to interconnect: peering and transit. The chapter discusses these models and the current pressures to move toward more differentiated forms of interconnection, including forms of asymmetric and paid peering. The discussion is anchored in the need to find new and innovative arrangements in a network environment that is increasingly dominated by real-time entertainment traffic.

1.5 ECONOMICS AND MANAGEMENT OF APPLICATIONS AND SERVICES

Radical and disruptive Internet technologies require appropriate business models and strategies to fully utilize their potential. This is the common theme of the chapters in Part IV. Chapter 17 by Johann J. Kranz and Arnold Picot shows differences in doing business off- and online, referring, for example, to the platformization of markets, to scalability, ubiquity, universality and customer engagement. The authors provide a classification of business models and identify core elements of successful Internet business strategies.

Internet search is one of the most successful, highly profitable, generic Internet businesses. It is an example of a two-sided market supported by advertising, as Hal R. Varian explains in Chapter 18. He describes the history of information retrieval and the business model of Internet search. Selling advertisements that are related to the search queries is the primary source of revenues for this business, characterized by high fixed costs, low marginal costs and low switching costs. The author rates learning-by-doing as the most important economic factor determining search engine success, and he foresees much progress in the field of marketing based on the massive amounts of data generated, among others, by search engines.

Search engines are an indicator of how algorithms on the Internet increasingly shape our lives and realities. They are the most prominent example of a fast-growing Internet phenomenon called algorithmic selection, which is defined by automated selection of information elements and the assignment of relevance to them. Applications range from recommender systems to social scoring and predictive policing. In Chapter 19,

Michael Latzer, Katharina Hollnbuchner, Natascha Just and Florian Saurwein explain their economics, the operational model, market structures and business models. They also show how economic benefits and social risks of algorithmic selection co-evolve, and indicate governance choices for business and political strategies that boost economic and social welfare effects.

Computational advertising is another example of advanced algorithmic selection markets, yet only one example of the massive changes in the economics of advertising. In Chapter 20 Wenjuan Ma and Steven S. Wildman review the economic literature on Internet advertising. While advertising was present on the Internet early on, the rapid expansion started with the commercialization of the Internet since the mid-1990s. After a brief historical review, the chapter focuses on the two main bodies of research – targeted advertising and search advertising. The chapter concludes with a critical assessment of the state of research and possible future research trajectories.

These massive changes in advertising contributed to a substantial crisis and shake up of the news business, which went online with the diffusion of the World Wide Web in the early 1990s. In Chapter 21 Lucy Küng, Nic Newman and Robert G. Picard analytically distinguish between two eras of online news, 'Digital Publishing – Web 1.0' and 'Participation and Multimedia', and three subsectors of the media: print, broadcasting and pure players. Based on selected cases, they provide an overview of strategic, organizational and editorial implications of online news in these industries. The authors conclude with a discussion of the challenging combination of increasing competition, a bleak financial outlook for online news and the associated threats to high-quality news journalism.

The next three chapters take a closer look at the economics of online entertainment. Ryland Sherman and David Waterman focus in Chapter 22 on the fast-growing 'over-the-top' (OTT) markets for streaming and downloading professionally produced and user-generated videos to Internet-connected devices. The authors compare the economics and technology of online and offline media delivery systems, explore the empirical development of online video, and analyze business models and programming.

Business strategies of OTT services are also the focus of Chapter 23 by Yu-li Liu. Based on case studies and a literature review, she presents ten different business strategies and six revenue models for converged Internet services. Bundling, flexible pricing and various forms of content differentiation are among the strategies pursued by OTT players. Similar to the news industry, OTT suppliers are challenged by the reluctance of users to pay for online content. However, the author describes conditions under which subscription models, freemium strategies and revenue sharing appear as viable options for the financing of converged video services. Case studies of OTT service providers from North America, Europe and Asia illustrate the conceptual arguments.

Online video games are another important and fast-growing part of Internet entertainment. They create virtual worlds, and their specific systems of production, distribution and trade can be analyzed as virtual economies. In Chapter 24 Isaac Knowles and Edward Castronova review the history of virtual worlds and explain their economics. They emphasize the catalyzing role of real-money trade – the exchange of virtual goods, currencies and services for real money. Further, the authors discuss the possibilities of using virtual worlds as large-scale laboratories for (political) experiments.

The final chapter in this part examines the economics of big data, a topic that is rapidly attracting considerable attention in politics and research. Chapter 25 by Claudio Feijóo, José-Luis Gómez-Barroso and Shivom Aggarwal is an introduction to the economic issues raised by the big data ecosystem, pointing out that big data is a field with more challenges than answers. The authors explain the relationships between players, discuss the economic value of data, and assess their impact on growth and jobs. They conclude with potential avenues for further research, highlighting the importance of governance options for future developments.

1.6 PAST AND FUTURE TRAJECTORIES

The enormous diversity and rapid growth of the Internet greatly complicates the formulation of a comprehensive theory of its development. Complexity often begets attempts to simplify, sometimes at the expense of mistaking selected elements and relationships for the whole phenomenon. The Internet is no exception, as the growing number of analyses demonstrates. These are often inspired by exuberant enthusiasm for the benefits of the Internet and the fundamental transformations it enables (Tapscott and Williams, 2006; Shirky, 2010; Rifkin, 2014; Diamandis and Kotler, 2015) or by a rather gloomy view of the downsides of our increasingly Internet- and social media-driven culture (Lanier, 2013; Taylor, 2014; Ford, 2015; Keen, 2015).

The two chapters of Part V provide integrative analyses of the longer-term development of the Internet, seeking to weave a multitude of considerations into a coherent picture. Chapter 26 by D. Linda Garcia analyzes the history of the Internet through an organizational field perspective. This approach examines the embeddedness of economic and market activities in institutional arrangements and in society at large. Looking at four distinct periods of Internet development (the unified telephone regime; ARPANET and the emergence of TCP/IP; the NSF era; and the increasing commercialization of the Internet) the chapter discusses the respective actor constellations and the organizational fields in which they interact. This makes it possible to construct a detailed yet overarching socio-economic account of Internet evolution.

Chapter 27 by Eli M. Noam is also linked to the broad historical developments yet focuses on the ongoing transformation of the Internet from the Internet of Science to the Internet of Entertainment. With a keen eye for the broader emerging trends and their economic drivers, the chapter provides an alternative take on the past and future of the Internet and its economics.

The chapters in the *Handbook* synthesize the state of knowledge as of early 2016. Given space and other constraints, some important issues could not be addressed. Topics such as the economics of the Internet in low- and middle-income countries, the economics of the Internet of Things (IoT) and the industrial Internet, and the effects of the Internet on trade will have to await a complementary volume. The Internet is also intricately related to transformations of labor markets, employment, and the global and national distribution of incomes. In all these areas important and controversial public debates are unfolding although rigorous theoretical and empirical knowledge is often lacking. These emerging questions and the numerous theoretical and empirical challenges identified in this volume suggest that Internet economics will remain a vibrant field of inquiry for the foreseeable future.

NOTES

1. Important contributions in these volumes are the chapters on the economics of the Internet backbone (Economides, 2005), the economic geography of the Internet (Greenstein, 2005) and the economics of domain names (Mueller, 2005).
2. The terms 'next-generation network' (NGN) and 'all-IP' network are often used interchangeably, referring to a network architecture built around the Internet Protocol (IP) and related protocols (e.g., TCP/IP, UDP/IP, Ethernet/IP). These networks have a distinct vertical layered architecture in which a core transportation network supports a broad range of applications and services. They integrate communication flows from formerly separate networks, therefore allowing the retirement of legacy networks such as the voice networks. It is likely that these architectures are but one choice in a longer-term evolution of the future Internet.
3. There is no widely agreed definition of 'broadband'. Technically speaking, broadband is the capability to transmit multiple signals and types of traffic simultaneously. As user and communication needs change, it is impossible to define 'broadband' once and for all. The US National Research Council's Computer Science and Telecommunications Board (CSTB, 2002) has delineated broadband as the download speed that supports the development of advanced applications and services, which implies it is a moving target. The Organisation for Economic Co-operation and Development (OECD) includes download speeds above 256 Kbps in its Broadband Portal and the International Telecommunication Union (ITU) considers download speeds above 1.5–2.0 Mbps are broadband. The US Federal Communications Commission (FCC) used 256 Kbps until 2010, when it increased the threshold for download speeds to 4 Mbps and upload speeds to 1 Mbps. In 2014 it further increased these numbers to 25 Mbps download and 3 Mbps for uploads.

REFERENCES

Armstrong, M. (2006), 'Competition in two-sided markets', *RAND Journal of Economics*, **37** (3), 668–91.
Bauer, J.M., G. Madden and A. Morey (2014), 'Effects of economic conditions and policy interventions on OECD broadband adoption', *Applied Economics*, **46** (12), 1361–72.
Börner, K., S. Sanyal and A. Vespignani (2008), 'Network science', *Annual Review of Information Science and Technology*, **41** (1), 537–607.
Brandenburger, A.M. and B.J. Nalebuff (1996), *Co-opetition*, New York: Currency Doubleday.
Bresnahan, T.F. and M. Trajtenberg (1995), 'General purpose technologies: "engines of growth"?', *Journal of Econometrics*, **65** (1), 83–108.
Briglauer, W. (2014), 'The impact of regulation and competition on the adoption of fiber-based broadband services: Recent evidence from the European union member states', *Journal of Regulatory Economics*, **46** (1), 51–79.
Brynjolfsson, E. and A. McAfee (2014), *The Second Machine Age: Work, Progress, and Prosperity in a Time of Brilliant Technologies*, New York: W.W. Norton and Company.
Büchi, M., N. Just and M. Latzer (2015), 'Modeling the second-level digital divide: A five-country study of social differences in Internet use', *New Media & Society* (published online 9 September, doi: 10.1177/1461444815604154).
Cambini, C. and Y. Jiang (2009), 'Broadband investment and regulation: A literature review', *Telecommunications Policy*, **33** (10–11), 559–74.
Cortada, J.W. (2001), *21st Century Business: Managing and Working in the New Digital Economy*, Upper Saddle River, NJ: Financial Times/Prentice Hall.
Coyle, D. (1997), *The Weightless World: Strategies for Managing the Digital Economy*, Cambridge, MA: MIT Press.
CSTB (2002), *Bringing Home the Bits*, Washington, DC: National Research Council, Computer Science and Telecommunications Board.
Diamandis, P.H. and S. Kotler (2015), *Bold: How to Go Big, Create Wealth, and Impact the World*, New York: Simon & Schuster.
Dutton, W.H. (ed.) (2013), *The Oxford Handbook of Internet Studies*, Oxford, UK: Oxford University Press.
Easley, D. and J. Kleinberg (2010), *Networks, Crowds, and Markets: Reasoning About a Highly Connected World*, Cambridge, UK: Cambridge University Press.
Economides, N. (2005), 'The economics of the Internet backbone', in S. Majumdar, I. Vogelsang and M. Cave (eds), *Handbook of Telecommunications Economics, Volume 2: Technology Evolution and the Internet*, Amsterdam: Elsevier, pp. 375–412.

Ford, M. (2015), *Rise of the Robots: Technology and the Threat of a Jobless Future*, New York: Basic Books.

Greenstein, S. (2005), 'The economic geography of Internet infrastructure in the United States', in S. Majumdar, I. Vogelsang and M. Cave (eds), *Handbook of Telecommunications Economics, Volume 2: Technology Evolution and the Internet*, Amsterdam: Elsevier, pp. 287–372.

Greenstein, S. (2015), *How the Internet Became Commercial. Innovation, Privatization, and the Birth of a New Network*, Princeton, NJ: Princeton University Press.

Groenewegen, J., R.W. Künneke and J.F. Auger (eds) (2009), *The Governance of Network Industries: Institutions, Technology and Policy in Reregulated Infrastructures*, Cheltenham, UK and Northampton, MA, USA: Edward Elgar Publishing.

Gruber, H. and P. Koutroumpis (2013), 'Competition enhancing regulation and diffusion of innovation: The case of broadband networks', *Journal of Regulatory Economics*, **43** (2), 168–95.

Hall, W. and T. Tiropanis (2012), 'Web evolution and web science', *Computer Networks*, **56** (18), 3859–65.

Illing, G. and M. Peitz (eds) (2006), *Industrial Organization and the Digital Economy*, Cambridge, MA: MIT Press.

ITU (2015), *ICT Facts and Figures: The World in 2015*, Geneva: International Telecommunication Union, accessed 8 August 2015 at http://www.itu.int/en/ITU-D/Statistics/Documents/facts/ICTFactsFigures2015.pdf.

Jackson, M.O. (2008), *Social and Economic Networks*, Princeton, NJ: Princeton University Press.

Jackson, M.O. and Y. Zenou (eds) (2013), *Economic Analyses of Social Networks*, Cheltenham, UK and Northampton, MA, USA: Edward Elgar Publishing.

Keen, A. (2015), *The Internet is Not the Answer*, New York: Atlantic Monthly Press.

Koutroumpis, P. (2009), 'The economic impact of broadband on growth: A simultaneous approach', *Telecommunications Policy*, **33** (9), 471–85.

Künneke, R., J. Groenewegen and C. Ménard (2010), 'Aligning modes of organization with technology: Critical transactions in the reform of infrastructures', *Journal of Economic Behavior & Organization*, **75** (3), 494–505.

Lanier, J. (2013), *Who Owns the Future?* New York: Simon & Schuster.

Latzer, M. (1998), 'European mediamatics policies: Coping with convergence and globalization', *Telecommunications Policy*, **22** (6), 457–66.

Latzer, M. (2013), 'Media convergence', in R. Towse and C. Handke (eds), *Handbook on the Digital Creative Economy*, Cheltenham, UK and Northampton, MA, USA: Edward Elgar Publishing, pp. 123–33.

Lessig, L. (1999), *Code and Other Laws of Cyberspace*, New York: Basic Books.

Madden, G. (ed.) (2003), *The International Handbook of Telecommunications Economics (3 vols)*, Cheltenham, UK and Northampton, MA, USA: Edward Elgar Publishing.

Majumdar, S.K., I. Vogelsang and M. Cave (eds) (2005), *Handbook of Telecommunications Economics, Volume 2: Technology Evolution and the Internet*, Amsterdam: Elsevier.

Mansell, R. (2012), *Imagining the Internet: Communication, Innovation, and Governance*, Oxford: Oxford University Press.

McKnight, L.W. and J.P. Bailey (eds) (1997), *Internet Economics*, Cambridge, MA: MIT Press.

Mueller, M. (2005), 'Toward an economics of the domain name system', in S. Majumdar, I. Vogelsang and M. Cave (eds), *Handbook of Telecommunications Economics, Volume 2: Technology Evolution and the Internet*, Amsterdam: Elsevier, pp. 442–85.

Newman, M., A.-L. Barabasi and D.J. Watts (eds) (2006), *The Structure and Dynamics of Networks*, New York and Cambridge, UK: Cambridge University Press.

Noam, E.M. (2009), *Media Ownership and Concentration in America*, New York: Oxford University Press.

Nora, S. and A. Minc (1978), *L'informatisation de la Société* [The Computerization of Society], Paris: La Documentation française.

Pastor-Satorras, R. and A. Vespignani (2004), *Evolution and Structure of the Internet: A Statistical Physics Approach*, Cambridge, UK: Cambridge University Press.

Peitz, M. and J. Waldfogel (eds) (2012), *The Oxford Handbook of the Digital Economy*, Oxford, UK: Oxford University Press.

Ragnedda, M. and G.W. Muschert (2015), *The Digital Divide: The Internet and Social Inequality in International Perspective*, London: Routledge.

Reidenberg J.R. (1998), 'Lex Informatica: The formulation of information policy rules through technology', *Texas Law Review*, **76** (3), 553–93.

Rifkin, J. (2014), *The Zero Marginal Cost Society: The Internet of Things, the Collaborative Commons and the Eclipse of Capitalism*, New York: Palgrave Macmillan.

Robinson, L., S.R. Cotten and H. Ono et al. (2015), 'Digital inequalities and why they matter', *Information, Communication & Society*, **18** (5), 569–82.

Rochet, J.-C. and J. Tirole (2003), 'Platform competition in two-sided markets', *Journal of the European Economic Association*, **1** (4), 990–1029.

Rochet, J.-C. and J. Tirole (2006), 'Two-sided markets: A progress report', *RAND Journal of Economics*, **37** (3), 645–67.

Röller, L.-H. and L. Waverman (2001), 'Telecommunications infrastructure and economic development: A simultaneous approach', *American Economic Review*, **91** (4), 909–23.

Sandvine (2011), *Global Internet Phenomena Report Fall 2011*, Waterloo, ON: Sandvine.

Sandvine (2015), *Global Internet Phenomena Report 1H2014*, Waterloo, ON: Sandvine.

Shapiro, C. and H.R. Varian (1999), *Information Rules: A Strategic Guide to the Network Economy*, Boston, MA: Harvard Business School Press.

Shirky, C. (2010), *Cognitive Surplus: Creativity and Generosity in a Connected Age*, New York: Penguin.

Shy, O. (2001), *The Economics of Network Industries*, Cambridge, UK: Cambridge University Press.

Tapscott, D. and A.D. Williams (2006), *Wikinomics: How Mass Collaboration Changes Everything*, New York: Penguin.

Taylor, A. (2014), *The People's Platform: Taking Back Power and Culture in the Digital Age*, New York: Metropolitan Books.

Tiropanis, T., W. Hall, J. Crowcroft, N. Contractor and L. Tassiulas (2015), 'Network science, web science, and Internet science: Comparing interdisciplinary areas', *Communications of the ACM*, **58** (8), 76–82.

Williamson, O.E. (2000), 'The new institutional economics: Taking stock, looking ahead', *Journal of Economic Literature*, **38** (3), 595–613.

PART II

THEORETICAL FOUNDATIONS

2. The industrial organization of the Internet

Günter Knieps and Johannes M. Bauer

2.1 INTRODUCTION

Outlining the elements of an industrial organization of the Internet requires an operational delineation of its boundaries and reliance on theoretical frameworks appropriate to its rapid pace of change. We respond to the first challenge by examining the Internet as a multi-layered socio-technical system. Embracing an inclusive perspective of the entire Internet ecosystem we differentiate, where appropriate, network infrastructure from applications and services based on this infrastructure. We analyze the economic characteristics of these layers, their interaction, and the emerging overall economic properties of the Internet. The conceptual challenges are addressed by grounding our approach in the economics of technologically dynamic industries with rapidly evolving markets.

Narrowly construed, the Internet can be operationalized as a physical and logical network of networks based on open shared protocols that enable digital information flows among an increasing number of individuals, organizations and devices. From this vantage point attention is directed to issues such as technological change in the Internet; network platforms and their economic characteristics; or the structure and performance of component, access, backbone, and storage markets. The analysis may focus on particular segments of this infrastructure (e.g., the industrial organization of access markets or the economics of cloud infrastructure) or at emergent properties at an aggregated level such as the overall patterns of innovation or the effects of the Internet on productivity and employment (in a particular country, region, or the world).

Concentrating on the network infrastructure sharpens the focus but it also excludes important aspects of the Internet that are critical for its overall organization. Additional theoretical and empirical questions emerge by widening the perspective to broader Internet ecosystems, including applications and the proliferating number of services offered over the Internet. This enables us, for example, to examine organizational innovations such as new forms of intermediation, vertical and multi-sided market and non-market relations, and the repercussions of the Internet on the economy as a whole. While appealing, this approach also faces challenges. Aside from the sheer complexity of the domain to be studied, it may not be analytically meaningful to distinguish Internet-based services and applications, such as streamed video or a voice application, from related, traditionally organized markets such as cable TV, over-the-air broadcasting, and voice services. Moreover, it may be difficult to delineate the Internet in this broad sense from firms that use the Internet as an integral part of their business model, such as eBay or Amazon.

We combine these two perspectives to examine the economics of the Internet from micro and macro perspectives. At a 'lower' micro level we see multiple technologies and market segments (e.g., access, backbones, Internet exchanges, hosting, and specific services) (Comer, 2006) with specific economic characteristics. With the transition from narrowband to broadband Internet the evolution of alternative fixed and mobile access infrastructures and the services they enable becomes particularly relevant. At a 'higher' level we see properties that emerge from these component markets, such as investment and innovation patterns at the sectoral level. This multi-pronged way allows systematic economic theorizing on how decisions and behavior at lower levels of the Internet contribute to (emergent) properties at higher levels of the system.

A second challenge is the selection of theoretical frameworks appropriate for analyzing this dynamic system of interrelated technologies, markets, and non-market activities. At a first glance many of the issues arising in the Internet economy look similar to those of traditional industrial economics and the economics of networks. Nonetheless, the tight combination of high fixed and low incremental cost, the pervasive presence of increasing returns, the rapidity and frequency of entry and exit, high rates of innovation, and economies of scale in consumption (positive network externalities) have created unique economic conditions that have inspired the term 'new economy'.[1] One approach is to apply concepts of traditional industrial organization to the Internet, building on insights from game theory, the economics of networks, and institutional economics, among others. This route has been taken by several contributors and has yielded numerous valuable insights as evidenced in the chapters in Majumdar et al. (2005) and Peitz and Waldfogel (2012).[2]

However, the methodological conventions of these approaches, such as the analysis of market equilibria and the treatment of technological change as exogenous, while allowing analytical rigor, may not reflect the unique dynamics of the Internet with sufficient accuracy. An alternative route is to seek radically new frameworks that allow better capture of the new attributes of the Internet economy. Interesting strands of research have emanated from evolutionary and complexity theory (e.g., Dorogovtsev and Mendes, 2003; see also Schultze and Whitt, Chapter 3 in this volume) and from network theory (e.g., Jackson, 2008; Easley and Kleinberg, 2010; see also Schneider and Bauer, Chapter 4 in this volume). Promising avenues are also opened by computational and agent-based approaches that allow the simulation of highly non-linear systems such as the Internet.

We opt for a middle ground by combining insights from traditional industrial organization with concepts rooted in the works of Schumpeter (1934), who emphasized the dynamic forces of innovation, and an evolutionary view of markets as dynamic mechanisms of discovery and coordination (e.g., Hayek [1968] 2002). As several authors have recognized, digital technology has changed and accelerated the process of innovation by allowing continuous experimentation, rapid feedback and evaluation, and imitation and scaling of successful business models (Brynjolfsson, 2011; Brynjolfsson and McAfee, 2014). The Internet is an integral driver of these developments and is affected itself similarly. Not surprisingly, digital industries have also inspired new research on the role of competition and antitrust in interrelated markets (e.g., Posner, 2000; Farrell and Weiser, 2003; Evans and Schmalensee, 2007).

A basic message of much of this research is that dynamic markets like the Internet should neither be exempted from general competition policy nor do they justify new and specific regulatory and antitrust policies. Moreover, theory and evidence suggest that market participants can explore their innovation and efficiency potentials, including the creation of new markets (e.g., Katz and Shapiro, 1999; Shapiro and Varian, 1999). At the same time, while there is considerable evidence that technologically dynamic industries flourish in the absence of government intervention, there is also evidence of the complementarity of public policy and the performance of high-tech markets. Arguments include the failure of markets to generate sufficient innovation in basic research, the need to facilitate coordination among many participants in complex systems, and the existence of strong spillover and public good effects (e.g., Block and Keller, 2011; Atkinson and Ezell, 2012; Mazzucato, 2013). In fact, the Internet itself is a product of public initiative, emerging from ARPANET, the US Department of Defense's Advanced Research Projects Agency (DARPA) computer networking project (see Tanenbaum and Wetherall, 2011, pp. 55–9; Garcia, Chapter 26 in this volume).

Since legal entry barriers have been lifted in network industries worldwide, end-to-end vertically integrated network systems owned and operated by legal monopolists have been replaced by liberalized markets for network services differentiated from the markets for network infrastructures capacities. Consequently, horizontal and vertical coordination issues arise, including interconnection and mutual compensation, that are addressed in innovative ways and open new opportunities for innovative entrepreneurial bundling and unbundling decisions (Knieps, 1997b). Since the different components of the Internet (e.g., computers, software) are not isolated but connected via networks, questions regarding the system character of networks and the boundaries of markets in network industries have to be considered. The study of other large technical systems (e.g., Mayntz and Hughes, 1988) shows that an analytical separation of networks into individual components and decision-makers risks neglecting important system interdependencies. This is particularly problematic in systems undergoing dynamic change.

This velocity of change is visible in the changing focus of the overarching paradigm of the Internet, which has shifted from characterizing it as a 'network of networks' to a 'network of platforms' (Greenstein, 2009, 2012b) and an 'Internet of Internets' (Noam, Chapter 27 this volume). Several authors have pointed to the increasing role of communication processes and transactions outside of the public Internet (e.g., in private Internets and in darknets; see claffy and Clark, 2014). Apart from illegal activity that seeks to avoid the public Internet, this development seems to be primarily a response to the quest of finding sustainable business models (a walled garden facilitates establishing a payment system), to challenges of information security (keeping sensitive information behind secure walls), and a desire to escape more stringent regulation imposed on the public Internet. A key dynamic is the interdependent innovation process unfolding between the vibrant applications and services sector and the network infrastructure.

To fully understand these economic and technological dynamics a closer look at the interplay of innovations in application services (at the logical edge)[3] and innovations for traffic services (at the core) is required. The capabilities supported by the core network enable and constrain the types and variety of innovation possible at the edge. At the same time, the diversity and number of innovative services at the edge influence the value of the network and have implications for innovation and investment incentives at the core layers. Whereas much of the public debate focuses on edge innovations, innovations at the core are also relevant. With heterogeneous applications and user groups it is useful to look at markets for Internet traffic services as a separate market, providing platforms for Internet application service providers and end users. From a technical vantage point, platforms facilitate the building of related products and services; from an economic perspective, they facilitate transactions between related players and the internalization of externalities (Gawer and Cusumano, 2002; Hagiu and Wright, 2012). Understanding the evolution of open versus proprietary platforms requires taking into account issues like platform governance, design and coordination of platforms as well as competition between and upgrades of platforms (Greenstein, 2012b). It also raises new issues and research questions. Examples are the role of platform competition from the perspective of network economics, the theoretical relations between platforms and two- (multi-)sided markets, the role of network externalities and complementarities, the role of experimentation and learning, the role of path dependency and network evolution, and the question of whether platform competition is a special case of competition in networks (Bauer, 2014).

In this historical development the search for appropriate governance mechanisms, particularly the 'proper' role of markets, the state, and forms of networked governance (e.g., standardization committees) is an ongoing process. Non-government and non-market organizations of networked governance such as the Internet Corporation for Assigned Names and Numbers (ICANN), the Internet Governance Forum (IGF), and other voluntary organizations such as the Internet Society address coordination tasks across the entire Internet ecosystem (Mueller, 2010). An important example is the changing role of the Internet Engineering Task Force (IETF) as a forum to achieve universality and interconnectivity in the best-effort Internet and the development of innovative quality of service (QoS) differentiated traffic architectures (Knieps, 2015b). At the same time, traditional government players, including national regulatory agencies, legislatures, and intergovernmental organizations like the International Telecommunication Union (ITU) have increasingly asserted a role in addition to decentralized markets.

The remainder of the chapter is organized as follows. Section 2.2 briefly discusses the development and unique attributes of the Internet through an economic lens. With this background, section 2.3 focuses on the industrial organization of the dynamic environment of the Internet. Section 2.4 discusses technology and cost conditions followed by an exploration of demand and pricing in section 2.5. Section 2.6 focuses on the interplay of innovation and service quality in the Internet. The chapter returns to one of the opening questions – what can and cannot be coordinated by market forces – in section 2.7. An outlook on possible future developments and emerging research questions concludes.

2.2   DEVELOPMENT AND UNIQUE ECONOMIC ATTRIBUTES OF THE INTERNET

Important economic characteristics of the Internet developed interdependently with its technological basis, its organization, and the level of adoption (see also Chapter 26 by Garcia, this volume). During the initial attempts to network a small number of computer centers and find a technical solution to route traffic across heterogeneous wire and radio networks, the Internet and its components were a special niche within the broader field of computing and data communications. Although the number of nodes on the network and the number of users increased, the early Internet remained largely complementary to other forms of telecommunications (voice, data, audio, and video) until the 1980s. Funding by the public sector of these initial developments relieved Internet pioneers of the pressures to sustain operations from revenues in the market place.

2.2.1   The Emergence of the Commercial Internet

The first commercial providers of public Internet access emerged in the late 1980s. In the USA, The World and PSINet started operations in 1989 but were initially not allowed to access many university and government installations. This situation changed when an agreement with the National Science Foundation (NSF) was reached.[4] The development by Tim Berners-Lee and his collaborators of the components of the World Wide Web (WWW) – including the Hypertext Transfer Protocol (HTTP), the Hypertext Markup Language (HTML) and a first web browser – were additional steps toward moving the Internet beyond a specialized community of researchers. Adoption accelerated with the release of the graphical user interface-based browser Mosaic in 1993 and Netscape Navigator in 1994.

Early commercial online networks offered services to closed user groups and employed proprietary technology. CompuServe (founded in 1969) built its initial customer base around the time-sharing of computing resources. Computers were linked using modems operating on the telephone network and leased lines. America Online (founded in 1983 as Control Video Corporation) similarly offered its online services only to subscribers. Given their large user base, these networks already exhibited some of the distinct economic features of the later Internet, such as economies of scale and scope as well as network effects on the supply and demand side. Because they relied on a walled garden business model, these effects were more limited than in the later open Internet. Moreover, closed access allowed generating a direct revenue stream for the companies.

After a short period during which such access was based on measured hourly prices, America Online and other Internet service providers (ISPs) introduced flat monthly rates that further facilitated adoption. Because the US telephone network was organized as a common carrier and flat local telephone pricing was widely adopted by subscribers, it was relatively easy for ISPs to offer dial-up Internet access as a service configured on top of the existing, ubiquitously available telephone network. At peak, nearly 6000 ISPs offered dial-up service and within a few years Internet access via the phone network spread rapidly (see the excellent discussion in Greenstein, 2015).

2.2.2   Migration Toward Broadband

The migration from narrowband to broadband access started in the 1990s and enabled vast innovations in application services in a virtuous cycle of improvements in the network and in applications. Upgrades from narrowband to access speeds above 256 kbps are often referred to as first-generation broadband. Subsequent generations of technology that can support access speeds up to the gigabit range are commonly labeled as ultra-broadband or next-generation networks (NGNs). First-generation broadband could be deployed by upgrading existing networks but the more advanced next-generation networks require more significant upgrade investment and the increasing rollout of new fiber-optic networks in combination with advanced wireless technology that supports access speeds up to the gigabit range. Because broadband networks build on the Internet Protocol (IP), we will use the more generic term 'all-IP' networks.

Network and service upgrade patterns vary greatly between countries and regions and show strong forms of path dependence. In countries where investment in the commercial

Internet is the outcome of entrepreneurial decisions, multiple alternative upgrading paths are visible, leading to different technology mixes in first- and second-generation broadband. In the USA, cable TV service providers seeking to mitigate the competitive pressures of a saturated multi-channel video market introduced faster broadband Internet access during the second half of the 1990s. US telephone companies initially invested only slowly in digital subscriber loop/line (DSL) technology but accelerated their investment in response to the rollout strategy of cable systems and regulatory changes that reclassified DSL and mobile Internet access as information services, creating regulatory parity with cable (Bauer, 2005). In response to concerns about preserving an open Internet this trend toward less regulation was reversed in February 2015 when the Federal Communications Commission (FCC) again reclassified all broadband Internet access, independently of the technical platform, as common carrier services (FCC, 2015). Whereas there are many concerns about this approach, it offers for the first time a symmetric regulatory model. In countries where cable TV did not have such a strong early market position, such as in many European Union member states, regulators retained unbundling rules for broadband. This often resulted in xDSL (all types of DSL lines) remaining the leading platform for broadband Internet access (Cave and Shortall, 2011). In some Asian countries, such as Japan, South Korea, and Singapore, fiber deployment was prioritized by public policy.

The gradual migration to fixed and wireless broadband enabled increasingly higher access speeds and went hand in hand with declines in the price per unit of data for users.[5] Together with advances in computing, signal compression, and dramatic declines in the costs of information storage, these developments unleashed a broad range of new applications and services and further altered the economic characteristics of the Internet toward a layered architecture and vertically related markets. Divergent national policies and entrepreneurial upgrading strategies resulted in different technology mixes in the Internet infrastructure (Bauer, 2010; Shortall and Cave, 2015). While access has improved across high- and low-income countries, these differences nonetheless are visible in highly varying performance along other attributes, such as access speeds and prices (Bennett et al., 2013; OECD, 2013).

2.2.3   Evolving Network Topology and Convergence

Thus, within a relatively short period of time the Internet evolved from the ARPANET of the 1960s to the narrowband Internet in the 1970s and 1980s, the subsequent migration towards broadband Internet from 1990s onwards, and the ongoing convergence to an all-IP platform, in which multiple technologies are seamlessly integrated by logical protocols, especially TCP/IP (Transmission Control Protocol/Internet Protocol). Despite this transformation from a government-funded to a largely commercially funded network, many stakeholders retained the original vision of the Internet as a commons in which traffic capacity is a non-rival good. However, the migration from narrowband to broadband Internet and the different funding models have resulted in a reassessment of the paradigm of universal connectivity using a best-effort network. Congestion and asymmetric traffic flows as well as increasing demand for traffic quality differentiation resulted in the development of more complex interconnection arrangements between carriers, such as asymmetric and paid peering arrangements in which payments are exchanged for traffic volumes exceeding certain thresholds (Besen et al., 2001; Laffont et al., 2001; Faratin et al., 2008).

In this process the mix of technologies employed in access, middle mile, and backbone networks changed driven by the relative costs and capabilities of different network platforms. Dial-up and first-generation broadband technology essentially utilized the existing networks. The topology of the telephone, cable, and wireless networks had been optimized based on the relative costs of transmission, switching/routing and storage (e.g., Egan, 1996). Cable modems and subsequent generations of xDSL services essentially were incremental investments to enhance the capabilities of these networks. Logical layers integrated these diverse physical networks, most importantly TCP/IP but also numerous other protocols that integrate and homogenize them into a seamless web. This logical layer also provided a transparent and standardized interface for applications and services at higher layers of the advanced communications system. The end-to-end principle guiding the engineering architecture of the Internet facilitated innovations and services at the edge of the network, an approach contributing to the tremendous dynamics of the Internet (van Schewick, 2010). This experience of rapid and continuous innovation was markedly different from the slow and incremental innovations known from the telephone monopoly era. Many experts looked at the infrastructure supporting the Internet as a highly standardized transportation network. Arguing that additional capacity was cheap they saw the best response to expanding traffic volumes in the extra provision of such capacity.

The migration to broadband and ultra-broadband further changed the economics of the Internet. First, incremental network upgrades were increasingly insufficient to keep pace with the growing demand for capacity. Rather, new network capacity had to be deployed in backbone and access networks at much higher costs than the migration from dial-up to first-generation DSL or the rollout of first-generation cable modem service. Creating proper incentives for network infrastructure investment became a major challenge for national regulatory agencies, who had designed unbundling and open access rules for environments in which networks had already been installed (Cambini and Jiang, 2009; Gruber and Koutroumpis, 2013; Briglauer et al., 2013). Second, services and applications configured over-the-top (OTT) of the network, such as Skype or Netflix, and increasingly heterogeneous user demand required a broader range of QoS support. Third, decreasing costs of storage and of connectivity in conjunction with the higher demand for high-quality services facilitated new network topologies and configurations, among them the emergence of overlay networks such as content delivery networks (CDNs) like Akamai and of cloud-based services such as 'infrastructure as a service' (IaaS).

These changes accelerated the decade-long process of convergence between telecommunications, computing, and media content. Digital multi-purpose networks with broadband and ultra-broadband capacity allowed the integration of formerly separated networks and services on an all-IP network so that network operators can use fixed and wireless technologies in complementary ways to grant users seamless access independently of device and location. While all-IP networks are not necessarily the most efficient technical solution, changing user demand and habits, such as the expectation to get access to content anytime and anywhere, added additional momentum to these developments.[6] These technical and economic developments contributed to a new wave of innovation in the core network infrastructure in addition to the vibrant innovation activity on the edges of the network. Furthermore, the changing economic structure contributed to strong pressures toward industry consolidation and vertical integration.

2.2.4 Modularity, Layering and the End-to-end Principle

The Internet is built around a particular set of design principles that influence its economic attributes and organization. Of particular importance are modularity, layering, and the end-to-end principle. Modular design of technical systems seeks to reduce the interdependence of components so that they are only loosely coupled (Saltzer et al., 1984; Yoo, 2013). It allows individual components to be designed, produced, and possibly used independently (van Schewick, 2010, p. 39). Modularity facilitates certain types of innovation processes, as individual modules may be changed without having to alter the entire system. This is very visible in the app economy, where innovative software can be configured to reside on the edges of the network, thus avoiding time-consuming and potentially costly changes in the core of the network. All that needs to be known to an app developer is the application programming interface (API) to the operating system and the network. Interoperability and standardization are therefore critical for modular systems to work well. Modular innovation processes will often flourish in a competitive market environment (Baldwin and Clark, 2000; Langlois, 2002; Bourreau et al., 2007). However, not all socially beneficial innovations are modular. For example, the first smartphones required considerable efforts to coordinate the value network that could not be delivered by decentralized markets (Ehrlich et al., 2010). Coordination across modules may be difficult in systems that are governed in a decentralized fashion so that more systemic types of innovation may be complicated to achieve. Coupled innovations, such as smartphones or smart grids, in which applications and service innovations are contingent on network innovations (and vice versa), may require other forms of coordination such as exclusive contracts or forms of joint ventures and alliances.

One widely recognized attribute of the Internet related to the modular nature of information technology is its layered architecture. Layering is a hierarchical technological design feature. The specific setup can be largely explained by its historical evolution and the technical choices made by the engineers involved in its early design but it also turned out to be a robust and scalable solution. Authors have delineated these layers differently. Moreover, the dynamic evolution of the Internet may change them (claffy and Clark, 2014). The most basic distinction is between the physical network layer (link layer), logical layers allowing traffic to seamlessly flow over these heterogeneous networks (IP layer, and transport layer) and application and services layers configured on the former two (Lemley and Lessig, 2001, Yoo, 2013, pp. 1742). Others have devised more finely differentiated layer models (e.g., Whitt, 2007; Fransman, 2010). In this vertical division of labor the Internet layer serves as an integrative layer that homogenizes differences at the physical link layer, where fiber, copper, coaxial cable, wireless, and satellite networks are used to transport signals. Engineering conventions in the Internet allow for higher layers to make use of lower layers down to the Internet layer (but not below that layer). Lower layers are not allowed to make use of higher layers. Thus, the Internet layer functions as a portability layer within a framework of relaxed layering (van Schewick, 2010, p. 88). The end-to-end design is related to these features. Expressed in various ways, it is a convention that places commonly used functionality in the logical core of the Internet whereas other functions, applications, and services are configured at the logical edges and in higher layers of the network (see van Schewick, Chapter 14 in this volume for a detailed discussion).

2.2.5   Multi-sided Platforms and Plasticity

Two related bodies of research on technological and economic platforms focus on these pervasive interdependencies. The management literature looks at platforms as 'technological foundations upon which other products, services, and systems are built' (Gawer and Cusumano, 2002). This technological perspective is related to but not identical to definitions that emphasize the economic features of platforms as linking different sides of a market (Rysman, 2009). A technology-centric view starts from the realization that important high-tech industries, including computing and telecommunications, have adopted modular technological architectures since the 1960s to facilitate coordination between increasing numbers of components. Platforms enable the assembly of complementary modules into the systems needed to create value. In a complex socio-technical system such as the Internet, multiple platforms co-exist, often arranged in a nested way. Semiconductors enable operating systems, which in turn function as platforms for applications and services. Physical communication networks serve as platforms for information transportation services, which in turn enable applications and services. Likewise, mobile devices can be seen as platforms that enable mobile data communications and the multitude of applications and services built on them. Some platforms are sufficiently flexible to support a wide range of complementary modular technologies and services. Hence they are examples of general purpose technologies (GPTs) (Bresnahan and Trajtenberg, 1995; Helpman, 1998) with a high generative potential (Zittrain, 2008).

Economic models of platform markets recognize these characteristic technological features but broaden the perspective. Hagiu and Wright (2011, p. 1) provide a particularly compelling definition of multi-sided platforms (MSPs), and view them as 'an organization that creates value primarily by enabling direct interactions between two (or more) distinct types of affiliated customers'. Although there is some variation in what are considered their key economic attributes, all contributors conceptualize platform markets (often also referred to as two- or multi-sided markets) as special type of intermediation. Early contributions emphasized the presence of direct and indirect network effects between the market sides (Rochet and Tirole, 2006; Armstrong, 2006; Evans and Schmalensee, 2007) but more recent papers point out that such network effects, while often present, are not a necessary condition for an intermediary to be a platform (Hagiu and Wright, 2011). One important economic function of platforms is to reduce transaction costs between participants in different market sides. Where externalities are present, platforms can facilitate internalizing them. In this sense, platforms are institutional arrangements to help overcome forms of market failure and obstacles to market transactions.

Taken together, modularity and flexible layering have greatly increased the plasticity and generativity of digital production technology. Plasticity allows the production of digital services and applications with multiple factor combinations at often radically different costs (e.g., online video via best-effort Internet connections, peer-to-peer communications [P2P], and CDNs). Within limits, most products and services can be produced with alternative technologies but in a digital environment in which many products and services are software-based the flexibility abounds. The resulting greater plasticity allows new, non-traditional players to enter the market swiftly and hence may significantly alter patterns of competition in digital and traditional markets. A recent example is the rapid intrusion of WhatsApp (owned by Facebook) in the market for voice and messaging services. Generativity refers to the greatly expanded space of innovation opportunities opened up by digital technology and the accelerated pace at which it is being explored. It also has direct consequences for the intensity and dynamics of competition.

2.3   INDUSTRIAL ORGANIZATION OF THE DYNAMIC INTERNET

2.3.1   Technological Basics and their Dynamics

During the initial phase of Internet evolution it was meaningful from an economic perspective to distinguish between Internet periphery and service provision (Knieps, 2003, p. 218). Elements that were viable on their own were considered as part of the periphery (e.g., terminal equipment, content, local telecommunications network infrastructure, and long-distance telecommunications infrastructure). In contrast, Internet traffic services (based on telecommunication infrastructure capacities and Internet logistics) as well as Internet application services (based on Internet traffic) could be considered to form the nucleus of the Internet. The convergence towards all-IP networks has rendered the distinction between telecommunication infrastructure and the Internet untenable as both are seamlessly integrated. Instead all-IP network infrastructures are better conceptualized as GPTs.

These developments point to the need for a more general approach towards the evolution of Internet architectures: the choice between where to place functionality and 'intelligence', on the edges, in the network core, or a hybrid. The optimal configuration depends on the relative costs of different solutions, path dependency of technological decisions, alternative entrepreneurial business models and so on. As broadband infrastructures are becoming part of an all-IP network in which different levels of service quality are differentiated to properly support services such as Voice-over-IP (VoIP), the traditional specialized high-quality networks (e.g., PSTN [Publicly Switched Telephone Network], ISDN [Integrated Services Digital Network]) are phased out. In this all-IP environment an industrial organization of the Internet can build on a disaggregated representation distinguishing all-IP broadband infrastructures, markets for Internet traffic and markets for application services.

Broadband access networks use different types of fixed network technology, including copper wire, coaxial cable, and fiber. Moreover, several mobile access network technologies are available and increasingly integrated with fixed networks into seamless access infrastructures (ITU, 2014; OECD, 2014; Tripathi and Reed, 2014). The specific technology mix of access networks varies and is to some degree path dependent on the upgrading strategies chosen by the network operators (Knieps and Zenhäusern, 2015). Various generations of DSL technologies configure broadband connections based on copper wire. Innovations such as vectoring have expanded the capacity of copper access loops far beyond initial constraints. Cable systems also were able to increase data rates by improving the protocols used for data transportation, most recently DOCSIS 3.1 (Data

Over Cable Service Interface Specification), which allows access speeds up to the gigabit range. Presently, different fiber optical network solutions including fiber to the curb (FTTC) and fiber to the home (FTTH) allow the highest data rates.

These fixed network technologies are complemented by wireless access technologies, which became available in the 1990s and offered new options to connect at the edges of the network. Wireless local area networks (WLANs, particularly Wi-Fi) and wireless personal area networks (WPANs, particularly Bluetooth) facilitate seamless connectivity at different scales. Mobile Internet access became available using 2G (e.g., GSM, CDMA) wireless technology although data throughput was low. With the advent of 3G (e.g., UMTS), 4G wireless networks (e.g., LTE [long-term evolution] and WiMax [Worldwide Interoperability for Microwave Access]) and presently 5G platforms, data rates in the 100 Mbps range can be supported and have greatly expanded the uses of mobile broadband, including live video streaming, mobile games, and other data-intensive applications.

All-IP access infrastructures increasingly combine these component technologies. Because the alternative network platforms have different costs, this allows configuring a least-cost network infrastructure by rolling out an appropriate mix of technologies. A growing number of network operators take advantage of this flexibility by integrating various fixed and wireless network elements into a seamless access infrastructure. Upgrading costs of DSL acceleration technologies like vectoring are much lower than investment costs to establish FTTH (Zhao et al., 2014, p. 11). Capacity and speed over cable networks depends on the type of upgrading investments to provide bidirectional communication, often achieved by replacing coaxial parts of the network with fiber plant. Fixed access technologies are increasingly complemented by wireless platforms with a growing number of users opting for wireless only access. The development of access networks does not seem to converge toward a dominant platform, due to heterogeneous irreversible investments in alternative access technologies and heterogeneous consumer demands. Rather, the pervasive use of IP-based transmission supports the coexistence of a variety of access network infrastructures that are integrated by the IP layer (Knieps and Zenhäusern, 2015).

2.3.2 The Dynamics of Internet Traffic Management

Given the nature of the Internet as a network of networks, interconnection among the proliferating number of ISPs is critical (Noam, 2001). Interconnection has evolved considerably from the initial arrangements. Earlier public peering via network access points (NAPs) was often plagued by congestion and delay due to rapidly growing traffic volumes. Consequently, private peering arrangements evolved soon after the transition to a commercial Internet. In the mid-1990s two basic forms of incentive-compatible contracting between different Internet traffic providers dominated: transit and peering. Under transit, a traffic provider is selling data packet transmission to its customers to and from any Internet destination. Under peering, bilateral or multilateral arrangements between traffic providers on a barter trade (bill and keep) basis without payments are provided. With the increasing asymmetries and heterogeneity of traffic flows, additional arrangements such as paid peering have emerged (see also Clark, Lehr and Bauer, Chapter 16 in this volume). Only data packets between the customers of peering traffic providers (as well as data packets of transit customers of their customers) are transmitted

(European Commission, 1998, p. 7). Data packets to and from customers of non-peering networks that are served by other peering partners are not transmitted.

2.3.2.1   The traditional universal connectivity paradigm

The pursuit of universal Internet connectivity has resulted in a hierarchical network structure with peering and transit arrangements (e.g., European Commission, 1998, p. L116/6; Laffont and Tirole, 2000, p. 268; Besen et al., 2001; Crémer et al., 2000, p. 443). Consequently, interconnection of networks in various institutional arrangements has been a major driver of the traditional Internet. Internet exchange points (IXPs) emerged as central switching platforms that allow networks to interconnect directly (Vanberg, 2009, p. 81). Initially, a set of typically larger traffic providers had peering arrangements with each other and enjoyed universal connectivity without the necessity of transit arrangements (called tier 1 or top-level traffic providers).

ISPs not belonging to the 'club' of tier 1 networks could benefit from their universal connectivity by buying transit from one of them. Within the traditional Internet, top-level providers were considered to compete in an upstream ('backbone') market distinct from the downstream market for Internet access (Besen et al., 2001, p. 292). If traffic is symmetric between some traffic service providers and asymmetric between others, combinations of peering and transit arrangements may be chosen. Secondary peering traffic providers offer their customers a mix of their own peering-based connectivity combined with transit to and from the remaining destinations. Incentives may arise for non-tier 1 providers to peer with another non-tier 1 provider to exchange data packets between these two networks and thereby bypassing the transit options provided by the tier 1 providers. Indeed, during the past decade the historical hierarchical arrangements have started to change with an increasing number of peering arrangements among tier 2 and even tier 3 networks. This has considerably reduced the role and power of tier 1 networks (claffy and Clark, 2014).

2.3.2.2   The evolution of partial transit and paid peering

The transition from narrowband to broadband has gone hand in hand with a diversification of services and a reconfiguration of the architecture of hosting and service provision. As a result, traffic flows among networks have become increasingly asymmetrical. Thus incentives arise to develop more flexible contract arrangements between traffic providers dealing with heterogeneous traffic demand (Faratin et al., 2008, p. 58). Paid peering increases the flexibility of peering arrangements if asymmetric traffic flows between two potential peering partners are to be compensated by side payments. Partial transit limits universal connectivity by restricting the scope of sender and/or receiver addresses and thereby reducing the opportunity costs of transit obligations.

2.3.2.3   Overlay networks

Overlay networks are designed to enhance or modify the basic functions of traffic handling on top of the traditional best-effort TCP/IP Internet architecture. They include routing overlay networks, CDNs, P2P, and security overlay networks. Overlay networks may be commercial, cooperative, or peer-to-peer based. Whereas commercial overlay network providers (e.g., Akamai) create successful business models, a large scope for non-commercial activities evolves where peers are both suppliers and consumers (prosumers). CDNs consist of caches of content copies distributed across the Internet in order to economize response time and server loads and to reduce bandwidth costs. The purpose of routing overlay networks is to reduce routing delays of the best-effort TCP/IP Internet by running the overlay protocol software. Although a routing overlay network cannot change the TCP routing procedure, it can optimize the sequence of overlay nodes that a data packet traverses to its destination. A popular example of a peer-to-peer overlay network is file sharing among equally privileged peers acting as prosumers (Clark et al., 2006, p. 3). Overlay networks can to some extent fulfill complementary functions of traffic management not provided within the TCP/IP Internet. However, overlay networks cannot substitute for active traffic management within all-IP networks.

2.3.2.4   The challenge for active traffic management

In the following subsection only a short preview for active traffic management focusing on negative externalities due to congestion is provided whereas a further analysis of QoS-based traffic management is provided in section 2.6.1. Different definitions of congestion are applied by network engineers, which differ from an economic definition of congestion (Bauer et al., 2009, p. 8). Queuing theory considers traffic as congested if within a time interval the arrival rate into a system exceeds the service rate. Alternatively, a network operator may define congestion as the (average) load on a network over a particular period of time exceeding a specified level. Within TCP congestion control the focus is on packet dropping and the impact of send-rate reduction on queuing. In contrast an economic definition of congestion is based on the welfare economic concept of negative externalities, already analyzed by Pigou (1920). When an increase in the use of a facility imposes a cost (negative externality) on the existing users the facility is considered to be congested.

This economically well-founded concept is widely accepted in network economics and can be applied to any network architecture (e.g., Knieps, 2015a, Chapter 3). In the context of packet data transmission it has been analyzed by MacKie-Mason and Varian (1995b). A congestion charge can be assessed to avoid overusage of a facility, thus mitigating congestion externalities. The socially optimal congestion fee reflects congestion cost. Since TCP controls each traffic flow individually, a differentiation between heavy and light users of capacity is not possible. TCP allocates a higher share of capacity to intense users and a lower share to light users. Moreover, TCP cannot provide prioritization of data packets and quality of service guarantees (Knieps, 2011, p. 27). As long as active traffic management with price and quality differentiation is not implemented, network usage restrictions aiming to limit capacity consumption of heavy users are to be expected. Moreover, network operators may pursue a bifurcation of the network into a public and a private Internet. It is doubtful whether, within all-IP networks, such a market split can be a stable configuration in the long run (Knieps and Stocker, 2015).

2.4   TECHNOLOGY AND COSTS

Technology and cost characteristics can be observed in each of the complementary market segments: infrastructure capacity, Internet traffic, as well as Internet applications and services. The convergence of specialized network infrastructures into all-IP networks will likely create increasing demand for active traffic management (congestion management and QoS differentiation) as this is a precondition for a wide range of heterogeneous Internet application services.

2.4.1   Specialized Technologies Versus General Purpose Technologies (GPTs)

The Internet historically resided on the specialized network technologies that were in use to provide telecommunications services. Although fixed and wireless networks both exhibit economies of scale and scope as well as network effects, they differ in their unique cost structures. Historically, wireless networks exhausted economies at a lower scale of operations than fixed networks. Moreover, the regulatory framework influenced technology choices and the extent of scale economies. Networks built in an era of monopoly regulation were designed to reach minimal costs at a much higher scale than networks rolled out in an era of competition. As existing networks are gradually integrated into all-IP platforms and new IP-based networks are deployed, old and new networks become GPTs for Internet traffic. The transition from specialized traffic networks (ISDN voice and best-effort Internet) towards multi-purpose QoS Internet with active traffic management is a time-consuming process. While GPTs will handle the bulk of traffic, specialized networks built for specific services such as financial transactions will likely continue to coexist with multi-purpose technologies.

2.4.2   Economies of Scale, Scope, and Density

Important economic characteristics such as economies of scale, economies of scope, and economies of density are visible at the level of individual ISPs and firms in the higher layers. They are driven by high upfront costs but, probably more importantly, also by rapid cost-reducing technological change. At an aggregate system level, characteristics may emerge that replicate these properties or that are qualitatively different.

2.4.2.1   Economies of scale and economies of scope on the supply side
Economics of scale are typical for the supply side of Internet markets, including markets for infrastructure capacity, Internet traffic (where multiplexing can achieve high economies of scale), and Internet application services (e.g., software markets). Economies of scale prevail if a proportional increase of all input factors causes a disproportionally higher increase of output. In the single-product case economies of scale manifest themselves in declining average costs. In digital markets such as software, declining average costs are mainly driven by the high development costs. This large intellectual property component of new digital products contributes to large upfront costs. Consequently, the average costs of production, which include the development costs, are then significantly higher than the marginal costs. Markets with this unique cost structure are typically characterized by high market concentration. Forms of price differentiation will be needed to recover total costs (Katz and Shapiro, 1998, p. 6).

The markets for Internet traffic consist of a combination of Internet logistics and infrastructure capacities. These traffic service markets can realize economies of scale and scope by bundling different types of traffic. In the past these cost characteristics of networks have been of particular relevance in local telecommunications access networks (local loops), which were regarded as 'natural' monopolies with typically only one active provider. After market liberalization an increasing number of formerly monopolistic market segments, such as long-distance and wireless communications, developed effective competition with several active network providers. Due to technological innovations and strongly growing demand economies of scale became exhausted (Knieps, 1997a, p. 328, Laffont and Tirole, 2000, p. 98). Thus, despite advantages of traffic bundling, competing traffic service networks evolved in response to the heterogeneous preferences of users for traffic network variety (e.g., Knieps and Zenhäusern, 2008, p. 124). Similar forces are at work in all-IP networks.

2.4.2.2   Network effects and positive externalities

Network effects exist if the utility of participating in a network is dependent on the number of users. They can be direct (e.g., the benefits of having more communication options in larger networks) or indirect (e.g., the benefits of the availability of more complementary goods and services in networks with a larger user base). Network effects can be positive and negative (e.g., the disutility of congestion). Positive network effects may also be characterized as economies of scale on the demand side: as an increasing number of users choose a technology its benefits increase. Suppliers often take such network effects into account when pricing their services. However, if interdependencies are not reflected in market transactions network externalities may prevail (Liebowitz and Margolis, 2003). Examples are positive effects of network size on innovation or negative effects on other users of insufficient protection against malware.

The theory of compatibility standards has been developed during the past decades, using standards competition as a metaphor for rivalry between competing technologies (Liebowitz and Margolis, 1996, p. 290). Katz and Shapiro (1994, p. 100) point out that positive adoption externalities are not limited to communication networks but also affect hardware and software, These effects may be (fully or partly) internalized through network sponsorship, integration, or contracts. Taking into account heterogeneous preferences for alternative technologies, a trade-off between network externalities and variety has been considered in analogy to the traditional theory of monopolistic competition (Farrell and Saloner, 1986). Free entry within a dynamic world leads to an important additional dimension, namely, the search for new technologies. This provides a strong argument in favor of leaving the evolutionary search for new technological solutions unhampered by restrictive regulations. Market-driven committees of stakeholders play an important role in solving coordination activities within the standard-setting processes (Blankart and Knieps, 1993). In addition, alternative forms of decentralized governance, including organizations without voting procedures, may become relevant, for example in developing open source software, or in the development of gateways (e.g., David and Bunn, 1988; Economides, 1996). Interoperability in all-IP networks mitigates the trade-off problems between network externalities and variety in particular at the level of network infrastructure. Even with heterogeneous technology, network effects of a specific platform are mitigated if cheap converter technology is available (e.g., Gottinger, 2003).

2.4.3   Path Dependence and Critical Mass Phenomena

The analysis of the conditions under which technologies reach a critical mass of users and become viable has a long tradition in telecommunications (Rohlfs, 1974; Oren and Smith,

1981). A key question is whether such a critical mass of users can be reached via market strategies or whether public policy intervention is required. In evolutionary economics, the notion of path dependence refers to a situation in which earlier decisions constrain later decisions. Technology upgrade paths therefore may show signs of path dependence. In a more narrow sense, the question has been examined of whether an already implemented technology can prevail even if superior technologies become available. In this context a highly controversial debate has unfolded: Arthur (1989) and David (1985) argue and illustrate with the historical example of the QWERTY keyboard that a specific standard may persist due to positive network effects and externalities, even if it is technically inferior.

Liebowitz and Margolis (1990) subsequently raised doubts whether specific historical examples can 'prove' the survival of inferior technologies as a consequence of path dependence. For the case of heterogeneous preferences of users regarding the superiority of a new technology, a trade-off exists between a network effect related to the size of the user base and the utility difference between the new technology and the old technology (technology effect). This trade-off may lead to a partial switching of a subset of users to a new technology, whereas other users may prefer to stay with the old technology. If a critical mass of users for a new technology cannot be reached, only the old technology will be used. Such path-dependent lock-in of an old technology would, however, be the outcome of heterogeneous user preferences for technologies (Farrell and Saloner, 1986).

2.4.4 Standardization and Path-dependent Technology Choice

Many studies on compatibility standards focus on standards for single products. Within large technical systems such as the Internet, standards for complementary components and layers gain particular relevance. Considering the layered technical architecture of the Internet, a logical relation between standards can be established in which basic standards form preconditions for more specific standards (Blankart and Knieps, 1993, p. 40). Applied to the Internet, the all-IP physical infrastructure layer consists of alternative network infrastructures (including mobile, fixed telecom, and cable access networks) (Knieps and Zenhäusern, 2015). Based on such all-IP infrastructures, a variety of heterogeneous standards for Internet traffic management have evolved in addition to the best-effort TCP/IP, which has historically been dominant. For applications and services, a proliferating variety of standards for content delivery, video streaming, VoIP, and so on, are in use and being developed.

Path-dependent technology choice can become relevant on all physical network infrastructures. Depending on the existing stock of sunk investment, businesses face decisions to upgrade established networks, build new network infrastructures, or lease access from other players (Bourreau and Doğan, 2006). Such forms of path dependence are neither a result of historical accidents nor necessarily a signal for inefficient behavior and exercise of market power. Under competitive pressure firms can only survive if they pursue successful price, product and investment strategies. With durable capital equipment in networks this requires taking path dependence into explicit consideration.

Path dependence is also relevant in markets for network services. Under competitive conditions consumers can choose between different providers of network services and thereby reveal their preferences for network effects, variety and new technologies. Consumers with strong preferences for an established technology and a large user base are rather prepared to adhere to the established technology, whereas consumers with weak preferences for network effects and strong preferences for novelty will choose the advantages of a new technology. If firms were to neglect network effects of their services when making their price and product policies, they would not survive competitive pressures. Path dependence has also played an important role in the history of the public Internet. One example is the durability of the best-effort TCP that does not provide for active traffic management. With the transition to all-IP networks, the importance of variety and search for innovative traffic architectures in markets for Internet traffic services greatly increases. Although traffic networks are software defined and can be configured easily, experience suggests that it is difficult to initiate a bandwagon effect to introduce active traffic management more widely.

2.5   INTERNET DEMAND AND PRICING

Internet access and traffic services are provided as inputs to the production of goods and services and to final users. Given the large number of players in the Internet system and the historical reliance on decentralized forms of coordination, numerous non-market and market transactions take place. A wide range of prices and pricing models exists for transit, peering, interconnection at Internet exchanges and other connection points, access of content providers to ISPs, CDNs, arrangements between content provider and access providers, hosting, and many more. Due to the multi-sided nature of many market relations, prices between any two players may be positive, with payments flowing in either direction, or zero (as in traditional peering). As many of the prices at the wholesale level are negotiated in private contracts and agreements, only limited information is available in the public domain. Aspects of interconnection and peering are discussed by Clark, Lehr and Bauer in Chapter 16 in this volume and will not be explored further here. Rather, we will focus on the pricing of access for consumers and (by analogy) business users.

The literature on network pricing has historically differentiated prices of access and prices of usage. In the widespread unlimited usage models the latter is zero. Like in other communication markets, such as mobile services, Internet access services have been priced in response to demand- and supply-side conditions as well as the institutional environment in which Internet services developed. These choices had clear implications for the adoption and use of services. In the USA, local telephone service was historically offered at both flat and measured prices, with most subscribers opting for flat rates (even if measured rates would have been associated with lower total spending). This allowed early dial-up users to go online without concerns about high phone bills. After a brief period during which ISPs such as AOL charged measured prices they also adopted flat pricing. Unlimited use probably had a positive effect on the larger Internet ecosystem, stimulating both demand and supply in a virtuous cycle. It also led to congestion and the (temporary) dubbing of the World Wide Web as the 'World Wide Wait'.

During the late 1990s, an increasing number of experts argued in favor of measured rates or some other forms of congestion pricing (e.g., MacKie-Mason and Varian, 1995a, 1995b; MacKie-Mason et al., 1997; Crémer and Hariton, 1999) but as the capacity of networks and routers was expanded and with the migration to broadband services that were initially less capacity constrained, flat unlimited pricing remained the dominant model. Beginning in the late 1990s, mobile voice service providers adopted multi-part self-selection pricing and gradually designed more and more complex bundles of services. With the growing importance of video traffic, network operators in high-income countries claim to face capacity constraints and are increasingly relying on volume-based multi-part pricing approaches in which the lower service tiers come with data caps. This may again be a short-lived phenomenon. Odlyzko (2014) argues that multi-part and volume-based pricing are best understood as attempts by network operators to extract rents while flat rates would be better suited to help fill the available network capacity.

Consumers typically pay for access to the Internet and they may pay for usage depending on the specific plan they subscribe to. Unlimited plans do not have any incremental usage charge but plans with data caps may require overage fees. Some network operators have implemented other responses, such as degrading service or even suspending it. While multi-part pricing and especially data caps are rather unpopular among avid Internet users, they may actually be welfare enhancing (e.g., Bauer and Wildman, 2012). Such pricing schemes are a workable approach to recovering high fixed and shared costs of network access services in ways that are responsive to demand. Initial estimates of the price elasticity of broadband demand suggest that it is inelastic (Rappoport et al., 2003; Rosston et al., 2011). Price differentiation also allows introducing low-priced plans or even zero-priced options ('sponsored data') and thus to expand adoption to additional user groups. However, to assure a workable market such models require sufficient price and quality transparency.

Consumers also pay for content and other online services, but often indirectly and in somewhat disguised form. An increasing number of OTT services, such as Netflix, Amazon Prime, or providers of online games charge a flat or per-use price. Likewise, many apps, music, and videos can be bought from online stores. In other cases, transactions are organized in multi-sided markets and the flows of payments are more complex. For example, music streaming services such as Spotify, Deezer, or Pandora offer free tiers that periodically interrupt the service for commercials or require participating in sponsor activities. In these cases advertisers and the companies enlisting their services generate the revenue flow. Online services such as Google Search or Facebook monetize aspects of their users' online behavior by harvesting massive amounts of online data from users, sometimes without their explicit knowledge and consent. The pervasive nature of multi-sided markets raises new and challenging competition issues for which antitrust does not yet have clear answers (see Haucap and Stühmeier, Chapter 9 in this volume).

Internet traffic service providers are platform providers serving end users as well as application providers. Congestion and quality of service differentiation not only play a role in access networks but also in the markets for traffic capacity in the entire Internet. They are a response to heterogeneous demand for traffic qualities such as prioritization offered to application service providers as discussed in the following section.

2.6   INNOVATION AND QUALITY OF SERVICE

The implementation of active traffic management and related traffic capacity allocations diverges from the homogeneous best-effort TCP/IP model (Knieps, 2011, p. 28;

Yoo, 2013, pp. 1741, 1757). The TCP/IP stack is an integral concept of the end-to-end architecture. Within the best-effort Internet the TCP/IP stack differentiates between five complementary layers: the physical layer, the data link layer (switch-to-switch), the network layer (router-to-router), the transport layer (host-to-host), and the applications layer (process-to-process). The applications layer and the transport layer have functions executed by the host at the top of the TCP/IP stack. The introduction of QoS differentiation requires active traffic management carried out by routers and switches on the data link and network layers, thereby shifting the transport layer function from the top of the stack (the 'edges') to the lower network layers (the 'core').

Contrary to much of the public debate that focuses primarily on innovations at the 'edge' of the Internet, innovations at higher layers and at lower layers unfold in a dynamically interdependent relationship. The capabilities supported by the network enable and constrain the types and variety of innovation possible at higher layers. At the same time, the diversity and number of innovative services at higher layers influence the value of the network and have implications for innovation and investment decisions at the network layer. Thus, in order to understand the ongoing high dynamics of the Internet, a closer look on the interplay of innovations in applications and services as well as innovations in network infrastructure and traffic services is required. As discussed with heterogeneous applications and user groups, markets for Internet traffic services can be conceptualized as platforms for Internet application services providers and end users. The following sections explore the future role of active traffic management, which becomes even more important within the future all-IP networks.

2.6.1 Active Traffic Management of Internet Traffic Service Networks

The provision of time-sensitive applications like Voice-over-IP, video conferences, and video games demands guaranteed timely and steady packet delivery. In turn, active traffic management requires a consistent incentive-compatible allocation of traffic capacities and incentive-compatible prices for network services (Knieps and Zenhäusern, 2008, p. 123). Given the complementarities between lower and upper layers, innovations in application service markets may become drivers for innovations in markets for traffic services and vice versa. Innovations at the network layer include, but are not limited to, QoS differentiation in data packet transmission such as the control of delay, jitter, and packet loss.

2.6.1.1 Congestion prices and QoS differentiation

Network operators primarily make the decisions about traffic capacity investment and allocation based on the perceived business cases. Active entrepreneurial traffic management takes into account the opportunity costs of capacity usage. Within a capacity-constrained network an additional data packet may increase delay costs for all other packets. Price signals to internalize congestion externalities are well known from other fields within economics (e.g., transportation economics). For homogeneous traffic quality in the Internet they have been derived by MacKie-Mason and Varian (1995a). Different traffic classes can be provisioned relying on the differentiated services (DiffServ) architecture (Chen and Zhang, 2004, p. 370). Based on this approach it becomes possible to implement QoS differentiation by means of interclass externality pricing in IP networks. For example, in the special case of three traffic classes all data packets with the highest priority are assigned to the premium traffic class, all data packets with medium priority to the medium traffic class, and all other data packets belong to the 'best-effort' traffic class. The implementation of strict priority scheduling provides a hierarchical structure to deal with congestion externalities. If the network is capacity constrained, the transmission of each additional data packet in the premium class increases delay of all lower-class data packets, thereby causing interclass externalities. Since the highest traffic class causes the highest opportunity costs for the data packets in lower traffic classes, the users of the top priority traffic class are required to pay the highest congestion fee (Knieps, 2011, p. 32).

2.6.2   Vertically-related Markets

A basic characteristic of all-IP networks is the decoupling of application services and traffic management such that service-related functions are independent from underlying traffic-related technologies. Since all transmissions are IP-based there may be a combination of interconnected broadband infrastructures involved. Although application services and traffic management services are technically separated, vertical relations between application service providers and traffic service providers may exist. The question arises whether application service providers owned or tightly cooperating with a traffic service provider or paying for QoS will be granted higher traffic priority ('access tiering'). If so, do such arrangements constitute forms of unfair competition and/or a violation of the vision of a 'neutral' and 'open' Internet?

During the past decades the IETF has evolved as a forum for developing standards for basic building blocks (e.g., IntServ/RSVP, DiffServ, combination versus integration of DiffServ and IntServ) as a basis for flexible open traffic architectures that enable the provision of a variety of traffic qualities within multi-purpose traffic networks. Instead of standardization of a specific QoS differentiation architecture, the IETF only proposes configuration guidelines for DiffServ classes, based on the standardized building blocks. This provides freedom to entrepreneurs to implement a specific QoS traffic architecture derived from the applications' quality requirements. The open set of flexible multi-purpose QoS architectures capable of supporting a variety of traffic qualities required for different application services can be considered as a 'meta-architecture', termed Generalized DiffServ architecture (Knieps, 2015b, p. 739).

The entrepreneurial selection of a specific QoS differentiated architecture as an implementation of the Generalized DiffServ architecture provides a flexible common multi-purpose traffic architecture that can support time and non-time-sensitive applications and services. QoS differentiated pricing, taking into account the opportunity costs of traffic capacities, is incentive compatible because discrimination between application services on the basic of traffic capacity requirements is avoided. The general principle of rivalry for network resources for different traffic classes is applied. Under QoS-differentiated pricing the minimal traffic quality of the lowest traffic class results endogenously. It differs from the best-effort average traffic quality of TCP. Consequently, an artificial market split between best-effort TCP and specialized services within Generalized DiffServ architecture would not be incentive compatible and unstable. Within the Generalized DiffServ architecture the use of best-effort TCP with passive traffic management at the edges (hosts) conflicts with the active traffic management required for the provision of heterogeneous traffic qualities (Knieps, 2015b).

2.6.3　Network Neutrality

Openness has long been seen as one of the key drivers of Internet-based innovation. With the migration to all-IP networks and the differentiation of applications, services and demand, the traditional best-effort approach to traffic management has come under considerable strain. A long debate exists on whether the openness of the Internet needs safeguarding by means of regulatory interventions into active traffic management (Schwartz and Weiser, 2009; Sidak and Teece, 2010; Schuett, 2010; Krämer et al., 2013). Conducted under the label of network neutrality, arguments usually point to the ambiguous incentives of ISPs for whom some applications are complementary while others compete with their own services. Economic concerns related to the implications of quality of service differentiation on innovation and investment and political concerns related to the freedom of speech are articulated and often poorly separated (Bauer and Obar, 2014). Few specific cases of discrimination are known, with the BitTorrent case in 2008 the most visible instance, revealing that Comcast had engaged in practices to throttle certain types of traffic (FCC, 2008). The case illustrated the problems caused by overuse by some user groups and by intransparent rationing by network operators (Wu, 2003). In the USA, two issues drove the debate. First, there was a concern that unregulated market power in broadband access networks would be shifted to the markets for Internet access services and subsequently abused to exploit Internet application service providers (Economides, 2008, p. 210). At the same time there were concerns that quality differentiation in the Internet would undermine its vibrant, 'permission-free' innovation system. While such concerns are not entirely invalid, the major arguments against network neutrality regulation have been that general competition law and consumer protection laws apply to competition in the Internet. Instead of prohibiting price and quality differentiation by ISPs, it seems a more appropriate strategy to regulate market power at its roots, that is, where monopolistic bottlenecks in broadband infrastructures prevail (Knieps and Zenhäusern, 2008, p. 127).

A related question is whether it would be beneficial from a welfare point of view to allow QoS differentiation but require the provision of a minimal quality to restrict quality of service limitations imposed by other broadband providers. A crucial advantage of minimum quality regulation is that in contrast to network neutrality requirements it is consistent with charging content providers for carriage and that it does not preclude transmission qualities higher than the minimum quality, although presumably supplied at higher prices. A minimum quality standard, however, would not be without potential drawbacks, among others bearing the risk of suppressing some competition through quality differentiation. Compared to enforced uniformity through net neutrality rules the cost of minimum standards would appear far smaller (Brennan, 2011, p. 69). From the perspective of all-IP Internet, guaranteed high traffic quality becomes crucial for highly time-sensitive applications. Other applications only need low priority transmission. If regulators would prescribe a minimum traffic quality the freedom of Internet entrepreneurs to choose traffic service classes would be hampered and a demand for low traffic quality might go unfulfilled (Knieps and Stocker, 2015, p. 51).

The entrepreneurial flexibility to individually develop tailored QoS traffic architectures may result in a large variety of QoS differentiation strategies. In a fast-paced technological environment, preserving this evolutionary search for improving QoS differentiation depends on the flexibility of entrepreneurs envisioned in the implementation of the Generalized DiffServ architectures. Regulatory interventions will likely impede this type of discovery process.

One important argument within the network neutrality debate has been that the best-effort principle of the TCP/IP – which implies a zero-price rule for transactions between ISPs and content providers and the recovery of network costs from end users – promotes content and application service innovation. There is considerable evidence for such a process but it is not the only type of innovation relevant in the Internet ecosystem. A ban on charging termination fees to content providers would effectively subsidize the creation of new application services. The prohibition of fees facilitates entry of new application service providers and also empowers consumers to participate via user-generated applications and content. Due to the trade-off between possible welfare gains if content production is increased and potentially higher access or usage fees to consumers, the final answer to the highly controversial question of network neutrality regulation remains open (Lee and Wu, 2009, p. 66). As outcomes are highly contingent on specific modeling assumptions no clear-cut conclusion about the relationship between net neutrality regulation and the innovation incentives of Internet traffic service providers or content providers has emerged (Choi and Kim, 2010).

The conclusion from the controversial literature on network neutrality regulation seems to be that a regulatory implementation of a zero-price rule is not well justified. The opposite may be the case because of the potential importance of 'innovational complementarities' (Bresnahan and Trajtenberg, 1995, p. 84). Since the Generalized DiffServ architecture has the characteristics of flexible multi-purpose technologies the (derived) demand for specific traffic qualities to enable new application services can be successfully matched, which strongly stimulates the entrepreneurial search of innovative application services and related application software. Moreover, innovations in Internet traffic architectures that facilitate more differentiated transmission qualities can also cause the search for new application services. Consequently, the innovation potential for application services and Internet traffic are interrelated. A key challenge for the policy framework is therefore to balance these two interdependent innovation dynamics, one facilitated by non-discriminatory access to network and the other dependent on differentiation.

2.6.4   The Entrepreneurial Search for Active Traffic Management Architectures

The interactive dynamics of complementary general (multi-) purpose technologies and applications within the Internet can build on the GPT literature. Although this research has focused on the role of key technologies on aggregate economic growth, its overall framing of 'innovational complementarities' is relevant for understanding the dynamics of the Internet. According to Bresnahan and Trajtenberg (1995, p. 83) innovation in the upstream GPT increases the productivity of R&D in downstream application markets. In turn, innovations and improvements in applications raise the return to further advances in the GPT.

This perspective re-emphasizes the analysis provided above that the major driver of innovations within the Internet is not limited to applications (Simcoe, 2012). Innovation may also be stimulated by positive feedback effects from the all-IP infrastructure and Generalized DiffServ architecture, which function as GPTs for applications and services. Therefore, it is important that the GPTs, both on the broadband infrastructure level as well as on the traffic architecture level, remain open for innovative evolution, taking into account requirements of the application side. Although complementarities between different GPTs as well as between GPTs and application services are important, the entrepreneurial search process on the specific markets for all-IP infrastructure capacities, for Internet traffic provision (combining infrastructure capacities with Internet logistics) as well as Internet applications (search engines, content, PC software etc.) is also vital.

2.7   ROLES AND LIMITATIONS OF MARKETS

2.7.1   From Regulated Public Utilities Towards Liberalized Network Industries

The emergence and evolution of markets in a dynamic environment such as communications and the Internet creates a challenging environment for competition policy and sector-specific regulation. In the past century the state has played an important role as actor in infrastructure sectors like electricity, railroads, air transport, postal delivery and telecommunications. As a result of deregulation and privatization the traditional public utilities developed into the present network industries. Legally protected entry barriers were largely replaced by free market entry. The economics of network industries became a vibrant yet challenging field, focusing on the peculiarities of markets for network industries and generating new insights pertinent to these unique sectors (Shy, 2001; Knieps, 2015a). Cost characteristics like economies of scale, economies of scope, high fixed costs combined with low marginal costs are typical for network industries in general. A large body of research exists addressing industries with few suppliers and their market strategies (Tirole, 1988; Scherer and Ross, 1990; Carlton and Perloff, 2005). A key insight is that competition may unfold in many forms even though the general equilibrium theory of perfect competition does not hold. Market participants should exhaust the potentials of dynamic markets including the emergence of new markets, undisturbed by government interventions. Remaining market power problems are left within the competency of antitrust authorities based on general competition policy (e.g., Geroski, 1998; Katz and Shapiro, 1999; Shapiro and Varian, 1999; Shy, 2001).

There are, however, peculiarities within network industries that suggest a role for governance mechanisms other than markets. Network externalities, public good aspects, and possibly failures to coordinate the systemic interdependencies in the Internet limit the ability of decentralized markets to coordinate effectively. Other forms of governance, including government regulation, co-regulation (e.g., public–private partnerships such as computer emergency response teams in the area of cybersecurity), and self-regulation (e.g., forums such as the IETF) may be able to address these problems.

In liberalized network industries the traditional goals of consumer protection and of competition policy also hold without apology. Moreover, ex ante sector-specific regulations may be justified although the goals during the past decades were to focus these interventions to minimize the scope of regulation as well as the possible distortions created by regulatory interventions. The concepts of natural monopoly and irreversible costs can be applied to help regulatory agencies localize and discipline network-specific market power. Two kinds of potential errors are associated with government intervention. A false positive or Type I error occurs when an agency intervenes although there is no need for such intervention. A false negative or Type II error arises when there is no intervention although there is a need for active competition or other type of policy. The relevance of such Type II errors cannot simply be defined away but each situation needs careful examination.

For example, owners of civil engineering infrastructure do often possess the characteristics of monopolistic bottlenecks (due to the combination of natural monopolies and irreversible costs) so that competition on the markets for network services may be impeded (Knieps, 2015a, p. 135). Type II errors can sometimes be recognized ex post and then be corrected. Unfortunately, Type I errors do not allow such self-correcting processes. Shortall and Cave (2015) provide an interesting illustration for European next-generation access markets, where regulatory decisions in some countries cemented monopolistic structures. Obviously, discretionary interventions, applied case by case, are strongly susceptible to the impact of rent-seeking activities. Instead, the development of generic solutions seems necessary that are reasonably robust to variations in the details of individual markets and firms but applicable to classes of cases. The starting point of such a disaggregated competition and regulatory policy model should be the localization of market power. In sub-markets where market power can be localized government agencies have a clear case for regulatory intervention.

2.7.2 Consumer Protection in Innovative Industries

Consumer protection issues are important in markets for Internet applications as well as Internet traffic services. This includes issues of security, deterrence of cybercrime, market transparency of price conditions, and so on. A major focus of consumer protection is on market and information transparency related to price and quality conditions. Within the traditional TCP/IP Internet the actual transmission quality remains unspecified. Depending on demand and the provided transmission capacity, quality attributes such as speed result endogenously. An ex ante quality guarantee would conflict with the best-effort slow-start congestion avoidance mechanism. If a packet is dropped because the receiver cannot handle the traffic flow the sending computer halves its rate (Jacobson, 1988). From the perspective of consumer protection a transparent provision of TCP does not raise problems even though, given the protocols implemented at routers, heavy users of capacity are favored compared to light users. Transparent contractual broadband usage restrictions as described in Wu (2003, p. 158) likewise do not raise concerns. However, intransparent ad hoc traffic management procedures aiming to reduce congestion or favoring specific applications are incompatible with consumer protection. One well-known example has been the intransparent traffic management of Comcast when interfering with its customers' use of the peer-to peer networking protocol BitTorrent. A precondition for non-discriminatory active traffic management is the requirement that the providers make available their congestion pricing and quality differentiation strategies in a transparent manner. This includes traffic service classes and related quality guarantees as well as prices, including penalties in case the contracted transmission qualities are not delivered.

Consumer protection is also relevant in markets for applications and services, for example guaranteed Voice-over-IP quality. Whereas in the past quality characteristics have been specified based on ITU standards, in the future an evolutionary search for heterogeneous end-to-end qualities can be expected. The role of data protection and individual privacy may become an even greater challenge for the future developments towards the Internet of Things (Klein and Rao, 2014). See also Chapter 12 by Ian Brown in this volume.

2.7.3   Competition and Antitrust Policy in Innovative Industries

Important antitrust cases in innovative industries have been the IBM and the Microsoft cases (Fisher et al., 1983; Fisher, 2000a, 2000b; Economides, 2001) and the various cases against Google in the USA and the EU (see Chapter 9 by Haucap and Strühmeier, this volume). A controversial question has been whether traditional antitrust analysis is also applicable to innovative industries or whether their dynamic nature would exempt them from such scrutiny. However, despite the difficulties to operationalize workable competition in dynamic industries, 'To do otherwise is to provide a license to destroy competition under the excuse that a firm is innovative' (Fisher, 2000a, p. 564). Controversial questions during these long-lasting cases have been whether and at which layers (components, hardware, services) market power could be identified and if so whether such market power had been extended to complementary activities using bundling as a tying strategy, whether predatory pricing strategies had been applied, as well as the role of predatory inventions.

A key lesson from these cases is that market power is very difficult to establish. The definition of the relevant markets and their boundaries, the definition and measurement of market shares, and the role of entry barriers are highly controversial and complex issues without clear-cut answers. Due to the innovational dynamics, market boundaries are blurring, entry strategies by competing platforms become important and innovative product design is hard to distinguish from strategic innovations intended to thwart competition. Even if market power could be identified (e.g., IBM's 360 series computer generation or Microsoft's operating system) traditional antitrust instruments cannot identify the abuse of market power. For example, anti-competitive price setting on the browser markets with high fixed and low variable costs cannot be identified with the traditional Areeda-Turner and other tests.

2.7.4   Regulation in Innovative Industries

Similar to the role of antitrust policy in innovative markets the labeling of a network industry as innovative can by no means serve as a blanket justification for absence of market power regulation. The relevant questions are in which part of a network industry network specific market power continues to exist after liberalization and how adequate regulatory instruments could be designed that are not conflicting with the evolution of network dynamics. The role of sector-specific market power regulation in network industries changed over time in response to the degree of market opening.

It is useful to differentiate between the phases of 'static regulation', 'comparative static regulation' and 'dynamic regulation'. Whereas during the period of legal entry barriers, static regulation and the control of market power subject to given technological constraints was the predominant approach, during the period of gradual entry deregulation comparative static approaches were applied to take into account technological change when applying adaptions to regulatory instruments. In the meantime 'dynamic regulations' evolved, taking into account proper incentives for innovations and related investments in an environment of gradual network evolution and facilitating dynamic efficiency (Bauer and Bohlin, 2008, p. 38). With the emergence of new markets, network-specific market power becomes less severe. To the extent that technological progress leads to active competition, the area of monopolistic bottlenecks is shrinking and potential market power regulations should be phased out. Ex ante regulation of access to ducts and conduits may be justified if alternative infrastructure platforms are not available (Blankart et al., 2007, p. 425). The case for intervention to promote a specific network access technology is much less clear where path-dependent upgrading strategies are an outcome of entrepreneurial decisions (Knieps and Zenhäusern, 2015).

2.8   CONCLUSION

This chapter provided an overview of key industrial organization aspects of the Internet. In contrast to earlier contributions to the field, it focused less on single market segments but emphasized the unique technological attributes and technological dynamics of the Internet. The Internet has evolved as the prime driver of convergence of telecommunications, media and information technology sectors. Much of future communications will be carried out via general purpose all-IP networks. Specialized communication networks (ISDN, PSTN, etc.) are being phased out. The underlying physical all-IP broadband infrastructures as well as the complementary QoS differentiated traffic architectures are both flexible multi-purpose technologies that can be adapted to the demand for heterogeneous application services.

The inherent dynamics of the Internet requires focusing on the interdependence of the innovation potential for application services and traffic services. With heterogeneous applications and heterogeneous user groups it is analytically useful to consider markets for Internet traffic services as platforms for Internet application services providers as well as end users. The basic message of industrial economics is that dynamic markets like the Internet should neither be exempted from general competition policy nor do they justify new and specific antitrust policies. Entrepreneurial decision-making is a powerful force to explore the potential of dynamic and emerging markets.

In liberalized network industries the traditional goals of consumer protection policies as well as general competition policy also hold. Similar to the role of antitrust policy in innovative markets the labeling of a network industry as innovative can by no means serve as a blanket justification for the elimination of market power regulation. Ex ante sector-specific regulations of network specific market power are justified. With the help of dynamic approaches the scope of regulation and distortions created by regulatory interventions can be minimized. However, regulatory fallacies can be particularly costly in dynamic markets. Potential examples are misguided interventions to eliminate quality of service differentiation or the regulatory intervention to deploy a specific access technology, such as fiber to the home, as currently discussed within the EU.

The Internet also raises fundamental theoretical problems for economics. For one, industrial organization does not yet have a good set of theories to model highly interdependent systems. Given interdependence, plasticity of technology and dynamic technological change, core notions of economics – the definition and operationalization of a 'market', the operationalization of competition – are increasingly difficult if not impossible. This has potentially far-reaching implications for public policy, given that regulation and antitrust are rooted in a clear understanding of relevant markets and the effectiveness of competition in these markets. Moreover, given the interdependencies among different actors, the non-linear relations that characterize the Internet, and the pervasive presence of increasing returns, many basic assumptions of equilibrium-oriented economics are violated. In highly interconnected and interdependent systems actors' perceptions and optimization calculus may become endogenous and evolve with the state of the Internet. Thus the assumptions of stable preferences, the existence of a stable optimum, and many other key economic concepts may have to be reassessed.

There is interesting theoretical and empirical research in many areas that may eventually help in overcoming these challenges (some of it discussed in subsequent chapters of this Handbook). Research in the areas of the economics of networks, in the emerging field of network science, and in innovation economics is coming to grips with the dynamics of highly connected systems characterized by a high rate of technological change. Work on new institutional arrangements, such as peer production, the economics of standards within a system of networked governance, and on antitrust in high-tech markets, all contribute to this emerging literature. As empirical data are generated, there will be more opportunities to test new theoretical models. At the same time, data collection in an environment where massive amounts of data can be harvested online poses daunting problems. However, we are confident that rapid advances in big data analytics and in the empirical modeling of these processes open a new frontier of innovative research. Empirical analysis will find a strong complement in computational modeling approaches ranging from agent-based models to advanced simulation models. The Internet has greatly re-energized the field of industrial organization but many challenging problems remain unanswered.

NOTES

1. The term 'new economy' was initially used in the 1990s and associated with many exuberant claims such as the emergence of an economy without business cycles and with unlimited growth prospects. Many of these expectations have since been replaced by more realistic assessments but the notion retains some of its appeal.
2. Economides (2005); Greenstein (2005, 2012a); Church and Gandal (2005); Gans et al. (2005); as well as Hoernig and Valletti (2012) provide overviews of the economics of Internet infrastructure. Benkler (2006) is an innovative discussion of market and non-market dimensions of the Internet and their fundamental economic and social consequences. See also Chapter 5 by Benkler in this volume.

3. From the perspective of the Internet layer scheme, one may further differentiate into application and services at the edge. Where justified without loss of generality we will refer to application services as including both.
4. The National Science Foundation permitted Barry Stein, the founder of The World, to sell Internet to ordinary people as opposed to 'bona fide researchers'. See 'Thanks, Al Gore', accessed 18 April 2015 at http://technology.ie/thanks-al-gore-podcast-30/.
5. The price of mobile data declined from nearly $10 per megabyte in 2006 to a few cents per megabyte in 2012. See 'The truly personal computer', *The Economist*, 28 February–6 March 2015, p. 19.
6. For TV distribution, over-the-air broadcasting is technically much more efficient than streaming over fixed or mobile networks.

REFERENCES

Armstrong, M. (2006), 'Competition in two-sided markets', *RAND Journal of Economics*, **37** (3), 668–91.
Arthur, W.B. (1989), 'Competing technologies and lock-in by historical small events: The dynamics of allocation under increasing returns', *The Economic Journal*, **99** (394), 116–31.
Atkinson, R.D. and S. Ezell (2012), *Innovation Economics*, New Haven, CT: Yale University Press.
Baldwin, C.Y. and K.B. Clark (2000), *Design Rules, Volume 1: The Power of Modularity*, Cambridge, MA: MIT Press.
Bauer, J.M. (2005), 'Unbundling policy in the United States: Players, outcomes and effects', *Communications & Strategies*, **57** (1), 59–82.
Bauer, J.M. (2010), 'Regulation, public policy, and investment in communications infrastructure', *Telecommunications Policy*, **34** (1–2), 65–79.
Bauer, J.M. (2014), 'Platforms, systems competition, and innovation: Reassessing the foundations of communications policy', *Telecommunications Policy*, **38** (8–9), 662–73.
Bauer, J.M. and E. Bohlin (2008), 'From static to dynamic regulation: Recent developments in US telecommunications policy', *Intereconomics: Review of European Economic Policy*, **43** (1), 38–50.
Bauer, J.M. and J.A. Obar (2014), 'Reconciling political and economic goals in the net neutrality debate', *The Information Society*, **30** (1), 1–19.
Bauer, J.M. and S.S. Wildman (2012), *The Economics of Usage-Based Pricing in Broadband Markets*, accessed 10 April 2015 at http://i.ncta.com/ncta_com/PDFs/Wildmanreport_web.pdf.
Bauer, S., D. Clark and W. Lehr (2009), 'The evolution of Internet congestion', paper presented at the 37th Research Conference on Communication, Information and Internet Policy, Arlington, VA, September, accessed 10 April 2015 at http://ssrn.com/abstract=1999830.
Benkler, Y. (2006), *The Wealth of Networks: How Social Production Transforms Markets and Freedom*, New Haven, CT: Yale University Press.
Bennett, R., L.E. Stewart and R.D. Atkinson (2013), *The Whole Picture: Where America's Broadband Networks Really Stand*, Washington, DC: The Information Technology & Innovation Foundation.
Besen, S., P. Milgrom, B.M. Mitchell and P. Srinagesh (2001), 'Advances in routing technologies and Internet peering agreements', *American Economic Review, Papers and Proceedings*, **91** (2), 292–6.
Blankart, C.B. and G. Knieps (1993), 'State and standards', *Public Choice*, **77** (1), 39–52.
Blankart, C.B., G. Knieps and P. Zenhäusern (2007), 'Regulation of new markets in telecommunications: Market dynamics and shrinking monopolistic bottlenecks', *European Business Organization Law Review (EBOR)*, **8** (3), 413–28.
Block, F. and M.R. Keller (eds) (2011), *State of Innovation: The U.S. Government's Role in Technology Development*, Boulder, CO and London: Paradigm Publishers.
Bourreau, M. and P. Doğan (2006), '"Build-or-buy" strategies in the local loop', *American Economic Review*, **96** (2), 72–6.
Bourreau, M., P. Doğan and M. Manant (2007), 'Modularity and product innovation in digital markets', *Review of Network Economics*, **6** (2), 175–93.
Brennan, T.J. (2011), 'Network neutrality or minimum quality standards: Network effects vs. market power justifications', in I. Spiecker and J. Krämer (eds), *Network Neutrality and Open Access*, Baden-Baden: Nomos, pp. 61–80.
Bresnahan, T.F. and M. Trajtenberg (1995), 'General purpose technologies: Engines of growth?', *Journal of Econometrics*, **65** (1), 83–108.
Briglauer, W., G. Ecker and K. Gugler (2013), 'The impact of infrastructure and service-based competition on the deployment of next generation access networks: Recent evidence from the European member states', *Information Economics and Policy*, **25** (3), 142–53.

Brynjolfsson, E. (2011), 'Innovation and the e-economy', unpublished paper, MIT, Sloan School of Management, October.

Brynjolfsson, E. and A. McAfee (2014), *The Second Machine Age: Work, Progress, and Prosperity in a Time of Brilliant Technologies*, New York: W.W. Norton & Company.

Cambini, C. and Y. Jiang (2009), 'Broadband investment and regulation: A literature review', *Telecommunications Policy*, **33** (10–11), 559–74.

Carlton, D.W. and J.M. Perloff (2005), *Modern Industrial Organization*, 4th edition, Reading, MA: Addison-Wesley.

Cave, M. and T. Shortall (2011), 'The extended gestation and birth of the European Commission's recommendation on the regulation of fibre networks', *Info*, **13** (5), 3–18.

Chen, J.-C. and T. Zhang (2004), *IP-Based Next-Generation Wireless Networks: Systems, Architectures, and Protocols*, Hoboken, NJ: John Wiley & Sons.

Choi, J.P. and B.-C. Kim (2010), 'Net neutrality and investment incentives', *RAND Journal of Economics*, **41** (3), 446–71.

Church, J. and N. Gandal (2005), 'Platform competition in telecommunications', in S.K. Majumdar, I. Vogelsang and M.E. Cave (eds), *Handbook of Telecommunications Economics, Volume 2: Technology Evolution and the Internet*, Amsterdam: Elsevier, pp. 117–53.

claffy, kc and D.D. Clark (2014), 'Platform models for sustainable internet regulation', *Journal of Information Policy*, **4**, 463–88.

Clark, D.D., W. Lehr and S. Bauer et al. (2006), 'Overlay networks and the future of the Internet', *Communications & Strategies*, **63** (3), 1–21.

Comer, D.E. (2006), *Internetworking with TCP/IP Principles, Protocols and Architecture*, 5th edition, Englewood Cliffs, NJ: Pearson.

Crémer, J. and C. Hariton (1999), 'The pricing of critical applications in the Internet', *Journal of the Japanese and International Economies*, **13** (4), 281–310.

Crémer, J., P. Rey and J. Tirole (2000), 'Connectivity in the commercial Internet', *Journal of Industrial Economics*, **48** (4), 433–72.

David, P.A. (1985), 'Clio and the economics of QWERTY', *American Economic Review*, **75** (2), 332–7.

David, P.A. and J.A. Bunn (1988), 'The economics of gateway technologies and network evolution: Lessons from electricity supply history', *Information Economics and Policy*, **3** (2), 144–65.

Dorogovtsev, S.N. and J.F.F. Mendes (2003), *Evolution of Networks: From Biology to the Internet and WWW*, Oxford, UK: Oxford University Press.

Easley, D. and J. Kleinberg (2010), *Networks, Crowds, and Markets: Reasoning About a Highly Connected World*, Cambridge, MA: Cambridge University Press.

Economides, N. (1996), 'The economics of networks', *International Journal of Industrial Organization*, **14** (6), 673–99.

Economides, N. (2001), 'The Microsoft antitrust case', *Journal of Industry, Competition and Trade*, **1** (1), 7–39.

Economides, N. (2005), 'The economics of the Internet backbone', in S.K. Majumdar, I. Vogelsang and M. Cave (eds), *Handbook of Telecommunications Economics, Volume 2: Technology Evolution and the Internet*, Amsterdam: Elsevier, pp. 375–410.

Economides, N. (2008), '"Net neutrality", non-discrimination and digital distribution of content through the Internet', *I/S: A Journal of Law and Policy for the Information Society*, **4** (2), 209–33.

Egan, B.L. (1996), *Information Superhighways Revisited: The Economics of Multimedia*, Boston, MA and London: Artech House.

Ehrlich, E.M., J.A. Eisenach and W.A. Leighton (2010), 'The impact of regulation on innovation and choice in wireless communications', *Review of Network Economics*, **9** (1).

European Commission (1998), *Commission Decision of 8 July 1998 declaring a concentration to be compatible with the common market and the functioning of the EEA Agreement, Case IV/M.1069-WorldCom/MCI, C(1998) 1887 final–EN*, accessed 4 June 2015 at http://ec.europa.eu/competition/mergers/cases/decisions/m1069_19980708_600_en.pdf.

Evans, D.S. and R. Schmalensee (2007), 'Antitrust analysis of multi-sided platforms: The industrial organization of markets with two-sided platforms', *Competition Policy International*, **3** (1), 151–79.

Faratin, P., D. Clark and S. Bauer et al. (2008), 'The growing complexity of internet interconnection', *Communications & Strategies*, **72** (4), 51–71.

Farrell, J. and G. Saloner (1986), 'Standardization and variety', *Economic Letters*, **20** (1), 71–4.

Farrell, J. and P.J. Weiser (2003), 'Modularity, vertical integration, and open access policies: Towards a convergence of antitrust and regulation in the Internet Age', *Harvard Journal of Law and Technology*, **17**(1), 85–134.

FCC (2008), 'In the matter of formal complaint of free press and public knowledge against Comcast Corporation for secretly degrading peer-to-peer applications', *EB-08-IH-1518 (FCC 08-183)*, *Memorandum Opinion and Order*, adopted 1 August 2008, Washington, DC: Federal Communications Commission.

FCC (2015), 'In the matter of protecting and promoting the open Internet, report and order on remand, declaratory ruling, and order', *GN Docket No. 14–28*, adopted 26 February, Washington, DC: Federal Communications Commission.

Fisher, F.M. (2000a), 'Antitrust and innovative industries', *Antitrust Law Journal*, **68** (2), 559–64.

Fisher, F.M. (2000b), 'The IBM and Microsoft cases: What's the difference?', *American Economic Review, Papers and Proceedings*, **90** (2), 180–83.

Fisher, F.M., J.J. McGowan and J.E. Greenwood (1983), *Folded, Spindled and Mutilated: Economic Analysis and U.S. v. IBM*, Cambridge, MA: MIT Press.

Fransman, M. (2010), *The New ICT Ecosystem: Implications for Policy and Regulation*, Cambridge, UK: Cambridge University Press.

Gans, J.S., S.B. King and J. Wright (2005), 'Wireless communications', in S.K. Majumdar, I. Vogelsang and M. Cave (eds), *Handbook of Telecommunications Economics, Volume 2: Technology Evolution and the Internet*, Amsterdam: Elsevier, pp. 241–85.

Gawer, A. and M.A. Cusumano (2002), *Platform Leadership: How Intel, Microsoft, and Cisco Drive Industry Innovation*, Boston, MA: Harvard Business School Press.

Geroski, P.A. (1998), 'Thinking creatively about markets', *International Journal of Industrial Organization*, **16** (6), 677–95.

Gottinger, H.-W. (2003), *Economies of Networks*, London: Routledge.

Greenstein, S. (2005), 'The economic geography of Internet infrastructure in the United States', in S. Majumdar, I. Vogelsang and M. Cave (eds), *Handbook of Telecommunications Economics, Volume 2: Technology Evolution and the Internet*, Amsterdam: Elsevier, pp. 287–372.

Greenstein, S. (2009), 'A network of platforms', *Micro Economics*, **29**(6), 2–3, accessed 10 December 2015 at https://www.computer.org/csdl/mags/mi/2009/06/mmi2009060002.pdf.

Greenstein, S. (2012a), 'Internet infrastructure', in M. Peitz and J. Waldfogel (eds), *The Oxford Handbook of the Digital Economy*, Oxford, UK: Oxford University Press, pp. 3–32.

Greenstein, S. (2012b), *The Lexicon of Network Economics in Evolving Markets: An Applied Guide*, accessed 23 April 2015 at http://cis.ier.hit-u.ac.jp/English/society/111206ws.pdf.

Greenstein, S. (2015), *How the Internet Became Commercial: Innovation, Privatization, and the Birth of a New Network*, Princeton, NJ: Princeton University Press.

Gruber, H. and P. Koutroumpis (2013), 'Competition enhancing regulation and diffusion of innovation: The case of broadband networks', *Journal of Regulatory Economics*, **43** (2), 168–95.

Hagiu, A. and J. Wright (2011), 'Multi-sided platforms', *Working Paper No. 12–024*, Harvard Business School.

Hayek, F.A. ([1968] 2002), 'Der Wettbewerb als Entdeckungsverfahren', *Kieler Vorträge gehalten im Institut für Weltwirtschaft an der Universität Kiel, Neue Folge 56*, Kiel, reprinted as 'Competition as a discovery procedure', trans. Marcellus S. Snow, *The Quarterly Journal of Austrian Economics*, **5**(3), 9–23.

Helpman, E. (ed.) (1998), *General Purpose Technologies and Economic Growth*, Cambridge, MA: MIT Press.

Hoernig, S. and T. Valletti (2012), 'Mobile telephony', in M. Peitz and J. Waldfogel (eds), *The Oxford Handbook of the Digital Economy*, Oxford, UK: Oxford University Press, pp. 136–59.

ITU (2014), *The State of Broadband 2014: Broadband for All. A Report by the Broadband Commission*, Geneva: International Telecommunication Union.

Jackson, M.O. (2008), *Social and Economic Networks*, Princeton, NJ, Princeton University Press.

Jacobson, V. (1988), 'Congestion avoidance and control', in *Proceedings of SIGCOMM '88*, August, ACM, Stanford, CA.

Katz, M.L. and C. Shapiro (1994), 'Systems competition and network effects', *Journal of Economic Perspectives*, **8** (2), 93–115.

Katz, M.L. and C. Shapiro (1998), 'Antitrust in software markets', prepared for presentation at the Progress and Freedom Foundation conference, 'Competition, Convergence and the Microsoft Monopoly', 5 February 1998.

Katz, M.L. and C. Shapiro (1999), 'Antitrust in software markets', in J.A. Eisenach and T.M. Lenard (eds), *Competition, Innovation and the Microsoft Monopoly: Antitrust in the Digital Marketplace*, Boston, MA: Kluwer Academic Publishers, pp. 29–81.

Klein, J.A. and P.M. Rao (2014), 'Competition and consumer protection in the cyberspace market place', paper presented at the 20th Biennial Conference of the International Telecommunications Society, Rio de Janeiro, Brazil, November, accessed 13 July 2015 at http://econpapers.repec.org/paper/zbwitsb14/106857.htm.

Knieps, G. (1997a), 'Phasing out sector-specific regulation in competitive telecommunications', *Kyklos*, **50** (3), 325–39.

Knieps, G. (1997b), 'The concept of open network provision in large technical systems', in M. Holler and E. Niskanen (eds), *EURAS Yearbook of Standardization, Volume 1*, Munich: Accedo, pp. 357–69.

Knieps, G. (2003), 'Competition in telecommunications and Internet services: A dynamic perspective', in C.E. Barfield, G. Heiduk and P.J.J. Welfens (eds), *Internet, Economic Growth and Globalization: Perspectives on the New Economy in Europe, Japan and the US*, Berlin: Springer, pp. 217–27.

Knieps, G. (2011), 'Network neutrality and the evolution of the Internet', *International Journal of Management and Network Economics*, **2** (1), 24–38.

Knieps, G. (2015a), *Network Economics: Principles–Strategies–Competition Policy*, Cham, Switzerland: Springer.

Knieps, G. (2015b), 'Entrepreneurial traffic management and the Internet Engineering Task Force', *Journal of Competition Law & Economics*, **11** (3), 727–45 (first published online 9 July, DOI: 10.1093/joclec/nhv018).

Knieps, G. and V. Stocker (2015), 'Network neutrality regulation: The fallacies of regulatory market splits', *Intereconomics*, **50** (1) 46–51.

Knieps, G. and P. Zenhäusern (2008), 'The fallacies of network neutrality regulation', *Competition and Regulation in Network Industries*, **9** (2), 119–34.

Knieps, G. and P. Zenhäusern (2015), 'Broadband network evolution and path dependency', in: *Competition and Regulation in Network Industries*, **16** (4), 335–53.

Krämer, J., L. Wiewiorra and C. Weinhardt (2013), 'Net neutrality: A progress report', *Telecommunications Policy*, **37** (9), 794–813.

Laffont, J.-J. and J. Tirole (2000), *Competition in Telecommunications*, Cambridge, MA: MIT Press.

Laffont, J.-J., S. Marcus, P. Rey and J. Tirole (2001), 'Internet peering', *American Economic Review, Papers and Proceedings*, **91** (2), 287–91.

Langlois, R.N. (2002), 'Modularity in technology and organization', *Journal of Economic Behavior and Organization*, **49** (1), 19–37.

Lee, R.S. and T. Wu (2009), 'Subsidizing creativity through network design: Zero-pricing and net neutrality', *Journal of Economic Perspectives*, **23** (3), 61–76.

Lemley, M.A. and L. Lessig (2001), 'The end of end-to-end: Preserving the architecture of the Internet in the broadband era', *UCLA Law Review*, **48** (4), 925–72.

Liebowitz, S.J. and S.E. Margolis (1990), 'The fable of the keys', *Journal of Law and Economics*, **33** (1), 1–25.

Liebowitz, S.J. and S.E. Margolis (1996), 'Should technological choice be a concern of antitrust policy?', *Harvard Journal of Law & Technology*, **9** (2), 283–318.

Liebowitz, S.J. and S.E. Margolis (2003), 'Network effects', in M.E. Cave, S.K. Majumdar and I. Vogelsang (eds), *Handbook of Telecommunications Economics*, Amsterdam: Elsevier, pp. 75–96.

MacKie-Mason, J.K. and H.R. Varian (1995a), 'Pricing congestible network resources', *IEEE Journal on Selected Areas in Communications*, **13** (7), 1141–9.

MacKie-Mason, J.K. and H.R. Varian (1995b), 'Pricing the Internet', in W. Sichel and D.L. Alexander (eds), *Public Access to the Internet*, Cambridge, MA: MIT Press, pp. 269–314.

MacKie-Mason, J.K., L. Murphy and J. Murphy (1997), 'Responsive pricing in the Internet', in L.W. McKnight and J.P. Bailey (eds), *Internet Economics*, Cambridge, MA: MIT Press, pp. 279–303.

Majumdar, S.K., I. Vogelsang and M.E. Cave (eds) (2005), *Handbook of Telecommunications Economics, Volume 2: Technology Evolution and the Internet*, Amsterdam: Elsevier.

Mayntz, R. and T.P. Hughes (eds) (1988), *The Development of Large Technical Systems*, Frankfurt am Main: Campus.

Mazzucato, M. (2013), *The Entrepreneurial State: Debunking Public vs. Private Sector Myth*, London: Anthem Press.

Mueller, M.L. (2010), *Networks and States: The Global Politics of Internet Governance*, Cambridge, MA: MIT Press.

Noam, E.M. (2001), *Interconnecting the Network of Networks*, Cambridge, MA: MIT Press.

OECD (2013), *Communications Outlook 2013*, Paris: OECD Publishing.

OECD (2014), 'The development of fixed broadband networks', *OECD Digital Economy Papers, No. 239*, Paris: OECD Publishing.

Odlyzko, A. (2014), 'Will smart pricing finally take off?', in S. Sen, C. Joe-Wong, S. Ha and M. Chiang (eds), *Smart Data Pricing*, New York: John Wiley & Sons, pp. 3–33.

Oren, S.S. and S.A. Smith (1981), 'Critical mass and tariff structure in electronic communications markets', *Bell Journal of Economics*, **12** (2), 467–87.

Peitz, M. and J. Waldfogel (eds) (2012), *The Oxford Handbook of the Digital Economy*, Oxford, UK: Oxford University Press.

Pigou, A.C. (1920), *The Economics of Welfare*, London: Macmillan.

Posner, R.A. (2000), 'Antitrust in the new economy', *University of Chicago Law & Economics, Olin Working Paper No. 106*.

Rappoport, P.N., D.J. Kridel, L.D. Taylor, J.H. Alleman and K.T. Duffy-Deno (2003), 'Residential demand for access to the Internet', in G. Madden (ed.), *Emerging Telecommunications Networks. The International Handbook of Telecommunications Economics, Volume II*, Cheltenham, UK and Northampton, MA, USA: Edward Elgar Publishing, pp. 55–72.

Rochet, J.-C. and J. Tirole (2006), 'Two-sided markets: A progress report', *RAND Journal of Economics*, **35** (3), 645–67.

Rohlfs, J. (1974), 'A theory of interdependent demand for a communications service', *The Bell Journal of Economics and Management Science*, **5** (1), 16–37.

Rosston, G.L., S.J. Savage and D.M. Waldman (2011), 'Household demand for broadband Internet in 2010', *The B.E. Journal of Economic Analysis & Policy*, **10** (1), Article 59.

Rysman, M. (2009), 'The economics of two-sided markets', *Journal of Economic Perspectives*, **23** (3), 125–43.

Saltzer, J.H., D.P. Reed and D.D. Clark (1984), 'End-to-end arguments in system design', *ACM Transactions on Computer Systems (TOCS)*, **2** (4), 277–88.

Scherer, F.M. and D. Ross (1990), *Industrial Market Structure and Economic Performance*, 3rd edition, Boston, MA: Houghton Mifflin.

Schuett, F. (2010), 'Network neutrality: A survey of the economic literature', *Review of Network Economics*, **9** (2), 1–13.

Schumpeter, J.A. (1934), *The Theory of Economic Development: An Inquiry Into Profits, Capital Credit, Interest, and the Business Cycle*, Cambridge, MA: Harvard University Press.

Schwartz, M. and P.J. Weiser (2009), 'Introduction to a special issue on network neutrality', *Review of Network Economics*, **8**(1), 1–12.

Shapiro, C. and H.R. Varian (1999), *Information Rules: A Strategic Guide to the Network Economy*, Boston, MA: Harvard Business School Press.

Shortall, T. and M. Cave (2015), 'Is symmetric access regulation a policy choice? Evidence from the deployment of NGA in Europe', *Communications & Strategies*, **98**, 1–26.

Shy, O. (2001), *The Economics of Network Industries*, Cambridge, UK and New York: Cambridge University Press.

Sidak, J.G. and D.J. Teece (2010), 'Innovation spillovers and the "dirt road" fallacy: The intellectual bankruptcy of banning optional transactions for enhanced delivery over the Internet', *Journal of Competition Law & Economics*, **6** (3) 521–94.

Simcoe, T. (2012), 'Standard setting committees: Consensus governance for shared technology platforms', *American Economic Review*, **102** (1), 305–36.

Tanenbaum, A.S. and D.J. Wetherall (2011), *Computer Networks*, 5th edition, Boston, MA: Prentice Hall.

Tirole, J. (1988), *The Theory of Industrial Organization*, Cambridge, MA: MIT Press.

Tripathi, N.D. and J.H. Reed (2014), *Cellular Communications: A Comprehensive and Practical Guide*, Hoboken, NJ: John Wiley & Sons.

Vanberg, M. (2009), *Competition and Cooperation among Internet Service Providers: A Network Economic Analysis*, Baden-Baden: Nomos.

van Schewick, B. (2010), *Internet Architecture and Innovation*, Cambridge, MA: MIT Press.

Whitt, R.S. (2007), 'Adaptive policymaking: Evolving and applying emergent solutions for U.S. communications policy', *Federal Communications Law Journal*, **61**(3), 483–589.

Wu, T. (2003), 'Network neutrality and broadband discrimination', *Journal on Telecommunication & High Technology Law*, **2** (1), 141–79.

Yoo, C.S. (2013), 'Protocol layering and Internet policy', *University of Pennsylvania Law Review*, **161** (6), 1707–71.

Zhao, R., W. Fischer, E. Aker and P. Rigby (2014), 'Creating a brighter future: Broadband access technologies', White Paper, Brussels, FTTH Council, accessed 23 August 2015 at http://www.ftthcouncil.eu/documents/Publications/DandO_White_Paper_2_2013_Final.pdf.

Zittrain, J. (2008), *The Future of the Internet and How to Stop It*, New Haven, CT: Yale University Press.

3. The Internet as a complex layered system*
Stephen J. Schultze and Richard S. Whitt

3.1 INTRODUCTION

Mainstream discussions of Internet economics often rely on assumptions that were already seriously in doubt by the middle of the twentieth century. As it turns out, the rise of new economic thinking, along with new technology platforms culminating in the Internet, directly challenge many of those chief assumptions. In this chapter, we examine two features of the Internet – that it is a 'complex adaptive system', and that it is a layered, end-to-end platform – and we describe the effect of these features on our understanding of the economics of this unique network.

Twenty years ago, no one would have anticipated the Internet as we know it today. Consumer-grade computer modems were still in their infancy, and the few dial-up online communities that existed were a far cry from the globally connected 'network of networks' that now pervades so much of what we do. In many ways, the Internet was a happy accident. What started out as isolated islands – universities, bulletin board systems, and commercial services – linked together and grew unexpectedly as the result of the actions of millions of unaffiliated people. The underlying software protocols opened up the ability to interact and speak freely across thousands of interconnected networks.

Even with the benefit of hindsight, traditional economics does not allow us to fully understand what led to this success. The digitization of information, dramatic increases in computing power, and declines in the cost of computer storage were all necessary conditions. Nevertheless, they alone are insufficient to explain how the Internet exploded into the thriving marketplace of innovation and economic growth that now pervades the daily life of an increasing number of individuals and organizations worldwide.

Many have tried to explain these phenomena in the language of traditional economic theory. We begin by describing some of the principles of neoclassical economics, and suggest ways in which it fails to fully capture the Internet's dynamics and growth. We then outline the wave of new economic thinking referred to as 'complexity economics', and discuss how it helps to explain why highly networked systems often experience explosive growth. We show that the Internet can properly be understood as a complex adaptive system that also possesses a layered, end-to-end architecture – making it exceptionally well suited to promoting cascades of innovation.

3.2 NEOCLASSICAL ECONOMICS IN PERSPECTIVE

In this section, we describe some of the principles of neoclassical economic theory, with two caveats. First, our characterization is a necessarily simplified version of a diverse body of work that does not always fit into neat categories. Second, our characterization emphasizes principles that have evolved significantly in recent years in reaction to, among

other things, some of the subsequent thinking that we describe. Nevertheless, the principles that we describe below arise out of a fundamentally different way of understanding
economic activity than prevails to varying degrees today.

Neoclassical economics generally tries to understand economies by way of models
that posit rational actors interacting through competition, reaching equilibrium in which
supply and demand intersect in an optimally efficient manner. As more complications to
the operations of real-world markets became evident, this strain of economics developed
ever-more complicated models to compensate. A chief critique of this trajectory of thinking has been that as models increasingly rely on esoteric mathematics, they more easily
diverge from reality. Even as they become more complicated, they maintain reductionist
assumptions and even introduce new abstractions. This issue alone is not cause enough
to reject what has become mainstream economic theory, but closer scrutiny of its foundational principles in the context of the Internet era yields sufficient reason for realignment.
The neoclassical line of reasoning proceeds from its traditional roots in Adam Smith and
Léon Walras to transitional figures like Kenneth Arrow, Friedrich A. Hayek and – in
retrospect – Joseph Schumpeter.

3.2.1 Market Equilibrium

Neoclassical economic theory states that the economy is a static equilibrium system, existing at rest, and moving from one equilibrium point to another as it seeks balance. Under
this view, the economy is a closed system (Taylor, 2004, pp. 239–40). Neoclassical theory
sees an 'invisible hand' – as first articulated by Adam Smith in 1776 – at work in competitive markets. In such a free market, supply equals demand, resources are put to their
most efficient use, and the resulting balance optimizes social welfare. Economic processes
are dominated by dampening, negative feedback that keeps things contained. The theory
typically assumes indeterminacy away by means of econometric models (Ormerod, 2005,
pp. 79–80). The business cycle of boom and bust is determined *exogenously* – that is, by
occasional shocks originating from *outside* the system itself. Léon Walras, champion of
economic equilibrium theory, famously noted, 'For, just as a lake is, at times, stirred to its
very depths by a storm, so also the market is sometimes thrown into violent confusion by
crises, which are sudden and general disturbances of equilibrium' ([1874] 1954).

The idea that the market tends toward optimally efficient equilibrium runs head-
long into reality. Lawrence Summers (1986) has noted that careful analysis, 'call[s] into
question the theoretical as well as empirical underpinnings of the Efficient Market
Hypothesis'. Shiller et al. (1984) claim that, 'the efficient markets hypothesis represents
one of the most remarkable errors in the history of economic thought'. These critics
decry the inapt metaphor appropriated from the Industrial Revolution – the economy as
a human-made machine like a steam engine, whose behavior is fixed, stable, predictable,
and controllable (Axelrod and Cohen, 2001, pp. 28–31).

3.2.2 Perfect Competition

According to the traditional view of economic dynamics, 'perfect competition' compels
free markets to allocate scarce resources in the most efficient manner possible. In this
view, perfect competition will allow free markets to squeeze as many useful goods and

services as possible out of the available resources (maximal output at minimal prices); anything that interferes with the price system's ability to do so is a detriment to social well-being (Case, 2007). When the supply of every traded good or service is precisely equal to the demand for it at prevailing prices, the economy rests in perfect equilibrium. The theory sees diversity of products, locally contingent factors, and variation in motivation of market actors as all interfering with this idealized state of affairs.

Unfortunately for this theory, competition is rarely, if ever, perfect. The theory posits an inherently top-down view of the world, in which the market conditions are static, and the actors all play by the same set of rules. As Friedrich A. Hayek observed, 'When we deal, however, with a situation in which a number of persons are attempting to work out their separate plans, we can no longer assume that the data are the same for all the planning minds' (1948, p. 93). Indeed, these market actors are shaping the market from the inside out through their individual goals, innovations, and connections with others.

3.2.3 Rational Actors

In traditional neoclassical economics, individuals rationally pursue their self-interest on the basis of utility. For decades, many economists assumed that people are 'representative agents' who are perfectly rational and consistent in their behaviors (Hartley, 1997). This casts agents as *homo economicus* (Thaler, 2000). University of Chicago professor Frank Knight stated emphatically in 1946 that economics must assume that actors possess 'rational and errorless choice, presupposing perfect foresight' and 'foreknowledge free from uncertainty' (cited in Parker, 2005, p. 197).

In the real world, barriers to decision-making almost always exist. Information is costly, incomplete, and rapidly changing. At best, we employ bounded rationality, by making decisions in the face of obvious constraints and motivations. Ormerod observes that every individual decision involves massive complexity and defies the orderly application of the rational calculations of traditional economic theory (2005, p. 125). That is not to say that market participants are not acting 'rationally' in the colloquial sense, but rather that they do not uniformly follow a single deterministic set of rules.

3.2.4 Abstract Models

Traditional economic theory has proven inadequate in terms of the two standard criteria for a scientific theory: prediction and explanation. The theory's models often use simplifying and highly restrictive assumptions. Famously, Milton Friedman has insisted that unrealistic assumptions in economic theory do not matter so long as the theories make correct predictions (1953, pp. 30–31).

Such optimism seems misplaced. Assumptions must be appropriate for the purpose of the model, and must not affect the answers the model provides for that purpose. In econometrics, statistical correlations do not provide a causal explanation of the phenomena, and assumption without verifiable explanation is mere faith. As Philip Ball (2006, p. 181) explains: 'economic models have been augmented, refined, garlanded, and decorated with baroque accoutrements. Some of these models now rival those constructed by physicists in their mathematical sophistication. Yet they still lack their "Newtonian" first principles: basic laws on which everyone agrees'.

3.2.5   The Turn to Innovation Economics and Endogenous Growth

By the middle of the twentieth century, certain economists had turned their attention to the source of economic growth, reframing Adam Smith's 'invisible hand' hypothesis in the context of entrepreneurial innovation. Whereas Smith theorized that firm efficiencies would lead to optimally efficient pricing, these economists pondered why markets often grow beyond this in bursts that defy the predictions of static equilibrium. Joseph Schumpeter, an unorthodox Austrian economist, pointed out that often one firm battles another in order to unseat it in a process he called 'creative destruction'. He observed that the critical advantage of a winning new entrant is its improved technology. Through this process, innovations occur in a stair-step fashion rather than a continuous line. These innovations spur fundamentally new ways of producing wealth rather than incrementally improving efficiency (Schumpeter [1942] 1976).

Much of economic growth theory has focused on how best to encourage development of these technologies – with 'technology' defined broadly to mean any innovative means of production or organization. Robert Solow (2007) observed that Schumpeter:

> [. . .] worked out his conception of the entrepreneur, the maker of 'new combinations,' as the driving force and characteristic figure of the fits-and-starts evolution of the capitalist economy. He was explicit that, while technological innovation was in the long run the most important function of the entrepreneur, organizational innovation in governance, finance, and management was comparable in significance . . . I think that this is Schumpeter's main legacy to economics: the role of technological and organizational innovation in driving and shaping the growth trajectory of capitalist economies.

Schumpeter's insight would nevertheless lie somewhat dormant until the 1980s, when a new generation of economists began to consider where these innovations came from. Traditionally, economists thought of production in terms of land, labor, and capital. They assumed that human knowledge and new ideas were factors outside of the economic model. In 1990, then-unheralded economist Paul Romer released a paper in which he concluded that the new factors of production should be classified as people, ideas, and things (Romer, 1990). Most importantly, new ideas emerged from the economic actors themselves – an activity that is *internal* or *endogenous* to the economy. This helped to spawn 'new growth theory'. This theory indicates that the fastest-growing economies are those that feed ideas back into the system, allowing others to adopt, adapt, and innovate in a way that multiplies productivity (Warsh, 2006).

3.2.6   Internet Economics as Evolutionary and Generative

We now live in a highly networked economy, formed bottom-up by interactions between individuals in a globally connected marketplace. Some basic rules govern these interactions, but for the most part the system emerges freely and unpredictably. Economic actors become nodes of growth, and the structure of the market evolves based on their collective practices. Whereas neoclassical economics defined these relationships statically, the Internet economy thrives on experimental evolution. New ideas emerge and technologies are constantly refined. In section 3.3 we describe this as an instance of a 'complex adaptive system'.

The mechanism for growth is innovation, and these innovations serve as a platform for further growth. While neoclassical economics tells us that productivity comes simply from adding more capital or generating greater efficiency, we now see that new technologies are essentially better recipes for production. Economists use the phrase 'virtuous circle' to describe systems that contain such positive feedback loops. Rather than moving toward equilibrium, these economies are self-reinforcing and have the potential to multiply their effects. The Internet – its software protocols, social norms, and polycentric governance – is structured in such a way that innovators are free to make use of this 'generative' platform in unexpected ways (Zittrain, 2008). In section 3.4, we describe how this platform facilitates highly productive interactions within and between different 'layers'.

Yet, the dynamics present in the Internet economy are not entirely new – particularly in the case of communications-based technology sectors. Indeed, 'the forces at work in network industries in the 1990s are very similar to those that confronted the telephone and wireless industries in the 1890s' (Varian et al., 2004, p. 3). Many of the elements at play in today's economy have been present to some extent for decades, but are becoming dominant in the highly networked Internet economy.

3.3   THE INTERNET AS A COMPLEX ADAPTIVE SYSTEM

By the late 1970s a community of economists had begun grappling with the role of 'complexity' in the field of economics. These scholars distinguish complex systems from merely 'complicated' systems, explaining that it is not possible to understand the whole simply by better grasping each of the parts. As Miller and Page (2007, p. 27) note: 'As the parts begin to connect with one another and interact more . . . we move from the realm of complication to complexity, and reduction no longer gives us insight into construction'.

The Austrian critique of neoclassical equilibrium, initiated by thinkers like Hayek, paved the way for economists to consider theories in which diverse economic agents interact in this complex and networked fashion (Koppl, 2009). In recent years, 'neo-Schumpeterian' approaches have emphasized the evolutionary nature of these dynamics (Langlois and Everett, 1994).

A group of scholars affiliated with the Santa Fe Institute have done much of the seminal work in this area. This interdisciplinary group of thinkers draws heavily from biological and evolutionary models in order to inform their approach to economics. The canonical output of their thinking is catalogued in a three-part series of edited volumes entitled *The Economy as an Evolving Complex System* (Anderson et al., 1988; Arthur et al., 1997; Blume and Durlauf, 2006).

Eric Beinhocker has summarized these developments as what he calls simply 'complexity economics' (2006). In place of traditional economics' conventional wisdom of equilibrium and the market's 'invisible hand', Beinhocker emphasizes a notion of 'fitness functions'. Various emergent structures may be more or less fit for the environment and the task at hand. The best chance of finding good fitness functions lies in leaving the emergent system open to subsequent experimentation, adaptation, and emergence.

Holland and Miller describe economies that function as 'complex adaptive systems' consisting of a 'network of interacting agents' that exhibit 'a dynamic, aggregate behavior that emerges from the individual activities of the agents'. Each of these agents 'behaves so as to increase this value over time' – that is, their behavior evolves (1991, p. 365).

In the following four subsections, we describe these essential characteristics of complex adaptive systems and give examples of how the Internet exhibits each.

3.3.1   Agents

Agents are economic actors, and they are individual nodes in a network. Whether acting as consumers or investors, CEOs or government officials, all of us play this interactive role in the economy. The term *agent* is preferred to either *consumer* or *user*, both of which tend to reduce humans to a one-way transactional relationship.

Whereas the usual economic model of human behavior posits 'incredibly smart people in unbelievably simple situations' (Leijonhufvud, 1996), the agent-based view admits that we have diverse motivations and limited knowledge. We are not 'homogeneous billiard balls or gas molecules' (Taylor, 2004, p. 273). We have a variety of motivations, including those that are non-pecuniary and non-proprietary (Benkler, 2008, pp. 460–73). We utilize not just reason but imagination, intuition, and creativity. We are altruistic, cooperative, and sharing creatures. We can use intelligent action to 'tip' the world in certain directions. Perhaps most importantly, we learn – that is, we have 'evolved the adaptation of adaptability' (Shermer, 2008, p. 190).

Agents throughout the Internet ecosystem exhibit these characteristics. The billions of humans that use the network daily each have their own motivations and adaptive ways of achieving their goals. This includes a tremendous amount of creating and sharing of culture in a participatory fashion that was far more difficult in one-way broadcast media. Likewise, adaptation on the Internet is cheap relative to markets that are constrained by physical commodities. Start-ups can try, fail, and adapt in a matter of weeks. The general purpose protocols at the heart of Internet software and hardware (which we discuss at more length in subsection 3.4) allow more entities to try their hand at being a productive agent – at any layer of the network.

3.3.2   Networks

Economic agents do not exist in a vacuum. The full productive potential of agents comes from their interactions with each other, which facilitate sharing of information and effort. Any particular agent may have a link to several other agents, who in turn link to others through lines of communication, common tasks, market agreements, or any number of other relationships. In the language of network science, the agents are 'nodes' and the links are 'edges'. The connections between agents can be unpredictable and ephemeral, helping to create complexity in the overall system. Network science explores how networks form and attempts to explain why certain dynamics in networks arise that do not appear in more static, linear systems (Johnson, 2001; Barabási, 2002; Watts, 2003).

In many systems, individual actors end up having indirect positive effects on others. Economists call these effects 'positive externalities' and often describe the benefits that accrue to others as 'spillovers' (Frischmann and Lemley, 2006). For example, I may invent a new method for scanning bar codes that yields me great profit, but you might adopt or adapt this technology to your own benefit (provided that the law allows). Furthermore, to the extent that different agents share this standard – say, a manufacturer using bar codes for inventory management and a retailer using the same codes to automate checkout – the system benefits exceed the sum of the parts, becoming 'network effects'. In complex networks, all of these benefits flow more freely than in disconnected islands. Each new node creates added value for the existing nodes.

These forces are strongly at work on the Internet, where new innovations are immediately available to the entire network of agents. An improvement in the core Internet Protocols benefits all users, and an app built on top of layers of others' work can grow exponentially overnight. This phenomenon is strikingly evident in the case of social networking tools like Facebook or with platforms like iOS or Android, but many of the same forces are at work throughout the Internet economy. The Internet's engineers understand that more complex systems like the Internet display more non-linearities, which occur (and are 'amplified') at large scales (Bush and Meyer, 2002). Moreover, more complex systems often exhibit increased interdependence between components, due to 'coupling' between or within protocol layers.

Arthur (2000, p. 1) notes that 'the network is the dominant pattern of the new digital economy', subject to increasing returns. This extends beyond the bounds of the Internet itself to all technologies touched by networked economic dynamics. In the language of neo-Schumpeterian evolutionism:

> A network is useful, increases efficiency and systemic performance, but is *altruistic* in the sense of 'systemic interests' . . . Networks are not institutions. The behavior of network units may be influenced by institutional parameters, but the emergent knowledge base of the network is basically *open* with regard to the *future*. (Dopfer, 1994, p. 154; original emphasis)

This helps to shift our focus from the 'firm' to the network-enabled configurations of and interactions between agents. Ronald Coase explained that firms are created in order to reduce transaction costs – the costs of finding and negotiating interactions with partners (1937). By bringing many entities together under a single umbrella, an organization can limit the transaction costs required. In complex networks, these units need not be literal 'firms', and the multitude of links can reduce transaction costs in a more dynamic fashion.

3.3.3   Evolution

To Schumpeter, 'the essential point to grasp is that in dealing with capitalism we are dealing with an evolutionary process' ([1942] 1976, pp. 82–3). '[Economics] is the study of how humans choose. That choice is inescapably a biological process' (Glimcher, 2004, p. 336). Evolution is the algorithm for change in economic systems (Vermeij, 2004), and the iterative process of experimentation by agents contributes to optimal growth. Hayek noted that markets involve the 'evolutionary formation' of 'highly complex self-maintaining orders' (1988, p. 9). Evolutionary economists use 'replicator dynamics' to represent how heterogeneous agents innovate, interact, and evolve in the Darwinian spirit of 'survival of the fittest' (Cantner, 2009).

On Beinhocker's analysis, the first step of evolution is 'differentiation', in which intelligent agents identify various possible approaches. Next, through experimentation, these agents sort through the variations in order to select the most fit solutions – to decide what works and what does not. Finally, the agents share and iterate on the most success-ful approaches, throwing out the others and amplifying the effects (2006, pp. 213–16). In other words, natural selection both 'weeds out' what fails and 'weeds in' ('nurtures') what works.

Complexity economists describe evolution as operating on 'technologies'. One way of viewing this is that evolution operates on two broad types of technologies, which Richard Nelson refers to as 'physical technologies' and 'social technologies' (Nelson, 2003). Physical technologies are means or recipes for producing objects or ideas; they consist of specifications, instructions, shareable practices, and other ways of transforming materials to serve a goal. These technologies have a modular, building-block character consisting of components and architecture. Social technologies, on the other hand, are methods and designs for organizing people in service of a goal, and instilling order in the social realm.

Technological breakthroughs can come from unexpected directions. Perhaps most important is the process of adaptive tinkering. Chance and accident produce such effi-cient systems that we often forget that their logic is often the result of non-linear trial and error. As Taleb has observed, 'The reason free markets work is because they allow people to be lucky, thanks to aggressive trial and error, not by giving rewards or "incentives" for skill. The strategy is, then, to tinker as much as possible' (2007, p. xxi).

The Internet has, at all layers, evolved according to such trial-and-error. The Internet Engineering Task Force (IETF) is an example of a flexible 'social technology' premised on 'rough consensus and running code' with input from anyone who cares to participate. The IETF generates 'physical technologies' in the form of specifications – some of which are adopted widely and survive as the 'fittest', and others that fail to gain adoption. Likewise, the Internet has served as a platform for tinkerers, innovators, and entrepre-neurs who constantly experiment with new business models. Amidst endogenous waves of boom and bust, transformative technologies and businesses emerge.

3.3.4   Emergence

Economic agents interact and evolve via networks, ultimately yielding macro systems – that is, emergence. The value generated by this emergent structure is more than the sum of its parts, and the fact that it is complex means that its form is hard to pin down or to predict. The scholarship on this phenomenon spans the physical sciences, social sciences, economics, and interdisciplinary studies (Holland, 1998; Johnson, 2001; Morowitz, 2002).

Emergent systems have no single ideal structure. They exist in an ever-changing envi-ronment and consist of complex interactions that continuously reshape their internal relationships. The many independent actions of agents unify, but they do not necessarily work toward one particular structure or equilibrium. For example, emergent systems can be robust to change, and they can be far better at evolving toward efficiency than top-down systems. On the other hand, emergent structures can fall apart when their basic conditions are altered in such a way that they work against the health of the system as a whole.

Agents' actions in turn affect the other agents, setting off both positive and negative feedback loops. Fortunately, we have developed some understanding of what types of conditions lead away from such negative feedback loops, and towards more productive emergence. Generally speaking, a greater ability of agents to connect and explore new modes of production will facilitate the chance connections that a top-down designer might not foresee. Better global information sharing and feedback between agents facilitates better local decisions. The system as a whole can leap forward when new innovations come out of this process and are replicated throughout the network. Inductive tinkering by a single agent can lead to breakthroughs with widespread payoff.

Emergent systems are often described as being organism-like. One canonical example is the ant colony. Each ant follows rules for when and how to forage, leaving pheromone trails to food. In one strikingly literal parallel to the Internet, a team of biologists and computer scientists found that harvester ants employ congestion control techniques that mirror those of the Internet's Transmission Control Protocol (TCP) (Prabhakar et al., 2012). Beyond this compelling anecdote of a real-world 'anternet', the Internet exhibits widespread emergent structure. For instance, the Border Gateway Protocol (BGP) that controls network routing at the core of the Internet relies on information passed on from neighbors, adapting dynamically to changes in network structure (with the help of human network operators when things go awry). The economic relationships between these interconnecting entities are the subject of constant individual negotiation and adaptation. Nevertheless, the Internet continues to function largely as a single unified network.

The Internet is not, however, merely the routing of traffic and the negotiation of interconnections. It is a modular, layered system, in which the core standards in the 'middle' of the Internet allow others to build on top of the network to create their own standards and applications. Applications may themselves facilitate follow-on innovation – technologically via something like an application programming interface (API) or simply as a matter of agents finding new ways of using a tool. For instance, Twitter relies on the emergent structure of the Internet – globally interconnected wired and wireless networks, protocols like HTTP, and the 'agent base' of millions of Internet users. Others have built on top of Twitter's API to create new applications, or have used it to establish new cultural practices or form political movements. The flexibility at the heart of the Internet is reflected to varying degrees in all of the technologies built on top of its core protocols. The more that these technologies permit evolution and experimentation, the more complex the emergent Internet becomes. At each layer, and within each layer, complex adaptive systems may develop and influence each other. In this sense, the Internet can be seen as a complex adaptive system of complex adaptive systems – a constellation of emergent structures.

3.4   THE INTERNET AS A LAYERED, END-TO-END PLATFORM

The Internet is a uniquely vast emergent system – a platform for untold forms of economic, social, and personal interaction. Holland and Miller note that 'complex adaptive systems usually operate far from a global optimum or attractor. Such systems exhibit many levels of aggregation, organization, and interaction, each level having its own time scale and characteristic behavior' (1991, p. 365). The Internet's technical and organizational architecture exhibits these types of distinct levels, and its layered structure is imbued with a set of guiding principles (Solum and Chung, 2003). This section discusses four fundamental architectural principles inherent in the Internet – principles that make it not only more complex, but also more likely to facilitate productive adaptation and experimentation. Engineers have created the Internet's architecture collaboratively over many years, with an eye to these principles. This architecture is what gives the Internet its exceptional value and ability to promote growth (Whitt, 2013).

The technical architecture of the Internet is at once simple and complex. The relatively simple Internet Protocol (IP) sits in the 'middle' of all Internet communications. Any device or application that connects to the Internet will ultimately have its communications translated into this lingua franca of the network. However, IP is highly extensible because it allows for new virtual protocols to be built 'above' its layer, or for new physical devices to implement ways to transport IP traffic 'below' its layer. Higher-layer protocols include HTTP (a standard for web traffic), and lower-layer protocols include Ethernet (a standard for wired devices). This is what makes up the so-called 'hourglass' structure of the Internet. As Bush and Meyer (2002) explain:

> In this model, the thin waist of the hourglass is envisioned as the (minimalist) IP layer, and any additional complexity is added above the IP layer. In short, the complexity of the Internet belongs at the edges, and the IP layer of the Internet should remain as simple as possible.

Organizationally, there is no single governing body or process that directs the development of the Internet's architecture. Instead, we have multiple bodies and processes of consensus. Much of the 'governance' of the Internet is carried out by so-called multistakeholder organizations, such as the Internet Society (ISOC), the World Wide Web Consortium (W3C), and the Internet Corporation for Assigned Names and Numbers (ICANN) (Sieh and Hatfield, 2012). Over the last two decades, although these entities have largely established the norms and standards for the global Internet, 'they are little known to the general public, and even to most regulators and legislators' (Waz and Weiser, 2012, p. 1). The IETF operates under the auspices of ISOC, and its stated goal is 'to make the Internet work better' (Alvestrand, 2004, p. 1). It is the institution that has developed the core networking protocols for the Internet, including IP, TCP, UDP (User Datagram Protocol), and countless others. The IETF is open to any interested individual, and conducts activities through working groups in various technical areas.

The IETF Requests for Comments (RFCs) were first established in April 1969 by Steve Crocker at UCLA. The memos were intended as an informal means of distributing shared ideas among network researchers on the ARPANET project, the precursor to the Internet. 'The effect of the RFCs was to create a positive feedback loop, so ideas or proposals presented in one RFC would trigger other RFCs' (Leiner et al., 1997). Once consensus came together within the IETF, a specification document would be created in order to serve as the basis for implementation by various research teams. Many RFCs have become de facto standards for core Internet Protocols. It is well established that:

> Internet Protocols not only serve critical technical functions but can have significant political and economic implications . . . The open publication of Internet standards with minimal intellectual property restrictions has enabled rapid innovation and has generally produced the market effect of full competition among companies developing products based on those standards. (DeNardis, 2010, p. 7)

Many scholars have attempted to articulate the principles embedded in the Internet's architecture (Bernbom, 2000; Barwolff, 2010; van Schewick, 2010; Doria, 2011). RFC 1958 provides perhaps the best workable foundation: 'In very general terms, the community believes that the goal is connectivity, the tool is the Internet Protocol, and the intelligence is end to end rather than hidden in the network' (Carpenter, 1996). It is likewise clear that 'modularity' – or layering – is the logical scaffolding that makes it all work together.

3.4.1 Modularity

The use of layering means that functional tasks are divided up and assigned to different software-based protocol levels. For example, the 'physical' layers of the network govern how electrical signals are carried over physical wiring. Independently, the 'transport' layers deal with how data packets are routed to their correct destinations, and what they look like. The 'application' layers control how those packets are used by an email program, web browser, or other user application or service.

This simple and flexible system creates a network of modular 'building blocks' that can be adapted and evolved. Applications or protocols at higher layers can be developed or modified with little impact on lower layers, while lower layers can adopt new transmission and switching technologies without requiring changes to upper layers. Innovations at each layer are thus unconstrained and independent, while at the same time being interdependent on the functions of the other layers. Therefore, it is important that there exist stable interfaces between the layers, and that a particular bug or feature be addressed at the appropriate layer. Computer engineers call this type of segmented functionality 'abstraction'. In the case of the Internet, this approach has facilitated tremendous experimentation and innovation throughout the system.

The Internet succeeded where other attempts at large-scale networks failed. Not only did the Internet overtake commercial ventures like AOL, CompuServe, and Prodigy, it proved far more amenable to adaptation than similarly situated governmental initiatives. By the early 1980s, the French government had launched a project called 'Minitel', which sought to establish a nationally networked system of personal computers. Each device would call in to a set of centralized 'Kiosques', while France Telecom billed for usage. Five million Minitel units were distributed free of charge to citizens and businesses, and the system became pervasive in French society. However, as Alcouffe and Alcouffe (2009, p. 213) note:

> As successful as the widespread acceptance of the Minitel was, it effectively set a new technological standard that was not open to competitors. This locked in a technology that failed to keep up with other technological developments such as packet-switching protocols (e.g. TCP/IP) and protocols that are broadly interoperable across a wide variety of communication service providers with other network providers.

In the language of complexity economics, Minitel simply did not allow enough evolutionary experimentation. In the language of Internet engineering, it was unitary and monolithic rather than modular and layered. By the 1990s Minitel was rapidly losing ground to the Internet, and it was finally shut down on 30 June 2012.

In all engineering-based models of the Internet, the fundamental point is that the horizontal layers, defined by code or software, serve as the functional components of an end-to-end communications system (Whitt, 2004).

3.4.2   End-to-end

RFC 1958 states that 'the intelligence is end to end rather than hidden in the network' with most work 'done at the fringes'. The function of the middle portion of the IP hourglass is simply to deliver communications – without processing, changing, or discriminating between traffic. This 'end-to-end principle' arose in the academic communities of the 1960s and 1970s. It took hold when the US government compelled adoption of the TCP/IP, mandated a regulated separation of conduit and content, and granted non-discriminatory network access to computer device manufacturers and dial-up online companies (Whitt, 2009, pp. 507–8). Consequently, these end-to-end arguments 'have over time come to be widely considered the defining if vague normative principle to govern the Internet' (Barwolff, 2010, p. 134).

End-to-end tells us where to place the network functions within a layered architecture. Layers that are closer to the 'middle' of the network should serve merely to connect, rather than to make decisions on behalf of the nodes. The Internet has thrived as a complex system because the agents using the system can rely on the network to connect them without hindrance. This maximizes their evolutionary options, and increases the degree of overall emergence.

The end-to-end principle is reasonably straightforward to apply at the core of the network, even when some reasonable exceptions can be made for firewalls and traffic shaping (Whitt, 2009, p. 453, n. 199). Moving up to the application and content layers, there is considerably more discretion. Application developers and content producers are themselves adaptive agents. Thus, the end-to-end principle has become a general mandate to make the basic Internet Protocols simple, general, and open, leaving room for innovation at higher layers.

3.4.3   Interconnection

RFC 1958 puts it plainly: the goal of the Internet is 'connectivity'. Unlike the earlier ARPANET, the Internet is a collection of IP networks owned and operated by private telecommunications companies, governments, universities, individuals, and others – each of which needs to connect with others. Kevin Werbach has pointed out that, 'the defining characteristic of the Net is not the absence of discrimination, but a relentless commitment to interconnectivity' (Werbach, 2007, p. 1273). Jim Speta agrees that the Internet's utility largely depends on, 'the principle of universal interconnectivity, both as a technical and as an economic matter' (Speta, 2003, p. 17). The early Internet was designed with an emphasis on internetworking and interconnectivity, and moving packets of data transparently across a network of networks. Steve Crocker reports that even in the pre-Internet environment all hosts would benefit from interconnecting, but that 'the interconnection had to treat all of the networks with equal status' with 'none subservient to any other' (Crocker, 2012).

Today's Internet embodies a key underlying technical idea: open-architecture networking. Under this design principle, network providers can freely interwork with other networks through 'a meta-level "internetworking architecture"' (Leiner et al., 1997, p. 103). Critical ground rules include that each distinct network must stand on its own, communications will be on a best-effort basis, and there is no global control at the operations level.

The interconnecting of disparate networks has direct economic implications. 'Interconnection agreements do not just route traffic in the Internet, they route money' (Clark et al., 2011, p. 2). Likewise, a healthy flow of money from end users to Internet service providers (ISPs) – absent market power abuses by the ISPs – is essential for sustained infrastructure investment.

More broadly, it is clear that the Internet's interconnection principle supports the observation that complex systems have the greatest opportunity to grow when they are highly networked. Agents have more avenues for collaboration, learning, and adaptation as their universe grows beyond their local network. A densely connected set of nodes has more chances for novel innovation, and greater means to 'route around' market failures.

3.4.4   Agnosticism

RFC 1958 states that, in order to achieve connectivity, 'the tool is the Internet Protocol'. By design, IP is completely indifferent to both the underlying physical networks, and to the countless applications and devices using those networks. In particular, IP does not care what underlying transport is used (such as fiber, copper, cable, or radio waves), what application it is carrying (such as browsers, email, instant messaging, or MP3 packets), or what content it is carrying (text, speech, music, pictures, or video). Thus, IP enables any and all user applications and content. This enables incredible diversity of use. 'The system has standards at one layer (homogeneity) and diversity in the ways that ordinary people care about (heterogeneity)' (Palfrey and Gasser, 2012, p. 108).

RFC 172, discussing the File Transfer Protocol, says that the network should 'assume nothing about the information and treat it as a bit stream . . . whose interpretation is left to a higher level process, or a user' (Bhushan et al., 1971, p. 5). As Barwolff puts it, IP creates 'the spanning layer' that creates 'an irreducibly minimal coupling between the functions above and below itself' (2010, p. 136). Not only does IP separate the communications peers at either end of the network, it generally maintains a firm separation between the entities above and below it.

As a result of this core agnosticism, the Internet – like other highly complex systems – can generate surprising outcomes. As one neo-Schumpeterian puts it, 'The contemporary technological paradigm generates novelty, uncertainty, and surprise in an unprecedented way' (Dopfer, 1994, p. 159). Economists and policy-makers should embrace this agnosticism, rather than trying to predict or impose specific outcomes on the system.

We must keep in mind that these four principles describe the Internet in its native environment, with no alterations or impediments imposed by other agents in the larger ecosystem. Where laws, regulations, or other activities would curtail these design attributes, the Internet may become less than the sum of its parts. It is only when the design features are able to work together that we see the full emergent phenomenon of the Internet (Whitt, 2013).

3.5   THE INTERNET INFRASTRUCTURE: A GENERAL PURPOSE TECHNOLOGY

Far from what traditional economic theory would tell us, we cannot treat the Internet as a top-down market that will reach equilibrium. Its value derives from the actions of billions of individually motivated agents, collaborating and innovating in unexpected ways. This network is facilitated by some wise – and lucky – design principles that go back to the earliest days of the Internet's development. The Internet emerged as the 'most fit' technology for global networking, and now itself serves as a platform for further evolution and growth. The fact that it has become the infrastructure for countless economy-growing activities calls for an infrastructure-oriented understanding of its value (Frischmann, 2012).

Some economists have identified a special class of technologies that serve as platforms for endogenous growth because they allow a great deal of follow-on innovation. Steam power and electricity are classic examples. The concept of a 'general purpose technology' (GPT) was first articulated by Bresnahan and Trajtenberg (1995), and has been the subject of considerable subsequent scholarship (Lipsey et al., 2005; Bresnahan, 2010). GPTs play a role of 'enabling technologies' by opening up new opportunities rather than offering complete, final solutions. The result is 'innovational complementarities', meaning that 'the productivity of R&D in downstream sectors increases as a consequence of innovation in the GPT technology' (Bresnahan and Trajtenberg, 1995, p. 84).

Looking back at the development of the IT industry more than ten years after his key GPT paper, Bresnahan (2007, pp. 114, 118) noted:

> The lesson here for Schumpeterian Economics is far more general than the narrow and specific point about 'open architecture,' which seems like a technical concept from computing. Instead, the point is about the role of a permissive, forward-looking system of innovation in which inventions can come from multiple sources ... The most economically important use of a general purpose technology need not be determined by the inventors of the GPT, but rather by the inventors of complements, applications.

The economic value of the Internet derives in large part from its general-purpose nature. It has great 'capacity to produce unanticipated change through unfiltered contributions from broad and varied audiences' (Zittrain, 2008, p. 70). The lesson for economists and policy-makers is to preserve this open platform – most often by refraining from government interference, but occasionally by discouraging those who would seek to make it less 'general'.

3.6   CONCLUSION: ON THE INTERNET, 'MORE IS DIFFERENT'

Complexity economics warns against attempts to synthesize the dynamics of a system by reference to reductionist universal laws. Theorists of complexity often point to physicist Philip Anderson's 1972 essay, 'More is different' in the journal *Science* (Anderson, 1972). There, he explains that although we can describe individual components of a complex system, we cannot predict with certainty what will happen when they interact. That is not to say that trying to understand the Internet through the lens of complexity theory is a lost cause. As Anderson (1972, p. 396) notes: 'In general, the relationship between the system and its parts is intellectually a one-way street. Synthesis is expected to be all but impossible; analysis, on the other hand, may be not only possible but fruitful in all kinds of ways'. He then notes that by observing certain principles or phenomena – often cross-pollinated from one discipline to another – scholars can obtain a far more accurate understanding of systems than from reductionist approaches. In this spirit, we have highlighted here the most enduring technological design principles of the Internet in order to elucidate why it has been such a remarkable economic catalyst.

The Internet Protocol has helped to fashion a 'virtuous hourglass' from disparate activities at the different network layers. The Internet drives convergence at the IP (middle) layer, while at the same time facilitating divergence at the physical networks (lower) and applications/content (upper) layers. The interconnected, end-to-end nature of the network allows innovations to build upon each other in self-feeding loops.

The result is not just more activity and growth, but the flourishing of many different ways for humans to innovate and interact. This layered network of relationships and interconnected technologies relies upon and creates a self-feeding infrastructure, driven by principles that are simultaneously simple and complex.

NOTE

*   The ideas expressed here are those of the authors alone, and do not reflect the opinion of Princeton University or Motorola Mobility LLC/Google Inc. (the organizational affiliations of the authors at the time of writing). This chapter draws significantly from Whitt and Schultze (2009) and Whitt (2013).

REFERENCES

Alcouffe, A. and C. Alcouffe (2009), 'French industrial policy', in A. Pyka, U. Cantner, A. Greiner and T. Kuhn (eds), *Recent Advances in Neo-Schumpeterian Economics*, Cheltenham, UK and Northampton, MA, USA: Edward Elgar Publishing.

Alvestrand, H. (2004), 'RFC 3935 – a mission statement for the IETF', *Internet Requests for Comments*, accessed 29 April 2015 at https://www.ietf.org/rfc/rfc3935.txt.

Anderson, P.W. (1972), 'More is different', *Science*, **177** (4047), 393–6.

Anderson, P.W., K.J. Arrow and D. Pines (1988), *The Economy as an Evolving Complex System*, Reading, MA: Addison-Wesley.

Arthur, W.B. (2000), 'Myths and realities of the high-tech economy', talk given at Credit Suisse First Boston Thought Leader Forum, 10 September, Boston, MA, accessed 1 May 2015 at http://tuvalu.santafe.edu/~wbarthur/Papers/Credit_Suisse_Web.pdf.

Arthur, W.B., S.N. Durlauf and D.A. Lane (eds) (1997), *The Economy as an Evolving Complex System II*, Reading, MA: Addison-Wesley.

Axelrod, R. and M.D. Cohen (2001), *Harnessing Complexity*, New York: Simon and Schuster.

Ball, P. (2006), *Critical Mass: How One Thing Leads to Another*, New York: Farrar, Straus and Giroux.

Barabási, A.-L. (2002), *Linked: The New Science of Networks*, New York: Basic Books.

Barwolff, M. (2010), 'End-to-end arguments in the Internet: Principles, practices, and theory', dissertation submitted to the Department of Electrical Engineering and Computer Science at Technical University of Berlin.

Beinhocker, E. (2006), *The Origin of Wealth: Evolution, Complexity, and the Radical Remaking of Economics*, Cambridge, MA: Harvard Business School Press.

Benkler, Y. (2008), *The Wealth of Networks*, New Haven, CT: Yale University Press.

Bernbom, G. (2000), 'Analyzing the Internet as a common pool resource: The problem of network congestion', presentation at the International Association for the Study of Common Property, IASCP 2000, 29 April.

Bhushan, A., B. Braden and W. Crowther et al. (1971), 'RFC 179 – the File Transfer Protocol', *Internet Requests for Comments*, accessed 1 May 2015 at https://tools.ietf.org/html/rfc172.

Blume, L. and S.N. Durlauf (eds) (2006), *The Economy as an Evolving Complex System III*, Oxford, UK: Oxford University Press.

Bresnahan, T. (2007), 'Creative destruction in the PC industry', in F. Malerba and S. Brusoni (eds), *Perspectives on Innovation*, Cambridge, UK and New York: Cambridge University Press, pp. 105–40.

Bresnahan, T.F. (2010), 'General purpose technologies', in B.H. Hall and N. Rosenberg (eds), *Handbook of the Economics of Innovation, Volume 2*, Amsterdam: Elsevier, pp. 761–91.

Bresnahan, T.F. and M. Trajtenberg (1995), 'General purpose technologies: Engines of growth?' *Journal of Econometrics*, **65** (1), 83–108.

Bush, R. and D. Meyer (2002), 'RFC 3439 – some Internet architectural guidelines and philosophy', *Internet Requests for Comments*, accessed 1 May 2015 at https://www.ietf.org/rfc/rfc3439.txt.

Cantner, U. (2009), 'Competition in innovation', in A. Pyka, U. Cantner, A. Greiner and T. Kuhn (eds), *Recent Advances in Neo-Schumpeterian Economics*, Cheltenham, UK and Northampton, MA, USA: Edward Elgar Publishing, pp. 13–33.

Carpenter, B.E. (1996), 'RFC 1958 – architectural principles of the Internet', *Internet Requests for Comments*, accessed 1 May 2015 at https://www.ietf.org/rfc/rfc1958.txt.

Case, J. (2007), *Competition: The Birth of a New Science*, New York: Hill and Wang.

Clark, D.D., W. Lehr and S. Bauer (2011), 'Interconnection in the Internet: The policy challenge', paper presented at TPRC 2011, Alexandria, VA, accessed 1 May 2015 at http://ssrn.com/abstract=1992641.

Coase, R.H. (1937), 'The nature of the firm', *Economica*, **4** (16), 386–405.

Crocker, S. (2012), 'Where did the Internet really come from?, *TechPresident*, accessed 1 May 2015 at http://techpresident.com/news/22670/where-did-internet-really-come.

DeNardis, L. (2010), 'The emerging field of Internet governance', *Yale Information Society Project Working Paper Series*.

Dopfer, K. (1994), 'The phenomenon of economic change: Neoclassical vs. Schumpeterian approaches', in L. Magnusson (ed.), *Evolutionary and Neo-Schumpeterian Approaches to Economics*, Boston, MA: Kluwer Academic Publishers, pp. 125–71.

Doria, A. (2011), 'Study report: Policy implications of future network architectures and technology', presented at the 1st Berlin Symposium on Internet and Society.

Friedman, M. (1953), 'The methodology of positive economics', in M. Friedman, *Essays in Positive Economics*, Chicago, IL: University of Chicago Press, pp. 3–43.

Frischmann, B.M. (2012), *Infrastructure: The Social Value of Shared Resources*, New York: Oxford University Press.

Frischmann, B.M. and M.A. Lemley (2006), 'Spillovers', *Columbia Law Review*, **107** (1), 257–301.

Glimcher, P.W. (2004), *Decisions, Uncertainty, and the Brain: The Science of Neuroeconomics*, Cambridge, MA: MIT Press.

Hartley, J.E. (1997), *The Representative Agent in Macroeconomics*, New York: Routledge.

Hayek, F.A. (1948), *Individualism and Economic Order*, Chicago, IL: University of Chicago Press.

Hayek, F.A. (1988), *The Fatal Conceit: The Errors of Socialism*, Chicago, IL: University of Chicago Press.

Holland, J.H. (1998), *Emergence: From Chaos to Order*, Reading, MA: Addison-Wesley.

Holland, J.H. and J.H. Miller (1991), 'Artificial adaptive agents in economic theory', *American Economic Review*, **81** (2), 365–70.

Johnson, S. (2001), *Emergence: The Connected Lives of Ants, Brains, Cities, and Software*, New York: Scribner.

Koppl, R. (2009), 'Complexity and Austrian economics', in J.J. Barkley Rosser (ed.), *Handbook of Research on Complexity*, Cheltenham, UK and Northampton, MA, USA: Edward Elgar Publishing, pp. 393–409.

Langlois, R.N. and M.J. Everett (1994), 'What is evolutionary economics?' in L. Magnusson (ed.), *Evolutionary and Neo-Schumpeterian Approaches to Economics*, Boston, MA: Kluwer Academic Publishers, pp. 11–48.

Leijonhufvud, A. (1996), 'Towards a not-too-rational macroeconomics', in D. Colander (ed.), *Beyond Microfoundations: Post-Walrasian Macroeconomics*, Cambridge, UK and New York: Cambridge University Press, pp. 39–55.

Leiner, B.M., V.G. Cerf and D.D. Clark et al. (1997), 'The past and future history of the Internet', *Communications of the ACM*, **40** (2), 102–8.

Lipsey, R.G., K.I. Carlaw and C.T. Bekar (2005), *Economic Transformations: General Purpose Technologies and Long-Term Economic Growth*, Oxford and New York: Oxford University Press.

Miller, J.H. and S.E. Page (2007), *Complex Adaptive Systems: An Introduction to Computational Models of Social Life*, Princeton, NJ: Princeton University Press.

Morowitz, H.J. (2002), *The Emergence of Everything: How the World Became Complex*, Oxford, UK: Oxford University Press.

Nelson, R.R. (2003), 'Physical and social technologies, and their evolution', *LEM Working Paper Series No. 2003/09*, accessed 1 May 2015 at http://www.sssup.it/UploadDocs/5735_2003_09.pdf.

Ormerod, P. (2005), *Why Most Things Fail*, Hoboken, NJ: Random House.

Palfrey, J. and U. Gasser (2012), *Interop: The Promise and Perils of Highly Interconnected Systems*, New York: Basic Books.

Parker, R. (2005), *John Kenneth Galbraith: His Life, His Politics, His Economics*, New York: Farrar, Straus and Giroux.

Prabhakar, B., K.N. Dektar and D.M. Gordon (2012), 'The regulation of ant colony foraging activity without spatial information', *Computational Biology*, **8** (8), e1002670.

Romer, P.M. (1990), 'Endogenous technological change', *Journal of Political Economy*, **98** (5), Part 2, S71–S102.

Schumpeter, J.A. ([1942] 1976), *Capitalism, Socialism, and Democracy*, New York: Harper & Row.

Shermer, M. (2008), *The Mind of the Market. Compassionate Apes, Competitive Humans, and Other Tales from Evolutionary Economics*, New York: Times Books.

Shiller, R.J., S. Fischer and B.M. Friedman (1984), 'Stock prices and social dynamics', *Brookings Papers on Economic Activity*, **15** (2), 457–510.

Sieh, K.A. and D.N. Hatfield (2012), 'The Broadband Internet Technical Advisory Group (BITAG) and its role in Internet governance', paper presented at TPRC 2012, accessed 1 May 2015 at http://ssrn.com/abstract=2032233.

Solow, R.M. (2007), 'Heavy thinker', *The New Republic*, 21 May, accessed 1 May 2015 at http://www.newrepublic.com/article/heavy-thinker.

Solum, L.B. and M. Chung (2003), 'The layers principle: Internet architecture and the law', *University of San Diego School of Law, Public Law and Legal Theory Research Paper No. 55*.

Speta, J.B. (2003), 'FCC authority to regulate the Internet: Creating it and limiting it', *Loyola University Chicago Law Journal*, **35** (15), accessed 1 May 2015 at http://lawcommons.luc.edu/luclj/vol35/iss1/3.

Summers, L.H. (1986), 'Does the stock market rationally reflect fundamental values?' *Journal of Finance*, **41** (3), 591–601.

Taleb, N.N. (2007), *The Black Swan: The Impact of the Highly Improbable*, New York: Random House.

Taylor, M. (2004), *Confidence Games*, Chicago, IL: University of Chicago Press.

Thaler, R.H. (2000), 'From homo economicus to homo sapiens', *Journal of Economic Perspectives*, **14** (1), 133–41.

van Schewick, B. (2010), *Internet Architecture and Innovation*, Cambridge, MA: MIT Press.

Varian, H.R., J. Farrell and C. Shapiro (2004), *The Economics of Information Technology: An Introduction*, Cambridge, MA: Cambridge University Press.

Vermeij, G.J. (2004), *Nature: An Economic History*, Princeton, NJ: Princeton University Press.

Walras, L. ([1874] 1954), *Elements of Pure Economics*, trans. W. Jaffe, George Allen and Unwin Ltd.

Warsh, D. (2006), *Knowledge and the Wealth of Nations: A Story of Economic Discovery*, New York: W.W. Norton.

Watts, D.J. (2003), *Six Degrees: The Science of a Connected Age*, New York: W.W. Norton.

Waz, J. and P. Weiser (2012), 'Internet governance: The role of multistakeholder organizations', *Silicon Flatirons Roundtable Series on Entrepreneurship, Innovation, and Public Policy*, accessed 1 May 2015 at http://ssrn.com/abstract=2195167.

Werbach, K. (2007), 'Only connect', *Berkeley Technology Law Journal*, **22** (4), 1233, accessed 1 May 2015 at http://scholarship.law.berkeley.edu/btlj/vol22/iss4/1.

Whitt, R.S. (2004), 'A horizontal leap forward: Formulating a new communications public policy framework based on the network layers model', *Federal Communications Law Journal*, **56** (3), 587–672.

Whitt, R.S. (2009), 'Evolving broadband policy: Taking adaptive stances to foster optimal internet platforms', *CommLaw Conspectus*, **17** (2), 417–534.

Whitt, R.S. (2013), 'A deference to protocol: Fashioning a three-dimensional public policy framework for the Internet era', *Cardozo Arts & Entertainment Law Journal*, **31** (1), 689–768.

Whitt, R.S. and S.J. Schultze (2009), 'Emergence economics', *The Journal of Telecommunications and High-Technology Law*, **7** (2), 217–315.

Zittrain, J. (2008), *The Future of the Internet and How to Stop It*, New Haven, CT: Yale University Press.

4. A network science approach to the Internet
Volker Schneider and Johannes M. Bauer

4.1 INTRODUCTION

During the past decades considerable progress has been made in developing research methods that are particularly suited to examine network relations in the Internet and their consequences for outcomes such as the diffusion of applications and services, the winner-take-all dynamics of digital markets, and the spread of malware. Social scientists have long recognized the importance of interdependencies among agents in social systems and the need for coordination in an economy with division of labor. Network science provides powerful tools to analyze both topics in innovative ways. It needs to be distinguished from two other emerging fields – Internet science and web science – which share common interests but do not primarily use network science tools. This chapter provides an overview of network science methods and their potential to study the Internet and its economic effects.

The Internet profoundly affects economic and social interactions while enabling novel forms of coordination. Weaving individuals, organizations and devices into new, wider and denser networks of interaction, it also creates new interdependencies. For example, contacts on social media platforms and Web 2.0 services such as Facebook, Twitter, YouTube, Snapchat or Digg likely affect individuals' perceptions and preferences. Thus, in an economy with dense connectivity, the preferences of agents may evolve in response to other agents' choices and revealed preferences. Such endogenous preference formation may require a rethinking of the notion of rational, independent decision-makers that continues to be at the heart of much economic analysis (Gintis, 2009). Another example is the complex value network of the Internet economy, in which complementarity and platform relations between firms abound. These developments change the nature of competition in ambiguous ways, often requiring companies to compete and cooperate with their rivals (Brandenburger and Nalebuff, 1996; Christensen, 1997; Farrell and Weiser, 2003; Anderson, 2009). Moreover, the ability to innovate using digital technology has accelerated the process of innovation. Competition is further intensified by the ability of new players to enter and exit digital markets with relative ease. Last but not least, the Internet has contributed to a global synchronization of economic events that might eventually increase the volatility of the economy (Noam, 2006).

As communication flows between individuals and devices are increasingly computer-mediated, the Internet allows the collection of highly granular and detailed data on information flows between agents, networked relations, agent behavior, and on Internet-mediated economic transactions. This is a significant departure from the past, when such information was difficult and expensive to collect in a reliable way (Newman et al., 2006, p. 5). Consequently, new and innovative forms of inquiry have evolved that take advantage of this massive empirical base. Given the early state of the field's development, different trajectories of investigation can be distinguished, although they may eventually become more integrated. Analytical network science often relies on game theory to model the behavior of individual nodes and combines it with insights from graph theory. New agent-based and other computational approaches allow applying game theory to situations for which no analytical solution can be devised (Tesfatsion, 2003; Judd and Tesfatsion, 2005). Much of empirical network science uses computational techniques that are spreading rapidly in the social sciences (Lazer et al., 2009). There is enthusiasm about the opportunities offered by 'big data' analytics (Mayer-Schönberger and Cukier, 2013; Siegel, 2013; Pentland, 2014), although the early experience has revealed the need to develop careful theoretical and empirical models to take advantage of the abundant information (Monge and Contractor, 2003; Easley and Kleinberg, 2010; boyd and Crawford, 2012; Doornik and Hendry, 2015).

These developments have led to an invigoration of research applying network theory perspectives to better understand the Internet and other networks. This chapter briefly discusses these approaches with a focus on network science and its relevance for studying the Internet and its economic effects. It discusses the uses and limits of network theory models and whether they offer new answers to the questions and challenges raised by the Internet economy. The following section describes the emergence of network science and discusses its precursors in mathematical graph theory and the social sciences. Section 4.3 develops basic concepts of network models and section 4.4 applies them to explain the Internet's global structures. Section 4.5 discusses several selected areas in which network science enriches the analysis of Internet economics, including the use of network models to develop a better understanding of dynamic processes in the Internet. Section 4.6 summarizes key points.

4.2   THE EVOLUTION OF NETWORK SCIENCE

Even though the term network science was used only sporadically and colloquially before the 1990s, network thinking can be traced back to developments in the eighteenth century (Freeman, 2004). Which scientists and philosophers ought to be treated as forerunners of network research depends on how its core ideas are defined. If the use of terms such as 'connections' and 'relationships' already qualifies for a precursor role, then social scientists such as Montesquieu, Marx, and Comte need to be included (Emirbayer, 1997; Freeman, 2004). The first mathematical conceptualizations of relational configurations can be found in the work of Leonhard Euler, solving the famous 'Königsberg Bridges Problem' (Wilson, 2004), and Francis Galton developing stochastic kinship mathematics (Freeman, 2004).

The school of network studies becomes more exclusive if systematic concept development and an explication of research methods are seen as the relevant threshold. The first steps in method-based network analysis began with Leopold von Wiese and Jacob Moreno, who developed simple statistical methods to describe relations, albeit without advanced mathematical foundations. Similar developments happened in social anthropology and industrial sociology (Scott, 1991; Freeman, 2004). Kurt Lewin's application of physical and mathematical concepts to interpersonal psychological relations can be considered a next step (Lewin, 1936). This also supported the development of modern graph theory, which contributed to a kind of 'breakthrough' (Raab, 2010) in social network

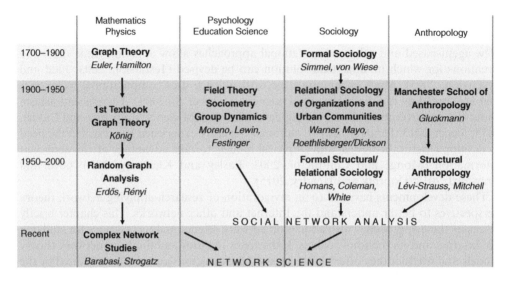

	Mathematics Physics	Psychology Education Science	Sociology	Anthropology
1700–1900	**Graph Theory** *Euler, Hamilton*		**Formal Sociology** *Simmel, von Wiese*	
1900–1950	**1st Textbook Graph Theory** *König*	**Field Theory Sociometry Group Dynamics** *Moreno, Lewin, Festinger*	**Relational Sociology of Organizations and Urban Communities** *Warner, Mayo, Roethlisberger/Dickson*	**Manchester School of Anthropology** *Gluckmann*
1950–2000	**Random Graph Analysis** *Erdős, Rényi*		**Formal Structural/ Relational Sociology** *Homans, Coleman, White*	**Structural Anthropology** *Lévi-Strauss, Mitchell*
			SOCIAL NETWORK ANALYSIS	
Recent	**Complex Network Studies** *Barabasi, Strogatz*		NETWORK SCIENCE	

Sources: Scott (1991); Freeman (2004); Wilson (2004).

Figure 4.1   The development of network science and network research

research at Harvard and MIT with a range of new methods and techniques during the 1970s (Scott, 1991; Freeman, 2004). Completely independent of social network analysis were the advances in mathematical graph theory at the end of the 1950s, spurred by the development of random graph models for global network structures that were developed by Paul Erdős and Alfred Rény in the 1950s and 1960s (Harary, 1969). The proliferation of computational methods and models based on these concepts and algorithms facilitated the emergence of the current version of 'network science' (Barabási and Frangos, 2002; Jungnickel, 2005). In parallel, under the notion of 'social network analysis', network approaches have been booming in the social sciences since the 1970s and 1980s (Wasserman and Faust, 1994; Borgatti et al., 2009; Hennig et al., 2012). Figure 4.1 outlines the main lines of development of network science and network research.

In network science, roads, rivers, communications circuits and social relations are no longer described as systems, as was popular during the 1960s and 1970s, but as networks in which 'systemness' is emerging from a network of relations. Notions such as the 'web of life' (Capra, 1996) or the 'network society' (Castells, 1996) have become widely used descriptors of ecological and social reality. Although the concepts of 'system' and 'network' have similar meanings – at least in a mathematical sense, as interrelated components within a boundary separating them from their environment – the network concept does not imply equilibrium orientation, and involves much lower integration. Rather, it emphasizes precariousness and vulnerability of social and biological configurations. Complexity and complex interdependence are important related concepts. Networked reality is non-linear, with only a few one-to-one relations and multiple and multiplex dependencies in most cases (Capra, 1996). In such systems, small local incidences may have global ramifications.

Although many studies in network science are related to the Internet, network science is much broader than Internet science or web science (Dorogovtsev and Mendes, 2003; Pastor-Satorras and Vespignani, 2004; Wright, 2011; Shadbolt et al., 2013; Tiropanis et al., 2015). Network scientists try to find similar network characteristics in all natural and social phenomena – networks of proteins, people, words, or websites. Their ultimate goal is to find general patterns and laws that are effective in networks of any kind. From this perspective, network science is rather a subfield of mathematics that uses graph theory to model network topologies and analyzes empirical network data to explore the phenomenon of 'networkness'. This can be done in many physical, biological and social networks that are unrelated to the Internet. From this broad research program, network science has developed powerful tools and methods to analyze networks and their implications for outcomes, aptly summarized by Newman (2012) in his comprehensive textbook on streams and directions of network science.

Networked complexity suggests distributed control. In a political sense network configurations are new institutional arrangements that disperse power and control. In contrast to hierarchical control, networks are based on autonomous interaction of components. This idea of non-hierarchical but all-embracing connectedness became a technical reality through the World Wide Web, in which not only states and organizations, but also people and increasingly 'things' became globally interconnected. The provision of universally open technical network infrastructures created new forms of social interaction, new media and public spheres, new forms of scientific cooperation, new electronic economic sectors and new forms of governmental organization (e-government and e-democracy) and public services. The penetration of the Internet into almost all spheres of life created a new academic industry studying these socio-technical processes of adoption, diffusion and their actual and future impact. Network science offers a unique set of methods to model and understand these relations and their effects.

During the past decade Internet science and web science have emerged as fields that are related to but not identical with network science. Moreover, these areas connect with the much broader domain of Internet studies, which predominantly employs social science approaches to examine a wide array of issues related to the Internet, its effects, and governance (Dutton, 2013). Tiropanis et al. (2015) examine the relations between network science, web science and Internet science in detail and identify multiple overlaps but also areas of differentiation. Of the three approaches, network science has the broadest scope as it analyzes networks beyond the Internet. Thus it provides a broader canvas to examine the economic consequences of the pervasive adoption of the Internet. At the same time, because of its reliance on network science approaches it is methodologically more narrowly construed than Internet science or web science. Both Internet science and web science focus on the specific domain of the Internet, with many overlaps between them and with network science (in as far as the latter focuses on the Internet). Within the recently formed Internet science community, many contributions approach the Internet as a socio-technical system with an emphasis on the infrastructural layer of the web and the implications of different protocols and designs for the openness and dynamics of the Internet.

Web science is a hybrid of the two research paradigms embedded in physics and computer science. It seeks scientifically to understand the macroscopic laws operating in the web while also synthetically designing systems in ways that are compatible with fundamental human values such as privacy and freedom of speech. In the words of Berners-Lee et al. (2006a), 'Web science, therefore, must be inherently interdisciplinary; its goal is to both understand the growth of the web and to create approaches allowing new powerful and more beneficial patterns to occur'. Thus, 'Web science is about more than modeling the current web. It is about engineering new infrastructure protocols and about understanding the human society that uses them and creates the Web, and it is about the creation of beneficial new systems' (Berners-Lee et al., 2006a, p. 771; see also Berners-Lee et al., 2006b; Hendler et al., 2008; Wright, 2011; Shadbolt et al., 2013). It remains to be seen whether these fields will continue to cross-fertilize and coalesce around a shared interest in the Internet or whether the differences in methods and primary interests will lead to segmentation into separate communities.

4.3   MAJOR CONCEPTS OF NETWORK SCIENCE

In order to systematically describe and analyze networked configurations, graph theory and network analysis have developed a proper 'language', a coherent body of concepts. One of the key pursuits of network science is the uncovering of stable relationships between network structure and outcomes. Attributes of a network, such as its density or the centrality of nodes, influence the flows of information and hence may have predictable consequences for outcomes. It is therefore necessary to briefly explain the key concepts used to describe networks.

4.3.1   Elementary Concepts

Networks and graphs are sets of nodes (vertices, points) and edges (links). The various concepts are illustrated in Figure 4.2 using a graph designed by Brandes and

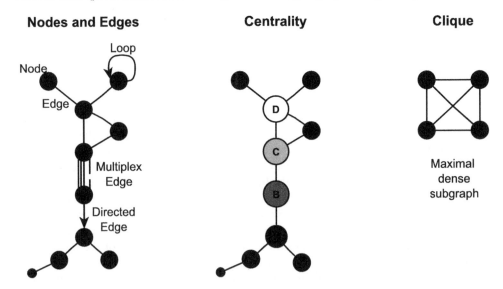

Source: Based on Brandes and Hildenbrand (2014).

Figure 4.2   Elementary concepts of network research

Hildenbrand (2014) for didactic purposes. Edges can be directed (arcs) or undirected, weighted (positive or negative, and strong or weak), or unweighted (binary). A reflexive edge is also called a loop. If a graph contains multiple edges of different quality it is called multiplex.

Nodes are adjacent if they are directly connected by an edge. A node's degree is the number of edges to which it is related. In-degree measures the number of incoming and out-degree the number of outgoing edges. An isolate node is not adjacent to any other node and has a degree of 0. A walk in a graph is an alternating sequence of nodes and edges, and the length of a walk is the number of edges (including repetitions). A trail in a graph is a walk in which no edge occurs more than once. A Eulerian trail is a walk that contains each edge only once – the formalization of the above-mentioned Königsberg Bridges Problem. A path is a trail in which no vertex is repeated. The distance between two nodes in a graph is the length of the shortest walk between them, also called geodesic. A graph is connected if there is a walk between every pair of nodes.

Graphs may contain different sets of nodes. A bipartite graph can be partitioned into two sets in such a way that no edge connects two nodes in the same set. In social network analysis such a configuration is also called a two-mode network. Based on these different concepts the topology of graphs and networks can be described in a systematic way. A complete graph is one in which every node is connected to all other nodes, that is, every pair of nodes is connected by an edge (also referred to as a fully connected network). Such a graph has maximal density of 1.0, as density is the number of edges in a graph expressed as a proportion of the maximum possible number of edges. In a complete bipartite graph every node of one set is connected to every node in the other set.

A graph is regular when every node is of the same degree; it is k-regular if every node is of degree k. A k-regular graph of k = 2 is a ring. A 4-regular graph is a hexagram combined with a hexagon. Another well-structured form is a star, which is defined as a connected graph in which only one node has a degree greater than 1. A star graph is a maximally centralized graph where the node with multiple degrees is located at the most central position.

Centrality is a topological concept for the description of relative positions of nodes. In social network analysis there are many different ways to specify node centrality. The most basic one equates centrality with degree. In this perspective, node D in the Brandes and Hildenbrand graph is most central. Another concept is centrality based on closeness developed by Bavelas (1948) where the most central node(s) have the shortest path lengths to all other nodes (node C). Freeman (1977) developed a centrality concept based on betweenness, where such nodes are most central that are most frequently located on geodesic distances between all pairs of nodes (node D). Connectivity of a graph is described by the average length of the shortest paths between all pairs of nodes in the network.

Graphs can also be described with respect to their internal grouping or 'clustering'. A part of a graph is a subgraph. A clique in an undirected graph is a subgraph in which all nodes of the subgraph are connected to all other nodes of the subgraph. A clique of four, for instance, is a subgraph with four nodes that are all connected (see Figure 4.2). The degree to which subgraphs come close to a clique can be specified by the local clustering coefficient (Watts and Strogatz, 1998). At global network level clustering can be measured on the basis of triplets of nodes, that is, three nodes that are connected by either two (open triplet) or three (closed triplet; clique) undirected ties. Watts and Strogatz's (1998) global clustering coefficient is the number of closed triplets over the total number of triplets (both open and closed).

At least three levels of analysis and various concepts that are related to these levels can be distinguished in network studies. Density, centralization and clustering concepts describe characteristics of global networks, that is, macro structures of graphs. Subgraphs, cliques and components describe the meso structure of a graph. Centrality describes the individual positions of nodes, that is, the micro structure. Almost all these concepts have been the basis of social network analysis for decades. However, some are recent innovations for which the network scientists from mathematics and physics (Strogatz, 2001; Barabási and Frangos, 2002; Watts, 2004; Newman, 2012) have to be credited. One of their main contributions was the discovery of specific forces and mechanisms behind network evolution and network formation.

4.3.2   Network Formation and Evolution

Against this theoretical background, from the perspective of a general network theory, network science raises the question: what forces are shaping network development and creating specific network structures? Are there general principles and mechanisms that can be found in networks of any kind? A major finding of network science is that empirical networks are neither regular nor random. Most exhibit small-world features (Watts, 2004) in the sense that densely connected subgraphs are interlinked by a few edges, creating the typical feature of organized complexity that Simon (1962) had already noticed. In a small world network a few hub-nodes connect multiple clustered subgraphs so that geodesics in the global networks are shortened. Experiments have shown that (almost) every person on the planet is linked to everybody else in the world by relatively few edges. The eminent task of network scientists was then to use computer simulation to show how such networks grow out of local interactions rather than global design.

A key mechanism for network growth is 'preferential attachment'. In creating new links, nodes prefer to connect to other nodes with high degrees. Based on a simple example in which a network starts from scratch and grows in each sequence by a new node establishing two additional links, Barabási and Frangos (2002, p.86) state this dynamic more formally:

> The probability that [the new node] will choose a given node is proportional to the number of links the node has. That is, given the choice between two nodes, one with twice as many links as the other, it is twice as likely that the new node will connect to the more connected node.

Such a rich-get-richer mechanism has been known for more than 2000 years. Merton (1968) called it 'the Matthew effect', after a passage in the Bible: 'For unto every one that hath shall be given, and he shall have abundance: but from him that hath not shall be taken away even that which he hath' (Matthew 25:29, King James Version). In economics these types of interdependency are discussed as network effects and externalities. Their implications for market structures have been discussed for the telecommunications sector (Katz and Shapiro, 1985) and more recently for information industries (Noam, 2009).

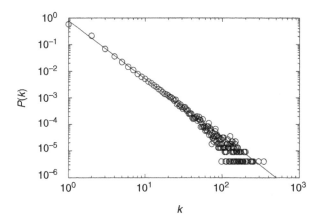

Source: Pastor-Satorras and Vespignani (2007, p. 45).

Figure 4.3 Power-law distribution: probability P(k) that any given vertex has degree k

Network scientists attribute this outcome to the pervasive presence of 'power laws'. When these are in play, networks develop a hierarchical structure: a few nodes have many links, and many nodes exhibit few links. The overall degree distribution follows an exponential decay curve. If the distribution pattern is presented in logarithmic scales (log-log plots) it becomes linear, as Figure 4.3 shows. In economics such patterns are familiar from the distribution of incomes (Pareto law) or city sizes (Zipf law or rank-size property) (Reed, 2001).

This pattern also is called 'scale-free,' denoting 'invariance under rescaling' (Mitchell, 2009). Many network scientists claim that all or most networks display similar distributions (many nodes with few links, few hub-nodes with many links), governed by a power law, regardless of the scale in which they are presented (Barabási and Frangos, 2002). Preferential attachment and power laws would thus be a universal dynamic governing all networks. Clauset et al. (2009) present dozens of datasets on different items such as words in novels, interaction links in cells, telephone calls, numbers of customers affected in electricity blackouts, numbers of adherents of religious groups, co-authorships or citations in science, and so on. The most prominent examples are related to the Internet, for example, where nodes are websites and edges are directed URL hyperlinks, or IP addresses and Internet connections, and so on. This topic will be treated in more detail in the next section, where network science is applied to the topology of the Internet. Clauset et al. (2009, p. 689) conclude that the 'study of power laws spans many disciplines, including physics, biology, engineering, computer science, the earth sciences, economics, political science, sociology, and statistics'.

At a general level, however, it is still a matter of debate as to whether this is really an iron and universal law (e.g., see the skeptical statements by Mitchell, 2009). Willinger et al. (2010) go so far to call the universality of the scale-free feature in the Internet a myth. One reason is that many factors influence network evolution, not only preferential attachment. Another strong mechanism is homophily, denoting the tendency of nodes to create connections to other nodes with similar attributes, as expressed in the proverb 'birds of a feather flock together' (McPherson et al., 2001; Monge and Contractor, 2003). There is a range of other motives for nodes to be connected to other nodes, which are not always relational but may also depend on intrinsic characteristics of nodes or legal rules. In political life, for instance, there are institutional rules establishing that some political actors (nodes) are only allowed to communicate with particular other classes of actors. Leifeld and Schneider (2012) test multiple driving forces of network formation.

4.4 INTERNET GLOBAL STRUCTURES

One of the basic tenets of network science is that the structure of a network not only shapes the behavior of its components but also contributes to emergent properties at an aggregate level. Important features are reliability and robustness, the ability to absorb dysfunctions, and the capacity to survive partial failures. Simulation studies in this research tradition show that both properties are functions of the network structure. In the following paragraphs we will therefore first discuss studies on various network topologies, and then address the issue of network robustness.

4.4.1 Network Topologies

Network science has been widely used to study the topology of the physical network infrastructures of the Internet and the economic and social networks formed on them. Using graph theory concepts outlined above, and strongly influenced by the work of Erdős and Rény, network scientists have highlighted the difference between regular and random networks in contrast to scale-free networks that are governed by power laws. The term 'scale free' is derived 'from the simple observation that power-law node degree distributions are free of scale – most nodes have small degree, a few nodes have very high degree, with the result that the average node degree is essentially non-informative' (Willinger et al., 2010, p. 588).

As we have outlined above, in regular networks all nodes have an equal degree, in random networks it depends on the specific network model. In all networks relative degree frequency can be taken as the probability that a randomly chosen node will have a particular number of links. In a normal distribution the relative degree frequency follows a bell curve in which the average degree lies at the peak of the distribution, but in a power-law distribution the curve begins with a peak and decreases exponentially.

Network scientists applied these concepts in empirical studies of real-world big data in nature, society, and technology and discovered that many relations exhibit power-law distributions. Similar structures were found in various social networks, although the findings suggest considerable diversity (Adamic and Adar, 2003; Jackson, 2008; Easley and Kleinberg, 2010; Leskovec et al., 2011). Despite the pervasive presence of power laws their universal application to communication networks and their usefulness remain under debate (Clegg et al., 2010). Simon Knight et al. (2011, p. 10) describe a dataset that includes information on 232 networks. The authors demonstrate a broad variety of network topologies in the 'Internet topology zoo'. They conclude that there is:

[. . .] evidence for or against many phenomena, for instance: against power-law degree distributions; for hub-and-spoke like behavior; for hierarchy; but the evidence is never completely convincing, reflecting the sheer variety in the networks. If there is any message in this data, it is that there are as many types of networks as there are network designers.

There is a widespread perception that the Internet is a fully connected and widely open virtual space. However, a closer examination of the link structure of the Internet, the World Wide Web, and of other services reveals a more multi-faceted picture. Such a topology can be constructed from various aspects of the Internet, including the link structure among nodes, the flow of data, the control arrangements among autonomous systems (AS), and the management of the Internet. Research dating back to the pioneering work of Broder et al. (2000) reveals that at the core of the Internet is a giant strongly connected component (SCC) within which sites are mutually reachable. In addition, there is a large in-component (sites that are linked to the SCC but cannot be reached from it) and an out-component (sites that can be reached from the SCC but are not connected to it). Furthermore, there are 'tendrils' that are linked to the in- and out-components and disconnected components. Work at the Center for Applied Internet Data Analysis (CAIDA) represents these structures in concentric circles outward from the nodes with highest degree, creating jellyfish-like visualizations[1] that reveal a similar multi-faceted topology.

4.4.2 Internet Robustness

An important discovery of network science was the effect of alternative network topologies on network robustness in cases of accidental failure or deliberate attack. Robust networks continue to function even if some nodes or components fail, and experience blackouts only in extreme situations. Robust networks are also highly resilient in that they quickly recover after a serious breakdown. While the distributed nature of the Internet is inherently designed for robustness – in contrast to traditional hierarchical telecommunication networks – the degree of robustness ultimately depends on the topology, that is, the layout of a network. Network research methods can convincingly answer questions regarding which kind of network structures are particularly robust.

A conventional wisdom in organizational research is that redundant structures are less prone to disruption. In an overview Mitchell (2009) points to a similar observation, summarizing that a very important property of scale-free networks is their resilience to the deletion of nodes. If a set of random nodes and their links are deleted from a large scale-free network, the network's basic properties would not change. However, Albert et al. (2000) show that scale-free networks also imply some vulnerabilities. Using formal modeling and computer simulation, they demonstrate that not all redundant systems but only scale-free networks (such as the Internet and social and biological networks) are error tolerant. However, they also find that error tolerance of these networks comes at a price as they are extremely vulnerable to attacks targeting and deliberately removing a few central nodes. Robustness is studied by the simulation of random removal of nodes in different network structures and its effects on connectedness. The latter is measured as change in the diameter (i.e., the shortest path between the two most distant nodes in a network) of a given network as a function of the fraction of the removed nodes. Albert et al. (2000)

compare a heterogeneous scale-free network with a homogeneous Erdős-Rény (ER) network in which most nodes have approximately the same number of links.

When nodes are removed, many groups of nodes are cut off from the main cluster. When nodes with the highest degree are eliminated, the diameter of the scale-free network increases rapidly. It doubles its original value if only 5 percent of the nodes are removed. This vulnerability stems from the heterogeneous degree distribution, where connectivity is based on a few highly connected nodes. Their overall finding is that scale-free networks display a surprisingly high degree of tolerance against random failures, a property not shared by the ER network. But error tolerance would come at the price of attack survivability. This finding highlights topological weaknesses of the current communication networks.

Crucitti et al. (2004) followed a similar research track with a more extended methodology using also a centrality concept developed in social network analysis. The effects of errors and attacks on different network topologies have been studied with respect to the efficiency of a graph, that is, the length of communication-link sequences measured as the average geodesic path length. Removal of nodes was simulated with respect to accidental errors but also deliberate attacks on central nodes, where centrality was measured by degree and betweenness centrality. Their findings were similar to those by Albert et al. (2000): homogeneous ER graphs exhibit some tolerance with respect to errors and attacks whereas heterogeneous scale-free networks are robust to errors but vulnerable to attacks. Crucitti et al. (2004) conclude that great effort would be necessary in order to protect many real-world networks such as the Internet from attacks.

4.5   CONTRIBUTIONS TO INTERNET ECONOMICS

Network science approaches offer additional analytical and empirical tools that can be used to examine the interrelations in the digital economy and the effects of increasing connectivity. These approaches build upon the earlier literature on the economics of network industries (e.g., Economides, 1996; Shy, 2001) but enhance it in several ways.

4.5.1   New Analytical and Methodological Frameworks

Economics has established a successful research program by analyzing representative decision-makers in situations that they understand well or that are repeated so that choices can converge to the best alternative in a few iterations. This has resulted in the wide use of rational choice models not only in economics but also in other social sciences (Gintis, 2009). Despite numerous weaknesses and criticism the model remains highly influential. Even the broad critique based on findings in behavioral economics and cognitive science that challenges the ability of individuals to be rational in the model sense have thus far mainly led to modifications at the margin and have not challenged the basic premise that individuals seek to achieve best outcomes. However, these alternative approaches place much greater emphasis on the role of information constraints, the framing of the decision problem, systematic biases especially involving risk, habits, and concerns about others ('other-regarding', social preferences) (Kahneman et al., 1982; Simon, 1982–97; Kahneman and Tversky, 2000; Fehr and Fischbacher, 2002; Sunstein et al., 2002; Kahneman, 2011). In a highly connected world, the role and effect of these concerns will require further analysis.

Network science offers a framework and a variety of modeling approaches that can help shed light on these issues with the potential to support the development of overarching new theoretical foundations. Because it makes it possible to integrate micro-level perspectives, such as the examination of individual nodes in a network and the uni- and bi-directional connections to and from this node, with analyses of the emergent behaviors at various levels of aggregation (sub-networks, the entire network), network science has the potential to offer a novel approach to create a microfoundation for macroeconomic processes. Such an endeavor could build on and integrate with existing efforts in related theoretical and empirical areas. For example, since the 1950s, economics has widely used game theory to study decision-making by individual agents in situations in which the consequences of an actor's actions are dependent on other actors' actions and strategies. A rich literature has shed light on non-cooperative games, cooperative games, and evolutionary games, among others (Fudenberg and Tirole, 1991; Fudenberg and Levine, 1998; Camerer, 2003; Gintis, 2009). One of the surprising results from this line of research was that the well-known Prisoner's Dilemma – situations in which cooperation would make it possible to achieve a better outcome but coordination problems let each agent act selfishly, resulting in a worse outcome for all – can be overcome. Robert Axelrod (1984) found that in simple computer tournaments the simple strategy of 'tit-for-tat' (each player does what the other player does) wins. Subsequent research revealed that the slightly more complicated strategy of 'win-stay, lose-shift' is even more successful in longer types of tournaments and interactions. Moreover, it is also more stable and leads to successful cooperation. These processes are widely observable in biological evolution and in cultural evolution (Nowak, 2006; Nowak with Highfield, 2011). Network science promises new insights into such interdependent decision-making processes.

The fundamental importance of network relations has also been recognized by economic sociology, including the work of Granovetter (1985) on the effects of strong and weak ties on economic activities and outcomes, the work of White (2001), who developed an innovative approach explaining markets from network relations, and the research by Padgett and Powell (2012) on the emergence of organizations and markets. These insights from the fields of game theory and of economic sociology are ripe for further integration with network analysis into new theoretical and empirical frameworks for the study of social and economic processes in multi-layer socio-technical systems, including but not limited to the Internet. One promising path in this direction is the use of agent-based modeling (ABM) techniques, which are increasingly deployed to model the economy as a dynamic system (Judd and Tesfatsion, 2005). ABM makes it possible to replace the widely used assumption of maximizing agents in equilibrium with boundedly rational agents adapting to other agents and to their environment and studying the emergent economic processes. This could eventually lead to a new paradigm of explaining social and economic processes from the bottom up (Epstein and Axtell, 1996; Epstein, 2006). Despite its potential this approach faces considerable challenges as the options for explaining outcomes multiply greatly so that model validation becomes excruciatingly complicated. Nonetheless, these are promising approaches and the availability of highly granular and detailed network data harvested from the Internet should provide an enormous boost to this research agenda.

4.5.2   Dynamic Economic and Social Processes

Coordinating the actions of distributed agents is one of the central challenges of economies (North, 1990). Telecommunication technologies have facilitated such coordination
by reducing the costs of message exchange across ever-larger geographic distances.
The telegraph allowed communication with distant territories, shortening the time
of message delivery from months and weeks to hours and minutes. Telephones, fax
machines and e-mail further reduced communication delays. As a platform-independent
technology that can provide cheap communications as an application over the top of
the network, the Internet has greatly expanded the reach of these instant forms of communications to more than three billion people worldwide. Moreover, it has affordances
that support more complex forms of communication than prior telecommunications
technologies and services. For example, the ability to interact with a communication
partner via video, document sharing and chat simultaneously increases the potential to
engage in transactions that are contingent on high levels of relationship-specific investment and historically required repeated personal interactions (Chattopadhyay, 2013).
Consequently, the Internet and the social media it enables have greatly affected economic and social processes, although the welfare outcomes are sometimes ambiguous
and not always positive.

The economic model of decision-making under information and resource constraints
has been regarded as fairly robust in explaining individual- and aggregate-level outcomes.
However, how preferences form and how knowledge about constraints and potential
outcomes (payoffs) is obtained is rarely modeled (Wildman, 2008). Network analytical
approaches have the potential to fill this gap with explicit models of information flows
and their influence on individual decisions as well as their consequences for emergent
phenomena at an aggregate level. Advances are possible in several areas. First, economists have long had a hunch that preferences are not immutable but are influenced by
interactions among agents. Behavioral economics has found strong evidence for social
preferences among decision-makers (Fehr and Fischbacher, 2002; Camerer and Fehr,
2006). Individuals regard others, often differentiated by in-group and out-group relations. In a densely networked environment, these groups may change dynamically and
they will likely be influenced by the network structure of relations. In highly connected
networks these social relations may have predictable consequences for preferences and
decisions (Christakis and Fowler, 2009; Gomez Rodriguez et al., 2013). At an abstract
theoretical level, preferences may become endogenous and adaptive (von Weizsäcker,
2005) requiring a rethinking of the traditional approach of assuming given individual
preference orderings.

Second, it is possible to use network theory approaches to gain a better understanding of whether and how an agent's knowledge, decisions and behavior are related to
the information flows it is exposed to. In networked environments with incomplete and
asymmetrically distributed information it may be rational to base decisions on the behavior of other agents. One example is the existence of direct and indirect network effects.
In the case of direct network effects, the benefits of a choice such as the adoption of a
technology or device are contingent on the number of other adopters. In the case of indirect network effects, the number of adopters influences the availability of complementary
technologies and services. A second example is information cascades or herding effects.

Even if an agent's private information were to suggest another choice, in situations with sequential decision-making observing prior choices of other individuals conveys information on what they may know. Following earlier choices may be a rational response but also an outcome of social pressures. Thus, information cascades can be wrong, can be based on very limited information, and are often fragile (Easley and Kleinberg, 2010, p. 442). In contrast to situations in which the aggregation of independent assessment can lead to accurate outcomes at the population level, in information cascades decisions are made sequentially and that aggregation effect may not hold. In highly networked environments, cascade-like behavior may affect many types of economic and social processes from the dynamics of financial markets to fashion, moral panics and other trends.

Network science approaches have stimulated the development of alternative approaches and deeper insights into processes of dynamic change and diffusion. Such processes can be observed at the level of entire populations, subgroup and components, and at the level of individual decision-makers. Pioneering studies by Ryan and Gross (1943), Rogers (1962), and Coleman et al. (1966) examined the factors that facilitated and blocked the adoption of innovations. Among the factors that Rogers (1962) identified as critical for the success of an innovation were its relative advantage, complexity, observability, trialability and the compatibility with the social system in which it was introduced. Network approaches allow the modeling of these aspects in a highly granular fashion. In such a perspective, nodes can be seen as responding to neighboring nodes either due to informational effects or due to network effects (Easley and Kleinberg, 2010, p. 499). Such processes can be modeled as coordination games that percolate through the nodes of a network. Consequently, the choices of each node are contingent on the choices of all connected nodes. This framework can also be used to understand the extent to which competing technologies can coexist in a network and the conditions under which a network might tip toward adopting just one of the alternatives. Furthermore, network analyses have revealed that clusters of similar nodes (an outcome of homophily in network formation) may form barriers to the adoption of innovations.

4.5.3   Network Structure, Governance and Outcomes

An important question pursued by network analysis approaches is whether the structure of the network, reflected in metrics such as the degree and centrality of nodes or the density of the network, has predictable consequences for the outcomes of the interactions at an aggregated level. An increasing number of findings suggest such patterns. Early models studied epidemics, but similar issues arise in the study of product purchases, fashions, and in marketing. The dynamics of contagion processes is related to the node structure and topology of the network. For example, all else being equal, if contagion starts at nodes with high degree then information will spread more rapidly (Duan et al., 2005). In their study of Digg and Twitter, Lerman and Ghosh (2010) found evidence that the structure of the underlying networks influences the information diffusion process. Because Digg networks are dense and highly connected, news initially spreads quickly but the process slows down once a story is exposed to a larger number of unconnected users. In contrast, stories in the less connected Twitter network spread slower than on Digg but continue to spread at the same rate, so eventually reach further than Digg stories. Similar effects of the network structure were found in other areas, such as viral marketing and recommender systems (e.g., Leskovec et al., 2007), social movements (González-Bailón et al., 2011), online and local communities (Toral et al., 2009; Yardi and boyd, 2010), and for user-generated content (Susarla et al., 2008).

Network analytical models also offer novel perspectives for the theory of innovation. Evolutionary approaches recognize that innovation is an experimental process of combination and recombination of knowledge (see Antonelli and Patrucco, Chapter 15 in this volume). Consequently, the structure of the pertinent social and economic networks will influence the available innovation opportunities. This is explicitly theorized in Ronald S. Burt's theory of 'structural holes' (Burt, 1992; Borgatti et al., 2009), which examines the role of gaps in networks of complementors as opportunities for entrepreneurs to innovate and develop market niches. Recent studies have found evidence of the role of structural holes as a driver of innovation in information and communication markets (Hitt and Ireland, 2014).

A third area in which network analytical models offer new perspectives to better understand the Internet economy is issues of income distribution and winner-takes-all dynamics. In recent years, concerns have been growing that the unique economic characteristics of Internet-based markets, including high initial costs combined with low incremental costs, have contributed to high income gains for a very small group of companies and individuals. This rich-get-richer phenomenon is related to the preferential attachment dynamics that result in the familiar power law distributions of nodes, popularity, and many other phenomena on the Internet. While the dynamics is well understood once a node has a higher degree, the initial process is highly unpredictable (Easley and Kleinberg, 2010, p. 484). Nonetheless, the effects are visible in increasing industry concentration in many high-tech and digital economy markets as well as mounting evidence of an increasing share of income gains flowing to top earners and entrepreneurs (Bauer, 2015).

Last but not least, network science allows unique insights for network governance. Spulber and Yoo (2005, 2009) offer an integrated approach rooted in network and complexity theory to the regulation of telecommunications. It is a widely shared view that the networked structure of Internet governance has contributed to its global success (Mueller, 2010). While seen as an alternative to traditional forms of state and market governance, the details of how such networked coordination affects outcomes remain often opaque. Recent work in network science is helping to shed light on the underlying processes (Padovani and Pavan, 2011; Pavan, 2012). The influence of the network topology and structure has also been examined in more specific areas such as cybersecurity (e.g., Van Mieghem et al., 2009), where the density of a network was identified as a critical factor in the spread of viruses.

4.6   CONCLUSION

Network science originated in the social sciences and in mathematical graph theory in the eighteenth century, with major new contributions made since the mid-twentieth century. It has developed a unique language, concepts and metrics to represent and measure networks. These tools have made it possible to analyze the topology of the Internet in novel ways. Because it allows the modeling of the structure and connectedness among the nodes in a network, network science offers a powerful conceptual and methodological framework to study the Internet and its effects on economic and social outcomes. Social scientists, computer scientists, and physicists have made important contributions to this eminently interdisciplinary field. Much of the theoretical and empirical work is in an early stage with significant ongoing innovations. The integration of social science theory, game theory and computational methods with the availability of large granular datasets promises fruitful insights. Moreover, the cross-fertilization of economic approaches with models from communications holds considerable potential. Although network science has facilitated important insights and innovations, much work remains to be done. Further impulses may come from the exchanges between network science, Internet science, web science and Internet studies. The overlaps and synergies between network science and complexity theory are fertile ground for theoretical and empirical innovation. At the same time, network science has some weaknesses. The focus on network structures comes, to a certain extent, at the expense of addressing important features of social systems, such as differences in the power attributable to agents, the specific social relations embedded in laws and norms, and the political economy of Internet governance and policy. These are not fundamental weaknesses, though, as network science, in principle, should be able to accommodate such concerns in richer models.

NOTE

1. See http://www.caida.org/tools/visualization/walrus/, accessed 15 December 2015.

REFERENCES

Adamic, L.A. and E. Adar (2003), 'Friends and neighbors on the web', *Social Networks*, **25** (3), 211–30.
Albert, R., H. Jeong and A.-L. Barabási (2000), 'Error and attack tolerance of complex networks', *Nature*, **406** (6794), 378–82.
Anderson, C. (2009), *Free: The Future of a Radical Price*, New York: Hyperion.
Axelrod, R.M. (1984), *The Evolution of Cooperation*, New York: Basic Books.
Barabási, A.-L. and J. Frangos (2002), *Linked: The New Science of Networks*, Cambridge, MA: Perseus Books.
Bauer, J.M. (2015), 'The Internet and inequality', paper presented at the 27th Conference of the Society for the Advancement of Socio-Economics, London, 2–4 July.
Bavelas, A. (1948), 'A mathematical model for group structure', *Human Organization*, **7** (3), 16–30.
Berners-Lee, T., W. Hall, J.A. Hendler, N. Shadbolt and D.J. Weitzner (2006a), 'Creating a science of the web', *Science*, **313** (August), 769–71.
Berners-Lee, T., W. Hall and J.A. Hendler et al. (2006b), 'A framework for web science', *Foundations and Trends in Web Science*, **1** (1), 1–130.
Borgatti, S.P., A. Mehra, D.J. Brass and G. Labianca (2009), 'Network analysis in the social sciences', *Science*, **323** (5916), 892–5.
boyd, d. and K. Crawford (2012), 'Critical questions for big data: Provocations for a cultural, technological, and scholarly phenomenon', *Information, Communication & Society*, **15** (5), 662–79.
Brandenburger, A.M. and B.J. Nalebuff (1996), *Co-opetition*, New York: Doubleday.
Brandes, U. and J. Hildenbrand (2014), 'Smallest graphs with distinct singleton centers', *Network Science*, **2** (3), 416–18.
Broder, A., R. Kumar and F. Maghoul et al. (2000), 'Graph structure in the web', *Computer Networks*, **33** (1), 309–20.
Burt, R.S. (1992), *Structural Holes: The Social Structure of Competition*, Cambridge, MA: Harvard University Press.

Camerer, C.F. (2003), *Behavioral Game Theory: Experiments in Strategic Interaction*, New York and Princeton, NJ: Russell Sage Foundation and Princeton University Press.

Camerer, C.F. and E. Fehr (2006), 'When does "Economic Man" dominate social behavior?' *Science*, **311** (5757), 47–52.

Capra, F. (1996), *The Web of Life: A New Scientific Understanding of Living Systems*, New York: Anchor Books.

Castells, M. (1996), *The Rise of the Network Society*, Cambridge, MA: Blackwell Publishers.

Chattopadhyay, T. (2013), 'Reshaping institutions: Effects of ICT on bilateral trade', PhD dissertation, Michigan State University, East Lansing, Michigan.

Christakis, N.A. and J.H. Fowler (2009), *Connected: The Surprising Power of Our Social Networks and How They Shape Our Lives*, New York: Little Brown & Company.

Christensen, C.M. (1997), *The Innovator's Dilemma: When New Technologies Cause Great Firms to Fail*, Boston, MA: Harvard Business School Press.

Clauset, A., C.R. Shalizi and M. Newman (2009), 'Power-law distributions in empirical data', *SIAM Review*, **51** (4), 661–703.

Clegg, R.C., C. di Cairano-Gilfedder and S. Zhou (2010), 'A critical look at power law modelling of the Internet', *Computer Communications*, **33** (3), 259–68.

Coleman, J.S., H. Menzel and E. Katz (1966), *Medical Innovations: A Diffusion Study*, Indianapolis, IN: Bobbs-Merrill Co.

Crucitti, P., V. Latora, M. Marchiori and A. Rapisarda (2004), 'Error and attack tolerance of complex networks', *Physica A: Statistical Mechanics and its Applications*, **340** (1), 388–94.

Doornik, J.A. and D.F. Hendry (2015), 'Statistical model selection with "big data"', *Cogent Economics & Finance*, **3** (1) [online], accessed 4 January 2016 at http://www.tandfonline.com/doi/abs/10.1080/23322039. 2015.1045216.

Dorogovtsev, S.N. and J.F.F. Mendes (2003), *Evolution of Networks: From Biology to the Internet and WWW*, Oxford, UK: Oxford University Press.

Duan, W., Z. Chen, Z. Liu and W. Jin (2005), 'Efficient target strategies for contagion in scale-free networks', *Physics Review E*, **72** (2), 026133.

Dutton, W.H. (ed.) (2013), *The Oxford Handbook of Internet Studies*, Oxford, UK: Oxford University Press.

Easley, D. and J. Kleinberg (2010), *Networks, Crowds, and Markets: Reasoning About a Highly Connected World*, Cambridge, UK: Cambridge University Press.

Economides, N. (1996), 'The economics of networks', *International Journal of Industrial Organization*, **14** (6), 673–99.

Emirbayer, M. (1997), 'Manifesto for a relational sociology', *American Journal of Sociology*, **103** (2), 281–317.

Epstein, J.M. (2006), *Generative Social Science: Studies in Agent-Based Computational Modeling*, Princeton, NJ: Princeton University Press.

Epstein, J.M. and R. Axtell (1996), *Growing Artificial Societies: Social Science from the Bottom Up*, Washington, DC and Cambridge, MA: Brookings Institution Press/MIT Press.

Farrell, J. and P.J. Weiser (2003), 'Modularity, vertical integration, and open access policies: Towards a convergence of antitrust and regulation in the Internet age', *Harvard Journal of Law and Technology*, **17** (1), 85–134.

Fehr, E. and U. Fischbacher (2002), 'Why social preferences matter – the impact of non-selfish motives on competition, cooperation and incentives', *The Economic Journal*, **112** (478), C1–C33.

Freeman, L.C. (1977), 'A set of measures of centrality based on betweenness sociometry', *Sociometry*, **40** (1), 35–41.

Freeman, L.C. (2004), *The Development of Social Network Analysis. A Study in the Sociology Science*, Vancouver, BC: Empirical Press.

Fudenberg, D. and D.K. Levine (1998), *The Theory of Learning in Games*, Cambridge, MA: MIT Press.

Fudenberg, D. and J. Tirole (1991), *Game Theory*, Cambridge, MA: MIT Press.

Gintis, H. (2009), *The Bounds of Reason: Game Theory and the Unification of the Behavioral Sciences*, Princeton, NJ: Princeton University Press.

Gomez Rodriguez, M., J. Leskovec and B. Schölkopf (2013), 'Structure and dynamics of information pathways in online media', in *Proceedings of the Sixth ACM International Conference on Web Search and Data Mining (WSDM'13)*, pp. 23–32.

González-Bailón, S., J. Borge-Holthoefer, A. Rivero and T. Moreno (2011), 'The dynamics of protest recruitment through an online network', *Scientific Reports*, **1** (197) [online], accessed 4 January 2016 at http://www. nature.com/articles/srep00197.

Granovetter, M. (1985), 'Economic action and social structure: The problem of embeddedness', *American Journal of Sociology*, **91** (3), 481–510.

Harary, F. (1969), *Graph Theory*, Reading, MA: Addison-Wesley Publishing Co.

Hendler, J.A., N. Shadbolt, W. Hall, T. Berners-Lee and D.J. Weitzner (2008), 'Web science: An interdisciplinary approach to understanding the web', *Communications of the ACM*, **51** (7), 60–69.

Hennig, M., U. Brandes, J. Pfeffer and I. Mergel (2012), *Studying Social Networks: A Guide to Empirical Research*, Frankfurt am Main: Campus.

Hitt, M.A. and R.D. Ireland (2014), *Formal and Informal Alliances in the Telecommunications Industry and their Outcomes*, Phase 2 Final Report, Texas A&M University.

Jackson, M.O. (2008), *Social and Economic Networks*, Princeton, NJ: Princeton University Press.

Judd, K.L. and L. Tesfatsion (eds) (2005), *Handbook of Computational Economics, Volume 2: Agent-based Computational Modeling*, Amsterdam: North-Holland.

Jungnickel, D. (2005), *Graphs, Networks, and Algorithms*, Berlin and New York: Springer.

Kahneman, D. (2011), *Thinking, Fast and Slow*, New York: Farrar, Straus and Giroux.

Kahneman, D. and A. Tversky (eds) (2000), *Choices, Values, and Frames*, New York and Cambridge, UK: Russell Sage Foundation/Cambridge University Press.

Kahneman, D., P. Slovic and A. Tversky (eds) (1982), *Judgment Under Uncertainty: Heuristics and Biases*, Cambridge, UK; New York: Cambridge University Press.

Katz, M.L. and C. Shapiro (1985), 'Network externalities, competition, and compatibility', *American Economic Review*, **75** (3), 424–40.

Knight, S., H.X. Nguyen, N. Falkner, R. Bowden and M. Roughan (2011), 'The Internet topology zoo', *IEEE Journal on Selected Areas in Communications*, **29** (9), 1765–75.

Lazer, D., A.S. Pentland and L.A. Adamic et al. (2009), 'Life in the network: The coming age of computational social science', *Science*, **323** (5915), 721–3.

Leifeld, P. and V. Schneider (2012), 'Information exchange in policy networks', *American Journal of Political Science*, **56** (3), 731–44.

Lerman, K. and R. Ghosh (2010), 'Information contagion: An empirical study of the spread of news on Digg and Twitter social networks', in *Proceedings of the Fourth International AAAI Conference on Weblogs and Social Media*, 23–26 May, Washington, DC, pp. 93–7.

Leskovec, J., L.A. Adamic and B.A. Huberman (2007), 'The dynamics of viral marketing', *ACM Transactions on the Web (TWEB)*, **1** (1), Article 5 [online], accessed 4 January 2016 at http://dl.acm.org/citation.cfm?id=1232727.

Leskovec, J., D. Huttenlocher and J. Kleinberg (2011), 'Predicting positive and negative links in online social networks', in *Proceedings of the 19th International Conference on World Wide Web (WWW'10)*, 26–30 April, Raleigh, NC, pp. 641–50.

Lewin, K. (1936), *Principles of Topological Psychology*, New York: London: McGraw-Hill.

Mayer-Schönberger, V. and T. Cukier (2013), *Big Data: A Revolution That Will Transform How We Live, Work, and Think*, Boston, MA: Houghton Mifflin Harcourt.

McPherson, M., L. Smith-Lovin and J.M. Cook (2001), 'Birds of a feather: Homophily in social networks', *Annual Review of Sociology*, **27**(1), 415–44.

Merton, R.K. (1968), 'The Matthew effect in science', *Science*, **159** (3810), 56–63.

Mitchell, M. (2009), *Complexity: A Guided Tour*, Oxford, UK: Oxford University Press.

Monge, P.R. and N.S. Contractor (2003), *Theories of Communication Networks*, New York: Oxford University Press.

Mueller, M.L. (2010), *Networks and States: The Global Politics of Internet Governance*, Cambridge, MA: MIT Press.

Newman, M. (2012), *Networks. An Introduction*, Oxford, UK: Oxford University Press.

Newman, M., A.-L. Barabási and D.J. Watts (eds) (2006), *The Structure and Dynamics of Networks*, New York and Cambridge: Cambridge University Press.

Noam, E.M. (2006), 'Fundamental instability: Why telecom is becoming a cyclical and oligopolistic industry', *Information Economics and Policy*, **18** (3), 272–84.

Noam, E.M. (2009), *Media Ownership and Concentration in America*, New York: Oxford University Press.

North, D.C. (1990), *Institutions, Institutional Change and Economic Performance*, Cambridge, UK: Cambridge University Press.

Nowak, M.A. (2006), *Evolutionary Dynamics: Exploring the Equations of Life*, Cambridge, MA: Belknap Press of Harvard University Press.

Nowak, M.A. with R. Highfield (2011), *SuperCooperators: Altruism, Evolution, and Why We Need Each Other to Succeed*, New York: Free Press.

Padgett, J.F. and W.W. Powell (eds) (2012), *The Emergence of Organizations and Markets*, Princeton, NJ: Princeton University Press.

Padovani, C. and E. Pavan (2011), 'Actors and interactions in global communication governance: The heuristic potential of a network approach', in R. Mansell and M. Raboy (eds), *The Handbook of Global Media and Communication Policy*, London: Wiley-Blackwell, pp. 543–63.

Pastor-Satorras, R. and A. Vespignani (2004), *Evolution and Structure of the Internet: A Statistical Physics Approach*, Cambridge, UK: Cambridge University Press.

Pavan, E. (2012), *Frames and Connections in the Governance of Global Communications: A Network Study of the Internet Governance Forum*, Lanham, MD: Lexington Books.

Pentland, A. (2014), *Social Physics: How Good Ideas Spread – The Lessons from a New Science*, New York: The Penguin Press.

Raab, J. (2010), 'Der "Harvard Breakthrough"', in C. Stegbauer (ed.), *Handbuch Netzwerkforschung*, Wiesbaden: Springer, pp. 29–37.

Reed, W.J. (2001), 'The Pareto, Zipf and other power laws', *Economics Letters*, **74** (1), 15–19.

Rogers, E.M. (1962), *Diffusion of Innovations*, New York: Free Press of Glencoe.

Ryan, B. and N.C. Gross (1943), 'The diffusion of hybrid seed corn in two Iowa communities', *Rural Sociology*, **8** (1), 15–24.

Scott, J. (1991), *Social Network Analysis. A Handbook*, London: Sage.

Shadbolt, N., W. Hall, J.A. Hendler and W.H. Dutton (2013), 'Web science: A new frontier', in *Philosophical Transactions of the Royal Society of London A: Mathematical, Physical and Engineering Sciences*, **371** (1987), 20120512, accessed 4 October 2015 at http://dx.doi.org/10.1098/rsta.2012.0512.

Shy, O. (2001), *The Economics of Network Industries*, Cambridge, UK: Cambridge University Press.

Siegel, E. (2013), *Predictive Analytics: The Power to Predict Who Will Click, Buy, Lie, or Die*, Hoboken, NJ: John Wiley & Sons.

Simon, H.A. (1962), 'The architecture of complexity', in *Proceedings of the American Philosophical Society*, **106** (6), 467–82.

Simon, H.A. (1982–97), *Models of Bounded Rationality*, 3 vols, Cambridge, MA: MIT Press.

Spulber, D.F. and C.S. Yoo (2005), 'On the regulation of networks as complex systems: A graph theory approach', *Northwestern University Law Review*, **99** (4), 1687–722.

Spulber, D.F. and C.S. Yoo (2009), *Networks in Telecommunications: Economics and Law*, Cambridge, UK and New York: Cambridge University Press.

Strogatz, S.H. (2001), 'Exploring complex networks', *Nature*, **410** (6825), 268–76.

Sunstein, C.R., D. Kahneman, D. Schkade and I. Ritov (2002), 'Predictably incoherent judgments', *Stanford Law Review*, **54** (6), 1153–215.

Susarla, A., J.-H. Oh and Y. Tan (2008), 'Social networks and the diffusion of user-generated content: Evidence from YouTube', *Information Systems Research*, **23** (1), 23–41.

Tesfatsion, L. (2003), 'Agent-based computational economics: Modeling economies as complex adaptive systems', *Information Sciences*, **149** (4), 263–9.

Tiropanis, T., W. Hall, J. Crowcroft, N. Contractor and L. Tassiulas (2015), 'Network science, web science and Internet science: Comparing interdisciplinary areas', *Communications of the ACM*, **58** (8), 76–82.

Toral, S.L., M.R. Martínez-Torres, F. Barrero and F. Cortés (2009), 'An empirical study of the driving forces behind online communities', *Internet Research*, **19** (4), 378–92.

Van Mieghem, P., J. Omic and R. Kooij (2009), 'Virus spread in networks', *Transactions on Networking*, **17** (1), 1–14.

von Weizsäcker, C.C. (2005), 'The welfare economics of adaptive preferences', *MPI Collective Goods Preprint No. 2005/11*, accessed 12 December 20115 at http://ssrn.com/abstract=771904.

Wasserman, S. and K. Faust (1994), *Social Network Analysis: Methods and Applications*, Cambridge, UK: Cambridge University Press.

Watts, D.J. (2004), *Six Degrees: The Science of a Connected Age*, New York: Norton & Company.

Watts, D.J. and S.H. Strogatz (1998), 'Collective dynamics of "small-world" networks', *Nature*, **393** (6684), 440–42.

White, H.C. (2001), *Markets from Networks: Socioeconomic Models of Production*, New Haven, CT: Princeton University Press.

Wildman, S.S. (2008), 'Communication and economics: Two imperial disciplines and too little collaboration', *Journal of Communication*, **58** (4), 693–706.

Willinger, W., D. Alderson and J.C. Doyle (2010), 'Mathematics and the Internet: A source of enormous confusion and great potential', in M. Pitici (ed.), *The Best Writing on Mathematics 2010*, Princeton, NJ: Princeton University Press, pp. 109–33.

Wilson, R.J. (2004), 'History of graph theory', in J.L. Gross and J. Yellen (eds), *Handbook of Graph Theory*, Boca Raton, FL: CRC Press, pp. 29–49.

Wright, A. (2011), 'Web science meets network science', *Communications of the ACM*, **54** (5), 23.

Yardi, S. and d. boyd (2010), 'Tweeting from the town square: Measuring geographic local networks', in *Proceedings of the Fourth International AAAI Conference on Weblogs and Social Media (ICWSM-10)*, 23–26 May, Washington, DC, pp. 194–201.

5. Peer production and cooperation
Yochai Benkler

5.1 INTRODUCTION AND OVERVIEW

Peer production is the most significant organizational innovation that has emerged from Internet-mediated social practice. Organizationally, it combines three core characteristics: (1) decentralization of conception and execution of problems and solutions, (2) harnessing diverse motivations, and (3) separation of governance and management from property and contract. Functionally, these components make peer-production practices highly adept at learning and experimentation, innovation, and adaptation in rapidly changing, persistently uncertain and complex environments. Under high rates of technological innovation, and the high diversity of sources of uncertainty typical of early twenty-first-century global markets, the functional advantages of peer production have made it an effective organizational model in diverse domains. From free software, through Wikipedia to video journalism, peer production plays a more significant role in the information production environment than predicted by standard models at the turn of the millennium.[1]

Free and open-source software (FOSS) and Wikipedia are the most recognized instances of peer production. FOSS is responsible for the development of most of the basic utilities on which the Internet runs. Firms have recognized this, and have been adopting FOSS as a strategic option for 15 years. The beginning of this period was marked by the 1999 initial public offering (IPO) of Red Hat, the first successful commercial Linux distribution, IBM's announcement in 2000 that it would invest $1 billion in its FOSS strategy, and the decision by Netscape, the company that had created the web browser market but lost its early dominance to Microsoft (as a result of strategies that formed the basis of the antitrust adjudication against the firm), to make its browser FOSS and create the Mozilla Foundation to shepherd what would become Firefox. Most recently, Google's strategic choice to develop Android as FOSS allowed Android to catch up and overtake Apple's iOS as the dominant smartphone operating system. Wikipedia was laughable – a curiosity at best, a theoretical impossibility at worst, for mainstream economic theory of 1999. And yet it has developed into one of the most important knowledge utilities of our time.

Much of the early economic analysis of peer production focused on software (Ghosh, 1998; Lerner and Tirole, 2002; Bessen, 2005), but FOSS was understood by some from the start as an aspect of online cooperation (Ghosh, 1998; Kollock, 1999; Moglen, 1999) with a strong emphasis on the comparative advantages of peer production as an organizational and institutional model of collaborative innovation and information production (Benkler, 2001, 2002; Von Hippel and Von Krogh, 2003; Weber, 2004; Bauwens 2005). Since then there has been a gradually expanding literature on FOSS and peer production.

Peer production refers to open collaborative innovation and creation, performed by diverse, decentralized groups organized principally by neither price signals nor organizational hierarchy, harnessing heterogeneous motivations, and governed and managed based on principles other than the residual authority of ownership implemented through contract. Work has largely fallen in the categories of motivation, organization, and effectiveness or value to innovation. Here I will particularly emphasize the lessons for the importance of (1) diversity of human motivation, (2) innovation, experimentation, and tacit knowledge under conditions of uncertainty and change, and (3) transaction and organization costs, in making these decentralized models stable and self-sustaining, effective, and in some cases superior to the traditional models of production – markets, firms (both for-profit and non-profit), and governments.

The implications of peer production are broader than the direct economic impact of the practice. Beyond the magnitude of its effects on innovation and knowledge production in the networked economy and participation in the networked society, the success of peer production and online cooperation has several implications for economics more generally. It requires that we refine our ideas about motivation or incentives; it recalibrates the roles of property and contract, as opposed to commons and social organization, in the growth-critical domains of knowledge-dependent production and innovation; and it requires adaptations to the theory of the firm.

5.1.1   Definitions: Peer Production Distinguished from Crowdsourcing, Online Labor Markets, Prizes or Competitions, and Open, Collaborative Innovation

Peer production is an organizational innovation along three dimensions:

- Decentralized conception and execution.
- Diverse motivations, including a range of non-monetary motivations, are central.
- Organization (governance and management) is separated from property and contract:
  - Inputs and outputs mostly governed as open commons or common property regimes.
  - Organizational governance and managerial resource and task definition and allocation utilize combinations of participatory, meritocratic (do-ocracy) and charismatic, rather than proprietary or contractual, models. In firm-hosted peer production, however, property and contract are often retained, but contract structure is designed to simulated freedom to operate features of the absence of property and contract. The retention of control over platforms does influence the dynamics, capabilities, and potential tensions faced by firm-based peer production.

Section 5.2 will explain the centrality of these three to the particular advantages of peer production as an information, innovation, and knowledge production system. For now, take Wikipedia or FOSS as the core examples, where conception and execution (of a feature needing development, or an article that needs writing) are decentralized; where contributors rely on diverse motivations, many (about half in FOSS, all in Wikipedia) non-monetary; where the copyright licenses used make ownership or contract irrelevant to the core organizational question of who does what, when, with what resources and which collaborators; and where task construction generally is collaborative, though in some cases may be merely coordinated/collated. Property and contract play a somewhat larger role in copyleft[2] licenses than non-copyleft licenses. However, even in copyleft licenses the property/contract aspects supply a minimal baseline set of constraints rather than providing the basis for either signaling or authority to direct and coordinate action.

The phenomenon most often confounded with peer production (see Table 5.1 for all the phenomena discussed here) is 'crowdsourcing' (Howe, 2006), whose clearest instance is Amazon Mechanical Turk (MTurk). MTurk is an online labor market that allows anyone to offer distributed workers monetary rewards in exchange for completing discrete, usually highly granular, tasks for low per-task payment. One common use is image tagging. Visual comprehension is extremely difficult for machines to perform well but highly intuitive for people. 'Human computing' is a developing field in computer science that tries to solve machine-hard, human-easy tasks. This includes, for instance, interpreting visual images by building platforms that harness human beings to perform these tasks in ways that can then be recombined as a solution. To provide a concrete example, let us look at ReCAPTCHA, a project developed by Luis van Ahn that uses optically scanned book fragments as gateways to secure services. Because vision is computer-hard, human-easy, requiring human beings to identify and type in the letters in a visually blurry string of letters is a good mechanism for telling humans apart from bots on the Net. These 'CAPTCHAs' are therefore a good gateway device for services, such as online subscription services, or security questions, to filter out bots – automated scripts programmed to look human to the service they access. By using scanned books or newspapers as the captcha, ReCAPTCHA harnesses the human beings who need to access the service to clean up digitized archives (Van Ahn et al., 2008).

Crowdsourcing is distinct from peer production because the tasks it involves are highly regimented and pre-specified by the task designer. It comes in two flavors – monetary and non-monetary. MTurk is the most widely used monetary crowdsourcing platform (Horton, 2010). Non-monetary crowdsourcing platforms, whose lead innovator has been Van Ahn, use fun, as in games with a purpose (GWAP),[3] or necessity, as with ReCAPTCHA, to harness distributed human action to achieve the predefined goal. The critical distinction between crowdsourcing and peer production is in the location of conception of tasks and solutions. 'Crowdsourcing' would most usefully be applied to instances where cost reduction, rather than distributed exploration of a resource and opportunity space, is the core function of the system. This would properly apply to situations where the task is conceived and defined by a given entity, and then put out to distributed individuals whose actions are limited to performing the preconceived task. In this regard, it harnesses undifferentiated human labor, rather than judgment, creativity, experience, tacit knowledge, or talent. From an organizational perspective, crowdsourcing represents a relatively small innovation. It harnesses thousands of independent contractors to perform tightly specified tasks. However, it does not affect governance or ownership, does not restructure innovation, learning, and adaptation for the organization or the task, and does not generally harness any new motivational vectors beyond standard hedonic gains, through payments (MTurk), fun (GWAP), or as a precondition to access desired services (ReCAPTCHA). The task construction itself generally relies on the coordinated output of many contributors. Unlike online labor markets or prize systems, no single contribution by itself is a potentially complete, however imperfect, solution to the task or problem addressed. Some citizen science projects have this characteristic, like the Mars Clickworkers that originated the practice, distributed computing, like SETI@ Home or Folding@Home, which harnessed thousands of volunteers to contribute excess computation cycles of their home computers to compute highly complex problems at speeds that rival the largest supercomputers, or open government projects that harness citizens to monitor their governments by performing very low-level regimented data input from diverse forms to convert them into computable form.

'Online labor markets' are yet a different model of decentralization. Upwork (combining Elance and ODesk), for example, is a platform that allows computer programmers from around the world to bid on contracts to execute on orders proposed by customers. The innovation is in creating a much more efficient, global market for high-quality services, which allows firms to harness distributed talent from around the world. Organizationally, these represent a significant incremental improvement in the efficiency of markets for skilled labor, harnessing dramatic declines in market transactions cost to reduce the need for firm-based labor organization. Online labor markets adopt some degree of decentralized conception and execution, more the latter than the former, and in this regard are very different from crowdsourcing. They usually result in individual, rather than collaborative or even coordinated, production: the person who gets the contract generally performs it as an individual contractor. They rely on monetary motivations as the sole motivator and generally maintain the nexus between ownership and governance and management, using contract and property to govern inputs, outputs, processes, and role allocation associated with the task.

'Prize systems' include TopCoder, a platform that enables about one million registered coders to enter competitions for designing the best solutions to problems posed by clients. InnoCentive, Kaggle, and other firms provide similar platforms for either general purpose or field-specific competition and prize systems to be deployed to harness creative problem-solving effort toward problems posed by firms or governments. Prize systems are similar to online labor markets, but they emphasize decentralization of conception and execution even more forcefully, leaving even the design of the task to a highly distributed pool of innovative, skilled workers. Because prize systems need not pay for effort or outcome of every participant, unlike online labor markets, they can afford much wider and more diverse experimentation with alternative solution approaches than can online labor markets. This, in turn, allows them to capture extreme value solutions in areas where the problem definition and path of execution are highly uncertain (Boudreau et al., 2011). Even more than online labor markets, prize systems engage parallel efforts of competitors, and the ultimate output is generally the output of a single competing person or entity, as opposed to offering even complementarity between solutions offered. I call this task construction 'parallel-competitive', as distinguished from 'parallel-complementary' task organization models that allow each discrete contribution to offer a complete solution to the problem, but depend on complementarity between the alternative solutions to attain the best outcome.

'Open collaborative innovation' is a set of productive practices that have developed among firms in various complex product- and innovation-rich markets for some time, and received a boost from networked communications (Powell, 1990, 1996; Chesbrough, 2003; Gilson et al., 2008, 2010). These practices share with peer production the recognition that the smartest and best people to solve any given problem are unlikely to work in a single firm, such as the firm facing the challenge. Further, they recognize that the

Table 5.1   Peer production distinguished from other models of decentralized production and innovation

	Task Conception Decentralized	Task Execution Decentralized	Social Motivations Significant	Governance/ Management Separated from Ownership	Task Structure
Crowdsourcing	0	1	~	0	Coordination
Online labor markets	~	1	0	0	Individual; parallel
Prize systems	1	1	~	0	Parallel-competitive
Open collaborative innovation	~	~	0	0	Collaboration
Firm-hosted peer production	1/~	1	1	0/~	Collaboration; coordination; parallel-complementary
Commons-based peer production	1	1	1	1	Collaboration; coordination; parallel-complementary

Note: 1 = characteristic present; 0 = characteristic absent; ~ = present in some instances or only to a degree.

models of innovation and problem-solving that allow diverse people, from diverse settings, to work collaboratively on the problem will lead to better outcomes. By contrast, production models that enforce strict boundaries at the edge of the firm and do not allow collaboration based on fit of person to task rather than based on employment contract and ownership of the problem will be less innovative and productive. There are strong overlaps between open collaborative innovation and peer production from policy perspectives, primarily in implications for intellectual property, but this category does not include the separation of ownership from governance and management, or the inclusion of participants who are not part of any of the set of mutually cooperating firms, or those motivated by non-monetary motivations. A firm facing a complex software development problem could enter into contracts with several of its suppliers and even competitors, adopt open standards at the core of its strategy, and place some of its workers in other firms, and receive those of others in its own, as part of an open collaborative strategy. Or, that same firm could partly develop the software it requires and license it as FOSS and use SourceForge or GitHub to manage the repository. In the former case, the firm would be engaged in open collaborative innovation. The latter would be the firm engaging peer production.

Peer production itself has, over the past decade, developed into two quite distinct flavors. Commons-based peer production (CBPP), the original model of FOSS and Wikipedia, includes all attributes I ascribed to peer production. Firm-hosted peer production, such as Yelp or TripAdvisor, deviates in a critical way from CBPP, or full peer production, in that the governance and management are based in proprietary claims to exclusion from the site to enforce terms of use with regard to user contributions. These are anchored in firm control over the infrastructure or platform that is used to host and coordinate the peer-production effort (Fuster Morell, 2010). Yelp is a clear example of this approach. The firm depends on its users to select restaurants, businesses, and so on to be reviewed, and depends on them to provide reviews. At the same time, the contributions are governed by terms of use that retain proprietary claims over the database, and outline certain acceptable use constraints as contractual obligations of the users. Task conception (who should be reviewed) is more distributed than in crowdsourcing, and social motivations are salient, as users are not paid for their reviews. These firm-hosted peer-production models need to rely on contract terms that simulate the absence of property and contract. Firms do so by retaining and providing to users non-exclusive licenses to all user content, rather than asserting full ownership over it. Further, they make contributions flow into the system without permission, and they limit their own assertion of contractual and property rights to rare occasions. On those rare occasions, firms will justify their actions by reference to shared norms, not merely to firm interest or legal right.

Not all firms that engage with peer production necessarily deviate from commons-based peer production. When IBM participates in Apache (which is not an IBM-hosted or -initiated project) development, or even when Google distributes Chromium (a Google project) under a FOSS license, the organization of development, despite the formal ownership of the code, is severed from the firm's ownership. Where the property and contract remain separated from ownership and operation of the site, the fact that a firm owns the site does not make a commons-based peer-production enterprise into a firm-hosted peer-production enterprise. For example, when peer editors of Wikitravel came to dislike the policies of the site/trademark owner, Internet Brands, they were able to leave, take all the content they had developed, which was under a Creative Commons License, and start afresh as Wikivoyage. Despite its corporate ownership and the presence of for-profit advertising on the site from 2006 to 2012, the property and contract structure of management and governance maintained the nature of the site as CBPP or full peer production. It is whether contract and property are separated from governance and management, not ownership of the site or the trademark associated with it, that marks a site as firm-hosted peer production or commons-based peer production. In terms of the information quality attributes, a firm-hosted peer-production process will only share the exploration and discovery characteristics of commons-based peer production if it avoids using contract or property to steer and constrain avenues of exploration and experimentation by the peers. In terms of motivational harnessing attributes, firm-based peer production will only replicate the attributes of commons-based peer production if the host firm can authentically and credibly bind itself, or by practice instill trust in the peers whose work it facilitates, that it will not undermine community norms. The host firm must assure users that it will not assert its contractual or proprietary authority in ways visibly at odds with management and coordination practices commonly observed in commons-based peer-production enterprises or with normative understanding among the peers about the proper role of the firm with regard to the peer community.

5.1.2 How Significant is Peer Production in the Actual Economy?

Measuring the direct economic significance or impact of peer production is difficult. One approach is to observe adoption of information goods, in various verticals, that are the outputs of peer production. The most obvious cluster of utilities is the web itself. Netcraft web survey has been collecting data on web server software adoption since the middle of 1995. At that point, academically developed and a range of 'other' servers were competing for adoption. By March of 1996, Sun Microsystems and the FOSS project Apache were the main competitors, as Microsoft joined the field. Within a year, Microsoft caught up with and eclipsed Sun, and since then has been the primary competitor to Apache. Nonetheless, Apache never lost its dominance in terms of share of adopted web server platforms connected to the Net. As of January of 2013, Apache held a 55 percent market share, Microsoft 17 percent; NGINX, an alternative FOSS platform, 13 percent; Google's servers for its own machines, 4 percent; and the remainder was held by platforms bunched as 'other' (Netcraft, 2013).

Server side scripting languages are the primary languages used for programming functions on the web. PHP, an open source language, is used by 78 percent of websites, while Microsoft's ASP.NET holds the remaining 20 percent. Most of the remaining languages, like Ruby or Python, are also open source (W3Techs, 2013). Web browser statistics are less clearly in favor of open source. Historically, Microsoft's Internet Explorer (IE) held over 95 percent of the market after it squeezed Netscape Navigator out of the market (illegally, according to antitrust adjudications in both the USA and EU). Netscape then spun out Navigator to a non-profit, the Mozilla foundation, as FOSS. Over time, Firefox gradually captured market share over the 2000s, and in 2008 Google also released Chrome, and at the same time a parallel, FOSS project, Chromium. As of January 2013, competing methods identify IE as either having 55 percent of the desktop browser market or 31 percent; and Chrome and Firefox having either 18 percent and 20 percent, respectively, or 36 percent and 22 percent, respectively (Vaughan-Nichols, 2013). By a different measure, almost 40 percent of firms engaged in software development reported spending development time on developing and contributing to FOSS software (Lerner and Schankerman, 2010). Others have suggested that FOSS has higher quality or innovativeness by various measures. Considering the adoption patterns and the literature it appears clear that, at least in software, FOSS is an economically significant organizational and institutional strategy (Bonnacorsi and Rossi, 2003; Von Krogh, 2003; Lorenzi and Rossi Lamastra, 2007). Additionally, software, as an industry, accounts for somewhere between $350 billion and $400 billion per year in the United States (on one model, one could combine computer services: NAICS[4] 5415 [$245 billion] software publishing NAICS 5112 [$135 billion]/Internet publishing NAICS 51913 [$31 billion]; Forrester Research suggests $208 billion in software sales and $188 billion in IT integration and consulting services) (Datta, 2012).

Software adoption is more widely and consistently measured than other information production sectors. Wikipedia is by far the most successful, largest, and most diverse peer-production project. The subject of several books and over 5000 articles, Wikipedia is among the top six to eight sites in the world,[5] and has become the basic knowledge utility of networked life, alongside Google search. Frischmann et al. (2014) collect a series of chapters describing a wider range of peer-production practices. Maurer (2010) describes case studies of instances where distributed, non-state, non-market action was able to deliver discrete but meaningful public goods, ranging from nanotech safety standards to a synthetic DNA anti-terrorism code. Online, in a range of specific product areas, business models that depend on peer production have outcompeted businesses that depend on more traditional, price-cleared or firm-centric models of production. Flickr, Photobucket, and Google Images, all of which are peer-production platforms capable of delivering stock photography, have overshadowed Corbis, the primary firm using the traditional model in this field. YouTube, Google video, and Vimeo are all more highly ranked as online video sites than the proprietary models of HULU, Vevo, or even Netflix (though Netflix, the most widely used among these, is roughly equal to Vimeo). TripAdvisor is more popular than Lonely Planet, Fodor's, or Frommers in travel guides, and Yelp in restaurant reviews. In all, organizations, both for-profit and non-profit, who have found ways of organizing their core production function on a peer-production model have thrived in the networked environment, often overcoming competition from more traditional, market- and firm-based models. However, there have been no formal measurements of the relative contribution of peer production to the Internet economy, or efforts to measure performance of firms that have adopted these strategies. The closest efforts we have are De Jong and Von Hippel (2009), who seek to assess the level of innovation by user firms, as opposed to producer firms, and Von Hippel et al. (2010), who use survey methods to elicit innovation among individuals in the UK population generally. This is related, but not direct evidence. For our purposes here, it is perhaps sufficient to accept that peer production has played a significant role over the course of the first 20 years of the commercial Internet, and continues to do so today. The dearth of work suggests that formal measurement of the productivity and contributions of peer production in well-defined studies is an important avenue for future research.

5.1.3   Core Economic Questions

Three major questions occupy the literature on the economics of peer production, mostly discussed in the domain of free and open source software. The broad overarching question is that of effectiveness and innovation: what are the conditions for the emergence of sustained peer production, and what are the relative advantages of this networked organizational model over more traditional models: firms, government, and pure market clearance? Two more discrete questions inform that broader question: motivations and governance. For motivations, much of the initial question in economics has been why individuals would volunteer their efforts toward producing a product in which they then claim no exclusion rights, and later this work also focused on why firms would invest in such efforts and adopt their outputs. The forward-looking question, however, should be whether or not we can use our knowledge of the microfoundations of diverse motivations to design organizational forms that better harness and direct these diverse motivations. In other words, can we move from mechanism design to cooperative human systems design? The second question is one of governance and management: how do networks of collaborators organize their affairs once exclusive ownership and formal contract are excluded as the foundation of organizational governance (questions of who gets to make what kinds of decision in the organization) and management (questions of who does what with which resource sets)?

5.2 INNOVATION AND LEARNING: WHY WOULD PEER PRODUCTION EMERGE NOW, AND WHAT ARE ITS ADVANTAGES AS A MODE OF PRODUCTION?

Peer production (including FOSS) is an organizational innovation. It marks a new organizational form that expands on the more traditional market/hierarchy dichotomy in the study of organizations (Benkler, 2002, 2006; Osterloh et al., 2003; Elsner et al., 2010; Baldwin and Von Hippel, 2010). It is the clearest instance of the rise of networks as an alternative organizational model to markets and hierarchies (Powell, 1990). To understand this organizational innovation, in turn, requires an explanation of the advantages that loosely coupled networks of diversely experienced and motivated individuals have over firms or markets as innovation and knowledge production models.

The basic model is a straight transactions cost model. Production requires the coordination of people (agents), resources, and projects. In a classic perfect market, prices on each of these three components lead to matching. A firm expecting a given price for project P will be able to determine how much it can afford to pay for agents and resources for the project, which converts resources and agents bought in that market into the output that will be sold at some price p in the market. The values of the competing projects, the value of the various people and resources to competing projects, will determine the market-clearing price for any given resource or person, and in turn will decide whether, when, and at what quality the project can be pursued given the market valuation of its output. Coase's new institutional theory of the firm (Coase, 1937) posited that for some resources, people, and projects, the cost of managerial allocation plus potential misallocation was lower than the cost of market clearance, leading to the creation of firms but also limiting their size when managerial costs outweigh price-system costs. Once one understands that social exchange is also a transactional framework widely used for a broad range of goods and services (Benkler, 2004 provides a series of NAICS categories that denote market provision of services alongside their commonly used social exchange) (childcare, home healthcare, entertainment, carpooling, being the most intuitively visible services for which social exchange is widely used in modern economies), it is trivial to expand the same analysis to social exchange transactional networks. Where information inputs, whose marginal cost is zero, can be combined with highly distributed low-cost physical capital (computers and communications networks) and human capital that is widely underemployed (TV watching hours, at least), a substantial amount of distributed information production using these widely distributed inputs can effectively compete with market, firm, or state-based transactional models (Benkler, 2002).

A simple, elegant model in this vein is Baldwin and Von Hippel (2010). Baldwin and Von Hippel posit a two-dimensional space made of communications costs and design costs for innovation. Where communications costs are extremely high (e.g., unique needs of a single farmer) but design costs are very low, the communication necessary for producers to work on the problem will fail, and only single-user developers will innovate. Where design costs are high, and communications costs are high, only producer innovators will develop, because the capital cost of innovating will be too high for the user innovator to undertake alone, and the high communication costs will prevent peer production from spreading the design cost among many contributors. Where design costs are extremely high and communications costs extremely low, open collaborative innovation, or peer production, will be dominant, because peer producers can spread the design costs over many developers, at a low communications cost. There are various levels of design cost/communications cost where two or three of the approaches will be sustainable.

The simple transactions cost model can be supplemented with a more specific view of information and learning that explains why distributed innovation, creativity, or problem-solving would have a transactions costs advantage over proprietary and managed systems. A less crisp but more complete explanation requires a clearer model of how organizations learn. Both managerial control and price clearance require formalization of descriptions of resources, people (i.e., their diverse capabilities and availabilities for a given project at a given juncture/time), and projects into units capable of transmission through the communications system these organizational models represent. To economize on transactions and organization costs, both managerial control and pricing require abstraction, generalization, and standardization of what are in reality heterogeneous and changing characteristics of the people, resources, and projects that could be combined in a project or transaction. In that abstraction process, both administrative descriptions and prices are 'lossy': the formalization strips information out of the real world characteristics of the relevant resources and projects. The lost information, in turn, leads systems whose functioning depends on discarding the information to underperform relative to systems able to bring a more refined fit of potential resources and agents to better-defined projects. Complexity and uncertainty make the information problem of matching people, resources, and projects less amenable to managerial or price-based solutions. Complexity and uncertainty (Knightian uncertainty of unknown probabilities of outcomes or unknown potential outcomes, as opposed to risk, with known probabilities of a known range of outcomes) put pressure on both neoclassical and new institutional models, because the actual properties of resources, people, and projects are highly diverse and interconnected; and the interactions among them are complex, in the sense that small differences in initial conditions or perturbations over time can significantly change the qualities of the interactions and outcomes at the system level. This leads to the known phenomenon of path dependence, both technological and institutional (David, 1985; North, 1990; Arthur, 1994), suggesting that these divergences can persist in the face of systematic observed inefficiency. The fine-grained, diverse qualities of people, projects, and resources, and the relatively significant divergences that can occur because of relatively fine-grained differences in input combinations or local interactions, mean that it is impossible to abstract and generalize the process into communications units available for a managerial decision or price clearance without significant loss of information, control, and, ultimately, effectiveness.

Note that 'knowledge' and 'learning' in the presence of complexity and uncertainty refer to more than a classic notion of innovation, such as creating a new way of doing something that was impossible to do before. Importantly, they also include problem-solving, or iterative improvement in how something is done given persistent absence of complete knowledge about the problem and the solution that comes with complexity and uncertainty. If creating the WWW or writable web software like Wiki was 'innovation' on a commons-based model, Wikipedia's organizational innovation is in problem-solving more than innovation: how to maintain quality contributions together with potentially limitless expansion, a problem that scarcity absolved *Britannica* from solving. User-generated content similarly serves more diverse tastes than a more centralized system can;

user-created restaurant or hotel accommodation reviews solve a complexity in implementation problem, with highly diverse sites to review and tastes of people who may want to use the places reviewed. In each case, the peer approach allowed the organizations to explore a space of highly diverse interests and tastes that was too costly for more traditional organizations to explore.

In this model, a critical part of the advantage of peer production incorporates the importance of incontractible knowledge, either because it is tacit knowledge or because the number and diversity of people with knowledge that needs to be brought to bear on an implementation problem is too great to contract for. Tacit knowledge is knowledge people possess, but in a form that they cannot communicate. Once you learn how to ride a bicycle, you know how to do so. Yet, if you were to sit down and write a detailed memorandum, your reader would not know how to ride a bicycle. It is increasingly clear that tacit knowledge is critical in actual human systems. Peer production allows people to deploy their tacit knowledge directly, without losing much of it in the effort to translate it into the communicable form (an effort as futile as teaching someone how to ride a bike by writing a memo) necessary for decision-making through prices or managerial hierarchies. Where knowledge is explicit, but highly distributed in forms that need to be collated to be effective, the barrier is a simple transactions costs problem. A system that allows agents to explore their environment for problems and solutions, experiment, learn, and iterate on solutions and their refinement without requiring intermediate formalizations to permit and fund the process will have an advantage over a system that does require those formalizations; and that advantage will grow as the uncertainty of what path to follow, who is best situated to follow it, and what class of solution approaches are most promising become less clearly defined.

Consider the original, single-person version of user innovation as originally developed by Von Hippel (e.g., Von Hippel, 1988). There, Von Hippel showed how in diverse settings lead users were able to identify new uses that required an innovation, the limitations of existing devices or systems to address these uses, and were able to experiment with diverse solutions until they hit on an innovation that solved a problem that producers did not even know existed. Examples of this distributed search for problems and solutions range as wide as the first heart-lung machines, developed by physicians who had reached the boundary of innovation in surgical techniques that required that improvement, or self-moving irrigation systems developed by leading farmers. In both cases, the diversity of practices in medicine, and the divergence of practices and needs of local farming, created a knowledge gap between emerging needs and the companies that would ultimately stabilize the solution. Innovative users, who applied themselves to the problem, solved the basic innovation outlines, and freely shared their innovations, filled that vacuum. Only once the practice had reached a level of crystallization that could be transmitted to a firm did firms enter and ultimately improve on the original design. But the diversity and complexity of problems, resources, and experiments on potential solutions was driven by decentralized actors that were not operating within either price or managerial structures for the production of the innovations they developed. Von Hippel documented this phenomenon repeatedly regarding users exploring problem and solution spaces while firms generalize and standardize, you might say 'productize', a solution developed by one of these many and diverse individuals.

Peer production more generally, in particular when it relies on commons – that is, on symmetrical access privileges (with or without use rules) to the resource without transaction – allows (1) diverse people, irrespective of organizational affiliation or property/contract nexus to a given resource or project, (2) dynamically to assess and reassess the available resources, projects, and potential collaborators, and (3) to self-assign to projects and collaborations. By leaving all these elements of the organization of a project to self-organization dynamics, peer production overcomes the 'lossiness' of markets and bureaucracies, whether firm or governmental. It does so, of course, at the expense of incurring new kinds of coordination and self-organization costs. Where the physical capital requirements of a project are either very low, or capable of fulfillment by utilizing pre-existing distributed capital endowments, where the project is susceptible to modularization for incremental production pursued by diverse participants, and where the diversity gain from harnessing a wide range of experience, talent, insight, and creativity in innovation, quality, speed, or precision of connecting outputs to demand is high, peer production can emerge and outperform markets and hierarchies (Benkler, 2002, 2004).

The effectiveness of the distributed search and experimentation model was increased dramatically when the cost of communication and 'material' dropped, so that diverse individuals could share problem definitions, potential solutions, and experimental models (Baldwin and Von Hippel, 2010). The first person to identify a need or problem worth solving may not be the best to offer a tentative solution, or the best to identify the incremental improvement on that tentative solution to move the solution to a usable stage. This collaboration then substantially increased the scale and scope of problems and solutions that communities of users could approach (Raymond, 1999; Benkler, 2002; Von Hippel, 2005; Baldwin and Von Hippel, 2010). An early version that connected the benefits of this approach specifically to the complexity of software projects was Bessen (2005).

To model the importance of learning under uncertainty to organizational models, we can map the organizational approaches described here along three dimensions. These are: (1) the degree of uncertainty in the project space, (2) the degree to which the human knowledge input is important, as well as the degree to which it is formalizable, explicit, and routine as opposed to tacit, intuitive, or creative, and (3) the degree of capital concentration required to execute the project (Figure 5.1). The more uncertain, as opposed to routine, the problem and solution space is, and the more tacit, creative, intuitive, or knowledge-intensive the human dimensions, the harder it is to define the required human, material, and knowledge resources necessary, as well as to define the best project to pursue. As uncertainty and creativity, tacit knowledge, intuition increase, the benefits of managerial control and explicit pricing decrease relative to their costs. As uncertainty increases along these two dimensions, so too do the advantages of peer production specifically, and more generally of open innovation strategies, over proprietary, closed models that limit the range of actors and resources in order to improve appropriability. The third dimension, the degree to which the capital costs of execution are high and concentrated (the steam engine, the assembly plant), as opposed to low (writing a song) or susceptible to fulfillment by aggregating diffuse capital (personal computers already distributed in the population), creates an efficient limit on the more open, diverse strategies. Aggregating, managing, and renewing an expensive and concentrated capital base will tend to favor managerial hierarchies, either state or market-based as necessary, and will place a limit on the degree to which a project can embrace freedom to operate by diverse

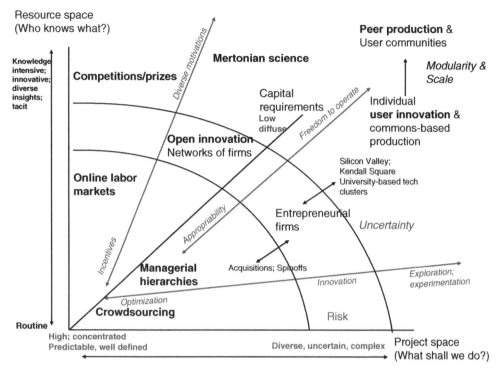

Figure 5.1   Organizational models as a function of uncertainty, knowledge, and capital

actors over appropriability of the project outputs. To the extent that capital formation does not present a barrier, we see strategies migrate toward the more exploratory and less price mediated. The part of the map where projects and resources and human knowledge necessary are relatively routine and well understood, and capital concentrated, hierarchical managerial firms are at their best is also the space where crowdsourcing can lower the cost associated with production (although it depends on distributed capital necessary for participation – that is, computers in the hands of the crowd harnessed), but only where problem spaces and human inputs can be defined in advance with some precision. Online labor markets still require sufficient certainty on the problem definition to assure payment for labor, but greater uncertainty of who can do the job and a higher degree of diversity in capabilities. It also allows for applying labor to less modular problems.

As we move out from the origin, the organizational models trade off clear, well-understood monetary incentives for a need to harness more diverse motivations. In particular, because the required skills and combinations are increasingly uncertain, the required effort becomes increasingly incontractible in that you do not know who to contract with, what to contract them to do, or how to measure what they have done. Here, intrinsic and non-monetary motivations that do not require crisp contracting and monitoring become critical. Moreover, as the project and human space becomes more uncertain, appropriability becomes less certain, and its expected value is overshadowed by the expected learning and exploration benefits of freedom to operate in the resource and problem space; similarly, well-managed optimization of such an uncertain project and human scope becomes futile and wide open exploration and experimentation become more important. As we move out to a band with less certain but still well-understood risk–reward tradeoffs, we see two types of solutions. Where the question of 'what is worth doing' is very risky, we see entrepreneurial firms using the market to raise risk capital and deploy, failing or succeeding with little global systemic cost. Where the project space is better understood, but the talent pool is uncertain, we see networks of firms embracing open innovation and collaboration as a mechanism to reach across firm boundaries to apply diverse talent to a range of problems, but retaining manageability and appropriability by keeping the set of actors well-defined, in well-managed, usually long-term contractual relationships, applied to what are more clearly defined problems than those where we see peer production at its more effective. The particular advantage of user innovation, competitions/prizes, and peer production lies outside these relatively well-understood boundaries of routine or even well-understood risky development. Similarly, the classic literature on the tradeoff between basic academic science and applied commercial science (Nelson, 1959), and the role of universities alongside pharmaceuticals and entrepreneurial firms in biotechnology (Powell, 1996) is easy to locate on the map to orient it toward already well-known phenomena.

The broad openness of the model to contributions from anyone, with freedom to operate without having to translate one's ideas or initiatives into someone else's decision over purse strings or authority structures, enables rapid and diverse exploration and experimentation in a highly uncertain scape – where neither the relevant insights and knowledge that human beings possess is well understood, nor the range of plausible projects well defined. Because competitions and prizes still require a 'client', a payor who defines the goal, and because the competitors in a prize system usually seek the prize, and hence seek to maintain some level of control or appropriability, these systems will tend to be single person or managed group entrants, and are therefore closer to the origin than peer production. Fully distributed search and experimentation that characterizes user innovation and peer production varies based on the scale of the problem and the modularity of the project. As the scale, complexity, or novelty of the problem grows, identifying solutions individually becomes less likely. As long as the solution or project aimed at solution retains its decomposability into modules, these larger-scale projects will draw user communities and peer production rather than depending solely on individual distributed innovation or commons-based production. The ability to harness a more diverse set of eyes to look at the problem gives these collaborative projects their advantage over distributed, purely parallel search.

Before turning to the question of motivation, it is worthwhile noting the development of evolutionary models to explain the organizational distinctness of FOSS specifically, and peer production more generally (e.g., Elsner et al., 2010). Landini (2012) offers an evolutionary game-theoretic model that complements the new institutionalist model of Benkler and Baldwin and Von Hippel. In addition to the technological effects driving decentralization of capital, reduction of communications cost, and modularization making peer production more efficient and feasible, Landini develops a model of two alternative stable equilibria based on bidirectional causality – where the form of rights can determine the type of technological development path chosen as well as vice versa. Thus, closed proprietary and non-modular, relatively high labor cost production is stable given proprietary control, because of its superior rent-extraction properties (whether efficient in context of not), and open, modular, low incremental labor cost contributions are similarly stable because of their cost, learning, and efficiency advantages. Landini's model explains well the observed relative stability of software projects – those that start open, remain open, and those that start closed, remain closed – rather than convergence on one model or another. It integrates the cost of peer production, in terms of its rent-extraction properties, to those who choose it as a development path into a stable equilibrium model that makes no claim to superior welfare or innovation properties.

In conclusion to this section, the primary organizational innovation of peer production is that it represents the confluence of technological, organizational and institutional innovations that permit diverse individuals who would not have been able to communicate and coordinate in advance to explore collaboratively an opportunity space made of resources, problems, people, and potential solutions. Peer production further allows them to self-assign and harness their tacit, creative, or otherwise hard-to-communicate knowledge or facility to identify or contribute to defining a problem or solution. Last, they can do so by relying on diverse, often non-monetary motivations that do not incur the limitations imposed by the need to formalize and standardize their insights, efforts, or experimental successes for transmission into formalized channels of markets or hierarchies.

5.3   THE PROBLEM OF DIVERSE MOTIVATIONS AND THE SUCCESS OF PEER PRODUCTION

Given complexity, uncertainty, and the pervasiveness of tacit knowledge, a core advantage of peer production is its capacity to enable action without requiring translation into a system of formalized carrots and sticks. A system better able to engage self-motivated action will be better able to attract this kind of decentralized, non-price, non-command-mediated discovery of projects, resources, and solutions (Osterloh et al., 2002). This perspective would suggest that the critical question of motivation is how to design for diverse interdependent motivations; that is, monetary and non-monetary, intrinsic and extrinsic motivations that are subject to crowding out. While there has been some work on this problem, to which I will return later in this section, the core initial question that most work in economics focused on was whether it was feasible to collapse the diverse motivations apparently exhibited in peer production back to relatively well-defined models of self-interest.

Early work by Ghosh (1998) and an early canonical statement by Lerner and Tirole (2002), based on case studies of FOSS projects, asserted that FOSS developers are motivated by several incentives that can mostly be assimilated into standard models of economic motivation. These included: (1) the use value of the software to the contributing developer, (2) hedonic pleasure from the coding involved, (3) enhanced employment prospects from reputation gains or human capital accumulated, and (4) social status gains within the community of peers (Ghosh, 1998; Lerner and Tirole, 2002; Lakhani and Von Hippel, 2003; Von Krogh, 2003). Early non-economists added more diverse motivational considerations. Kollock emphasized reciprocity, reputation, a sense of efficacy, and collective identity (Kollock, 1999), and Benkler emphasized that the combination of material and social-psychological, extrinsic and intrinsic gains makes interdependence of motivations, or crowding out, an important constraint on the organization of peer production (Benkler, 2002, 2004).

Much of the work on individual motivation then moved to focus on surveys. The most influential survey work included the European FLOSS study headed by Rishab Ghosh (Ghosh et al., 2002) (FLOSS is sometimes used instead of FOSS, particularly in Europe, adding the French '*libre*' to 'free' and 'open source' but there is no substantive difference), the Boston Consulting Group Hacker Survey (Lakhani et al., 2002; Lakhani and Wolf, 2005), and the US study by Paul David and Joseph Shapiro (David and Shapiro, 2008). Lakhani et al. emphasized the self-reported motivations of intellectual stimulation, or hedonic gain, and skills building (Lakhani et al., 2002), while Ghosh et al. found reciprocity as the core motivation, alongside skills development (Ghosh et al., 2002). Despite their differences in emphasis, all these early surveys supported the claim that motivations were diverse and heterogeneous, and that they included all the hypothesized motivations, as well as a significant number of contributors who earned a living directly or indirectly from writing free and open source software. The break-down of self-reported motivations was roughly similar even where the responses were segmented between students and hobbyists as compared to salaried contributors (Hars and Ou, 2002). Belenzon and Schankerman (2008), using contributions to differently licensed projects, supported the finding that contributors are heterogeneous in their motivational profiles, but argued that contributors self-sorted among projects, such that those who were more responsive to extrinsic motivations, primarily reputation and employment opportunities, tended to contribute more to larger and more corporate-sponsored projects. An excellent recent formal literature review on the literature on motivations in FOSS covers these and other sources (Von Krogh et al., 2012). Note that there is a separate and significant literature on why *organizations*, firms and governments in particular, choose to adopt open source software (Lerner and Schankerman, 2010; Schweik and English, 2012). Schweik and English in particular offer a richly detailed analysis, using the institutional analysis and development framework developed by Elinor Ostrom to explain the advantages of adopting peer-produced outputs to governments, companies, and individuals. These focus on the rate of innovation and the capacity to collaborate with other firms, as well as the avoidance of dependence on sole-source providers. Another major organizational advantage is that participating in a peer-production enterprise can allow the firm to develop in-house expertise in a tacit knowledge–rich innovation system; it increases the absorptive capacity of the firm (Lakhani and King, 2011).

The diversity of motivational drivers (experience by each individual) and motivational profiles (the mix of motivational drivers that characterize a given individual; or one's baseline taste for prosociality, which is heterogeneous among individual contributors) find support in more recent work on Wikipedia as well, work that combines full observational data on behavior in Wikipedia with experimental observations of Wikipedians in lab experiments. Combining observational data on the full contribution history of 850 Wikipedians with the performance of these individuals in a battery of lab experimental games with social signaling measures based on how users edit their user page and display barnstars, Algan et al. (2013) show that while a taste for reciprocity as measured by contributions to public goods games and trustworthy behavior in the trust game predicts increased contributions in the real world of Wikipedia, a taste for reciprocity as measured in anonymous experimental settings does not explain contributions of the group of highest contributors. A taste for social signaling does predict levels of contributions, but these high-contributing social signalers do not exhibit particularly prosocial behavior in the abstracted setting of the lab. The growing evidence that individuals themselves are driven by diverse motivations, and that individuals are different from each other in the mix of motivational drivers that characterize them, makes the problem of designing a well-functioning peer-production system more complex. Trying to develop the equivalent of mechanism design for a population of individuals who have diverse motivations within each agent, and are diverse between agents, is complex. This difficulty is compounded substantially by the fact that the effects of any given design intervention focused on a given motivational driver (most commonly, material rewards and punishments) are non-separable from their effects on the prosocial motivational drivers. Experimental and observational data has exhaustively documented that the effects of explicit material rewards and punishments, the standard economic incentives tools, are not separable from the effects of these interventions on social-motivational vectors (major reviews are Frey, 1997; Frey and Jegen, 2001; Bowles and Hwang, 2008; Bowles and Polanía-Reyes, 2013). Adding a monetary reward to an activity may undermine the sum of motivations across the target population if it reduces the magnitude of prosocial motivations to perform the act more than it increases the magnitude of self-interested monetary incentives to perform the act in a sufficient proportion of the population in which the activity is to be increased. Positive (negative) monetary rewards (punishments) can (1) drive the total sum of motivations for any given individual in the opposite direction, and (2) lead to substitution in the population of agents from individuals driven by prosocial motivations to individuals driven by monetary motivations. Managing the tension, first between explicit, direct material rewards and prosocial motivations, and second, among diverse prosocial rewards, is a critical design challenge of peer-production systems. FOSS in particular has shown that, with the appropriate normative framing, it is possible to combine both paid and unpaid contributions without causing crowding out (Alexy and Leitner, 2010). Nonetheless, managing this tension is hardly a trivial achievement, and there are no good studies of successful integration of material rewards and prosocial rewards in other areas of peer production. Most prominently, Wikipedia does not combine material and social rewards, and sites, like Weblogs Inc., that have tried to improve on peer-production systems precisely by offering material rewards to top contributors have failed. Beyond mechanism design, the diversity of motivational profiles and the potential for complex interactions between the design of the system and the social behavior it elicits has been translated into calls for evidence-based social design in computer science (Kraut and Resnick, 2011) or more generally to cooperative human system design (Benkler, 2010, 2011).

In addition to effecting levels of cooperation statically, it is possible, though not yet empirically investigated, that pro-social, cooperative preferences are endogenous to cooperative practices. That is, that participating in cooperative practices can have long-term feedback effects on levels of cooperation by participants in similar practices. If true, whether one succeeds in achieving cooperative dynamics in the short term can influence whether the task becomes harder or easier over time, as participants internalize virtues and values associated with the cooperative or non-cooperative model. With habituation and practice, internalized habitual compliance with norms and practices (encapsulated in the term 'virtues') may lead people to adopt a more, or less, cooperative stance in contexts based on their interpretation of the appropriate social practice, its rightness, and its coherence with their own self-understanding of how to live their lives well. That is, through practice coupled with a set of normative commitments, people's preferences over discrete elements of a cooperative utility function – their taste for fairness, reciprocity, or altruism/generosity – will be endogenous to the degree of cooperativeness of the practice they undertake. This would be an economists' characterization of what in virtue ethics would be understood as the development of virtues through self-conscious practice (see Benkler and Nissenbaum, 2006; Von Krogh et al., 2012). Practice, in other words, can shift the proclivity to cooperate, at least in what is seen as a situationally appropriate context, of participating individuals, and make the work or the organizational framework easier.

In section 5.4 below, I discuss the observed patterns of governance in peer-production enterprises. Here, it is important to note that the governance mechanisms and technical platforms of peer production can play a motivational role in eliciting sustained levels of prosocial contributions, in addition to providing integration and coordination. These include the following:

- *Communication:* A critical design focus of cooperative human systems is to assure extensive communications. Communications systematically improve cooperation in experimental set-ups (Sally, 1995); human, unstructured exchanges, rather than canned messages, are important (Putterman, 2009); and face-to-face, or more humanized exchanges, are important too. Low-cost communication has been a pervasive feature of economic models of peer production (Baldwin and Von Hippel, 2010), and the persistent role of open and continuous communications has been a core feature of anthropological and sociological descriptions of peer production (Coleman, 2005; Kelty, 2008; Reagle, 2010).
- *Fun:* A repeated finding in surveys of FOSS developers is that fun, and a sense of self-efficacy, or the ability to do something well under one's own direction, are important motivators (Lakhani and Von Hippel, 2003; Lakhani and Wolf, 2005; Van Ahn et al., 2008). While fun is not a prosocial motivation, it is a fuzzy, intrinsic motivation that will drive behavior without requiring that it be formalized into price or command allocation mechanisms.
- *Normative framing and norm setting:* How a situation is framed normatively affects the set of motivations most salient to an interaction. Framing cannot, in the long term, be an exercise in manipulation, because participants learn when the framing is inauthentic. Rather, the normative framing of an interaction must be authentic and sustained in order to permit the relevant motivations to develop and become fixed in the interaction. Both Kelty and Coleman make normative negotiation and self-creation central to their accounts of FOSS (Coleman, 2005; Kelty, 2008), and Reagle (2010) locates normative negotiation at the heart of Wikipedia governance. Moreover, in the case of FOSS, normative framing has been described as permitting a mixture of monetary and non-monetary rewards, as long as monetary rewards are separated from governance of the project (Alexy and Leitner, 2010). A less explicit model involves behavioral patterning of norms. In particular, social network analysis has shown that people pattern even basic behaviors, like

overeating, on observed near nodes (Christakis and Fowler, 2007). Setting standards for 'normal' behavior can lead to prosocial behavior when that behavior is perceived as normal.

- *Reciprocity, reputation, transparency:* Reciprocity has long been understood as a central mechanism for sustained cooperation (Bowles and Gintis, 2002, 2011). Over time, evolutionary biology in particular has shown that looser and looser definitions of indirect and network reciprocity can sustain cooperation in a population of strangers (Nowak, 2006). The surveys of FOSS programmers have long placed reciprocity at the heart of FOSS practices (Ghosh et al., 2002). Algan et al. (2013) show that a behaviorally measured proclivity for reciprocity indeed predicts a substantial amount of contributing behavior among Wikipedians. As the set of people who engage in reciprocity increases, reputation mechanisms that enable some persistence of identity across contexts, and a level of transparency regarding past behavior of participants can all improve levels of contribution.
- *Fairness:* Extensive experimental and observational work has documented the importance of perceived fairness of outcomes, intentions, and processes to maintaining levels of prosociality (Fehr and Schmidt, 2001). Repeated studies of FOSS and Wikipedia emphasize the suspicion of power ('There is no cabal': TINC), and continuous negotiation of assuring that participants accept the processes, outcomes and intentions of participants, and leaders in particular, as fair (Colman, 2005; Kelty, 2008; Reagle, 2010).
- *Empathy and solidarity:* Cooperative systems perform better when they emphasize other-regarding motivational vectors. In particular, systems that allow an agent to see and interact with, or take the perspective of, other individuals improve cooperation. They effectively include an argument in each agent's utility function that takes the payoffs of the other into account (albeit, mostly discounted). Moreover, in-group bias, or solidarity, is a distinct motivational driver that triggers higher degrees of contributions to public goods and cooperative games where present. Measures to develop collective identity, sometimes as simple as naming a team or wearing a uniform, can significantly affect contribution levels (Haslam, 2000). The clearest instance of in-group–out-group solidarity used in FOSS relates to the long-standing conflict particularly among those FOSS developers who associate more with the more political interpretation of FOSS development, that is, the 'free software' movement as distinct from 'open source' development.

To conclude, peer production and FOSS development successfully elicit contributions based on diverse prosocial motivations. Because elicitation of prosocial motivations is a central part of their organizational advantage over firms, governments, and markets, a central challenge of peer-production enterprises is the design of systems that elicit prosocial motivations in the presence of within-agent diversity of motivations, across-agent diverse motivational profiles, and the non-separability of motivational vectors. Early work exists, both theoretical and empirical, separating out and documenting the different motivational vectors, the different profiles, and the effects of discrete interventions on these different motivations. However, this work is in early stages of development and offers a rich area of future research into cooperative human systems design.

5.4   GOVERNANCE IN PEER-PRODUCTION COMMUNITIES: DIVERSE REDUNDANT MECHANISMS

Governance of peer production must (1) provide freedom to operate for an open class of agents, who may have something to contribute to the common project, (2) elicit prosocial motivations, and (3) permit coordination and steerage of the collective output without undermining prosocial motivations. The first requirement flows from the advantages of peer production as an innovation and learning process, discussed in section 5.2. If the advantage is the capacity to permit diverse individuals, with diverse perspectives, insights, capabilities, and opportunities, to define, experiment with, and act on a collective project without seeking permission or pre-clearance, then the governance structure must assure freedom to operate, and must avoid techniques that constrain in the absence of clearance by a manager or property owner. The second requirement flows from the fact that the informational and diversity advantages of self-motivation and self-monitoring require a system that can elicit intrinsic motivations in order to harness that effort without necessitating monitoring and explicit reward/punishment structures. The third requirement comes from the potential tension between the definition of governance as that set of organizational and institutional mechanisms that allow groups to coordinate their actions, combined with the recognition that the two most widely used models, hierarchical authority and price signals, can have a negative impact on prosocial motivations and therefore undermine the second desideratum of peer-production governance design.

5.4.1   Freedom to Operate: Commons-based Production

The core benefit of peer-production systems is their capacity to elicit self-directed action from diverse sources of human talent, experience, tacit knowledge, opportunity and availability, productive interactions, and so on, and to bring these to bear on a wide and diversely defined set of projects using a diverse set of materials and knowledge resources. In order for that core advantage to be operative, actors within the action arena must have freedom to operate with resources in that arena on projects. It is precisely the lack of need of actors to seek permission or await direction before acting that allows peer production to avoid the information and diversity losses associated with price-cleared and hierarchical systems.

The major institutional form available to create this kind of freedom to operate in contemporary market economies is commons. These commons are not the more widely known common property regimes that were the subject of study in the Ostrom school of commons studies. Commons property regimes are available only to constrained and predefined groups of users, under well-understood use and access limitations. Rather, these are open commons: roads, highways, and major shipping channels, common carrier telecommunications networks and WiFi radio systems, and most importantly the public domain in information, knowledge, and culture (see Benkler, 2014). The core institutional feature of such commons is the fact that anyone can use the resource on symmetrical terms, without requiring permission from any single property owner or administrator. This is precisely the institutional framework that allows access to and use of resources in the distributed, self-directed form typical of peer production.

Most resources that are the subject of peer production and FOSS are created under a default regime of property. They are granted copyright automatically, as soon as they are fixed. The commons institutional framework therefore needs to be constructed from within the background property system. This 'reconstructed commons' (Reichmann and Uhlir, 2003; Madison et al., 2010) is techniques, some based in contract theories, others in property, that allow the default owners to license the materials on terms that functionally replicate the freedom to operate characteristic of commons. This was the great institutional innovation that Richard Stallman, the father of free software, created. The two major families of such licenses are the software-related licenses that flow out of the FOSS communities and the Creative Commons Licenses, developed by a non-profit to permit the commons licensing of non-software copyrightable materials.

The primary division within the various commons licensing frameworks is between those that permit use of the resources in the commons for any purpose, including reappropriation, and those that seek to limit uses of the resources, primarily either to limit the uses to non-commercial uses (observed mostly in Creative Commons licensing, and rarely in FOSS licensing) or to require those who make derivative works from the commons-licensed materials to license their own derivations on the same open terms as they themselves received access to the materials, what is often called 'copyleft'. There has been some attention within economics to this choice (Lerner and Tirole, 2002), suggesting a tradeoff between the breadth of for-profit firms and profit-seeking individuals who can be brought in to work on a project (larger with the less-restricted license) and the motivation-preserving effects of an assurance that one's work will not be reappropriated by another to produce materials that a present contributor will not be able to build on in the future. Many of the major projects are subject to copyleft, such as Wikipedia or Linux. Other major projects such as Apache or the academic literature project PloS are not. Whether one or the other systematically translates into more creative, productive, or stable peer-production efforts requires further empirical investigation, but no clear answer to that question presently exists.

5.4.2 Governance Without Property or Contract: Diversity of Constraint and Affordance

Peer production and FOSS enterprises are left with the question of how to govern their practices while abjuring exclusive control through property and contract in the absence of other sources of legally binding formal authority. Studies of FOSS projects (Coleman, 2005; O'Mahony and Ferraro, 2007; Kelty, 2008) and Wikipedia (Reagle, 2010; for a review see Fuster Morell, 2011) identify a series of shared characteristics of the internal, norms-based governance structures that peer-production enterprises have in fact developed to deal with these competing goals under the institutional and motivational constraints characteristic of peer production. Contrary to early work in economics that suggested the potential of a reassertion of hierarchy (Weber, 2004), or focused on the increasing prevalence of firm-adopted FOSS, what the work in sociology, anthropology, and management studies suggests is that the complexity of governance without property and contract is solved not by re-emergence of hierarchy, but by the utilization of flexible, overlapping, indeterminate systems of negotiating difference and permitting parallel inconsistencies to co-exist until a settlement behavior or outcome emerges. This system is less determinate; its lines of authority or determination are less clear, its components share a role as non-exclusive mechanisms for dispute resolution and the targeting of action, and it preserves freedom of action to the participants for much longer than would likely be thought efficient under either of the more traditional systems. It permits for prolonged experimentation and debate, rather than reaching closure earlier. Its elements are the following:

- *Meritocracy:* Individuals gain partial local authority over particular sub-areas of the shared enterprise based on their contributions to it and the perceived quality of those contributions. This is viewed most crisply in the high-visibility role of charismatic founders of projects, but then is replicated in nested forms throughout the collaborative networks as individuals who make significant contributions to particular projects within clusters of contributors receive greater meritocratic deference.
- *Leadership as coordination, not control:* Those who emerge in the meritocratic process as leaders, in turn, serve a role as coordinators of that bit of the network, rather than as hierarchically superior sources of task allocation. Dahlander and O'Mahony (2011), for example, using GNOME data (a graphical user interface to Linux), show that progression in networked collaboration involves not a move 'up' a hierarchy that involves greater authority over other individuals (who continue to self-assign to tasks) but a move 'to the center' of a network of contributions, where those who move to the center begin their rise in lateral authority through contributions and quality, but then (1) increase their efforts after their increase in authority, and (2) shift their role toward spending more time on coordination of contributions and efforts.
- *Organizational formalization:* Several of the larger projects, such as Apache or Wikipedia, have developed more traditional organizational models to manage some of the governance functions. These foundations, however, do not exercise formal rights to manage the workflow, and have limited roles in the management of the work itself, and conflicts among the peer contributors, as opposed to managing the infrastructure of the projects (Fuster Morell, 2010).
- *Norms:* Wikipedia is the clearest and earliest example of the extensive use of written norms as a governance mechanism, with internal community enforcement. However, the definition of norms and the use of transparent records of prior disagreement have been a central part of peer-production communities in FOSS as elsewhere (Coleman, 2005; Kelty, 2008).
- *Transparency:* Decisions, disagreements, and so on are almost entirely transacted in media that keep public open records of the interactions. This radical transparency underwrites the procedures that depend on continued debate, communication, and voting, and allows for the creation of a degree of trust that the shared enterprise is not being hijacked by any subset of participants.
- *Rough consensus and non-determinative voting:* The Internet Engineering Task Force famously relied on 'rough consensus and running code' (Clark, 1992). The 'running code' part of the definition goes to a shared sense of common purpose that has measurably or defined 'better'/'worse' outcomes, and that appeal to that

outcome is critical. This shared understanding of the possibility of better/worse is foundational to the meritocratic aspect of governance. The 'rough consensus' aspect is an important voting rule that mediates two competing risks: first, the risk that full consensus will create veto points, second, the risk that strict majoritarian voting will lead to (1) disaffection by repeated minorities and (2) weakened discourse or communication over what the 'right answer' is, that is, whether the 'code' is running, which is harder to achieve in non-functional settings, such as Wikipedia. As a result, projects range from very structured majoritarian voting (see Debian model in O'Mahony and Ferraro, 2007) to the very fuzzy non-binding straw polls used in Wikipedia (Reagle, 2010). In all events the results of voting are not really the binding decision. Instead, as described below, there are redundant governance paths and even after a vote substantial play remains for resistance, avoidance, and continued negotiation of the proper projects, resources, and outcomes.

- *Humor, mockery, irreverence:* Coleman first focused on TINC ('There is no cabal') as a core feature of these systems of governance (Coleman, 2005). This feature is important in preserving the looseness of coupling between decisions and action. It serves as a social mechanism to constrain the capacity of majorities, or charismatic leaders, or formal organizational organs like the foundations created to manage the platform from over-reaching.

- *Charismatic leadership:* Some of the projects remain importantly influenced by their founders: Linus Torvalds in Linux; Jimmy Wales in Wikipedia. Some projects use these 'benevolent dictators for life' as last-resort Gordian Knot breakers, but they can only perform that function relatively rarely, and with appropriate humility and publicly performed reluctance. Founder-leaders range in power from those who carry a title but whose role is rare and minimal (Drupal) to quite substantial (Linux kernel), with intermediate models of the quite legalistic Debian that has formal constraints on leadership.

- *Redundancy of governance pathways:* Perhaps the most remarkable aspect of governance in peer-production enterprises is that it is rarely definitive. In FOSS, for example, the fact that most projects over the past five years have come to be version controlled by Git means that even where there is a centralized foundation or leader who maintains the official version, every version is hosted independently by every developer, and forking[6] is technically easier than it was until the mid-2000s, when most projects used centralized depositories. In Wikipedia, a central overarching rule is 'Ignore All Rules'. It is foundational to the process that individuals see themselves as having the freedom to act against the rules, or against the decisions of others. Wikipedia Administrators can apply their administration powers in ways that contradict those of others who have acted on the same matter.

These characteristics of the governance of peer-production systems contribute both to the freedom to operate and to the maintenance of intrinsic motivations. They make determinative exclusions of paths of exploration and experimentation rare and difficult to achieve. They provide substantial room for peers to maintain a sense of self-efficacy even when their actions are rejected, or when the process points to a direction of action that one or some peers have not chosen. They allow for mixed motivations to co-exist, and they provide the mechanism for normative framing, establishment of the bounds of fairness, transparency and reciprocity, and social signaling of actions and contributions. Together, these jointly solve the problem of coordination and motivation that is commonly seen as the task of governance systems.

The flexibility of governance mechanisms replicates within the range of peer-production practices the tradeoffs discussed in section 5.2 between hierarchical systems and decentralized networked systems. That is, the extent to which the governance mechanisms are flexible, redundant, and non-determinative trades off freedom to operate for manageability, intrinsic self-direction for extrinsic control over actions within the project, and unstructured exploration for a more directed search of predictable enhancements or developments. In Linux distributions, for example, we see for-profit firm-based distributions, like Red Hat or Novell, and non-profit foundation distributions, like Ubuntu, developing to serve the needs of companies or unsophisticated users, respectively, by replacing some flexibility with a more managed, directed approach focusing on assuring the availability of particular features and a predictable release cycle, or the integration with proprietary platforms. By contrast, the standard-setting cutting-edge distribution, Debian, retains its highly flexible governance mechanism. New empirical work that critically assesses the internal governance structures of peer-production enterprises is developing, and as that work advances we will be able to refine our understanding of the extent to which the fully flexible, decentralized governance model prevails, and the extent to which hybrids that trade off flexibility and the networked form for various flavors of hierarchy and structure that improve survival and effectiveness (Benkler et al., 2013).

Despite the potential limitations of fully flexible governance mechanisms, the extent to which non-determinative governance systems are in fact observed in successful peer-production enterprises in the wild provides support for the theoretical claim that the particular advantage of these systems is the freedom to operate they offer. The governance system's diversity and redundancy is clearly exhibiting the success of costly systems for the maintenance of diversity and divergent behavior well beyond what one might expect in a relatively predictable and well-behaved environment, where the efficiency costs would not be outweighed by the exploration and experimentation benefits.

5.5   CONCLUSION

Peer production and FOSS represent a new mode of production. Its defining characteristics include (1) decentralization of conception and execution of problems and solutions, (2) diverse motivations, and (3) separation of governance from property and contract. These characteristics make peer-production practices adept at learning and experimentation, innovation, and adaptation in rapidly changing, persistently uncertain and complex environments.

The core advantage of peer production is its capacity to harness diversely motivated and capable individuals in the context of persistent uncertainty and complexity. The freedom to operate that marks peer production, and the full organizational permeability of the practices, allow anyone with a potential to contribute to self-assign, experiment with resources, projects, and collaborations, and test the improvement produced in these experiments. This freedom to operate is purchased at the cost of rent extraction or appropriability. It is most effective when the costs of experimentation are relatively low, or susceptible to collaborative investment of small or pre-existing increments of capital, physical and human; when communication costs are low; and when the work can be performed with high modularity. These characteristics, all present in Internet-mediated production, explain the relatively high salience of these practices in the networked environment. Coupled with the high uncertainty and complexity introduced by a global, rapidly innovating effective market, the advantages of peer production are at their clearest.

Peer production successfully harnesses diverse and primarily intrinsic and self-policed motivations. This is important because it avoids the necessarily lossy (and costly in terms of transactions costs) process of formalization of information about individual capabilities and opportunities into prices or information packets susceptible to managerial decision-making, particularly where tacit knowledge or high diversity of experience and perspective are important, the lossiness of markets and hierarchies is pronounced, and the advantages of intrinsically motivated action clearest.

In order to preserve the relatively loose organization and freedom to operate, while permitting coordination and collaboration without triggering the dysfunctions of motivation crowding out or interdependence of motivations, peer-production processes avoid the authority of property and contract. They implement, instead, overlapping, incomplete systems of governance, adapted dynamically to the particular instances of potential conflict or practical decision-making faced by the enterprise. These mechanisms are diverse, and their successful implementation depends on communication and recursive adaptation of practice to context.

NOTES

1. For example, Shapiro and Varian (1999) is an excellent example of the best understanding at the time. It characterizes the core dynamics of information and network production as related to high fixed, low marginal cost, lock-in, network effects, and the experience good nature of information goods. Free and open-source software (FOSS) or what would become peer production; the role of diverse motivations – these play no role in the book, which uses the threat of Microsoft's *Encarta* to *Britannica* as a core instance of the new models of network-based and information production.
2. A 'copyleft' license is one that uses copyright to assure that derivative works made from the work so licensed are themselves available to anyone under the same terms as the original work. It conditions the permission to use the work to create a derivative work (such as by improving or adding functionality to FOSS software), without which it would be illegal for the downstream developer to write that modification or development, on a provision that makes the derivative work (the modification or improvement) available under the same terms as they themselves relied on when they used the original license.
3. Games with a purpose was a platform created at Carnegie Mellon University by Van Ahn, which, between 2008 and 2011, harnessed the work of over 200 000 users to play games and, in the process, solve problems that computers could not solve. See http://www.gwap.com/.
4. North American Industry Classification System.
5. A search in Google Scholar on 2 August 2014 retrieved 4120 articles in which Wikipedia appeared in the title. Global rankings of websites can be based on different metrics. Based on the one-month Alexa traffic rank, a combination of average daily visitors and page views over the past month, Wikipedia ranked sixth as of 16 August 2014. See http://www.alexa.com/topsites; accessed 4 January 2016.
6. 'In software engineering a project fork happens when developers take a copy of source code from one software package and start independent development on it, creating a distinct and separate piece of software'; see https://en.wikipedia.org/wiki/Fork_%28software_development%29; accessed 4 January 2016.

REFERENCES

Alexy, O. and M. Leitner (2010), 'A fistful of dollars: Financial rewards, payment norms, and motivation crowding in open source software development', accessed 16 August 2014 at http://ssrn.com/abstract=1007689.

Algan, Y., Y. Benkler, M. Fuster Morell and J. Hergueux (2013), 'Cooperation in a peer production economy: Experimental evidence', unpublished manuscript, accessed 16 August 2014 at http://www.parisschoolofeconomics.eu/IMG/pdf/hergueux_paper-2.pdf.

Arthur, W.B. (1994), *Increasing Returns and Path Dependence in the Economy*, Ann Arbor, MI: University of Michigan Press.

Baldwin, C. and E. von Hippel (2010), 'Modeling a paradigm shift: From producer innovation to user and open collaborative innovation', *MIT Sloan School of Management Working Paper No. 4764–09*, accessed 2 August 2014 at http://papers.ssrn.com/sol3/papers.cfm?abstract_id=1502864.

Bauwens, Michel, 'The Political Economy of Peer Production', *CTheory*, 12/1/2005. http://www.ctheory.net/articles.aspx?id=499.

Belenzon, S. and M. Schankerman (2008), 'Motivation and sorting in open source software innovation', *CEPR Discussion Paper No. DP7012*, accessed 16 August 2014 at http://ssrn.com/abstract=1311136.

Benkler, Y. (2001), 'The battle over the institutional ecosystem in the digital environment', *Communications of the ACM*, **44** (2), 84–90.

Benkler, Y. (2002), 'Coase's Penguin, or, Linux and *The Nature of the Firm*', *Yale Law Journal*, **112** (3), 369–446.

Benkler, Y. (2004), 'Sharing nicely: On shareable goods and the emergence of sharing as a modality of economic production', *Yale Law Journal*, **114** (2), 273–358.

Benkler, Y. (2006), *The Wealth of Networks: How Social Production Transforms Markets and Freedom*, New Haven, CT: Yale University Press.

Benkler, Y. (2010), 'Law, policy and cooperation', in E.J. Balleisen and D.A. Moss (eds), *Government and Markets: Toward A New Theory of Regulation*, Cambridge, MA: Cambridge University Press, pp. 299–331.

Benkler, Y. (2011), *The Penguin and the Leviathan: How Cooperation Triumphs over Self-Interest*, New York: Crown Business.

Benkler, Y. (2014), 'Between Spanish huertas and the open road: A tale of two commons', in B.M. Frischman, M.J. Madison and K.J. Strandburg (eds), *Governing the Knowledge Commons*, New York: Oxford University Press, pp. 69–98.

Benkler, Y. and H. Nissenbaum (2006), 'Commons-based peer production and virtue', *The Journal of Political Philosophy*, **14** (4), 394–419.

Benkler, Y., B.M. Hill and A. Shaw (2013), 'Peer production: A modality of collective intelligence', in M. Bernstein and T. Malone (eds), *Collective Intelligence*, forthcoming, draft, accessed 16 August 2014 at http://mako.cc/academic/benkler_shaw_hill-peer_production_ci.pdf.

Bessen, J.E. (2005), 'Open source software: Free provision of complex public goods', accessed 13 December 2015 at http://ssrn.com/abstract=588763.

Bonnacorsi, A. and C. Rossi (2003), 'Why open source software can succeed', *Research Policy*, **32** (7), 1243–58.

Boudreau, K.J., N. Lacetera and K.R. Lakhani (2008), 'Incentives and problem uncertainty in innovation contests: An empirical analysis', *Management Science*, **57** (5), 843–63.

Bowles, S. and H. Gintis (2002), '*Homo reciprocans*', *Nature*, **415** (6868), 125–8.

Bowles. S. and H. Gintis (2011), *A Cooperative Species: Human Reciprocity and its Evolution*, Princeton, NJ: Princeton University Press.

Bowles, S. and S.A. Hwang (2008), 'Social preferences and public economics: Mechanism design when social preferences depend on incentives', *Journal of Public Economics*, **92** (8–9), 1811–20.

Bowles, S. and S. Polanía-Reyes (2012), 'Economic incentives and social preferences: Substitutes or complements?', *Journal of Economic Literature*, **50** (2), 368–425.

Chesbrough, H.W. (2003), *Open Innovation: The New Imperative for Creating and Profiting from Technology*, Boston, MA: Harvard Business School Publishing.

Christakis, N.A. and J.H. Fowler (2007), 'The spread of obesity in a large social network over 32 years', *New England Journal of Medicine*, **357** (4), 370–79.

Clark, D.D. (1992), 'A cloudy crystal ball – visions of the future', in M. Davies, C. Clark and D. Lagare (eds), *Proceedings of the Twenty-Fourth Internet Engineering Task Force (IETF)*, Massachusetts Institute of Technology, NEARnet, Cambridge, MA, 13–17 July, pp. 539–43, accessed 16 August 2014 at https://www.ietf.org/proceedings/24.pdf.

Coase, R.H. (1937), 'The nature of the firm', *Economica*, **4** (16), 386–405.

Coleman, E.G. (2005), 'Three ethical moments in Debian', working paper, NYU, Department of Media, Culture and Communication, accessed 16 August 2014 at http://ssrn.com/abstract=805287.

Dahlander, L. and S. O'Mahony (2011), 'Progressing to the center: Coordinating project work', *Organization Science*, **22** (4), 961–79.

Datta, S. (2012), 'Analytics, cloud computing challenge flat growth in Forrester's tech market outlook for 2012', *Social Media Today*, 5 January, accessed 26 April 2015 at http://www.social mediatoday.com/content/analytics-cloud-computing-challenge-flat-growth-forresters-tech-market-outlook-2012.

De Jong, J.P.J. and E. von Hippel (2009), 'Measuring user innovation in Dutch high tech SMEs: Frequency, nature and transfer to producers', *MIT Sloan Working Paper No. 4724–09*, accessed 16 August 2014 at http:// ssrn.com/abstract=1352496.

David, P.A. (1985), 'Clio and the economics of QWERTY', *American Economic Review, Papers and Proceedings*, **75** (2), 332–7.

David, P.A. and J.S. Shapiro (2008), 'Community-based production of open-source software: What do we know about the developers who participate?', *Information Economics and Policy*, **20** (4), 364–98, accessed 16 August 2014 at http://ssrn.com/abstract=1286273.

Elsner, W., G. Hocker and H. Schwardt (2010), 'Simplistic vs. complex organization: Markets, hierarchies, and networks in an organizational triangle – a simple heuristic to analyze real-world organizational forms', *Journal of Economic Issues*, **44** (1), 1–30.

Fehr, E. and K.M. Schmidt (2001), 'Theories of fairness and reciprocity – Evidence and economic applications', in M. Dewatripont, L.P. Hansen and S.J. Turnovsky (eds), *Advances in Economics and Econometrics: Theory and Applications, Eighth World Congress, Volume 1*, Cambridge, UK: Cambridge University Press, pp. 208–57.

Frey, B.S. (1997), 'A constitution for knaves crowds out civic virtues', *The Economic Journal*, **107** (443), 1043–53.

Frey, B.S. and R. Jegen (2001), 'Motivation crowding theory: A survey of empirical evidence', *Journal of Economic Surveys*, 15 (5), 589–611.

Frischmann, B.M., M.J. Madison and K.J. Strandburg (eds) (2014), *Governing the Knowledge Commons*, New York: Oxford University Press.

Fuster Morell, M. (2010), 'Governance of online creation communities: Provision of infrastructure for the building of digital commons', PhD thesis, Department of Political and Social Sciences, Florence, Italy: European University Institute.

Fuster Morell, M. (2011), 'The Wikimedia foundation and the governance of Wikipedia's infrastructure: Historical trajectories and its hybrid character', in G. Lovink and N. Tkacz (eds), *Critical Point of View: A Wikipedia Reader*, Amsterdam: Institute of Network Cultures, pp. 325–41.

Ghosh, R.A. (1998), 'Cooking pot markets: An economic model for the trade in free goods and services on the net', *First Monday*, **3** (3), accessed 16 August 2014 at http://firstmonday.org/ojs/index.php/fm/rt/ printerFriendly/580/501.

Ghosh, R.A., R. Glott, B. Krieger and G. Robles (2002), *Free/Libre and Open Source Software: Survey and Study*, International Institute for Infonomics, University of Maastricht, accessed 26 April 2015 at http://web.archive.org/web/20021203011411/http://www.infonomics.nl/FLOSS/report/.

Gilson, R.J., C.F. Sabel and R.E. Scott (2008), 'Contracting for innovation: Vertical disintegration and inter-firm collaboration', *Law Working Paper No. 188/2008*, accessed 13 December 2015.

Gilson, R.J., C.F. Sabel and R.E. Scott (2010), 'Braiding: The interaction of formal and informal contracting in theory, practice and doctrine', *Stanford Law and Economics Olin Working Paper No. 389*.

Hars, A. and S. Ou (2002), 'Working for free? Motivations of participating in open source projects', *International Journal of Electronic Commerce*, **6** (3), 25–39.

Haslam, S.A. (2000), *Psychology in Organizations: The Social Identity Approach*, Thousand Oaks, CA: Sage.

Horton, J.J. (2010), 'Online labor markets', paper at the 6th Workshop on Internet and Network Economics (WINE), accessed 16 August 2014 at http://ssrn.com/abstract=1689743.

Howe, J. (2006), 'Crowdsourcing: A definition', *Crowdsourcing Blog*, accessed 2 January 2013 at http://crowd-sourcing.typepad.com/cs/2006/06/crowdsourcing_a.html.

Kelty, C.M. (2008), *Two Bits: The Cultural Significance of Free Software*, Durham, NC: Duke University Press.

Kollock, P. (1999), 'The economies of online cooperation: Gifts and public goods in cyberspace', in M. Smith and P. Kollock (eds), *Communities in Cyberspace*, London: Routledge.

Kraut, R.E. and P. Resnick with S. Kiesler et al. (2011), *Building Successful Online Communities: Evidence-Based Social Design*, Cambridge, MA: MIT Press.

Lakhani, K.R. and E. von Hippel (2003), 'How open source software works: "Free" user-to-user assistance', *Research Policy*, **32** (6), 923–43.

Lakhani, K. and A. King (2011), 'The contingent effect of absorptive capacity: An open innovation analysis', *Harvard Business School Working Paper No. 11–102*, accessed 10 September 2014 at http://www.hbs.edu/ faculty/Publication%20Files/11-102_054a5f12-8925-4a87-ba79-270820c13417.pdf.

Lakhani, K. and R. Wolf (2005), 'Why hackers do what they do: Understanding motivation and effort in free/

open source software projects', in J. Feller, B. Fitzgerald, S. Hassam and K.R. Lakhani (eds), *Perspectives on Free and Open Source Software*, Cambridge MA: MIT Press, pp. 3–22.

Lakhani, K., R. Wolf, J. Bates and C. DiBona (2002), 'The Boston Consulting Group hacker survey', accessed 16 August 2014 at http://mirror.linux.org.au/linux.conf.au/2003/papers/Hemos/Hemos.pdf.

Landini, F. (2012), 'Technology, property rights and organizational diversity in the software industry', *Structural Change and Economic Dynamics*, **23** (2), 137–50.

Lerner, J. and M. Schankerman (2010), *The Comingled Code: Open Source and Economic Development*, Cambridge, MA: MIT Press.

Lerner, J. and J. Tirole (2002), 'Some simple economics of open source', *The Journal of Industrial Economics*, **50** (2), 197–234.

Lorenzi, D. and C. Rossi Lamastra (2007), 'Innovativeness of free/open source solutions: Evidence from an alternative methodology', accessed 16 August 2014 at http://ssrn.com/abstract=1077107.

Madison, M.J., B.M. Frischmann and K.J. Strandburg (2010), 'Constructing commons in the cultural environment', *Cornell Law Review*, **95** (4), 657–709.

Maurer, S. (2010), 'Five easy pieces: Case studies of entrepreneurs who organized private communities for a public purpose', *Goldman School of Public Policy Working Paper No. GSPP10–011*, accessed 16 August 2014 at http://ssrn.com/abstract=1713329.

Moglen, E. (1999), 'Anarchism triumphant: Free software and the death of copyright', *First Monday*, **4** (8), accessed 16 August 2014 at http://journals.uic.edu/ojs/index.php/fm/article/view/684/594.

Nelson, R.R. (1959), 'The simple economics of basic scientific research', *Journal of Political Economy*, **67** (3), 297–306.

Netcraft (2013), 'January 2013 web server survey', accessed 16 August 2014 at http://news.netcraft.com/archives/2013/01/07/january-2013-web-server-survey-2.html.

North, D.C. (1990), *Institutions, Institutional Change and Economic Performance*, Cambridge, MA: Cambridge University Press.

Nowak, M.A. (2006), 'Five rules for the evolution of cooperation', *Science*, 314 (5805), 1560–63.

O'Mahony, S. and F. Ferraro (2007), 'The emergence of governance in an open source community', *Academy of Management Journal*, **50** (5), 1079–106.

Osterloh, M., S. Rota and B. Kuster (2003), 'Open source software production: Climbing on the shoulders of giants', Working Paper, Institute for Research in Business Administration, University of Zurich, accessed 16 August 2014 at http://citeseerx.ist.psu.edu/viewdoc/download;jsessionid=C9D63177125F0BCE717D8A4BBEAE9647?doi=10.1.1.12.3183&rep=rep1&type=pdf.

Powell, W.W. (1990), 'Neither market nor hierarchy: Network forms of organization', in B.M Staw and L.L. Cummings (eds), *Research in Organizational Behavior, Volume 12*, pp. 295–36.

Powell, W.W. (1996), 'Interorganizational collaboration in the biotechnology industry', *Journal of Institutional and Theoretical Economics*, **120** (1), 197–215.

Putterman, L.G. (2009), 'Heterogeneous predispositions and the effects of sorting, voting, and communication in collective action dilemmas', *Context and the Evolution of Mechanisms for Solving Collective Action Problems Paper*, accessed 16 August 2014 at http://ssrn.com/abstract=1368879.

Raymond, E. (1999), *The Cathedral and the Bazaar*, Sebastopol, CA: O'Reilly & Associates.

Reagle, J.M., Jr. (2010), *Good Faith Collaboration: The Culture of Wikipedia*, Cambridge, MA: MIT Press.

Reichman, J.H. and P.F. Uhlir (2003), 'A contractually reconstructed research commons for scientific data in a highly protectionist intellectual property environment', *Law and Contemporary Problems*, **66** (1/2), 315–462.

Sally, D. (1995), 'Conversation and cooperation in social dilemmas', *Rationality and Society*, 7 (1), 57–92.

Schweik, C.M. and R. English (2012), *Successful Internet Collaboration: A Study of Open Source Commons*, Cambridge, MA: MIT Press.

Shapiro, C. and H.R. Varian (1999), *Information Rules: A Strategic Guide to the Network Economy*, Boston, MA: Harvard Business School Press.

Van Ahn, L., B. Maurer, C. McMillen, D. Abraham and M. Blum (2008), 'ReCAPTCHA: Human-based character recognition via web-security measures', *Science*, **321** (5895), 1465–8.

Vaughan-Nichols, S.J. (2013), 'The web browser wars continue, and #1 is . . . well, that depends on whom you ask', *ZDNET*, 2 January, accessed 16 August 2014 at http://www.zdnet.com/article/the-web-browser-wars-continue-and-1-is-well-that-depends-on-whom-you-ask/.Von Hippel, E. (1988), *The Sources of Innovation*, New York: Oxford University Press.

Von Hippel, E. (2005), *Democratizing Innovation*, Cambridge, MA: MIT Press.

Von Hippel, E. and G. von Krogh (2003, 'Open source software and the "private-collective" innovation model: Issues for organization science', *Organization Science*, **14** (2), 209–23.

Von Hippel, E., J.P.J. de Jong and S. Flowers (2010), 'Comparing business and household sector innovation in consumer products: Findings from a representative study in the UK', accessed 16 August 2014 at http://ssrn.com/abstract=1683503.

Von Krogh, G. (2003), 'Open-source software development: An overview of new research on innovator's incentives and the innovation process', *Sloan Management Review*, **44** (3), 14–18.

Von Krogh, G., S. Haefliger, S. Spaeth and M.W. Wallin (2012), 'Carrots and rainbows: Motivation and social practice in open source software development', *MIS Quarterly*, **36** (2), 649–76.

Weber, S. (2004), *The Success of Open Source*, Cambridge, MA: Harvard University Press.

W3Techs (2013), 'Usage of server-side programming languages for websites', accessed 16 August 2014 at http://w3techs.com/technologies/overview/programming_language/all.

6. The Internet and productivity
*Carol Corrado and Bart van Ark**

> The Internet was originally built to facilitate collaboration. By contrast, personal computers, especially those meant to be used at home, were devised as tools for individual creativity. For more than a decade, beginning in the early 1970s, the development of networks and that of home computers proceeded separately from one another. They finally began coming together in the late 1980s with the advent of modems, online services, and the Web. Just as combining the steam engine with ingenious machinery drove the Industrial Revolution, the combination of the computer and distributed networks led to a digital revolution that allowed anyone to create, disseminate, and access any information anywhere.
>
> (Walter Isaacson, 2014, p. 2)

6.1 INTRODUCTION

The subtleties of how the Internet impacts productivity growth, once a boost to investment concludes, are not entirely evident in macroeconomic data and traditional methods of accounting for the contribution of information and communication technology (ICT) to economic growth. ICT investments make the Internet and wireless connectivity possible, and new technologies for high-speed digital communication (as opposed to computing per se) give rise to new possibilities that impact how firms do business and how households use time. How are these changes reflected in economic growth and productivity? In this chapter we will address how the growth in digital communication technology – particularly the Internet – has impacted productivity and living standards from a national and international point of view. The next section outlines the general approach. Section 6.3 discusses the Internet, ICT and productivity and section 6.4 addresses network and ICT externalities. A recap of main points and conclusions is offered in section 6.5.

6.2 APPROACH

A national and international comparative point of view – a view from 30 000 feet – does not address the precise nature of the impacts of digital technology on individual firm and consumer behavior. But it is a fitting place to begin given the importance of understanding the technological forces shaping future opportunities for growth in business and household incomes. Figure 6.1 shows that the trend in global labor productivity growth has been declining since the mid-2000s, stymied by the impact of the global financial crisis and its aftermath in Europe and the USA, and also by weakening performance among large emerging economies such as China and Brazil.

Will ICTs boost US productivity growth again as they did with the emergence of the

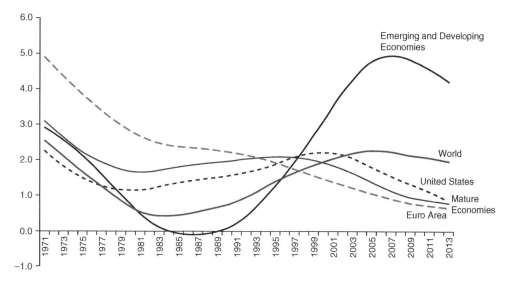

Source: The Conference Board Total Economy Database™ (The Conference Board, 2015).

Figure 6.1   H-P (Hodrick-Prescott) filter trend growth in labor productivity (GDP per person employed), 1970–2013

Internet in the 1990s? Can Europe's Horizon 2020 strategy to realize the potential of ICT spur its long-term growth? To answer these questions one needs to appropriately frame the mechanisms through which the Internet, and technologies spawned by the Internet, impact economies. In the mainstream productivity and sources-of-growth (SOG) literature, assessments center on the impact of ICT capital investments on labor productivity and the rate of increase in total factor productivity (TFP): are these the appropriate metrics? Where in the data does one 'go' to see the impact of the Internet? What about the unmeasured consumer surplus or, for that matter, why not consider jobs?

We rely primarily on the SOG framework for the analysis reported in this chapter. The advantages of the growth accounting framework are well known, chief of which is its general equilibrium perspective. New technologies inevitably displace some existing economic activity, and the SOG framework naturally accounts for these effects (unlike many microeconomic analyses or case studies of specific innovations). Against this advantage, the data requirements are steep (Griliches, 1994), suggesting that Solow's famous 1987 quip could be paraphrased for today's times as, 'You see the Internet/Smartphone/Cloud Computing age everywhere but in the productivity statistics'. Let us begin, then, by reviewing and analyzing these statistics.

6.3   THE INTERNET, ICT AND PRODUCTIVITY

Productivity measures the output produced by companies, sectors, and countries relative to the inputs required to produce that output. It therefore provides a simple but powerful indicator of economic efficiency and innovation. For the economy as a whole, labor productivity (or output per hour) is the most widely used metric. Labor productivity is related to measures of living standards such as per capita income, but labor productivity alone cannot distinguish between gains from more capital per worker versus gains from innovation. An SOG decomposition does just that, however. It computes increases in capital per worker (movements along a production frontier) and derives as a residual change in total factor productivity (shifts of a production frontier) the famous 'Solow residual' of growth accounting.

By reflecting the combined efficiency of labor and capital inputs relative to the growth in gross domestic product (GDP), total factor productivity (TFP) is a widely accepted metric for assessing the net effects of innovative activity within a country, sector, or firm.[1] In practice, the measurement of different types of labor and capital inputs allows for the identification of productivity change due to composition shifts to higher-performing types. But even so, much is not captured by the conventional decomposition: the impact of unmeasured inputs, such as intangible capital; the influence of imperfect competition, increasing returns to scale, and knowledge spillovers.

Many issues stand at the intersection of these caveats to growth accounting and determining the impact of the Internet on economic growth, issues that are an active area of research: ICT capital and uncounted intangible capital as complementary assets (Brynjolfsson et al., 2002; Basu et al., 2004); network effects and Internet externalities as drivers of measured productivity change (Corrado, 2011); and ICT spillovers, for example, due to open-source Internet software (Greenstein and Nagle, 2014), as potentially large contributors to TFP growth, to name a few.

We first report and analyze SOG results based on the traditional approach, then consider measurement issues and relevance of the above-mentioned indirect channels.

6.3.1   ICT and Productivity in the EU and USA

Table 6.1 reports estimates of productivity for the EU-27 and USA from 1995 to 2013.[2] Looking first at the pre-crisis results for the USA and comparing the late 1990s (column 4) with the 2000s (column 5), we see that output and output per hour growth (rows 1 and 3) decelerated rather sharply between these two periods. The main supply-side culprit behind this drop off is a slowdown in the rate at which US workers were equipped with capital, especially ICT capital (the circled item in row 5). Turning to the EU-27, Europe's output and output per hour growth was not as robust as activity in the USA in the late 1990s, and Europe's economic activity did not slow so much in the early 2000s relative to the late 1990s.

On balance, the portrait of European growth and its sources was rather similar to the USA during the early 2000s. In both Europe and the USA, a slowing rate of ICT capital deepening (the circled items in row 5) detracted from growth in output per hour during the 2000s, whereas growth of total factor productivity (row 7), a proxy for the net economic impact of innovative activity, remained brisk – contributing more than 0.5 percentage points per year, on average, to growth in Europe and 0.75 percentage

Table 6.1 Productivity growth, 1995 to 2013

Item		EU-27			United States		
		1995–2001 (1)	2001–07 (2)	2007–13 (3)	1995–2001 (4)	2001–07 (5)	2007–13 (6)
1.	Output (total real GDP)	20.8	20.5	−0.1	30.8	20.7	10.0
2.	Hours	0.9	0.8	−0.5	10.3	0.9	−0.2
3.	Output per hour	20.0	10.7	0.4	20.5	10.7	10.2
Contribution of:[a]							
4.	Labor composition	0.3	0.3	0.1	0.3	0.2	0.1
5.	ICT capital (per hour)	0.5	(0.3)	0.4	0.8	(0.4)	0.4
6.	Non-ICT capital (per hour)	0.6	0.5	0.6	0.6	0.4	0.3
7.	Total factor productivity	0.6	0.6	(−0.7)	0.8	0.7	(0.3)
Contribution of:[b]							
8.	ICT-producing industries[c]	−0.1	0.3	0.2	0.3	0.5	0.3
8a.	Manufacturing	0.1	0.2	0.1	0.5	0.2	0.1
8b.	Services	−0.2	0.1	0.1	−0.2	0.4	0.2

Notes:
Rows 1–3 are average annual rates of growth (percent). Rows 4–7 are percentage points.
a. Contributions in rows 4–7 are to growth in output per hour.
b. Contributions in row 8 are to growth in total factor productivity.
c. Rows 7 and 8 are not strictly comparable. EU contributions in row 8 are based on eight countries (Austria, Finland, France, Germany, Italy, Netherlands, Spain, and United Kingdom), and are derived from different sources. Also, the estimates in row 8 for the last period are to 2011 for Europe (column 3) and to 2012 for the United States (column 6).

Sources: Lines 1–7, The Conference Board Total Economy Database, January 2014. Line 8, columns 1–3, EUKLEMS as extended in Corrado and Jäger (2014); columns 4–6, Rosenthal et al. (2014) with backcasts by authors using EUKLEMS.

points per year in the USA – from 1995 to 2007. ICT-producing industries accounted for a large fraction of the gains in the 2000s (row 8, columns 2 and 5).

The picture of productivity growth and its sources, especially the measured contribution of innovative activity, changed greatly after the onset of the global financial crisis. In the USA (column 6), growth in output per hour slowed to essentially the rate that prevailed during the much-discussed extended period of slow productivity growth from 1972 to 1995 (1.3 percent per year), well below its very long-term trend of about 2 percent per year (Gordon, 2014a). Europe's economic performance since 2007 has been utterly dismal (column 3). The main villain among Europe's post-2007 growth detractors is total factor productivity, which fell a whopping 0.75 percent per year, whereas TFP growth remained positive in the United States (the circled items in row 7). As discussed in more detail in Van Ark (2014a, 2014b), virtually no European economy exhibited positive TFP growth during this period.

As argued more fully below, one channel whereby Internet technology affects economic growth is TFP in ICT services-producing industries – and in this regard, the most interesting row in Table 6.1 is row 8b. Innovation in ICT service-producing industries contributed more than half of the gains estimated for the total economy of the USA from 2001 to 2013. And for eight EU countries where we have industry-level productivity estimates, albeit only to 2011, ICT producers also contributed positive changes to aggregate TFP, on average, during the early crisis period – all the more remarkable when one considers that, in these same countries, the contribution of all market services industries was the major drag on market sector TFP change and economic growth (Van Ark, 2014b).

Many analysts believe that the recent weak EU and US productivity performance – and the lack of resilience of these economies to shocks incurred – stems from structural factors and poor policy response rather than a result of EU and US innovation mechanisms suddenly grinding to a halt. Still, there is much concern, for example, over the low rate of new business formation and lack of financing opportunities for small and medium-size enterprises. While innovative activity is generally thought to emanate from ecosystems with certain dynamics of their own, most observers agree that innovative activity depends on a healthy business environment to be self-sustaining (Jackson, 2011). At the risk over-simplification, then, one could say that what separates the growth pessimists such as Robert Gordon from optimists such as Erik Brynjolfsson and Andrew McAfee (2014) – where the latter two base their arguments on the potential of Internet and digital technology to spur economic growth – is how strong a force for innovation (i.e., TFP growth) can Internet and digital technology possibly be? We review the trajectory of these trends, and their measurement, in the next section.

6.3.2   Internet Technology

Internet technology is not a single identifiable invention, but rather a suite of communications technologies, protocols, and standards for networking computers and increasingly mobile devices (Greenstein, 2000, p. 391). Advances in Internet technology have been very rapid in the past 25 years and continue to increase at blistering rates to this day. Indeed, without continued increases in Internet capacity, the world could not have achieved the estimated 30+ percent per year increase in IP (Internet Protocol) traffic and 100+ percent per year increase in wireless data traffic from 2010 to 2015 (see Figure 6.2(a)). Growth in IP traffic has been driven by the Internet second wave (social networks, smart phones, app stores, and e-readers), cloud services adoption, and spread of machine-to-machine communications (the Internet of Things, or IoT). All told, the Internet markets of the G-20 are projected to reach $4.2 trillion in 2016 – nearly double the size they were in 2010; three out of four data center workloads are expected to be processed in the cloud in 2018; and IoT devices attached to the Internet – most of them wirelessly – are expected to increase more than 25-fold, from nearly one billion units in 2010 to 26 billion units by 2020.[3]

These projections cannot be realized without continued, rapid increases in Internet capacity, especially wireless capacity, and prospects seem very bright on this score. Figure 6.2(b) shows that by one measure, the rate at which wireless-related patents are filed, the pace of change of late is as brisk as it was in the late 1990s. A recent analysis of the pace of communication technology from the perspective of price change for the equipment and products that determine Internet and wireless network capacity supports that assessment (Byrne and Corrado, 2015a, b).

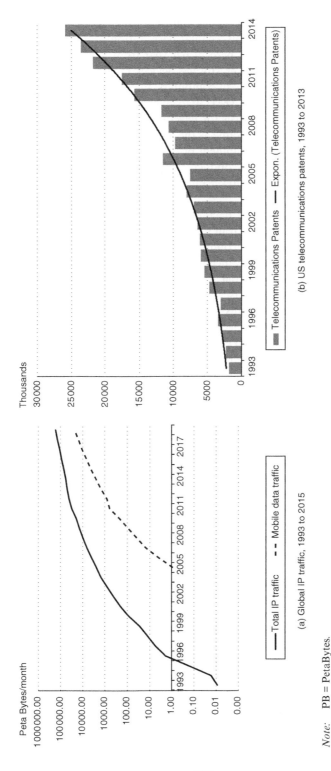

Peta Bytes/month

Thousands

(a) Global IP traffic, 1993 to 2015

(b) US telecommunications patents, 1993 to 2013

Note: PB = PetaBytes.

Sources: (a) Cisco's Visual Networking Index 2010–15 (2011) and Global Mobile Data Forecast Update 2011–16 (2012). (b) US Patent and Trademark Office, Part I, Patent Counts by Class by Year (sum of classes 370, 379 and 455).

Figure 6.2   Global IP traffic and US telecommunications patents

Byrne and Corrado (2016) report that quality-adjusted prices for three types of telecom equipment (data networking equipment, cellular base station equipment, and local loop transmission equipment) fell 12 to 14 percent per year from 1985 to 2013 – faster than declines in official prices for computer storage devices (7 percent) but less than half that of semiconductors used primarily in computers, microprocessor units (MPUs) and dynamic random access memory (DRAM) (30 to 40 percent). Quality-adjusted prices for cell phones fell more rapidly than prices for telecom equipment – about 20 percent per year from 1985 to 2013 – roughly the same as the average annual decline in official prices for PCs over this period. Telecom equipment price declines also have been steadier than price declines for computers and semiconductors since 1995, that is, telecom equipment prices have not fallen at a materially slower rate since 2003, as have prices for computers and semiconductors.

What explains the large sustained declines in prices of communication products? Communication technology benefits from semiconductor and computer technology, for example, the miniaturization of semiconductors speeds up computation functions on communication devices, computer advancement is used to improve digital signal quality and storage improvements are essential for increasing smartphone functionality. But more fundamental to achieving increases in traffic capacity are improvements in transmission techniques (e.g., signal compression, multiplexing, and waveforms that increase spectral efficiency). The ability to squeeze more information through a band of radio wave spectrum or single cable has been absolutely instrumental in achieving the increases in data and voice traffic that have occurred.[4]

For one reason or another, and notwithstanding the invention of the Internet and World Wide Web (much less Internet browsers and smartphone apps), the technical and engineering advances that drive increases in communication capacity tend to be less heralded than advances in computing and semiconductor technology. The wireless world is thinking now about standards and protocols for 5G.[5] But who outside the wireless community speaks of multiple-input and multiple-output (MIMO) techniques, a technology anticipated to be vital in the design of standards for 5G mobile broadband platforms?

If the pace of communication technology and declines in related equipment prices are not slowing down, one would expect that official price statistics for all things related to communication – Internet services (access and cloud), telecom services, and complementary manufactured ICT products – are also still declining as fast as they once did. Unfortunately, this conclusion cannot be drawn that simply for at least three reasons. First, and most basic, one must drill pretty far into available statistics to see the direct footprints of Internet and wireless technology. Second, the discussion is further complicated because one cannot ignore the argument by Robert Gordon that the exceptional US economic performance during the late 1990s and early 2000s was due to temporary productivity gains from one-time developments in computing and software technology (Gordon, 2014a, 2014b).

Third, inasmuch as the Internet facilitates the creation of new markets characterized by scalability, customization, and collection and use of detailed consumer and market data to meet previously unmet needs (Levin, 2011) we must consider that the defining feature of these markets is innovation, particularly the incremental type of innovation that occurs continuously. As this may manifest as a form of returns to scale, or process innovation, there may be little or no discernable impact on price change due product innovation as previously so evident with computers and other electronic products. And because the spread of new Internet platforms tends to be about new uses of ICT (in truth, new web uses), unlike the 1990s' ICT-induced productivity wave, the distinction between ICT users (e.g., financial institutions) and producers (computer and chip makers) is no longer so clear-cut. The growth and popularity of elastic cloud services makes that abundantly clear.

We address the first two issues outlined above in subsection 6.3.3. As some of this material digs rather deep into the statistics, the reader can skip the detail and go straight to the recap and implications in section 6.3.4. The third issue leads naturally to exploring the indirect ways in which Internet markets leave their footprints in the productivity data. This is taken up in section 6.4 by incorporating network effects and other externalities into the standard model.

6.3.3   ICT Prices

6.3.3.1   Investment prices

ICT investment includes communications equipment (mainly, telecommunication and broadcast equipment) and, of course, computers and software. Real ICT investment prices indexes for the USA are plotted in Figure 6.3(a).[6] The real price index for communication equipment (the solid black line) fell below its simple long-term trend after 2000 and has remained below it since then.[7] By contrast, the combined price index for computers and software (the solid gray line), which was below its similarly calculated trend for an extended period of time, returned to trend by about 2004 and continued to flatten further. Computers and software greatly outweigh communications equipment in ICT investment – see Figure 6.3(b) – and thus overall ICT investment prices follow a similar, albeit muted, trend as prices for computers and software. This then would appear to solve part of the puzzle of why trends in communication technology do not seem to show through in the usual macro productivity data – they do not because the weight that is directly attached to them in ICT investment is rather small. Note, however, that according to The Conference Board's Total Economy Database, telecom equipment spending is now the largest component of global ICT investment. Indeed, while software is the primary driver of US ICT investment, both software and telecom equipment drive ICT investment globally.

Figure 6.3 thus shifts the question of what is happening to technology primarily to computers and software. With regard to computers, most analysts agree that a slowing in the pace of change in performance occurred after 2003 (Flamm, 2007; Hilbert and López, 2011).[8] The slowing in performance is indeed reflected in real computer prices: from 2003 to 2008, the annual decline in real computer prices was 7.25 percentage points slower than it was from 1995 to 2003. Official data record another, equally sharp slowdown (that is, another 7.25 percentage points per year) in computer prices beginning in 2008 however, and the jury is still out on the validity of these figures. Related work that looks at microprocessor prices finds substantial upward biases in official semiconductor price indexes after 2008 (Byrne et al., 2015), a finding that also undermines official estimates of computer price declines since then. If the pace of decline in computer prices that prevailed from 2003 to 2008 had been maintained after 2008, labor productivity and the contribution of ICT capital deepening would each be about a 0.04 percentage point

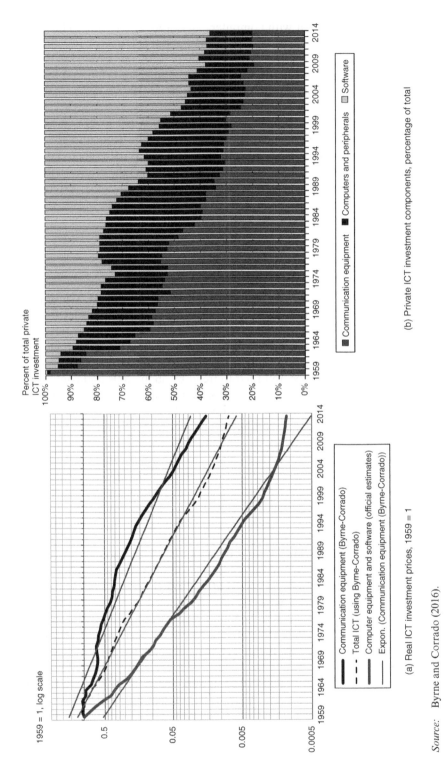

Percent of total private
ICT investment

■ Communication equipment ■ Computers and peripherals □ Software

(b) Private ICT investment components, percentage of total

1959 = 1, log scale

— Communication equipment (Byrne-Corrado)
- - Total ICT (using Byrne-Corrado)
— Computer equipment and software (official estimates)
— Expon. (Communication equipment (Byrne-Corrado))

(a) Real ICT investment prices, 1959 = 1

Source: Byrne and Corrado (2016).

Figure 6.3   Real ICT investment prices and shares, 1959 to 2013

stronger per year from 2007 to 2013 – not inconsequential but also not a game changer for the analysis of recent economic growth.[9]

New research on the determinants of software prices by type of application – Internet platform apps, systems for cloud services, and so on – is needed to inform the analysis of recent price change for ICT software investment. From 2001 to 2007, software prices declined nearly 3 percent per year, whereas from 2007 to 2013, they fell a bit less than 1.5 percent per year. Increasing prices for enterprise and network software in the PPI for application software may be a culprit in this acceleration, but it is hard to know because the component was newly introduced into the PPI in June 2006.[10] The increases in this index since mid-2006 may of course be accurate, but only having data from then on does not identify when the price increases for network software began. To place the reported acceleration in context consider the following: had the real price of software not accelerated after 2007, labor productivity and ICT capital deepening would have been stronger by another 0.05 percentage points and 0.03 percentage points per year, respectively – the same rough magnitudes associated with the 2008 computer price acceleration.

When the two thought experiments are combined, the impacts are 0.08 percentage points per year on labor productivity and 0.07 percentage points per year on ICT capital deepening. The difference between the output effect (labor productivity) and the investment effect (capital deepening) – 0.016 percentage points – is a small boost to the change in total economy TFP via the contribution attributed to ICT services-producing industries. These are verging on consequential impacts.

6.3.3.2 Consumption prices

Researchers developed quality-adjusted prices for cellular telephone and Internet access services from emergence of these markets in the USA in the mid/late 1980s to the late 1990s (Hausman, 1999; Stranger and Greenstein, 2007). The US Bureau of Economic Analysis (BEA) incorporated these research price indexes into the US national accounts in the early 2000s. For the household sector, the research indexes were linked with consumer price indexes (CPIs) for these services, which the US Bureau of Labor Statistics newly introduced in December 1997. The BLS' CPI indexes for cellular telephone and Internet access services reportedly are quality adjusted (Fixler et al., 2001).

The BEA's published series are converted to real terms and plotted in Figure 6.4(a). As may be seen, real cellular services prices (the thick solid line) decline relatively steadily whereas declines in the price index for Internet services (the dashed line) occur in fits and starts until 2007, after which the real price for Internet access services barely budges. The accelerating rate of decline in quality-adjusted prices for cell phones, much less the advent of mobile broadband, does not leave a footprint on telecom services prices but, without additional research, it is hard to know what may be going on. On the other hand, it seems reasonable to ask: how can Internet access prices be flat in real terms since 2007?

A recent analysis suggested a hedonic model would yield somewhat larger price declines than currently reported by the Internet access CPI prior to 2007 (Williams, 2008), and the large dots plotted on the figure underscore this possibility for subsequent years. They show a simple characteristic price measure obtained by dividing an Internet service provider (ISP) performance measure into BEA's estimates of household expenditure on Internet access for Q1 of each year.[11] The characteristic price measure lies close to a simple trend line (the thin solid line) based on BEA history, which falls 5.6 percent

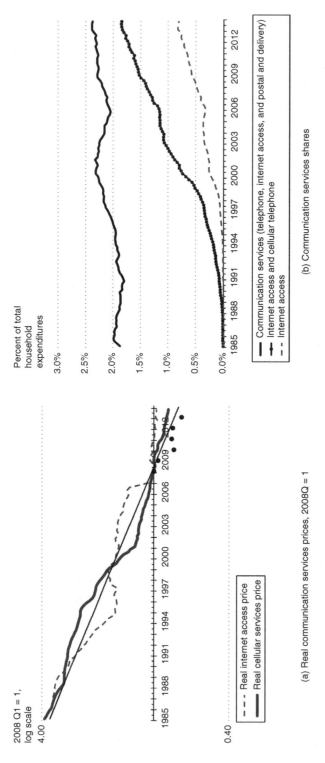

2008 Q1 = 1,
log scale

4.00

1985 1988 1991 1994 1997 2000 2003 2006 2009

0.40

--- Real internet access price
— Real cellular services price

(a) Real communication services prices, 2008Q = 1

Percent of total
household
expenditures

3.0%

2.5%

2.0%

1.5%

1.0%

0.5%

0.0%

1985 1988 1991 1994 1997 2000 2003 2006 2009 2012

— Communication services (telephone, internet access, and postal and delivery)
↕ Internet access and cellular telephone
-- Internet access

(b) Communication services shares

Note: The large dots are the OOKLA implied real price for Q1 of each year. The thin dashed line is the trend in BEA's real Internet access price index to 2008, and OOKLA thereafter.

Sources: (a) US BEA NIPS Table 2.4.4U and www.netindex.com for OOKLA net index. (b) US BEA NIPA Table 2.4.5U.

Figure 6.4   Real communication services prices and shares, 1985Q1 to 2013Q4

per year. A thought experiment in which the post-2007 history of consumer prices for Internet access is rewritten to show real declines 5.5 percentage points per year faster than currently shown adds 0.04 percentage points per year to the growth of real GDP, and by implication to growth of TFP via a larger contribution from ICT services producers, in this case telecommunications (NAICS [North American Industry Classification System] 517), which includes Internet access services.

6.3.4 Implications

That the rapid increase in IP traffic and continued advances in communication technology are not regularly featured in macroeconomic productivity discussions is perhaps unsurprising as one cannot easily drill into the data to 'see' the change that is going on. We examined a new research price index for communications equipment, which supported the view that advances in communication technology are proceeding at historically rapid rates. On the other hand, advances in computer and semiconductor technology have slowed since 2003.

Our examination of ICT services prices in national accounts data found the picture incomplete or lacking in detail: where is Internet software technology and how much is its use increasing? With total ICT services production now more than 4.5 percent of GDP in the USA (Figure 6.5) and nearly that in Europe (not shown), accurate and more detailed ICT services prices are needed to fully understand how value created by Internet and digital technologies leads to increases in living standards. All told, new research on

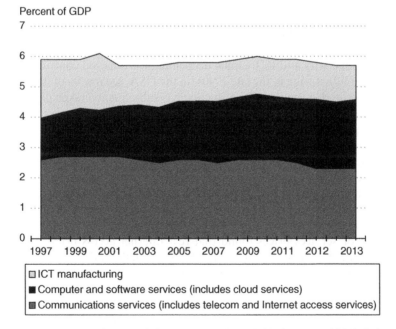

Source: Authors' elaboration of US BEA's data on gross value added by industry, which includes R&D.

Figure 6.5   Value-added share of US ICT-producing industries, 1997 to 2013

high-tech communication services prices – mainly, all forms of cloud services made possible by high-speed communication systems – is needed for a thorough analysis of the impact of the Internet on productivity and economic growth.

Turning to the ICT-related productivity issues raised by Gordon, it is important to note first that the computing and semiconductor developments of the 1990s are very evident in the pace of nominal ICT investment and growth in worldwide semiconductor consumption prior to 2001. Figure 6.6 supports Gordon's view that the rate of ICT investment was temporarily elevated heading into, but also including, the year 2000. On this basis, Gordon would have us discount the 1995 to 2001 US productivity experience when thinking about the influence of ICT on productivity trends going forward. Even though a literal read of available ICT data may lead to some pessimism, we hope to have made abundantly clear that the slowing of ICT price declines in official measures does not signal an end to advances in communication and Internet technologies.

Our analysis of ICT prices revealed an inexplicable acceleration in price change for computers and software after 2008; recall, they also slowed after 2003 but this is not disputed. If the second acceleration had not occurred, labor productivity and ICT capital deepening would be a tad stronger (nearly 0.1 percentage point) after 2008, but the post-2001 labor productivity growth experience would still look disappointing – 1.1 percent per year in Europe and 1.5 percent per year in the USA.[12] Note that ICT capital deepening stands at rates that, if sustained, are not strong but not growth detractors either (between 0.4 and 0.5 percentage points per year). To achieve 1.5 percent growth in output per hour going forward, both Europe and the USA would need to post annual TFP gains in the neighborhood of 0.5 percent per year. This was accomplished prior to the global financial crisis (and after the tech boom), so it would appear that the real stretch is thinking TFP growth could be strong enough to boost labor productivity growth back to 2 percent. But how much of a stretch?

Like labor productivity and ICT capital deepening, the outsized contribution of innovation in ICT manufacturing in the late 1990s (in the USA, see row 8a of Table 6.1) seems unlikely to be repeated, given the offshoring that has subsequently taken place. Gordon in fact makes this point, supporting his argument with figures indicating a massive drop in manufacturing production capacity for ICT products in the USA after 2000.[13]

From the perspective of this review and future relevance of ICT, it seems natural to focus on ICT services as the locus of future innovation and change. What are the prospects for sizable contributions to total economy TFP growth from ICT-producing services industries harnessing the power of high-speed communication networks to deliver customers the services and information they demand (security, data analytics, etc.)? We pointed to the already outsized contribution of this sub-sector in our review of Table 6.1, and our review of services prices found that real Internet access prices were flat after 2007. If such prices had indeed continued to fall on a quality-adjusted basis, the impact would flow through an increase in the contribution of ICT services to total economy TFP, suggesting the sub-sector may have even contributed a bit more to growth than currently attributed. This assessment can be applied to Europe as well as the USA.[14] All told, then, the combined contribution of ICT impacts via investment and production accounts for two-thirds of the total growth in output per hour in the Europe and the USA after 2001.

To identify the underlying sources of ICT services industries' TFP performance or determine whether their performance will continue in the future is beyond the power

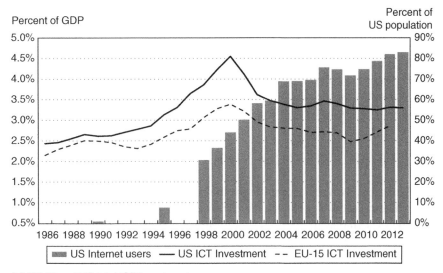

(a) EU-15 and US total ICT investment

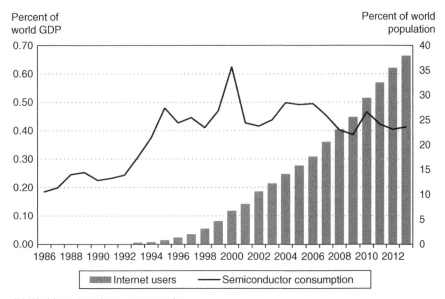

(b) World semiconductor consumption

Note: EU-15 excludes Luxembourg.

Sources: (a) EUKLEMS (EU-15 ICT Investment), US BEA (US ICT investment) and ITU (Internet users, 2000 on). (b) ITU (world Internet users as % of populations), WSTS (world semiconductor billings) and IMF (world GDP).

Figure 6.6   *ICT investment and semiconductor consumption, 1986 to 2013*

of growth accounting. If rapid expansion of Internet markets and unique character of Internet platform businesses are underlying drivers, the contribution to TFP growth from this sector might even pick up with improving conditions in the wider economy. Studying this sub-sector of the economy and its linkages with other sectors is a high priority for future research. For example, Brynjolfsson et al. (2014) study the role of user-generated content on firm-level performance using a panel of Internet platform businesses; also, Levin (2011) theorizes on how they price and compete. Perhaps they and others will soon achieve new insights on the mechanisms sustaining innovation and value creation in this important sector of modern economies.

6.4   NETWORK EFFECTS AND ICT EXTERNALITIES

The traditional approach to accounting for the contribution of ICT to economic growth follows neoclassical economic theory, which makes clear predictions about the magnitude of the impact of a change in an input on output: if markets are competitive and returns are constant, the impact of 1 percentage point change in an input is the input's share of income generated by all productive inputs. Factor income shares are relatively easy to measure compared with an approach that determines impacts via econometric estimation of a production function, and the non-parametric nature of neoclassical SOG analysis is one of the major reasons why it is such a powerful tool.

6.4.1   Externalities and Productivity

The traditional approach does not consider, indeed it cannot completely identify, network effects as part of the contribution of ICT capital to growth. The potential importance of network effects is most clearly explained by Metcalfe's Law that states that the value of a network increases with the square of the number of users of the network and implies that stocks of ICT capital within a sector or country are disproportionately beneficial to growth as the number of users expands (for a given quantity of capital).[15] The extra kick, the disproportionate benefit that accrues as additional users join a network, is commonly referred to as network externalities in economics, and micro-, industry and cross-country studies have confirmed the presence of these externalities in productivity.[16] In growth analysis terms, the externalities might be called returns to scale, but that does not connote as clearly that we are dealing with a property of a network or a system, not a firm's production function.

A recent study took direct aim at analyzing and quantifying the macroeconomic impact of network effects due to increased use of the Internet and wireless networks within a traditional SOG framework (Corrado, 2011). Corrado's results stemmed from working through the ways in which network effects might be expected to leave their footprints in an SOG analysis. Table 6.2 shows the main elements of this analysis.

The establishment of a network has certain phases for which Metcalfe's Law is a good shorthand.[17] The first is a build-out phase characterized by high investment and capacity building, followed by a take-up phase, during which utilization of the installed capacity rises and returns to scale accrue. And because investments in communication capital create networks inextricably linked to computing, Internet, and wireless technologies,

Table 6.2   Internet and wireless networks in SOG empirics

Process	Description (Metcalfe's Law)	Where to Find?
1. Network build-out	High investment and capacity	Communication capital
2. Network take-up	Utilization of installed capacity rises	Communication capital contribution
3. Network Externalities	a. Returns to scale	TFP
	b. Innovative adaptations (Internet and wireless)	TFP

Source: Corrado (2011).

the capital embodies the general purpose nature of these technologies. General purpose technologies (or GPTs) have characteristics such as high fixed costs, low reproduction costs, and a ready ability to be adapted to new uses (Bresnahan and Trajtenberg, 1995).

Communication capital thus has the ability to generate high marginal returns when widely dispersed, usage rises, and innovation adaptation occurs. The synergy between the GPT nature of network technology and the scale effects of Metcalfe's Law suggest communication capital has significant potential for creating network externalities. In SOG analysis, the direct effects of the establishment of a network are attributed to capital formation and capital's contribution, including ICT capital's contribution, and if the spread of high-speed networking and wireless communication through the wider economy creates network externalities via returns to scale, the conventional framework will attribute them to TFP, not capital. Excess net returns to new uses of existing networks – innovative adaptations – are pure TFP.[18]

Although the events depicted in Table 6.2 do not evolve in strict sequence in real time (i.e., capacity is always being added to networks), the perspective offered by the explicit modeling of network effects leads naturally to a reconsideration of the underlying forces behind the ICT investment boom in the 1990s. Because Internet and wireless communication technologies obtain economic value from complementary investments in ICT, much of the increase in these investments can arguably be attributed to the expansion of networks and the possibilities they created for competitive advantage (Greenstein, 2000; Forman et al., 2003a), that is, that the demand for Internet access was the primary driving force behind the ICT investment boom of the late 1990s.[19] Once that boom concluded, and as Internet and wireless use continued to rise, the utilization of capital associated with Internet and wireless networks (mostly ICT capital) rose sharply even though the capital stock did not. Although some of the impact of the pure rise in usage was captured in capital's contribution through a higher income share, the network externalities and innovative adaptation effects appeared as increased TFP in the 2000s.[20]

To estimate network effects as set out in Table 6.2, it seems reasonable to begin by defining and measuring communication capital. One might take communication capital to be the 'C' in ICT capital (where, note, 'C' should include wireless spectrum assets), and then one might consider, in addition, all other types of capital deployed in communications and Internet services firms, that is, their server farms, network management software, public transmission lines, etc.). Finally, one might also consider how well non-ICT producers were poised to use the Internet for competitive advantage, say, by having installed advanced software typically used to enhance internal and customer-facing business processes. Corrado (2011) directly measured the first two types of communication capital for the USA, using new quality-adjusted deflators for communications equipment capital (discussed previously), and included wireless spectrum in investment. She was also able to exploit industry-level differences in the end purpose of the installed software base (e.g., email vs business process enhancement) using measures developed in Forman et al. (2003b). All told, Corrado concluded that, in addition to the direct contribution of communication capital, more than half of the 1.0 percentage point acceleration in total factor productivity growth estimated by the Bureau of Labor Statistics for the non-ICT business sector from 2000 to 2005 (relative to 1995 to 2000) could be explained by network externalities.

A related study covering the market sector of eight EU countries developed estimates of network effects in SOG percentage point terms for each of the items in Table 6.2 (Corrado and Jäger, 2014); the estimates, which are contributions to real value-added growth in the market sector of these economies, are plotted in Figure 6.7. The contributions due to ICT use and TFP are growth accounting estimates consistent with the figures shown in Table 6.1. The contributions of network externalities are based on an econometric analysis that attributed a portion of TFP to (1) returns-to-scale effects from more intensive use of communication capital throughout an economy and to (2) effects due to innovative adaptations, proxied by spillovers from IT stocks at the industry level; the sum of these

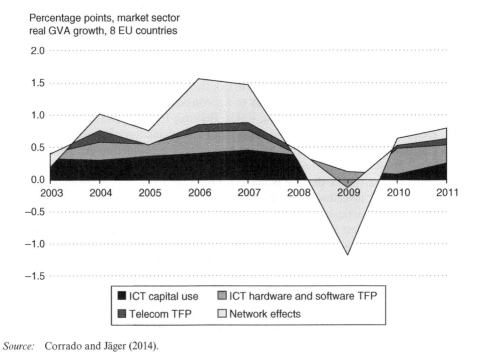

Source: Corrado and Jäger (2014).

Figure 6.7   Contributions of network effects to real GVA growth, 2003–11

two effects are what is plotted on the figure. The econometric analysis covered the years 2003 to 2011, when network effects associated with take-up were most likely in play.

The estimated contribution of network externalities to TFP in these 8 EU economies is rather large prior to the onset of the global financial crisis and European sovereign debt crises. Although not apparent from Table 6.1, the market sector of these economies was growing rapidly during these years, especially during 2006 and 2007; rapid increases in network usage accompanied this growth, and so did the estimated contribution of network effects to that growth. But as usage pulled back sharply in 2008 and 2009, the normally welfare-enhancing impacts of networks effects reversed sign. The estimated innovative adaptions effect remained a small positive (IT stocks did not decline) but was insufficient to offset the negative drag from the usage effect.

All told, the Internet – more precisely, the demand for connectivity and the externalities that accompany the spread of connectivity – offers a consistent story for how ICT capital contributed to economic growth and productivity from the 1990s through much of the 2000s. Even if the first-order externalities due to pure usage spread are tapering off in economies such as Europe and the USA, Figure 6.6(b) suggests there is a long way to go in many other areas of the world.

6.4.2   Externalities and Complementarities

If communication capital, the Internet, and Internet markets play a special role in productivity change via externalities, what about computers and computing technology (or IT) per se? And what about complementarity between ICT capital and intangible capital?

Given the vast number of studies that have looked at the special role of ICT capital in growth and productivity change, it is worth reminding readers that the search for externalities to ICT in country- and industry-level growth accounts data usually depends on whether above-average TFP growth is experienced by countries or industries with above-average ICT intensities and/or growth contributions from ICT capital. On balance, the literature that uses such datasets fails to uncover externalities to ICT, with the exception of studies that look at telecom capital and/or broadband alone, discussed in the previous section.[21]

Our earlier discussion commented on the recent and projected increases in adoption of cloud services, which suggests future industry-level ICT research will need to factor purchased ICT services into the usual analysis, but this consideration does not necessarily apply to the corpus of previous work. Evidence developed from firm- and plant-level data suggests that IT use per se plays a very important role explaining productivity differences across firms, suggesting the underlying productivity-enhancing IT mechanism operates powerfully within industries. For example, Syverson (2011) notes that Bartelsman et al. (2010) develop the notion that IT shifts the mean and the variance of the distribution of innovation outcomes and that Faggio et al. (2010) find the greatest increase in productivity dispersion occurs in industries with the largest growth in IT capital intensity.

Two other key takeaways from microeconomic studies of productivity change are that: (1) the link from firm-level IT adoption to productivity growth is complex, requiring co-investments in training and organizational change (Brynjolfsson and Hitt, 2000; Black and Lynch, 2001; Caroli and Van Reenen, 2001), and (2) human resource and management practices play an important role in explaining productivity differences across firms (Ichniowski and Shaw, 2003; Bloom and Van Reenen, 2007, 2010). Interestingly, these effects surface in industry-level growth accounting datasets augmented to include intangible capital following Corrado et al. (2005, 2009). The availability of macroeconomic data for a wide range of countries, including the availability of sector and industry estimates for a subset of countries, for example, at www.INTAN-Invest.net, is a relatively recent development.[22]

Studies exploiting intangible capital-augmented datasets have found (1) complementarity between ICT and intangible capital in production for eight market sub-sectors (Chen et al., 2014; Corrado et al., 2015), and (2) sizable spillovers from private investments in non-R&D intangible capital to market sector TFP growth at the country level (Corrado et al., 2014).[23] By asset type, the complementarity is with design, firm-specific training, and organizational structure, suggesting several possible indirect channels through which private IT investments augment the productivity performance of countries.[24] A complementary relationship between R&D capital and other intangible investments also is found (albeit a weak one), as are spillovers from private investments in R&D to market sector TFP growth at the country level. A large literature has of course documented productivity spillovers from the conduct of R&D at firm, industry, and country levels. All told, excluding network effects, the evidence-based indirect links among these three types of knowledge capital – IT, non-R&D intangibles, and R&D – and TFP at the industry and country level are sketched in Figure 6.8.

The exploration of non-R&D intangible knowledge flows is still in its infancy, but at some point in the near future improved and more detailed data may yield more refined

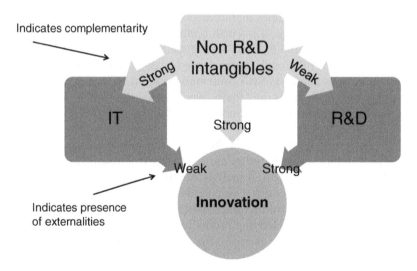

Note: IT includes software. Network effects are excluded.

Source: Adapted from Corrado et al. (2015).

Figure 6.8   *Indirect links between knowledge capital types and TFP: evidence on externalities/spillovers and complementarities in country and industry-level studies*

and/or richer specifications of IT spillovers and IT/intangible capital complementarities, in which case a clearer and more definitive picture of indirect impact of IT capital on productivity change may emerge.

6.4.3   Summary

All told, we conclude that (1) spillovers from increases in communication capital to TFP growth due to network effects are well documented in the literature, (2) recent estimates of the impacts in Europe and the USA are sizable, yet (3) the literature on the whole has not estimated these impacts with much precision (Holt and Jamison, 2009). The presence of network effects could be attributed in an economic sense to the spread of the use of ICT, in which case it is a form of spillover in one of the senses that the word has been used in the literature (see Cardona et al., 2013 for a discussion). When thinking about the Internet and productivity, however, it seems more appropriate to call these effects network externalities. Addressing how these effects can be modeled and estimated in ways that summarize their contribution to economic growth is the most direct and straightforward way to complete the picture of the Internet and productivity.

We also argued here that the same scale efficiencies that generated spillovers from telecom capital in the age of the telephone (Röller and Waverman, 2001) likely drove the sizable spillovers estimated for the period during which the Internet and wireless networks reached large fractions of the population of advanced countries (Corrado, 2011; Corrado and Jäger, 2014). That the same mechanisms may repeat again with the spread of a new wave of ICT services delivered via high-speed communication systems does not seem especially far-fetched. In any event, the use of ICT services for competitive advantage will in all likelihood continue to require co-investments in organizational change and human resource and management practices.

6.5   CONCLUSION

Strategy& reports:[25]

> By the year 2020, an entire generation, Generation C (for 'connected'), will have grown up in a primarily digital world. Computers, the Internet, mobile phones, texting, social networking – all are second nature to members of this group. And their familiarity with technology, reliance on mobile communications, and desire to remain in contact with large networks of family members, friends, and business contacts will transform how we work and how we consume.

Some observers assume such 'transformations' automatically translate to major, positive impacts on economic growth and productivity. But do they?

Before we reprise our answer to this question – which is essentially the same question as the subject of this chapter, the impact of the Internet on productivity – we need to underscore that we have discussed and analyzed ways in which measured living standards, as reflected by increases in labor productivity, are impacted by the direct and indirect channels of Internet-related economic activity. We did not discuss impacts on consumer surplus or what Greenstein and Nagle called 'digital dark matter', economic activity that cannot be seen because it is beyond the production boundary set by national accountants when they tally up GDP. This would take us to non-market uses of household time, where changes due to connectivity may indeed be dramatic but for which economic implications are unclear.

Household and business connectivity has increased dramatically since the late 1990s, however, suggesting that the economic impacts of the diffusion of digitization are creeping into the statistics. By analyzing the productivity experience of the last dozen or so years and discounting the extraordinary productivity experience of the late 1990s (as Gordon would have us do), we are able to rely on trends established during the period described by some as the Internet second wave. Because roughly half of this period is affected by the global financial crisis and its aftermath, this is difficult terrain. Outcomes are a blend of supply and demand (and short- and long-term) influences, and because we also must delve rather deep into the statistics to see what is going on, it is not a straightforward exercise to discern the trends that will influence productivity in the future.

We sorted through this terrain in two steps. First we relied on an analysis of ICT price change that revealed a central finding, namely that prices of products that determine the capacity of Internet and wireless networks suggest that advances in communications technology are not slowing down. The analysis also revealed slowdowns in price declines for (1) computer and software investments and (2) Internet access services after 2007 that were difficult to explain. Altogether these factors are rather consequential for assessing the size and significance of recent tech-driven contributions to productivity growth.[26] Contributions from ICT capital deepening and TFP in ICT-producing industries accounted for a noteworthy fraction (two-thirds) of the growth in labor productivity in Europe and the USA from 2001 to 2013. If trends in the components underlying ICT continue at post-2001 average (adjusted) rates, ICT will contribute between 0.66 (Europe) and 1 (US) percentage points per year to labor productivity growth going forward.[27]

How much of a stretch is it to assume that other major sources of growth – increases in labor composition, non-ICT capital deepening, and productivity growth in non-ICT producing industries – will contribute another 0.66–1.0 percentage point, thereby raising labor productivity growth to between 1.5 and 2 percent per year?[28] Put differently, consider whether the Internet and/or ICT use contributes an extra punch to productivity growth via externalities, spillovers, or complementarities and ICT thereby boosts economic growth even further. This was the second step in our analysis.

After setting out how network effects might be expected to leave their footprints in an SOG analysis, we reframed the story of the 1990s and 2000s to center on the Internet and the demand for connectivity as the impetus for change, not on the microprocessor as an independent supply-side driver of change. Rather, following Metcalfe's Law, the ICT contributions that were so evident in the 1990s were just part of a story that played itself out via network effects (TFP gains) in the early and mid-2000s (prior to the financial crisis). The available evidence suggests that TFP in non-ICT-producing industries was boosted via network effects by 0.25 percentage points per year in the market sector of eight major EU economics from 2002 to 2007 and by 0.5 percentage points in the private business sector of the USA from 2001 to 2005. As noted in our discussion, not all of these gains are sustainable; indeed, some might argue against building them into trends to the extent they were part of an already played out process of computerization that began in the 1990s. The impetus to innovation stemming from connectivity and the availability of high-speed communication platforms has not played out, however, and this is part of the just-quoted estimates. To answer the question originally posed at the conclusion of section 6.2.1, then, we believe that Internet and digital technology remain a supply-side force for future TFP change, and that the potential impact is relatively strong: if such technology contributed about 0.1 to 0.2 percentage points per year to market sector TFP change during the mid-2000s via innovative adaptations of networks, then we would expect this force to be at least as strong, if not stronger, going forward.[29]

The network effects framework we offered in Table 6.2, itself drawn from Corrado (2011), Corrado and Jäger (2014), and based in part on Bresnahan and Trajtenberg (1995), sets out a way of thinking about production and innovation due to the Internet. It was derived in order to provide a consistent story for the 1990s and early 2000s, but it also provides an additional dimension for the decomposition of productivity growth and can be applied to the ICT issues of today. For example, social networks surfaced in the mid-2000s, where, note, their build-out is not very evident in conventional statistics, and we are currently in a period during which innovative adaptions of social media are taking place. Has (or will) much TFP change come from this? This is hard to say because impacts are diffuse, but the subject of competition in Internet markets is an active area of research. The shift to cloud services and growth of the IoT are other developments that can be analyzed with the network effects framework set out in Table 6.2 as, note, changes in the utilization of IT and other durable goods stocks are also part of the story. We leave this to future work.

All told, many subtleties are involved in how the Internet and investments in networks impact productivity growth, and one of the chapter's main messages was to underscore that, if the Internet and wireless networks are the highways of the modern age (on which traffic is growing at explosive rates worldwide), we need to use models and data that are up to the task of analyzing their macroeconomic impacts. We believe the source-of-growth framework works well in this regard, provided one agrees with how we 'fit' the Internet and networks into it. As to the data required for this analysis, we will not reprise specific comments on ways that existing data fall short for an analysis of ICT developments since the early 2000s, but another conclusion of this chapter is that filling those gaps is an important subject of future research.

NOTES

*   We thank Abdul Erumban and Kirsten Jäger for the growth accounting estimates reported in this chapter.
1.   TFP thus includes the impacts of implementing knowledge and technology 'borrowed' from elsewhere. In noting this, we are underscoring the important distinction between scientific invention and innovation, where the latter includes the economic value created by all activities associated with the commercialization of knowledge and technology. It has been said, 'If invention is a pebble tossed in the pond, innovation is the rippling effect that pebble causes. Someone has to toss the pebble. That's the inventor. Someone has to recognize the ripple will eventually become a wave. That's the [innovator/] entrepreneur' (Tom Grasty for PBS Idea Lab, 29 March 2012).
2.   EU-27 excludes Croatia, which joined the European Union as its 28th member on 1 July 2013.
3.   IoT devices *exclude* PCs, tablets and smartphones. The sources for these forecasts are Boston Consulting Group (accessed 3 July 2015 at http://www.marketwired.com/press-release/g-20s-internet-economy-is-set-reach-42-trillion-2016-up-from-23-trillion-2010-as-nearly-1611718.htm), Cisco's Global Cloud Index (2013–18) (accessed 3 July 2015 at http://www.cisco.com/c/en/us/solutions/service-provider/global-cloud-index-gci/index.html) and Gartner (accessed 3 July 2015 at http://www.gartner.com/newsroom/id/2636073).
4.   In this regard, Byrne and Corrado's assessment of price change for communications equipment is in

sync with Hilbert and López's compilation of figures on the world's capacity to compute, store, and communicate information (Hilbert and López, 2011). Hilbert and López cover fewer years, 1986 to 2007, but also consider broadcasting; Byrne and Corrado (2015a) cover telecommunications only, but from 1963 to 2013. See Byrne and Corrado (2015b) for further discussion.

5. See, for example, the keynote by Seizo Onoe, CTO and EVP and Member of Board of Directors, NTT DOCOMO, '5G technology' at the workshop 'Can Mobile Broadband Realize its Full Potential?', sponsored by the Wireless Technology Association (WTA), Mobile Computing Promotion Consortium of Japan, and Georgetown University, Washington DC, 29 October 2014.

6. Even though the remainder of this section mostly discusses the US Bureau of Economic Analysis (BEA) price deflators, the BEA computer price index is used to harmonize ICT capital measures in EUKLEMS, and price measures for all ICT components for non-EUKLEMS countries are harmonized to US prices in The Conference Board's Total Economy Database, the source for the growth accounting results reported in Table 6.1.

7. The communications equipment price index plotted is a research series originally developed by Byrne and Corrado in 2007 to include wireless equipment and to update earlier work by Doms (2005). The original Byrne-Corrado indexes continue to be maintained and updated by Federal Reserve Board staff. BEA incorporated some of this work into the National Income and Product Accounts (NIPA) in 2011. The overall ICT index plotted in the figure is constructed by aggregating the Byrne-Corrado research price index for communication equipment for all years with BEA's official prices for computers and software, thereby providing a consistent historical series for total ICT investment prices from 1959 to present. Real prices are constructed using the price index for business output.

8. The story as reported in Byrne and Corrado (2016) goes like this: In the early 2000s computer chip makers found that pushing the performance envelope by increasing clock speed got harder due to power and heat considerations. Following standard practice of pulling circuit design innovations from the high-performance computing (HPC) world onto personal workstations, the computer industry turned to parallel processing via a multicore architecture. Note that the move toward parallel processing thus shifted the computing challenge from creating faster computer microprocessors to designing computer systems and software that utilized large numbers of processors efficiently – a problem then on the cutting edge of academic supercomputing R&D.

9. Note that the estimated impact on labor productivity is the same as private investment because, after adding in other components of final demand and subtracting imports, the average GDP weight of computer final sales is essentially the same as the GDP weight of computer investment (2007 to 2013). See US Bureau of Economic Analysis (BEA) National Income and Product Accounts (NIPA) Table 9.2U.

10. The producer price index (PPI) for application software has two published components from June 2006 on, desktop and portable device application software and other application software. The first component is flat and the second increases 10 percent between mid-2006 and mid-2014. According to Census Bureau data for 2010 to 2013, enterprise or network software is 73 percent of application software revenues excluding PC software, suggesting roughly 1.0 percentage point per year increases in application software price change stem from prices of enterprise and network software.

11. The measure used is from OOKLA, a company that tests and benchmarks ISP speed and performance, and which also compiles global metrics on broadband performance. The OOKLA net index of US metrics is available since January 2008. It is based on ISP-reported upload and download speeds, actual measures of connection stability, and survey-based estimates of median broadband costs in megabits per second and median ratio of actual download speed to promised/advertised speed. Note further that a characteristic price is a form of hedonic approach implying a simple, linear function through the origin of the hedonic price-single characteristic plane (Triplett, 2004). The OOKLA characteristic price measure reflects both commercial and residential customers (we have no way to separate the two segments) and will not be strictly comparable to the CPI to the extent mix shifts or differential hedonic surfaces prevail across segments.

12. See note 6 for why we apply the results of an analysis of US ICT prices to Europe.

13. Figure 6.5 does not show a particularly large drop off in national accounts value added in ICT manufacturing, in part, because a sharp pullback in purchased services and increases in R&D and software investment on own-account offset a 22 percent drop in the value of factory production in computer and electronic manufacturing (NAICS 334) in the United States between 2000 and 2007.

14. See Karamti (2007) for results of a hedonic model of telecom pricing in France.

15. Metcalfe's Law is named for a researcher once at Xerox's famed Palo Alto Research Center. See 'Beyond the ether' in the *Economist* magazine's Technology Quarterly, 12 December 2009, p.23 for more information on Metcalfe and Metcalfe's Law.

16. See Brynjolfsson and Kremerer (1996); Mun and Nadiri (2002); Röller and Waverman (2001), respectively, for examples of these types of studies.

17. To be clear, we do not take Metcalfe's Law literally; it is based on certain assumptions, such as equal value of all connections, that may overstate the benefits from networks.
18. To the extent increases in consumer welfare occur via network effects (i.e., via the number of users on a network), then economic theory suggests a cost of living index should take these welfare-enhancing effects into account. But the number of users does not play into the computation of consumer price indexes; indeed no externalities do. For example, as noted in Fixler et al. (2001), the CPI for auto alarms is not adjusted according to the rate of car thefts deterred, and so on.
19. That impetus behind the late 1990s investment boom was the demand for Internet access, not the microprocessor, is argued more fully in Corrado (2011).
20. As a theoretical matter, Berndt and Fuss (1986) showed that to the extent capital productivity (which varies directly with capital utilization) is proportional to the marginal product of capital, capital utilization is absorbed in capital income and capital services as conventionally calculated. For further discussion and caveats see Hulten (2009).
21. Some key studies that looked for externalities from ICT capital in growth accounting datasets but were unable to find them are Stiroh (2002), who used industry-level data for the United States, and Inklaar et al. (2008), who used industry-level data for ten EU countries and the United States. For recent reviews, see Biagi (2013) and Cardona et al. (2013). Note that the IT spillover estimated in the Corrado and Jäger (2014) study mentioned in the previous section and attributed to network effects applied only to the period after 2002; testing for the same effects in the same dataset using observations before 2002 failed to uncover a statistically significant spillover coefficient for IT. In view of this finding, and the earlier literature that also could not detect spillovers to IT capital investments, Corrado and Jäger argued that what they found was related to network effects.
22. In addition to developments at national statistical offices, this is owed to work by researchers too numerous to mention and to the support given to them by, among others, the European Commission, NESTA, Organisation for Economic Co-operation and Development (OECD), Research Institute of Economy, Trade and Industry (RIETI), The Conference Board, UK Intellectual Property Office, US National Science Foundation, and World Intellectual Property Office.
23. The latter is a cross-country econometric study of ten European countries using intangible capital augmented growth accounts data from 1995 to 2007. The study included the possibility of productivity spillovers from investments in ICT capital but none were found. In both sets of findings, computer software is included in ICT, that is, ICT is the conventional definition in the economics literature, and non-R&D intangibles refers to all intangibles (Corrado et al., 2005, 2009) except software and scientific R&D, that is, it includes (1) other new product development expenditures, for example, on artistic and entertainment originals and industrial design, and (2) investments in economic competencies, for example, brands, organization structure, and firm-specific training.
24. The findings on complementarities by asset type refer to the Corrado et al. (2015) study.
25. Accessed 3 July 2015 at http://www.strategyand.pwc.com/global/home/what-we-think/digitization/megatrend.
26. As previously noted, the price and tech analysis is drawn from other works (Byrne and Corrado, 2015a, b, 2016).
27. Some observers may be surprised to see such similar figures for Europe and the United States, but the dismal EU productivity performance of late does not have its roots in the quantity of its ICT investments or productivity of its ICT producers. That said, policies directed at ICT are a path forward, as argued in Van Ark (2014a).
28. The average rate of growth in output per hour in the United States for the past 63 years is about 2 percent.
29. The estimate of 0.1 is the point estimate from the EU study, and the estimate of 0.2 is obtained by applying the same model to parse the US study's estimate of total network externalities.

REFERENCES

Bartelsman, E.J., P.A. Gautier and J. de Wind (2010), 'Employment protection, technology choice, and worker allocation', *De Nederlandsche Bank Working Paper No. 295*, accessed 3 July 2015 at http://ssrn.com/abstract=1951839.

Basu, S., J.G. Fernald, N. Oulton and S. Srinivasan (2004), 'The case of the missing productivity growth: Or, does information technology explain why productivity accelerated in the United States but not in the United Kingdom?', in M. Gertler and K. Rogoff (eds), *NBER Macroeconomics Annual 2003*, Cambridge, MA: The MIT Press, pp. 9–82.

Berndt, E.R. and M.A. Fuss (1986), 'Productivity measurement with adjustments for variations in capacity utilization and other forms of temporary equilibrium', *Journal of Econometrics*, **33** (1), 7–29.

Biagi, F. (2013), 'ICT and productivity: A review of the literature', *JRC Technical Reports Digital Economy Working Paper No. 2013/09*, Institute for Prospective Technological Studies, Seville, Spain, accessed 4 July 2015 at http://publications.jrc.ec.europa.eu/repository/handle/JRC84470.

Black, S.E. and L.M. Lynch (2001), 'How to compete: The impact of workplace practices and information technology on productivity', *Review of Economics and Statistics*, **83** (3), 434–45.

Bloom, N. and J. van Reenen (2007), 'Measuring and explaining management practices across firms and countries', *Quarterly Journal of Economics*, **122** (4), 1351–408.

Bloom, N. and J. van Reenen (2010), 'Why do management practices differ across firms and countries?', *Journal of Economic Perspectives*, **24** (1), 203–24.

Bresnahan, T.F. and M. Trajtenberg (1995), 'General purpose technologies: "Engines of growth?"', *Journal of Econometrics*, **65** (1), 83–108.

Brynjolfsson, E. and L.M. Hitt (2000), 'Beyond computation: Information technology, organizational transformation and business performance', *Journal of Economic Perspectives*, **14** (4), 23–8.

Brynjolfsson, E. and C.F. Kremerer (1996), 'Network externalities in microcomputer software: An econometric analysis of the spreadsheet market', *Management Science*, **42** (12), 1627–47.

Brynjolfsson, E. and A. McAfee (2014), *The Second Machine Age*, New York: Norton.

Brynjolfsson, E., L.M. Hitt and S. Yang (2002), 'Intangible assets: Computers and organizational capital', *Brookings Papers on Economic Activity*, **1**, 137–98.

Brynjolfsson, E., S.T. Kim and J. Oh (2014), 'User-generated capital and firm value: Theory and evidence from Internet firms', paper presented at the 2014 NBER Summer Institute Digitization Workshop, Cambridge, MA.

Byrne, D.M. and C.A. Corrado (2015a), 'Prices for communications equipment: Rewriting the record', FEDS Working Paper 2015-069 (September), Federal Reserve Board, Washington, D.C.

Byrne, D.M. and C.A. Corrado (2015b), 'Recent trends in communications equipment prices', FEDS Notes (29 September), Federal Reserve Board, Washington, D.C.

Byrne, D.M. and C.A. Corrado (2016), 'ICT prices and ICT services: What do they tell us about productivity and technology?', forthcoming working paper.

Byrne, D.M., S.D. Oliner and D.E. Sichel (2015), 'How fast are semiconductor prices falling?', NBER working paper No. 21074 (April), Cambridge, MA.

Cardona, M., T. Kretschmer and T. Strobel (2013), 'ICT and productivity: Conclusions from the empirical literature', *Information Economics and Policy*, **25** (3), 109–25.

Caroli, E. and J. van Reenen (2001), 'Skill-biased organizational change? Evidence for a panel of British and French establishments', *The Quarterly Journal of Economics*, **116** (4), 1449–92.

Chen, W., T. Niebel and M. Saam (2014), 'Are intangibles more productive in ICT-intensive industries? Evidence from EU countries', *ZEW Discussion Papers No. 14-070* (September), Centre for European Economic Research (ZEW), Germany.

Corrado, C. (2011), 'Communication capital, Metcalfe's law, and US productivity growth', *Economics Program Working Paper No. 11-01*, New York: The Conference Board, Inc.

Corrado, C., J. Haskel and C. Jona-Lasinio (2014), 'Knowledge spillovers, ICT, and productivity growth', The Conference Board, CEPR, and IZA Working Paper (June).

Corrado, C., J. Haskel and C. Jona-Lasinio (2015), 'Intangibles, ICT and industry productivity growth: Evidence from the EU', forthcoming in D. Jorgenson, K. Fukao and M. Timmer (eds), *The World Economy: Growth or Stagnation?* Cambridge, UK: Cambridge University Press.

Corrado, C., C. Hulten and D. Sichel (2005), 'Measuring capital and technology: An expanded framework', in C. Corrado, J. Haltiwanger and D. Sichel (eds), *Measuring Capital in the New Economy, Studies in Income and Wealth, Volume 65*, Chicago, IL: University of Chicago Press, pp. 11–46.

Corrado, C., C. Hulten and D. Sichel (2009), 'Intangible capital and US economic growth', *Review of Income and Wealth*, **55** (3), 661–85.

Corrado, C. and K. Jäger (2014), 'Communication networks, ICT, and productivity growth in Europe', *Economics Program Working Paper No. 14-04*, New York; The Conference Board, Inc.

Doms, M. (2005), 'Communication equipment: What has happened to prices?', in C. Corrado, J. Haltiwanger and D. Sichel (eds), *Measuring Capital in the New Economy, Studies in Income and Wealth, Volume 65*, Chicago, IL: University of Chicago Press, pp. 323–62.

Faggio, G., K.G. Salvanes and J. van Reenen (2010), 'The evolution of inequality in productivity and wages: Panel data evidence', *Industrial and Corporate Change*, **19** (6), 1919–51.

Fixler, D., J.S. Greenlees and W.J. Lane (2001), 'Telecommunications indexes in the US Consumer Price Index', paper presented at the Sixth Meeting of the International Working Group on Price Indices (April), Canberra, Australia.

Flamm, K. (2007), 'The microeconomics of microprocessor innovation', paper presented at 2007 NBER Summer Institute Productivity Workshop.

Forman, C., A. Goldfarb and S. Greenstein (2003a), 'The geographic dispersion of commercial Internet use', in S. Wildman and L. Cranor (eds), *Rethinking Rights and Regulations: Institutional Responses to New Communication Technologies*, Cambridge, MA: MIT Press, pp. 113–45.

Forman, C., A. Goldfarb and S. Greenstein (2003b), 'Which industries use the Internet?', in M.R. Baye (ed.), *Organizing the New Industrial Economy, Advances in Applied Microeconomics, Volume 12*, Amsterdam: Elsevier, pp. 47–72.

Gordon, R.J. (2014a), 'The demise of US economic growth: Restatement, rebuttal, and reflections', *NBER Working Paper No. 19895*, Cambridge, MA: NBER.

Gordon, R.J. (2014b), 'A new method of estimating potential real GDP growth: Implications for the labor market and the debt/GDP ratio', *NBER Working Paper No. 20423*, Cambridge, MA: NBER.

Greenstein, S. (2000), 'Building and delivering the virtual world: Commercializing services for Internet access', *Journal of Industrial Economics*, **48** (4), 391–411.

Greenstein, S. and F. Nagle (2014), 'Digital dark matter and the economic contribution of Apache', *Research Policy*, **43** (4), 623–31.

Griliches, Z. (1994), 'Productivity, R&D and the data constraint', *American Economic Review*, **81** (1), 1–23.

Hausman, J. (1999), 'Cellular telephone, new products, and the CPI', *Journal of Business & Economic Statistics*, **17** (2), 188–94.

Hilbert, M. and P. López (2011), 'The world's technological capacity to store, communicate, and compute information', *Science*, **332** (6025), 60–65.

Holt, L. and M. Jamison (2009), 'Broadband and contribution to economic growth: Lessons from the US experience', *Telecommunications Policy*, **33** (10–11), 575–81.

Hulten, C. (2009), 'Growth accounting', *NBER Working Paper No. 15341*, Cambridge, MA: NBER.

Ichniowski, C. and K. Shaw (2003), 'Beyond incentive pay: Insiders' estimates of the value of complementary human resource management practices', *Journal of Economic Perspectives*, **17** (1), 155–60.

Inklaar, R., M.P. Timmer and B. van Ark (2008), 'Market services productivity across Europe and the US', *Economic Policy*, **23** (53), 139–94.

Isaacson, Walter (2014), *The Innovators*, New York: Simon & Schuster.

Jackson, D.J. (2011), 'What is an innovation ecosystem?', White Paper, Arlington, VA: NSF Engineering Research Center.

Karamti, C. (2007), 'Hedonic price indexes for mobile telephony services in France', *Working Paper No. ESS-07-07*, Paris: Telecom Paris.

Levin, J.D. (2011), 'The economics of Internet markets', *NBER Working Paper No. 16852*, Cambridge, MA: NBER.

Mun, S.B. and M.I. Nadiri (2002), 'Information technology externalities: Empirical evidence from 42 US industries', *NBER Working Paper No. 9272*, Cambridge, MA: NBER.

Röller, L.H. and L. Waverman (2001), 'Telecommunications infrastructure and economic development: A simultaneous approach', *American Economic Review*, **91** (4), 909–23.

Rosenthal, S., M. Russell, J. Samuels, E.H. Strassner and L. Usher (2014), 'Integrated industry-level production account for the United States: Intellectual property product and the 2007 NAICS', paper presented at the Third WORLD KLEMS conference, Tokyo, Japan, 19–20 May.

Solow, Robert M., (1987), 'We'd better watch out', review in the *New York Times Book Review*, 12 July 12, p. 36.

Stiroh, K.J. (2002), 'Are ICT spillovers driving the new economy?', *Review of Income and Wealth*, **48** (1), 33–57.

Stranger, G. and S. Greenstein (2007), 'Pricing on the on-ramp to the Internet: Price indexes for ISPs during the 1990s', in E.R. Berndt and C.R. Hulten (eds), *Hard-to-Measure Goods and Services: Essays in Honor of Zvi Griliches, Studies in Income and Wealth, Volume 67*, Chicago, IL: University of Chicago Press, pp. 197–233.

Syverson, C. (2011), 'What determines productivity?', *Journal of Economic Literature*, **49** (2), 326–65.

The Conference Board (2015), The Conference Board Total Economy Database™ May 2015. The Conference Board, accessed 1 March 2016 at http://www.conference-board.org/data/economydatabase/.

Triplett, J.E. (2004), 'Handbook on hedonic indexes and quality adjustments in price indexes: Special application to information technology products', *STI Working Paper No. 2004/9*, Paris: Organisation for Economic Co-operation and Development.

Van Ark, B. (2014a), 'Productivity and digitalization in Europe: Paving the road to faster growth', Policy Brief, Brussels and New York: The Lisbon Council and The Conference Board.

Van Ark, B. (2014b), 'Total factor productivity: Lessons from the past and directions for the future', *Working Paper Series No. 271*, Brussels: National Bank of Belgium.

Williams, B. (2008), 'A hedonic model for Internet access service in the Consumer Price Index', *Monthly Labor Review*, **131** (7), 33–48.

7. Cultural economics and the Internet*
Christian Handke, Paul Stepan and Ruth Towse

7.1 INTRODUCTION

Cultural economics is concerned with the supply, demand and markets for creative goods and services.[1] As suppliers of information goods and services, the arts, heritage organizations and cultural industries are greatly involved in the changes accompanying the diffusion of ever-new Internet-based services and digitization. Much Internet traffic consists of reproducible cultural works, such as music recordings and movies. Moreover, the Internet has had an impact on cultural services that require 'live' participation. Accordingly, this chapter addresses changes in the production, consumption and distribution of the output of the cultural sector due to the Internet.

Cultural economics is relevant to the Internet era for another reason: this literature has long discussed a combination of market characteristics that are present online and, more generally, in the contemporary IT sector. The cultural sector exhibits: radical uncertainty and unpredictable changes in demand; challenges with incentivizing investments in the supply of goods and services that have external benefits and public good characteristics; superstar effects and highly skewed earnings; as well as informal and flexible employment of creative workers. Nevertheless, there is little work in cultural economics on digital ICT and the Internet in the creative economy, and only a few cultural economists have done research on the economics of copyright.[2]

Therefore, this chapter addresses two fundamental issues. First, it points out a number of longstanding and inspirational insights in cultural economics (on topics such as the pricing of information goods and services, or intrinsic motivation), and discusses how the concepts and practice of cultural economics could inform the study of the economics of the Internet. Second, this chapter highlights gaps and unfulfilled potential for research on technological change in cultural economics.

The chapter has seven further sections. Section 7.2 gives an overview of the realm of cultural economics. Section 7.3 considers the impact of the Internet on the production and consumption of cultural goods and services. Section 7.4 deals with the Internet's impact on the distribution of cultural goods and services. The Internet and the industrial structure of the creative economy are addressed in section 7.5. Section 7.6 reviews pricing models for the distribution of cultural goods and services on the Internet. Section 7.7 is about the supply of professional and user-generated content on the Internet, and section 7.8 offers some conclusions.

7.2 AN OVERVIEW OF CULTURAL ECONOMICS AND RELATED TOPICS

Cultural economics developed in the 1960s from a concern about the sustainability of subsidies to performing arts organizations and museums, which led to analysis of the costs and benefits of the arts. The leading model for empirical research was that proposed by Baumol and Bowen (1966) and Baumol (1967), who asserted that live performances and cultural services, which are labor intensive, could not achieve productivity increases that matched those in sectors in which labor productivity could be improved by investment in technology. The conditions of the so-called 'Baumol's cost disease' were subsequently found and studied in a wide range of public services beyond the cultural sector (Towse, 1997). Given increasing relative costs, financing the performing arts through the box office would become more difficult over time, and there would be greater calls for state subsidy and other sponsorship. In the economic debate, it was recognized from the start that the case for state subsidy must be made through establishing net social benefit. Therefore, welfare economics became the other dominant model of cultural economics (Blaug [1976] 1992).

Cultural economics was initially concerned with the operation of non-profit organizations, public finance and welfare economics. It was essentially only after the turn of this century that interest extended to what are now called the cultural industries – those producing commercial 'recorded' versions of music, film, broadcasts and so on, primarily in for-profit firms. Cultural economics has yet to develop a literature on the Internet per se, though there is increasing awareness of the opportunities presented to 'traditional' art forms by digitization and the Internet (Rochelandet, 2011).

The arts (theatre, opera, dance, literature, visual art) and cultural heritage (tangible items like museums, built and human-made structures and objects as well as intangibles like traditional knowledge and skills) are not normal goods: they are *experience goods* that have external benefits of consumption and production and other characteristics of public goods. The presence of these features is widely accepted, though their extent has been disputed. Accordingly, one important research topic in cultural economics is the willingness to pay and valuation of the private and social benefits of these services, and cultural economists have used contingent valuation studies and participation studies to illuminate the issue. Another central issue in cultural economics is the effect of quality and other success factors in markets for highly diversified goods and services. Furthermore, economic impact studies have estimated spillover effects of a range of goods and services from individual theatre and museum buildings to festivals.[3] Other topics have been the economic organization of the cultural and creative industries and studies of specialized markets, such as the art market. A useful overview is found in Towse (2011a).

It became clear early on in the study of cultural economics that analysis of the production and consumption of cultural goods and services demanded the adaptation of traditional economic models. Two areas of interest in cultural economics in particular have led to modifications of existing economic theory: taste formation on the part of consumers and intrinsic motivation of artists and other creators. Cultural economics has developed models that incorporate these issues by importing concepts from social psychology.

An important aspect of the arts is that they change people's tastes and perceptions (and that is indeed a major reason for subsidizing them), which is associated with bandwagon effects and fashions in the cultural and social environment. In addition, as cultural goods are experience goods, consumers need information and education in order to make effective choices. Some cultural economists argue that the arts are rationally addictive, as past consumption and learning seems to increase the utility of some artistic works (Becker and Murphy, 1988). Addiction is also invoked for Internet use, even though with a more conventional, negative connotation.

On the supply side, empirical work on artists' labor market behavior produced two particularly noteworthy insights. First, creators and performers tend to accept below average pecuniary rewards. The human capital model based on economically rational (that is, financially rewarding) behavior breaks down when applied to artists: though artists have higher than average education, they earn, on average, less than other workers and an unquantifiable factor of talent makes earnings and career success unpredictable using the standard model (Towse, 2006). Second, most artists do both arts and non-arts work. According to the 'work preference' model (Throsby [1994] 2007), artists 'buy time' with income from non-arts work to finance time spent on their preferred arts work. Overall, artists' labor markets exhibit the effects of excess supply. Many hopefuls seek to make a career, and most are unlikely to succeed. All but the most successful artists are in a weak bargaining position when dealing with intermediary firms such as publishers. Cultural economists' work on intrinsic motivation has resonance for understanding the explosion of user-generated content on the Internet.

Furthermore, consumer behavior in markets for creative goods and services as well as artists' labor markets gives rise to 'winner-takes-all' or superstar effects: a small minority of suppliers captures most of the revenues, often without an apparent explanation in terms of talent or the quality of the works supplied, and dominates markets. No method has yet been developed for predicting success not only for individual artists but also for many of the products of the creative industries. Uncertainty rules –summed up in the phrase 'nobody knows' (Caves, 2000). The discussion among cultural economists on uncertainty, superstars, as well as fads and fashions provides a useful framework in which to study the impact of the Internet on markets for creative works.

7.2.1   Cultural and Creative Industries

Though political economists and cultural sociologists had turned their attention to the cultural and media industries from the mid-1970s, cultural economists were until quite recently primarily concerned with the subsidized arts and heritage ('high art'). Initially, the incorporation of the arts and cultural industries into the present day conception of the creative industries and the creative economy was essentially politically motivated (see UNCTAD, 2010). Nevertheless, it coincided with the extension of cultural economics into this area, with research on film, sound recording and broadcasting (especially public service broadcasting). Other areas are still little explored, including publishing and games, for example. The art market has had a considerable share of attention in cultural economics, with its huge databases of prices attracting the econometricians (Ashenfelter and Graddy, 2011); there has also been some work on art fakes and counterfeiting, which chimes in with the wider issue of illegal copying (Frey, 2000). The creative industry concept has broadened to embrace cultural tourism and cultural clusters, as well as cultural districts. For the latter, Santagata

(2011) documents that goods specific to a geographical area are often held in collective property.

There are various ways of defining the creative industries and of identifying what falls into the 'sector' (UNCTAD, 2010). A 'typical' list consists of the following: advertising, architecture, the art and antiques market, crafts, design, fashion, film, games, heritage services/museums and libraries, publishing, software, television and radio, and other educational or entertaining audiovisual media content. Copyright law has figured so prominently in the conceptualization of the creative industries that they are often designated as 'copyright based' or just 'copyright' industries. Though the vast majority of the output of the creative industries is undoubtedly protected by copyright this does not mean that copyright is the *sine qua non* of value added in this sector.

The concept of the creative industries embraces both the creation of content and its processing and distribution. Firm sizes range from one-person operations, such as self-employed creators (for instance authors, artists, and composers), to big multinational media conglomerates. Caves (2000) observes that the more creative and innovative work associated with the generation of novel content tends to occur under small, flexible organizational set-ups, whereas the dissemination of finished creative works is often conducted in large oligopolies. Digitization may alter the industry structure to some extent. On the one hand, it facilitates the distribution of creative works and related information, which could erode the position of large corporations. However, there is little indication that creators at large would have gained financially from 'going it alone' or from a stronger negotiation position with intermediary firms (Farchy, 2011). On the other hand, digitization has enabled many amateurs to create works of reasonable quality, often by adapting and building on existing copyright works. Though much of this 'user-generated content' is not made with financial reward in mind, some has considerable market value.

7.2.2   Economic Importance of the Creative Industries

In many countries, the creative industries are now regarded as a significant sector of the economy (Towse, 2010). Much work, however, remains to be done in national income accounting to bring all relevant items into a suitable system of industrial classification. Despite a lack of standardization of products and consistent designation of creative industries, there have been many studies (often by consultants) measuring their size and growth (for example, UNESCO, 2012). Estimates of the contribution of the cultural industries to GDP typically range between 2 percent and 7 percent for highly developed economies but many difficulties remain in delineating cultural industries and developing valid results.

These estimates are often referred to in policy debates. One case in point is the debate on copyright policy, which also illustrates some pitfalls in using such data.

7.2.3   Unauthorized Copying

Even before digitization, creative industries were characterized by high sunk costs of product creation and relatively low marginal costs of delivery (Caves, 2000). This cost structure makes it hard for those investing the creation of new works to compete with free-riders, who generate copies without financing development costs. An effective copyright system may mitigate that problem and that is the economic rationale for copyright. By giving authors and publishers the exclusive right to control uses of their works, copyright law enables them to protect the initial investment outlay in creating new works (Towse et al., 2008).

Over the centuries copyright law has adapted to new technologies for producing and disseminating creative works, while retaining the same underlying principles. Copyright may have worked well enough as long as creative works were disseminated in association with tangible carriers such as printed books or vinyl records. It seems to have floundered with the purely digital dissemination of creative goods and services as downloads and streams online. Copyrights are infringed upon or circumvented on a massive scale online. There is a burgeoning literature on the economics of digital copying and copyright, much of which falls into the realm of applied econometrics (Handke, 2012). This literature has little association with cultural economics, however (Towse, 2008), and tends to sideline issues like intrinsic motivation or taste formation.

While some progress has been made recently on the measurement of investment in copyright assets (Farooqui et al., 2011), none of the work on the economic import of creative industries and the effect of unauthorized copying has been able to establish the extent to which copyright is an economic incentive to authors and publishers in the creative industries. That copyright applies to many creative works does not mean that the supply of such work hinges on copyright protection. Measures of the contribution to GDP of the creative industries are inappropriately adopted as estimates of the 'impact' or value of copyright and, conversely, of the value lost due to unauthorized copying. The subject has become increasingly politicized as the sector is seen as a major source of growth, especially in post-industrial developed countries but also for developing countries.

This is all too familiar to cultural economists who lived through the era in the 1980s of measurement of the 'value' of the arts and the economic importance of the arts to the national economy. The implication was always there (often made explicit) that if resources – regularly meaning state subsidy in that context – were not devoted to the arts, the 'loss' would reduce national income. Exactly the same line has been spun for the economic importance of the creative industries and the need for ever-greater copyright protection. Thus, cultural economists have been well armed to resist these assertions, though lobbyists have mostly managed to grab the attention of policy-makers, not the dismal scientists (Towse, 2011b).

7.3 THE RANGE OF IMPACT(S) OF THE INTERNET ON THE PRODUCTION AND CONSUMPTION OF CULTURAL GOODS AND SERVICES

The Internet is a prime example of a general purpose technology that lowers production costs for a multitude of different activities and enables the emergence of many new products and markets. Like most firms, enterprises in the cultural sector use Internet-based services to run back-office tasks. However, the most fundamental impact of digitization on the creative economy is that goods and services that were previously rival and excludable, at least to some extent, have become in effect public goods for Internet users. Many new ways of disseminating creative works via the Internet have been developed. A vast range of reproducible cultural products is available at no financial costs. Technical restrictions on access have become less important, and the copyright system, the possibility of technical protection methods, and perhaps user ethics are the only barrier to 'free' use.

Digitization and the Internet have together had an impact on all manner of cultural goods and services; the obvious cases are where services are put in digital form at the point of production by the adoption of digital technology – sound recording, film, books and games being leading examples. The Internet also affects the creation of cultural works – product innovation from the perspective of specialized suppliers of arts and culture. Many video games use the Internet to link consumers and generate shared experiences, for example. The Internet enables not only access to, but also the modification and dissemination of many variations of cultural products, as discussed below. So far, this development has not generated many widely recognized new cultural genres, in contrast to the application of other aspects of digital ICT in the market for music, for instance, which was key to the development of electronic music and musical styles such as hip-hop. Product innovation per se does not feature prominently in the literature on cultural economics though there has been work on measuring cultural diversity. The related debate on Internet-based retailing and the diversity of supply is discussed later on in this chapter.

Perhaps surprisingly, even live performances of opera, ballet, spoken theatre and orchestral concerts have felt the impact of digitization and Internet, as they are digitally streamed and delivered by satellite in virtually simultaneous time to computers and, for better sound and visual quality, to venues such as cinemas, enabling audiences to access distant events that they could not otherwise attend. Moreover, these 'performances' generate access for a significantly wider paying audience than the 'original' venue could accommodate. As theatres and concert halls typically have limited seating capacity, these developments offer additional sources of 'box office' revenues for organizations that have previously had to rely heavily on public subsidy. It remains to be seen whether online dissemination will stimulate interest in these elite art forms. Little has so far been written on these developments and it is too early to generalize about the overall effect. The Metropolitan Opera is the oldest of these ventures and has been offering live performances in cinemas throughout the world since 2006, reaching over 3 million viewers; it is said that it took several years before it broke even (Bakshi and Throsby, 2010) and hearsay evidence has it that attendances are falling in the home theatre, that is, the transmissions are 'cannibalizing' them, but there are no firm data. Other than that, Internet selling of tickets and bookings has also made 'real' box offices more efficient for producers and consumers (Towse, 2013).

These are cases where traditional pricing models work because access is controlled and restricted to paying audiences. Even so, some of these services are provided 'for free', and free delivery occurs often in creative industries. One example is the Gutenberg Project, which embraces the idea of providing free access to digital sources of literary works in the public domain. Another case in point are the various efforts of national libraries and museums to digitize their collections and the European digitalization project Europeana. These efforts are held back by the costs of obtaining permissions from copyright holders on works that are still in copyright. Clearing of copyrights is a particular problem with so-called 'orphan works' for which there is no traceable rights holder. This is one reason why digital archives of the cultural heritage in museums, libraries and audiovisual archives, such as those of broadcasting organizations and film institutes, are not as yet open to the public. Broadly speaking, digitization of the content of large cultural institutions has long been limited to content produced before the twentieth century. Much of the twentieth century, and even some more recent intangible heritage, is largely inaccessible online. Little work has so far been done in cultural economics on these developments and problems.

7.4   INTERNET AND DISTRIBUTION IN THE CREATIVE INDUSTRIES

The use of the Internet and other aspects of digital ICT not only affect the costs of producing and consuming creative goods and services, they also affect the costs of disseminating and making them available. From the perspective of producers of cultural products, novel e-commerce applications are mainly process innovations that reduce costs of production, in particular regarding distribution and retailing. There is no direct effect on the characteristics of the core product. (Of course, changes in markets due to e-commerce can affect incentives to produce different types of goods and services. This is what we would refer to as an indirect effect.)

7.4.1   Online E-commerce and Cultural Products

E-commerce comes in several variants in the creative industries. For non-reproducible cultural products such as original paintings or performances, e-commerce is mostly limited to retailing. Examples are the services provided by online trading platforms for live performance tickets, such as Ticketmaster, and online auctions for art works, which reduce transaction costs substantially and make markets more efficient (albeit with the risk of the rise of central intermediaries wielding market power). In any case, the impact of ICT is less immediate than in markets for reproducible cultural products.

For reproducible cultural products, such as sound recordings, movies or literary texts, a hybrid version is the sale of physical copies via online shops. The initial service provided by Amazon was to sell physical books via the Internet, for example. The more completely 'digital' version of e-commerce is to sell access to streams or downloads via retail outlets online. Sales of e-books and music downloads via Amazon are a case in point. Even better known is the iTunes Store that became the largest e-retailer for music downloads in most major markets after 2004. E-commerce requires a standing ICT infrastructure. On this basis, it can substantially reduce the costs of reproducing, distributing and retailing creative works.

The completely 'digital' version of e-commerce is associated with debundling and rebundling of former 'analogue' products. In the market for music downloads, for example, consumers can purchase almost any individual track rather than entire albums. Debundling has also occurred for news items or academic articles that are often available individually online. At the other end of the spectrum are subscriptions, where users acquire temporary access to a wide variety of works. A typical example is subscriptions to 'pay TV' channels (also discussed below). Another case in point is subscriptions to large catalogues of music recordings that have become more popular since 2010.

Moreover, in conjunction with some video games, consumers purchase temporary access to virtual gaming environments, which allow for interactions between consumers. As with other aspects of e-commerce, there is no specific standard model by which creative goods and services are distributed and sold online, and that is also the case with pricing models, which are discussed later in this chapter.

It is an open question to what extent a single, standard way of distributing and retailing cultural products will emerge, and how much variety will remain. At the moment, traditional means of distribution and retailing still tend to generate the bulk of revenues in the creative industries.

7.4.2   Retailing and Distribution Costs

In the traditional system of selling cultural products, much of the reproduction costs and some distribution costs had to be borne in advance of sales. Suppliers needed to predict demand and the number of copies produced and shipped to retail outlets. This was usually approximated by several runs of reproduction, shipping and restocking. By contrast, downloads are available on demand, which reduces the need to predict sales and thus some of the risks of supplying cultural products (Rochelandet, 2011).

Under competitive pressure, lower risks and costs will usually be associated with lower retail prices. However, as long as traditional marketing remains important, even relatively cheap new ways of distribution and retailing may not reduce total costs as suppliers need to incur the costs associated with each type of distribution. For whatever reason, prices for commercial downloads are at present often not much lower than those for copies on physical media formats. This may also reflect some market power on the supply side.

7.5   INTERNET AND INDUSTRY STRUCTURE OF THE CREATIVE ECONOMY

The cultural sector is characterized by extensive product differentiation, albeit with a small minority of hits accounting for the bulk of the market. Over recent years, a number of articles have discussed the effect of digitization on concentration in the cultural industries. Roughly speaking, an application of superstar theory (Rosen, 1981) predicts greater concentration of sales on a few superstar suppliers whereas the long tail hypothesis predicts some fragmentation (Anderson, 2004).

7.5.1   Superstar Theory[4]

Rosen (1981) observed that the labor markets for talented individuals tend to bring up a small minority of high-earning superstars. He argued that disproportionate earnings for superstars occur where small differences in talent have an amplified effect on demand, and where technologies allow superstars to reach a large audience. This theory has been well established and adopted in cultural economics (Adler, 1985; Chung and Cox, 1994; Cox et al., 1995; Caves, 2000).

Besides differences in talent, bandwagon effects may explain concentration of sales on particular creators (Leibenstein, 1950), as consumers follow each other to reduce the risk of purchasing inferior products. There may also be network externalities as consumers value more popular works because the shared experience becomes the subject of desirable social interaction.

According to superstar theory, stars will come to dominate more of the market where digital distribution and retailing enables the most outstanding creators to supply a greater number of consumers. The result would be an even more highly skewed distribution of attention and earnings in favor of a few superstars, and perhaps reduced diversity of creative works supplied.

7.5.2   The Long Tail Hypothesis

By contrast, the long tail hypothesis (Brynjolfsson et al., 2003; Anderson, 2004) predicts that niche products will account for an increasing share of sales with the diffusion of digital ICT. E-commerce reduces the marginal costs of distributing and retailing reproducible cultural products. E-commerce also has the potential to integrate markets irrespective of geographical distance. It thus can become profitable to supply a greater diversity of cultural products. Also, with more abundant pre-purchase information online, consumers may find it easier to search for niche products that suit individual preferences.

There is some empirical evidence consistent with the long tail hypothesis from markets for cultural products such as books, movies and recorded music (Brynjolfsson et al., 2003, 2006; Anderson, 2004; Moreau and Peltier, 2004; Elberse and Oberholzer, 2007; Benhamou and Peltier, 2007). Online retailers tend to offer a much greater number of different titles than traditional retailers, and the share of top hits in total sales tends to be lower online than offline. Some studies suggest that the overall market share of niche products has increased significantly with the diffusion of digital ICT. This point could be exaggerated, however. Despite some fragmentation, sales for cultural products are still highly concentrated on a small proportion of them. Furthermore, measuring changes in sales concentration is tricky: there is no clear boundary between the long tail and the top end of the market. Should one count the top ten titles as the 'hits' or the top 1000, for example? Different aspects of the distribution may be affected differently, say some mid-range versus the far end of the tail. It also remains to be seen to what extent the long tail consists of back catalogue or of new works, or how works from different types of suppliers are affected.

Superstar (winner-take-all) theory and the long tail are often discussed in the analysis of other markets but a substantial number of examples are drawn from markets for cultural products. Many academic works seem to be forthcoming on the long tail and other aspects of the impact of digitization on concentration in the creative economy.

7.5.3   Market Power

Another interesting aspect is the effect of digitization on competition in the cultural sector. Pivotal parts of many creative industries are organized in narrow oligopolies. A number of studies illustrate that e-commerce is associated with greater competition (Brynjolfsson and Smith, 2000; Brynjolfsson et al., 2011). The same factors that drive the long-tail effect could be associated with greater contestability and inter-firm competition.

This could adversely affect growth of major incumbent firms relative to fringe suppliers and newcomers. It could also strengthen creators in their relationship with more concentrated intermediary firms such as record companies and literary publishers.

E-commerce seems to play an ambiguous role. On the one hand, online retailing platforms make it possible for more fringe suppliers to extend the size of the market they can serve. The alternative outlet of e-commerce may also diminish the market power of major incumbents in the traditional market. On the other hand, digital retailing of many cultural products is even more concentrated than offline distribution and retailing has ever been. The effect of digitization on competition in the cultural industries should become an important topic in the future.

7.6   PRICING MODELS FOR INTERNET DISTRIBUTION OF CREATIVE GOODS AND SERVICES

For a long time, economists have suggested new forms of pricing strategies and business models in order to adapt to the diffusion of digital ICT (Shapiro and Varian, 1999). Traditional creative industries have often had difficulties in adjusting to digitization. By now, technological innovation and e-commerce have affected business models in the cultural and creative industries, particularly in those industries that cater for the end user market and for goods that are in digital form. The public goods characteristics of online distribution often make the traditional price per unit model used for most cultural products unworkable, and new models have developed for Internet access to them. Not all types of transactions in the creative industries are changing, however. In the business-to-business sectors of industrial design and commercial graphic design, for example, there is no apparent trend to new business models (3D-printing may come to instigate extensive change, however). In the film industry, business-to-business deals with TV broadcasters remain largely unchanged.

7.6.1   Two-sided and Multi-sided Markets

A long-standing business model in the creative industries is the two-sided market model, widely employed, for example, by commercial broadcasters. TV or radio stations often make programs available to viewers without direct payment. The broadcasting stations then finance themselves by selling airtime to advertisers and sponsors. The market value of advertising depends on the number of users of the 'free' service, and roughly speaking, this makes the market two-sided (Armstrong, 2006; Rysman, 2009). More recently, two-sided or even more complex, multi-sided markets are being developed for many applications on the Internet such as search engines, social networks, illegal download platforms and others (Farchy, 2011; Rochelandet, 2011).

Two-sided markets are associated with positive network effects, where the individual utility of a bundle of goods and services increases with the number of other users.[5] The optimal pricing scheme may then be to supply some services free of charge to attract users on one side, while charging on the other side for access and information on a large user base. The search engine Google illustrates the principle. Google provides its search engine service for free and charges for advertisements, ratings and advertorials (entries that look like regular entries but are, in fact, advertisements). Information gathered on users allows for more targeted advertising and may also become a commodity in its own right. What is more, the search engine improves with use. The search results are based on a ranking influenced by the individual consumer's behavior as well as by the behavior of the masses and therefore every entrance to the search engine influences future results. The more people use a particular search engine, the more accurate the results get: every entry to the search engine benefits not only the person searching but also other Google users and the company itself.

Some of the most successful Internet-based services – the social media sites Facebook and Twitter, as well as the Google search engine – operate in two-sided or multi-sided markets and exploit the associated network effects. The principle is familiar from older parts of the creative industries, and they are gradually becoming more important throughout the creative economy. Online newspapers, for example, are experimenting with user postings and other means to foster community building around their core products. Nevertheless, incumbent firms in the traditional creative industries have found it hard to develop sustainable business models based on multi-sided markets.

Network effects are associated with entrenched large incumbents (Liebowitz and Margolis, 1998). If the value of a bundle of services per user increases with the number of users, large firms enjoy a productivity advantage over smaller competitors. The point is that smaller competitors cannot exploit network effects to the same extent. Thus business models based on multi-sided markets and network effects may bolster the superstar and winner-takes-all features already observed in the consumption of cultural products.

7.6.2   Subscription Models

Subscription models have become more important in some markets for creative works. Some subscription models allow members/subscribers access to a narrow range of club goods. In the cultural sector, this model has long been used for book clubs and for clubs that support arts institutions ('friends of' associations). It has been applied in a digital environment by a couple of music bands such as the German band Einstürzende Neubauten, who sold live streams and allowed direct interaction with the band during the creative process. Subscribers further received the CD prior to the public release and packaged as a special edition.

Subscription models that allow access to a much broader catalogue of content have been more important in markets for cable TV, mail-order DVD rentals, and streamed video. However, so far they do not account for a large market share for any general type of creative products. Nokia launched one prominent example under the title 'Nokia comes with music'. In 2007, the company started to sell an optional music subscription service with their mobile phones. Subscribers were able to access and download the catalogues of the major music companies and some independent labels. The project failed to attract many subscribers, probably because of tight usage restrictions. The initial idea had been that downloads could be used indefinitely. In practice, downloads were only accessible for the period of the subscription. Other restrictions were that the service could only be used with a Nokia mobile phone, and the music could only be played on the phone and one computer. More recently, enterprises like Rdio, Rhapsody or Spotify have offered similar music subscription services, some of which are financed through charging music users and some are financed through advertising. Whether this way of marketing music can significantly contribute to creators' income remains to be seen.

In the film industry, comprehensive subscription models are fairly new.[6] Online video stores such as LoveFilm and Netflix initially developed a business model where subscribers can order a certain number of (physical) DVDs.[7] Customers can keep these DVDs as long as they want, but needed to send them back through mail in order to get new movies. It is a permanent rental contract for a flat rate one-off payment and provides access to a wide range of titles. Many pure online subscription models for commercializing a broad range of films are either illegal or located in a legal limbo. Rapid Share, Megaupload (now replaced by Mega) or other such services sell downloading capacities on a so-called 'freemium' basis: with some restrictions, downloading is free of charge, while users can pay for a 'premium' subscription with fewer restrictions. While such enterprises try to limit their legally relevant involvement with copyright infringements, the services are widely used to download movies, which seems to work more reliably and faster than in most free P2P file-sharing networks. Copyright holders are not remunerated and rights are infringed in most jurisdictions, even though it is unclear whether the supplier of the downloading capacity is accountable. That these subscription models do attract paying members, suggests that the movie industry proper may have a chance to sell convenient access to movies online under current market conditions. This is the niche that Amazon, Netflix and other online (subscription) services have been cultivating with considerable success (see Sherman and Waterman, Chapter 22 in this volume).

7.6.3 Taxes and Levies

Though not a business model in the conventional sense, a mandatory flat rate charge is often applied in the cultural sector to finance the provision of public goods and to compensate for losses occasioned by unauthorized copying. Even before the development of the Internet, flat rate license fees were used (and still are) to finance public service terrestrial television (Maule, 2011). In some countries, a levy is charged for blank, recordable data carriers or photocopying. Such levies were introduced as a last resort to compensate creators and rights holders for unauthorized reproduction and use. The levy is typically collected from retail sales and paid to the relevant copyright collective rights organization for distribution to copyright holders. Levy systems have been criticized for distorting market outcomes, leading to the misallocation of resources. The copying technologies for which levies apply typically have uses other than copying of copyrighted materials, which makes it hard to set adequate rates. What is more, it is hard to develop adequate distribution schemes among rights holders, which would closely reflect the actual use of specific copyright works. In any case, levy systems vary substantially between different types of works and different territories (Kretschmer, 2011).

In some countries, more extensive use of levies, and statutory intervention to install them, are discussed as a means to mitigate current copyright conundrums online. This would probably involve the collective administration of copyright. However, copyright collecting societies have come under increasing scrutiny of late (Handke and Towse, 2007). In any case, most economists are skeptical regarding extensive use of levies, as such a system could choke the market mechanism (Liebowitz and Watt, 2006).

7.7   SUPPLY OF 'PROFESSIONAL' AND USER-GENERATED CONTENT ON THE INTERNET

One of the major consequences of Internet usage has been the outpouring of words, sounds and images on websites and on social networking sites. Some of this content is supplied by 'professionals' with the intention of eventual financial reward. Much content is also supplied by 'amateurs' or end users without pecuniary incentives, and related buzzwords are user-generated content and prosumption. Of course, a distinction between amateurs and professionals is difficult to make with any precision but there is some mileage in it. In cultural economics, research on artists' labor markets distinguishes between professional and amateur creators according to several criteria: payment for their work; use, performance or exhibition of their work; or the proportion of working time spent on creating. This research on artists' labor markets does provide a useful framework for research on content supply via the Internet.

For professional artists, the Internet has opened up the opportunity to promote their careers and to interact with their audiences or fans more extensively. In some (likely few) cases, the creation of their work has taken place interactively with potential consumers, which may make success on the market more likely. Casting shows illustrate the promise as well as the apparent limitations of the procedure.

For both established artists and those trying to break into the arts professionally, the Internet has enabled them to advertise their work and to sell it directly to consumers without the presence of an intermediary, such as a record label, publisher or art gallery. However, no systematic research has yet been done on whether disintermediation is a sustainable model for generating income. Traditionally, intermediary firms provide upfront finance for the creation of works, promotion and distribution. If digital ICT decreases development and marketing costs, this may enable artists to more easily go it alone. However, there may still be economies of scale in promotion and distribution of creative works. What is more, the evidence on artists' labor markets in general has shown that the success of both works and careers is subject to radical uncertainty. Markets for creative works on the Internet will probably remain volatile and uncertain. Intermediaries may then have a function in taking on market risks, as they can spread their investments over a larger repertoire of works than individual creators can.

Intermediaries also act as certifiers, selecting the artists whose work they deem to be marketable (or culturally significant in the case of non-profit promoters), thus restricting and guiding consumer choice of works and creators. The Internet has undoubtedly increased the output of accessible and diverse material. What proportion of it has a substantial value is not known, however. Again, intermediaries may have an important role to play in helping to generate positive attention for creators, and in providing some orientation to consumers.

Unauthorized use may undermine pecuniary rewards to creators. The extent of the problem is hard to gauge. Moreover, the transmission mechanism from pecuniary rewards and the quality and quantity of supply has hardly been assessed empirically. Rights holders may adapt their business models to unauthorized, digital copying by selling more excludable complements to digital copies (as discussed above in the context of multi-sided markets). A radical solution is crowdfunding, where the production of a creative work is subject to the provision of up-front finance from private individuals. It is an open question whether any of this can sustain pecuniary incentives to create in the presence of digital copying.

Furthermore, there is extensive evidence for non-pecuniary incentives to create. Amateur production of material on the Internet – which brings about so-called user-generated content – documents this well. Some of that material may later take on monetary value and be paid for. What is more, user-generated content often impinges on professional output, through mash-ups, collages and other such alteration of original works. This invokes the older question whether parody and other transformative uses of creative works, such as appropriation art, harm the creator of the original (Landes, 2000; Favale et al., 2013). What is more, even if a user-generated work embodies unauthorized use of the work of others, it enjoys protection within the scope of copyright law. Then user-generated content via the Internet can create a confusion of rights that are often anyway unenforceable. Overall, it is tricky to establish whether we gain more from unrestricted user-generated content, than we lose from any adverse consequences for professional suppliers. At this point, there is little documentation as to whether 'amateur' content drives out 'professional' content at all; a study by Erickson et al. (2013) suggests it does not. Even ignoring the ambiguity of these terms, these are challenging questions for empirical research. Nevertheless, it is something that cultural economics should try to tackle. All this suggests that there is considerable scope here to extend research on artists' labor markets to investigate the impact of digitization on creators' working practices and productivity and on any displacement of labor by the Internet.

7.8   CONCLUSION

The cultural sector exhibits market characteristics that are typical for all types of information goods and services, and much of it is immediately affected by the diffusion of Internet-based services. Cultural economics has a strong empirical tradition in research on the performing arts, heritage and increasingly on the wider creative industries. Empirical work in this field has also supported theorizing on topics that are central in new academic work on the Internet and the production, dissemination and consumption of information goods and services. This includes taste formation and supplier induced demand, intrinsic motivation, the industrial organization of non-profit organizations and decision-making under extensive uncertainty, superstar effects, and the social value of non-excludable and non-rival goods and services (Blaug, 2001). The literature on cultural economics provides rich pickings for researchers on markets for information goods and services and the Internet, including user-generated content, the private provision of quasi-public goods, the value and valuation of goods and services with extensive external effects, demand formation and superstar effects, or the desirable level of copyright protection.

That being said, cultural economics is only beginning to directly engage with the Internet and the implications for the cultural sector. There is an urgent need for robust insights regarding the impact on various parts of the cultural sector of miniscule and non-increasing marginal costs of reproducing and disseminating works, new forms of user–producer and user–user interaction, customization, personalization and user innovation, media convergence, and the rise of highly concentrated suppliers of general purpose, Internet-based services, such as search engines, social media sites and online retailers.

Cultural economics has an important contribution to make to understanding the wider implications of the economic changes brought by the Internet for cultural welfare and the welfare of those who create it. There is greater scope for research on the Internet to draw on what we know about the more traditional markets for cultural information goods and services. It is also high time that cultural economists extended their repertoire to deal with technological change and its ambiguous effects.

NOTES

*   The final version of this chapter was submitted to the editors in August 2013, which is reflected in the selection of examples and the literature. The chapter identifies fundamental topics of cultural economics and how they relate to research on digitization and the Internet, which are as current as ever.
1.   By 'cultural economics' we mean in particular publications in the category Z11 (Economics of the Arts and Literature) according to the *Journal of Economic Literature* (JEL) classification system. This body of literature has developed over the last 50 years. Much of the related research has been presented at the biennial conferences of the Association of Cultural Economics International (www.culturaleconomics.org), and many articles are published in the *Journal of Cultural Economics*, as well as a number of authored and edited books.
2.   For recent surveys of the economics of copyright see Towse et al. (2008) or Handke (2010, 2012). On the impact of the Internet on mass media and creative industries, see Picard et al. (2008).
3.   Essentially, impact studies are empirical cost–benefit analyses. They fall relatively comfortably within the scope of the neoclassical welfare model, as applied in fields like environmental economics and the economics of health and education.
4.   Cultural economics has tended to stick with the superstar moniker; 'winner-take-all' is a similar concept applied to a wider range of market situations, though without the analysis of the role played by differences in talent.
5.   Cultural products tend to be non-rival in consumption – the consumption by one party does not diminish the value of the same work by others. If there are no problems with excessive use (congestion), network effects will usually be positive. There may be exceptions where cultural products are Veblen goods that are appreciated for their scarcity and the potential to demonstrate social status through conspicuous consumption.
6.   Pay TV subscriptions for selected – often exclusive – audiovisual content have been marketed for a long time.
7.   LoveFilm exited the rental business in 2009 and was acquired in 2011 by Amazon. Netflix is also a major, authorized supplier of on-demand video subscriptions in the USA, and has started operating in several countries.

REFERENCES

Adler, M. (1985), 'Stardom and talent', *American Economic Review*, **75** (1), 208–12.
Anderson, C. (2004), 'The long tail', *Wired Magazine*, **12** (10), accessed 23 August 2015 at http://www.wired. com/wired/archive/12.10/tail.html.
Armstrong, M. (2006), 'Competition in two-sided markets', *RAND Journal of Economics*, **37** (3), 668–91.
Ashenfelter, O. and K. Graddy (2011), 'Art auctions', in R. Towse (ed.), *A Handbook of Cultural Economics*, 2nd edition, Cheltenham, UK and Northampton, MA, USA: Edward Elgar Publishing, pp. 19–27.
Bakhshi, H. and D. Throsby (2010), *Culture of Innovation: An Economic Analysis of Innovation in Arts and Cultural Organizations*, London: NESTA.
Baumol, W.J. (1967), 'Macroeconomics of unbalanced growth: The anatomy of urban crisis', *American Economic Review*, **57** (3), 415–26.
Baumol, W.J. and W.G. Bowen (1966), *Performing Arts: The Economic Dilemma*, Hartford, CT: The Twentieth Century Fund.

Becker, G.S. and K.M. Murphy (1988), 'A theory of rational addiction', *The Journal of Political Economy*, **96** (4), 675–700.

Benhamou, F. and S. Peltier (2007), 'How should diversity be measured? An application using the French publishing industry', *Journal of Cultural Economics*, **31** (2), 85–107.

Blaug, M. (ed.) ([1976] 1992), *Economics of the Arts* [reprint] Aldershot, UK: Gregg Revivals.

Blaug, M. (2001), 'Where are we now on cultural economics?', *Journal of Economic Surveys*, **15** (7), 123–43.

Brynjolfsson, E. and M.D. Smith (2000), 'Frictionless commerce? A comparison of Internet and conventional retailers', *Management Science*, **46** (4), 563–85.

Brynjolfsson, E., Y. Hu and M.D. Smith (2003), 'Consumer surplus in the digital economy: Estimating the value of increased product variety at online booksellers', *Management Science*, **49** (11), 1580–96.

Brynjolfsson, E., Y. Hu and M.D. Smith (2006), 'From niches to riches: Anatomy of the long tail', *Sloan Management Review*, **47** (4), 67–71.

Brynjolfsson, E., Y. Hu and D. Simester (2011), 'Hello Pareto principle, hello long tail: The effect of search costs on the concentration of product sales', *Management Science*, **57** (8), 1373–86.

Caves, R.E. (2000), *Creative Industries: Contracts between Art and Commerce*, Cambridge, MA: Harvard University Press.

Chung, K.H. and R.A.K. Cox (1994), 'A stochastic model of superstardom: An application of the Yule distribution', *Review of Economics and Statistics*, **76** (4), 771–5.

Cox, R.A.K., J.M. Felton and K.H. Chung (1995), 'The concentration of commercial success in popular music: An analysis of the distribution of gold records', *Journal of Cultural Economics*, **19** (4), 333–40.

Elberse, A. and F. Oberholzer-Gee (2007), 'Superstars and underdogs: An examination of the long-tail phenomenon in video sales', *Working Paper Series No. 4*, Harvard Business School.

Erickson, K., M. Kretschmer and D. Mendis (2013), *Copyright and the Economic Effects of Parody: An Empirical Study of Music Videos on the YouTube Platform, and an Assessment of Regulatory Options*, report for the UK Intellectual Property Office (IPO), Newport, UK: IPO.

Farchy, J. (2011), 'The Internet: Culture for free', in R. Towse (ed.), *A Handbook of Cultural Economics*, 2nd edition, Cheltenham, UK and Northampton, MA, USA: Edward Elgar Publishing, pp. 245–53.

Farooqui, S., P. Goodridge and J. Haskel (2011), *The Role of Intellectual Property Rights in the UK Market Sector*, report for the UK Intellectual Property Office (IPO), Newport, UK: IPO.

Favale, M., M. Kretschmer and D. Mendis (2013), *The Treatment of Orphan Works Under Copyright Law in Seven Jurisdictions: A Comparative Review of the Underlying Principles*, report for UK Intellectual Property Office (IPO), Newport, UK: IPO.

Frey, B. (2000), *Arts & Economics: Analysis & Cultural Policy*, Berlin: Springer.

Handke, C. (2010), *The Economics of Copyright and Digitisation*, report for the Strategic Advisory Board for Intellectual Property Policy (SABIP) and the UK Intellectual Property Office, Newport, UK: IPO.

Handke, C. (2012), 'A taxonomy of empirical research on copyright: How do we inform policy?', *Review of Economic Research on Copyright Issues*, **9** (1), 47–92.

Handke, C. and R. Towse (2007), 'Economics of copyright collecting societies', *International Review of Intellectual Property and Competition Law*, **38** (8), 937–57.

Kretschmer, M. (2011), *Private Copying and Fair Compensation: An Empirical Study of Copyright Levies in Europe*, report for the UK Intellectual Property Office, Newport, UK: IPO, accessed 15 February 2015 at http://www.wipo.int/edocs/mdocs/mdocs/en/wipo_ip_econ_ge_1_12/wipo_ip_econ_ge_1_12_ref_kretschmer.pdf.

Landes, W. (2000), 'Copyright, borrowed images and appropriation art: An economic approach', *George Mason Law Review*, **9** (1), 1–24.

Leibenstein, H. (1950), 'Bandwagon, snob, and Veblen effects in the theory of consumers' demand', *Quarterly Journal of Economics*, **64** (2), 183–207.

Liebowitz, S.J. and S.E. Margolis (1998), 'Network and externalities', *New Palgrave Dictionary of Economics and the Law*, Basingstoke, UK: Macmillan, pp. 671–4.

Liebowitz, S.J. and R. Watt (2006), 'How best to ensure the remuneration of creators in the market for music? Copyright and its alternatives', *Journal of Economic Surveys*, **20** (4), 513–45.

Maule, C. (2011), 'Television', in R. Towse (ed.), *A Handbook of Cultural Economics*, 2nd edition, Cheltenham, UK and Northampton, MA, USA: Edward Elgar Publishing, pp. 413–19.

Moreau, F. and S. Peltier (2004), 'Cultural diversity in the movie industry: A cross-national study', *Journal of Media Economics*, **17** (2), 123–43.

Picard, R., L. Kueng and R. Towse (eds) (2008), *The Internet and the Mass Media*, London: Sage.

Rochelandet, F. (2011), 'The Internet: Economics', in R. Towse (ed.), *A Handbook of Cultural Economics*, 2nd edition, Cheltenham, UK and Northampton, MA, USA: Edward Elgar Publishing, pp. 254–60.

Rosen, S. (1981), 'The economics of superstars', *American Economic Review*, **71** (5), 845–58.

Rysman, M. (2009), 'The economics of two-sided markets', *Journal of Economic Perspectives*, **23** (3), 125–43.

Santagata, W. (2011), 'Cultural districts', in R. Towse (ed.), *A Handbook of Cultural Economics*, 2nd edition, Cheltenham, UK and Northampton, MA, USA: Edward Elgar Publishing, pp. 147–52.

Shapiro, C. and H.R. Varian (1999), *Information Rules*, Boston, MA: Harvard Business School Press.

Throsby, D. ([1994] 2007), 'A work-preference model of artist labour supply', reprinted in R. Towse (ed.) (2007), *Recent Developments in Cultural Economics*, Cheltenham, UK and Northampton, MA, USA: Edward Elgar Publishing, pp. 397–408.

Towse, R. (ed.) (1997), *Baumol's Cost Disease: The Arts and other Victims*, Cheltenham, UK and Lyme, NH, USA: Edward Elgar Publishing.

Towse, R. (2006), 'Human capital and artists' labour markets', in V. Ginsburgh and D. Throsby (2007), *Handbook of the Economics of the Arts and Culture*, Amsterdam: Elsevier, pp. 865–94.

Towse, R. (2008), 'Why has cultural economics ignored copyright?', *Journal of Cultural Economics*, **32** (4), 243–59.

Towse, R. (2010), 'Creativity, copyright and the creative industries paradigm', *Kyklos*, **63** (33), 483–500.

Towse, R. (2011a), *A Handbook of Cultural Economics*, Cheltenham, UK and Northampton, MA, USA: Edward Elgar Publishing.

Towse, R. (2011b), 'What we know, what we don't know and what policy-makers would like us to know about the economics of copyright', *Review of Economic Research on Copyright Issues*, **8** (2), 101–20.

Towse, R. (2013), 'Performing arts', in R. Towse and C. Handke (eds), *Handbook on the Digital Creative Economy*, Cheltenham, UK and Northampton, MA, USA: Edward Elgar Publishing, pp. 311–21.

Towse, R., C. Handke and P. Stepan (2008), 'The economics of copyright law: A stocktake of the literature', *Review of Economic Research on Copyright Issues*, **5** (1), 1–22.

UNCTAD (2010), *Creative Economy Report 2010*, Geneva, Switzerland: United Nations Conference on Trade and Development.

UNESCO (2012), *Measuring the Economic Contribution of Cultural Industries*, Montreal: United Nations Educational Scientific and Cultural Organization.

8. A political economy approach to the Internet
Patricia Mazepa and Vincent Mosco

8.1 INTRODUCTION

> The radio spectrum is to communications today as is land to crops and water to fish. It is a peculiar natural resource, one whose politico-economic and social aspects have been largely ignored by social scientists. Like all other features of the human environment, it must be looked at in its relationships with people . . . Like no other resource, the radio spectrum is the first form of world property. (Smythe, 1981, p. 300)

It may seem unusual to begin with a historical pronouncement on the radio spectrum, but this understanding of the means of communication as a world property – a public and globally shared resource – is fundamental to how a political economist approaches the Internet. Dallas Smythe, a founder of this approach, began from this standpoint to identify how such essential resources were the subject of constant power struggles, given relentless efforts to transform a world public property into one where private ownership and control dominates. Rather than taking this as an inevitable, acceptable or desirable outcome, political economists question what is generally taken for granted by orienting the focus on the social relations, social processes and social changes – and thus the power struggles – that constitute the Internet as one of today's most important forms of world property.

This chapter begins with a definition of political economy and explains four fundamental aspects that mark a political economy approach to the Internet. It then distinguishes between historical and current variations to provide an overview of examples moving from the general to specific. This is followed by an explanation of commodification, spatialization and structuration – three social processes that are central to the field – as applied to the Internet. It concludes with a discussion of major directions and distinctive advances in a political economy approach to the Internet today.

8.2 WHAT IS POLITICAL ECONOMY?

A general, but ambitious definition of political economy is the study of control and survival in social life. Control refers specifically to the internal organization of social group members and the process of adapting to change. Survival means how people produce what is needed for social reproduction and continuity. Control processes are broadly political, in that they constitute the social organization of relationships within a community, and survival processes are mainly economic, because they concern processes of production and reproduction.

Understanding the interactions between control and survival yields a more specific definition of political economy as the study of the social relations, particularly the power relations that mutually constitute the production, distribution and consumption of resources, including communication resources from the press to the Internet (Mosco, 2009). This distinguishes political economy from studies where the focus is primarily on the means of communication (e.g., radio, television and other information and communication technologies [ICTs]) or on various communication modes (e.g., interpersonal, organizational, or networked), to consider communication as inseparable from social relations of power. This means that a political economy of communication is necessarily critical in its consideration of historical and current articulations of power, whether experienced as social inequality, as manifest in struggles for knowledge legitimacy or in efforts to realize democracy more generally.

Political economy is distinguished from traditional economic theory in its insistence on the inseparability of the economic from the *social* (the combination of human thoughts and [inter]actions with each other and the natural environment), whether in theory or in practice. It also recognizes that what is social is never static, but is constituted through *power* dynamics (including harmony, negotiation, struggle, and conflict). Thus, whether the focus is on media, technology, the Internet, or even the philosophy of communication, identifying and explaining social relations, social processes, and social change in terms of these dynamics is part and parcel of the theory and methods of political economy.

Political economy has consistently placed in the foreground the goal of understanding social change and historical transformation. For classical political economists of the eighteenth and early nineteenth centuries such as Adam Smith ([1776] 1937), David Ricardo (1819) and John Stuart Mill (1848), this meant comprehending the great capitalist revolution, the vast social upheaval that transformed societies based primarily on agricultural labor into commercial, manufacturing and, eventually, industrial societies. For Karl Marx ([1867] 1976), it meant examining the conflicting and dynamic forces within capitalism and the relationship between capitalism and other forms of political economic organization, in order to understand the processes of social change that would, he contended, ultimately undermine the capitalist system. Orthodox economics, which began to coalesce against political economy in the late nineteenth century, tended to set aside this concern for the dynamics of history and social change, in order to transform political economy into the science of economics, which, like the science of physics, would provide general, if static, explanations.

Political economists of the Internet start by situating it in *history* through an examination of the interactions between social forces and technological instruments that have shaped the Internet over time. How has the Internet been influenced by and helped to change power relations and the systems of social class, gender and race relations in society? Beginning with histories of electrical power (Nye, 1990), the telegraph (Winseck and Pike, 2007), telephone (Martin, 1991), radio (Douglas, 1987), and television (Fisher and Fisher, 1996), political economists have identified several historical continuities between the use and development of these communication resources and the Internet. These indicate that power relations are not significantly altered by the Internet, but are extended online.

Foremost among the research findings is the general trend towards monopolies and oligopolies of corporate ownership and control affecting the full range of Internet use and development. Although not complete, this includes: 'entry' (hardware and software required for access and use); 'service provision' and 'infrastructure' (data carriage, processing and storage); content (extension of commercial media conglomerates and intellectual property regimes); 'content management' (search engines and databases); as well as 'content exchange' (through the so-called 'social media' used for data collection); the sum total of which is underpinned and promoted by advertising, marketing, and public relations (Fuchs, 2010, 2011; Sussman, 2011). In each case, with some national variations, only a handful of large corporations dominate globally. These include Apple, Google, Amazon, Microsoft, Facebook, and major media companies like News Corp., Disney, NBC, and CBS (Winseck and Jin, 2011). While the names may change periodically, the existing structures of corporate power remain largely the same (Schiller, 1999).

Another historical constant in Internet use and development is the significant role of Western nation-states and their militaries in supporting and directing specific trajectories. While it is common knowledge that the Internet was forged out of this nexus (with some debate as to whether government, corporations or peer networks were the lead innovators), the connections remain significant, as many of the world's largest communication corporations were established to fulfill, and continue to depend on, government procurement and military specifications and contracts (Schiller, 2011; Mazepa, 2015). This relationship is only intensifying as converging networks bring the state and military into intimate relationships with business in a mutual concern over network security.

The (re)creation of myths associated with technological change is also an historical accessory to the Internet. As each new form of technology is introduced, the death of the 'old' media is pronounced, and the 'new' media are heralded as providing the ultimate solution – promising an end to enduring political economic and social problems (Mosco, 2004). Glossy predictions offer the possibility of heretofore unrealized economic gains, and limitless freedom and democracy for all. While such myths are arguably possible and are undeniably attractive, they tend to gloss over the 'complexities and contradictions' of new technology, and in the case of digital media like the Internet, shield the *ideal* of cyberspace from 'the messiness of down-to-earth politics' (ibid., pp. 30–31).

Political economy is also characterized by an interest in examining the social whole, or the 'totality of social relations' that make up the economic, political, social, and cultural areas of life. From Adam Smith, whose interest in understanding social life was not constrained by the disciplinary boundaries that mark academic life today, to Karl Marx, and contemporary institutional, conservative and neo-Marxian theorists, political economists have consistently aimed to build on the unity of the political and the economic by accounting for their mutual influence and for their relationship to wider social and symbolic spheres of activity. Accordingly, the political economist asks: how are power and wealth related? How do these influence our systems of communication, information, and entertainment?

Attending to the social totality means that the 'wealth of networks' (Benkler, 2006) can also be seen as 'networks of wealth', as digital divisions complement divisions of social class, gender, race, and other social inequalities following a long history of inclusions and exclusions. Political economists thus identify and question the extent of power conferred by profit priorities that significantly skew public access and participation away from those who can least afford it, or otherwise direct and contain Internet use and development under private ownership of the means and modes of communication.

This focus on social relationships means that the Internet is not driven by the 'invisible hand' of the market, or solely by either corporate decision-making or individual consumers. Instead, it is made up of the collective and changing networks of institutions, organizations, social movements, and other social aggregates that use and develop it. These networks are not considered random, objective or agentless connections, but instances and places where power coalesces and is exercised. A political economy approach thus pays close attention to the contested grounds of business decisions, government policy-making, legal challenges, and labor negotiations over the range of communication resources as primary sites where the relationship and extent of private and public ownership are negotiated, opposed and decided (Mosco and McKercher, 2008). These are important indications that the Internet is the result of continual and contentious political processes, while appreciating that research is itself a political process, and thus remains open to scrutiny and change (Fuchs, 2010).

Political economy is also noted for its commitment to 'moral philosophy', understood as both an interest in the values that help to create social behavior and in those moral principles that ought to guide efforts to change it. For Adam Smith, this meant understanding values like self-interest, materialism, and individual freedom, which he argued were contributing to the rise of commercial capitalism, whereas for Karl Marx moral philosophy meant reconciling the ongoing struggle over human agency between the innate drive to realize individual and social value in human labor and the push (in capitalism) to reduce labor to a marketable commodity.

Contemporary political economy tends to favor moral philosophical standpoints that promote the extension of democracy to all aspects of social life. This goes beyond the political realm, which guarantees rights to participate in government, to the economic, social and cultural domains where supporters of democracy call for income equality, access to education, full public participation in cultural production, and a guarantee of the right to communicate freely. Through attending to a moral philosophical position, political economists place the Internet at the center of questions about ethics and the public good. Political economy asserts that all organizations – public *and* private – are accountable for our collective well-being, as underpinned by the basic necessities of communication such as universalism, public service, and the right to privacy (McChesney, 2007).

Following from this view, 'social praxis', or the fundamental unity of thinking and acting, also occupies a central place in political economy. Specifically, in contrast to traditional academic positions which separate the sphere of research from that of social intervention, political economy traces its roots back to ancient Greek and Roman political philosophy (of Aristotle, Plato and Socrates) with its practice of providing advice and counsel to leaders. Accordingly, intellectual life is taken as a form of social transformation, and social intervention as a form of knowledge.

Taking collective responsibility and accountability seriously then, the political economy approach expressed through praxis is necessarily critical. As previously underscored, this last characteristic means questioning and challenging social relations of power; not as just an exercise of criticism or philosophy, but as a method of normative and practical evaluation with the objective of suggesting and advancing public alternatives in the use and development of the Internet, among other shared resources (Artz et al., 2006).

Starting at the individual level, this involves critical pedagogy that advances public education and research, not as justification and training to support the status quo, but as activism that facilitates public participation in decision-making, equitable resource distribution, and social and environmental health. This is advanced by the public nature of the research itself through avenues such as: education and information venues (ranging from universities and public conferences to newspapers and social media); direct activism and publicizing research via alternative media; publications in open-access journals (e.g., *Global Media Journal*, *triple C*, and *Democratic Communiqué*); online research-sharing sites (e.g., the Canadian Media Concentration Project); as well as policy involvement on local, regional, national and international levels (e.g., see Mansell and Raboy, 2011 and Padovani and Calabrese, 2014). These initiatives aim to take action on issues such as communication rights, public access, rural broadband development, net neutrality, privacy and lawful access, as links between local and global Internet use and development, and national and international policy (e.g., the University of Toronto Information Policy Research Program). Praxis-driven research includes identifying and working with the range of labor, feminist, environmental and other non-government organizations that have been part of the use, development and decision-making processes of the Internet from the start (Lee, 2006; Mosco, 2009, pp. 58–61; Mansell and Raboy, 2011, Chapters 8–14).

Political economists view democratizing the means and modes of communication as inseparable from movements to democratize politics and economics more generally (Hackett and Carroll, 2006). They question, for example, researchers and other stakeholders who foreground the Internet as an unlimited space for individual expression or democratic politics, while downplaying or ignoring other initiatives that could contribute to a democratic economy and facilitate meaningful public participation in national and international decision-making (Fuchs, 2011).

The many schools of thought that comprise the political economy approach guarantee the inclusion of a significant variety of viewpoints and vigorous internal debate. Arguably the most important divide in political economy emerged in response to the classical political economy of Adam Smith and his followers. One set of scholars, which eventually established the contemporary discipline of economics, focused on the individual as the primary unit of analysis and the market as the principle structure, both coming together through individuals' decisions to register wants or demands in the marketplace. Over time, this approach has dominated mainstream thought on the Internet and progressively eliminated classical political economy's concerns for history, the social totality, moral philosophy and praxis. It thus transformed classical political economy into the purportedly value-free 'science' of economics founded on the empirical investigation of marketplace behavior conceptualized in the language of mathematics. A second set of scholars opposed this as a limited and restricted methodology and refused to abandon the classical concerns, such that subsequent formulations continued to engage in a holistic method. The complexity of engaging in such a comprehensive approach to political economy leaves us with a dynamic and contentious range of contemporary formulations.

Beginning at one end of the political-economic spectrum, a 'neo-conservative political economy' thrives on the work of people like Stigler, Buchanan and Coase, all recipients of the Nobel Prize in Economics, who apply the categories of neoclassical economics to all social behavior with the aim of expanding individual freedom. In contrast, 'institutional political economy', primarily identified with the work of Galbraith (who drew principally on Veblen), argues that institutional and technological constraints help shape markets to the advantage of those corporations and governments large and powerful enough to control them.

With its attention to power differentials, institutionalists created a framework for media studies, documenting, for example, how large media companies can control the production and distribution of mass media products to restrict diversity of content, specifically by filtering out work that challenges pro-business views (Herman and Chomsky, 2002). Also attending to the concentration and networks of power relations underpinning capitalism, 'neo-Marxian' approaches, including those of the French Regulation School, world systems theory, and others engaged in the debate over globalization, continue to place social class at the center of analysis. These are principally responsible for debates on the relationship between monopoly capitalism, the automation and deskilling of work, and the growth of an international division of labor.

A number of social movements have also generated and invigorated schools of political economy. These include 'feminist political economy', which addresses the persistence of patriarchy and the dearth of attention to gender in political economy, distinguishing how gender is articulated in household labor, as well as media and technology production and consumption (Meehan and Riordan, 2002). Expanding the holistic approach in political economy to the ecosystem, 'environmental political economy' concentrates on the links between social behavior and the wider organic environment (see Mosco, 2009, pp. 60–61). Last, a political economy that melds the analysis of social movements and labor to identify alternative forms of organization and social change is advanced in the 'autonomous Marxist theoretical tradition' (Dyer-Witheford, 1999).

8.3   THE POLITICAL ECONOMY OF THE INTERNET: COMMODIFICATION, SPATIALIZATION, STRUCTURATION

One can also map the political economy of communication through three social processes that are central to the field: commodification, spatialization and structuration. Commodification has long been understood as the process of taking goods and services that are valued for their use or need, for example, food to satisfy hunger, water as necessary for life, or information required for problem-solving, and transforming them into commodities that are valued for what they can earn in the marketplace, for example, processed fast food, bottled and branded water, or intellectual property. The process of commodification holds a dual significance for communication research about the Internet.

First, communication practices and technologies contribute to the general commodification process throughout society. For example, the introduction of computer communication gives all companies, not just communication companies, greater control over the entire process of production, distribution, and exchange, permitting retailers to monitor sales and inventory levels with ever-improving precision. This enables firms to produce and ship only what they know is likely to sell quickly, thereby reducing or outsourcing labor, inventory requirements and unnecessary merchandise. Second, commodification is an entry point to understand specific communication institutions and practices. For example, the general, worldwide expansion of commodification in the 1980s, partly in response to global declines in economic growth, led to changes in government priorities, the increased commercialization of media programming, the privatization of once-public media and telecommunications institutions, and the liberalization of communication markets.

As a result, when the Internet started to expand rapidly in the 1990s, it was easier to make the case to develop it as a commercial medium, shaped by private markets, and used to advance the global market system. Although these principles were contested by those advancing the case for various ways of making the Internet a public information utility, it was, by then, much more difficult to advance this vision compared to previous battles for public libraries, public education and public postal communication, as historical research by McChesney (2007) and Murdock (2011) has demonstrated.

Even public regulation itself, which was considered essential to advance the democratic development of radio and television, was eschewed by corporate and government officials – convinced by economic arguments – that the private market was the best means to develop the Internet. Political economists therefore concentrate on how the Internet has been exploited for commercial purposes by measuring and monitoring, packaging and repackaging communication and information, thereby turning Internet content into a marketable commodity. Political economy has thus examined the ways patent, copyright, and trademark law has taken content – which is in principle freely available to anyone with Internet access – and restricted access to those with the ability to pay (McChesney, 2007; Schiller, 2007, 2011; Tian, 2009).

Political economists have also extended the analysis of commodification in Internet use as prefigured by the concept of the 'audience commodity' (Smythe, 1981). As applied to television for example, Meehan (2005) identified how audiences are assembled into categories and sold to advertisers. In the process this constructs artificial categories of people based on their market value – what Meehan (2005, pp. 34–5) calls 'consumer castes' – and this has both material and symbolic consequences. For instance, even though these categories are not actual social relations, the process reinforces social divisions of class, gender, race and ethnicity by catering only to those with the desired disposable income. This complements class divisions while at the same time drawing on and reinforcing existing stereotypes of what 'women', 'men' or 'Hispanics' want, in a continual feedback loop that reifies constructed differences. With the Internet, the under- or misrepresentation of women and marginalized people prevalent in commercial media are multiplied and extended on a global scale (Smith-Shomade, 2004, p. 70); whereas individual interests based on consumption are correspondingly magnified through personalization, narrowcasting and audience fragmentation (Biltereyst and Meers, 2011, Hirst et al., 2014).

In addition to examining the process of commodifying media content and audiences, it is important to consider the commodification of media labor. Braverman's (1973) now classic work directly confronted the transformation of the labor process in capitalism. According to him, general labor is constituted out of the unity of 'conception', the power to envision, imagine, and design work, and 'execution', the power to carry it out. Within the process of commodification, capital acts to separate conception from execution – to divide skill from the raw ability to carry out a task. This separation concentrates conceptual power in a managerial class that is either a part of capital or represents its interests, and reconstitutes the labor process with this new distribution of skill and power at the point of production.

The process of commodification is also extended in the labor of communication workers directly experienced as wage labor, a development that increases in significance throughout the technology-mediated workplace. In order to cut labor costs and expand revenue in the print media, for example, managers replaced mechanical with electronic systems to eliminate thousands of jobs in the printing industry as electronic typesetting did away with the jobs of linotype operators. Today's digital systems allow companies to expand and extend this process. Print reporters increasingly serve in the combined roles of editor and page producer. They not only report on a story, they also put it into a form for transmission to the printed, and increasingly, electronic page. Companies generally retain the rights to the multiplicity of repackaged forms and thereby profit from each use while the workers do not. Concentrated control of the production process is directly related to an increase in outsourced, piecemeal and freelance work. Moreover, as content is increasingly digitized, sophisticated computers and algorithms used to produce news and entertainment targeted to specific consumer groups can be used to replace journalists and journalism itself (see Chapter 21 in this volume).

Wage labor may also be reduced or eliminated in the software industry. Companies now sell software and apps well before they have been debugged with the understanding that customers will report errors, download and install updates, and figure out how to work around problems. This ability to eliminate labor, combine it to perform multiple tasks, and shift labor to unpaid consumers further expands the revenue potential as Huws (2003) and Mosco (2011) have documented for example. Additional research, such as Mosco et al. (2010), identifies how workers have resisted and responded by bringing together people from different media, including journalists, broadcast professionals, and technical specialists in the film, video, telecommunications and computer services sectors into trade unions that represent large segments of the communications workforce.

Commodification of the Internet also suggests a reconceptualization of labor, also as prefigured in political economy by the concept of the audience commodity. Smythe (1981) identified the time and attention audiences give to media as 'work'. In this view, the content – whatever its subjective use value (e.g., entertainment, information, and stress relief) – provides the metaphorical 'free lunch' designed to attract audiences since their time and attention is sold to advertisers (exchange value), which allows the media company to expand its profit. This put into question long-standing distinctions made between production (paid labor) and consumption (leisure, non-work or unpaid labor) at the center of feminist political economy, including debates around Marxism. Applied to the Internet, such distinctions are further eroded with user-generated content, where consumers can also produce content, with terms such as 'produsage' and 'prosumer' indicating converging relations of labor, as research from Cesareo (2011), Fuchs (2012) and Scholz (2012) explains.

While efforts to commodify the use and future development of the Internet continue, political economy's attention to power relations recognizes that this process is not complete without taking into account resistance, opposition, and the creation of alternatives. Historical and current evidence of alternative, autonomous, independent, radical, critical, and other variations of media all indicate the ways of negotiation or rejecting the processes of commodification (see Mazepa, 2007; McChesney, 2007; Feenberg and Friesen, 2011; Hands, 2011). This includes efforts to subvert commercial dominance of communication resources, with examples ranging from radio (e.g., the retaining of radio as a two-way communication device), to hacking into telephone monopolies (e.g., phreakers), to current digital alternatives such as the 'free software' movement. The latter – based as it is on the moral philosophy and ethics of public sharing, exchange and development of source code – is but one example (Stallman, 2002; Mansell and Berdou, 2010). As Milberry (2012, p. 116) points out, this is different from (the more commonly known) open software initiatives: it is not simply a question of using or developing technology in a particular way, or realizing one of the myths of the Internet such that capitalism remains intact; the ultimate goal is praxis – research and activism that sees communication resources as essential to progressive social change and inseparable from political economic change. These alternatives 'subvert the dominant social order' rather than mitigating, complementing, or extending it.

The second starting point for the political economy of communication is spatialization, or the process of overcoming the constraints of space and time in social life. In this regard, political economists have focused on upheavals in the international division of labor that have seen millions of jobs relocated to low-wage regions of the world, especially China and India (Stevens, 2011; Yu, 2011), creating conditions where nation-states (and various jurisdictions therein) compete for jobs by lowering or eliminating labor, health and safety laws, corporate taxes, and environmental protections.

Communication is central to spatialization because communication and information processes and technologies promote flexibility while simultaneously concentrating control throughout industry – but particularly within the communication and information sectors. Spatialization encompasses the process of globalization, the worldwide restructuring of industries and firms. Restructuring at the industry level is exemplified by the development of integrated markets based on digital technologies and, at the firm level, by the growth of the flexible or 'virtual' company, which makes use of communication and information systems to continuously change structure, product line, marketing, and relationships with other companies, suppliers, its own workforce, and customers.

The political economy of communication has traditionally addressed spatialization as the institutional extension of corporate power in the communication industry. This is manifested in the sheer growth in size of media firms, measured by assets, revenues, profit, employees and stock share values, a development that has accelerated since the development of the Internet (Downing, 2011). In addition to demonstrating how media firms have developed into transnational conglomerates that now rival, in size and power, firms in any industry (as well as some nation-states), political economists are addressing the development of flexible forms of corporate power as evident in term- and project-specific arrangements. In addition to international free trade agreements, these can take the form of informal or formal agreements – identified as synergies, joint ventures or strategic alliances – that take advantage of more flexible means of communication to unite and separate corporations according to mutual interests. As Hope (2011) explains, these create networks of supra-state corporations that can manage time and space to their own substantial advantage. Identifying how this control shapes labor on a worldwide scale, political economists of the Internet have also focused on how globalization is manifested in a new international division of labor that places China at the base of a network of commodity chains that embody both the power of capitalism to exploit labor and the challenges it faces. Such exploitation leads to the upheavals that regularly mark ICT companies such as in the Taiwan-based electronics company Foxconn, and as epitomized by its employees' suicides (Qiu, 2010; Yu, 2011; Zhao, 2011).

The third entry point for the political economy of communication is structuration, which, drawing from the work of Karl Marx and Anthony Giddens, describes the ways people actively make history, but not under conditions of their own making. Specifically, research based on structuration helps to balance a tendency in political economic analysis to concentrate primarily on structures, typically business and governmental institutions, by incorporating the ideas of agency, social process, and social practice into analysis.

The political economy of the Internet addresses social class in these terms by producing research that documents persistent inequities in communication systems, particularly in access to the means of communication, and the reproduction of these inequities in social institutions (Eubanks, 2011). Class structuration is taken as a central entry point for comprehending social life, and numerous studies have documented the persistence of class divisions in the political economy of the Internet. Nevertheless, there are other dimensions to structuration that complement and conflict with class structuration, including gender, race, and those broadly defined social movements, which, along with class, make up much of the social relations of communication (Castells, 2012). Political economy has also made important strides in addressing the intersection of feminist studies and the political economy of the media (Daniels, 2009; Eubanks, 2011). It has taken major steps in research on information technology, gender, and the international division of labor, which addresses the double oppression that female workers face in industries like microelectronics, where empirical evidence indicates that they have experienced the lowest wages and the most brutalizing working conditions (Huws, 2003; Ngai, 2005), and where unequal gender relations and power disparities between the Global North and South persist despite the introduction of new information technologies (Lee, 2011).

8.4   NEW DIRECTIONS AND ENDURING SIGNPOSTS

The final section of this chapter addresses three major trends in the political economy of the Internet, including the globalization of the field, the shift from an emphasis on traditional to new media, and the growth of activism connected to the political economy tradition. None of these are brand new tendencies, but rather build on existing ones that have often previously been submerged beneath the more dominant trends in the field.

The global extension of political economy research is proceeding rapidly. Some of this is the result of the sheer movement of scholars, a development that has sped up over the last two decades. For example, the Canadian political economist of the Internet Robin Mansell established a base for institutional political economy at the London School of Economics. Yuezhi Zhao (2011), who has provided the foundation for a political economy of China's media and telecommunications system, moved from that country to the United States and from there to Canada, establishing important connections among scholars in all three countries. One of her students, A.J.M. Shafiul Alam Bhuiyan came to Canada from Bangladesh and has produced important work on political economy of new media from the perspective of a postcolonial subject (Bhuiyan, 2008). The Korean political economist Dal Yong Jin (Winseck and Jin, 2011) moved to the University of Illinois at Urbana-Champaign and worked with political economist Dan Schiller to complete a dissertation on the political economy of telecommunications in South Korea. He has since joined Yuezhi Zhao and Robert Hackett to continue the historically strong presence of a political economy perspective at Simon Fraser University.

In addition to formal and informal movements of scholars across regions, universities with a strong political economy orientation have established an institutional base concentrating on international research. The International Association for Media and Communication Research (IAMCR) was founded in 1957 and, for many years, was the only global academic society that supported political economy research, making the political economy of communication one of its major sections. The organization continues to grow and to support political economic research with an international orientation. Under the leadership of renowned scholars such as Robin Mansell and Janet Wasko, the IAMCR demonstrates the global significance of the political economy tradition (Mansell, 2011; Wasko et al., 2011).

One might reasonably wonder what this expansion of scholarship means for the content of research in political economy. Aside from increasing the total volume of research – has this process of global expansion made a difference for what political economists of the Internet have to say? The primary difference is that current research addresses the profound integration of the global political economy and new media. Heretofore the focus was on how one (the USA), or just a handful of nation states (USA plus EU) and their corporations dominated weaker states and their nascent economies, in the process producing little more than dependency and underdevelopment. Today the emphasis of research is on the integration of corporations, nation-states and classes across national, regional and even developmental divides (Curtin, 2011; Ekecrantz, 2011; Mattelart, 2011). In the view of Chakravartty and Zhao (2008), for example, this involves the creation of a 'transcultural political economy', which they document in a book containing contributions from primarily non-Western scholars.

Where once corporations, including those in the communication industry, were based in one country and moved through the rest of the world as an external force, today they are increasingly integrated into the fabric of societies to the point where it is often difficult to determine their national origin. Operating as owners, partners, and in strategic alliances with companies based in the host country, they have led political economists to shift from addressing the power of multinational corporations to examining the rise of a worldwide transnational economy. Many of these companies originate in the West but the growth of other economies, especially those of China and India, renders simplistic many of the standard models of Western domination as being a predominantly unidirectional, and a US- or European-led process (Thomas, 2012).

Attending to the governance of the Internet, political economic research has importantly documented the restructuring of public authorities including nation-states, regional blocs and global governance organizations, and it has described their integration into the commercial sector to produce hybrids that blur the distinction between public and private at every level of government activity. Again, it is no longer just a question of demonstrating how a large corporation 'captures' a government by getting it to steer policies and resources to big business. Rather, we are witnessing the thorough integration of public and private decision-making in a transnationalization of political authority (Braman, 2007; Curtin, 2011), and a related shift in the global management of time and space that considerably favors concentrated private interests (Hope, 2009).

Nevertheless, the worldwide integration of capitalism with its corporate, government, and social structuring is a work in progress. The course is fraught with risks, tensions and contradictions, and there is considerable opposition. This is evidenced in the rise of social movements that have opposed its progression at meetings of international agencies like the World Trade Organization (WTO) and other international bodies such as the World Summit on the Information Society (WSIS) that have attempted to provide a relatively public forum in which opposition could be extended into the communication industry (Pickard, 2007). Political economists have not only examined these developments, they have also taken praxis seriously and participated at the political and policy levels (Mansell and Nordenstreng, 2007). In doing so, they acknowledge the importance of the trend to transnationalize the political economy of communication. They also recognize the need to create transnational democracy and a genuine cosmopolitan citizenship (Mansell, 2012; Thomas, 2012).

A second trend in the political economy approach to the Internet aims to distinguish key similarities and differences articulated by this current configuration of communication. Some political economists have responded by emphasizing continuities between old and new media. For them, history indicates the ways in which significant 'old' issues continue to endure in the world of new media. For others, the emphasis is on discontinuities, or the new connections that networked media make possible. Still others remain skeptical of the potential and the promise that new media pundits and techno-gurus promote, while some concentrate on identifying and addressing the latest issues that today's media raise.

In all of these cases, political economy continues to give considerable attention to analyzing and critiquing capitalism as an enduring and inherently exploitive system that turns workers, raw materials, land, technology, information, and communication itself into marketable commodities in order to earn profit for those who invest capital into the system. Political economists of communication have thus tended to focus on media, information, and audiences as resources, and charted the ways they are packaged into products for sale (Murdock and Wasko, 2007). Many who make the shift from the study of old media to the Internet emphasize the continuities between old and new media capitalism (Mansell, 2011). For them, new media deepen and extend tendencies found within earlier forms of capitalism by opening new possibilities to turn media and audiences into saleable commodities.

Examining the process of commodification on social media, for example, Fuchs (2012) has examined the creation of audience commodities by Facebook and Twitter. His findings demonstrate that users are essentially working for Facebook for free, that is, their labor is exploited to make a profit for Facebook as the data generated from their personal information, online behaviors, browsing and networking is sold to advertisers and marketers (and any other private or government entity), and without disclosure of who bought it, and for what purposes it will be used. This marks a distinction between old and new media, both in terms of conceptualizations and practices of labor and of privacy itself. In economic terms, media corporations no longer need to pay for the production of content, thereby eliminating dependence on wage labor as surplus value is accumulated from user input. In political terms, the constant surveillance of personal data and overall communication and social behaviors, collected by private owners of social media, attack individual privacy and undermine the social fabric. On the one hand, corporate control is strengthened (through intellectual property and private ownership and control over communication resources); on the other, matters of privacy are subordinated or eliminated entirely. Such findings call into question the purported benevolence of new projects like Internet.org, begun by Facebook, that seek to extend public access while retaining and extending private control over communication and technological infrastructure, as well as the ownership of data collected as a result of this access.

Other significant examples of the continuities and discontinuities in new media are Bermejo's (2009) and Lee's (2010) work that charts the rise of Google as a corporate power that has made commodification the center of its global strategy. Expanding its reach through vertical and horizontal ownership, the search giant follows the patterns of old media, and, together with social media corporations like Facebook, is using the data collected to build what can be called a 'surveillance economy' (Hirst et al., 2014, Chapter 12). In the meantime, however, Google is using the surveillance capabilities afforded by the new media to restructure information according to the necessities required by commodification and the security requirements of changing nation-states. In this variation of commodification, privacy is re-conceptualized so that it is no longer seen as a social right or a civil liberty to be exercised by the public; in the surveillance economy privacy becomes a means of exchange (ibid.). In the process, information is also reconstructed according to Google's priorities. Lee's (2010, 2011) work in particular identifies how Google reduces the possibilities of randomness or objectivity of online information and correspondingly alters how users interact with the information itself. The sheer amount of information amassed by Google through surveillance, whether through its search engine, Street View or Google Glass, gives political economists pause to ask what happens to this information should its private owners decide to exercise their capacity to control it; or if Google should go bankrupt or sell out to another company (Lee, 2010). The volatility of the digital economy has certainly taught us that new media is not immune to crises of capitalism.

The power structures that endure in new media can also be identified via the examination of 'web conglomeration' and corporate boards of directors. As Simmons's (2010, 2011) research indicates, corporate dominance strengthened by interpersonal and interorganizational networks has extended to the Internet where an increasingly small number of decision-makers have the power to influence decision-making on a global scale. Simmons's work demonstrates that boards of old media conglomerates are interlocked with new media to the extent that, in her words: 'the Web does not serve as an alternative to media consolidation' (Simmons, 2010, p. 105), but in fact, further facilitates it. Finally, Han (2012), following research by Bettig (1996) and McChesney and Schiller (2003), has documented how ownership and control is strengthened through the extension of copyright power to media labor. Han's research showing how international intellectual property rights were extended in China indicates the variations in state-specific negotiations with capitalism, while confirming that copyright operates as a key vector in the marketization of communication and culture industries and the exploitation of labor, whether in old media or in new (Schiller, 2007). In essence, the Internet may lead us to call it 'digital capitalism', but it is still capitalism, and there is no doubt about which is the more important term.

For other political economists, the emphasis is on discontinuity and departure from historical tendencies in capitalism. For Hardt and Negri (2000), Terranova (2004) and Dyer-Witheford and De Peuter (2009), for example, their central concern is still about the power relations that mutually constitute the production, distribution and exchange of resources. However, as a result of the growth of the Internet, they view those power relations differently than do those who focus on continuity in capitalist relations. Their 'autonomist' perspective, so named because it starts from the autonomy of the working class, maintains that capitalism is propelled by the energy and activity of those who work within it. From this perspective, the focus needs to be placed on the self-activity and self-organization of what Hardt and Negri refer to as 'the mass' or 'the multitude' – the vast majority of people typically viewed as exploited from other critical perspectives (Hardt and Negri, 2000, 2004). Their research findings identify alternatives to traditional labor union structures and models of social movement organization indicating that the social relations of capitalism are never static or unchallenged. Furthermore, it is argued that the growth of communication and information technology does not just serve capitalism – it significantly disrupts it (Scholz, 2012).

In addition to approaches emphasizing continuity and disjunction, the political economy of communication has responded to new media in a third way, by taking a skeptical view of the enthusiasm that inevitably accompanies it. As heretofore identified, this has been particularly important in historical work that demonstrates that much of what is considered new and revolutionary in new media was actually associated with every communication technology when present-day old media were new (Mosco, 2004; Flichy, 2007). Today, what Sussman (2011) calls the 'promotional culture' – the combination of media, public relations, advertising, marketing and spin – is increasingly effective in buttressing the myths and optimistic visions of technological utopia, much to the detriment of critical reflection and praxis in general.

The fourth response of political economy to the Internet is to address new problem areas that are particularly significant in this cycle of development in communication and information technology. One should be hesitant to call them new issues because they are really not unique to the Internet and have been distinguished by political economy in the past. Nevertheless, enduring issues of ownership and control are arguably more acute today given the increase and extension of intellectual property rights (May, 2009), surveillance (Brown, 2006; Lyon, 2009; Andrejevic, 2011), and the tendency toward what some call a 'network economy' (Melody, 2007; Mansell, 2011).

Last but not least, praxis – or the unity of research and action – remains fundamental to a political economy approach. Most political economists of the Internet have been activists as well as scholars, involved in media democracy, development communication, independent media and universal access work, as well as with labor, feminist, and anti-racist movements through organizations like the Union for Democratic Communication and the International Association for Media and Communication's working groups in communication, and its policy task force on Internet governance (www.iamcr.org). Important as these developments are, one of the most significant advances in public political activity has been the creation in 2002 of the Free Press by the political economist Robert W. McChesney (2007). The organization has been a focal point for the remarkably resurgent new media reform movement in the United States and is a model for reform movements around the world.

8.5   CONCLUSION

The political economy of the Internet encompasses a vast range of issues that are rigorously debated within the field. Nevertheless, scholars are united in their commitment to the view that political economy is vital because it brings together two fields that were historically separated in the academic division of labor. Moreover, it unites the political and the economic in the study of power in all of its forms, but with particular attention to how the Internet inflects, and is inflected by, social relations of power. In addition, political economists come together to recognize the importance of history, the social totality, moral philosophy and praxis as enduringly essential to its scholarship.

As reviewed here, there are many different schools and approaches to political economy, such that its theories and methods are not homogeneous, or absent of vigorous internal critique (e.g., see Babe, 2009; Mosco, 2009; Winseck and Yin, 2011). Moreover, given its focus on the social relations of capitalism as a primary factor in understanding communication and the Internet today, the approach is inherently oriented to staying dynamically in tune with them. Accordingly, political economy avoids the technological determinism expressed through studies that see the Internet itself as a 'revolution' and similar work that places communication at the very center of analysis to prioritize how interpersonal networks and meanings are made. Either of these approaches can take capitalism as a given, relegate it to the background, or render power so diffuse as to make it entirely dependent on individual interpretation.

Considering political, economic and social questions in terms of local and global concentrations and practices of power – and the interconnections between them – means that the approach is complex and challenging for researchers and lay people alike, both in terms of its breadth and historical reach and its consistent skepticism in the face of dominant theories or practices. Its explanations can be dense due to its insistence on empirical evidence, internal self-reflexivity, and dialogue with other approaches, as underpinned by its critical nature and central characteristics.

As the Internet continues to evolve, more issues will emerge to test the strength and the unity of the political economy perspective. For example, one field that is emerging is the expansion of cloud computing and 'big data' (Mosco, 2014). Cloud computing is the first step in building what one might reasonably call the 'Next Internet'. While it is far from fully formed and retains some of the same characteristics as the one born in 1989, the Next Internet is developing rapidly and already challenging its founders' vision of a pluralistic, decentralized and democratic digital world with one that privileges exclusive, centralized control and ubiquitous surveillance. In addition to cloud computing, the Next Internet is made up of big data analytics, and the Internet of Things. It promises companies and government agencies centralized data storage and services in vast digital factories that process and analyze massive streams of information gathered by networked sensors stored in every possible consumer, industrial, and office device, as well as in living bodies. But it is also encourages concentrations of political-economic power and data-driven decision-making, as well as posing major environmental, privacy and labor challenges (Mosco, 2015).

The global spread of massive facilities to house the infrastructure, platforms and applications that make up the cloud are just beginning to draw the attention of political economists concerned with the ecological (Maxwell and Miller, 2012) and the ethical dimensions of this development (boyd and Crawford, 2012). Such research demonstrates that political economy is a living tradition that will continue to bring an important critical voice to the study and future development of the Internet, and also serve as a vital contributor to realizing its democratic potential as a public resource.

REFERENCES

Andrejevic, M. (2011), 'Surveillance and alienation in the online economy', *Surveillance and Society*, **8** (3), 278–87.
Artz, L., S. Macek and D.L. Cloud (eds) (2006), *Marxism and Communication Studies: The Point is to Change It*, New York: Peter Lang.
Babe, R. (2009), *Cultural Studies and Political Economy*, Lanham, MD: Lexington Books.
Benkler, Y. (2006), *The Wealth of Networks*, New Haven, CT: Yale University Press.
Bermejo, F. (2009), 'Audience manufacture in historical perspective: From broadcasting to Google', *New Media and Society*, **11** (1–2), 133–54.
Bettig, R.V. (1996), *'Copyrighting Culture: The Political Economy of Intellectual Property'*, Boulder, CO: Westview Press.
Bhuiyan, A.J.M. (2008), 'Peripheral view: Conceptualizing the information society as a postcolonial subject', *The International Communication Gazette*, **70** (2), 99–116.
Biltereyst, D. and P. Meers (2011), 'The political economy of audiences', in J. Wasko, G. Murdock and H. Sousa (eds), *The Handbook of Political Economy of Communication*, New York: Blackwell, pp. 415–35.
boyd, d. and K. Crawford (2012), 'Critical questions for big data', *Information, Communication & Society*, **15** (5), 662–79.
Braman, S. (2007), *Change of State*, Cambridge, MA: MIT Press.
Braverman, H. (1973), *Labor and Monopoly Capital*, New York: Monthly Review.
Brown, F. (2006), 'Rethinking the role of surveillance studies in the critical political economy of communication', paper presented at the annual conference of the International Association for Media and Communication Research, Cairo, July.
Castells, M. (2012), *Networks of Outrage and Hope: Social Movements in the Internet Age*, London: Polity.
Cesareo, G. (2011), 'From the "work of consumption" to the "work of prosumers": New scenarios, problems, and risks', in J. Wasko, G. Murdock and H. Sousa (eds), *The Handbook of Political Economy of Communication*, New York: Blackwell, pp. 401–14.
Chakravartty, P. and Y. Zhao (eds) (2008), *Global Communication: Toward a Transcultural Political Economy*, Lanham, MD: Rowman and Littlefield.
Curtin, M. (2011), 'Global media capital and local media policy', in J. Wasko, G. Murdock and H. Sousa (eds), *The Handbook of Political Economy of Communication*, New York: Blackwell, pp. 541–57.
Daniels, J. (2009), 'Rethinking cyberfeminism(s): Race, gender, and embodiment', *WSQ*, **37** (1–2), 101–24.
Douglas, S. (1987), *Inventing American Broadcasting, 1899–1922*, Baltimore, MA: Johns Hopkins University Press.
Downing, J.D.H. (2011), 'Media ownership, concentration, and control: The evolution of debate', in J. Wasko, G. Murdock and H. Sousa (eds), *The Handbook of Political Economy of Communication*, New York: Blackwell, pp. 140–68.
Dyer-Witheford, N. (1999), *Cyber-Marx: Cycles and Circles of Struggle in High Technology Capitalism*, Urbana and Chicago, IL: University of Illinois Press.
Dyer-Witheford, N. and G. de Peuter (2009), *Games of Empire: Global Capitalism and Video Games*, Minneapolis, MN: University of Minnesota Press.
Ekecrantz, J. (2011), 'Media and communication studies going global', in J. Wasko, G. Murdock and H. Sousa (eds), *The Handbook of Political Economy of Communication*, New York: Blackwell, pp. 483–500.
Eubanks, V. (2011), *Digital Dead End*, Cambridge, MA: MIT Press.
Feenberg, A. and N. Friesen (eds) (2011), *Re-Inventing the Internet: Case Studies*, Rotterdam and Boston, MA: Sense Publishers.
Fisher, D.E. and M.J. Fisher (1996), *Tube: The Invention of Television*, New York: Counterpoint.
Flichy, P. (2007), *The Internet Imaginaire*, MA: MIT Press.
Fuchs, C. (2010), *Internet and Society: Social Theory in the Information Age*, New York: Routledge.
Fuchs, C. (2011), *Foundations of Critical Media and Information Studies*, New York: Routledge.
Fuchs, C. (2012), 'Dallas Smythe today – The audience commodity, the digital labour debate, Marxist political economy and critical theory: Prolegomena to a digital labour theory of value', *tripleC*, **10** (2), 692–740.
Hackett, R.A. and W.K. Carroll (2006), *Remaking Media: The Struggle to Democratize Public Communication*, New York and London: Routledge.
Han, D. (2012), 'Copyrighting media labor and production: A case of Chinese television', *Television & New Media*, **13** (4), 283–306.
Hands, J. (2011), *@ is for Activism: Dissent, Resistance and Rebellion in a Digital Culture*, London: Pluto Press.
Hardt, M. and A. Negri (2000), *Empire*, Cambridge, MA: Harvard University Press.
Hardt, M. and A. Negri (2004), *Multitude: War and Democracy in the Age of Empire*, New York: Penguin.

Herman, E.S. and N. Chomsky (2002), *Manufacturing Consent: The Political Economy of the Mass Media*, New York: Pantheon.

Hirst, M., J. Harrison and P. Mazepa (2014), *Communication and New Media: From Broadcast to Narrowcast*, Canadian edition, Toronto: Oxford University Press.

Hope, W. (2009), 'Conflicting temporalities: State, nation, economy and democracy under global capitalism', *Time & Society*, **18** (1), 62–85.

Hope, W. (2011), 'Global capitalism, temporality, and the political economy of communication', in J. Wasko, G. Murdock and H. Sousa (eds), *The Handbook of Political Economy of Communication*, New York: Blackwell, pp. 521–40.

Huws, U. (2003), *The Making of a Cybertariat: Virtual Work in a Real World*, New York: Monthly Review Press.

Lee, M. (2006), 'What's missing in feminist research in new information and information technologies', *Feminist Media Studies*, **6** (2), 191–210.

Lee, M. (2010), 'A political economic critique of Google Maps and Google Earth', *Information, Communication & Society*, **13** (6), 909–28.

Lee, M. (2011), 'A feminist political economic critique of the human development approach to new information and communication technologies', *The International Communication Gazette*, **73** (6), 524–38.

Lyon, D. (2009), *Identifying Citizens: ID Cards as Surveillance*, London: Polity.

Mansell, R. (2011), 'New visions, old practices: Policy and regulation in the Internet era', *Continuum: Journal of Media & Cultural Studies*, **25** (1), 19–32.

Mansell, R. (2012), *Imagining the Internet: Communication, Innovation and Governance*, Oxford, UK: Oxford University Press.

Mansell, R. and E. Berdou (2010), 'Political economy, the Internet and FL/OSS development', in J. Hunsinger, L. Klastrup and M. Allen (eds), *International Handbook of Internet Research*, New York: Springer, pp. 341–61.

Mansell, R. and K. Nordenstreng (2007), 'Great media and communication debates: WSIS and the MacBride Report', *Information Technologies and International Development*, **3** (4), 15–36.

Mansell, R. and M. Raboy (eds) (2011), *The Handbook of Global Media and Communication Policy*, New York: Blackwell.

Martin, M. (1991), *Hello, Central? Gender, Technology, and Culture in the Formation of Telephone Systems*, Montreal, QC and Kingston, ON: McGill-Queen's University Press.

Marx, K. ([1867] 1976), *Capital: A Critique of Political Economy, Volume 1*, trans. B. Fowkes, London: Penguin Classics.

Mattelart, A. (2011), 'New international debates on culture, information, and communication', in J. Wasko, G. Murdock and H. Sousa (eds), *The Handbook of Political Economy of Communication*, New York: Blackwell, pp. 501–20.

Maxwell, R. and T. Miller (2012), *Greening the Media*, New York: Oxford University Press.

May, C. (2009), *The Global Political Economy of Intellectual Property Rights: The New Enclosures*, 2nd edition, London: Routledge.

Mazepa, P. (2007), 'Democracy of, in and through communication: Struggles around public service in Canada in the first half of the twentieth century', *Info*, **9** (2–3), 45–56.

Mazepa, P. (2015), 'Manifest spatialization: Militarizing communication in Canada', *Global Media Journal, Canadian Edition*, **8** (1), 9–30.

McChesney, R.W. (2007), *Communication Revolution: Critical Junctures and the Future of Media*, New York: The Free Press.

McChesney, R.W. and D. Schiller (2003), *The Political Economy of International Communications: Foundations for the Emerging Global Debate about Media Ownership and Regulation*, Geneva: United Nations Research Institute for Social Development.

Meehan, E.R. (2005), *Why TV is Not Our Fault*, Lanham, MD: Rowman and Littlefield.

Meehan, E.R. and E. Riordan (eds) (2002), *Sex and Money: Feminism and Political Economy in the Media*, Minneapolis, MN: University of Minnesota Press.

Melody, W. (2007), 'Cultivating knowledge for knowledge societies at the intersections of economic and cultural analysis', *International Journal of Communication*, **1**, 70–78.

Milberry, K. (2012), 'Hacking for social justice', in A. Feenberg and N. Friesen (eds), *(Re)inventing the Internet*, Rotterdam and Boston, MA: Sense Publishers, pp. 109–30.

Mill, J.S. (1848), *Principles of Political Economy*, Boston: C.C. Little and J.B. Brown.

Mosco, V. (2004), *The Digital Sublime*, Cambridge, MA: MIT Press.

Mosco, V. (2009), *The Political Economy of Communication*, 2nd edition, London: Sage.

Mosco, V. (2011), 'The political economy of labor', in J. Wasko, G. Murdock and H. Sousa (eds), *The Handbook of Political Economy of Communication*, New York: Blackwell, pp. 356–80.

Mosco, V. (2014), *To the Cloud: Big Data in a Turbulent World*, Boulder, CO: Paradigm Publishers.

Mosco, V. (2015), 'Can the Internet of Things be democratized?', *The Monitor*, Ottawa: Canadian Centre for

Policy Alternatives, November/December, accessed 8 January 2016 at https://www.policyalternatives.ca/publications/monitor/can-internet-things-be-democratized.

Mosco, V. and C. McKercher (2008), *The Laboring of Communication: Will Knowledge Workers of the World Unite?*, Lanham, MD: Lexington Books.

Mosco, V., C. McKercher and U. Huws (eds) (2010), *Getting the Message: Communications Workers and Global Value Chains*, London: Merlin Press.

Murdock, G. (2011), 'Political economies as moral economies', in J. Wasko, G. Murdock and H. Sousa (eds), *The Handbook of Political Economy of Communication*, New York: Blackwell, pp. 11–40.

Murdock, G. and J. Wasko (eds) (2007), *Media in the Age of Marketization*, Cresskill, NJ: Hampton Press.

Ngai, P. (2005), *Made in China: Women Factory Workers in a Global Workplace*, Durham, NC: Duke University Press.

Nye, D. (1990), *Electrifying America*, Cambridge, MA: MIT Press.

Padovani, C. and A. Calabrese (eds) (2014), *Communication Rights and Social Justice: Historical Accounts of Transnational Mobilizations, Global Transformations in Media and Communication Research – A Palgrave IAMCR Series*, London and New York: Palgrave Macmillan.

Pickard, V. (2007), 'Neoliberal visions and revisions in global communications policy from NWICO to WSIS', *Journal of Communication Inquiry*, **31** (2), 118–39.

Qiu, J.L. (2010), 'Across the Great Wall we can reach every corner in the world: Network labour in China', in V. Mosco, C. McKercher and U. Huws (eds), *Getting the Message*, London: Merlin Press, pp. 111–25.

Ricardo, D. (1819), *On the Principles of Political Economy and Taxation*, London: G. Bell and Sons.

Schiller, D. (1999), *Digital Capitalism*, Cambridge, MA: MIT Press.

Schiller, D. (2007), *How to Think About Information*, Chicago and Urbana, IL: University of Illinois Press.

Schiller, D. (2011), 'Power under pressure: Digital capitalism in crisis', *International Journal of Communication*, **5**, 924–41.

Scholz, T. (ed.) (2012), *Digital Labor*, New York: Routledge.

Simmons, C. (2010), 'Weaving a web within the Web: Corporate consolidation of the Web, 1999–2008', *The Communication Review*, **13** (2), 105–19.

Simmons, C. (2011), 'Converging competitors? Board interlocks in the changing media landscape', *Journal of Media Economics*, **24** (4), 201–13.

Smith, A. ([1776] 1937), in E. Canaan (ed.), *An Inquiry into the Nature and Causes of the Wealth of Nations*, New York: Modern Library.

Smith-Shomade, B.E. (2004), 'Narrowcasting in the new world information order: A space for the audience?', *Television & New Media*, **5** (1), 69–81.

Smythe, D. (1981), *Dependency Road*, Norwood, NJ: Ablex.

Stallman, R. (2002), *Free Software, Free Society*, Boston, MA: Free Software Foundation.

Stevens, A. (2011), 'Calling for resistance: The political economy of Indian and Canadian call centre industries', doctoral dissertation, Queen's University, Kingston, ON.

Sussman, G. (2011), *The Propaganda Society: Promotional Culture and Politics in Global Context*, New York: Peter Lang.

Terranova, T. (2004), *Network Culture: Politics for the Information Age*, London: Pluto.

Thomas, P. (2012), *Digital India: Understanding Information, Communication and Social Change*, New Delhi: Sage Publications India.

Tian, G. (2009), *Re-Thinking Intellectual Property: The Political Economy of Copyright Protection in the Digital Era*, New York: Routledge.

Wasko, J., G. Murdock and H. Sousa (eds) (2011), *The Handbook of Political Economy of Communication*, New York: Blackwell.

Winseck, D. and D.Y. Jin (eds) (2011), *The Political Economies of Media*, New York: Bloomsbury.

Winseck, D. and R. Pike (2007), *Communication and Empire: Media Power and Globalization, 1860–1930*, Durham, NC: Duke University Press.

Yu, H. (2011), *Labor, Class Formation and China's Informationalized Policy of Economic Development*, Lanham, MD: Lexington Books.

Zhao, Y. (2008), *Communication in China: Political Economy, Power, and Conflict*, Lanham, MD: Rowman and Littlefield.

Zhao, Y. (2011), 'The challenge of China: Contribution to a transcultural political economy of communication for the twenty-first century', in J. Wasko, G. Murdock and H. Sousa (eds), *The Handbook of Political Economy of Communications*, New York: Blackwell, pp. 558–82.

PART III

INSTITUTIONAL ARRANGEMENTS AND INTERNET ARCHITECTURE

9. Competition and antitrust in Internet markets

Justus Haucap and Torben Stühmeier*

9.1 INTRODUCTION

The rapid rise, enduring growth and success of Internet markets and e-commerce platforms have spurred a lively and sometimes heated debate among academics and policy-makers: do Internet markets foster competition or are they prone to concentration, possibly to the point of monopolization?[1] Competition economists and lawyers vigorously discuss the peculiarities of these markets and whether traditional rules and interpretations of competition law are sufficient to deal with potential new competition problems. The cases against search engine Google have received most public and academic attention (e.g., Devine, 2008; Bork and Sidak, 2012; Haucap and Kehder, 2013; Lao, 2013; Manne and Rinehart, 2013; Lianos and Motchenkova, 2013; Edelman, 2015), closely followed by the e-book case against Apple (e.g., Johnson, 2013; Gaudin and White, 2014; De los Santos and Wildenbeest, 2014). In addition, numerous cases concerning vertical restraints in online sales have recently been brought before European courts (for overviews see Vogel, 2012; OECD, 2013; Buccirossi, 2015; ICN, 2015). These vertical restraints include across-platform parity agreements (APPAs), which are a special form of a most-favored customer clause, general bans on online sales or bans on particular platforms, dual pricing systems, and selective and exclusive distribution systems.

Among competition lawyers, the European Court of Justice's (ECJ) decision of 13 October 2011 in the Pierre Fabre case has received much attention. In that case the ECJ ruled that an outright ban on Internet sales constituted a hardcore restriction under European competition law or, to be more precise, an infringement by object of Article 101(1) of the Treaty on the Functioning of the European Union (TFEU). Following this decision, a discussion has emerged on the legal treatment of vertical restraints in Internet retail markets in general (e.g., OECD, 2013; Bundeskartellamt, 2013). In the USA, in contrast, vertical restraints in Internet commerce have played much less of a role, reflecting a more lenient approach towards vertical restraints compared to Europe. Instead, net neutrality has been a much more prominent issue than in most European countries. Common to the USA and the EU is the high attention paid to the antitrust proceedings (a) against Google and (b) against Apple in the e-book case.

This chapter will discuss recent antitrust cases related to online markets. Before we describe and comment on these cases we will very briefly summarize the particularities of online markets in order to provide a foundation for our analysis. The remainder of the chapter is organized as follows: section 9.2 describes the unique economic characteristics of online markets, before section 9.3 discusses the antitrust allegations and proceedings against Google. Section 9.4 discusses the most prominent cases related to vertical restraints, including the Apple e-book case and the ECJ Pierre Fabre case. Section 9.5 highlights competition issues at the infrastructure level, namely margin or price squeezing of incumbent operators vis-à-vis alternative Internet Service Providers (ISPs) and network neutrality. Policy conclusions and further research questions are discussed in the concluding section 9.6.

9.2   COMPETITION IN ONLINE MARKETS

9.2.1   Key Characteristics of Online Markets

The intensity of competition in Internet markets is often (but not always) influenced by direct and indirect network effects and switching costs (e.g., Evans and Schmalensee, 2007; Alexandrov et al., 2011). Many Internet markets operate as multi-sided platforms where a platform operator brings (at least) two different groups of customers together, for example, buyers and sellers or 'users' and advertisers. A market is typically called two-sided or even multi-sided if indirect network effects are of major importance (Rochet and Tirole, 2003, 2006; Wright, 2004; Armstrong, 2006; Evans, 2009; Rysman, 2009). Indirect network effects need to be distinguished from direct network effects which are directly related to the size of a network. Put differently, direct network effects imply that a user's utility from a particular service is directly affected by the number of other users (Rohlfs, 1974; Farrell and Saloner, 1985; Katz and Shapiro, 1985). The classical example is the telecommunication network. For example, as the user base of communications services such as Skype or WhatsApp grows they become more attractive by offering even more communication links with others. Similarly, if a large customer base is already using a certain social network such as Facebook or LinkedIn this tends to attract even more users to join, as a large customer base increases the probability of finding valuable contacts.

In contrast, indirect network effects arise if the number of users on one side of the market attracts more users on the other market side. Hence, users on one side of the market do not *directly* benefit from an increase in the number of users on their market side, but only *indirectly*, as an increase in users on their market side attracts more potential transaction partners on the other market side. While there is no direct benefit of an increase in users on the same market side (in fact there may even be negative direct effects via increased competition), the network effect unfolds indirectly through the opposite market side. Taking eBay or Amazon Marketplace as an illustration, more potential buyers attract more sellers to offer goods on these platforms as (1) the likelihood of selling their goods increases with the number of potential buyers and (2) competition among buyers of the goods will be more intense and, therefore, auction revenues are likely to be higher (Rochet and Tirole, 2003, 2006; Ellison and Ellison, 2005; Evans and Schmalensee, 2007). A higher number of sellers and an increased variety of goods offered, in turn, make the trading platform more attractive for potential buyers. With positive indirect network effects, more participants on one side of the market imply higher utility of participants on the other side of the market and vice versa. These indirect network effects are a key characteristic of two-sided markets. While these indirect network effects have always been present in market places such as fairs, exchanges and malls, capacity constraints and transport costs or travel times have limited the expansion of market places. In contrast, in online markets such constraints play virtually no role so that further concentration processes can be expected. The so-called 'death of distance' removes the natural barrier to expansion imposed by travel costs on traditional market places, while the virtual location on the Internet removes the barrier to expansion traditionally imposed on malls, fairs, and so on by space or capacity constraints.

Apart from eBay and Amazon Marketplace, prominent online platforms that exhibit indirect network effects are Uber, Lyft and similar ride-sharing platforms; Airbnb, Expedia, Booking.com and other travel-related booking platforms; Google, Bing, and other search engines; Craigslist, file-sharing networks and many other platforms and applications.

From a competition policy point of view, it is important to note that network effects often require large platform sizes to achieve efficient utilization of the platform. Hence, high concentration levels cannot simply be interpreted in the same manner as in conventional markets without network effects (e.g., Wright, 2004; Alexandrov et al., 2011; Evans and Schmalensee, 2015). In fact, the existence of one large market place may often be efficient, as it helps to reduce search costs for potential trading partners compared to a situation with a larger number of smaller market places.

From a business perspective, two-sided markets pose the challenge that it is not sufficient for the platform operator to convince only users of one market side to join the platform, as there is an interrelationship between the user groups on both market sides. Neither the buyer side nor the seller side of the market can be attracted to join the platform if the other side of the market is not sufficiently large. This is a realization of the well-known chicken-and-egg problem, where both sides of the market affect each other and no side can emerge without the other (Caillaud and Jullien, 2003). Consequently one side of the market is often 'subsidized' by the other (Wright, 2004; Parker and Van Alstyne, 2005). Products such as the Acrobat Reader, Microsoft's MediaPlayer, or the RealPlayer are available free of charge for consumers, as is searching with search engines and shopping on online trading platforms. These services are 'subsidized' by the market side that is less price sensitive than the other (see, e.g., Wright, 2004; Rysman, 2009; Kaiser and Wright, 2006; Weyl, 2010). As a result, platform operators generate most of their profits on the market side with the lower price elasticity of demand.

9.2.2 Concentration of Online Markets

As a consequence of indirect network effects platform markets may be more concentrated than other industries. However, this does not imply that every digital platform market is automatically highly concentrated (see, e.g., Haucap and Heimeshoff, 2014). Counter-examples are online real-estate brokers, travel agents, and many online dating sites, where several competing platforms (still) co-exist. Hence, the presence of indirect network effects is by no means sufficient for a monopoly or even high levels of market concentration to emerge. Moreover, competition between several platforms is not necessarily welfare enhancing when compared to monopolistic market structures. While, generally speaking, competition between several firms is almost always beneficial in 'traditional' markets (as long as the particular market under consideration is not characterized by natural monopoly conditions), this general wisdom does not always hold for two-sided markets.

Even if multiple platforms are not associated with a duplication of fixed costs, the existence of multiple platforms may not be efficient due to the presence of indirect network effects. As Caillaud and Jullien (2003) and Jullien (2006) have shown, a

Table 9.1   Determinants of concentration in two-sided markets

Driving Force	Effect on Concentration
Strength of indirect network effects	+
Degree of economies of scale	+
Capacity constraints	−
Scope of platform differentiation	−
Multi-homing opportunities	−

Source: Evans and Schmalensee (2008).

monopoly platform can be efficient because network effects are maximized when all agents manage to coordinate over a single platform. Hence, strong network effects can easily lead to highly concentrated market structures, but strong network effects also tend to make these highly concentrated market structures efficient (see Weyl, 2010; Chandra and Collard-Wexler, 2009). In contrast, capacity constraints (and the associated risk of platform overload), heterogeneous preferences (and the resulting potential for platform differentiation) and users' 'multi-homing' (i.e., the opportunity to participate in several platforms at the same time) tend to drive competition in digital markets. It is therefore not only unclear how market concentration and consumer welfare are related in these platform markets, but also whether the market is quasi-naturally converging towards a monopoly structure. Evans and Schmalensee (2008) have identified five driving forces that determine the concentration process and level in two-sided markets (Table 9.1).

It is relatively straightforward and immediately plausible that indirect network effects and economies of scale lead to increasing concentration. But it is difficult to draw general conclusions as to how indirect network effects influence market concentration, as their strength varies from platform to platform. The second driver of concentration is economies of scale, which are often the outcome of the cost conditions of online businesses. Many two-sided markets are characterized by a cost structure that combines a relatively high share of (fixed) set-up and maintenance costs with a relatively low share of variable costs (e.g., Jullien, 2006). For companies such as eBay, Expedia, and Booking.com most of the costs arise from managing the respective databases, while additional transactions within the capacity constraints of the databases cause very low additional costs. Increasing returns to scale are, therefore, not unusual, but rather typical for two-sided markets in the online world. While network effects and economies of scale both have a positive effect on market concentration levels, there are also three countervailing forces that facilitate market competition.

One important countervailing force is capacity constraints. While in offline two-sided markets such as shopping centers, trade fairs and nightclubs space is physically limited,[2] this does not necessarily hold for digital two-sided markets. However, advertising space is often restricted, since too much advertising is often perceived as a nuisance by users (e.g., Becker and Murphy, 1993; Bagwell, 2007) and therefore decreases the platform's value in the recipients' eyes.[3] In electronic two-sided markets, like online auction platforms or dating sites, capacity limits can also emerge as a result of negative externalities caused by additional users. If additional users make the group more heterogeneous, users' search costs may increase. In contrast, the more homogeneous the users are, the higher a given platform's value for the demand side. If, for example, only certain types of people visit a particular platform (some platforms are, for example, mainly visited by women, golf players, or academics), targeted advertising is much easier. Also note that some dating sites advertise that they only represent a certain group of clients (e.g., only academics). This reduces the search costs for all visitors. Additional users would make the user group more heterogeneous and would not necessarily add value, as increased heterogeneity increases the search cost for other users.

Directly related to the platforms' heterogeneity is the degree of product differentiation between platforms. For dating sites, magazines, and newspapers it is almost always evident that consumer preferences are heterogeneous, so some product differentiation emerges. Such differentiation can be vertical (e.g., high-income users may be more interesting for the advertising industry than a low-income audience) and horizontal (e.g., people interested in sailing, people interested in golf).

The higher the degree of heterogeneity among potential users and the easier it is for platforms to differentiate, the greater the diversity of platforms that will emerge in the marketplace and the lower the level of market concentration. The finding that increasing returns to scale foster market concentration while product differentiation and heterogeneity of user preferences work in the opposite direction is well known from other markets (e.g., Dixit and Stiglitz, 1977; Krugman, 1980). On two-sided markets increasing concentration will be driven by indirect network effects, but capacity limits, product differentiation, and the potential for multi-homing (i.e., the parallel usage of different platforms) will decrease concentration levels. How easy it is for consumers to multi-home depends, among other things, on (1) switching costs (if they exist) between platforms and (2) whether usage-based tariffs or positive flat rates are charged on the platform.

To illustrate this idea, consider online travel agencies such as Expedia. Switching from one online travel agency to another is usually associated with relatively low switching costs. Multi-homing is also simple, as travelers can easily search for flights, hotels, and so on, over more than one platform before actually booking. Likewise, airlines, hotels, and so forth, can easily be listed on more than one platform. With respect to search engines, users can also easily and without major costs switch away from Google to another general search engine such as Bing or even to specialized searches over Amazon, TripAdvisor, social networks (for people), library catalogs, travel sites, restaurant guides and so on if a switch appears to be attractive. In contrast, switching costs between social networks such as Facebook are generally much higher because of strong direct network effects and the effort needed to coordinate user groups. While there are no significant *direct* network effects for Google (i.e., it does not *directly* matter how many other people use Google) this is not true for social networks, such as Facebook, where the number of users is a very important factor for users' utility. Still, entry into the search engine business is not easy, due to the *indirect* network effects described above and the economies of scale that are (1) at least partly based on learning effects, which depend on the cumulative number of searches made over the network in the past, and (2) caused by substantial fixed costs of the technical infrastructure that result in decreasing average costs over a wide output range.

There is another form of switching cost on platforms such as eBay or Airbnb, where, apart from indirect network effects, the user's reputation is also highly relevant (e.g., Melnik and Alm, 2002; Bajari and Hortaçsu, 2004). As a user's reputation is a function of the number of transactions already conducted over the platform, it is typically platform specific (e.g., for eBay), so that changing platforms involves high switching costs, as it is difficult, if not impossible, to transfer one's reputation from one platform to another.

9.2.3   Market Definition for Platform Markets

Having discussed the determinants of concentration in two-sided markets, let us now discuss the peculiarities of defining markets for platform services, as the delineation of the relevant product market is typically the first step in any antitrust proceeding. Market definition concepts are based on actual and potential substitution patterns in order to determine the products and companies that actually or potentially compete with each other. The market definition process aims at revealing the products and companies that are likely to be affected by, for instance, a merger or an abuse of market power. A popular approach in the academic literature is the small but significant non-transitory increase in price (SSNIP) test. If a firm was (hypothetically) in the position to profitably and sustainably raise its price by 5 to 10 percent above the competitive price level, it is considered not to be effectively constrained by competition. If, in contrast, such a price increase is unprofitable, for example, because consumers switch to alternative products that they consider to be sufficiently good substitutes, these alternative products are considered to belong to the same product market. Hence, if a 5–10 percent price increase is estimated to be unprofitable there must be other products or firms in the relevant product market.

In online markets, this market definition process becomes much more complicated for two reasons. First, in many online markets consumers do not pay a positive price, at least not in monetary terms. Instead, consumers pay an implicit price in the form of personal data and/or attention (see Evans, 2013). Platforms compete for consumers' data and their attention in order to sell it to advertisers (tailor-made based on personal data). Clearly, the SSNIP test scenario of a 5–10 percent price increase cannot be computed as long as the starting price (in money) is zero. Even if one were to consider a 5–10 percent increase in the implicit price that consumers pay, namely their disclosure of personal data and/ or their exposure to advertising, it is unclear what such an increase of advertising exposure or data disclosure would mean in practical terms and how it could be measured in a meaningful way. This highly relevant practical problem of defining two-sided markets has thus far been largely ignored in the literature.

More attention has been paid to a second problem in defining two-sided markets, namely that the profitability of a price increase on one side of the market also depends on user reactions on the other side and the feedback effects induced as a consequence of the indirect network effects. As Evans (2003, p. 325) has pointed out, in two-sided markets 'market definition and market power analyses that focus on a single side will lead to analytical errors'. A price increase on one side of the market cannot be analyzed in isolation from the other side, as such separate treatment may define the relevant market too narrowly. A price increase that may be profitable on one side of the market – if looked at in isolation – may no longer be profitable once user reactions on the other market side are accounted for. To provide a simple example: it may appear profitable for an online shopping platform to increase the commission charged to the sellers listed if the additional revenues generated from the price increase exceed the loss in revenues that results from some sellers leaving the platform. However, having fewer listed sellers reduces the platform's value for buyers, so they may switch to a different online platform, in turn reducing the value of the platform for sellers. In total, the price increase may thus be unprofitable once feedback effects are accounted for, highlighting the importance of defining the market more broadly.

The two-sided market structure causes another problem for competition authorities. Since a platform sets prices (explicit or implicit) to at least two customer groups (e.g., advertisers and users) it is not clear which price(s) should hypothetically be increased in a market definition exercise. Should only the price on one market side be increased or all prices simultaneously? This problem is especially severe in situations with asymmetric substitution patterns. Advertisers may regard platforms as closer substitutes than users and may respond to a price increase for advertising more quickly than the user side. An alternative approach to market definition may be to predict how a price increase on either side will impact on the platform's transaction volume.

Argentesi and Filistrucchi (2007) and Filistrucchi et al. (2014) discuss the applicability of the SSNIP test in two-sided markets and propose modifying the test.[4] In order to measure market power, it is necessary to compute price–cost margins while taking into account its two-sided nature. For instance, on online news pages the publisher's optimal behavior depends on four different elasticities: the elasticity of readers' demand with respect to the price to access an article; the elasticity of readers' demand with respect to the quantity of advertising; the elasticity of advertising demand with respect to advertising prices (which are typically charged on a pay-per-click basis); and the elasticity of advertising demand with respect to the click conversion rate. In order to compute the price structure an empirical model has to include demand estimations on all sides of the markets taking interactions between the sides into account. This puts high requirements on the amount and detail of data needed and on the estimation techniques.

While the interrelatedness of the markets may, in theory, be resolved via more complex versions of the SSNIP test, data needs put practical limits on its use. Even more challenging is the fact that many Internet platforms are (seemingly) free for users, so that a 5–10 percent price increase can often not be calculated, as users do not pay with money, but with their data and their attention to the advertising shown. It is difficult to operationalize a hypothetical 5–10 percent increase of data disclosure requirements in practice (even though the issue may be examined theoretically if the simplifying assumptions that users are homogeneous and hold the same valuation for privacy are accepted). The value of personal data or privacy varies heavily in terms of monetary equivalents between users (e.g., Bendorf et al., 2015). Moreover, even a theoretical solution is unlikely to work in practice for antitrust agencies, given the enormous data requirements. Some relief may come from surveys about hypothetical consumer reactions and conjoint analysis techniques. Their major drawback, however, is that they use stated rather than revealed preferences and are therefore less reliable than data on observed consumer behavior.

9.3   COMPETITION AMONG SEARCH ENGINES AND THE ANTITRUST CASE AGAINST GOOGLE

Search engines such as Google or Bing are multi-billion-dollar businesses. At the same time, the market for online search is highly concentrated around the globe. While Google is the clear market leader in virtually all Western countries, Baidu in China, Yandex in Russia and to a lesser degree Yahoo! in Japan have dominant positions in these countries. In all of these markets, we observe a highly concentrated structure with a monopoly or at best a duopoly (in Japan) emerging. These high concentration levels are an outcome of the economies of scale as well as network effects that characterize search engines.

However, while it appears to be relatively easy to understand that large customer bases may be more attractive for advertising companies, this becomes less clear on second sight. If online advertising is charged on a pay-per-click basis, an online site that induces 10 000 clicks may be as attractive as ten smaller sites that induce 1000 clicks each (see Manne and Wright, 2011). Nevertheless, large search engines may still be more attractive than smaller ones, as (1) there can be a fixed cost per web page associated with monitoring advertising campaigns and (2) larger search engines may be better able to place targeted advertising, as they have access to a larger base of historical search data and past 'clicking behavior'. These two features can make larger search engines more attractive than smaller ones. In addition, Google has traditionally created (by means of contract) some artificial incompatibility between advertising campaigns on Google and other search engines, but this incompatibility issue has been largely resolved following investigations by the Federal Trade Commission (see FTC, 2013). Furthermore, since space is limited on web pages, a given web page that induces 10 000 clicks for a given ad generates more revenue per page than a page that only induces 1000 clicks. Given the largely fixed-cost nature of online content provision, the resulting economies of scale can induce market concentration.

It is much less clear, however, how important a search engine's size is for search engine users. While it is plausible that access to a large set of (historical) search data and consumer clicking behavior is beneficial to improve an engine's search results, there is some debate about how much data are needed to further refine the search mechanism before the marginal benefit of additional data exceeds the additional cost of processing it (see Manne and Wright, 2011). In fact, the literature is divided about whether it is Google's sheer size that allows it to maintain its market position (e.g., Pollock, 2010; Crane, 2012) or whether it is its superior innovation (see Manne and Wright, 2011; Bork and Sidak, 2012). Overall, it appears that Google's superior ability to place advertising, based on its analysis of large datasets of customer clicking behavior, and the fixed cost of placing and monitoring advertising, gives rise to indirect network effects from users to advertisers, which ultimately makes Google a two-sided market.[5]

In any case, switching costs between search engines are very modest for consumers, as the past has shown. When Google entered the market in 1998, Altavista was the leading search engine with Yahoo! closely following in second place in Western countries. Still Google managed not only to enter the market, but also to offer superior quality so that it even leapfrogged its competitors. Similarly, Rambler was the leading Russian search engine in the late 1990s before Yandex surpassed it. Many commentators therefore suggest that Google's success is also a result of its superior quality (e.g., Evans, 2008; Devine, 2008; Argenton and Prüfer, 2012).

Overall, the quality of search engines can be approximated by 'expected time a user needs to obtain a satisfactory result'. The time needed to find a satisfactory result in turn depends on several factors (Argenton and Prüfer, 2012), including search algorithm quality, hardware quality, and data quality, where data quality refers both to data freely available on the Internet and search engine–specific data that has been collected during previous search processes. In principle, the availability of hardware and Internet data should not differ between competitors, especially given the substantial financial resources available to companies such as Microsoft, Google and also Facebook, for which access to sufficient financial resources should be taken as given. It is argued that the main competition problem for those companies is the limited availability of high-quality search data that are company specific (ibid.). Due to its significant market share Google also has the best access to (also historical) search data and consumer clicking behavior. This is an important aspect for success in search engine markets, as search data are needed to refine the engines' search algorithms. The more search data an operator has, the better are the refinements of its search algorithm. In principle this process results in superior search engine quality and provides a competitive advantage for the market leader, Google. It is unclear, however, at which point or data quantity the marginal benefit of utilizing additional data exceeds the marginal cost of additional processing capacity. As some authors such as Manne and Wright (2011) argue, this point where the marginal cost exceeds the marginal benefit has not only been passed by Google, but also by other large search engines such as Yahoo! and Bing. In fact, it appears that most search engines only use subsets of their search data to further improve the search algorithm and not all their available data.

While the existence of a superior search engine is, of course, not a policy concern for competition authorities in itself, there have also been numerous complaints that Google abuses its dominant position, especially to favor its own subsidiaries (such as Google Maps, YouTube or Google Shopping) over competing platforms. More precisely the allegation is that Google biases its search results so that links to its own subsidiaries appear ahead of links to rival sites even though a rival's site may be a better fit for what the user is searching for. This search bias allegation (e.g., Goldman, 2006; Crane, 2011; Edelman, 2011; Ammori and Pelican, 2012) has – by and large – been the key to the antitrust investigations against Google (see FTC, 2013; European Commission, 2015), even though the European Commission's allegation is slightly different in that it also objects to Google advertising its own services, in particular Google Shopping, 'too prominently'.

In addition, other allegations have concerned Google's (unlicensed) use of content generated by competing specialized search engines (so-called vertical search engines) as well as the strategic incompatibility that Google introduced for third parties between advertising campaigns on Google platforms and other web pages. Both issues have largely been resolved through commitments accepted by the Federal Trade Commission (FTC, 2013) in January 2013. A fourth antitrust investigation concerns the exclusive or default contracts Google has used to incentivize mobile handset manufacturers (through exclusive contracts, rebates or potentially predatory prices) to use Google's Android operating system and Google as the default search engine (see, e.g., Manne and Wright, 2011; Bork and Sidak, 2012). Whether these contracts give rise to market foreclosure is, at the time of writing in 2015, being investigated by the European Commission and other competition agencies.

Regarding the most prominent allegation of search bias, in January 2013 the Federal Trade Commission (FTC, 2013) decided not to initiate formal proceedings. In contrast, after more than five years of investigation and analysis (which started in early 2010) and following a lengthy discussion of various commitments that Google had offered to undertake in order to mitigate the alleged search bias problem, in April 2015 the

European Commission issued a formal statement of objections (SO) against Google. The SO outlines the European Commission's preliminary view that Google is:

> [. . .] abusing a dominant position, in breach of EU antitrust rules, by systematically favoring its own comparison shopping product in its general search results pages in the European Economic Area (EEA). The Commission is concerned that users do not necessarily see the most relevant results in response to queries – to the detriment of consumers and rival comparison shopping services, as well as stifling innovation. (European Commission, 2015)

More specifically, the Commission's main preliminary conclusions are that (1) 'Google systematically positions and prominently displays its comparison shopping service in its general search results pages, irrespective of its merits'; (2) 'Google does not apply to its own comparison shopping service the system of penalties, which it applies to other comparison shopping services on the basis of defined parameters, and which can lead to the lowering of the rank in which they appear in Google's general search results pages'; and that (3) 'Google's conduct has a negative impact on consumers and innovation. It means that users do not necessarily see the most relevant comparison shopping results in response to their queries, and that incentives to innovate from rivals are lowered as they know that however good their product, they will not benefit from the same prominence as Google's product'. The SO suggests that:

> Google should treat its own comparison shopping service and those of rivals in the same way. This would not interfere with either the algorithms Google applies or how it designs its search results pages. It would, however, mean that when Google shows comparison shopping services in response to a user's query, the most relevant service or services would be selected to appear in Google's search results pages. (European Commission, 2015)

In addition, further proceedings are underway at US state level as well as in India, Argentina and South Korea.

Whether Google has in fact biased its search results in favor of its own subsidiaries is difficult to determine from the outside, as Google's search algorithm is naturally a business secret. Moreover, personalized search results (based on one's own search history and one's cookies) imply that different individuals may obtain different search results for the same keyword search. Bork and Sidak (2012) furthermore argue that Google's incentives to bias search results are limited, as users could easily switch to another search engine that may provide better (and less biased results), given that switching costs are low and multi-homing easy in case of search engines. As Bracha and Pasquale (2008) correctly point out, though, this implies that consumers notice that they are shown biased results – something not very likely given that consumers are searching for something they do not know where to find. Given that searching is becoming more and more personalized and that Google's estimate of what results consumers may want to see in which order may only be an (informed) opinion (see Grimmelmann, 2011), it is by no means easy to establish a search bias (e.g., Edelman and Lockwood, 2011) or to design appropriate remedies.

The European Commission's statement of objection also reveals how difficult it is to delineate the relevant product market. While the European Commission defines a distinct product market for general search, it is far from clear how consumers would substitute if Google were to charge for search requests. While some users may switch to other general search engines, other users may use Wikipedia, Amazon, IMDb, LinkedIn, Twitter and other websites with search functions for their searches for general information, books, movies, people and so on. In fact, the Commission appears to hold the view that users search for specific web pages, while one may also argue that users rather search for information. In its market delineation the Commission therefore exclusively focuses on technical aspects (how and which websites are crawled and listed), but does not analyze consumer behavior. Hence, it is completely unclear whether the Commission's market delineation is appropriate or not. Similarly, the Commission argues that comparison shopping services constitute a different product market from specialized search services, online retailers, and merchant platforms/market places. Again, the Commission bases its view entirely on technical and functional aspects, arguing that comparison shopping services constitute a market in their own right, since consumers cannot directly purchase the product from these sites. This means, of course, that Google shopping would belong to a different and more competitive market, if Google were to include one-click-purchase options in its ads. From an economic perspective, this is not immediately plausible, as a further vertical integration would imply that Google is no longer dominant with regard to eBay and Amazon. Again, user behavior has not been analyzed to delineate the market, which is somewhat troublesome.

In addition, the European Commission's statement of objections appears to suggest that, in the absence of an objective justification, discrimination and favoring one's own services is abusive by its very nature for dominant companies. Alternatively, the Commission may hold the view that Google Shopping is an essential facility or bottleneck for online retailers, even though the Commission does not use the term. In any case, given the presence of numerous market places such as eBay and Amazon, the view may be difficult to sustain.

Finally, the Commission argues that the success and growth of Google's services do not reflect its relative quality and attractiveness for users. The statement of objections suggests that Google's success is not the outcome of competition on the merits, although little evidence is provided to substantiate this claim. Given these shortcomings, an interesting question – also from a political economy of antitrust perspective – is why the Commission chose Google Shopping as its showcase and not any of the other services for which market definition may be much less contentious. For now, it is interesting to see how the case will evolve.

Even ignoring the practical problems of proving potential abuse, the next question concerns potential remedies to prevent any anticompetitive search biases in the future. A number of scholars have suggested mandating search neutrality (e.g., Pollock, 2010; Edelman, 2011; Ammori and Pelican, 2012; Crane, 2012; Manne and Wright, 2012). As has been pointed out though, search neutrality is, first of all, difficult to operationalize and, second, may inhibit further innovation, thereby harming consumers in the end (see Grimmelmann, 2011; Bork and Sidak, 2012; Crane, 2012). As a consequence, some policy-makers have proposed to unbundle or separate Google's search business from its content business. However, consequences for innovation and consumers may be even more adverse than with search neutrality requirements, as unbundling would imply that search engines would no longer be allowed to answer questions themselves, but only provide links to answers. Moreover, an unbundling remedy would become completely untenable in other cases as, for example, Amazon may also be considered the largest search engine for books. Obviously, unbundling does not make any sense here. Given that many websites have search functions and may be considered search markets, unbundling requirements become highly problematic.

Another suggestion has been to require Google to reveal its search algorithm, but such a measure would appear disproportionate, as has been argued in the literature, as it concerns the heart of Google's business and the main element of competitive rivalry (e.g., Argenton and Prüfer, 2012; Bork and Sidak, 2012). Others have proposed regulating Google's search algorithm and changes in it. However, practically, this is not without problems either. For example, Google changed its algorithm 665 times in 2012 alone.[6] Consequently, there is a risk that regulation will either be too slow or even retard innovation.

Instead, Argenton and Prüfer (2012) have suggested that Google should be required to share its specific search engine data to foster competition in search engine markets. This suggestion is based on the assumption that it is very difficult for competing search engines to catch up or even overtake Google, due to their lack of online search data to develop better search engine algorithms. Hence access to (historical) search data may help to enable Google's competitors to develop better search algorithms, thereby increasing competitive pressures in the market for search engines.

Another option, which is more light-handed, would be to mandate that Google colors the background or the links to its own subsidiaries in a manner similar to sponsored links. Once consumers clearly realize that some search results point to Google websites or services, they can better evaluate the quality of the results and, if they are not satisfied, switch to some other search engine. Increased transparency should resolve most of the problems associated with any potential discriminatory search bias in vertical search.[7]

The European Commission has been in discussions with Google since 2011 on how the concerns can be alleviated through binding commitments. In 2014,[8] Google proposed a threefold remedy for its current and future specialized services. First, users would be informed by a label indicating Google's own services. Second, Google services would be graphically separated from general search results. Third, Google would prominently display three links to three rival specialized search services in a format that is visually comparable to that of links to its own services. Joaquín Almunia, then European Commissioner for Competition, stated that the objective of the Commission is not to interfere in Google's search algorithm but to ensure that rivals can compete fairly with Google. The Commission, at that time, stated that the concessions 'are far-reaching and have the clear potential to restore a level playing-field in the important markets of online search and advertising'.[9] However, with the change of Commissioners, following the appointment of the new Commission in 2014, the European Commission has changed its view and issued the statement of objections, mentioned above.

9.4   VERTICAL RESTRAINTS IN INTERNET COMMERCE

Apart from the highly visible and hotly debated Google cases, there have been numerous cases in Europe regarding the use of vertical restraints in online markets. The development of the Internet as a powerful channel for the distribution of goods and services has created new platforms and sellers such as eBay, Amazon, Expedia, Booking.com and so on. The most common vertical restraints in online commerce are the following:

- general bans on online sales by manufacturers;
- agreements limiting the absolute quantity or percentage of online sales;
- dual pricing strategies with higher wholesale prices for online sales and lower wholesale prices for offline sales;
- selective distribution schemes; and
- across-platforms parity agreements (APPAs).

The most common restraint is probably the complete or partial restriction of online sales. One of the earliest cases was Yves Saint Laurent perfume. In this instance, in 2001 the European Commission approved that online sales could be restricted to retailers who were already operating brick-and-mortar stores.[10] The Commission recognized that certain products cannot be properly supplied without specialized distributors, especially if the product's quality needs to be preserved or its proper use ensured.

The French competition authority reached a very similar conclusion in 2006 and 2007, as did the appeals court, when a pure online retailer (Bijourama) wanted to enter the Festina France selective distribution system in the market for (expensive) watches. The authority and the court stressed that a manufacturer with a market share below 30 percent can limit online sales as long as the criteria are transparent and used consistently. Hence, the exclusion of a purely online dealer was ruled to be legal. A similar decision was reached in 2007 regarding several selective distribution systems for high-end cosmetics and hygiene products (Bioderma).

In 2002, a Belgian court ruled that even the complete ban on online sales that Makro imposed on its selective distribution networks of luxury perfumes and cosmetics was legal, because the products' nature required personal expert guidance and the sales methods could not be replicated over the Internet.

The most prominent case was the Pierre Fabre ruling, where in 2009 the European Court of Justice ruled that a de facto ban on online sales (through the requirement of a qualified pharmacist to assist the sale) should be regarded as an infringement 'by object' of Article 101(1) TFEU. Put differently, the ban on Internet sales is regarded as a hardcore restriction, even though the Paris court to which the case was referred noted Pierre Fabre's 20 percent market share and the lively inter-brand competition.

There are several other cases dealing with selective distribution systems, some of which are summarized in Buccirossi (2013, 2015), Dolmans and Leyden (2012), Vogel (2012), ICN (2015) and Dolmans and Mostyn (2015). In principle, European competition authorities tend to take a rather strict view, focusing on the protection of intra-brand competition without much analysis of the degree of inter-brand competition and the economic effects on consumers and the competitive process as such.

This is also reflected in proceedings against various companies for engaging in dual pricing. Dual pricing means that retailers are granted different wholesale prices depending on whether they intend to sell the product online or over the counter. While wholesale price discrimination between different retailers and different retail channels is perfectly in line with naive profit maximization in all but perfectly competitive industries, European competition authorities have – in contrast to the USA – viewed this pricing practice with great skepticism when applied to Internet commerce. For example, Bosch Siemens Home Appliances (BSH) introduced a new rebate system in 2013 with lower performance rebates for online sales. BSH argued that different rebate levels were aimed at compensating brick-and-mortar dealers and sales for their high-quality sales services in comparison with online dealers. However, the German Cartel Office took the view that lower rebates for online sales create incentives for hybrid dealers to sell less online, which reduces competition through online sales and is therefore without further analysis anticompetitive. The German Cartel Office also suggested that BSH should compensate brick-and-mortar sales through fixed payments, thereby largely ignoring the lack of incentive effects that fixed lump-sum payments have.

From an economic perspective the great attention paid to intra-brand competition is misguided, as long as there is active inter-brand competition. Moreover, it is unclear why excluding the Internet as a distribution channel should be considered a hardcore restriction. Many cases concern status products such as watches, perfumes, cosmetics and similarly expensive products. In these instances, consumers may actually purchase the product because of its (expensive) brand image. If online sales destroy the expensive image of the product, this may obviously harm the manufacturer, but also many consumers themselves, who buy status products exactly because they are expensive. However, given the current approach in Europe, it appears to be extremely onerous to prove such a case.

Dual pricing schemes are nothing but a form of price differentiation, which is common in almost all wholesale markets that are less than perfectly competitive. Prohibiting dual pricing and disallowing bans on online sales makes it much more difficult for companies to incentivize brick-and-mortar retailers and presence by which manufacturers can generate value from window-shopping effects, additional services that can be provided offline and the easier provision of after-sales services by bricks-and-mortar stores. All these features would contribute to maintaining a brand's value, thereby intensifying inter-brand competition.

Furthermore, preventing dual pricing can make manufacturers more reluctant to offer special discounts for offline sales in regions where a presence may be valued (e.g., in order to have a nationwide presence), but retailer profits are lower (e.g., due to lower demand), as a dual pricing ban in the presence of intense online competition basically prevents manufacturers from charging different wholesale prices to different retailers. Consequently, input price differentiation becomes much more difficult, even though the welfare effects are at best unclear (see Dertwinkel-Kalt et al., 2015, 2016). Hence, European competition agencies should revisit their overly strict approach to vertical restraints in the Internet and take a more lenient approach similar to the USA.

A final vertical restriction that has received much attention is across-platforms parity agreements (APPAs), illustrated in Figure 9.1. APPAs have most famously been used in the Apple e-book case and for travel and hotel booking platforms. With an APPA, a booking platform prohibits its content providers (e.g., e-book publishers or hotels) from offering their products at lower prices on any other platform. The standard theories of harm are either that this may lead to collusion among the content providers (e.g., publishers) or a foreclosure of the platform market, as no new platform can enter with lower prices. Other cases involve Amazon (in Germany and the UK) and motor insurance providers (in the UK).

Regarding the e-book case, when Apple entered the electronic books industry in 2010 it convinced book publishers (1) to adopt agency agreements under which final e-book prices are set by publishers, while retailers only receive a commission on every copy sold (in the case of Apple itself 30 percent), and (2) to adopt an APPA for their e-books that

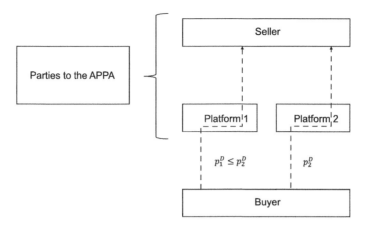

Source: Buccirossi (2013, p. 22).

Figure 9.1   An across-platforms parity agreement (APPA)

allowed Apple to sell e-books at its competitors' lowest price. The agency agreements replaced the previous wholesale agreements that left the retail pricing decision with retailers. Around this time, the retail price of e-books sold by Amazon, the dominant retailer with a 90 percent market share in 2010, rose by about 18.6 percent on average, and the price of *New York Times* bestsellers rose by about 42.7 percent.[11]

In April 2012, the US Department of Justice (DOJ) brought a case against Apple and a group of five major publishers for illegally conspiring to raise e-book prices, claiming that agency agreements played an instrumental role. The DOJ reached a settlement with the publishers and won the case against Apple. Both the court's order and the settlement prohibited further use of agency agreements.

Similar proceedings against Apple and the five publishers were opened in the EU in December 2011. The European Commission had doubts concerning the companies' joint switch from the wholesale model, where the e-book retail price is set by the retailer, to agency contracts that all contained the same key terms for retail prices – including an APPA, maximum retail price grids and the same 30 percent commission payable to Apple. The European Commission was particularly concerned 'that the joint switch to the agency contracts may have been coordinated between the publishers and Apple, as part of a common strategy aimed at raising retail prices for e-books or preventing the introduction of lower retail prices for e-books on a global scale. This would violate Article 101 of the TFEU that prohibits cartels and restrictive business practices' (European Commission, 2013). The Commission accepted commitments offered by Apple and four of the publishers in December 2012, while the fifth publisher settled on the same conditions in July 2013. The publishers and Apple offered commitments that contained the following three key provisions:

- Apple and the publishers terminate their then valid agency agreements.
- For a period of two years, the publishers cannot prevent e-book retailers from setting their own prices for e-books or, from offering discounts and promotions.

- For a period of five years neither the publishers nor Apple can set up agreements for e-books with retail-price APPAs (see European Commission, 2012).

In its defense Apple had claimed that its introduction of the iPad represented a major innovation that should be taken into account. Around the time Apple entered the e-book market it also introduced the iPad, thereby increasing competition in the market for e-book reading devices. In response, Amazon lowered the price of its reader, the Kindle, from $299 to $139 (and later even further) and also developed free software allowing its e-books to be read on the iPad and other devices.

In fact, the evidence on the e-book case is mixed. While De los Santos and Wildenbeest (2014) show that e-book prices increased following the APPA introduced by Apple, Gaudin and White (2014) also show that the e-book reader prices (the complementary asset) have fallen at the same time, making the overall effect less clear. Interestingly enough though, some European countries such as Germany are now about to introduce a legal resale price maintenance requirement for e-books.

With respect to hotel booking platforms and online travel agencies (OTAs), several European authorities have investigated the OTAs' APPA. Parallel investigations took place in several countries, including France, Germany, Italy, Sweden and the UK. In Germany, the Federal Cartel Office concluded that the APPA foreclosed the market and softened competition in the distinct market for searching, comparing and booking hotels online, as new entrant platforms would not be able to undercut existing platforms' hotel rates. While the OTA platforms argued that an APPA was needed to safeguard their platforms' investments, as hotels could otherwise free-ride on the platform's investment by charging lower prices in own channels, the German Federal Cartel Office did not accept this argument and ruled that APPAs were anticompetitive and a violation of competition law.

In contrast, the joint investigation started under the coordination of the European Commission, in Italy, France and Sweden, concluded in April 2015 with a commitment by Booking.com to abstain from using a general APPA and use a so-called narrow APPA (or NAPPA) instead. Under a NAPPA, price parity clauses will only apply to prices and other conditions publicly offered by the hotels through their own online sales channels (such as their own website), in order to prevent the most obvious possibility for free-riding. However, hotels are free to set prices and conditions to other OTAs and to offline channels. This decision appears to be more balanced than the rather strict prohibition by the German Cartel Office, especially since the office's theory of harm – namely that competition between platforms is not possible between OTAs in the presence of an APPA – must be called into question when it is noticed that the leading OTA, called Hotel Reservation Service (HRS), saw its market share reduced from more than 40 percent to almost exactly 30 percent over a period of two years. Even with APPAs, competition between platforms could occur through general rebates provided to users by the platform itself. In general, though, APPAs are an interesting new form of most-favored-customer clause, where more analysis is needed before robust results can be used.

9.5   COMPETITION ISSUES AT THE INFRASTRUCTURE LEVEL

At the infrastructure level two competition issues have received most attention: first, price- or margin-squeeze cases, where incumbent network providers charge retail prices for Internet access that make it unsustainable for competitors to operate in the market, given the incumbent's retail prices, and second the debate surrounding net neutrality and the risk that network operators or Internet service providers engage in price and/or quality discrimination with respect to different content providers or types of content.

9.5.1   Price and Margin Squeezes in Internet Access Markets

One of the most common allegations in Internet access markets is that vertically integrated incumbent network operators abuse their dominant position by engaging in so-called price or margin squeezing, that is by strategically lowering retail prices or raising access prices at the wholesale level in order to constrain reasonably or even equally efficient downstream competitors. In the academic literature one of the debates has been about the incentives for regulated companies to engage in price or margin squeezing at all (see, e.g., Bouckaert and Verboven, 2004). This debate is quite similar to well-known discussions about the rationality of predatory pricing in unregulated markets (see Hovenkamp and Hovenkamp, 2009). In principle, the regulated access price at the wholesale level reflects the incumbent's opportunity cost of serving a particular customer. While the economic logic of a margin squeeze largely resembles that of a predatory pricing strategy or, alternatively, refusal to deal, there is a lively legal debate as to whether price and margin squeezes should be treated as a separate competition policy concern or whether they should be subsumed as a particular case of predatory pricing or refusal to deal (e.g., Sidak, 2008).

Further policy debates concern the proper efficiency standard that an incumbent has to adhere to when setting its retails prices: Which competitors need to be able to survive in the retail market, reasonably efficient operators or only equally efficient operators? While most economists argue for the equally efficient operator test (e.g., Bouckaert and Verboven, 2004; Gaudin and Saavedra, 2014), Clerckx and De Muyter (2009) defend the reasonably efficient competitor standard and emphasize that incumbent network operators tend to have inherited their positions from a government enterprise or other forms of protection. Moreover, even though the reasonably efficient competitor test may lead to productive inefficiency, as it allows for the entry of inefficient competitors, the reasonably efficient competitor standard may alleviate allocative inefficiencies in imperfectly competitive markets. There is, however, another rather practical objection, namely that a reasonably efficient competitor standard would require the access provider to know or correctly guess the retail costs of its competitor to avoid violating competition law, while the equally efficient operator rule only requires that the access provider knows the costs of its own retail unit (see also Martin and Vandekerckhove, 2013).

The legal analysis of margin squeeze, furthermore, diverges into two different philosophies: some experts consider margin squeezes as a form of the classical refusal-to-deal abuse or predatory pricing, whereas others consider margin squeezes as a peculiar form of abuse warranting separate analysis and remedies.

In Europe, the four most prominent of the numerous price-squeeze cases have been Deutsche Telekom (2003/2010), Wanadoo (2003), Telefónica (2007) and TeliaSonera (2011), but there are several other cases in almost all EU member states. For detailed discussions, see Crocioni and Veljanovski (2003), Fernández Álvarez-Labrador (2006), Motta and de Streel (2006), Bravo and Siciliani (2007), Polo (2007), Clerckx and De Muyter (2009), Heimler (2010), Hay and McMahon (2012) as well as Gaudin and Saavedra (2014).

The general approach in the EU, following the Deutsche Telekom case, is that the European Commission as well as national competition or regulatory authorities tend to consider a price squeeze to be abusive per se and liable to prosecution under Article 102 TFEU, regardless of the economic effects on competition and consumers. When the European Union's Court of First Instance (CFI) endorsed the Commission's decision in the Deutsche Telekom case, it also clarified that an abusive margin squeeze can be discovered through the so-called imputation test. A price squeeze occurs whenever the retail arm of a vertically integrated operator cannot operate profitably if it had to pay the same wholesale access prices as its retail competitors. Hence, the 'equally efficient' or 'just as efficient' standard is used in the cases mentioned above, even though the Commission has also shown sympathy to the reasonably efficient standard in other cases.[12]

The formalistic approach of the imputation test contrasts heavily with the more economic or effects-based approach to which the European Commission has moved in other areas. Interestingly enough, all four cases were decided on grounds of predatory (retail) pricing, not on grounds of excessive (wholesale) pricing. The alleged margin squeeze did not result from an excessive wholesale/access price for an essential input (access to the fixed local loop) but from a retail access price that was considered too low.

The USA follows a rather different approach since Trinko and linkLine. The linkLine decision concerned four California Internet service providers (ISPs) supplying retail digital subscriber line (DSL) services. These ISPs purchased wholesale transmission services from the vertically integrated Pacific Bell (doing business as AT&T), which itself supplied DSL Internet access to the retail market. In July 2003, the ISPs brought a private antitrust suit against AT&T alleging that it had monopolized and attempted to monopolize the regional DSL market in violation of Section 2 of the Sherman Act in several ways, including the creation of a price squeeze. While the four ISPs prevailed in the District Court and the Circuit Court of Appeals, the US Supreme Court saw no need to view price squeeze as a distinct exclusionary strategy for antitrust purposes.[13] It decomposed vertical price squeeze into two parts: first, the high wholesale price is an exercise of monopoly power, and the exercise of lawfully obtained market power does not violate the Sherman Act Section 2 prohibition of monopolization. Second, the low retail price only violates the Sherman Act Section 2 prohibition of monopolization if the price is predatory (see Martin and Vandekerckhove, 2013). Similarly, the Trinko case has made clear that in the USA, price or margin squeezes are, in contrast to Europe, dealt with under the refusal-to-deal standard and not seen as an antitrust violation in their own right.[14] As a consequence, Sidak (2008) has proposed abolishing price or margin squeeze as a distinct theory of antitrust liability under Section 2 of the Sherman Act.

9.5.2   Net Neutrality

Traditionally, the Internet has developed within a non-discriminatory architecture. All data packages are treated equally (with so-called 'best effort'), independent of their content and origin. Recent technologies, however, enable network providers to distinguish and to differentiate and discriminate between different packages. Following the advent of new traffic management technologies a debate has emerged in policy circles and in academia – originally only in the USA (see Lessig, 1999; Wu, 2003), but subsequently spreading to Europe – on whether the traditional principle of 'net neutrality' would need to be secured by means of regulation.

The term net(work) neutrality is not clearly defined and has several meanings. As Krämer et al. (2013, p. 797) point out, the meaning 'is often ambiguous and can mean anything from blocking certain types of undesired or unaffiliated traffic (Wu, 2007), to termination fees (Lee and Wu, 2009), to offering differentiated services and taking measures of network management (Hahn and Wallsten, 2006)'.

One of the core elements of net neutrality in any case is the best-effort principle. As long as network operators do not identify the origins of the various packages, all packages are obviously treated equally (best-effort rule). In addition, network operators cannot charge the data sender as long as they do not identify them. This in turn implies zero prices for sending traffic (zero-pricing rule). Consequently, similar to the 'receiving-party-pays' principle in many telecommunications networks, data receivers (the typical Internet user) are charged for receiving and accessing online content, while content providers do not pay network operators for transmission services. As long as network operators cannot prioritize certain traffic, this implies non-discriminatory pricing of packages (non-discriminatory pricing rule). Any departure from one or more of these rules may be considered a violation of net-neutrality. Focusing on these three distinct rules, Schuett (2010) surveys the net-neutrality discussion in the economic literature.[15] Moreover, van Schewick (2012) offers an extensive report and framework on net neutrality with a special emphasis on non-discrimination rules adopted by the Federal Communications Commission (FCC).

From an antitrust policy perspective, the concept of net neutrality as a non-discrimination rule is of particular interest. Strict net neutrality then prevents ISPs from prioritizing any traffic from any origin. Advocates of strict net neutrality fear that any departure from this rule would induce vertically integrated ISPs to behave in anticompetitive fashion, for example by blocking or discriminating against rivals' content in terms of prices and quality of service. ISPs should thus be subject to a prophylactic regulation to prevent any such behavior right from the start.

We would like to shed light on the incentives of ISPs to engage in such behavior and on to the consequences for competition and welfare.

9.5.2.1   Blocking and degradation

Vertically integrated ISPs that own the network infrastructure and act, at the same time, as content providers may have an incentive to degrade the quality of rivals' content on their network or to entirely block services in order to reduce competition in the content market and enhance the demand for their own content. The concern is that ISPs will use their control over the last mile to favor their own proprietary content over content provided by competitors (see Krämer et al., 2013).

These are common examples of so-called vertical foreclosure practices. According to Rey and Tirole (2007) foreclosure is a dominant firm's denial of access to an essential facility with the intent of extending market power from one segment of the market (the bottleneck segment) to an adjacent segment (the competitive segment). By treating some groups of customers preferentially and offering less attractive terms to others, companies can achieve the same results as a vertically integrated company even without vertically integrating.

The theoretical findings on vertically integrated firms' incentives to foreclose rivals downstream are mixed. Bowman (1957) famously made the argument that there is only one monopoly rent in any vertical chain of production and, thus, a monopolist in the upstream market would have no incentive to monopolize the downstream market (and vice versa). According to the Chicago School's 'single-monopoly-rent hypothesis' a vertically integrated company can only earn a monopoly profit in one of the markets, either upstream or downstream, but not two separate monopoly rents in both markets. As a result, a monopolist either has no incentive to vertically integrate in order to leverage its dominant position from the upstream to its downstream market or, in the case of imperfect downstream competition, vertical integration would actually benefit consumers and increase welfare as it removes the inefficiencies from double marginalization.[16] Post-Chicago economists, however, have shown that the validity of the hypothesis depends, among other things, on the assumption that market participants have perfect information.[17] The modern economic literature identifies various circumstances where vertical foreclosure can be profitable (for an overview see Rey and Tirole, 2007).

In telecommunications markets, there is at least some evidence that ISPs may sometimes foreclose rival services in practice. In the USA, the net neutrality debate evolved in several steps. First, in 2005, the FCC took action against the Madison River Telephone Company.[18] Madison River Communications, a regional company offering both telephone and Internet services, blocked ports used for Voice-over-IP (VoIP) services, thus preventing its subscribers from using third party VoIP services. The FCC regarded this action as an infringement of principles of an open Internet, first expressed by then Chairman Michael Powell in 2004, which should generally enable customers to access any legal content.[19] Following the Madison River case, the FCC adopted the Open Internet Principles in 2005, establishing four consumer rights. However, these principles were not legally binding but were only a declaratory policy statement by the agency. When, in 2008, the cable network operator Comcast slowed BitTorrent peer-to-peer traffic in response to heavy usage by private customers,[20] the FCC required Comcast to disclose the details of its discriminatory network management practices to the Commission within 30 days. In addressing the BitTorrent case, the 2005 Open Internet Principles were applied but an appeals court overturned the decision. In response, the FCC adopted its 2010 Open Internet Order. This order was subsequently challenged by Verizon and referred back to the Commission by an appeals court. That court reiterated that the FCC had the authority to classify and reclassify broadband access services as information or telecommunication services (the two major US legal categories), that the agency had the authority to promulgate rules assuring non-discrimination in the Internet, and that there was concern that broadband access providers might abuse their market power. However, the court found that the 2010 order had applied common carrier principles to information service providers. After a lengthy political and legal process and many changes in direction, the FCC adopted a new order in February 2015, designed around the following core principles (see FCC, 2015):

- Bright line standards (no blocking, no traffic degradation, no paid prioritization).
- Broadband access services, both fixed and mobile, were reclassified as common carrier services according to Title II of the Communications Act.
- Additional safeguards for edge providers and customers (along the lines of the 2005 declaratory order) were adopted.

In Europe, broadband markets are less concentrated than in the USA (see Krämer et al., 2013). This may explain the European Commission's cautious view on any ex ante regulation of ISPs. In a less concentrated market there may be less potential for unlawful behavior of ISPs as long as consumers are able to figure out that certain services are blocked or degraded and can switch in a reasonable time. Moreover, European competition and telecommunications law already provides tools sufficient to deal with many of the problems of net neutrality. The risk of discrimination through (potentially) vertically integrated content and network providers can be addressed by means of sector-specific regulation, as an ISP with significant market power can be obliged to provide access to its facilities under current law. In this case, a regulation of access fees already prevents discrimination by (vertically integrated) ISPs.[21] Moreover, discrimination can be addressed by means of competition law. Article 102 of the TFEU prohibits the abuse by one or more undertakings of a dominant position within the internal market or in a substantial part of it. Hence, the European Commission's Universal Service Directive[22] acknowledges the positive effect of prioritization traffic and product differentiation, as long as consumers have a free choice of services and the conditions of these services are transparent to consumers.

9.5.2.2 Quality of service and price discrimination

Strict net neutrality prevents ISPs from prioritizing and discriminating against certain traffic. However, one of the main arguments against this best-effort principle is that services differ in their sensitivity to delay. Streaming services and VoIP are more sensitive to delay than, for example, web browsing and emails. Moreover, services like e-health may be highly sensitive to delay and require guarantees of prioritization. Hence, proponents in favor of price and quality differentiation and against net neutrality state that it makes sense to allow for traffic management by (1) offering different categories of quality of services and (2) price differentiate according to the sensitivity of delay. In contrast, advocates of strict net neutrality fear that this kind of traffic management may result in competition and welfare-distorting behavior by ISPs.

In the theoretical literature, there are arguments both in favor of and against discrimination. Hermalin and Katz (2007) and Litan and Singer (2007) widely acknowledge the positive effects of differentiation in service quality. In their model, ISPs only offer a single medium quality under net neutrality, whereas differentiation makes it possible to offer efficient high-quality to high-valuation providers. Moreover, due to the structure of the Internet one has to consider a further effect of strict net neutrality. All services use the network as a common resource. As stated above, services differ in their sensitivity to delay. Too much traffic of less sensitive services, such as file sharing, can cause capacity overload and delay or loss of data packages. This capacity overload, however, mainly affects the high-sensitive services like IP television. Finally, if this happens reasonably often, the high-sensitive services may be crowded out by low-sensitive services, which is a well-known phenomenon of the 'tragedy of the commons'. To avoid crowding out, ISPs have to manage traffic according to the sensitivity of delay and provide different quality class contracts (quality of service).

On the other hand, Economides (2008) points out that in such cases an ISP may abuse its market power and also force low valuation providers to accept priority pricing. Choi and Kim (2010) find ambiguous effects of prioritization on welfare. They state that for a large set of parameters a discriminatory regime may lead to lower short-run welfare. Bauer (2007) furthermore points to potential dynamic inefficiencies. Summarizing the theoretical literature, Schuett (2010) concludes that while welfare effects are not entirely clear, in many scenarios there are likely to be positive effects of non-neutrality.

Clearly on the other hand, service and price discrimination may carry the potential for ISPs to behave in an unlawful manner and distort competition and welfare. ISPs with significant market power, however, are subject to control of dominant behavior in Europe as well as in the USA. Article 102 of the TFEU prohibits discriminatory behavior by companies enjoying a dominant position. In the USA, Section 2 of the Clayton Act prohibits price discrimination if such discrimination substantially lessens competition or tends to create a monopoly. In a competitive environment, ISPs are free, as is any other company, to offer differentiated services. The parties will monitor whether the respective qualities promised are really maintained, and otherwise they are free to switch. Hence, the European Commission puts a special emphasis on transparency of providers' terms and condition. The EU Commission's Universal Service Directive forces national regulatory authorities to put transparency obligations into national law. According to the directive, providers with a significant market share have to provide the regulatory authority with the terms and conditions for access to and usage within their network. Moreover, all providers are to disclose information to consumers about their net neutrality policy. This should enable consumers to choose between providers. Practically, it may be questioned whether consumers are able to evaluate and compare the net neutrality policy or whether this requires great expertise. Finally, the EU Commission's Universal Service Directive entitles national regulators to secure a minimum quality level if necessary.

A case for strict net neutrality regulation is not compelling, as many violations are already recognized as cases subject to antitrust and competition law (see Yoo, 2005, 2007; Sidak, 2007). Strict net neutrality, where all services are treated equally, is economically inefficient, since services differ in their sensitivity to delay and users differ in their willingness to pay for these services. Although network management can provide incentives for discriminating, competition policy already provides sufficient tools to deal with many of the concerns and further ex ante regulation of net neutrality is not urgent. Finally, a departure from strict net neutrality may allow ISPs to deviate from the zero-pricing rule for content providers and split the charges between content providers and users. Economically, this seems to be more efficient than the current 'receiving-party-pays' principle since both parties share a benefit from the content.

9.6 CONCLUSION

In principle, online markets are prone to similar competition concerns as offline markets and competition policy can address many of the concerns by well-established competition policy tools. Some of the tools need to be adjusted to account for special characteristics of Internet markets such as their two-sidedness. Open questions concern, for example, whether the acquisition of data resources may require additional analysis in merger cases or whether increased price discrimination and, at the extreme, personalized prices may make market definition exercises practically infeasible.

In addition, Internet markets are typically more dynamic than long-established goods markets. Any intervention has to balance safeguarding a fair and level playing field against maintaining incentives for innovative players in the markets. We conjecture that competition concerns at the service level can be widely solved by competition policy, whereas there is some scope for regulation at the infrastructure level. The degree of regulation and competition policy intervention certainly depends on competitive conditions, which differ in Europe and in the USA.

Areas for future research include the precise effects of APPAs, which are less well understood than traditional best-price clauses. In addition, major research efforts are necessary to better understand the value of data for competitive processes and the conditions under which databases may become essential for competition. Under what circumstances do data become an essential facility? If data constitute a bottleneck, under what conditions should access be granted and how should the original data collector be compensated? Should data resources be specifically analyzed in merger proceedings? These questions lead to the further field of privacy and competition. While data sharing may be helpful to foster competition, if data are used as a resource, privacy concerns may arise, as subjects granting one company access to personal data may not be willing to do the same for another company. These questions again lead to more mundane and practical questions, such as how markets can be delineated and how market shares can be calculated if consumers do not generate sales but 'pay' with their data and/or attention. Other open questions concern (pricing) algorithms, following the US Department of Justice's indictment against Buy 4 Less, Buy For Less, and Buy-For-Less-Online for conspiring with third-party sellers to fix the prices of posters sold online via Amazon Marketplace: to what extent, therefore, can pricing algorithms serve as potential devices for facilitating collusion and under which circumstances? How should their adoption be treated under antitrust law? Hence, many open questions remain and the design for and application of competition rules to Internet markets will remain an interesting area for further research.

NOTES

*   We would like to thank Johannes Bauer for his extremely valuable comments on a draft of this chapter.
1. See, for example, Ellison and Ellison (2005), Evans and Schmalensee (2007, 2008), Evans (2013), Buccirossi (2013), Haucap and Heimeshoff (2014).
2. The capacity on one side of the market may be more limited than on the other. For example, the number of stands may be more limited at a trade show than the space for potential visitors.
3. This does not necessarily have to be the case though. Kaiser and Song (2009), for example, find in an

empirical study of the German magazine market that readers tend to appreciate advertising in women's magazines, business and politics magazines as well as in car magazines.
4. See also Evans and Noel (2008).
5. For a different conclusion see Luchetta (2014).
6. See 'Algorithms', accessed 22 August 2015 at http://www.google.com/insidesearch/howsearchworks/algorithms.html.
7. A much more detailed analysis of a potential antitrust case against Google and the costs and benefits of various remedies can be found in Pollock (2010), Manne and Wright (2011) and Bork and Sidak (2012).
8. See 'Antitrust: Commission obtains from Google comparable display of specialised search rivals – Frequently asked questions', accessed 22 August 2015 at http://europa.eu/rapid/press-release_MEMO-14-87_en.htm?locale=en.
9. See 'Statement on the Google investigation', accessed 22 August 2015 at http://europa.eu/rapid/press-release_SPEECH-14-93_en.htm.
10. See 'Commission approves selective distribution system for Yves Saint Laurent perfume', European Commission Press Release IP/01/713 of 17 May 2001, accessed 22 August 2015 at http://europa.eu/rapid/press-release_IP-01-713_en.htm?locale=en.
11. See *United States of America* v *Apple Inc*, 12 Civ. 2826 (DLC), Opinion & Order, p. 94, accessed 8 January 2016 at http://www.nysd.uscourts.gov/cases/show.php?db=special&id=306.
12. See, for example, European Commission Decisions EL/2010/1113 and IT/2010/1103.
13. See Supreme Court of the United States, *Pacific Bell Telephone Co.* v. *linkLine Communications, Inc.*, 555 U.S. 438 (2009).
14. See Supreme Court of the United States, *Verizon Communications Inc.* v. *Law Offices of Curtis V. Trinko, LLP* (02-682), 540 U.S. 398 (2004), 305 F.3d 89, reversed and remanded.
15. Further surveys are provided by Faulhaber (2012) and Krämer et al. (2013).
16. See, for example, Director and Levi (1956), Posner (1979) and Bork (1993).
17. See, for example, Whinston (1990, 2006). Ahlborn et al. (2004) and Rey and Tirole (2007) provide overviews of post-Chicago models challenging the one-monopoly-rent hypothesis.
18. FCC File No. EB-05-ICH-0110, 2005.
19. The investigation was dropped under terms of a consent decree.
20. FCC File No. EB-08-ICH-1518, 2008.
21. Similarly, according to Section 2 of the Sherman Act dominant companies can be obliged to provide access to essential facilities. However, different from Europe, the FCC characterizes broadband services as information services and thus, cable net operators in the USA are not part of the Common Carrier obligation.
22. Directive 2009/136/EC of the European Parliament and of the Council of 25 November 2009 amending Directive 2002/22/EC on universal service and users' rights relating to electronic communications networks and services, Directive 2002/58/EC concerning the processing of personal data and the protection of privacy in the electronic communications sector and Regulation (EC) No. 2006/2004 on cooperation between national authorities responsible for the enforcement of consumer protection laws (Universal Service Directive).

REFERENCES

Ahlborn, C., D.S. Evans and A.J. Padilla (2004), 'The antitrust economics of tying: A farewell to per se illegality', *Antitrust Bulletin*, **49** (1/2), 287–341.
Alexandrov, A., G. Deltas and D.F. Spulber (2011), 'Competition and antitrust in two-sided markets', *Journal of Competition Law & Economics*, **7** (4), 775–812.
Ammori, M. and L. Pelican (2012), 'Competitors' proposed remedies for search bias: Search "neutrality" and other proposals', *Journal of Internet Law*, **15** (11), 8–31.
Argentesi, E. and L. Filistrucchi (2007), 'Estimating market power in a two-sided market: The case of newspapers', *Journal of Applied Econometrics*, **22** (7), 1247–66.
Argenton, C. and J. Prüfer (2012), 'Search engine competition with network externalities', *Journal of Competition Law & Economics*, **8** (1), 73–105.
Armstrong, M. (2006), 'Competition in two-sided markets', *RAND Journal of Economics*, **37** (3), 668–91.
Bagwell, K. (2007), 'The economic analysis of advertising', in M. Armstrong and R. Porter (eds), *Handbook of Industrial Organization, Volume 3*, Amsterdam: Elsevier, pp. 1701–844.
Bajari, P. and A. Hortaçsu (2004), 'Economic insights from Internet auctions', *Journal of Economic Literature*, **42** (2), 457–86.

Bauer, J.M. (2007), 'Dynamic effects of network neutrality', *International Journal of Communication*, **1**, 531–47, accessed 22 August 2015 at http://ijoc.org/index.php/ijoc/article/view/156/79.

Becker, G.S. and K.M. Murphy. (1993), 'A simple theory of advertising as a good', *Quarterly Journal of Economics*, **108** (4), 941–64.

Bendorf, V., D. Kübler and H.-T. Normann (2015), 'Privacy concerns, voluntary disclosure of information, and unraveling: An experiment', *European Economic Review*, **75** (1), 43–59.

Bork, R.H. (1993), *The Antitrust Paradox: A Policy at War with Itself*, New York: Basic Books.

Bork, R.H. and J.G. Sidak (2012), 'What does the Chicago School teach about Internet search and antitrust treatment of Google?', *Journal of Competition Law & Economics*, **8** (4), 663–700.

Bouckaert, J. and F. Verboven (2004), 'Price squeezes in a regulatory environment', *Journal of Regulatory Economics*, **26** (3), 321–51.

Bowman, W. (1957), 'Tying arrangements and the leverage problem', *Yale Law Journal*, **67** (1), 19–36.

Bracha, O. and F. Pasquale (2008), 'Federal search commission? Access, fairness, and accountability in the law of search', *Cornell Law Review*, **93** (6), 1149–209.

Bravo, L.F. and P. Siciliani (2007), 'Exclusionary pricing and consumers harm: The European Commission's practice in the DSL market', *Journal of Competition Law & Economics*, **3** (2), 243–79.

Buccirossi, P. (2013), 'Background note', in *Vertical Restraints for Online Sales*, OECD Policy Roundtable, Document DAF/COMP(2013)13, Paris: Organisation for Economic Co-operation and Development, pp. 9–44, accessed 22 August 2015 at http://www.oecd.org/competition/VerticalRestraintsForOnlineSales2013.pdf.

Buccirossi, P. (2015), 'Vertical restraints on e-commerce and selective distribution', *Journal of Competition Law & Economics*, **11** (3), 747–773.

Bundeskartellamt (2013), 'Vertical restraints in the Internet economy', paper presented to the Meeting of the Working Group on the Internet Economy, Bonn, accessed 22 August 2015 at http://www.bundeskartellamt.de/SharedDocs/Publikation/EN/Diskussions_Hintergrundpapiere/Vertical%20Restraints%20in%20the%20Internet%20Economy.pdf?blob=publicationFile&v=2.

Caillaud, B. and B. Jullien (2003), 'Chicken & egg: Competition among intermediation service providers', *RAND Journal of Economics*, **34** (2), 309–28.

Chandra, A. and A. Collard-Wexler (2009), 'Mergers in two-sided markets: An application to the Canadian newspaper industry', *Journal of Economics and Management Strategy*, **18** (4), 1045–70.

Choi, J.P. and B.C. Kim (2010), 'Net neutrality and investment incentives', *RAND Journal of Economics*, **41** (3), 446–71.

Clerckx, S. and L. de Muyter (2009), 'Price squeeze abuse in the EU telecommunications sector: A reasonably or equally efficient test', *Competition Policy International*, April, accessed 22 August 2015 at https://www.competitionpolicyinternational.com/price-squeeze-abuse-in-the-eu-telecommunications-sector-a-reasonably-or-equally-efficient-test/.

Crane, D.A. (2012), 'Search neutrality and referral dominance', *Journal of Competition Law & Economics*, **8** (3), 459–68.

Crocioni, P. and C. Veljanovski (2003), 'Price squeeze, foreclosure and competition law, principles and guidelines', *Journal of Network Industries*, **4** (1), 28–60.

De los Santos, B. and M.R. Wildenbeest (2014), 'E-book pricing and vertical restraints', *NET Institute Working Paper No. 14-18*, accessed 22 August 2015 at http://ssrn.com/abstract=2506509.

Dertwinkel-Kalt, M., J. Haucap and C. Wey (2015), 'Raising rivals' costs through buyer power', *Economics Letters*, **126** (3), 181–4.

Dertwinkel-Kalt, M., J. Haucap and C. Wey (2016), 'Procompetitive dual pricing', forthcoming in *European Journal of Law and Economics*.

Devine, K.L. (2008), 'Preserving competition in multi-sided innovative markets: How do you solve a problem like Google?', *North Carolina Journal of Law and Technology*, **10** (1), 59–117.

Director, A. and H.E. Levi (1956), 'Law and the future: Trade regulation', *Northwestern University Law Review*, **51** (2), 256–81.

Dixit, A.K. and J.E. Stiglitz (1977), 'Monopolistic competition and optimum product diversity', *American Economic Review*, **67** (3), 297–308.

Dolmans, M. and A. Leyden (2012), 'Internet & antitrust: An overview of EU and national case law' (1), *e-Competitions: Competition Laws Bulletin, No. 45647*, accessed 6 August 2015 at http://www.cgsh.com/files/Publication/22db91b8-e716-4670-bdf8-f639e61d67b1/Presentation/PublicationAttachment/93706aee-0fdd-4cfe-bae3-f97cf5f17d9d/e-Competitions%20Article.pdf.

Dolmans, M. and H. Mostyn (2015), 'Internet & antitrust: An overview of EU and national case law' (2), *e-Competitions: Competition Laws Bulletin, No. 71276*, accessed 6 August 2015 at http://www.cgsh.com/files/Publication/e615db26-41a7-4093-8563-4da39381830a/Presentation/PublicationAttachment/540d6ed3-41ce-4c87-94bd-a195af768ab6/Internet%20%26%20Antitrust%20-%20An%20Overview%20of%20EU%20and%20National%20Case%20Law.pdf.

Economides, N. (2008), '"Net neutrality", non-discrimination and digital distribution of content through the Internet', *I/S: A Journal of Law and Policy for the Information Society*, **4** (2), 1–26, accessed 22 August 2015 at http://moritzlaw.osu.edu/students/groups/is/archives/volume-42/.

Edelman, B. (2011), 'Bias in search results? Diagnosis and response', *Indian Journal of Law and Technology*, **7**, 16–32.

Edelman, B. (2015), 'Does Google leverage market power through tying and bundling?', *Journal of Competition Law & Economics*, **11** (2), 365–400.

Edelman, B. and B. Lockwood (2011), 'Measuring bias in "organic" search', accessed August 6 2015 at http://www.benedelman.org/searchbias/.

Ellison, G. and S.F. Ellison (2005), 'Lessons from the Internet', *Journal of Economic Perspectives*, **19** (2), 139–58.

European Commission (2012), 'Statement on commitments from Apple and four publishing groups for sale of e-books', speech by Joaquín Almunia, Vice President of the European Commission responsible for Competition Policy, 13 December, *European Commission Press Release Database*, accessed 15 December 2015 at http://europa.eu/rapid/press-release_SPEECH-12-955_en.htm?locale=en.

European Commission (2013), 'Antitrust: Commission accepts legally binding commitments from Penguin in e-books market', *European Commission Press Release Database*, 25 July, accessed 15 December 2015 at http://europa.eu/rapid/press-release_IP-13-746_en.htm.

European Commission (2015), 'Fact sheet: Antitrust: Commission sends statement of objections to Google on comparison shopping service', *European Commission Press Release Database*, 15 April, accessed 15 December 2015 at http://europa.eu/rapid/press-release_MEMO-15-4781_en.htm.

Evans, D.S. (2003), 'The antitrust economics of multi-sided platform markets', *Yale Journal on Regulation*, **20** (2), 325–81.

Evans, D.S. (2008), 'The economics of the online advertising industry', *Review of Network Economics*, **7** (3), 359–91.

Evans, D.S. (2009), 'Two sided market definition', in ABA Section of Antitrust Law (ed.), *Market Definition in Antitrust: Theory and Case Studies*, Chapter XII.

Evans, D.S. (2013), 'Economics of vertical restraints for multi-sided platforms', *University of Chicago Institute for Law & Economics Olin Research Paper No. 626*, accessed 6 August 2015 at http://ssrn.com/abstract=2195778.

Evans, D.S. and M.D. Noel (2008), 'The analysis of mergers that involve multi-sided platform businesses', *Journal of Competition Law & Economics*, **4** (3), 663–95.

Evans, D.S. and R. Schmalensee (2007), 'The industrial organization of markets with two-sided platforms', *Competition Policy International*, **3** (1), 151–79.

Evans, D.S. and R. Schmalensee (2008), 'Markets with two-sided platforms', accessed 22 August 2015 at http://ssrn.com/abstract=1094820.

Evans, D.S. and R. Schmalensee (2015), 'The antitrust analysis of multi-sided-platform businesses', in R. Blair and D. Sokol (eds), *Oxford Handbook on International Antitrust Economics, Volume 1*, Oxford, UK: Oxford University Press, pp. 404–49.

Farrell, J. and G. Saloner (1985), 'Standardization, compatibility, and innovation', *RAND Journal of Economics*, **16** (1), 70–83.

Faulhaber, G.R. (2011), 'Economics of net neutrality: A review', *Communications & Convergence Review*, **3** (1), 53–64.

FCC (2015), 'FCC adopts strong, sustainable rules to protect the open Internet', *FCC News Release*, 26 February, Washington, DC: Federal Communications Commission, 26 February 2015.

Fernández Álvarez-Labrador, M. (2006), 'Margin squeeze in the telecommunications sector: An economic overview', *World Competition*, **29** (2), 247–67.

Filistrucchi, L., D. Geradin, E. van Damme and P. Affeldt (2014), 'Market definition in two-sided markets: Theory and practice', *Journal of Competition Law & Economics*, **10** (2), 293–339.

FTC (2013), 'Google agrees to change its business practices to resolve FTC competition concerns in the markets for devices like smart phones, games and tablets, and in online search' [press release], accessed 22 August 2015 at http://ftc.gov/opa/2013/01/google.shtm.

Gaudin, G. and C. Saavedra (2014), 'Ex ante margin squeeze tests in the telecommunications industry: What is a reasonably efficient operator?', *Telecommunications Policy*, **38** (2), 157–72.

Gaudin, G. and A. White (2014), 'On the antitrust economics of the electronic books industry', *DICE Discussion Paper No. 147*, accessed 22 August 2015 at https://ideas.repec.org/p/zbw/dicedp/147r.html.

Goldman, E. (2006), 'Search engine bias and the demise of search engine utopianism', *Yale Journal of Law and Technology*, **8**, 188–200.

Grimmelmann, J. (2011), 'Some skepticism about search neutrality', in B. Szoka and A. Marcus (eds), *The Next Digital Decade: Essays on the Future of the Internet*, Washington, DC: TechFreedom, pp. 435–59.

Hahn, R.W. and S. Wallsten (2006), 'The economics of net neutrality', The Economists' Voice, **3** (6), 1–7.

Haucap, J. and U. Heimeshoff (2014), 'Google, Facebook, Amazon, eBay: Is the Internet driving competition or market monopolization?', *International Economics and Economic Policy*, **11** (1–2), 49–61.

Haucap, J. and C. Kehder (2013), 'Suchmaschinen zwischen Wettbewerb und Monopol: Der Fall Google' [Search engines between competition and monopoly: The case of Google], in R. Dewenter, J. Haucap and C. Kehder (eds), *Wettbewerb und Regulierung in Medien, Politik und Märkten*, Baden-Baden: Nomos, pp. 115–54.

Hay, G.A. and K. McMahon (2012), 'The diverging approach to price squeezes in the United States and Europe', *Journal of Competition Law & Economics*, **8** (9), 259–96.

Heimler, A. (2010), 'Is a margin squeeze an antitrust or a regulatory violation?', *Journal of Competition Law & Economics*, **6** (4), 879–90.

Hermalin, B.E. and M.L. Katz (2007), 'The economics of product-line restrictions with an application to the network neutrality debate', *Information Economics and Policy*, **19** (2), 184–215.

Hovenkamp, E.N. and H. Hovenkamp (2009), 'The viability of antitrust price squeeze claims', *Arizona Law Review*, **51** (2), 273–303.

ICN (2015), *Online Vertical Restraints Special Project Report*, Canberra: International Competition Network.

Johnson, J.P. (2013), 'The agency and wholesale models in electronic content markets', working paper, accessed 22 August 2015 at http://ssrn.com/abstract=2126808.

Jullien, B. (2006), 'Two-sided markets and electronic intermediaries', in G. Illing and M. Peitz (eds), *Industrial Organization and the Digital Economy*, Cambridge, MA: MIT Press, pp. 272–303.

Kaiser, U. and M. Song (2009), 'Do media consumers really dislike advertising? An empirical assessment of the role of advertising in print media markets', *International Journal of Industrial Organization*, **27** (2), 292–301.

Kaiser, U. and J. Wright (2006), 'Price structures from the magazine industry', *International Journal of Industrial Organization*, **24** (1), 1–28.

Katz, M. and C. Shapiro (1985), 'Network externalities, competition, and compatibility', *American Economic Review*, **75** (3), 424–40.

Krämer, J., L. Wiewiorra and C. Weinhardt (2013), 'Net neutrality: A progress report', *Telecommunications Policy*, **37** (9), 794–813.

Krugman, P. (1980), 'Scale economies, product differentiation, and the pattern of trade', *American Economic Review*, **70** (5), 950–59.

Lao, M. (2013), '"Neutral" search as a basis for antitrust action?', *Harvard Journal of Law & Technology Occasional Paper Series*, July, accessed 22 August 2015 at http://ssrn.com/abstract=2245295.

Lee, R., and T. Wu (2009), 'Subsidizing creativity through network design: Zero-pricing and net neutrality', *Journal of Economic Perspectives*, **23** (3), 61–76.

Lessig, L. (1999), *Code and Other Laws of Cyberspace*, New York: Basic Books.

Lianos, I. and E. Motchenkova (2013), 'Market dominance and search quality in the search engine market', *Journal of Competition Law & Economics*, **9** (2), 419–455.

Litan, R. and H. Singer (2007), 'Unintended consequences of net neutrality', *Journal on Telecommunications & High Technology Law*, **5** (3), 533–72.

Luchetta, G. (2014), 'Is the Google platform a two-sided market?', *Journal of Competition Law & Economics*, **10** (1), 185–207.

Manne, G.A. and W. Rinehart (2013), 'The market realities that undermined the FTC's antitrust case against Google', *Harvard Journal of Law & Technology Occasional Paper Series*, accessed 21 August 2015 at http://mishkabobble.com/antitrust/articles/ManneRinehart.pdf.

Manne, G.A. and J.D. Wright (2011), 'Google and the limits of antitrust: The case against the antitrust case against Google', *Harvard Journal of Law and Public Policy*, **34** (1), 171–244.

Manne, G.A. and J.D. Wright (2012), 'If search neutrality is the answer, what's the question?', *Columbia Business Law Review*, **2012** (1), 151–239.

Martin, S. and J. Vandekerckhove (2013), 'Market performance implications of the transfer price rule', *Southern Economic Journal*, **80** (2), 466–87.

Melnik, M.I. and J. Alm (2002), 'Does a seller's ecommerce reputation matter? Evidence from eBay auctions', *Journal of Industrial Economics*, **50** (3), 337–49.

Motta, M. and A. de Streel (2006), 'Excessive pricing and price squeeze under EU Law', in C.-D. Ehlermann and I. Atanasiu (eds), *European Competition Law Annual 2003: What is an Abuse of a Dominant Position?*, Oxford, UK and Portland, OR: Hart Publishing, pp. 92–125.

OECD (2013), *Vertical Restraints for Online Sales* 2013, OECD Policy Roundtable, Document DAF/COMP(2013)13, Paris: Organisation for Economic Co-operation and Development.

Parker, G.W. and M. van Alstyne (2005), 'Two-sided network effects: A theory of information product design', *Management Science*, **51** (10), 1494–504.

Pollock, R. (2010), 'Is Google the next Microsoft? Competition, regulation in Internet search', *Review of Network Economics*, **9** (4), 1–31.

Polo, M. (2007), 'Price squeeze: Lessons from the Telecom Italia case', *Journal of Competition Law & Economics*, **3** (3), 453–70.

Posner, R.A. (1979), 'The Chicago school of antitrust analysis', *University of Pennsylvania Law Review*, **127**, 925–48.

Rey, P. and J. Tirole (2007), 'A primer on foreclosure', in M. Armstrong and R. Porter (eds), *Handbook on Industrial Organization, Volume 3*, North Holland: Elsevier, pp. 2145–220.

Rochet, J.-C. and J. Tirole (2003), 'Platform competition in two-sided markets', *Journal of the European Economics Association*, **1** (4), 990–1029.

Rochet, J.-C. and J. Tirole (2006), 'Two-sided markets: A progress report', *RAND Journal of Economics*, **37** (3), 645–67.

Rohlfs, J. (1974), 'A theory of interdependent demand for a communications service', *Bell Journal of Economics and Management Science*, **5** (1), 16–37.

Rysman, M. (2009), 'The economics of two-sided markets', *Journal of Economic Perspectives*, **23** (3), 125–43.

Schuett, F. (2010), 'Network neutrality: A survey of the economic literature', *Review of Network Economics*, **9** (2), 1–15.

Sidak, G. (2007), 'A consumer-welfare approach to network neutrality regulation of the Internet', *Journal of Competition Law & Economics*, **2** (3), 349–474.

Sidak, G. (2008), 'Abolishing the price squeeze as a theory of antitrust liability under Section 2 of the Sherman Act', *Journal of Competition Law & Economics*, **4** (2), 279–309.

van Schewick, B. (2012), 'Network neutrality and quality of service: What a non-discrimination rule should look like', Center for Internet and Society, Stanford, accessed 21 August 2015 at http://cyberlaw.stanford.edu/publications/network-neutrality-and-quality-service-what-non-discrimination-rule-should-look.

Vogel, L. (2012), 'EU competition law applicable to distribution agreements: Review of 2011 and outlook for 2012', *Journal of European Competition Law & Practice*, **3** (3), 271–6.

Weyl, E.G. (2010), 'A price theory of multi-sided platforms', *American Economic Review*, **100** (4), 1642–72.

Whinston, M.D. (1990), 'Tying, foreclosure and exclusion', *American Economic Review*, **80** (4), 837–59.

Whinston, M.D. (2006), *Lectures on Antitrust Economics*, MIT Press: Cambridge, MA.

Wright, J. (2004), 'One-sided logic in two-sided markets', *Review of Network Economics*, **3** (1), 42–63.

Wu, T. (2003), 'Network neutrality, broadband discrimination', *Journal on Telecommunications and High Technology Law*, **2** (1), 141–75, accessed 21 August 2015 at http://www.jthtl.org/content/articles/V2I1/JTHTLv2i1_Wu.PDF.

Wu, T. (2007), 'Wireless Carterfone', *International Journal of Communication*, **1**, 389–426, accessed 21 August 2015 at http://ijoc.org/index.php/ijoc/article/view/152/96.

Yoo, C.S. (2005), 'Beyond network neutrality', *Harvard Journal of Law and Technology*, **19** (1), 1–77.

Yoo, C.S. (2007), 'What can antitrust contribute to the network neutrality debate?', *International Journal of Communication*, **1**, 493–530, accessed 21 August 2015 at http://ijoc.org/index.php/ijoc/article/view/153/97.

10. The economics of Internet standards
*Stanley M. Besen and George Sadowsky**

10.1 INTRODUCTION

Internet standards permit users to have access to a wide variety of compatible software, to exchange documents, to combine the use of products made by different vendors, and to communicate directly. The Internet standardization process that eventually came to be carried out under the auspices of the Internet Engineering Task Force (IETF) has been remarkably successful both in achieving a high degree of acceptance by users and in adapting to significant growth in the number of Internet users and changes in the amount and nature of Internet traffic.[1]

After a brief discussion of the economics of standards, this chapter describes how this process came into existence and how and why it survived challenges both from an alternative standard that had been developed by the International Organization for Standardization (ISO) and from a number of proprietary technologies. Next, it addresses whether the technocratic nature of the IETF standards process can continue to remain largely immune from the increasing commercialization of the Internet. The chapter proceeds with a discussion of the recent controversy between the IETF and the International Telecommunication Union (ITU) over the standard for Multiprotocol Label Switching (MPLS). Finally, it explores a new challenge to the IETF standards process that has arisen because certain governments are seeking to have a larger role in the operation and governance of the Internet.

10.2 THE ECONOMICS OF STANDARDS

The economics of standardization largely began with work by David (1985), Farrell and Saloner (1985) and Katz and Shapiro (1985), although Rohlfs anticipated some of the analysis in an article (1974) on telecommunication networks. Fundamental to this analysis is the concept of network externalities, or network effects, which exist when the value of a product to any user is greater the larger the number of other users of the same product. *Direct* network externalities exist when an increase in the size of a network increases the number of others with whom one can 'communicate' directly. *Indirect* network externalities exist when an increase in the size of a network expands the range of complementary products available to the members of the network. Both of these are present in the Internet.

Where technologies are unsponsored, so that users choose among competing technologies but the suppliers of those technologies either cannot, or choose not to attempt to influence the nature or pace of adoption, several things may occur. First, network effects may outweigh preferences for intrinsic product characteristics so that, although a user would prefer the characteristics of one product to those of another if they were on networks of comparable size, he or she may choose to join the larger network in order to obtain its benefits. Second, network industries may exhibit 'tippiness', a tendency for a single technology to dominate because, as one network acquires more users, this increases the value of that network to other users, inducing them to join, and so on. Third, when consumers choose sequentially, 'stranding' may occur because adopters of a technology that 'loses' may either obtain few network benefits or may have to incur the substantial costs of switching to the winning network. Fourth, network industries may exhibit path dependence, so that the behavior of early adopters may have a disproportionate influence on the equilibrium outcome. Fifth, consumer expectations may be critical to the final equilibrium because users must often choose among technologies before those technologies have reached their ultimate network size. Finally, lock-in may occur on the 'wrong' technology because if, for whatever reason, the wrong technology is chosen, it may be difficult to achieve the *coordinated* movement of large numbers of users required for the 'right' technology to become the standard.

When sponsors of competing technologies wish to influence the outcome of the standard-setting process, or, more generally, to determine which network 'wins', the focus is on the strategies and tactics adopted by sponsors.[2] When sponsors decide to engage in a standards 'battle' they may attempt to build an early lead by, for example, (1) making the product available to early adopters at low prices, in order to influence the expectations of late adopters; (2) attempting to attract the suppliers of complementary products by, for example, providing information that facilitates the development of compatible products; (3) pre-announcing products in order to discourage users from joining rival networks; (4) and/or they may commit to low future prices in order to assure adopters that they will not be stranded on a small network.

It is also important to observe that the winner of a standards 'battle' may choose to make it difficult for others to join its network if the benefits to the winner from a somewhat larger network that open membership makes possible are more than offset by the increased competition to which it will then be subject. Among the ways that the winner might deny access to its network are by enforcing intellectual property rights, thus making it illegal for rivals to produce compatible products, changing technology frequently so that rivals are unable to respond quickly enough to offer products that users can employ on the dominant network, and refusing to share information with rivals about changes in network design.

Finally, sponsors may choose not to engage in a standards 'battle' but instead they may agree on a standard and agree to low-cost or royalty-free licensing to all of their respective technologies in order to allow the benefits of standardization to be shared among competing firms. They may also agree on standards that combine aspects of their technologies so as to prevent any sponsor from being disadvantaged in future competition.

Whereas the analysis of standardization initially focused on de facto standards, standards that resulted in choices made through the 'market', more recent analyses have addressed the behavior of participants in standard-setting organizations (SSOs) where what are sometimes called *voluntary* standards are established.[3] Here, the focus has been on the procedures used by SSOs and on the behavior of their members in attempting to influence the outcome of the standards process.

One concern has been whether the process has been distorted either by strategically placed participants or by the 'stacking' of SSO voting. Another has been whether participants in SSOs have engaged in deceptive practices by, for example, failing to disclose fully their intellectual property rights to other members and attempting to engage in 'hold-up', that is, to demand high license fees, after a standard has been widely adopted and industry participants are 'locked in'. Finally, even where intellectual property rights have been disclosed, there has been considerable controversy about whether intellectual property owners have adhered to SSO policies that, in principle at least, require them to license their technologies on fair, reasonable and non-discriminatory (FRAND) terms, and even on what FRAND means.[4] For all of these reasons, standard-setting has increasingly become the subject of antitrust litigation.

10.3 EARLY HISTORY OF INTERNET STANDARDIZATION AND THE ROLE OF THE IETF[5]

The origins of the Internet standardization process can be traced to a series of informal meetings that were held over the period 1968–72. These meetings initially involved four computer science contractors to the Department of Defense's Advanced Research Projects Agency (DARPA),[6] but they quickly expanded to include individuals from other computer network research groups from industry and universities and they eventually led to the establishment of protocols for communications over a packet-switched network. By the end of this period, there were a number of linked machines on what had come to be called the ARPANET and a significant number of documents, some of which contained standards, which were referred to as Requests for Comments or RFCs.

The RFC process eventually came to be organized under the auspices of the Network Working Group in 1972 and in 1979 the Internet Configuration Control Board (ICCB) was established to advise DARPA on 'the technical evolution of the protocol suite' (Cerf, 1990). The ICCB was reorganized as the Internet Activities Board (IAB) in 1983, and in 1986 the IAB created the Internet Engineering Task Force (IETF), which became 'the main forum in which the [Internet] technical standards were proposed, tested, and debated' (Froomkin, 2003, p. 787).[7] In 1992, the Internet Society was formed and subsequently undertook a number of actions in support of the IETF standards process (Cerf, 1995).

Contributions to the IETF standards process are accepted from those with the interest, time, and ability to make them and decisions are made by consensus. The process can be described as 'meritocratic' – decisions are based largely on the quality of proposals, 'democratic' – there is little or no hierarchy, 'informal' – decisions are based on broad agreement among the participants, and 'pragmatic' – whether something actually works is critical to its acceptance. In the words of David Clark, 'We reject: kings, presidents and voting. We believe in rough consensus and running code' (Clark, 1992, p. 543).

The IETF is generally seen as an organization in which decisions are made solely or primarily on technical grounds, that is, they are made largely without regard to commercial considerations.[8] Drake has noted, for example, that:

> [t]he 'new paradigm' standardization . . . process is controlled less by [Public Telecommunications Operators] and large equipment manufacturers and more by a plethora of advanced users, specialized suppliers, systems integrators, research institutions, and so on . . . This new model is

emerging in a variety of specialized industry fora outside the 'official' multilateral bodies like the ITU and ISO, and has been most thoroughly realized in the TCP/IP based Internet community. (Drake, 1993, p. 644)

Similarly, as one of us has observed, 'The basic Internet protocols were developed in the 1970s and 1980s and, to coordinate their development, called the Transmission Control Protocol/Internet Protocol (TCP/IP) family, the IETF was formed in the 1980s as a voluntary, unincorporated, non-governmental meritocracy open to anyone capable of contributing to their goals' (Sadowsky et al., 2004).[9] As some of the founders of the Internet put it, 'by 1990 . . . TCP had supplanted or marginalized most other wide-area computer network protocols worldwide, and IP was well on its way to becoming THE bearer service for the Global Information Infrastructure' (Leiner et al., 2003).

10.4   CHALLENGES TO TCP/IP

The TCP/IP protocols, and the process that created them, have not been without their challenges. One came from the Open Systems Interconnection (OSI) protocol suite, which had been developed by the ISO. The other came from proprietary protocols, including IBM's System Network Architecture and Digital Equipment Corporation's DECnet. These challenges were significant for somewhat different reasons.

The simultaneous existence of TCP/IP and OSI raised two possibilities. One was that the Internet would have 'tipped' and only one of the two competing standards would have survived. Alternatively, the Internet could have become fragmented, with both TCP/IP and OSI being in use at the same time.[10] Which of these two outcomes was more likely depended on whether users placed greater value on being on a large 'network' or on the intrinsic characteristics of the alternative standards. It also depended on the success of the tactics employed by the sponsors of the competing alternatives.

The challenge from proprietary protocols not only raised the possibility that TCP/IP would be displaced but also that a small number of commercial entities might dictate Internet standards. If that were the case, those entities could have charged for access to their intellectual property or denied rivals access to their standards altogether, or they could have obtained a competitive advantage through their superior knowledge of the standards and control of their further development.

As it turned out, both challenges to TCP/IP, and to the IETF process, were repulsed. Exactly why is subject to some interpretation. Some believe that the outcome of the TCP/IP-OSI 'war' was largely the result of the fact that TCP/IP was deployed first and developed an early lead, which, through network effects, created a 'bandwagon' that OSI could not overcome.[11] Others have argued that TCP/IP was, in many ways, superior to the OSI model, so that its 'victory' reflected this superiority, not only TCP/IP's head start. For example, Maathuis and Smit point out that 'TCP/IP products were readily available whereas one had to wait long . . . for OSI products. Further, when it came to actual implementation of OSI protocols, these were carried out in great variety, often resulting in new incompatibilities' (Maathuis and Smit, 2003, p. 172).[12] Similarly, Cargill argues:

The problem with the OSI protocol was that it was a technically driven revolutionary change to current practice, was highly complex, and required a great deal of expertise to implement correctly. Additionally, reference implementations and test suites were lacking when initial deployments were made, which caused severe interconnection problems. The IETF with its concept of 'rough consensus, running code, and dual implementations' provided a much simpler solution to the problem that could be implemented by all vendors. (Cargill, 2011)

Finally, some observers have emphasized the importance of the fact that TCP/IP had been incorporated into a number of versions of the popular Unix operating system. According to Hafner and Lyon, 'When Sun included network software [which included the Berkeley version of Unix] as part of every machine it sold and didn't charge separately for it, networking exploded' (Hafner and Lyon, 1996, p, 250). Similarly, Mowery and Simcoe note:

The TCP/IP protocols became an integral part of [the implicit standard based on the Unix operating system], since the networking protocol was included in the 4.2 BSD version of Unix that was available at a nominal cost and was widely used in the academic research computing community. (Mowery and Simcoe, 2002, p. 1373; footnote omitted)

It should also be noted that even those who predicted the eventual success of OSI noted the problems that it faced in dislodging TCP/IP as an industry standard. For example, Cashin claimed that '[b]y the year 2000, the OSI model may be the only one supporting completely open processing requirements' (Cashin, 1989). He noted, further, that 'TCP/IP will wane as we progress through the next decade' and that 'its eventual demise . . . will be related to the superior functionality associated with OSI protocols and services'. Nonetheless, he observed that 'This venerable protocol grouping [TCP/IP] is actually in ascendancy as we close out the last year of this decade' and that 'the rationale for TCP/IP's ongoing success is fundamental: it works, it is available on numerous hardware platforms, and it supports a heterogeneous networking environment'.

Five years later (in 1994), Cashin's view seems to have changed substantially. He noted that 'While still largely unimplemented, OSI does have pockets of support. OSI adherents, however, rail about the lack of software supporting the model' (Cashin and Frye, 1994).[13] The following is a list of factors that Cashin and Frye identified as undermining OSI:

- Products were developed only after the standard was developed and, as a result, 'No one detects errors in specification logic until long after the process begins'.
- 'Standards committees try to solve almost every conceivable problem their members envision. Because many different committees . . . carried OSI standards development forward, delays became common'.
- There was 'a lack of a migration path . . . migrating to OSI requires some interim steps due to its complexity and unique nature. For many of those who looked to TCP/IP as one of those interim steps, it became the final one'.
- 'OSI's lack of stability presented another obstacle . . . In view of OSI's complexity, stability is a must if vendors are to build products'.
- 'OSI products were too long in coming to market'.[14]

Although TCP/IP did not always work smoothly at first, and had to undergo a 'shakedown', that process took place via direct communications and collaborations among implementers without the need to propose changes to a standards organization before undertaking the needed technical work. In the end, TCP/IP's 'rough consensus and running code' triumphed over a system that took a long time to develop standards that did not always function as anticipated. As Cashin and Frye put it: 'Unlike the OSI effort, in which developers created a model on paper before undertaking any practical development, TCP/IP developers built and proved the networks before assuming a dominant position. As a result, TCP/IP works and is now the de facto standard for open systems' (Cashin and Frye, 1994).[15]

The United States government was a major player on both sides of the standards dispute. On the one hand, because DARPA had supported the development of the Internet and the TCP/IP protocols, these protocols were widely used within the scientific and research communities. On the other hand, in an attempt to standardize networking protocols for the Federal government, the National Institute of Standards and Technology (NIST) in the Department of Commerce succeeded in requiring all computer systems acquired by the Federal government to use the OSI protocol set (GOSIP).[16] However, after considerable turmoil, this decision was reversed in 1995 through FIPS PUB 146-2, which provided 'guidance for the acquisition and use of networking products implementing open, voluntary standards such as those developed by the Internet Engineering Task Force (IETF), the International Telecommunication Union, Telecommunication Standardization Sector (ITU-T; formerly the Consultative Committee on International Telegraph and Telephone [CCITT]), and the International Organization for Standardization (ISO)' (National Institute of Standards and Technology, 1995).

As Cerf noted recently:

As the new president of the Internet Society, I wrote to the US National Institutes of Standards and Technology in 1992, requesting that an evaluation be performed to determine whether TCP/IP protocols could be an acceptable alternative to the OSI protocols that were, at that time, formally preferred by the U.S. government and other governments around the world. A Blue Ribbon panel was formed, and a year later it was concluded that the TCP/IP protocols were an acceptable alternative. (Cerf, 2012)

This effectively ensured the dominance of TCP/IP protocols in both government and private networks and established them as the dominant and de facto wide area networking standards.

The dominance of TCP/IP over DECNET and SNA/APPN can be largely explained by: (1) the increasing rejection of manufacturer-dominated, that is, proprietary, standards; (2) the increasingly widespread demonstration of the benefits and ease of use of open standards; and (3) the failure of some major industry players to adapt to the new more decentralized environment.[17]

Many of the computing and networking industries before 1990 were dominated by a plethora of incompatible proprietary standards, symbolized by phrases such as 'IBM compatible'. This led to charges that firms such as IBM and AT&T were able to extract monopoly rents from buyers by subjecting manufacturers of competing products to changes in specifications that limited their ability to compete. Although technological progress had led to the downsizing of information and communications technology

(ICT) devices and a rapidly expanding market for such products, the existence of proprietary standards continued to be seen as an impediment to competition and a number of actions had been taken by the US government to lower the barriers to entry that proprietary standards had created.[18]

The creation of Interop in 1986 provided an important illustration of the benefits of the new open TCP/IP standards. Billed as a trade show, volunteers built a bare bones TCP/IP network in less than 48 hours and exhibitors were then invited to attach their TCP/IP-compatible devices to it and test and demonstrate the interoperability of their products. Attendance grew from 50 exhibitors and 5000 attendees in 1988 to 600 exhibitors and 70 000 attendees in 1993.[19] These events, by demonstrating the benefits of open standards, gave a major impetus to their adoption.

Finally, the major computer manufacturer at the time, IBM, failed to make the shift to the newer, more distributed environment. As late as 1997, IBM described its APPN offering as 'an open data networking architecture that is easy to use, has decentralized control with *centralized network management*, allows arbitrary topologies, has connection flexibility and continuous operation, and requires no specialized communications hardware' (IBM Corporation, 1997, p. x; emphasis added). Central management was seen as increasingly inappropriate for a network that depended for its growth and value on its becoming increasingly heterogeneous and public.[20]

Finally, it is important to observe that, regardless of which standard eventually 'won', it was widely accepted that there would be only one standard, and thus a single Internet. That is, although different participants favored different standards, all preferred compatibility to incompatibility. Once it became clear that TCP/IP would 'win' the competition to become the standard, the use of competing standards for public networks effectively ceased.[21]

10.5   THE COMMERCIALIZATION OF THE INTERNET AND THE STANDARDS PROCESS

A number of observers have pointed out that the decisions of the IETF are, or can be, influenced by commercial considerations. For example, Crocker has noted that, '[t]he IETF's growth is proving a fundamental challenge to its style of operation . . . Internet technology now represents a multi-billion dollar business. Hence, IETF decisions have significant financial impact and that can raise the heat of a debate quite a bit' (Crocker, 1993). Similarly, Froomkin (2003, p. 795) has observed that, 'Decisions regarding standards now have important financial consequences for would-be providers of Internet hardware and software, and tempers can flare when tens of millions of dollars are at stake'. Russell has noted that, 'As it embodied the new style of standardization, the Internet standards community constantly dealt with problems that stemmed from the tensions between centralized authority and grassroots initiatives, as well as the rising influence of commercial values' (Russell, 2006, p. 56).[22]

Lerner and Tirole make a similar point when they note that:

> [. . .] while in the first decades, engineers largely did participate in the IETF as objective individual experts, regardless of their corporate affiliations, and the agendas of these firms and

decisions were largely driven by technological considerations, today this has changed somewhat. The much greater stakes associated with the adoption of particular standards . . . implies that pressure is put on engineers in some cases to conform to corporate priorities in the decision-making process. (Lerner and Tirole, 2004, note 6)

However, they conclude that 'efforts by corporations to shape the [IETF] standard-setting agenda were often less successful' than similar efforts to affect the ITU standards process. Weiser goes even further by claiming that:

[. . .] it is important to understand that the common conception of the Internet rests in large part on a community that can enforce norms committed to open architecture and nonpro-prietary development. In today's Internet, however, the conditions that once nurtured that environment – considerable government support, a small community of stakeholders, and the absence of proprietary development – are increasingly no longer in place . . . the increasing number of interested parties and diversity of interests suggest that solutions like open source development and the creation of common, nonproprietary standards *will become the exception, not the norm.* (Weiser, 2003, p. 534; emphasis added)

Simcoe indicates that the standard-setting process will slow 'when SSO participants favor specific technologies because of development lead times, proprietary complements, or intellectual property rights' (Simcoe, 2012, pp. 305–6).[23] Specifically, he notes that 'the empirical results suggest that the IETF's evolution from a quasi-academic institution into a high-stakes forum for technical decision-making led to increased politics and a slow-down of consensus decision-making' (ibid., p. 330).[24] He also concludes that:

[. . .] low level protocols, such as IP, were already established by time of rapid IETF commer-cialization and remained relatively stable as higher level protocols were built on top of them. Rent-seeking was most pronounced at higher levels because that was the locus of innovation, where new applications created demand for new protocols which threatened the profits (or sunk investments) associated with proprietary solutions. (Simcoe, 2012, pp. 329–30)[25]

Finally, several of the founders of the Internet noted that:

[. . .] the architecture of the Internet has always been driven by a core group of designers, but the form of that group has changed as the number of interested parties has grown. With the success of the Internet has come a proliferation of stakeholders – stakeholders with an economic as well as an intellectual investment in the network. (Leiner et al., 2003)

The increased importance of commercial interests in the Internet standards process raises three potential issues. First, factors other than technical superiority can affect the choice of the standard. Although this is not necessarily undesirable – it is legitimate and, indeed, efficient for an SSO to consider factors such as the relative costs of implementing alternative standards – it does mean that the outcome of the standard process may not be the same as when such considerations are absent.[26]

Second, the presence of competing commercial interests within the IETF can make achieving 'rough consensus' more difficult, thus slowing the standards process. Moreover, firms that are dissatisfied with the outcome of the standards process can either attempt to have their technologies become de facto standards, by encouraging their adoption by other firms, or seek out other standards organizations that may be more amenable to adopting their preferred alternative, an activity that Lerner and Tirole have referred to as 'forum shopping'. Although this is an unlikely outcome in the case of the Internet – and, as we have noted, attempts to have proprietary technologies adopted as standards have failed in the past – this outcome cannot be excluded entirely. Indeed, there are a variety of strategies that a firm can pursue that have succeeded in other contexts. These include, as outlined in the introduction: (1) building an early lead over competing standards, perhaps by offering low prices to early adopters, in order to influence the choices of later adopters; (2) attracting the suppliers of complementary products to the standard in order to increase the attractiveness of the standard relative to its rivals; and (3) committing to low future prices in order to provide assurance that the standard will be widely adopted.[27] Vendors whose technologies have not been chosen by the IETF may attempt to pursue these strategies.[28]

Finally, the standards process can be distorted for anticompetitive purposes. Among the ways in which such behavior has been alleged to have occurred in the past are: (1) exploiting an employee's position in an SSO to favor a particular technology;[29] (2) 'packing' meetings of an SSO with new members in order to influence the outcome of a voting process;[30] and (3) disclosing the existence of intellectual property rights only after industry participants are 'locked in' to a technology that is included in the standard.[31] Moreover, even the threat of antitrust liability can affect the standard setting process if an SSO fears a legal challenge to its decisions by sponsors of technologies that have not been included in a standard.[32] Although the IETF has attempted to anticipate these concerns, they cannot be ruled out altogether.

Most fundamentally, the increasing commercialization of the Internet, which implies that standardization decisions can have significant economic effects, has significantly affected the informal, meritocratic, technocratic, and democratic character of the traditional IETF standards process. Although that process has had a remarkable run, commercial considerations are coming to play an increasingly important role in IETF deliberations.

10.6 THE CONTROVERSY OVER THE MULTIPROTOCOL LABEL SWITCHING (MPLS) STANDARD

In 2011, a major controversy developed between the ITU and the IETF over the MPLS standard. According to the Internet Society, the MPLS standard:

> [. . .] assigns labels to data packets, which can then operate across multiple different protocols. Forwarding or switching decisions for MPLS packets from one network node to another are made on the basis of the label (i.e., without requiring equipment to examine the packet's content) facilitating easy to create end-to-end circuits. MPLS is commonly used to create Virtual Private Networks (VPNs) and it can be used to deliver different levels of quality of service (QoS) for different types of data. It also gives service providers flexibility in routing; for example, to avoid broken links or failures. (Internet Society, 2012b)

In 2007, the IETF and the ITU had agreed to base the next-generation transport network of the Internet on MPLS technology that had been developed within the IETF and they had agreed to work together to extend MPLS functionality to the network.

In announcing this agreement, the Internet Society noted that, 'The work will move forward with the recognitions that the sole design authority for MPLS resides within the IETF and that expertise for Transport Network Infrastructure resides within the ITU-T Study Group (SG) 15' (Andersson and Bryant, 2008). It also quoted the Director, ITU Telecommunication Standardization Bureau, as saying:

> Given the complexity of today's networks, it is inevitable that we will, from time to time, see conflicts in approaches. This is natural. Quickly agreeing on a common way forward is imperative. And that we have done so is an indication of the great spirit of cooperation between IETF and ITU that has been built over many years of collaboration.[33]

Notwithstanding this 'great spirit of cooperation', according to the Internet Society, the ITU-T Study Group 15:

> [. . .] determined a Recommendation that defines operations, administration, and management (OAM) for MPLS transport networks. The determined Recommendation is at odds and not interoperable with the IETF standard being developed, in spite of an agreement put in place by the ITU and the IETF two years ago to avoid such an outcome. (Internet Society, 2012b)

According to the Internet Society, this 'sets the stage for a divergence of MPLS development; it creates a situation where some vendors will use the IETF standard for MPLS OAM while other vendors implement the ITU-T Recommendation for OAM. This situation ensures that the two product groups will not work together' (Internet Society, 2011).
According to the Counselor for SG15:

> Packet/optical transport network management requires carrier-grade protocols that can ensure fault detection and repair within strict time limits. It is also important that the OAM solution fits into the existing operational model to minimize the need for staff retraining. The ITU OAM protocol clearly addresses these strict requirements. The IETF OAM tools are still under development.[34]

Thus, in this view, the choice by the ITU reflects its judgment that the IETF process is not currently meeting the requirements of telecommunications carriers. An earlier IETF document had made a similar point: 'not all of MPLS's capabilities and mechanisms are needed and/or consistent with transport network operations. There are also transport technology characteristics that are not currently reflected in MPLS' (IETF, 2009).[35] Van Beijnum summarized the situation as follows:

> Two groups of vendors had proposed two different protocols for Transport MPLS/MPLS Transport Profile (T-MPLS/MPLS-TP), and especially its network management (NM), also known as Operations, Administration, and Management (OAM) . . . The IETF adopted that protocol that is closer aligned with the way it normally does things, much to the dismay of the ITU, which has a proposal that fits better within the traditional telecom environment. After failing to get any traction in the IETF, the second group of vendors petitioned the ITU-T to adopt its protocol in addition to the one being worked on in the IETF . . . the ITU-T . . . decided to go ahead with the second proposal. (Van Beijnum, 2011b)[36]

Although these descriptions suggest that technical differences, or at least a delay in resolving them, led to the split between the IETF and the ITU, other forces may also have been at work. For example, some carriers, most notably China Mobile, and some equipment manufacturers, most notably Alcatel Lucent and Huawei, had already adopted a different standard from the one being developed by the IETF and, as a result, they may have been reluctant to incur the costs of switching to a different standard.[37] At the same time, other vendors may have made significant investments in the approach being taken by the IETF and may also have been reluctant to incur the costs of adapting that standard to the needs of the telecom carriers. For example, one author noted that: 'Cisco and Juniper Networks, the largest providers of network devices, chose to work with and extend an IETF standardized protocol, RSVP, rather than develop a new label distribution protocol. Developing a new protocol involves huge efforts in designing, standardizing, developing, deploying and debugging' (Goyal, n.d.). Similarly, Juniper noted that, 'One of the design goals of MPLS-TP is to keep the MPLS architecture intact and reuse as many of the existing components of MPLS as possible' (Juniper Networks, 2011, p. 7).

Finally, a possible source of disagreement involved differences in the procedures that are used to set standards. The Chair of the IETF described the differences as follows: 'The IETF believes strongly in technical excellence, so a single solution is adopted when rough consensus emerges . . . In the ITU, optional extensions are added until nobody objects anymore' (Housley in Van Beijnum, 2011a). In this interpretation, the 'rough consensus' approach of the IETF is in conflict with the more formal international treaty–based approach of the ITU.[38]

Subsequently, at the 2012 meeting of the World Telecommunication Standardization Assembly (WTSA), participants 'approved key standards . . . on a technology for multiprotocol label switching – transport profile (MPLS_TP)' (International Telecommunication Union, 2012). According to the ITU, 'Recommendation ITU-T G.8113.1, "Operations, Administration and Maintenance mechanism for MPLS-TP in Packet Transport Network (PTN)" is an extension of the IETF's MPLS protocol developed in cooperation with the Internet Engineering Task Force (IETF)' (ibid.). Based on a previous understanding, the IETF agreed to award a code point[39] to the standard that was approved by the WTSA.[40]

Notwithstanding this development, the controversy over the two MPLS standards, and the disagreement between the two standards institutions, is likely to persist for some time. That is because the standards are incompatible so that, for example, packets that travel through routers that implement only the IETF version of MPLS will not be able to travel seamlessly through routers that implement the ITU version. This raises several possibilities.

First, as the IETF Chair noted, some router manufacturers may develop 'dual-mode' products, ones that implement both standards, so that their users will be able to communicate with others regardless of the standard that they have implemented (Housley in Lawson and Ricknas, 2011). However, we understand that this would be costly and time consuming, so that manufacturers may be reluctant to pursue this approach. Second, manufacturers or network operators may develop 'translators' in order to facilitate transmissions between networks using incompatible MPLS standards. Finally, packets may continue to flow between networks that have implemented different standards but they may not benefit from the additional functionality that MPLS would have otherwise provided.

The two incompatible MPLS standards may coexist, perhaps for a long time, especially if each of them is strongly preferred by a different user group. That is, the situation just described could persist, with label-based routing capability on the Internet fragmented between two camps, each using a different standard. Alternatively, one of the MPLS standards could come to dominate either because its technical superiority is generally recognized or because it develops a sufficient lead for the market to 'tip' through the type of process described by Arthur (1989).[41] If that were to occur, users that had employed the losing standard would be 'stranded' with the 'wrong' technology.

10.7 GOVERNMENT CHALLENGES TO THE IETF PROCESS

The IETF standards process may be facing an even more significant challenge than it has in the past as a result of the desire of some governments to play a larger role in Internet governance in general, and the standardization process in particular. Waz and Weiser (n.d.) note, for example, that 'The future of this unusual and largely successful form of Internet governance is far from assured'. An important manifestation of this development is a proposal to make it compulsory for member states of the ITU, an international treaty organization, to impose ITU-T standards on Internet service providers in their respective countries.[42] If this proposal were adopted, it would effectively shift much of the influence over Internet standards from the IETF to the ITU.[43]

According to former Federal Communications Commissioner (FCC) Robert M. McDowell, this would 'subsume under intergovernmental control many functions of the Internet Engineering Task Force, the Internet Society and other multistakeholder groups that establish the engineering and technical standards that allow the Internet to work' (McDowell, 2012). The proposal, along with ones that would deal with the Internet Domain Name System, electronic mail abuse, cybersecurity, and peering, among others, was initially scheduled to be considered at the World Conference on International Telecommunications [WCIT] to be held in Dubai in December 2012. Gross and Lucarelli have noted:

> For some governments, the WCIT presents an opportunity to significantly expand the jurisdiction and role of the ITU into previously unregulated, lightly regulated or domestically regulated aspects of the emerging digital economy. . . Several countries have proposed to move oversight or 'control' of aspects of the Internet and Internet development from the non-governmental multi-stakeholder mechanisms such as ICANN and replace them with the ITU.[44]

Although it is not alone, the United States government has opposed the proposal. For example, according to Lawrence E. Strickling, Assistant Secretary of Commerce for Communications and Information:

> The United States strongly supports the use of a multistakeholder process as the preferred means of addressing Internet policy issues . . . We expect that some states will attempt to rewrite the regulation in a manner that would exclude the contributions of multi-stakeholder organizations and instead provide for heavy-handed governmental control of the Internet, including provisions for cybersecurity and granular operational and technical requirement for private industry. We do not support any of these elements. (Strickling, 2011)

More recently, the Majority Staff of the Committee on Energy and Commerce of the US House of Representatives issued a memorandum expressing concern about proposals that 'seek to authorize regulation of the Internet by an international governmental body within the ITU, replacing the multi-stakeholder model that has served the Internet and the world so well'.[45] At about the same time, several members of the House of Representatives proposed that the US government should 'continue working to implement the position of the United States to promote an Internet free from government control and preserve and advance the successful multi-stakeholder model that governs the Internet today'.[46]

The Internet Society has also expressed strong concerns about the effect of these developments on the Internet standardization process. It notes that the proposals to modify Articles 1.4 and 3.5 of International Telecommunication Regulations (ITRs):

> [. . .] would have the effect of making it compulsory for states to impose ITU-T standards . . . on telecom/Internet service providers in their countries. This approach would be counterproductive for global communications and is counter to the international collaborative standards development process that is place today. The Internet Society believes that ITU-T Recommendations should continue to be voluntary. (Internet Society, 2012a)

The Society argues that:

> [t]he ITRs should enshrine a commitment to the use of open and voluntary international standards. Interoperability, mutual agreement, and collaboration are invariable requirements for the Internet's survival. Many standards development organizations contribute to the smooth functioning of the Internet, and new standards development organizations have emerged over time, so it is potentially damaging to impose a preference for some standards development organizations (SDOs) over others. (Ibid.)

At the same time that some countries are proposing changes that would alter substantially the current mode of Internet governance, including of the Internet standards process, there appears to be considerable support for retaining the arrangements, albeit with a somewhat larger role for governments. For example, a European Advisory Group has proposed, as one of its Internet Governance Principles that:

> [t]he decentralized nature of the responsibility for the day-to-day management of the Internet should be preserved. The private sector should retain its leading role in technical and operational matters while ensuring transparency and accountability to the global community for those actions which impact on public policy. (Council of Europe, 2011)

Similarly, the OECD has observed that:

> [t] Internet's openness . . . stems from globally accepted, consensus driven technical standards that support global product markets and communications. The roles, openness, and competencies of the global multi-stakeholder institutions that govern standards for different layers of Internet components should be recognised and their contribution should be sought on the different technical elements of public policy objectives. (OECD, 2011, p. 6)

It seems clear that the Internet standards process would change substantially if the current structure, which is dominated by private voluntary standards organizations, were replaced by one under the auspices of the ITU, where governments are able to block the adoption of standards. Such a change would likely mean that Internet standardization would no longer be a primarily technical activity and instead would accord a much larger role to commercial and political considerations, especially the interests of traditional tele-communications carriers, as well as to the interests of governments themselves. Although it seems unlikely that major changes to the Internet standards process will occur any time soon, the proposals before the World Conference on Telecommunications nonetheless represented a potential challenge to that process. Although they did not get a significant hearing at WCIT, such proposals are certain to be raised in future ITU-led international meetings. Thus, we expect the challenge to the current Internet standards process to continue, and we anticipate that it will be a long time before its outcome will be known.

NOTES

*   The authors wish to acknowledge the helpful comments of Lyman Chapin, Stephen D. Crocker, Timothy Simcoe and Philip L. Verveer on earlier drafts. The views expressed in this chapter are the authors' own and do not necessarily represent the views of any organizations with which they are affiliated.

1.   This chapter focuses on standards for the basic communication protocols of the Internet. It does not address the multiplicity of standards at higher layers, such as those developed by the World Wide Web Consortium (W3C) and others.

2.   For a fuller treatment see Besen and Farrell (1994).

3.   See Farrell and Saloner (1988), Lerner and Tirole (2004) and Simcoe (2012) for important contributions to this literature.

4.   For a discussion of these issues see Besen and Levinson (2012).

5.   For descriptions of the development of the Internet in its earliest days see Leiner et al. (2003) and Cerf (1993).

6.   The Advanced Research Projects Agency (ARPA) changed its name to the Defense Research Projects Agency (DARPA) in 1971, back to ARPA in 1993, and back to DARPA in 1996.

7.   For brief descriptions of the entities involved in the IETF standards process and of the process itself see Jakobs (2000).

8.   As we discuss below, however, recent developments suggest that this statement may now be less true than it was in the past.

9.   Some of the same people who were involved in the development of TCP/IP were also part of the International Packet Network Working Group (INWG), which was developing an alternative protocol. McKenzie (2011) argues that 'DARPA had a bigger research budget than any of the other research organizations, and for this reason, its protocol choice [TCP/IP] became dominant over time'.

10. For a model in which both types of outcomes are possible see Katz and Shapiro (1985). Balkanization could have involved either two 'Internets' between which users could not communicate or the development of (probably costly and imperfect) 'translators' that would permit users of one network to communicate with users of the other.

11. The classic article on how a small early lead can result in a permanent advantage when network effects are present is Arthur (1989).

12. It is important to note, however, that one of the advantages that the authors identify for TCP/IP is 'Availability of wide-spread technical expertise on TCP/IP (due to extensive deployment, i.e., large "installed base"), which resulted from TCP/IP's early lead' (Maathuis and Smit, 2003, p. 173).

13. Note, however, that Cashin significantly underestimated the amount of support available for OSI. In 1994 most or all of the OSI protocols were implemented in the standard software releases of every major computer and router manufacturer. They were just not being used very much.

14. Borthick (1991) attributes many of these problems to the fact that 'the standards committees are often populated by public network types and entrenched big suppliers, many of whom ignored the existence of private local and wide area networks for as long as possible. Technical developments have continually outpaced many of the very standards they were meant to embody, and multiple standards, subject to numerous interpretations and additions, have been approved'.

15. Many United States government agencies had purchased TCP/IP products despite a mandate that network procurements comply with OSI under the Government OSI Profile (GOSIP). Eventually, the US government withdrew the mandate and recommended acceptance of TCP/IP.

16. The influence of the Federal government was used successfully in this way in 1961, when it required use of the COBOL language for all procurements, assuring a quick death for IBM's competitive COMTRAN language.

17. Bresnahan and Greenstein (1999) argue that there is no inconsistency between the dominance of a standard such as TCP/IP and significant entry by, and competition among, firms that produce products that are based on that standard. Indeed, the success of a standard may well depend on the extent to which it receives support from different firms. Interestingly, TCP/IP has been incorporated both in proprietary operating systems, such as Windows, and public domain operating systems, such as BSD.

18. For example, in order to resolve a concern that IBM had manipulated interface standards in order to injure competitors, the company agreed to disclose information about these interfaces prior to the date at which it shipped new products (*United States* v. *IBM*, 69 Civ. 200 [S.D.N.Y. 1969]. Under the Modified Final Judgment that settled the US government's antitrust case against AT&T, the Bell operating companies were 'prohibited from discriminating between AT&T and other companies in . . . the establishment of technical standards' (*United States* v. *American Telephone and Telegraph Company*, 552 F. Supp. 131 [1982]).

19. Personal communication from Dan Lynch, CEO of Interop, 26 July 2003.

20. The tepid acceptance of DECnet Phase V, which was a solid implementation of the ISO/OSI model, was doomed both by the rapid adoption of TCP/IP, which created a bandwagon effect, and by the growing rejection of proprietary standards.

21. For a discussion of the trade-off between a vested interest in a particular standard and an interest in promoting the universal adoption of any standard see Besen and Saloner (1989, pp. 178–84). Besen and Farrell (1994) refer to the case in which compatibility is the preferred outcome for everyone as the 'Battle of the Sexes'.

22. Russell (2006, p. 54) also claimed that: 'The informal character of the IAB's oversight of the IETF had created problems in the past, especially when IETF engineers perceived that IAB decisions favored the commercial interests of vendors over the technical consensus of the IETF'.

23. Standards-setting organizations are sometimes referred to as standards-developing organizations (SDOs).

24. The empirical results refer to a comparison of the time that the IETF took to approve standards and the time that it took to approve what Simcoe referred to as 'non-standards'. Although the time-to-consensus has increased for both tracks, Simcoe finds that the increase is greater for standards and that the difference is statistically significant. One of the variables that Simcoe considers is the 'suit-to-beard ratio', which is based on the sources of contributions to an IETF Working Group listserv. Simcoe characterizes this as a measure of the extent to which an IETF working group 'is creating commercially relevant technology' (Simcoe, 2012, p. 319). Maher (1998) earlier noted a slowdown in the IETF process, although he attributed it to the increase in the number of participants, not to the fact that commercial considerations had become more important.

25. Lyman Chapin (private communication) notes that almost all of the protocols in the TCP/IP suite were well established even before the IETF was even created.

26. Of course, especially when there are many dimensions of performance, firms may have different views about what is the technically 'best' solution. Thus, a firm may favor a particular standard even if doing so does not provide it with a competitive advantage.

27. For more details on these strategies see Besen and Farrell (1994).

28. See the discussion below of the attempt by some vendors to have the ITU adopt their MPLS standard during the period when the IETF had not yet adopted its MPLS standard.

29. See, for example, *American Society of Mechanical Engineers* v. *Hydrolevel Corporation*, 456 U.S. 556 (1982).

30. See, for example, *Allied Tube & Conduit Corp.* v. *Indian Head, Inc.*, 486 U.S. 492 (1988). Waz and Weiser (n.d.) observe that that 'With greater openness to members [multistakeholder] bodies must minimize the risk of forum-packing, which can become a challenge when an organization's ground rules permit disproportionate representation that may introduce dimensions of politics into the processes. When broad industry participation takes place, [multistakeholder] bodies must manage potential antitrust and competition concerns, not overstepping appropriate bounds of cooperation intentionally or inadvertently'.

31. See, for example, *Rambus* v. *Fed. Trade Comm'n*, 522 F.3d 456, 469 (D.C. Cir. 2008) and Commission Decision of 9.12.2009 relating to a proceeding under Article 102 of the Treaty on the Functioning of the European Union and Article 54 of the EEA Agreement: Case COMP/38.636 – Rambus.

32. For example, Besen and Johnson (1986, p. 47) report that the National Association of Broadcasters declined to adopt a standard for AM stereo in part because it feared that its actions might be challenged in the courts.

33. See Andersson and Bryant (2008) and International Telecommunication Union (2007), 'ITU-T Newslog – T-MPLS agreement: ITU_T and IETF', 16 October, accessed 19 July 2014 at http://www.itu.int/ITU-T/newslog/default,date,2007-10-16.aspx.

34. Greg Jones, quoted in Van Beijnum (2011b).

35. An earlier trade press report makes this point even more strongly: 'Carriers do not believe that IP/MPLS can deliver the levels of network resilience and equipment reliability that define 'carrier-class'

performance. And carriers have serious reservations about the lack of operations, administration, and maintenance (OAM) systems in IP/MPLS switches and routers . . . Without carrier-grade resilience and reliability in place, service providers will not be able to offer the 'five-nines' class of network reliability for which corporate customers are willing to pay a steep premium' (Bennett, 2004). On the other hand, one vendor had suggested that the needs of carriers could be met by adding 'a few enhancements' to the MPLS Transport Profile (Juniper Networks, 2011).

36. In this regard, it is interesting that Lerner and Tirole (2004, p. 7) note that 'it has been argued that the ITU is a much more sympathetic venue [than is the IETF] for proposals by large telephone companies'.

37. Matsumoto (2011) reported that 'ITU-T Study Group 15 apparently passed a recommendation for using the ITU Y.1731 standard for operations, administration and management (OAM) in transport networks . . . The side that got their way includes AlcaLu, China Mobile Ltd . . . , Huawei and Telecom Italia'.

38. Curiously, one of the complaints that were apparently raised by the ITU was that a standard was urgently needed and that the IETF had failed to complete its work on schedule. On this point see Lawson and Ricknas (2011).

39. Code points in this context are identifiers assigned by the IETF for formally recognized protocols and administered by IANA (Internet Assigned Numbers Authority). They allow network objects on both ends of a data transmission to agree on and ensure a common protocol for transmission.

40. The IETF had conditioned the award of a code point on the existence of a stable normative reference, which the WTSA decision provided.

41. One possible interpretation of the behavior of those vendors who prevailed on the ITU to adopt their standard is that they sought to obtain an early, and possibly insurmountable, lead in a forthcoming standards 'war'.

42. See International Telecommunication Union (2012, p. 9, Option 1 MOD1 [Source: TD Rev. 1 and Russian Federation]) and Internet Society (2012a, Annex 2, Comment on Proposal to MOD Art. 1.4 and 3.5), accessed 8 January 2016 at https://info.publicintelligence.net/ITU-TD43.pdf and http://www.internet society.org/sites/default/files/Internet%20Society%20comment%20to%20the%20WCIT%20Preparations-%20February%202012.pdf respectively.

43. For an analysis of an earlier attempt by the ITU to maintain its historic pre-eminence in setting international telecommunications standards in the face of challenges from regional standards organizations see Besen and Farrell (1991).

44. Gross and Lucarelli (2012) also note that 'Some governments would also like the ITU to play a greater role in regulating peering, termination charges for data traffic, and other Internet-related rate issues to, among other things, potentially lower certain Internet backbone costs and to capture for domestic coffers some of the value of international VoIP services entering their countries'.

45. 'Memorandum, To: Members and Staff, Subcommittee on Communications and Technology, U.S. House of Representatives Committee on Energy and Commerce, From: Majority Committee Staff, Re: Hearing on International Proposals to Regulate the Internet, 29 May 2012'. See also Testimony of Ambassador Philip Verveer, Hearing on International Proposals to Regulate the Internet, 31 May 2012.

46. 'Proposed Concurrent Resolution, Expressing the sense of Congress regarding actions to preserve and advance the multistakeholder governance model under which the Internet has thrived, 30 May 2012'.

REFERENCES

Andersson, L. and S. Bryant (2008), 'Working with ITU-T: The MPLS transport profile case', *IETF Journal*, accessed 19 July 2014 at http://www.internetsociety.org/articles/working-itu-t-mpls-transport-profile-case.

Arthur, W.B. (1989), 'Competing technologies, increasing returns, and lock-in by historical events', *The Economic Journal*, **99** (394), 116–31.

Bennett, G. (2004), 'Resilience, reliability, and OAM in converged networks: A *Heavy Reading* competitive analysis', *Heavy Reading*, accessed 19 July 2014 at http://www.heavyreading.com/details.asp?sku_id=528&skuitem_itemid=558&promo_code=&aff_code=&next_url=%2Fdefault.asp%3F.

Besen, S.M. and J. Farrell (1991), 'The role of the ITU in standardization: Pre-eminence, impotence or rubber stamp?', *Telecommunications Policy*, **15** (4), 311–21.

Besen, S.M. and J. Farrell (1994), 'Choosing how to compete: Strategies and tactics in standardization', *Journal of Economic Perspectives*, **8** (2), 117–31.

Besen, S.M. and L.L. Johnson (1986), *Compatibility Standards, Competition, and Innovation in the Broadcasting Industry*, Santa Monica, CA: The RAND Corporation, accessed 19 July 2014 at http://www.rand.org/content/dam/rand/pubs/reports/2007/R3453.pdf.

Besen, S.M. and R.J. Levinson (2012), 'Introduction: The use and abuse of voluntary standard-setting processes in a post-*rambus* world: Law, economics, and competition policy', *The Antitrust Bulletin*, **57** (1), 1–16.

Besen, S.M. and G. Saloner (1989), 'The economics of telecommunications standards', in R.W. Crandall and K. Flamm (eds), *Changing the Rules: Technological Change, International Competition, and Regulation in Communications*, Washington, DC: Brookings Institution, pp. 177–220.

Borthick, S.L. (1991), 'SNA vs. OSI vs. TCP/IP? There is no winner!', *Business Communications Review*, accessed 19 July 2014 at http://www.highbeam.com/doc/1G1-11400962.html.

Bresnahan, T.F. and S. Greenstein (1999), 'Technological competition and the structure of the computer industry', *Journal of Industrial Economics*, **47** (1), 1–40.

Cargill, C.F. (2011), 'Why standardization efforts fail', *The Journal of Electronic Publishing*, **14** (1), accessed 19 July 2014 at http://quod.lib.umich.edu/j/jep/3336451.0014.103?rgn=main;view=fulltext.

Cashin, J. (1989), 'In network politics, OSI has upper hand; IBM, DEC both support OSI in different ways', *Software Magazine*, April, accessed 19 July 2014 at http://www.highbeam.com/doc/1G1-7242506.html.

Cashin, J. and C. Frye (1994), 'Messaging strength may send OSI up to the major leagues', *Software Magazine*, September, accessed 19 July 2014 at http://www.highbeam.com/doc/1G1-16253812.html.

Cerf, V. (1990), 'The Internet Activities Board', *RFC 1160*, May, accessed 19 July 2014 at http://www.ietf.org/rfc/rfc1160.txt.

Cerf, V. (1993), 'How the Internet came to be', as told to Bernard Aboba, accessed 26 June 2014 at http://www.virtualschool.edu/mon/Internet/CerfHowInternetCame2B.html.

Cerf, V. (1995), 'IETF and the Internet Society: A bit of history', *Internet Society*, 18 July, accessed 19 July 2014 at http://www.internetsociety.org/internet/internet-51/history-internet/ietf-and-internet-society.

Cerf, V. (2012), 'Keynote address', Global INET, Geneva, 24 April, accessed 19 July 2014 at http://www.elon.edu/docs/e-web/predictions/isoc_20th_2012/Vint%20Cerf%20INET%202012%20Keynote.pdf.

Clark, D.D. (1992), 'A cloudy crystal ball: Visions of the future', in *Proceedings of the Twenty-Fourth Internet Engineering Task Force, Massachusetts Institute of Technology, NEARnet, Cambridge, 13–17 July 1992*, accessed 19 July 2014 at http://www.ietf.org/old/2009/proceedings/prior29/IETF24.pdf.

Council of Europe (2011), *Internet Governance Principles*, proposal by the Council of Europe Ad Hoc Advisory Group on Cross-border Internet for a draft Council of Europe Committee of Ministers Declaration on Internet Governance Principles, Council of Europe conference, Strasbourg, 18–19 April, accessed 19 July 2014 at http://www.umic.pt/images/stories/publicacoes5/Internet%20Governance%20Principles.pdf.

Crocker, D. (1993), 'Making standards the IETF way', *Standard View*, **1** (1), 48–56.

David, P.A. (1985), 'Clio and the economics of QWERTY', *American Economic Review*, **75** (2), 332–7.

Drake, W.J. (1993), 'The Internet religious war', *Telecommunications Policy*, **17** (9), 643–9.

Farrell, J. and G. Saloner (1985), 'Standardization, compatibility, and innovation', *Rand Journal of Economics*, **16** (1), 70–83.

Froomkin, A.M. (2003), 'Habermas@Discourse.Net: Toward a critical theory of cyberspace', *Harvard Law Review*, **116** (3), 749–873.

Goyal, S. (n.d.), 'RSVP-TE: Choice of signaling protocol', *MPLS Tutorial*, accessed 21 July 2014 at http://mplstutorial.com/choice-signalling-protocol-rsvp-te.

Gross, D.A. and E. Lucarelli (2012), 'The 2012 world conference on international telecommunications: Another brewing storm over potential UN regulation of the Internet', accessed 19 July 2014 at http://www.whoswholegal.com/news/features/article/29378/the-2012-world-conference-international-telecommunications-brewing-storm-potential-un-regulation-internet/.

Hafner, K. and M. Lyon (1996), *Where Wizards Stay Up Late: The Origins of the Internet*, New York: Simon and Schuster.

IBM Corporation (1997), *Inside APPN: The Essential Guide to the Next-generation SNA*, Document SG24-3669-03, June, accessed 19 July 2014 at http://www.redbooks.ibm.com/redbooks/pdfs/sg243669.pdf.

IETF (2009), 'Requirements of an MPLS transport profile', *RFC 5654*, September, accessed 19 July 2014 at http://tools.ietf.org/html/rfc5654.

International Telecommunication Union (2012), 'Working group to prepare for the 2012 World Conference on International Telecommunications', CWG-WCIT Temporary Document 43, draft compilation of options, 27–29 February, Com-ITU 11(073), Geneva: ITU.

Internet Society (2011), 'IETF and Internet Society statement relating to today's ITU_T SG15 decision that will lead to non-interoperability in MPLS development', 25 February, accessed 19 July 2014 at http://www.internetsociety.org/node/190.

Internet Society (2012a), 'Comment to the WCIT preparations', 9 February, *CWG-WCIT12 Contribution*, accessed 19 July 2014 at http://www.internetsociety.org/sites/default/files/Internet%20Society%20comment%20to%20the%20WCIT%20Preparations-%20February%202012.pdf.

Internet Society (2012b), 'ITU decision Q&A', accessed 19 July 2014 at http://www.internetsociety.org/articles/itu-decision-qa.

Jakobs, K. (2000), 'Trying to keep the Internet's standards setting process in perspective', accessed 19 July 2014 at http://tnc2000.terena.org/proceedings/8A/8a1.pdf.

Juniper Networks (2011), 'MPLS transport profile (MPLS-TP)', White Paper, accessed 24 July 2014 at http://opti500.cian-erc.org/opti500/pdf/sm/mpls-tp%20Juniper.pdf.

Katz, M.L. and C. Shapiro (1985), 'Network externalities, competition, and compatibility', *American Economic Review*, **75** (3), 424–40.

Lawson S. and M. Ricknas (2011), 'ITU, IETF push dueling standards on MPLS features', *TechWorld*, accessed 19 July 2014 at http://www.techworld.com.au/article/print/378429/itu_ietf_push_dueling_standards_mpls_features/.

Leiner, B.M., V.G. Cerf and D.D. Clark et al. (2003), 'Brief history of the Internet', accessed 19 July 2014 at http://www.internetsociety.org/internet/internet-51/history-internet/brief-history-internet/.

Lerner, J. and J. Tirole (2004), 'A model of forum shopping, with special reference to standard setting organizations', *NBER Working Paper No. 10664*, Cambridge, MA: NBER.

Maathuis, I. and W.A. Smit (2003), 'The battle between standards: TCP/IP vs. OSI, victory through path dependency or by quality', paper at the 3rd IEEE Conference on Standardization and Innovation in Information Technology, 22–24 October, Delft, accessed 19 July 2014 at http://doc.utwente.nl/46343/.

Maher, M. (1998), 'An analysis of Internet standardization', *Virginia Journal of Law and Technology*, **3** (5), 1522–687.

Matsumoto, C. (2011), 'MPLS argument leads to split standard', *Light Reading*, 28 February, accessed 19 July 2014 at http://www.lightreading.com/ethernet-ip/mpls-argument-leads-to-split-standard/d/d-id/684530.

McDowell, R.M. (2012), 'The U.N. threat to internet freedom', *The Wall Street Journal*, 21 February, accessed 19 July 2014 at http://online.wsj.com/article/SB10001424052970204792404577229074023195322.html?mod=WSJ_article_comments#articleTabs%3Darticle.

McKenzie, A. (2011), 'INWG and the conception of the Internet: An eyewitness account', *IEEE Annals of the History of Computing*, **33** (1), 66–71.

Mowery, D.C. and T. Simcoe (2002), 'Is the Internet a US invention? An economic and technological history of computer networking', *Research Policy*, **31** (8–9), 1369–87.

National Institute of Standards and Technology (1995), 'Profiles for open systems internetworking technologies (POSIT)', *Federal Information Processing Standards Publication No. 146-2*, 15 May, accessed 8 January 2016 at https://www.gpo.gov/fdsys/pkg/FR-1995-05-15/html/95-11917.htm.

OECD (2011), *OECD Council Recommendation on Principles of Internet Policy Making*, 13 December, accessed 21 July 2014 at http://www.oecd.org/sti/interneteconomy/49258588.pdf.

Rohlfs, J. (1974), 'A theory of interdependent demand for a communications service', *Bell Journal of Economics and Management Science*, **5** (1), 16–37.

Russell, A.L. (2006), '"Rough consensus and running code" and the Internet-OSI standards war', *IEEE Annals of the History of Computing*, **28** (July–September), 48–61.

Sadowsky, G., R. Zambrano and P. Dandjinou (2004), 'Internet governance: A discussion document', in D. MacLean (ed.), *Internet Governance: A Grand Collaboration*, New York: United Nations, pp. 183–226.

Simcoe, T. (2012), 'Standard setting committees: Consensus governance for shared technology platforms', *American Economic Review*, **102** (1), 305–36.

Strickling, L.E. (2011), 'Remarks by Lawrence E. Strickling, PLI/FCBA Telecommunications Policy & Regulation Institute', 8 December, accessed 21 July 2014 at http://www.ntia.doc.gov/speechtestimony/2011/remarks-assistant-secretary-strickling-practising-law-institutes-29th-annual-te.

Van Beijnum, I. (2011a), 'ITU bellheads and IETF netheads clash over transport networks', *Ars Technica*, 3 March, accessed 21 July 2014 at http://arstechnica.com/tech-policy/news/2011/03/itu-bellheads-and-ietf-netheads-clash-over-mpls-tp.ars.

Van Beijnum, I. (2011b), 'Divide between ITU and IETF on MPLS MOA runs deep', *Ars Technica*, 13 March, accessed 21 July 2014 at http://arstechnica.com/tech-policy/news/2011/03/divide-between-itu-and-ietf-take-on-mpls-moa-runs-deep.ars.

Waz, J. and P. Weiser (n.d.), 'Internet governance: The role of multistakeholder organizations', *Silicon Flatirons Roundtable*, accessed 21 July 2014 at http://www.silicon-flatirons.org/documents/publications/report/InternetGovernanceRoleofMSHOrgs.pdf.

Weiser, P.J. (2003), 'The Internet, innovation, and intellectual property policy', *Columbia Law Review*, **103** (3), 534–613.

11. The economics of copyright and the Internet
*Sacha Wunsch-Vincent**

11.1 INTRODUCTION

Technology and the Internet have triggered important changes to how creative works are created and accessed, and how creators and copyright-based industries generate their revenues. During the past decade, digital content markets have exhibited double-digit growth rates across industry sectors and increasing shares of total revenues. In addition, new types of content, novel content producers and innovative ways of manipulating and modifying digital content are burgeoning.

This chapter reassesses the economics of copyright in the light of these changes. Section 11.2 provides an introduction to the economics of copyright. Section 11.3 gives an overview of the changes to the baseline copyright economics model. Section 11.4 summarizes the existing economic literature and resulting data needs. While this chapter focuses on copyright, it is worthwhile noting that other forms of intellectual property rights (IPRs) such as patents, industrial designs and trademarks also matter in the digital economy, both for physical products such as smartphones and tablet computers and for intangible products such as software and social networks. Furthermore, although this chapter exclusively refers to copyright, it is worthwhile clarifying that in addition to copyright vested in authors, international treaties also recognize related rights, vested in performers, phonogram producers and broadcasting organizations.

11.2 THE ECONOMICS OF COPYRIGHT – THE BASELINE MODEL BEFORE DIGITIZATION

At the outset, it makes sense to briefly restate the main economic rationales behind copyright law. Legally speaking, copyright law grants moral and economic rights to the creator of a work, such as a song or a movie. At the international level the minimum term of protection is 50 years, plus the life of the creator, but in many countries this term has been extended often to 70 years after the death of the creator. Although there are significant differences among national laws in the way they accord protection to moral rights, authors are usually granted the right to claim authorship and the right to object to any distortion or other modification that would be prejudicial to their honor or reputation.

Copyright consists of a bundle of exclusive economic rights that enable authors to control, and therefore license the use of, their creations. These economic rights include: rights to reproduce and distribute (e.g., in form of DVDs or books); rights to publicly perform and communicate to the public (e.g., the broadcast of a movie or the performance of a song in a concert); the right of making available the work on digital networks (e.g., downloading and streaming); and the right to control adaptations and translations. Because these rights are independent of each other, each commercial and non-commercial use can be licensed or transferred independently. In practice they can be managed directly by the original rights holder, by those to whom a right or rights have been transferred (e.g., producers or publishers), or by collecting societies entrusted to that end (WIPO, 2004). It must be noted that economic rights are subject to certain limitations or exceptions. In fact, certain actions normally restricted by copyright may, in circumstances specified in the law, be done without the authorization of the copyright owner (e.g., reproduction exclusively for private use or short quotations from a protected work).

This legal set-up is grounded in the economics of copyright, which sees this intellectual property right as an instrument to stimulate the production and dissemination of creative works (Landes and Posner, 1989; WIPO, 2003). Economists view creative works as non-excludable goods that can be reproduced at low marginal cost and enjoyed in a 'non-rival' way by many consumers. However, if creative works were to be provided at their low marginal costs or copied for free, creators and the associated industries would have no direct incentive to undertake the investments to create such works. In this case, the supply of creative works – in terms of quantity, quality or diversity – could fall below a level that is socially desirable. Indeed, the fixed cost of producing content and the risks associated with financing the production, marketing and distribution of creative works tend to be high in many content sectors.

The establishment of a copyright system is seen as the solution to the market failure scenario described above. As with other intellectual property (IP) rights, however, a trade-off among costs and benefits that merits careful consideration is involved (Table 11.1). The specific provisions of copyright seek to strike a balance between the short-term

Table 11.1   Effects of the copyright system – a conceptual framework

	Potential Upside Impacts	Potential Downside Impacts
Effect on creative supply	Positive incentive for creators and rights holders to create, supply and finance creative works induced by the prospect of remuneration Positive effect on follow-on creators as more creative works act as inspiration. Copyright also provides for a framework clarifying how to license and reuse creative works of others	Reduced follow-on creativity induced by fact that copyright might reduce access, increase price, and outlaw unauthorized adaptations and other reuses of creative works
Effect on access by the end user	The above positive effect on creative supply will positively influence the availability of creative works	Increased cost of access for the end user and limitations on if, how and when the content can be accessed
Institutional and administrative effects	The copyright system allows transactions and collaborations between the authors of creative works and publishers, distributors and other players involved in the copyright value chain with IP as the main coordination vehicle	Administration and transaction costs created by the copyright system, often referred to as deadweight loss, as costs are incurred that are nobody's gains

gratification of immediate consumption and the long-term process of providing eco-nomic incentives that reward creativity and foster a dynamic culture (Gurry, 2011).

On the one hand, the creator of a work is rewarded with the grant of exclusive rights for having invested the necessary time and effort in cultural creation (Plant, 1934). As outlined above, besides any moral rights conferred by copyright law, the economic rights grant the creator exclusive control over his or her work for follow-on activities. First, theoretically at least, these rights allow the creator to set the market price at a 'monopoly' rather than at a competitive level, and second, they allow the creator to price discrimi-nate with regard to the other market participants according to different levels of access (WIPO, 2003). The exclusive rights conferred by copyright are intended to stimulate the supply of creative works, both directly as authors are incentivized and indirectly as the created works might stimulate follow-on creativity by others.

Importantly, copyrights play a fundamental role in the economic organization of creative activities and the creative industries. Copyrights are a vehicle for transaction and cooperation, as rights can be transferred and bundled. Rarely do consumers enjoy creative works directly from a 'lone creator', as is often implied in economic treatises or studies relating to copyright. A musician will often rely on a record company to invest in his or her recording, to market it, to arrange for broadcasts, and so on. He or she will also rely on a collective management organization (CMO) to generate revenues for him or her through collective licensing of his or her music to radio stations and other outlets. Many creative works also require the participation of many creators with potential rights to their performance that need to be negotiated and bundled in one piece of work. A movie, for instance, has a scriptwriter, a director, actors, camera people and the like, who all share in the creation and potentially hold separate rights.

Copyright-based industries are often the rights holders responsible for financing, supporting, distributing and marketing creative works. They also often shoulder and manage the risk involved in the production of creative works; it is well demonstrated that only a limited number of copyright works generate the bulk of industry revenues, cross-subsidizing other less successful creations. On the other hand, the impact on follow-on creation and the access by end users can also be negatively affected.

When it comes to access by end users, the exclusive rights conferred by copyright law allow the rights holder to control the work, its accessibility, its pricing, its modification, and so forth. It is expected that this will raise the price of the said work, in particular when works can be shared through copying or rentals (Varian, 2005).

In reality, of course, creators or artists cannot set prices while ignoring market forces. The price elasticity of demand, the availability of other competing content products, and other factors rein in the power to control prices, which is more theoretical than real. In addition, it is not the creators themselves who decide on the pricing of their work in most cases, but intermediaries, (e.g., the movie studio, the collective management organiza-tion, etc.) and distributors, (e.g., record shops, supermarkets).[1] It also needs to be noted that in many creative posts, such as computer programmers, journalists, and others, the copyright is never attributed to the actual creator but to his or her employer, when these activities are treated as 'work for hire'. However, the point about potentially higher prices remains valid. Access to the creative work will certainly not be free and ubiquitous.

When it comes to the impact on follow-on creation, the limitations on accessing, reusing and modifying creative works – all of which can inspire the creation of new works – can, at the same time, potentially have a negative effect on follow-on creation. As compared to patents that offer protection to inventors for 20 years, copyrighted works fall in the public domain much later, and potential follow-on creators – either of original works or adaptations – can be negatively affected (Landes, 2002). This holds particularly true when copyright exceptions and limitations to exclusive rights (e.g., fair use provisions, exceptions for educational purposes) are not applicable, for instance in the case of mashing of different copyrighted songs to produce a new music track for commercial purposes.

Finally, while the existence of copyright facilitates transactions and collaborations, it can also hinder making works available and impose costs on intermediaries keen to invent new forms of access and new business models.

First, copyright by definition means exclusivity and territoriality depending on the country and its legal regime. Thus, rights holders could refuse to license and make the work accessible to particular actors or transmission channels, or to particular jurisdictions.[2] In particular, when new entrants would like to make content available in new ways, the refusal to offer or broadcast certain copyright works might disable new forms of accessing content. The daunting process telecom providers experienced in trying to secure the rights to broadcast soccer matches over mobile phones is one example of this kind of refusal. At times, such refusals to license copyrighted content can result from rights holders' anticompetitive motives (Wunsch-Vincent, 2010a).

Second, the nature of scattered and unregistered rights and their territorial nature can complicate the identification of rights holders and the construction of new business models. Indeed the complexity and costs of the legal processes and the fees involved can be so high as to discourage new market entrants. Small players in particular might face insurmountable obstacles. This became apparent in the online context, with new entrants – no matter how large their size – initially having a hard time securing rights for many territories in a timely manner. As posited in earlier OECD studies (2005, 2008) and documented more recently in KEA and Vrije Universiteit Brussel (2012), licensing music for online music platforms entails dealing with the copyrights granted to a spectrum of people involved in composing, performing, recording and exploiting musical works. The licensing process depends on a multiplicity of layers of protection for rights holders, a variety of management practices and the involvement of different management entities. Problems are caused by the way collecting societies work – irrespective of the category of rights holders they represent or the category(ies) of rights they manage – and by difficulties specific to the provision of multi-territory licenses for the online exploitation of musical works.[3] Consequently, it is challenging to propose an online video platform where videos can be watched in many legal jurisdictions alike, due to the difficulties of obtaining rights.[4] The difficulty of securing the rights to orphan works – creative works where the author can no longer be identified – is also a recurrent policy issue.

In addition, maintaining a copyright system is not without cost. Similar to other forms of statutory intervention, a copyright system also creates considerable administration, enforcement and transaction costs that lead to a so-called 'deadweight loss' (Watt, 2000).[5] As copyrights are never examined or renewed, no related efforts or fees have to be incurred.[6] As a result, in contrast to the patent system, the costs at this end are rather low. Still, private parties have to keep records, and transact, negotiate, clear, and enforce rights. Policy-makers must identify the right scope and duration of copyright protections.

Courts are necessarily involved in settling disputes, and police, border authorities and others – including private firms on their own or others' behalf – regularly participate in copyright enforcement.

In light of the above, there is recognition among economists that copyrights alone might not create optimal incentives and economic rewards for creators. Given the multiplicity of rights holders, copyright markets and institutions such as CMOs are needed to create more efficient markets, to mediate between creators, licensors and licensees, and hence to reduce transaction costs related to search, bargaining, and other licensing processes. Such arrangements become ever more important in the digital era (Wunsch-Vincent, 2010a, 2010b).

In order to better understand the impact of copyrights on economic outcomes and social welfare, economists have to disentangle the various above effects on creators and performers, rights holders, the industry, consumers and society at large while taking the parameters of the particular copyright system and possible alternatives into account.[7] Parameters include the definition of protectable subject matter; the scope of exclusive rights, exceptions and limitations; duration of protection; and the level of enforcement. Other concerns are mechanisms to create copyright markets and exchanges, as well as how these parameters are put into practice or modified by law or behavior in an online context.

Importantly, and to connect to the topic of copyright in the digital age, the outcome of this analysis is largely empirical and not theoretical. The analysis should seek to answer the following questions. Is the current legal and administrative copyright set-up guaranteeing an optimal supply of creative goods, new genres and related innovation and diversity? Is the term of protection long enough to stimulate these policy objectives, particularly compared to the access barriers it might create?

11.3   TRANSPOSING COPYRIGHTS TO THE INTERNET

How do the above trade-offs and the potential costs and benefits of the copyright system change in an online environment? At the outset, it can be said that the basic trade-offs and associated questions behind the copyright system remain unchanged. The basic tenets of the economics of copyright, and hence the motivation for copyright laws and regulations, remain valid in an Internet age. Yet, there are a few important factors brought about by the development of digital technologies that fundamentally change (1) how content is created, (2) how it is accessed, and (3), potentially, how copyrights are administered. The empirical economic evaluation of the associated trade-offs induced by copyright law is affected.

First, the increased availability of digital technologies, and the Internet in particular, have arguably and at first sight significantly lowered the costs to create, copy and distribute creative works on a global scale in a quasi-instantaneous fashion (Varian, 2010; Gurry, 2011). Undoubtedly, this paradigm shift has the potential to stimulate access and creativity. By many accounts, a promise of ubiquitous and more universal access to content and creativity should materialize. Lower content creation and distribution costs should eventually also lead to wider distribution of creative works or higher profit margins for creators and associated industries. Arguably, it has never been easier to create and reuse or adapt content. Amateur content creators are certainly now recognized as a new creative force (OECD, 2007). All in all, a wider range of potential authors and creators stands to be incentivized by the copyright system.

These above points need to be put into perspective, however, when looking at professionally produced content (see Wager, 2008).[8] Many content sectors have actually experienced increased costs of production in a digital context. For example, online video and computer games and new digitally shot cinema movies are multiple times more expensive than their offline equivalents. Similarly, creating a professional news report based on field research in a natural disaster zone still entails significant costs. Essentially, it is the distribution costs of content – and thus a relatively minor share of overall costs[9] – that have plummeted thanks to digitization and the Internet. Novel digital distribution costs have also arisen, as discussed later in this chapter.

At the same time, these developments also facilitate the piracy of creative works, as the cost of copying and disseminating unauthorized copies is reduced to nearly zero. Authors of creative works and associated content industries might benefit less as their revenues from paid copies could effectively be reduced. Costly policing of copyright infringements will ensue, and copyright holders will seek enforcement of their rights via private means and public courts to restore the original trade-off intended by the copyright system. Rampant unauthorized copying and the inability to enforce private copyrights might thus reduce the incentive effect of copyright.

Second, the rise of the Internet as a new distribution channel has introduced a change in how works are made accessible and how revenues are generated and shared. Digital content markets have experienced double-digit growth rates and increasing shares of total revenues. Many offline transactions have moved online. To illustrate, Figure 11.1 depicts the online share and growth of content sectors such as games, music, film and newspapers. The online share of computer games is greatest, whereas the share of revenues generated online by films and newspapers is still relatively

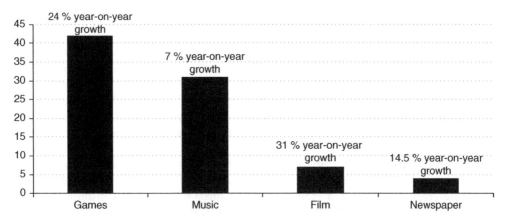

Source: Author, based on data from PricewaterhouseCoopers, updated from OECD (2008, 2010); see also OECD (2012).

Figure 11.1   Revenues generated online as a share of total revenues (%)

modest. The generation of online revenues is growing fastest for films, followed by games. In addition, new forms of content, new content producers and new ways of manipulating and modifying ('meshing') digital content are emerging that are not tracked by publicly available data.

Value chains and business models – and associated revenue opportunities and incentives – have changed in the face of uncertain impacts on the supply of and access to creative works. Initially it was expected that content creators could largely 'disinter-mediate' intermediaries, potentially generating more profits from themselves. The instant migration from a restricted offline model to a more liberated online model with access to content 'everywhere, on every device and at ever time of day' was not foreseen. In the process, additional incentives for creators and the content industry to cultivate and finance creativity would see the light of day.

Developments since have proven experts of these early days wrong. The development of workable online content business models has been slower than expected. Ten years ago nobody imagined the complexity of putting these online distribution and business models together. Roadblocks have included technological issues, the legitimate fear of online piracy and – amongst others – the difficulty of agreement on adequate revenue sharing and business models.

Direct relations between content creators and consumers, and thus full disintermedia-tion, are still the exception rather than the norm (e.g., musicians offering music for free to obtain revenue from donations and film writers offering short or feature films on video-sharing platforms for sale). Instead, the role of intermediaries and aggregators for digital content seems to be growing. The notions that the costs of content production will drop to zero, that creators can do away with the content industry or that user-created content will supplant professional content are now also largely discarded. A co-existence of mutually enriching professional and amateur content now seems to be the more likely scenario.

The position of creators, rights holders and cultural industries in this new configura-tion has changed following changes in their expected revenues and the economic function of copyright. Transformed digital content values and distribution chains exist, with new important intermediaries,[10] online platforms and, potentially, hardware devices required to access content;[11] in fact, reintermediation rather than disintermediation is now taking place. It is currently unclear who is extracting most value from commercial digital content transactions and where the bargaining power lies: does it lie with the creators, the content industry (i.e., the content), infrastructure providers (i.e., the 'pipes'), online intermediar-ies and aggregators (e.g., online content store-fronts, search engines, social networks), or device manufacturers that are able to tie content to their particular device? Rights holders still exercise distribution and price control. Yet, while hard to demonstrate with available numbers and economic analysis, this control is diminished by new distribution models and certainly also by the interest in luring consumers to legal content offerings. The power to extract revenues from copyright is thus affected, and new intermediaries and device manufacturers start having significant clout in the content value and distribu-tion chain.

At the same, time we are witnessing the proliferation of new revenue models (Box 11.1), which potentially also impact the expected economic benefit from copyright; the control of creators in how content revenue is generated and shared is challenged. More

---

BOX 11.1   DIGITAL BROADBAND CONTENT REVENUE MODELS

1. Voluntary donations and contributions.
2. Digital content sales (pay-per-view, pay-per-track, pay-per-game etc.)
3. Subscription-based revenues.
4. Advertising-based revenues.
5. Selling goods and services (including virtual items) to the audience.
6. Selling of user data and customized market research.
7. Licensing content and technology to other providers.

Source: Author, based on OECD (2008).

---

information about new forms of content revenue distribution models would be helpful. It is increasingly known how Apple's App Store, for instance, pays the creators of smartphone applications. According to data released by Apple, of the roughly US$19 billion generated by the App Store in 2012, roughly 70 percent was paid to the software developers.[12] Similar breakdowns, however, are hard to obtain for other existing or novel digital content services.

Indeed, often the direct link between a consumer's payment and their access to a given work by an artist is severed, with uncertain outcomes for artists and the content industry's revenue structure. In many advertising-, donation- or subscription-based models consumers no longer purchase one particular creative work.[13] For example, online music subscription services that are available for a few dollars or euros per month deliver unlimited music across a wide range of musicians.

An unbundling of content that has only been sold in bundled form for the last three decades is also taking place. The fact that consumers can now purchase individual newspaper articles rather than a whole newspaper, selected scientific articles rather than a full journal subscription, or individual songs rather than a full album has had an impact on expected copyright-based and other revenues. This is not to say that the revenues of content creators, the content industry or others need be negatively affected. If the overall price of revenues increases, potentially original creators, both amateurs and professionals, stand to benefit. It is again an empirical question whether revenues for creators – and hence, in part, the financial incentive triggered by copyright – have increased or decreased. On the one hand, incentives for creation might increase as costs are lower. New revenue sources and mechanisms (e.g., micropayment) can be discovered, and niche artists and genres can reach a more receptive audience. On the other hand, the redistribution of bargaining power along the value chain and the rise of different business models might also bring into question the sustainability of creative supply in the future. In other words: is copyright still a guarantee of generating sufficient revenue for artists and the associated content industries in this new context?

At the moment, the scarce information available regarding online digital business models does not convincingly demonstrate that copyright holders definitely benefit from new digital content value chains and business models. In OECD (2005), the authors tried to assess the revenue implications for artists from pay-per-track and other new subscription schemes, showing that the profits that go to the creators might be lower, but generally concluding that the data situation is too unsatisfactory to produce a conclusive finding on this point. Press articles have also surfaced with more anecdotal but revealing insights that streaming services do not generate much income for musicians.[14]

Looking at indirect revenue streams via collective management, a clear-cut assessment of what the online future holds for creators' revenues is also difficult. The annual reports of the International Confederation of Authors and Composers Societies (CISAC) show that in 2011 only 2.2 percent of revenues generated globally by public performance were collected via digital sources and the underlying rights (CISAC, 2012). At the same time, digital rights are the second most important driver of public performance revenues after television and radio. Despite the migration from offline to online channels CISAC's global collections have continuously increased throughout the last decade.

Finally, one could have expected that technology will make the administration of copyrights (i.e., the identification of a rights holder, the clearing of rights, the redistribution of revenue, etc.) easier, more efficient and more transparent. This is because it is generally assumed that digital transactions make it much simpler to gather detailed records on content consumption and to pay out a corresponding, and fair, remuneration.

So far, however, the administration of copyrights has not yet been significantly affected by the digital revolution. As Gurry (2011, p. 2) put it, 'important pressures for the copyright system are trapped in a territorial cage, whereas economic and technological behavior burst out of that cage some time ago'. The costs involved in managing legitimate transactions of copyrighted material are continuing to pose entry barriers, in particular for the international development of new creators or creative works worldwide or for new Internet-based, borderless distribution platforms (Varian, 2010). The scarcity of reliable information on copyright status and licensing conditions remains (Lanteri, 2012, 2013). Finding out whether the direct or indirect (i.e., via collective rights management) remuneration of artists has been made more efficient or precise is a challenge. This holds true despite the improvements in data work by CMOs. The latter necessarily cover their collection revenue only, and hence are biased towards certain sectors and indirect revenue sources. Also, in many countries several CMOs exist and not all of their data are equally accessible, making the compilation of meaningful national or international databases impossible.

Changes to the technical and institutional copyright infrastructure might thus be needed to reinstate the financial function of copyright, which is to allow the generation of revenue in return for authorized consumption (Gurry, 2011).

The enforcement of copyrights, a necessary condition to ensure the incentive effect of copyright law, has also become significantly more challenging in the online context (ibid.). Many years have passed, and still the legal certainty about digital consumption on the Internet has not improved. Knowing what is legal and what is not remains challenging for consumers and courts alike (e.g., unauthorized streaming versus downloading, uploading of unauthorized material versus the downloading). If one introduces the country-specific and case-specific heterogeneity of the matter, things become even more difficult.[15] To simplify research of this area, in their studies economists often lump together things that should not be grouped in such a manner, for example, treating all activity or files on peer-to-peer networks as illegal.

Finally, in response to the opportunities offered by the digital environment and responding to some challenges generated by new models such as Creative Commons, open source licenses and open distribution models for publishing that build on copyright have emerged. Research now needs to be undertaken to assess the economics of these new models and their impacts on content access and creation.

11.4   WHAT HAS THE ECONOMIC LITERATURE PRODUCED SO FAR, AND WHAT DATA ISSUES REMAIN AS OBSTACLES?

The empirical literature on copyright is admittedly relatively nascent. Economists have thus far largely focused their empirical work on the economics of the patent system.

Indeed, even independent of the impacts of new technologies and models as described in section 11.2, the basic effects of copyright on sector outcomes remain largely untested. It has been hard for economists to assess the actual incentive effect of copyright in an offline context and its impacts on access and creative supply that could serve as a useful benchmark by which to assess the changed incentives and access costs in the digital environment.

As outlined in Towse (2011) and Handke (2011) as well as in Chapter 7 of this volume, all excellent reviews of the empirical work on copyright, the literature on copyright as an economic incentive and hence as a motivator for content creators is not particularly rich.[16] Little empirical evidence is available concerning the effect on economic incentives of the current or proposed duration of rights, with some quarters believing it is too long and others thinking it too short (Akerlof et al., 2002). While economists criticize the 'one-size-fits-all' aspect of copyright that does not reflect the differences between creative sectors, no concrete recommendations on more appropriate copyright length(s) or sector-specific variations of copyright terms have been proposed. A few economists have made some headway in estimating the earnings of artists from copyright, which is significant for answering questions about the importance of the incentives it offers to creators (Kretschmer, 2002; Watt, 2000, 2004). Yet, more work on the creators' remuneration is needed. Likewise, few attempts have been made to estimate the costs of copyright to users or final consumers in terms of higher prices or reduced accessibility. Studies on the transaction costs of searching and clearing the rights to protected materials and related entry barriers are scarce, as discussed in more detail below.

How then has the economic literature reacted to the role of copyright in an era of digitization and electronic networks? In a somewhat unfortunate turn of events, the majority of empirical economic studies since the advent of the Internet have focused on the effects of unauthorized downloading of creative works on the sales of the creative industries, with a particular focus on music and more recently films (OECD, 2005; Png, 2006; Liebowitz, 2007; Handke, 2010). In this strand of research the focus is almost exclusively on creative industry revenues and not on the individual creator or his or her ability to make a living, or on the actual production of creative works, the nurturing of new talent, or innovation in the process of creativity.

This new 'peer-to-peer download and copyright' economics literature has produced some tentative but ambiguous results and two camps of economists: those who assert that unauthorized file-sharing has substantially decreased music industry revenues and those who argue the opposite (for reviews see OECD, 2005; Fink et al., 2010; Handke,

2011; Towse, 2011). In terms of quantity, the largest body of work confirms the negative effect of unauthorized downloads or streaming on music sales (i.e., displacement is taking place). At the same time, the literature also shows that the effect is not a one-to-one replacement of unauthorized downloads for purchased songs; some downloads do not harm music industry revenues, and some indeed have a sampling and tasting effect. In other words, free access to music via unauthorized downloading creates follow-on music purchases or offsetting increases in demand for complementary income streams such as concerts (Oberholzer-Gee and Strumpf, 2009).

A significant number of methodological issues are also at stake, such as the difficulty in causally linking declining industry revenues to increased peer-to-peer network activity and determining whether lower music industry revenues due to falling CD sales are or are not made up for by increased concert revenues. At a more philosophical level it is difficult to establish whether decreased overall music industry revenues have negatively impacted the creative supply of music from composers, musicians, and other creators. Also, the overall effects of copyright piracy on the producers of creative works, employment in creative industries, as well as on consumers and welfare remain ambiguous.

Transposing what happens in the field of music to other creative sectors is also a stretch as the lessons learnt could be sector specific.[17] With technology changing swiftly the question is whether throwing darts at this moving target, that is, conducting research on it, is a worthwhile pursuit. More fundamentally, and stepping outside of the peer-to-peer literature, the effects of the new digital set-up on creative supply – and thus the long-term sustainability of this digital ecosystem – have hardly been assessed from a solid empirical point of view (Wunsch-Vincent, 2010a, 2010b). However, this knowledge gap needs to be closed to better inform policy-making.

Based on these observations, a large research task lies ahead of economists when it comes to assessing copyright law in the context of digitization and the Internet. What are the obstacles that need to be overcome to further this research agenda on copyright in the digital age? This chapter concludes by pointing out five main data challenges on our way to assessing the motivational/incentive function of copyright and the main costs and benefits relating to copyright in the digital age.[18]

First, reliable statistics are missing on the number of copyrighted works and hence the supply of creative works that is meant to be positively stimulated by copyright law remains unknown. As suggested earlier, no formalities are involved when obtaining copyright; the recognition of copyright ownership is automatic.[19] It is true that some countries can oblige or give procedural advantages to national creators who register their work,[20] yet, at the moment, the data available in a few jurisdictions are generally not used for economic analysis, since they are often not accessible in the right format or the data themselves might not be representative.

An alternative route to estimating the number of existing original works could be to obtain unit counts of the number of creative works produced in a country or in a given subsector. In reality, data on units of creative works produced (whether sold or not) are also hard to obtain. For instance, internationally, it is nearly impossible to identify the number of books or the number of songs written in a given country in a valid and internationally comparable fashion.[21]

This problem is compounded in the Internet age, where no central entity exists that could monitor and report the production of creative works. Indeed, statisticians and economists have been struggling with trying to assess the true extent of user-created content online (OECD, 2007). Using simple count data (e.g., the number of online videos uploaded on popular video platforms) is misleading. Amateur videos or uploads to online video platforms are not always original creative works; some videos are unauthorized copies of television series or other protected works. Likewise, amateurs create or remix content over various decentralized and sometimes overlapping online platforms, causing problems of double-counting uploads. Also, new genres of content emerge that are unaccounted for, and thus difficult to categorize and count (Bruegge, 2011; INSEAD and WIPO, 2012). Finally, data on the uptake and intensity of the use of streaming services, the number of works accessed and revenues generated are unavailable.

Second, the quality and 'value' of copyrighted works are hard to objectively assess, in particular when one moves beyond economic value for the content industry alone, for instance if one is required to assess the economic value for the creator or the artistic value for society at large. A Hollywood movie that cost several million US dollars to produce, a Czech movie shot on a shoestring budget, or a home-made video put on an online platform might generate similar copyright entitlements. Yet, the varying quality of these different films and their overall economic and societal values are hard to account for in regular unit counts. While professionally produced content might have more value on average, some online videos or amateur productions are dramatically more popular than most professionally made movies and can attract millions of views within days or weeks. A simple association of production costs to the value of the creative work in question is often misplaced; that is, in the world of art and creativity more expensive works are not automatically better.

Third, data are missing on the revenues generated on the basis of copyright and the respective distribution of these revenues between creators, the creative industries, and other intermediaries. Admittedly, private sector associations have made tremendous progress in accounting for sales revenues generated by particular content sectors. The International Federation of the Phonographic Industry (IFPI), for instance, has been making available detailed data on sales – and more recently online sales and subscription revenues.[22]

International organizations are measuring the economic contribution of the copyright-based industries, including their value-added and their contribution to international trade. WIPO's Creative Industries Division undertakes activities to better conceptualize and measure the creative industries, and measures their contribution to economic growth, trade and development based on the methodology outlined in the *2003 WIPO Guide on Surveying the Economic Contribution of the Copyright-Based Industries*.[23]

Obtaining a clear picture from these figures on who earns what (i.e., what the creator or performer, the creative industries, other intermediaries such as online music stores and online video platforms earn from a given copyrighted work), and hence deducing something on the incentive effect of copyright, is hard. Indeed, determining the revenue of artists is challenging, as some is based on contractual income negotiated with the content industry, some earnings are based on collectively negotiated contracts from CMOs, and some income is based on the exploitation of copyright (such as income from concerts, readings, and, to use legal terms, performing, mechanical and other rights). Artists today may prefer to give away their music for free on their social media page (in which case the official music revenue statistics would show zero income), while subsequently generating concert-based revenues, a new phenomenon documented by numerous articles in the trade press but for which no official data or studies are available.

Similarly, in the online context revenues are not generated from the sale of songs via music platforms alone. Watching a video or listening to a song on a streaming service, like YouTube or Spotify (be it based on a subscription payment or supported by advertising) will technically generate a stream of revenue that is hard to elucidate in the current data context (Lanteri, 2013). Online videos often do not generate direct revenues for their creator, and if they do, the money generated does not show in traditional content industry revenue statistics, but rather in data such as revenues reported by CMOs. Certain music subscription services pay the rights holders in advance (advance payment) before any music is streamed and consumed, part of which – in principle – reaches the artist.

Conducting research on the artist and industry split has been complex in the past, and determining the revenue splits between creators, various industries and distributors requires true detective work.[24] Each artist's or creator's contract is different, and individual cases gleaned from private contracts – be it for exploitation of the work online or offline or on all media – cannot be generalized. In the case of films or online multiplayer games, rights are owned across the board and payments are not associated with rewards for owning the copyright.

Importantly, more detailed information about the cost structure of different content industries and creators is required to assess the motivational and incentive effects of copyright on the revenue generated (Merrill and Raduchel, 2013). As outlined earlier, the costs of the creative sector can be high at times. Artists rely on the financial and organizational capacity of the content industry to leverage the risk of the sector. The high cost of content production and delivery is particularly timely with respect to the online distribution of content. While earlier assumptions were of a costless, immediate and free global distribution in the digital age, reality has shown that many new costs have emerged (e.g., costs related to digital rights management, online payments, revenue shares paid to online platforms, and so forth).

Interestingly, artists and the creative sector as such also have non-monetary incentives that have to be factored in. While one could see non-monetary motives as a competing incentive to copyright, they are indeed often linked: for example, when a creator foregoes remuneration for the viewing of their works or their particular creative contribution, they might rely on attribution, and thus moral rights to build their reputation, generate other revenue streams or achieve non-monetary rewards.

Fourth, and related to the point on costs, few credible data are available on the administrative and transaction costs related to copyright, and the ways in which the system facilitates or creates barriers. Arguably the transaction costs have to be set against the potential incentive effect of copyright across the economy, which is difficult. One would want to assess the relative costs and benefits of various arrangements for managing transaction costs (Merrill and Raduchel, 2013). Moreover, one should assess the existing and potential effect of new technologies on current licensing procedures and collective rights management institutions.

At the moment the data situation does not allow this easily. A few studies and policy reports have stressed the difficulty of securing rights across the board, and one study in the European context has even put a figure on it, namely that services available in several countries and that offer more than one million titles can face transaction costs of several hundred thousand euros, requiring significant human resources and time (KEA and Vrije Universiteit Brussel, 2012). Any assessment of the administrative effect also has to factor in the economic and other implications of the exceptions and limitations that copyright law foresees. Technically, the latter decreases the costs of copyright as an access barrier. It is precisely the function of exceptions and limitations to make works accessible for various purposes such as parody, education, and other functions.

Finally, data on the pricing and the consumption of creative works would be needed to assess the access constraints potentially imposed by copyrights. These data do not exist beyond broad industry revenue aggregates or have not yet been used in solid economic studies.[25]

11.5 CONCLUSION AND AVENUES FOR FURTHER RESEARCH

Copyright law establishes an important trade-off between the incentives for creators and creative industries, on the one hand, and the potential new access restrictions on the other. This chapter has assessed the baseline model of copyright economics against the current realities of the online context. As a first step, it described the basic copyright economics as encountered in standard textbook analysis, while trying to overcome simplifications or short-cuts that are often taken by the economic community. In the second step, the chapter asked how this baseline model can be transposed to an online setting. In other words, the author described how the above trade-offs change in an online environment. In doing so it identified the three major areas where change has taken place, potentially affecting the economics of copyright, namely (1) how content is created, (2) how it is accessed, and, (3) how copyrights are administered. Finally, in a third step the chapter identified what the economic literature on copyright, with and without digitization, has delivered so far. The statistical obstacles to better empirical research on the matter were also identified.

The discussion revealed that the additional economic work required and the statistical challenges to be overcome are formidable. Economists and policy-makers have a long journey ahead of them. The absence of data; the complex financial and legal linkages between composers, creators, performers, editors, and other sectors of the creative industries; new online intermediaries; and the way revenues are generated and split complicate the matter. That the various content sectors operate differently complicates the situation and questions the validity and comparability of results across sectors.

To conclude on a positive note, however, economists and policy-makers have become more focused on these shortcomings and are now actively working on overcoming them. On a national level, a number of parliamentary hearings, reviews, and committees have been set up to study the effects of digitization and the role of copyright in the digital age.[26] Many of these activities orient the work of economists in the right direction. At the level of academic and other economic research, positive developments are also on the way with the creation of new research centers and continued work by international organizations on the topic.[27] An important determinant of success will be how well the data-related obstacles discussed above can be overcome. These observations promise that progress will happen more swiftly even though the target will continue to move rapidly for the foreseeable future.

NOTES

* The authors would like to thank Arno Hold (World Trade Institute, University of Bern) for providing help with background research on an earlier version of this chapter, and Paolo Lanteri (Culture and Creative Industries Sector, World Intellectual Property Organization, WIPO) for invaluable legal assistance throughout the drafting process. Comments on earlier drafts from Dimiter Gantchev (WIPO), Hannu Wager (Intellectual Property Division of the World Trade Organization), Prof. Martin Kretschmer (CREATe – RCUK Centre for Copyright & New Business Models, University of Glasgow), Stephen A. Merrill (Science, Technology, and Economic Policy, The National Academies), and Verena Weber (Directorate for Science, Technology and Innovation, OECD) are gratefully acknowledged. All remaining errors are the responsibility of the author. The views expressed are personal and do not necessarily reflect those of WIPO or its member states.
1. I am grateful to my colleague Paolo Lanteri (WIPO) for this important point.
2. This point greatly depends on the circumstances in question. For instance, CMOs often have the obligation of non-discriminatory practice, that is, nobody can be prevented from using particular content; indeed, no direct authorization from the rights holder is required. But even in this case, digital exploitation is often not included in CMO contracts.
3. See European Commission (2012) and 'Management of copyright and related rights', accessed 25 July 2015 at http://ec.europa.eu/internal_market/copyright/management/index_en.htm for a detailed explanation of the problems in clearing rights for the online environment.
4. Many online video platforms make content available in one or two jurisdictions only, in particular in the United States; the same content is often not accessible from a European or Asian country. For instance, Pandora is available in the USA, but not in Europe. The European music streaming service Spotify, in turn, took years to be able to launch its service in the USA.
5. A deadweight loss is a cost to society in terms of welfare without an offsetting gain to anybody.
6. Article 5(2) of the Berne Convention provides for formality-free protection of creative works. That said, some countries can oblige or give preference to national creators who register their copyright works. See the discussion in section 11.4.
7. From an economist's perspective, there are several alternatives to a copyright: one strand of literature argues that in the absence of a copyright system, markets would simply adapt and resort to alternative business models, such as first-mover advantages (Boldrin and Levine, 2002), the joint sale of complements, creating product lines (what Varian, 2005 called 'versioning'), price discrimination among different groups of customers (Liebowitz, 1985) or network effects (i.e., where the benefits of a good increase when more consumers use it). Another strand of literature prefers alternative statutory interventions such as charging levies on copying technologies to award prices, stipends or direct subsidies to creators. However, all these alternatives have the disadvantage of relying at least partly on central control, whereas in a copyright system, the decision-making is decentralized and based on market mechanisms.
8. Section three of Wager's article discusses the balance between original creators and follow-on creators.
9. See OECD (2005) for a breakdown of costs in the music sector.
10. For example, digitization, digital rights management, hosting of content, content aggregation and distribution.
11. Often particular content is now tied to particular platforms or devices (i.e., a new form of vertical integration with games tied to certain consoles, music tied to certain online platforms and/or MP3 players, online news content tied to certain tablets, user-created content tied to certain sharing platforms, and so forth), and in the face of lacking (commercial) interoperability and 'lock-in' third parties or new entrants cannot compete.
12. Information released at the Apple Media Event on 22 October 2013.
13. As my colleague Hannu Wager points out, with respect to music this is the return to the past where – before the invention of 'long play' vinyl records – songs were purchased individually.
14. 'As music streaming grows, royalties slow to a trickle showing that streaming services generate hardly any income for musicians', *New York Times*, 28 January 2013.
15. See the discussion on the Global INET 2012 'Digital Content, Intellectual Property and Innovation' expert panel session, 24 April 2012, accessed 25 July 2015 at http://www.elon.edu/e-web/predictions/isoc_20th_2012/intellectual_property_innovation.xhtml.
16. Further excellent reviews are Png (2006), Watt (2000, 2004), Waldfogel (2011) and Kretschmer and Towse

(2013). The *Review of Economic Research on Copyright Issues*, the Society for Economic Research on Copyright Issues (SERCI) and the International Association of Cultural Economics have all devoted much effort in recent years to improving the economic literature in the field.

17. There has been uneven industry coverage, with a great deal of attention to music, moderate attention to scientific publishing and film, and much less attention to news and book publishing and software. Variations across industries, countries, and time are poorly understood. See the studies on digital content sectors on the 'OECD work on digital content' portal, accessed 25 July 2015 at www.oecd.org/sti/digital content. For similar calls on the need for sector-specific studies see Merrill and Raduchel (2013).

18. A similar exercise has recently been conducted in the US context. See Merrill and Raduchel (2013).

19. Article 5(2) of the Berne Convention provides for formality-free protection of creative works.

20. See WIPO (2011).

21. The UNESCO Institute for Statistics has, in recent years, aimed to improve cultural and related statistics, notably by developing a 'Framework for Cultural Statistics' in 2009. The different sectors treated are: Cultural and Natural Heritage; Performance and Celebration; Visual Arts and Crafts; Books and Press; Audio-Visual and Interactive Media; and Design and Creative Services. Clearly, these statistics relate to cultural outputs such as films. While coverage is improving, little data are available for recent years for a broad set of countries. This situation will surely improve through new surveys and activities of the UNESCO Institute for Statistics (on cinemas, library statistics, and broadcasts); see Deloumeaux (2013) and Wunsch-Vincent (2011).

22. See, for instance, the IFPI's 'Recording Industry in Numbers 2013' and its 'Digital Music Reports', and other statistics accessed 25 July 2015 at http://www.ifpi.com/content/section_statistics/index.html.

23. From the WIPO Project on Measuring the Economic Contribution of the Copyright-Based Industries and Relevant National Projects.

24. See again OECD (2005), which was based on painstaking attempts to get access to various artists' contracts to conduct a meaningful quantitative analysis.

25. Encouragingly, a few credible papers are now emerging that assess the linkage between copyright and the price of creative works. Yet the one that comes to mind relates to the eighteenth century rather than the twenty-first, and is hard to transpose to the contemporary context. See Moser et al. (2012).

26. See, for instance, the Hargreaves Review (2011). See also the last chapter in Merrill and Raduchel (2013), which sets out research priorities and data needs.

27. See, for example, the recent inauguration of the RCUK Centre for Copyright and New Business Models in the Creative Economy (CREATe) at the University of Edinburgh, accessed 25 July 2015 at http://www.create.ac.uk/. See also the continued empirical work of the OECD on the matter, accessed 25 July 2015 at www.oecd.org/sti/digitalcontent and the studies commissioned by the European Commission as well as the work of its Joint Research Centres on the matter, for instance on the dynamics of media and content industries, accessed 25 July 2015 at http://is.jrc.ec.europa.eu/pages/ISG/MCI/conference.html. The WIPO studies on copyright in the context of the Committee for IP and Development also make important contributions.

REFERENCES

Akerlof, G.A., K.J. Arrow and T. Bresnahan et al. (2002), *The Copyright Term Extension Act of 1998: An Economic Analysis*, Washington, DC: AEI-Brookings Joint Center for Regulatory Studies.

Boldrin, M. and D. Levine (2002), 'The case against intellectual property', *The American Economic Review: Papers and Proceedings*, **92** (2), 209–12.

Bruegge, C. (2011), 'Measuring digital local content', *OECD Digital Economy Papers No. 188*, Paris: Organisation for Economic Co-Operation and Development.

CISAC (2012), *On the Lookout for Growth, Authors' Royalties in 2011*, Paris: International Confederation of Societies of Authors and Composers (CISAC).

Deloumeaux, L. (2013), 'UNESCO cultural and creative trade data', Chapter 1 (Annex 1) in *The Global Innovation Index 2013, The Local Dynamics of Innovation*, Ithaca, NY, Paris and Geneva: Cornell, INSEAD and WIPO.

European Commission (2012), 'Impact assessment – accompanying the document proposal for a Directive of the European Parliament and of the Council on collective management of copyright and related rights and multi-territorial licensing of rights in musical works for online uses in the internal market', Commission Staff Working Document, COM (2012) 372-final.

Fink, C., K. Maskus and Q. Yi (2010), 'The economic effects of counterfeiting and piracy: A literature review', prepared for the WIPO Advisory Committee on Enforcement, 6th session, WIPO/ACE/6/7, Geneva.

Gurry, F. (2011), 'The future of copyright', speech at the Blue Sky Conference: Future Directions in Copyright Law, Queensland University of Technology, Sydney, 25 February, 2011, accessed 25 July 2015 at http://www. wipo.int/about-wipo/en/dgo/speeches/dg_blueskyconf_11.html.

Handke, C. (2010), *The Economics of Copyright and Digitisation, Report for the Strategic Advisory Board for Intellectual Property Policy (SABIP) and the Intellectual Property Office*, London: UK Intellectual Property Office, accessed 25 July 2015 at http://webarchive.nationalarchives.gov.uk/20140603093549/http://www.ipo. gov.uk/ipresearch-economics-201005.pdf.

Handke, C. (2011), *Economic Effects of Copyright – The Empirical Evidence So Far*, report for the National Academy of Sciences, Washington, DC: NAS.

Hargreaves, I. (2011), *Digital Opportunity – A Review of Intellectual Property and Growth*, accessed 25 July 2015 at https://www.gov.uk/government/uploads/system/uploads/attachment_data/file/32563/ipreview-final report.pdf.

INSEAD and WIPO (2012), 'Online creativity in the Global Innovation Index 2012', Chapter 1 (Annex 1, Box 2) in *The Global Innovation Index 2012*, Paris and Geneva: INSEAD and WIPO.

KEA and Vrije Universiteit Brussel (2012), *Licensing Music Works and Transaction Costs in Europe*, accessed 25 July 2015 at http://www.keanet.eu/docs/music%20licensing%20and%20transaction%20costs%20-%20full. pdf.

Kretschmer, M. (2002), 'Copyright societies do not administer individual rights: The incoherence of institutional traditions in Germany and the UK', in R. Towse (ed.), *Copyright in the Cultural Industries*, Cheltenham, UK: Edward Elgar Publishing, pp. 140–63.

Kretschmer, M. and R. Towse (eds) (2013), *What Constitutes Evidence for Copyright Policy? Digital Proceedings of the ESRC Symposium*, accessed 25 July 2015 at www.copyrightevidence.org/create/ esrc-evidence-symposium/.

Landes, W.M. (2002), 'Copyright', in R. Towse (ed.), *The Handbook of Cultural Economics*, Cheltenham, UK and Northampton, MA, USA: Edward Elgar Publishing.

Landes, W.M. and R.A. Posner (1989), 'An economic analysis of copyright law', *The Journal of Legal Studies*, **18** (2), 325–63.

Lanteri, P. (2012), 'Asset management in the digital age: Beyond copyright (as we know it)', presentation on behalf of WIPO at the Dynamics of the Media and Content Industries international conference, Brussels, 26 October, accessed 25 July 2015 at http://is.jrc.ec.europa.eu/pages/ISG/MCI/documents/ Lanteri.pdf.

Lanteri, P. (2013), 'A digital agenda in search of evidence: Issues and trends', presentation on behalf of WIPO at the EuroCPR Conference, 22 March, Brussels.

Liebowitz, S.J. (1985), 'Copying and indirect appropriability: Photocopying of journals', *Journal of Political Economy*, **93** (5), 945–57.

Liebowitz, S.J. (2007), 'How reliable is the Oberholzer-Gee and Strumpf paper on file-sharing?', accessed 25 July 2015 at http://ssrn.com/abstract=1014399.

Merrill, S.A. and W.J. Raduchel (2013), *Copyright in the Digital Era: Building Evidence for Policy*, Committee on the Impact of Copyright Policy on Innovation in the Digital Era, Washington DC: National Research Council.

Moser, P., M. Macgarvie and X. Li (2012), 'Dead poet's property – The copyright act of 1814 and the price of literature in the romantic period', presented at the WIPO Seminar Series on the Economics of Intellectual Property, 17 December, accessed 25 July 2015 at http://www.wipo.int/edocs/mdocs/mdocs/en/wipo_ip_econ_ ge_5_12/wipo_ip_econ_ge_5_12_ref_zmoser.pdf.

Oberholzer-Gee, F. and K. Strumpf (2009), 'File-sharing and copyright', in J. Lerner and S. Stern (eds), *Innovation Policy and the Economy, Volume 10*, Cambridge, MA: NBER, pp. 19–55, accessed 25 July 2015 at http://www.nber.org/chapters/c11764.

OECD (2005), *Digital Broadband Content: Music*, Working Party on the Information Economy report, Paris: Organisation for Economic Co-operation and Development, accessed 25 July 2015 at http://www.oecd.org/ sti/ieconomy/34995041.pdf.

OECD (2007), *Participative Web and User-Created Content: Web 2.0, Wikis and Social Networking*, Paris: Organisation for Economic Co-operation and Development.

OECD (2008), 'Digital content in transition', Chapter 5 in *OECD Information Technology Outlook 2008*, Paris: Organisation for Economic Co-operation and Development.

OECD (2010), 'The Internet economy in the post-crisis era and recovery', Chapter 4 in *OECD Information Technology Outlook 2010*, Paris: Organisation for Economic Co-operation and Development.

OECD (2012), *Innovating for Economic Growth and Sustainability: Review of the Areas of Digital Content and Green ICTs*, Paris: Organisation for Economic Co-operation and Development.

Plant, A. (1934), 'The economic aspects of copyright in books', *Economica*, **1** (2), 167–95.

Png, I. (2006), 'Copyright: A plea for empirical research', *Review of Economic Research on Copyright Issues*, **3** (2), 3–13.

Towse, R. (2011), 'What we know, what we don't know and what policy-makers would like us to know about the economics of copyright', *Review of Economic Research on Copyright Issues*, **8** (2), 101–20.

Varian, H.R. (2005), 'Copying and copyright', *The Journal of Economic Perspectives*, **19** (2), 121–38.

Varian, H.R. (2010), 'Transactions costs and copyright', *WIPO Seminar Series on the Economics of Intellectual Property*, September, accessed 25 July 2015 at.

Wager, H. (2008), 'Copyright and the promotion of cultural diversity', in H. Schneider and P. van den Bossche (eds), *Protection of Cultural Diversity from an International and European Perspective*, Antwerp: Intersentia, pp. 193–218.

Waldfogel, J. (2011), 'The debate on copyright: What have we learned from empirical evidence?', draft for discussion, *Dialogue on Scenarios for Global Copyright Reform and Public Interest IP Agenda*.

Watt, R. (2000), *Copyright and Economic Theory: Friends or Foes?* Cheltenham, UK and Northampton, MA, USA: Edward Elgar Publishing.

Watt, R. (2004), 'The past and the future of the economics of copyright', *Review of Economic Research on Copyright Issues*, **1** (1), 151–71.

WIPO (2003), 'The economic fundamentals of copyright', Chapter 3 in WIPO (ed.), *Guide on Surveying the Economic Contribution of the Copyright-based Industries*, Geneva: World Intellectual Property Organization, pp. 18–22, accessed 25 July 2015 at http://www.wipo.int/freepublications/en/copyright/893/wipo_pub_893.pdf.

WIPO (2004), 'Fields of intellectual property protection', Chapter 2 in WIPO (ed.), *WIPO Intellectual Property Handbook: Policy, Law and Use*, Geneva: World Intellectual Property Organization, pp. 17–156.

WIPO (2011), 'WIPO summary of the responses to the questionnaire for survey on copyright registration and deposit systems', Thematic Project on Intellectual Property and the Public Domain, WIPO Committee on Development and Intellectual Property (CDIP) (CDIP/4/3), Geneva: World Intellectual Property Organization, accessed 25 July 2015 at http://www.wipo.int/export/sites/www/copyright/en/registration/pdf/registration_summary_responses.pdf.

Wunsch-Vincent, S. (2010a), 'Testimony to the German National Parliament on the evolution of copyright in the digital society', *Enquete-Kommission Internet und Digitale Gesellschaft*, 29 November 2010, Berlin: Deutscher Bundestag, available at http://gruen-digital.de/wp-content/uploads/2010/10/A-Drs.-17_24_009_G-Stellungnahme-Dr.-Wunsch-Vincent.pdfhttp://www.bundestag.de/internetenquete/dokumentation/Sitzungen/20101129/A-Drs_17_24_009_G-_Stellungnahme_Dr__Wunsch-Vincent.pdf.

Wunsch-Vincent, S. (2010b), 'Copyright and competition: An evolving relationship', comments at the Facilitating Access to Culture in the Digital Age – WIPO Global Meeting on Emerging Copyright Licensing Modalities, 4–5 November, accessed 25 July 2015 at http://www.wipo.in t/edocs/mdocs/copyright/en/wipo_cr_lic_ge_10/wipo_cr_lic_ge_10_ref09_wunsch_vincent.pdf.

Wunsch-Vincent, S. (2011), 'Accounting for creativity in innovation: What we should be measuring and related difficulties', Chapter 6 in S. Dutta (ed.), *The Global Innovation Index 2011 – Accelerating Growth and Development*, Paris: INSEAD, pp. 107–13, accessed 25 July 2015 at http://www.globalinnovationindex.org/userfiles/file/gii-2011_report.pdf.

12. The economics of privacy, data protection and surveillance*

Ian Brown

12.1 INTRODUCTION

In his pioneering research, political scientist Alan Westin defined privacy as 'the claim of individuals, groups, or institutions to determine for themselves when, how and to what extent information about them is communicated to others' (1967, p. 7). Institutional privacy is usually now discussed as part of commercial confidentiality, while a broader concept of individual privacy is often used in public debate, taking in other concepts such as autonomy and emotional release. But Westin's information-focused definition is particularly appropriate for individuals in the information economies that have developed since the late twentieth century. It is also the focus of the 'data protection' laws and regulations that have emerged globally since their development in Europe during the 1970s.

Economists have investigated a range of questions regarding individual and business decisions related to the use of personal information, as well as the possible contours and effects of privacy regulation. This has included analyses of the incentives that motivate individuals to disclose personal information in different situations, and firms to use that information to create personalized marketing and products. Both parties can suffer harm if this personal data is abused, leading to pressure for regulatory requirements such as disclosure and liability for security breaches, transparency about data use, and baseline security protections.

More recently, behavioral economists have tried to understand the factors underlying the 'privacy paradox' – that individuals commonly claim to be concerned about privacy, but behave in ways that seemingly contradict that claim (Spiekermann et al., 2001). Individual privacy decision-making seems to be particularly susceptible to some of the cognitive biases identified by Daniel Kahneman, Amos Tversky and others, again leading to pressure for regulation to help individuals protect their own long-term interests.

This chapter first describes the standard economic analysis of privacy, data protection and surveillance, looking at the costs and benefits to different parties and the incentives each therefore has, as well as the aggregate social welfare impacts of their decisions. It then considers the market failures that can lead to non-optimal outcomes, including information asymmetries, negative externalities, and cognitive biases of individual decision-makers. Finally, it analyzes the economic impact of various regulatory options for correcting these market failures, an important consideration given that most advanced and many emerging economies now have extensive systems of regulation in this area.

12.2　THE COSTS AND BENEFITS OF PRIVACY

The standard economic analysis of privacy looks at its costs and benefits to different parties in a transaction, and their resulting incentives. Generally, consumers want producers to know which products and services they are interested in – to reduce their own search costs – and producers have an incentive to provide this information. However, consumers do *not* want producers to know how much they are willing to pay. Otherwise, the producer's interest would be to price discriminate – to charge a price as close as possible to the amount each buyer is willing to pay (Varian, 1997).

Producers might also use wish to use knowledge of other consumer characteristics to charge higher prices – for example, a health insurer who wishes to charge more to smokers. While a smoker has an incentive to hide this information, a non-smoker has an incentive to reveal it and receive a lower price. The seller is therefore likely to structure the transaction so that the information is disclosed, such as through a discounted price for non-smokers (ibid.).

The growth of e-commerce has made it much easier for sellers to customize their offers, including price, to each buyer based on their revealed characteristics and behavior (Odlyzko, 2003). However, buyers are still able to use technical tools (such as cookie blockers) to conceal previous interactions from sellers and reduce the potential for price discrimination. Sellers therefore need to provide buyers with an incentive to reveal their identities – especially those with a higher willingness to pay. This explains the profusion of 'enhanced' services to regular customers, such as site personalization (including recommendations and saved addresses and payment information) and discount vouchers (common in loyalty clubs) (Acquisti and Varian, 2005).

Curtis R. Taylor (2004) demonstrated that when individuals are aware that details of purchasing behavior at one firm may be sold to other companies, affecting offered prices, this will undermine the market for customer information and increase the price elasticity of demand at the first firm. Under this condition, firms will prefer a regime preventing the sale or transfer of customer information.

Individuals can suffer tangible and intangible indirect costs if their personal data is misused. They may suffer from identity fraud, which can be damaging to their future ability to get credit as well as often taking significant time and expense to put right. If they are notified of data loss, individuals have to expend cognitive resources assessing risk and deciding on a course of action, as well as worrying about negative outcomes. Individuals may also feel shame at having private details of their lives exposed, and suffer stigma and discrimination as a result (Romanosky and Acquisti, 2009).

Organizations that lose personal data are likely to receive significant negative publicity and may be fined by regulators or lose future sales (ibid.) – although security breaches do not appear to have a long-run impact on companies' market value (Acquisti et al., 2006). In a survey of businesses across five industrialized countries, the Ponemon Institute (2010, pp. 3–7) estimated the average cost of a data breach incident to be $3.44 million, taking into account costs of detection and escalation, customer notification, incident response, and lost business.

As well as incurring costs if data is misused, consumers can also suffer from invasive unsolicited advertising communications. Varian (1997) characterized protection from junk letters, phone calls and e-mail as the 'right not to be annoyed'. Varian et al. (2004)

used US Federal Trade Commission (FTC) figures to suggest that even at 10 cents of annoyance per telemarketing call, US residents were suffering $3.6 billion per year of annoyance before the FTC introduced its 'do-not-call' opt-in list.

Many online services are provided free to consumers and financed through advertising revenues. Ads are commonly customized using 'behavioral targeting' systems that profile users based on their search and browsing history, in the latter case using 'third-party cookies' from advertising companies stored in their web browser software. More targeted ads can reduce consumer search costs, as well as spending wasted on showing ads to uninterested individuals.

Behavioral targeting can increase the (extremely small) likelihood that consumers will click on ads, and hence ad revenues, but is unpopular with users; one representative survey found that 66 percent of adult Americans did not want to receive tailored ads, and 73–86 percent rejected common tracking practices (Turow et al., 2009). This has led to an arms race where browser companies introduce new features to restrict tracking (such as Apple and Mozilla's default blocking of third-party cookies in their browsers) while advertising companies develop new technologies to track users (such as Flash and Silverlight cookies and device fingerprinting) (Hoofnagle et al., 2012). Tucker (2012) suggests that a better strategy is to give users more control over the use of their personal data in ad targeting, which in a natural experiment was found to double the likelihood of users clicking on targeted ads.

Law enforcement and intelligence agencies are intensive users of surveillance technologies and data gathered by third parties, especially as the technologies to perform such surveillance become ever cheaper (Brown and Korff, 2004). Much online interaction takes place in social 'spaces' such as mailing lists and social media; Danezis and Wittneben (2006) showed that low levels of surveillance can reveal information about large numbers of members of such spaces – in the network of political activists they studied, surveillance of the best-connected 8 percent of the network revealed the full network information. Even limited revelation of user 'friend lists' in social networks allows the approximation of degree and centrality of nodes, computation of small dominating sets and short paths between users, and detection of community structure (Bonneau et al., 2009). Also, personal characteristics can be revealed in many cases through these networks, due to homophily between family members, friends and colleagues (Xu et al., 2008). At the same time, Nagaraja (2008) showed that covert communities could avoid detection with a small investment in decentralized counter-surveillance techniques, while Danezis and Wittneben (2006) found that reliable detection of small, disconnected groups requires close to full-population surveillance.

While these results are also relevant to private sector actors, government surveillance is principally controlled through legal rather than economic mechanisms, and so is not considered further here.

12.2.1 Social Welfare Considerations

Whether or not certain individuals have a preference for privacy, what are the social impacts of controls on the flow of personal information? Posner (1981, p. 406) equated privacy to 'fraud in "selling" oneself', since there is evidence that 'people are rational even in non-market transactions such as marriage' and 'even in regard to such apparently emotional factors as race and sex'. Since disclosure of personal data increases the information available in the market, Posner argues that by definition this will increase the efficiency of resource allocation and hence maximize wealth. Training a healthy employee, for example, is a better investment for an employer; health privacy rules stop this discrimination. Preventing the revelation of individual ill health reduces the incentives for investment in increased productivity (Hermalin and Katz, 2006). Posner acknowledges the discriminatory impact increased information flows may have on individuals, but suggests that privacy merely shifts inequalities from one small group to another.

Hermalin and Katz (2006) describe three reasons why a more transparent society of better-informed parties transacting with each other is not necessarily wealth maximizing. First, privacy protection can enable insurance products – such as against catastrophic illness – that would be impossible if insurers could require purchasers to provide information, such as test results, that can at least partially predict the insured outcome. Welfare is increased by privacy rules that prevent socially wasteful testing and reduce the average risk borne by risk-averse individuals. Second, markets may not be able to adjust efficiently to additional information in the presence of price rigidities. Third, efficiency gains due to the availability of full information do not necessarily imply gains from partial information.

Non-economists have also criticized Posner's approach as utilitarian, ignoring other key social values, particularly equality, which are incommensurate with and cannot be traded against efficiency (Dworkin, 1980; Gandy, 2010). In most legal systems privacy is a fundamental right, and underpins other fundamental rights such as freedom of expression and association. There is an extremely broad legal and philosophy literature on this subject – some good starting points are Westin (1967), Solove (2008), Nissenbaum (2010) and Korff and Brown (2010).

12.3   MARKET FAILURES AND OTHER JUSTIFICATIONS FOR REGULATION

The European Union has had an extensive data protection regulatory framework since 1995, and has encouraged similar regulatory activity in nearly 50 non-EU countries. The USA has taken a more laissez-faire approach in the private sector, although the Obama administration launched a privacy 'Bill of Rights' in 2012 for consumers, and has encouraged the development of international privacy standards at the Asia-Pacific Economic Cooperation (APEC) intergovernmental group (Greenleaf, 2013). But beyond enforcing contracts and prosecuting fraud, why should regulators get involved in market transactions between willing buyers and sellers of personal information?

Economists recognize three main types of market failure that justify limited government intervention: negative externalities, asymmetric information, and anticompetitive market structures. A negative externality occurs when an actor takes an economic decision that imposes costs on a third party, such as the decision of a power station to dump polluted waste water in a local river. Since the actor suffers no negative consequences in the absence of regulation, they have a strong incentive to take such actions. The resale of personal data for marketing purposes is another example of such an action, since it imposes the cost of future invasive advertising on the data subject without compensation.

This is a strong argument for restricting third-party transactions in personal data to those authorized by the original consumer (Varian, 1997). More subtly, an individual that discloses information about themselves is also providing information about other individuals like them, which makes it harder for those individuals to mask their private characteristics (Moskowitz and Taylor, 2012).

The parties in a transaction often have asymmetric levels of information. In the case of privacy, consumers have limited knowledge of how their personal information will be used by producers. This is especially true of technology-mediated transactions, where personal data can be gathered ubiquitously and invisibly (Acquisti, 2004) in a way that few users – even young 'digital natives' – fully understand (Palfrey and Gasser, 2008, p. 285). For example, Debatin et al. (2009, p. 100) found in an online survey of students that while a majority reported they understood Facebook's privacy settings, this understanding was skewed.

To reduce information asymmetry, regulators commonly require companies to disclose how they will use personal information. Tsai et al. (2011) found some evidence that accessible privacy policies encourage consumers to purchase from online retailers with better privacy protection, and that some consumers are willing to pay a premium to buy goods from more privacy-protective websites.

In general, however, privacy policies are usually long and complex legalistic documents that few consumers read and even fewer understand. They are usually subject to change at any moment, especially if the business ownership is transferred (Greenstadt and Smith, 2005). Verification and enforcement is difficult, costly and has an unstable market equilibrium – when all firms respect privacy, no consumers will test those promises, encouraging firms to disregard their policies, which in turn encourages consumers to start testing policies and firms to respect privacy, ad infinitum (Vila et al., 2003). Finally, privacy is usually a secondary factor in an individual's decision to buy a product – there may be no good privacy-protecting alternative. If consumers have little reason to know about or believe in good privacy practices, no firm has an incentive to follow them (Greenstadt and Smith, 2005).

One widely used mechanism to improve consumer confidence in firms' privacy practices is the award of 'privacy seals' after an independent audit. However, these schemes often suffer from the problem of capture. If firms conducting audits earn income from the award of seals, they have an incentive to make them easy to obtain. The most popular scheme, TRUSTe, has been criticized for giving a seal to any firm that adhered to a stated privacy policy, however invasive that policy might be (ibid.). Edelman (2006) found that other 'trust' authorities issued seals without any substantial checks on the trustworthiness of recipients. This had the perverse effect that the sites seeking and obtaining seals were less trustworthy than those that did not.

Many early users of new social network sites are less concerned about privacy; the more privacy-concerned individuals join later in order to share information with their friends (Bonneau and Preibusch, 2009). Users that have invested a great deal of time in building profiles on one site will be reluctant to switch to a new site unless they can easily move their existing profile. There will therefore be limited competitive pressure for improved privacy practices in markets dominated by a small number of providers with high switching costs (Brown and Marsden, 2008).

Network effects tend to further encourage market concentration in communication markets: the value of such services increase with a growing customer base, since each new user increases the number of reachable users for all existing customers. Individuals want to be where their friends are, and are unlikely to leave popular sites such as Facebook unless all of their friends coordinate a move to another social networking site (ibid.).

12.3.1 Cognitive Biases

A broad range of behavioral economics research has found that individuals often do not behave in the calculating, rational manner assumed by classical economics. They do not have an unlimited amount of time and mental energy to carefully calculate the precise costs and benefits of every decision; they sometimes lack self-control and opt for immediate rather than delayed gratification; and they are often reluctant to overcome inertia, even when it would be to their benefit (Acquisti, 2004).

The risks that arise from disclosure of personal information are often highly probabilistic and difficult to calculate. Loss of data might lead to identity fraud, which can in turn result in the refusal of a small loan, a large mortgage, or a university place or job. Humans have finite cognitive resources; this 'bounded rationality' means that individuals can rarely obtain, remember and think through all of the information relevant to a privacy decision. Instead they rely on simplified mental models, approximate strategies and heuristics that will not have perfectly rational outcomes (Acquisti, 2002). For example, Acquisti and Grossklags asked respondents to a survey (all of whom were current or former university students) which parties had access to credit card details they had provided in an online purchase: 34.5 percent of survey respondents answered that only the merchant had access, while only 21.9 percent included 'my credit card company or bank', and just 19.3 percent answered 'hackers or distributors of spyware' (Acquisti and Grossklags, 2005, p. 31).

Individuals may only discover the payoffs of privacy protection or intrusion through infrequent experience (Acquisti, 2004). They are generally bad at judging cumulative risk, which is critical since personal data persists over time and total privacy risk is greater than the sum of its parts – a greater quantity of data makes it easier to identify the individual they refer to (ibid.). They also suffer from optimism bias, incorrectly estimating their own risks to be lower than those of other individuals under similar conditions (Acquisti, 2002).

Against these highly uncertain, subjective costs, individuals often receive some immediate benefit from information disclosure – sharing information with friends on a social network site, personalization of websites with recommendations and saved payment and delivery details, or discounts and coupons from loyalty schemes. Adults as well as children frequently make decisions that have an immediate benefit outweighed by longer-term costs, such as smoking or putting off a task that will take greater effort in future (Acquisti, 2004). This includes avoiding taking an action – such as opting out of a marketing program or changing default privacy settings (Edwards and Brown, 2009) – that has an immediate cost but only longer-term benefits.

Information disclosure behavior is highly situational, and can be strongly affected by the salience of privacy and other contextual factors such as anonymity and trust in the recipient. John et al. (2011) asked students a range of questions in a survey, with answers that could have significant consequences in a university setting – such as whether the student had cheated in an exam. Those who had been given an explicit assurance of con-fidentiality, thereby foregrounding privacy issues, were much *less* likely to admit cheating – 8 percent rather than 35.4 percent of participants. In a second experiment participants were asked more and less intrusive questions that they had to answer either explicitly or indirectly. Participants were 1.48 times more likely to admit intrusive behaviors when asked indirectly rather than explicitly.

Individuals sometimes need help to act in their own longer-term best interests (Thaler and Sunstein, 2008). They might wish to protect their privacy, but have difficulty in making the short-term decisions required to do so (Acquisti and Grossklags, 2003).

12.4   THE ECONOMIC IMPACT OF REGULATION

Given the various justifications for regulation described above, a key question is the eco-nomic impact of various forms of intervention. The most-studied interventions are creat-ing markets in personal information; requiring disclosure of the uses of data and security breaches; liability for data abuses; and requirements for organizational and technical baseline standards for privacy protection. The impact of privacy regulation on Internet innovation has been the subject of much debate and lobbying.

12.4.1   Markets in Privacy

If individuals 'owned' or were given property rights over data about them, they could choose to restrict its use or sell access. Given that different individuals and organizations have different preferences for the use of personal information and protection of indi-vidual solitude, property rights in privacy requiring negotiation between parties is a way to synchronize preferences and maximize overall welfare. However, this will only work with low transaction costs – if the parties to the transaction can be easily identified, and can negotiate, carry out and enforce an agreement without costs in time, attention and legal fees that outweigh the benefits of this flexibility. The legal environment and industry structure must support the transactions, and the classic market failures of asymmetric information and negative externalities must also be dealt with. An example of such a solution would be telephones that could block incoming marketing calls unless the caller agreed to pay a certain price, which could vary according to the receiver's willingness to be disturbed at different times of the day (Noam, 1996).

Noam (1996) suggests that a property-based approach is likely to fail. Second parties have very strong incentives to sell on personal data, since in doing so its value is hardly diminished to them. Privacy therefore would be extremely expensive to the data subject. Nor does this approach answer questions about the bundling of privacy with other serv-ices. Can data collected for purposes such as delivery of goods then be sold, with the consent of the purchaser? If so, and individuals have limited ability to refuse consent due to lack of competition, then much of their personal data is likely to be available to inter-ested parties without any need to purchase it directly from the data subject (Greenstadt and Smith, 2005). Hermalin and Katz (2006) further suggest that such an approach will lead to inefficient outcomes.

The concentrated industry structures commonly found in the communications and information industries hinder the efficiency of market approaches, since they reduce the bargaining power of consumers. Monopolists can extract almost the full value of privacy to their customers. This is particularly true of monopoly government services – where else can someone obtain a passport or driver's license? Market approaches are also of limited utility for managing employer–employee monitoring, since most employees have limited mobility and job choice is limited (Noam, 1996).

Because individuals have heterogeneous preferences for privacy, firms charging positive prices for the same product have an incentive to differentiate themselves from their competitors using privacy policies and thereby occupy a profitable niche, rather than face greater price competition for a consumer with more average privacy concerns. Conversely, when offering a product or service at no charge – common for advertising-supported websites – firms would be expected to cluster around the average consumer's preferences to maximize demand. Preibusch and Bonneau (2012) found evidence across five industry sectors to support these predictions: camera and DVD retailers, social networking sites, search engines, and blog hosts. In these sectors, websites facing little competition collected significantly more personal details from users.

12.4.2   Initial Allocation of Rights

If economic privacy rights are created, to which parties should they be initially allocated – the data subject, or organizations that wish to contact or profile that individual? Coase suggested that with low transaction costs, the same outcome would result even when parties' preferences differ – the only difference being in the resulting distribution of wealth. Therefore the most efficient solution is to distribute rights so as to minimize the cost of resolving the conflict (1960).

However, behavioral economists suggest an additional factor. Individuals generally value their own property at around twice the cost of acquiring the same property (the 'endowment effect'). Whether a data subject therefore 'owns' his or her data, or has to pay a data controller for it to be protected, could therefore result in a significantly different evaluation and outcome (Grossklags and Acquisti, 2007).

Bouckaert and Degryse (2006) modeled three common privacy regulations: that consumers should remain anonymous; that consumers are required to opt out of further data processing; or that personal data can only be processed with explicit consent from the data subject. The latter two conditions equate to initial allocation of rights to the consumer or the data controller. Bouckaert and Degryse found that these regulations affected firms' pricing strategy and market entry decisions, and that opt-out was most efficient, followed by anonymity and finally an explicit consent requirement.

12.4.3   Disclosure, Liability and Baseline Protections

Although new technology can reduce transaction costs in markets for personal information and attention, the other problems described above mean that this has not been a popular regulatory strategy. Much more common are three approaches that target the negative externalities and information asymmetry in privacy transactions. Mandatory information disclosure – of privacy practices and breaches – improves the informational position of the consumer, allowing him or her to make better-informed decisions about disclosing their personal data. Ex post liability allows consumers to claim damages from companies that have caused them harm by not adequately protecting their data. Ex ante regulation imposes basic standards of care for the processing of personal data, reducing the probability that it will be misused.

An ex post liability regime gives individuals harmed by misuse of their personal data a right of action against data controllers. This should force such organizations to take into account third-party costs potentially imposed by their decisions regarding personal data, thereby internalizing this negative externality. It also compensates individuals for losses. Liability provides an incentive for organizations to find efficient and effective mechanisms to protect data.

However, while economists recognize potential or probabilistic harms, courts generally do not. They are unlikely to award damages for an increased probability of experiencing invasive advertising or being subject to identity fraud, or suffering a decrease in the value of widely distributed personal data. It is also difficult for an individual to prove the origin of misused data, if it is in the possession of multiple organizations, or to retrieve damages for losses suffered long after a data breach has occurred (Romanosky and Acquisti, 2009).

The costs of taking legal action are often high. Privacy breaches commonly result in small damages suffered by a large number of individuals – suggesting that a right of collective action would be required. Liability is only efficient if consumers always succeed in winning damages for the full amount of harm caused by firms (ibid.).

Ex ante safety regulation imposes certain baseline security and privacy protection requirements on data controllers. This may be required if the probability of successful liability action against a firm is extremely low. As well as probabilistic harms, Kolstad et al. (1990) explain that this can include potentially serious new harms whose likely victims and consequences are unclear, or harm so small it is not recognized by individuals but still has a high aggregate impact across a large group. These are all true of privacy harms such as identity fraud. Monitoring security measure implementation can also be much easier than measuring privacy harms ex post (Romanosky and Acquisti, 2009).

Ex ante regulation can impose significant costs. The safety standards might not be relevant to a particular action, but compliance is still required. If standards are specified in detail, data controllers have little incentive to seek out the most efficient mechanisms to reduce harm. Regulators may not have the necessary information to set appropriate standards (ibid.) – especially in fast-moving information industries, where incentives for self-regulation may better engage industry expertise in setting standards (Rubinstein, 2011).

Rules mandating disclosure of the uses and protections afforded to personal data and incidents of data misuse are a third option. The aim of this type of rules is to reduce the information asymmetry between data subjects and controllers. They allow individuals to choose whether to disclose personal data to specific organizations in light of their practices, and to take remedial action if their data is lost.

The potential damage to their reputations caused by disclosure of data loss gives organizations an incentive to invest in protective systems and processes. In a survey of firms across the USA, UK, France, Germany and Australia, the Ponemon Institute (2010, p. 11) found that data breach incidents led to abnormal consumer churn rates between 3.4 and 4.5 percent. One survey found that California's security breach disclosure laws provided corporate Chief Security Officers with a justification for improving access controls, audit measures and the use of encryption, and improved security awareness generally within companies (Samuelson Law, Technology and Public Policy Clinic, 2007).

An FTC-sponsored survey found evidence that consumers that discovered incidents of identity fraud within six months suffered significantly less loss of time and money as a result (Synovate, 2007). Information disclosure reduces social harm if consumers take action to reduce their own losses. Disclosure is efficient if firms bear all consumer harm (Romanosky and Acquisti, 2009).

Of course, information disclosure rules face all of the challenges to perfectly rational consumer behavior identified by behavioral economists. Consumers may not have the time, interest or legal knowledge to understand all of a company's privacy policies and breach disclosures, or be able to use that to carefully compute the risk of disclosing a specific item of information. They will incur transaction costs in finding out more information about a breach, and acting to cancel credit cards or fraudulent transactions. By moving to a competitor, they are inevitably disclosing the information at risk to another party. There is also a concern among regulators that customers could quickly ignore a torrent of breach notifications (ibid.).

Using FTC panel data from 2002 to 2009, Romanosky et al. (2011) found that security breach disclosure laws in the USA reduced identity fraud losses on average by 6.1 percent. However, Jentzsch (2010) found that consumers do not benefit equally from information disclosure, because of rent-shifting behavior by firms and consumers.

Tang et al. (2005) modeled a range of markets and the corresponding impact of privacy protection regulation. They found the key variables to be the number of individuals affected by privacy losses, and the size of those losses. When few people are sensitive to privacy harms or when losses are low, then opt-out regimes are socially optimal. For intermediate levels of sensitivity and losses, privacy seals are socially optimal. When many people care strongly about privacy and face high losses, baseline protections are socially optimal.

Romanosky and Acquisti (2009) conclude that a combination of ex ante regulation and ex post liability would achieve better outcomes than each used separately. Acquisti (2004) suggests that technology, consumer awareness and regulation used together to generate and enforce liabilities and incentives will lead to the most socially optimal outcome.

12.4.4   Impact on Innovation

Many online businesses are both driven by and financially reliant upon user data, to the extent that personal information has been called the 'new oil' of the information economy (World Economic Forum, 2011). Such businesses are frequently critical of privacy regulation as a brake on innovation.

In a study for the European Parliament, Cave et al. (2011) found that in some cases, privacy regulation can lead to 'stranded investments' when products (such as Facebook's Beacon and Google's Street View) must be abandoned or significantly altered following ex post regulatory intervention. For this reason, they recommend an increased focus on ex ante regulatory mechanisms such as pressure on companies to include 'privacy by design' in new products and services. They also found weak business drivers for privacy-friendly products, correspondingly weak self-regulatory activity in industries such as online behavioral advertising, and hence a need for continued regulatory intervention in societies that value privacy as more than an individual preference in the marketplace.

Some limited empirical studies have shown that privacy regulation can have a significant impact beyond the direct costs to regulated firms. Goldfarb and Tucker (2011) used differences in EU member state privacy regulations to show that limits on using individual profiles to target online banner ads reduced their influence on purchase intent by 65 percent, particularly for smaller non-intrusive ads. This is a serious challenge for news websites and others that do not attract obvious communities of interest that can be shown related ads (such as sports or fashion sites).

Campbell et al. (2011) developed a model of the impact of regulations requiring customer opt-in for the use of personal data, suggesting this will disproportionately benefit incumbents and larger firms that are more likely to have an existing relationship with a given user. This anticompetitive effect can be reduced if standardized or global mechanisms for giving consent are provided. The model is extremely pertinent to the default cookie settings of Mozilla's Firefox browser, which block cookies from third parties such as advertising networks while allowing third-party cookies from sites that the user has visited directly. This gives companies such as Google, Facebook and Twitter (which all display ads based on users' previous browsing behavior across third-party sites) a significant advantage over competitors without direct customer relationships.

12.4.5 Examples of Privacy Regulation

Regulatory measures to protect privacy vary significantly between countries. In August 2012 the US National Conference of State Legislatures found that 46 states, the District of Columbia, Guam, Puerto Rico and the US Virgin Islands require companies that suffer data breaches involving personal information to notify affected consumers. Some skepticism has been expressed about the effectiveness of such rules; Calo (2013) concluded that 'the only thing piling up faster than examples of mandated disclosure as a regulatory strategy is the evidence it does not work ... time and time again, disclosure ends up helping few if any consumers or citizens actually make better decisions'.

The FTC and state attorneys general can take action against unfair or deceptive practices – as the FTC has done against Facebook for misleading privacy policies, Google for the flawed launch of its Buzz social network and resulting user data breaches, and Apple for bypassing privacy settings in its Safari web browser. Consumers can also take legal action against companies that have broken contractual privacy policies, although it can be difficult to quantify privacy-related losses. Additionally, the Children's Online Privacy Protection Act of 1998 (15 U.S.C. §§ 6501–6506) restricts the collection of personal information from children less than 13 years of age – although one study found that 38 percent of European 9–12-year-olds had social networking profiles, many on US-based services (Livingstone et al., 2011).

By contrast, the European Union has comprehensive rules covering almost all processing of personal data. While this ex ante approach is sometimes criticized as bureaucratic and stifling of innovation, it may well be appropriate given high levels of continuing privacy concern from a majority of Europeans, and the core constitutional role privacy rights play in most EU member states. A major revision of these rules took place in 2013 to improve their effectiveness and create a higher level of harmonization (European Commission, 2012).

The EU approach has apparently been persuasive to dozens of other states, which have introduced comprehensive data protection rules despite US attempts to encourage laissez-faire regimes through APEC and other international trade negotiations (Greenleaf, 2013). The EU regime encourages other states to develop comprehensive rules by restricting the export of personal data from Europe to countries that do not have such a legal framework. Even the laissez-faire USA has created a 'safe harbor' (enforced by the FTC) for firms that wish to voluntarily commit to follow EU-style privacy rules. This framework has been judged adequate by the European Commission (2000), and joined by major Internet companies including Facebook, Google and Microsoft.

12.5   CONCLUSION

Whether or not personal information is the 'new oil' of the information economy, the use of that information by economic actors is a central focus of Internet economists and regulators. An emerging privacy economics seeks to explain the actions of individuals and firms in disclosing and using personal data – to reduce search costs and pay for a broad range of 'free' online services, to target marketing and personalized offers, and to develop new products and services.

Behavioral economics research is improving the understanding of cognitive biases that can lead to non-optimal privacy decisions by individuals. Bounded rationality, time-inconsistent preferences, optimism bias and context-dependence have all been demonstrated to apply to information disclosure decisions. This is one, 'paternalistic', justification for regulation of the kind described by Thaler and Sunstein (2008). A second is the reduction of market failure resulting from information asymmetries, negative externalities, and market concentration. The third is non-economic, considering privacy as a vital underpinning of democracy, individual autonomy, and human rights including freedom of expression and association. These factors have all contributed to increased levels of privacy regulation worldwide, with many countries strongly influenced by the European Union's comprehensive system of data protection rules.

NOTE

*   This research was supported by the EU FP7 EINS project under grant agreement No. 288021.

REFERENCES

Acquisti, A. (2002), 'Protecting privacy with economics: Economic incentives for preventive technologies in ubiquitous computing environments', in *Proceedings from the Workshop on Socially-informed Design of Privacy-enhancing Solutions, 4th International Conference on Ubiquitous Computing*, accessed 3 April 2016 at http://www.academia.edu/2830436/Protecting_privacy_with_economics_Economic_incentives_for_preventive_technologies_in_ubiquitous_computing_environments.

Acquisti, A. (2004), 'Privacy in electronic commerce and the economics of immediate gratification', in *Proceedings from EC'04: The Fifth ACM Conference on Electronic Commerce*, New York: ACM Press, pp. 21–9, accessed 3 April 2016 at http://www.heinz.cmu.edu/~acquisti/papers/privacy-gratification.pdf.

Acquisti, A. and J. Grossklags (2003), 'Losses, gains, and hyperbolic discounting: An experimental approach to information security attitudes and behavior', in *Proceedings of the Second Annual Workshop on the Economics of Information Security (WEIS'03)*, accessed 3 April 2016 at http://www.heinz.cmu.edu/~acquisti/papers/acquisti_grossklags_eis_refs.pdf..

Acquisti, A. and J. Grossklags (2005), 'Privacy and rationality in individual decision making', *IEEE Security & Privacy*, **3** (1), 26–33.

Acquisti, A. and H.R. Varian (2005), 'Conditioning prices on purchase history', *Marketing Science*, **24** (3), 367–81.

Acquisti, A., A. Friedman and R. Telang (2006), 'Is there a cost to privacy breaches? An event study', in *Proceedings of the Fifth Workshop on the Economics of Information Security (WEIS'06)*, accessed 3 April 2016 at http://www.heinz.cmu.edu/~acquisti/papers/acquisti-friedman-telang-privacy-breaches.pdf.

Bonneau, J. and S. Preibusch (2009), 'The privacy jungle: On the market for data protection in social networks', in *Proceedings of the Eighth Workshop on the Economics of Information Security (WEIS'08)*, accessed 3 April 2016 at http://preibusch.de/publications/Bonneau_Preibusch__Privacy_Jungle__2009-05-26.pdf.

Bonneau, J., J. Anderson, R. Anderson and F. Stajano (2009), 'Eight friends are enough: Social graph approximation via public listings', in *Proceedings from SNS'09: The Second ACM EuroSys Workshop on Social Network Systems*, accessed 3 April 2016 at https://www.cl.cam.ac.uk/~rja14/Papers/8_friends_paper.pdf.

Bouckaert, J. and H. Degryse (2006), 'Opt in versus opt out: A free-entry analysis of privacy policies', in *Proceedings of the Fifth Workshop on the Economics of Information Security (WEIS'06)*, accessed 23 August 2015 at http://www.econstor.eu/handle/10419/25876.

Brown, I. and D. Korff (2004), *Technology Development and its Effect on Privacy and Law Enforcement*, Wilmslow, UK: Information Commissioner's Office.

Brown, I. and C.T. Marsden (2008), 'Social utilities, dominance and interoperability: A modest proposal', presentation at GikIII: Geek Law Workshop, accessed 3 April 2016 at http://www2.law.ed.ac.uk/ahrc/gikii/docs3/brown_marsden.pdf.

Calo, M.R. (2013), 'The disclosure crisis', *Concurring Opinions*, 2 March, accessed 3 April 2016 at http://www.concurringopinions.com/archives/2013/03/the-disclosure-crisis.html.

Campbell, J., A. Goldfarb and C. Tucker (2011), 'Privacy regulation and market structure', Working Paper, accessed 3 April 2016 at http://papers.ssrn.com/sol3/papers.cfm?abstract_id=1729405.

Cave, J., N. Robinson and R. Schindler et al. (2011), *Does It Help or Hinder?: Promotion of Innovation on the Internet and Citizens' Rights to Privacy*, Brussels: European Parliament Policy Department.

Coase, R. (1960), 'The problem of social cost', *Journal of Law and Economics*, **3**, 1–44.

Danezis, G. and B. Wittneben (2006), 'The economics of mass surveillance and the questionable value of anonymous communications', in *Proceedings of the Fifth Workshop on the Economics of Information Security (WEIS'06)*, accessed 3 April 2016 at http://freehaven.net/anonbib/cache/danezis:weis2006.pdf.

Debatin, B., J.P. Lovejoy, A.K. Horn and B.N. Hughes (2009), 'Facebook and online privacy: Attitudes, behaviors, and unintended consequences', *Journal of Computer-Mediated Communication*, **15** (1), 83–108.

Dworkin, R. (1980), 'Is wealth a value?' *Journal of Legal Studies*, **9** (2), 191–226.

Edelman, B. (2006), 'Adverse selection in online "trust" certifications', in *Proceedings of the Fifth Workshop on the Economics of Information Security (WEIS'06)*, accessed 3 April 2016 at http://www.benedelman.org/publications/advsel-trust-draft.pdf.

Edwards, L. and I. Brown (2009), 'Data control and social networking: Irreconcilable ideas?', in A. Matwyshyn (ed.), *Harboring Data: Information Security, Law and the Corporation*, Stanford, CA: Stanford University Press, pp. 202–27.

European Commission (2012), 'Proposal for a regulation of the European Parliament and of the Council on the protection of individuals with regard to the processing of personal data and on the free movement of such data (General Data Protection Regulation)', COM(2012)0011.

European Communities (2000), 'Decision of 26 July 2000 pursuant to Directive 95/46/EC of the European Parliament and of the Council on the adequacy of the protection provided by the safe harbour privacy principles and related frequently asked questions issued by the US Department of Commerce', *Official Journal of the European Communities*, *L 215*, 43, 7–47.

Gandy, O. (2010), 'Engaging rational discrimination: Exploring reasons for placing regulatory constraints on decision support systems', *Ethics and Information Technology*, **12** (1), 29–42.

Goldfarb, A. and C. Tucker (2011), 'Privacy regulation and online advertising', *Management Science*, **57** (1), 57–71.

Greenleaf, G. (2013), 'Global data privacy in a networked world', in I. Brown (ed.), *Research Handbook on Governance of the Internet*, Cheltenham, UK and Northampton, MA, USA: Edward Elgar Publishing, pp. 221–59.

Greenstadt, R. and M.D. Smith (2005), 'Protecting personal information: Obstacles and directions', in *Proceedings of the Fourth Annual Workshop on the Economics of Information Security (WEIS'05)*, accessed 3 April 2016 at http://infosecon.net/workshop/pdf/48.pdf.

Grossklags, J. and A. Acquisti (2007), 'When 25 cents is too much: An experiment on willingness-to-sell & willingness-to-protect personal information', in *Proceedings of the Sixth Workshop on the Economics of Information Security (WEIS'07)*, accessed 3 April 2016 at http://weis07.infosecon.net/papers/66.pdf.

Hermalin, B. and M. Katz (2006), 'Privacy, property rights and efficiency: The economics of privacy as secrecy', *Quantitative Marketing Economics*, **4** (3), 209–39.

Hoofnagle, C., J. Urban and S. Li (2012), 'Privacy and modern advertising: Most US internet users want "do not track" to stop collection of data about their online activities', *Amsterdam Privacy Conference Papers*, accessed 26 July 2014 at http://papers.ssrn.com/sol3/papers.cfm?abstract_id=2152135.

Jentzsch, N. (2010), 'A welfare analysis of secondary use of personal data', in *Proceedings of the Ninth Workshop on the Economics of Information Security (WEIS'10)*, accessed 3 April 2016 at http://weis2010.econinfosec.org/papers/session2/weis2010_jentzsch.pdf.

John, L., A. Acquisti and G. Loewenstein (2011), 'Strangers on a plane: Context-dependent willingness to divulge sensitive information', *Journal of Consumer Research*, **37** (5), 858–73.

Kolstad, C.D., T.S. Ulen and G.V. Johnson (1990), 'Ex post liability for harm vs. ex ante safety regulation: Substitutes or complements?', *The American Economic Review*, **80** (4), 888–901.

Korff, D. and I. Brown (2010), *New Challenges to Data Protection*, Brussels: European Commission DG Justice.

Livingstone, S., K. Ólafsson and E. Staksrud (2011), 'Social networking, age and privacy', *LSE Online*, accessed 3 April 2016 at http://eprints.lse.ac.uk/35849/.

Moskowitz, Y. and G. Taylor (2012), 'A theoretical model of externalities in anonymity decisions', unpublished working paper, Oxford Internet Institute.

Nagaraja, S. (2008), 'The economics of covert community detection and hiding', in *Proceedings of the Seventh Workshop on the Economics of Information Security (WEIS'08)*, accessed 3 April 2016 at http://weis2008.econinfosec.org/papers/Nagaraja.pdf.

Nissenbaum, H. (2010), *Privacy in Context: Technology, Policy, and the Integrity of Social Life*, Stanford, CA: Stanford University Press.

Noam, E. (1996), 'Markets in privacy', paper presented at the Second Aspen Summit on the Future of the Information Society, Washington, DC: Progress and Freedom Foundation.

Odlyzko, A. (2003), 'Privacy, economics, and price discrimination on the Internet', in *Proceedings from ICEC'03: The Fifth International Conference on Electronic Commerce*, New York: ACM Press, pp. 355–66.

Palfrey, J. and U. Gasser (2008), *Born Digital: Understanding the First Generation of Digital Natives*, New York: Basic Books.

Ponemon Institute (2010), *Five Countries: Cost of Data Breach*, accessed 3 April 2016 at http://www.symantec.com/content/en/us/about/media/pdfs/symantec_cost_of_data_breach_global_2010.pdf.

Posner, R. (1981), 'The economics of privacy', *American Economic Review*, **71** (2), 405–9.

Preibusch, S. and J. Bonneau (2012), 'The privacy landscape: product differentiation on data collection', in *Proceedings of the Tenth Annual Workshop on the Economics of Information Security (WEIS'11)*, accessed 3 April 2016 at http://preibusch.de/publications/Preibusch-Bonneau__privacy-landscape.pdf.

Romanosky, S. and A. Acquisti (2009), 'Privacy costs and personal data protection: Economic and legal perspectives', *Berkeley Technology Law Journal*, **24** (3), 1061–101.

Romanosky, S., R. Telang and A. Acquisti (2011), 'Do data breach disclosure laws reduce identity theft?', *Journal of Policy Analysis and Management*, **30** (2), 256–86.

Rubinstein, I.S. (2011), 'Regulating privacy by design', *Berkeley Technology Law Journal*, **26** (3), 1409–56.

Samuelson Law, Technology and Public Policy Clinic (2007), 'Security breach notification laws: Views from chief security officers', accessed 3 April 2016 at http://www.law.berkeley.edu/files/cso_study.pdf.

Solove, D. (2008), *Understanding Privacy*, Cambridge, MA: Harvard University Press.

Spiekermann, S., J. Grossklags and B. Berendt (2001), 'E-privacy in 2nd generation e-commerce: Privacy preferences versus actual behavior', in *Proceedings from EC'01: The Third ACM Conference on Electronic Commerce*, New York: ACM Press, pp. 38–47.

Synovate (2007), *Federal Trade Commission: 2006 Identity Theft Survey Report*, accessed 3 April 2016 at http://www.ftc.gov/os/2007/11/SynovateFinalReportIDTheft2006.pdf.

Tang, Z., Y. Hu and M.D. Smith (2005), 'Protecting online privacy: Self-regulation, mandatory standards, or caveat emptor', in *Proceedings of the Fourth Annual Workshop on the Economics of Information Security (WEIS'05)*, accessed 3 April 2016 at http://infosecon.net/workshop/pdf/31.pdf.

Taylor, C.R. (2004), 'Consumer privacy and the market for customer information', *The RAND Journal of Economics*, **35** (4), 631–50.

Thaler, R. and C. Sunstein (2008), *Nudge: Improving Decisions about Health, Wealth, and Happiness*, New Haven, CT: Yale University Press.

Tsai, J., S. Egelman, L.F. Cranor and A. Acquisti (2011), 'The effect of online privacy information on purchasing behavior: An experimental study', *Information Systems Research*, **22** (2), 254–68.

Tucker, C.E. (2012), 'The economics of advertising and privacy', *International Journal of Industrial Organization*, **30** (3), 326–9.

Turow, J., J. King, C.J. Hoofnagle, A. Bleakley and M. Hennessy (2009), *Americans Reject Tailored Advertising and Three Activities that Enable It*, Technical Report, Annenberg School for Communications, accessed 26 July 2014 at https://www.nytimes.com/packages/pdf/business/20090929-Tailored_Advertising.pdf.

Varian, H.R. (1997), 'Economic aspects of personal privacy', in National Telecommunications and Information Administration (ed.), *Privacy and Self-Regulation in the Information Age*, Washington, DC: US Department of Commerce.

Varian, H.R., F. Wallenberg and G. Woroch (2004), 'Who signed up for the do-not-call list?', in *Proceedings of the Third Annual Workshop on the Economics of Information Security (WEIS'04)*, accessed 26 July 2014 at http://www.dtc.umn.edu/weis2004/varian.pdf.

Vila, T., R. Greenstadt and D. Molnar (2003), 'Why we can't be bothered to read privacy policies: Models of privacy economics as a lemons market', in *Proceedings from ICEC'03: The Fifth International Conference on Electronic Commerce*, New York: ACM Press, pp. 403–7.

Westin, A.F. (1967), *Privacy and Freedom*, New York: Atheneum.

World Economic Forum (2011), *Personal Data: The Emergence of a New Asset Class*, accessed 26 July 2014 at http://www3.weforum.org/docs/WEF_ITTC_PersonalDataNewAsset_Report_2011.pdf.

Xu, W., X. Zhou and L. Li (2008), 'Inferring privacy information via social relations', in *Proceedings from ICDEW'08: IEEE Data Engineering Workshop*, Piscataway, NJ: IEEE, pp. 525–30.

13. Economics of cybersecurity
Hadi Asghari, Michel van Eeten and Johannes M. Bauer

13.1 INTRODUCTION

The Internet has enabled tremendous economic and social innovation yet the underlying systems, networks and services sometimes fail miserably to protect the security of communications and data. Security incidents occur in many forms, including but not limited to the leaking and theft of private information, unauthorized access to information, malicious alteration of data, or software and service unavailability. Enumerating all the technical ways in which security may be breached would generate a lengthy list as the network, devices, users, and services can all be attacked. A typical network runs hundreds of protocols and hosts devices operating thousands of applications consisting of millions of lines of code. Looking for solutions opens up an equally unwieldy range of ideas, technologies and complications. Not surprisingly, books on information security are typically voluminous. For example, Anderson's (2008) *Security Engineering* is over 1000 pages long. Despite its length the book can address most topics only briefly. Even research focusing on specific problems and solutions can be dauntingly complex. For example, the design and use of passwords has generated hundreds of papers but the jury on best practices is still out (Bonneau et al., 2012). Achieving cybersecurity under these conditions may appear like a hopeless endeavor and failure unavoidable.

Given the complexity of the problem, it seems improbable that security can be attained by eliminating all vulnerabilities. Moreover, preventative security measures are costly. Some level of uncertainty will therefore have to be accepted and choices need to be made, trading off competing objectives and limited resources. Recent research has developed approaches to better explain why certain security failures occur and others do not. These contributions clarified that security is not merely a technical problem that can be fixed with engineering solutions but that is also has important economic and behavioral dimensions that need to be addressed (Anderson and Moore, 2006). Examining the incentives of players in the information and communication technology (ICT) ecosystem has been particularly fruitful in explaining the landscape of vulnerabilities and attacks that can be observed. The core of this work is rooted in information security economics.

A key insight that catalyzed the development of this field is that many systems do not fail for technical reasons but because of the specific incentives shaping the behavior of individuals and organizations. For instance, if the individuals in charge of protecting a system do not have to bear any costs or other consequences in case of failure, they may exert insufficient care (ibid.). Attackers similarly respond to the set of pertinent incentives, for example by selecting targets and attack strategies based on expected financial or political benefits and risks. Technical tools to carry out attacks are often chosen opportunistically as attackers will use whatever means happen to work in a given scenario. These insights and the abundance of technical and non-technical vulnerabilities and attack vectors imply that it is more promising to approach cybersecurity as a defender–attacker dynamic with an emphasis on the incentives of players rather than with a focus on the vulnerabilities. Another consequence is that for the foreseeable future information systems will need to be defended against attacks with a combination of technology and human vigilance.

Given the abundance of interdependencies in the ICT ecosystem, cybersecurity at the individual and system levels is influenced by how the incentives of different actors align. Sometimes individual and group incentives are compatible with both the private and social costs and benefits so that decentralized decisions will be workable and effective to achieve desirable levels of security. However, more often such an alignment cannot be taken for granted and several questions arise. Are markets, networked governance, and individual organizational decisions – the predominant coordination mechanism in the Internet – sufficient to safeguard cybersecurity (Van Eeten and Mueller, 2012)? Or does such decentralized coordination fail because market and non-market players are not capable of or prepared for effectively dealing with the risks? If market failure is pervasive, the incentives of decentralized players will be systematically biased and may result in underinvestment or overinvestment in security (Lewis, 2005; Shim, 2006). A classical response to market failure is government intervention but the incentives of government actors are not necessarily aligned with the common good. Parts of government, including secret services and the military, may have an interest in exploiting vulnerabilities for surveillance purposes. Consequently, conflicts within government may prevent effective public sector responses to information security risks. Moreover, the global scale and connectivity of the Internet has created interdependencies that may require coordinated action beyond the national or global level to design effective responses, greatly compounding the challenges. Security economics has in the past decade successfully examined many of these questions and helped greatly in the design of rational responses.

Most of the work in the field has focused on information security as a means to fight criminal activities rather than on the protection of national security and cyberwar. The two topics, while at some level related, raise different theoretical and practical issues. It is important to understand the perspective used by each approach to conceptualize risk, costs and benefits, and the role of government (see, e.g., Singer and Friedman, 2013). Some scholars have argued that, due to its societal impact, cybercrime is more important than the hype-prone concept of cyberwar. Cybercrime is often discussed in a framework of risk management using cost–benefit and trial-and-error approaches, which makes it more amenable to empirical research. This approach typically results in tolerance for some level of risk and vulnerability. Protecting national security is more about scenarios and their potential impacts, often focusing on worst case circumstances, which typically imply massive economic and social disruption. Consequently, prevention and resilience are often the main emphases (Van Eeten and Bauer, 2009, 2013).

In this chapter, we set out to survey the state of the art of the existing research with a focus on the criminal threats to cybersecurity. The next section briefly outlines key topics addressed in economic analyses of information security. Sections 13.3 through 13.5 discuss software and platform security, end user and organizational security, and Internet intermediary security. Attacker behavior is addressed in section 13.6, followed by an exploration of policy options in section 13.7 and concluding remarks in section 13.8.

13.2   CYBERSECURITY AS AN ECONOMIC PROBLEM

Cybersecurity may refer to the technical, legal, and organizational measures directed at maintaining or enhancing the integrity and security of information assets. It can be assessed at the level of individuals, organizations, nations or cyberspace as a whole. Many of the Internet's technical and behavioral standards, conventions and norms emerge from decentralized repeated decisions of actors participating in it, ranging from component and hardware manufacturers to network operators, software vendors, application and service developers, content providers, and various users. These actors are heterogeneous and have different skill sets and motives. The architectural design adopted by Internet engineers created the specific socio-technical framework that constrains and enables these actors. While information security was initially not a pressing concern, the early choices that solidified the unique open design of the Internet inadvertently created later challenges of safeguarding cybersecurity (Lessig, 1999; Hofmann, 2010).

The field of economics of information security studies factors that actors perceive as relevant for security decisions ('incentives'), their influence on actions of individuals and organizations, and how these actions lead to emergent properties of the system. The early concepts and theories applied in the field originated from neo-classical microeconomics, and in particular the field of information economics. Economic sciences, however, constitute a wide discipline (Groenewegen, 2007; Colander, 2005). Concepts and theories from other fields, such as behavioral economics and new institutional economics, have also made their way into the economics of information security.

13.2.1   Public Goods, Externalities, Information Asymmetries and Property Rights

Cybersecurity has both private and public good characteristics: while investment in security protection entails private costs and benefits for the decision-maker, it may also benefit or harm other Internet actors. These interdependencies are called 'externalities', formally defined as the direct effect of the activity of one actor on the welfare of another that is not compensated by a market transaction (Rosen, 2004). Externalities can be negative or positive. In both cases the price of the direct market transaction will not reflect the full social costs or benefits of the product or service, because the third-party effects are not taken into account by the transaction partners. Consequently, systematic deviations from an optimal allocation of resources occur even in an otherwise functioning market economy (Musgrave and Musgrave, 1973). Individual security measures may have positive and negative externalities, depending on whether attacks are targeted or non-targeted and whether the associated risk is interdependent or not (Kunreuther and Heal, 2003). There are several ways to correct for such externalities and 'internalize' them into decision-making. A traditional response is collective action by government or the participants in an exchange. In information markets that are multi-sided ('platform' markets), the platform intermediary may have incentives to internalize the externalities caused by others, to improve its business case and competitiveness. Such platforms can be seen as institutional arrangements to reduce transaction costs and address externalities (Rysman, 2009).

Another key focus of the information security literature is the situation in which information is incomplete and unevenly distributed among actors, such as when buyers in a market do not have sufficient information to reliably separate between high-quality and low-quality products. For example, a subscriber looking to purchase Internet access may not be able to distinguish ISPs with strong security practices from those with lax ones. This makes buyers unwilling to pay a premium for the better product and consequently discourages suppliers from offering them – a situation dubbed a 'market for lemons' (Akerlof, 1970). Information asymmetry afflicts many Internet services when it comes to security and privacy, where it is impossible to determine how secure a service is.

Although rarely recognized explicitly in the literature, a fundamental economic problem at the heart of many information security issues may be the absence of clearly defined property rights in personal and other information (Branscomb, 1994). It is this absence that gives actors in the Internet more or less free reign to appropriate information from users and store large amounts of data. Moreover, it generates recurring challenges for the establishment of a clear legal definition of cybercrime.

13.2.2 Alignment of Incentives

Cybersecurity can be improved by introducing measures that align incentives of individual actors so that deviations between private and social costs and benefits are reduced. If successful, such strategies can reduce or even eliminate security-related market failures and deficiencies. Table 13.1 presents selected high-level options for aligning incentives among Internet actors. One can strengthen the incentives for security investment and other protective measures among defenders. One can also disincentivize attackers by increasing the costs or reducing the benefits of cybercrime and other malicious actions. Although the differentiation between defenders and attackers is sometimes muddied – government agencies with an interest in vulnerabilities to spy on others, white hat hackers who attack with the goal to improve defenses – the approach is useful in exploring principal options. In the next sections of this chapter we survey the security economics literature organized around these actors. We shall examine the incentives of each actor, their interactions with the ecosystem, and security issues that they create or resolve. Among the attackers, our focus will be on cybercriminals, economically motivated and by far the largest group.

Table 13.1   Improving cybersecurity by aligning incentives of actors

Improving Cybersecurity	
Incentivizing defenders	*Disincentivizing attackers*
Who:	*Who:*
Software vendors	Criminals
End users and organizations	Hacktivists
Internet intermediaries	Nation states
How:	*How:*
Reducing information asymmetries	Improved law enforcement
Addressing negative externalities	Reducing benefits of crime
Education and capacity building	Disrupting criminal resources

13.2.3   Approaches to Studying the Economics of Cybersecurity

The security economics literature can be categorized into analytical, empirical and experimental research. Analytical studies employ methods such as game theory to deduce theoretically how actors behave in security dilemmas. Key variables, such as prices, regulation and the type of competitive interaction, are parameterized. Determining cooperative and non-cooperative equilibria of the game allows researchers to explore the conditions under which cybersecurity improves or deteriorates. As it may be difficult to derive solutions to games analytically, researchers also use computational and simulation methods to approximate outcomes. These methods offer interesting results but their practical use may be limited by the required simplifying assumptions. Results are often highly stylized and application to more complicated real world situations may need careful and cautious interpretation.

Empirical studies start by collecting and observing actual cybersecurity behavior and performance. While many of the efforts are descriptive, additional insights may be gained by combining datasets of Internet measurements or surveys with data analysis to unveil how a market functions and how its actors behave. Empirical studies are a promising avenue but they also have their unique challenges, which include the dynamic nature of the phenomenon, insufficient or unreliable data, and problems of endogeneity that complicate establishing causality especially in cross-sectional comparative studies.

Experimental studies use lab or online experiments to test various hypotheses – with fewer assumptions and proxies than the other two methods. This raises challenges as to how generalizable the findings may be.

In subsequent sections of this chapter we look at all three categories of works. We focus mainly on the recent literature as it usually also relates to earlier work and point to classics and influential work in the field. We have chosen this approach to keep the material more manageable but also because much of the earlier research has been updated and extended in recent years. Moore and Anderson (2012) and Volume 3, Issue 1 of *IEEE Security & Privacy*, published in 2005 are earlier surveys of the field. For the purposes of this chapter, relevant literature has been drawn from papers presented at a number of leading security conferences, including the annual Workshop on the Economics of Information Security (WEIS), a detailed examination of journals where scholars of the field typically publish and through keyword search in other journals.[1]

13.3   SOFTWARE AND PLATFORM SECURITY

The Internet and its services are run by software. Many security issues arise because of poorly written or misconfigured software. The Common Vulnerabilities and Exposures database, a 'dictionary of common names for publicly known information security vulnerabilities', lists 60000 software vulnerabilities between 2005 and 2014 (CVE, 2015). They can be found in all operating systems and pieces of software. Anderson (2001) was one of the first to explore the fundamental economic reasons behind this phenomenon.

Software products share a number of interesting characteristics with other 'information goods' (Shapiro and Varian, 1998). High initial development and production costs are accompanied by close to zero incremental costs for additional copies. Information goods often exhibit direct and indirect 'network effects'. Direct network effects exist if the utility of a software product increases with the number of users (e.g., because documents can be shared with a larger group). Indirect effects exist if, as the user base grows, more complementary software and products become available, further increasing the utility of the software. In the absence of cheap and efficient converter technology, network effects can lead to switching costs and consequently 'lock-in' effects (Gottinger, 2003): the costs of equipping an organization with new hardware and software, the costs of switching from one solution or format to another including the associated costs of document conversion, and the costs of learning new skills all create rigidities that work in favor of sticking with the existing solution. This provides advantages for the first mover and disadvantages for competitors that enter a market late. Consequently, software markets have a 'winner-takes-all' dynamic that incentivizes vendors to move their products to market fast and to grow as quickly as possible.

In their battle for dominance, software vendors might initially give away their products for free or at a low price but change their pricing to generate a profit once they have a large user base and lock-in. Software vendors will attempt to lure developers to their platforms by making application programming interfaces (APIs) available for free or at a low cost as developers bring additional users. This might also imply that developers are given latitude and are permitted to work under lax rules for security technologies in the platform (Anderson and Moore, 2006). Vendors will lure customers with bells and whistles that are visible features or provide convenience. Security is rather intangible and does not easily fit into these considerations; it might even reduce functionality. That is why in the short term the market does not value security. After a firm gains dominance, the incentive structure changes: the costs of releasing software patches and mending brand damage incentivize firms to change course. An example is Microsoft whose reputation was tarnished after a series of spectacular worm attacks in the early 2000s. In response the company started an internal code-review campaign resulting in the release of Windows XP Service Pack 2 with many security enhancements in 2004 (Van Eeten and Bauer, 2008). Nowadays, Windows vulnerabilities make fewer headlines. Vulnerabilities have moved 'up the stack' to other applications, including open-source software. But, all in all, software vendors cause severe negative externalities as they do not bear much of the costs of insecure software.

Security software has an interesting extra hurdle. Since security is hard to measure, the average user basically has to take the word of a vendor claiming the product provides better security protection than another. Thus it becomes a classic lemons market (Schneier, 2007). A running joke states that antivirus software competes on every feature except security. Judging by the large sums spent on security products (Anderson et al., 2013) consumers demand security. If they are lacking clear and reliable information they will likely underinvest in some key areas and overinvest in hyped ones.

A number of ideas have been presented for aligning incentives of the players in the software market. To be fair the responsibility rests not solely on software vendors as they are not instigating the attacks. Even in a perfect market some users might choose software with a lower degree of security and remedy remaining problems using other countermeasures. Anderson et al. (2008) name an obligation to provide free and timely software patches for security products, mandating 'secure by default', and responsible vulnerability disclosure as policy options. Previously software certification has been suggested but this has not worked as anticipated. We look at these options later in the chapter.

Zittrain (2008) raised concerns that the market might evolve toward users preferring locked-down devices to reduce the threats from malware and other side-effects of insecure software. Given the rise of mobile devices there is some evidence to that effect as the major application stores are controlled by the respective firms or consortia (e.g., Apple's App Store, Google's Play Store, and Microsoft's Windows Store). Application stores for web browsers are another example. Application stores have their own share of security problems and exhibit a wide variation in their security mechanisms. Anderson et al. (2010) compared the incentives of ten different application stores and concluded that soft liability and signaling have the best chance for improving security without stifling innovation. The shift towards software as a platform and the rise of application stores means that some software vendors become Internet intermediaries who have different incentives (e.g., Fershtman and Gandal, 2012).

13.4   END USER AND ORGANIZATIONAL SECURITY

Users may be individual end users and organizations ranging from small to very large size. Our focus is on the incentives and decisions of organizations outside the IT security industry that need to protect information assets related to their core business. We start by looking at larger organizations with dedicated IT budgets and then turn our attention to smaller organizations and individuals with limited skills to assess and manage security risks.

13.4.1   Information Security Investment in Large Organizations

Rational large organizations would make security investment decisions based on several relevant factors, including the type of risk they are facing, the monetary and non-monetary consequences of failure, the resilience of their operations, and so on. In practice, the available budget is often a key determinant of their security investments (Cavusoglu et al., 2004). The total cost of security includes investment in technology, the hiring of experts, as well as the indirect productivity costs that might be caused by security controls. Although security spending figures tell little about the rationality of expenses they are a useful proxy for the total resources available. Framing security as an investment problem eases communication with upper management and helps set limits as it might make sense not to defend against certain threats.

Gordon and Loeb (2002) first explored optimal security investment conceptually. They proposed a model in which information assets are categorized based on their value, potential loss in case of a breach, and their vulnerability. The authors showed that under varying assumptions firms will be better off concentrating efforts on information assets with mid-range vulnerabilities as extremely valuable information may be 'inordinately expensive' to protect. To maximize expected benefits a firm should spend only a small fraction of the expected loss on securing an asset (except in cases when law requires an asset to be protected regardless of value).

A number of scholars have extended this simple and elegant model, for instance by looking at the timing of investment, by proposing different caps for security investment, and by relaxing model assumptions. Ioannidis et al. (2013a) show in a utility-theoretic model that security investment turns out to be cyclical when costly projects are deferred due to uncertainty related to the costs of future vulnerabilities. Böhme and Moore (2009) model the interaction between defenders that face investment decisions under uncertainty and attackers who repeatedly target the weakest link. They empirically validate their model and conclude that underinvestment can be reasonable under certain scenarios: when reactive investment is possible, when attacks are not catastrophic, and when uncertainty exists about attacker capabilities. Although difficult, quantifying cybersecurity risks and costs is an integral part of the investment models. Brecht and Nowey (2013) focus on establishing the costs of information security. They offer a comprehensive comparison of three alternatives to using surveys for determining such costs. Demetz and Bachlechner (2013) compared approaches using a configuration management tool as an example, and found that there is considerable potential for new approaches to complement existing ones. These selected findings illustrate the difficulties of operationalizing and implementing cost–benefit approaches to assessing security investment.

The level of investment aside, what security practices should an organization put into effect? A high-level distinction is between practices that have an observable impact on security and those that are adopted for compliance reasons, due diligence or keeping up with what are considered 'best practices'. The security benefits of alternative approaches also depend on the goals of an organization, which might include protecting the organization's intellectual property, finances and customers from attacks. Sometimes security solutions might be focused on other objectives than security, for instance on achieving customer lock-in, as is the case with security measures in printers designed to ensure that third-party ink cannot be used. In the case of best practices or standards, security measures are not adopted per se for their effectiveness, but rather for the sake of compliance. Standards such as the ISO 27000 series, the common criteria, or sector-specific security regulation may fall in this category if implemented mainly to disclaim liability in case of failure. From the perspective of policy-makers such measures can still be useful for the ecosystem as a whole if an evaluation of their aggregate results indicates that they have desired effects on security.

The security incentives of large organizations are, in short, mixed. Tolerating some level of insecurity is economically rational, and as long as the organization accepts the risks and compensates the direct and indirect costs it limits the externalities of its security decisions. An organization can also decide to transfer security risks to a third party via cyber insurance. But this arrangement has not been widely adopted thus far. Other policies are required if incident costs are not borne by the organization and externalities are created. One means is data breach disclosure laws (sometimes referred to as security breach notification laws) intended to mitigate harms to third parties caused by an organization's underinvestment in security. Organizations are required to notify all affected customers in cases of breaches leading to compromise of personal information. If they fail to do so they become liable for damages and face fines.

13.4.2   Security in the Healthcare Sector

Organizational security has also been studied in the context of particular sectors. The healthcare sector is a good example, illustrating many key aspects of security decisions. It deals with confidential and sensitive patient data and has been subject to sector-specific regulation such as the US Health Information Technology for Economic and Clinical Health (HITECH) Act and the Health Insurance Portability and Accountability Act (HIPAA). While confidentiality has considerable importance for earning the trust of patients and professionals, it is not the core business of health organizations. Consequently, attitudes towards such regulations might mainly be driven by a desire to be compliant. Given the interest in how an attitude of compliance affects security decisions, the healthcare sector has been studied in detail by researchers.

Gaynor et al. (2012) studied around 200 reported data breaches in hospitals from 2006 to 2011 and found that increased competition was associated with a decline in data protection. They suggest that hospitals in competitive markets may be inclined to shift resources to visible activities rather than data protection. Kwon and Johnson (2011) analyzed 2000 healthcare organizations and found that proactive security investments, associated with longer intervals between subsequent breaches, were most effective when voluntarily done. Miller and Tucker (2011) looked at encryption as a tool for increasing data security, in particular in states that provide safe harbors when it is used. They found that data breaches perversely increased after healthcare organizations adopted encryption software, possibly due to a false sense of security and/or a moral hazard problem. The effectiveness of sector regulation might be tied to the specifics of its formulation, as Kwon and Johnson (2013) suggest in a more optimistic study of the effects of the financial incentives created by the HITECH Act. They conclude that mitigating data breaches depends more on security resources and capabilities than regulatory compliance and reiterate that policy should provide guidelines to invest in a combination of security resources, capabilities, and cultural values, rather than impose single-solution requirements.

13.4.3   Individuals and Small Organizations

End users that lack dedicated IT staff often rely on a variety of heuristics to make security decisions. These decisions are prone to mistakes that fraudsters can exploit (Stajano and Wilson, 2011). The sheer number of such users means that even a small vulnerable fraction can cause major security risks for others and in the aggregate. An example is the market for fake anti-virus software: hundreds of thousands of users have been conned into paying for malware that claims to be an anti-virus product (Stone-Gross et al., 2013).

Psychology and behavioral economics provide explanations for such behaviors. Understanding how end users interpret error messages and make security decisions can be used to design user interfaces that nudge users towards better security choices (Sunshine et al., 2009; Camp, 2013). Bravo-Lillo et al. (2011) provide an enlightening example: novice users perceive 'saving' a file as being more dangerous than 'opening' it, as it implies persistent changes to the system. Similarly, Wash (2010) discusses 'folk models' formed by users about security threats and how they influence online behavior.[2] Given these difficulties, end users might be willing to pay for extra security services. Just as an example, Wood and Rowe (2011) estimated that customers of US Internet service providers are willing to pay $4 to $7 a month premium for mitigating malware harms. However, this willingness often does not translate into actual purchasing behavior due to information asymmetries and the market for lemons problem.

Users are not always wrong to ignore security advice (Herley, 2009). Typical advice concerning passwords is outdated, almost all certificate error warnings appear to be false positives, and if users spent even a minute a day reading URLs to avoid phishing, the costs would greatly outweigh phishing losses. Florêncio and Herley (2010) investigated password policies concluding that websites with the most restrictive policies are insulated from the consequences of poor usability: for example, universities have stricter password rules than Google and Facebook as they won't lose revenue if users have a hard time logging in. The latter defend against more attacks using other effective authentication controls that maintain convenience (such as the location of access). This example shows an interesting trade-off between different aspects of implementing security protections.

Due to carelessness and limits of human intuition end users can create considerable externalities for the Internet economy. However, they also fuel the Internet economy by shopping online and clicking on ads. Improving end user security at the expense of convenience might result in a negative net gain, an economic trade-off that possibly can be done away with by larger organizations. For example, when online merchants were pushed by Mastercard and VISA to adopt the 3D security anti-fraud measure or accept liability for the fraud losses, some found that the additional checks resulted in higher dropout rates during checkout. These exceeded the cost of accepting liability for the fraud, which led some merchants to opt out of the security program.

13.5   INTERNET INTERMEDIARIES

One of the most promising areas of security economics research has concentrated on Internet intermediaries. These entities provide the Internet's basic infrastructure and platforms, and enable communications and transactions between third parties and services. Players include Internet service providers (ISPs), hosting providers, payment systems, e-commerce platforms, search engines and participative platforms as shown in Figure 13.1 (Perset, 2010). The role of intermediaries has increased over the years, gradually modifying the original vision of an 'end-to-end' design of the Internet. Most intermediaries are private businesses and IT forms the core of their business. We will first make some general observations applying to all intermediaries, and then look at different types separately.

Intermediary markets are highly concentrated because of network effects and economics of scale. Network effects, as previously explained, reflect the increasing value of a service as more users adopt it. Economies of scale are cost advantages that firms gain due to their size. In many markets – for instance search engines, participative platforms or certificate authorities – a handful of companies control large market shares, sometimes up to 80 or 90 percent of the revenues or user base (Noam, 2009). Some of the largest Internet intermediaries are among the world's top firms and well-known brands – for example, Google, Facebook, eBay, Amazon, Apple and Microsoft.

Intermediaries raise interesting governance issues. They are in some sense gatekeepers

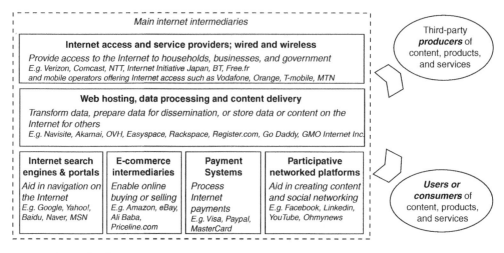

Source: Perset (2010).

Figure 13.1   Internet intermediary roles

of the Internet economy with direct access to end users. They become de facto stand-ardization bodies and their mundane technical choices frequently have more profound effects on outcomes than formal Internet governance structures (Van Eeten and Mueller, 2012). Their scale makes them focal points for regulation, whereas a network of thousands of organizations and millions of end users can hardly be regulated by traditional governance arrangements. However, as in the case of other players, the security incentives of Internet intermediaries are mixed. In some cases, security is a cost to avoid, in particular if it conflicts with business interests. In many cases, however, intermediaries take security seriously and are among the largest defenders of users against attacks, as they have incentives in maintaining trust in the Internet economy. Often, their role as multi-sided platforms that are enabling other market players will generate strong incentives to internalize some of the externalities in the system. Moreover, many intermediaries have the resources, knowledge and capabilities to provide security.

13.5.1   Internet Service Providers

Internet service providers (ISPs) are companies that connect subscribers to the global Internet. ISPs come in different sizes – from small regional ISPs to multinational tier 1 networks. There are several thousand ISPs worldwide but the 200 largest ones serve about 80 percent of broadband and mobile Internet markets (Van Eeten et al., 2010). Since ISPs have access to their subscribers' Internet traffic they are affected by and involved in policy debates on privacy protection, network neutrality, copyright enforce-ment, infrastructure resilience, the blocking of malware, and the disruption of botnets.[3] In many countries ISPs have historically been regulated in a less intrusive fashion than traditional telecommunications companies. In the USA they were historically classified as 'information service providers' and in other countries as value-added service providers. As part of these legal arrangements, they were shielded from liability for traffic carried on their networks as long as they followed certain required business practices (e.g., notice and take-down procedures).[4] We shall focus this section on the role and incentives of ISPs with regard to malware and botnets as some of the most pernicious cybersecurity threats.

Bots are computers infected with malware that puts them under remote control by attackers. The attackers may directly harm the owners of these machines through fraud or extortion. They may also combine infected computers into botnets of varying size or rent them out to other criminals. In either case they become platforms to launch attacks on other parts of the Internet and therefore are a serious problem for the whole Internet ecosystem. Numerous botnets remain active despite more than a decade of countervailing measures. Depending on whether one differentiates according to the malware families used or by the number of different attackers using them, their number ranges between tens and thousands. The largest botnets may at peak consist of millions of bots (Symantec, 2015).

The security community has had some success in seizing control over botnets through both technical infiltration and apprehension of the command and control infrastructure (Fryer et al., 2013). However, a key problem that remains is cleaning up the infected machines. Clayton (2011) contemplates alternative approaches to clean-up and concludes it might make sense for governments to subsidize ISPs or other third parties to clean up malware on end user machines. In the same vein, there have been calls to treat botnets by employing a public health approach. In this framework, a 'cybersecurity health agency' would provide education, monitoring (e.g., infections and intrusion trends), epidemiology (e.g., malware analysis), immunization (e.g., patch coordination), and incident response (Kelley and Camp, 2012; Sullivan, 2012).

Van Eeten et al. (2010) evaluated the role and incentives of ISPs in botnet mitigation by comparing spam-bots in 200 ISPs between 2005 and 2009. They found that large retail ISPs are indeed effective control points but that the number of infected machines per subscriber differs significantly among ISPs. This difference was relatively stable over time, suggesting that systematic differences exist in ISP policies and management practices as well as among users. The authors further found that larger ISPs have lower average infection rates, possibly due to automation of detection and clean-up that reduces the unit cost of providing security. Moreover, the data reveal that ISPs located in countries with an attentive regulator have cleaner networks. Other researchers have suggested that coordinated action by the largest networks can be very effective in stopping malware (Hofmeyr et al., 2013), and that a correlation exists between well-managed networks and end user security (Zhang et al., 2014). Different approaches to incentivize ISPs and other networks to improve security practices have been proposed. Tang et al. (2013) perform a shaming and faming experiment with networks that have high outgoing spam, a sign of botnet activity. They report that performance improved in a treatment group that was subject to information disclosure. In recent years, public–private partnerships between ISPs and a national anti-botnet center have been the most called upon model for clean-ups (OECD, 2012). By splitting costs these models recognize the role of ISPs and the public sector and that ISPs are not solely responsible for clean-ups. The jury on the effectiveness of these models is still out.

13.5.2 Hosting Providers

Hosting providers are organizations that operate servers used by customers to make content and services available to the Internet. Many hosting providers are also registrars: entities that sell and register domain names. As with virtually all services on the Internet, these businesses are abused by criminals. Phishing sites, command-and-control servers for botnets, and the distribution of child pornography, malware and spam all require such services. Like ISPs, hosting providers can thus play a key role in fighting cybercrime. Much of the criminal activity runs on compromised servers of legitimate customers but some run on servers rented by the criminals themselves. In either case, the hosting provider typically becomes aware of the problem only after being notified of the abuse. Responses to abuse reports vary widely, ranging from vigilant to slow to negligent (Stone-Gross et al., 2009; Canali et al., 2013; Bradbury, 2014). In a small number of cases, the hosting provider passively or actively facilitates the criminal enterprise and shields it from takedown attempts – a practice referred to as 'bulletproof hosting'.

While there is a wealth of research on security issues in hosting infrastructure, only a fraction has been done from an economic perspective. Moore and Clayton (2007) have studied hosting provider incentives to take down phishing sites. They found evidence for a 'clued-up' effect: it took time before a provider became aware and incentivized enough to start taking down sites. Once that effect occurred, takedown speed rapidly increased and stayed at this improved level. In a follow up study, Moore and Clayton (2009) expanded the research to other forms of Internet content and various notice and takedown regimes. The findings show that requester's incentives outweigh other factors in predicting takedown speed including the content, penalty, and evasion technology. Another study by Vasek and Moore (2012) looked at the responses of hosting providers to notifications of sites that were compromised with malware. It found that notifications that included comprehensive technical data of the detected problem were more likely to trigger takedown action on the side of the providers. This might be related to the competing incentives of providers: they do not want to disrupt service to their customers, while also protecting them and others from the negative consequences of compromised security. Extensive evidence helps them to legitimate countermeasures with regard to their customers.

The overall effects of takedown actions seem limited. Criminal activity might be concentrated at some providers or registrars. Getting those providers to act can dramatically reduce the level of abuse in those networks, but the attackers are prepared for this and merely migrate their activities to other providers (Levchenko et al., 2011; Liu et al., 2011). The result is a game of whack-a-mole. Organizing collective action against criminal activities in the hosting sector is made more difficult because this market is not nearly as consolidated at many other online markets. In the absence of reliable reputation signals, it seems unlikely that market incentives alone will result in higher security levels across the thousands of hosting providers.

13.5.3 Payment Service Providers and Certificate Authorities

Payment and other financial service providers (FSPs) are no strangers to attacks. Annual global losses from financial fraud amount to billions of dollars (Anderson et al., 2013). At the same time, these intermediaries have benefited tremendously from the growth of online payments, and in relative terms, fraud has been stable or diminishing (Financial Fraud Action UK, 2015). This is because they have become good at detecting fraud while maintaining convenience, for instance by profiling credit card transactions in real time in their back-end systems, rather than imposing additional security measures on the users directly. One advantage they have is that calculating the monetary gains and losses of certain trade-offs is easier for them than for other sectors. For example, after a data breach credit card issuers can calculate the relative cost of replacing cards or refunding victims of fraudulent cases (Graves et al., 2014). The FSPs have also been helped – perhaps paradoxically – by legal regimes in the USA and some European countries that limited the liability of consumers in cases of fraud. The burden of proof for fraud was put on the FSPs who actually had the capability to do something about it (Van Eeten and Bauer, 2008). In short, financial service providers are in a position to internalize some of the externalities in the sector and thus absorb and mitigate the sector-wide costs of fraud.[5]

Related to payment providers and e-commerce platforms are certificate authorities (CAs) – organizations that issue digital certificates. Such credentials are intended to enable secure online communications, assuring confidentiality and integrity of information and transactions. A series of high-profile breaches at CAs in recent years, most notably the breach and bankruptcy of DigiNotar in 2011, brought to light serious weaknesses in the current system (Arnbak and Van Eijk, 2012). Vratonjic et al. (2013) looked at how Transport Layer Security/Secure Sockets Layer (TLS/SSL) certificates are deployed on the top one million websites and found many misconfigurations. Durumeric et al. (2013) gathered all digital certificates in use on the public web and found hundreds of CAs with the authority to issue certificates that are recognized by browsers. If any of these CAs were to be breached, certificates could be maliciously issued for any other website, a serious negative externality. Arnbak et al. (2014) used the same data to calculate the market shares of CAs and connect them with their prices. Surprisingly, they found the market share of the most expensive CAs was much larger than cheaper CAs for identical certificates. This observation points to information asymmetries that create advantages for the largest players. A technical fix to the protocols is required, but their adoption is complicated as long as CAs benefit from the status quo. Other intermediaries, however, such as browser vendors and top websites, could play a role in pushing for new standards.

13.5.4   Search Engines and Participative Platforms

Search engines, portals and participative platforms are used to find content and connect to others. While these intermediaries have explored many different business models in the last decades, the market has converged on a business model in which users receive services for free while revenues are generated from targeted advertising. This development is driven by a combination of network effects and the 'economics of attention': in a world abundant with information, the scarcest resource is the attention of users (Shapiro and Varian, 1998). These platforms fight for user attention (Davenport and Beck, 2001). Since the marginal cost of information is close to zero, offering services at a low price or free is an economically rational strategy as it maximizes the size of the potential audience. Key players combine 'free' with a variety of nudging techniques to keep users on the platform (an interesting glimpse into this is the controversial study by Kramer et al., 2014 on changing the emotional content of Facebook newsfeeds to see how it effects users). Creating a revenue stream via advertisement is, of course, not new: broadcasting and newspapers have used the model for decades. The key difference is that targeted advertising can extract higher value (Goldfarb and Tucker, 2011).

In terms of cybersecurity, these platforms overall seem to internalize costs to keep their users satisfied. Just to illustrate, Google has a dedicated team to protect users against state-sponsored attacks (Grosse, 2012). This is not done out of nicety but as a competitive necessity: MySpace lost to Facebook partially as a result of increased spam and abuse on its network (Dredge, 2015). Another example is handling 'click fraud'. When a bot imitates a legitimate user clicking an ad to generate revenue, the advertisers and the platforms are harmed financially and by the erosion of confidence. Chen et al. (2012) suggest that platforms will likely pay the costs of click fraud investigations, thus internalizing some of the costs to the system at large. Schneier (2012) draws an analogy with 'feudal security' in the past: platforms provide users with security in exchange for allegiance. This approach has some benefits but it also comes with serious risks particularly with regard to privacy. Evidence of this tension is visible in how the platforms balance the interests of users and advertisers: Facebook Connect is preferred by many websites as a federated identity and password system over alternatives because of the user details it shares (Landau and Moore, 2012).

13.6　ATTACKER BEHAVIOR

Over the past years, cybercrime has become highly differentiated and professionalized with a vast 'underground' (illegal) market that supplies various services required for an attack (Franklin et al., 2007). The division of labor can be illustrated with Zeus, an effective financial malware that caused considerable damage. It was coded by competent programmers that sold it as a do-it-yourself (DIY) kit for several thousand dollars (Riccardi et al., 2013). Fraudsters customized the malware and distributed it to their victims by either renting spamming services, directly deploying it via 'pay-per-install' services, or via other methods. After the malware was distributed the attackers waited for victims and eventually managed to steal money and move it into other accounts. Finally, the money needed to be cashed out without leaving a trail. This was done using people known as 'money mules'. Thus four major types of players were involved in Zeus even though the different roles may be carried out by vertically integrated players.

Cybercrime is also affected by the social relations among criminals. Because there is a risk of being cheated by a fellow criminal, Herley and Florêncio (2010) argue that prices in the underground markets are driven down to reduce the risks for buyers. In turn, this makes it less attractive to offer valuable items and creates a cycle of decay. The authors suggest this leads to a two-tier structure with Internet relay chat (IRC) markets as the lower tier, filled with goods that are hard to monetize. Organization of criminal activities rather than ad hoc action is the route to profit. Repeated transactions also form a mechanism that incentivizes buyers and sellers to uphold their promises. Wondracek et al. (2010) looked at parts of the online adult industry employing practices that can be at best described as shady: acquiring traffic and infecting visitors for a fee. Their measurements showed that traffic brokers honored the amount and origin of traffic they were contracted for. Another mechanism, deployed in recent years on marketplaces active in the 'dark web', consists of seller ratings (Christin, 2013). Similar to eBay, criminal buyers rate criminal sellers after a transaction; the reputation effect increases the incentives of criminals to stay honest. Despite these differences, both tiers of the underground market generate large negative externalities for society.

To be economically rational, the anticipated success rate and monetary value of an attack need to outweigh its costs. Florêncio and Herley (2013b) use this insight to explain the large gap between potential and actual harm online – the fact that most users do not get their accounts hijacked despite using pet names and birthdates as passwords. Automating attacks to scale is hard because of user diversity; it is also hard to know in advance which users offer sufficient financial prospects to be worth an attack. Herley (2012) presents this as the reason why Nigerian scams – the prince with $5 million in dire need of your help – are so obvious. These scams are expensive to run and the attacker wants only the most gullible users. In short, many attacks cannot be made profitable on scale, which is one of the reasons why many doomsday scenarios did not unfold as predicted.

Focusing defender efforts on bottlenecks in the attacker monetization chain can be an ingenious way to reduce attacks. A monumental study has been the work of Levchenko et al. (2011) investigating the spam value chain. The team tracked a billion spam URLs and placed orders for the offerings (including Viagra). The study found that spammers fulfilled most purchases with real products (albeit generic versions). Interestingly, spammers refund unsatisfied customers to appease the scarcest resource in the spam value chain: the payment channel. Credit card companies put pressure on the acquiring banks who provide spammers with the ability to receive payments. Such financial relationships are very hard to replace, much harder than the technical infrastructure used for spamming and rogue pharmacies. Spam can be sent extremely cheaply via botnets, making conversion rates as low as one in 12.5 million viable (Kanich et al., 2008). Other elements are also readily available. But setting up relations within a credit card network turns out to be a bottleneck, as it requires legal documents, fees and time. Astonishingly, 95 percent of spam-advertised sales used merchant services from a handful of banks. After the study was released, Pfizer and Microsoft, two big targets of spam-advertised goods, asked VISA and MasterCard to act against these banks. This made a detrimental blow to spam profitability and production globally (Thomas et al., 2015).

Obviously, criminals do not like getting caught and paying a fine or spending time in jail reduces profitability. Law enforcement has been traditionally weak in cyberspace due to crimes crossing jurisdictions. This is gradually changing and law enforcement agencies are ramping up efforts, as evidenced by multiple high-profile arrests in recent years (Krebs, 2011). Anderson et al. (2013) believe investing in law enforcement abilities to arrest cybercriminals to be very efficient, as many attacks are run by a small number of gangs.

13.7   POLICY OPTIONS

We have so far looked at the incentives of various actors in the Internet economy and how these affect their security decisions. We have seen that actors impose positive and negative externalities on others and the problems caused by asymmetric information. These are classic examples of market failures that weaken security incentives and will typically lead to suboptimal investment in security. We also saw that some actors, notably among Internet intermediaries operating in multi-sided markets, are willing to bear the costs of mitigating security failures of others. The unique competitive position of this group puts it in a position to make trade-offs between security and other qualities, possibly bringing the entire sector closer to a social optimum. However, in many situations no such endogenous mechanisms are available. This raises the question of whether and how forms of market failure can be remedied and what could be done to strengthen incentives to provide security. A traditional response to market failure is government intervention but, given the conflicting incentives of the state, other forms of governance have been proposed as more effective (Moore and Anderson, 2012; Brown and Marsden, 2013). We continue with a brief discussion of theoretical and empirical contributions to the literature on policy options.

13.7.1   The Costs of Cybersecurity Breaches

Ideally, private and public policy measures would take the actual and potential cost of cybersecurity breaches into account. This is one of the preconditions of rational investment decisions by the private sector and of rational policy design. Unfortunately, while estimates and numbers abound, their reliability and representativeness is difficult to assess. Many reports are generated by players with a stake in inflating the numbers. They are often based on weak evidence and/or overly simplified strong assumptions. The employed methods typically are not publicly available, complicating an assessment of the validity and reliability of the information. Damage is typically assessed at a highly aggregated level and difficult to link to specific incidents. Florêncio and Herley (2013a) show that estimates are frequently biased by a few individual observations. Anderson et al. (2013) argue that the cost of prevention often exceeds the actual damage by orders of magnitude. With these caveats in mind, it is noteworthy that a joint study conducted by McAfee and the Center for Strategic and International Studies (CSIS) estimated the global costs of cybercrime at $445 billion, or about 0.6 percent of global GDP (CSIS and McAfee, 2014).

Absent systematic and reliable metrics, it is at least possible to identify the types of costs good metrics would include. Because of the highly interconnected nature of the Internet, security incidents not only affect the immediate targets of an attack but also have second- and third-round effects on other stakeholders. From a policy perspective, the relevant cost is the total cost to society, which also includes the costs incurred by stakeholders other than those immediately affected. A comprehensive assessment of the costs and benefits of cybersecurity therefore should include the entire ecosystem of players including: users, private sector organizations, public sector organizations, Internet infrastructure providers (software vendors, ISPs, hosting providers, registrars), incident response units, and society at large (including opportunity costs, lost efficiency gains, diminished trust and use of the Internet, etc.). It should also include revenues and profits made by cybercriminals, malevolent hackers, and all those seeking to profit from undermining the security of the Internet as these constitute 'bads' (i.e., costs) to society (Van Eeten et al., 2009).

13.7.2   Addressing Information Asymmetries

Several approaches can help address information asymmetries, including mandatory breach disclosure, vulnerability disclosure, certification schemes, and the publication of security metrics.

13.7.2.1   Mandatory breach disclosure

Data and security breach disclosure laws aim to reduce harms caused to consumers resulting from breaches, and to incentivize organizations to invest in security, by requiring them to notify all affected individuals when personal information has been compromised as a result of an attack or negligence. Critics of mandatory breach disclosure argue that they might perversely desensitize consumers or cause them to overreact. Breach disclosure laws have been enacted in past years across a number of countries and most US states. Romanosky et al. (2011) found only weak empirical evidence in support of the effectiveness of disclosure laws. Between 2002 and 2009 disclosure requirements reduced identity theft by a mere 6.1 percent. This might be related to a finding by Nieuwesteeg (2013) that the vast majority of security breaches remain unreported, possibly due to firms calculating the risks of being discovered as smaller than notification and reputation costs. These costs include impacts of disclosure on stock market valuations of firms (Gordon et al., 2011). As other countries are considering adopting similar laws, there are discussions on how to design the details of such requirements. Thomas et al. (2013), for instance, recommend estimating and communicating the severity of breaches.

13.7.2.2   Vulnerability disclosure

Should there be a mandate to publicly disclose a newly discovered software vulnerability? On the one hand, it forces vendors to acknowledge and prioritize releasing a patch; on the other hand it gives attackers information they might otherwise not have. Arora et al. (2010) looked at past evidence by analyzing the US National Vulnerability Database (NVD) from 2000 to 2003. The data suggest that disclosures accelerated patch release. Ransbotham and Mitra (2013) evaluated differences between immediate disclosure and 'responsible disclosure', a procedure for first revealing the vulnerability in private to vendors before making it public after a certain period. Combining a dataset of intrusion detections from several hundred clients with the NVD for 2006 and 2007, the findings cautiously suggest that responsible disclosure is indeed beneficial.

13.7.2.3   Certification schemes

Security certifications by trusted third parties have been proposed as fixes to the 'lemons market' problem affecting security aspects of products. Certification schemes have been tried for software (Anderson and Moore, 2006), for websites using various 'trust seals', and the ISO 27000 information security standards. The success of these schemes hinges on who pays for the certification, who bears the costs of errors and what the certificates actually measure. Product sellers paying for certification have incentives to go to lax certification authorities. Even worse, Edelman (2011) observes an 'adverse selection' problem in that fraudulent websites have a higher probability of purchasing trust seals. Some certificates only demonstrate compliance with legal provisions. A great example of this is that DigiNotar passed the WebTrust EV audit for CAs just months before its spectacular collapse, while forensics revealed serious security problems (Fox-IT, 2011). This is not to say that security certification is not useful. It can still guarantee a basic level of good practices. However, it will not fully solve information asymmetry.

13.7.2.4   Publishing security metrics

Other market signals have also been proposed that simultaneously reduce asymmetry and allow organizations to self-evaluate. Organizations often believe they are doing enough to safeguard security. If they are presented with evidence that they do worse than their peers, they might increase efforts (e.g., Tang et al., 2013). The need for reliable measurements in cybersecurity has been known for a long time (Geer et al., 2003; Pfleeger and Cunningham, 2010). However, getting security metrics or measurements right is not an easy task. One should take care not to confuse measurable properties with metrics that function as security indicators (Böhme, 2010 provides a systematic overview). Designing, measuring and reporting security metrics is a promising way to help markets produce security more efficiently.

13.7.3   Addressing Externalities

Among the instruments proposed to help mitigate externalities are cyber insurance, liability rules, and better law enforcement.

13.7.3.1   Cyber insurance

Insurance for cybersecurity incidents was proposed early on as a solution to align incentives, reduce information asymmetries, and enable firms to better manage risks (Schneier, 2004; Böhme, 2005). Scholars suggested that insurers would charge different premiums for different levels of cybersecurity and contingent on security practices, which would increase incentives for users to purchase more secure products and adopt better security policies. Nonetheless, these expectations did not materialize and the market for cyber insurance shrunk relative to the Internet economy (Böhme and Schwartz, 2010). Shetty et al. (2010) argue that quantifying cyber risks is fundamentally hard for insurers because of information asymmetries. In addition, the interdependent nature of cyber risks deviates from how risk is typically addressed in insurance markets, complicating the design of workable insurance policies.

13.7.3.2   Assigning liability

Making users, organizations and intermediaries liable for online harms caused by security breaches in their systems could tip security incentives toward higher investment. Fryer et al. (2013) examine the issue thoroughly by looking at liability theories and reviewing proposals in the security economics literature, for example, to make software vendors liable for bugs (August and Tunca, 2011) or early calls to make users of bots liable for negligence attacks. In general, 'hard liability' will be a difficult sell in cybersecurity. In cases of clear negligence it might make sense; however, tort law, existing 'duty to care' and consumer protection laws might be sufficient for the courts. Moreover, the forensics of establishing the facts of a case and measuring harm might not be easy. Due to the interdependencies, cascading harms might occur, implying that firms may go bankrupt, become extremely risk-averse innovators, or resolve to create 'shell' companies. 'Softer' mechanisms – such as peer pressure, reputation effects, and regulatory coordination – might be much more effective. An alternative approach suggested by Ioannidis et al. (2013b) is to have an 'information steward' value harms to the ecosystem and allocate costs derived from externalities fairly among targets. Certain intermediaries such as Amazon Marketplace might be doing exactly this.

13.7.3.3   Better law enforcement

An alternative way to reduce externalities – and cybercrime – is to increase costs for attackers. This can be achieved by improving defenses, stricter law enforcement and by increasing the punishment for cybercriminals. Looking at the direct, indirect and defense costs imposed by cybercrime, Anderson et al. (2013) conclude that a more balanced approach is to spend less in anticipation of crime and more in response to it. Given the trans-border nature of many forms of cybercrime, this will also require improved international collaboration among law enforcement agencies.

13.8   CONCLUSION

In this chapter we have seen that the economics of cybersecurity is a powerful tool to analyze security failures. By surveying the literature, we looked at the incentives of software vendors, organizations, end users, Internet intermediaries and attackers; where they align and produce security; and where the market fails. We highlighted the role of Internet intermediaries in securing the ecosystem. We then listed policy interventions proposed to address market failures. We further saw that the empirical evidence on policies is not always clear. In part, this is due to measurement difficulties, because aggregate outcomes are unclear, and because the responses of the dynamic system in which cybercrime develops are difficult to anticipate. For example, in the technology race between attackers and defenders tightened security may eventually lead to even more malicious forms of intrusion.

In the end, focusing on incentives rather than the technology helps to understand trade-offs and develop sound cybersecurity policy. Given the dynamic nature of cybersecurity, all the issues discussed in this chapter are the subject of ongoing research. Among emerging topics are security on mobile communications platforms, in the cloud, in the Internet of Things (IoT) and the industrial Internet, user behavior and education across life stages, the establishment of better national and international governance frameworks for security, and the development of better and more reliable metrics.

NOTES

1.   In addition to WEIS, proceedings of USENIX Security, IEEE S&P, ACM CCS, SOUPS were perused. Key journals that were reviewed in detail included *IEEE Security & Privacy*, *Communications of the ACM*, *Telecommunications Policy*, and *Information Systems Research*. Key search terms for other journals included 'economics, security' and 'internet, security'.
2.   Due to the scope of this chapter, we will not delve further into these topics. The interested reader is referred to works presented at the annual Symposium on Usable Privacy and Security (SOUPS).

3. These debates are all important for the Internet economy and a number of them are looked at explicitly in other chapters of this *Handbook*; we retain our focus on cybersecurity.
4. In the USA these safeguards were contained in the safe harbor provision of the Digital Millennium Copyright Act (DMCA) of 1998. While US ISPs were reclassified as common carriers early in 2015 (see Federal Communications Commission, In the Matter of Protecting and Promoting the Open Internet, GN Docket No. 14–28, adopted 26 February 2015), they are subject to similar protections under common carrier law. In the European Union, such protections are contained in the 'mere conduit' provision of the Electronic Commerce Directive.
5. Much research has been done into the technical aspects of online fraud, including analyzing malware, detecting fraudulent transactions and reverse engineering banking protocols. These topics touch upon economics but fall out of our scope. Cryptocurrency is another topic that has received much attention in the literature due to its technical, economic and regulatory aspects. The interested reader is referred to the conferences of the International Financial Cryptography Association (IFCA).

REFERENCES

Akerlof, G.A. (1970), 'The market for "lemons": Quality uncertainty and the market mechanism', *The Quarterly Journal of Economics*, **84** (3), 488–500.
Anderson, J., J. Bonneau and F. Stajano (2010), 'Inglorious installers: Security in the application marketplace', in *Proceedings of the Ninth Workshop on the Economics of Information Security (WEIS'10)*, Harvard University, 7–8 June, accessed 6 January 2016 at https://www.cl.cam.ac.uk/~fms27/papers/2010-AndersonBonSta-inglourious.pdf.
Anderson, R. (2001), 'Why information security is hard – an economic perspective', in *Proceedings of the 17th Annual Computer Security Applications Conference (ACSAC'01)*, IEEE Computer Society, December, accessed 11 July 2015 at http://www.acsac.org/2001/papers/110.pdf.
Anderson, R. (2008), *Security Engineering: A Guide to Building Dependable Distributed Systems*, 2nd edition, Tokyo and New York: Wiley.
Anderson, R. and T. Moore (2006), 'The economics of information security', *Science*, **314** (5799), 610–13.
Anderson, R., R. Böhme, R. Clayton and T. Moore (2008), *Security Economics and the Internal Market*, study commissioned by the European Union Agency for Network and Information Security (ENISA), accessed 12 July 2015 at http://www.enisa.europa.eu/publications/archive/economics-sec.
Anderson, R., C. Barton and R. Böhme et al. (2013), 'Measuring the cost of cybercrime', in R. Böhme (ed.), *The Economics of Information Security and Privacy*, Berlin: Springer, pp. 265–300.
Arnbak, A. and N. van Eijk (2012), 'Certificate authority collapse: Regulating systemic vulnerabilities in the HTTPS value chain', 40th Research Conference on Communication, Information and Internet Policy (TPRC), accessed 11 July 2015 at http://ssrn.com/abstract=2031409.
Arnbak, A., H. Asghari, M. van Eeten and N. van Eijk (2014), 'Security collapse in the HTTPS market', *Communications of the ACM*, **57** (10), 47–55.
Arora, A., R. Krishnan, R. Telang and Y. Yang (2010), 'An empirical analysis of software vendors' patch release behavior: Impact of vulnerability disclosure', *Information Systems Research*, **21** (1), 115–32.
August, T. and T.I. Tunca (2011), 'Who should be responsible for software security? A comparative analysis of liability policies in network environments', *Management Science*, **57** (5), 934–59.
Böhme, R. (2005), 'Cyber-insurance revisited', in *Proceedings of the Fourth Workshop on the Economics of Information Security (WEIS'05)*, Harvard University, accessed 12 July 2015 at http://infosecon.net/workshop/pdf/15.pdf.
Böhme, R. (2010), 'Security metrics and security investment models', in *Advances in Information and Computer Security*, Berlin: Springer, pp. 10–24.
Böhme, R. and T. Moore (2009), 'The iterated weakest link – A model of adaptive security investment', in *Proceedings of the Eight Workshop on the Economics of Information Security (WEIS'09)*, University College, London, 24–25 June, accessed 12 July 2015 at https://www.is.uni-muenster.de/security/publications/BM2009_IteratedWeakestLink_WEIS.pdf.
Böhme, R. and G. Schwartz (2010), 'Modeling cyber-insurance: Towards a unifying framework', in *Proceedings of the Ninth Workshop on the Economics of Information Security (WEIS'10)*, Harvard University, 7–8 June, accessed 14 July 2015 at http://www.icsi.berkeley.edu/pubs/networking/modelingcyber10.pdf.
Bonneau, J., C. Herley, P.C. van Oorschot and F. Stajano (2012), 'The quest to replace passwords: A framework for comparative evaluation of web authentication schemes', paper in *Proceedings of the 2012 IEEE Symposium on Security and Privacy (SP)*, 20–23 May, San Francisco, CA, pp. 553–67.

Bradbury, D. (2014), 'Testing the defences of bulletproof hosting companies', *Network Security*, **2014** (6), 8–12.

Branscomb, A.W. (1994), *Who Owns Information? From Privacy to Public Access*, New York: Basic Books.

Bravo-Lillo, C., L.F. Cranor, J.S. Downs and S. Komanduri (2011), 'Bridging the gap in computer security warnings: A mental model approach', *IEEE Security & Privacy*, **9** (2), 18–26.

Brecht, M. and T. Nowey (2013), 'A closer look at information security costs', in R. Böhme (ed.), *The Economics of Information Security and Privacy*, Berlin and Heidelberg: Springer, pp. 3–24.

Brown, I. and C.T. Marsden (2013), *Regulating Code: Good Governance and Better Regulation in the Information Age*, Cambridge, MA: MIT Press.

Camp, L.J. (2013), 'Beyond usability: Security interactions as risk perceptions', in *Proceedings of the Ninth Symposium on Usable Privacy and Security (SOUPS)*, 24–26 July, Newcastle, UK, accessed 14 July 2015 at http://citeseerx.ist.psu.edu/viewdoc/download?doi=10.1.1.385.7530&rep=rep1&type=pdf.

Canali, D., D. Balzarotti and A. Francillon (2013), 'The role of web hosting providers in detecting compromised websites', in *Proceedings of the 22nd International Conference on World Wide Web (WWW'13)*, 13–17 May, Rio de Janeiro, Brazil, pp. 177–88.

Cavusoglu, H., B. Mishra and S. Raghunathan (2004), 'A model for evaluating IT security investments', *Communications of the ACM*, **47** (7), 87–92.

Chen, M., V.S. Jacob, S. Radhakrishnan and Y.U. Ryu (2012), 'The effect of fraud investigation cost on pay-per-click advertising', in *Proceedings of the Eleventh Workshop on the Economics of Information Security (WEIS'12)*, 25–26 June, Berlin, accessed 14 July 2015 at http://weis2012.econinfosec.org/papers/Chen_WEIS2012.pdf.

Christin, N. (2013), 'Traveling the silk road: A measurement analysis of a large anonymous online marketplace', in *Proceedings of the 22nd International Conference on World Wide Web (WWW'13)*, 13–17 May, Rio de Janeiro, pp. 213–24.

Clayton, R. (2011), 'Might governments clean-up malware?', *Communication & Strategies*, **81**, 87–104.

Colander, David (2005), 'The making of an economist redux', *Journal of Economic Perspectives*, **19** (1), 175–98.

CSIS and McAfee (2014), 'Net losses: Estimating the global cost of cybercrime', accessed 14 July 2015 at http://www.cyberriskinsuranceforum.com/sites/default/files/pictures/rp-economic-impact-cybercrime2.pdf.

CVE (2015), 'Common vulnerabilities and exposures list master copy', accessed 14 July 2015 at https://cve.mitre.org/cve/cve.html.

Davenport, T.H. and J.C. Beck (2001), *The Attention Economy: Understanding the New Currency of Business*, Boston, MA: Harvard Business School Press.

Demetz, L. and D. Bachlechner (2013), 'To invest or not to invest? Assessing the economic viability of a policy and security configuration management tool', in R. Böhme (ed.), *The Economics of Information Security and Privacy*, Berlin and Heidelberg: Springer, pp. 25–47.

Dredge, S. (2015), 'MySpace – what went wrong: "The site was a massive spaghetti-ball mess"', *The Guardian*, 6 March, accessed 14 July 2015 at http://www.theguardian.com/technology/2015/mar/06/myspace-what-went-wrong-sean-percival-spotify.

Durumeric, Z., J. Kasten, M. Bailey and J.A. Halderman (2013), 'Analysis of the HTTPS certificate ecosystem', in *Proceedings of the 2013 Internet Measurement Conference (IMC'13)*, 23–25 October, Barcelona, pp. 291–304.

Edelman, B. (2011), 'Adverse selection in online "trust" certifications and search results', *Electronic Commerce Research and Applications*, **10** (1), 17–25.

Fershtman, C. and N. Gandal (2012), 'Migration to the cloud ecosystem: Ushering in a new generation of platform competition', *CEPR Discussion Paper No. DP8907*, accessed 14 July 2015 at http://ssrn.com/abstract=2034125.

Financial Fraud Action UK (2015), 'Scams and computer viruses contribute to fraud increases – calls for national awareness campaign', accessed 14 July 2015 at http://www.financialfraudaction.org.uk/cms/assets/1/2014%20annual%20fraud%20figures%20release%20-%20final.pdf.

Florêncio, D. and C. Herley (2010), 'Where do security policies come from?', in *Proceedings of the Sixth Symposium on Usable Privacy and Security (SOUPS)*, 14–16 July, Redmond, WA.

Florêncio, D. and C. Herley (2013a), 'Sex, lies and cyber-crime surveys', in B. Schneier (ed.), *Economics of Information Security and Privacy III*, New York and London: Springer, pp. 35–53.

Florêncio, D. and C. Herley (2013b), 'Where do all the attacks go?', in B. Schneier (ed.), *Economics of Information Security and Privacy III*, New York and London: Springer, pp. 13–33.

Fox-IT (2011), 'DigiNotar certificate authority breach – 'Operation Black Tulip'', accessed 14 July 2015 at http://www.rijksoverheid.nl/documenten-en-publicaties/rapporten/2011/09/05/diginotar-public-report-version-1.html.

Franklin, J., A. Perrig, V. Paxson and S. Savage (2007), 'An inquiry into the nature and causes of the wealth of internet miscreants', in *Proceedings of the ACM Conference on Computer and Communications Security (CCS'07)*, 29 October–2 November, Alexandria, VA, pp. 375–88.

Fryer, H., R. Moore and T. Chown (2013), 'On the viability of using liability to incentivise internet security', in *Proceedings of the Twelfth Workshop on the Economics of Information Security (WEIS'13)*, 11–13 June, Georgetown University, Washington, DC, accessed 15 July 2015 at http://weis2013.econinfosec.org/papers/ FryerMooreChownWEIS2013.pdf.

Gaynor, M.S., M.Z. Hydari and R. Telang (2012), 'Is patient data better protected in competitive healthcare markets?', in *Proceedings of the Eleventh Workshop on the Economics of Information Security (WEIS'12)*, 25–26 June, Berlin, accessed 15 July 2015 at http://weis2012.econinfosec.org/papers/Gaynor_WEIS2012.pdf.

Geer, D., K.S. Hoo and A. Jaquith (2003), 'Information security: Why the future belongs to the quants', *IEEE Security & Privacy*, **1** (4), 24–32.

Goldfarb, A. and C. Tucker (2011), 'Search engine advertising: Channel substitution when pricing ads to context', *Management Science*, **57** (3), 458–70.

Gordon, L.A. and M.P. Loeb (2002), 'The economics of information security investment', *ACM Transactions on Information and System Security (TISSEC)*, **5** (4), 438–57.

Gordon, L.A., M.P. Loeb and L. Zhou (2011), 'The impact of information security breaches: Has there been a downward shift in costs?', *Journal of Computer Security*, **19** (1), 33–56.

Gottinger, H.W. (2003), *Economies of Network Industries*, London: Routledge.

Graves, J., A. Acquisti and N. Christin (2014), 'Should payment card issuers reissue cards in response to a data breach?', in *Proceedings of the Thirteenth Workshop on the Economics of Information Security (WEIS'14)*, College Park, MD, accessed 23 July 2015 at http://weis2014.econinfosec.org/papers/GravesAcquistiChristin-WEIS2014.pdf.

Groenewegen, John (ed.) (2007), *Teaching Pluralism in Economics*, Cheltenham, UK and Northampton, USA: Edward Elgar Publishing.

Grosse, E. (2012), 'Security warnings for suspected state-sponsored attacks', *Google Online Security Blog*, 5 June, accessed 15 July 2015 at http://googleonlinesecurity.blogspot.com/2012/06/security-warnings-for-suspected-state.html.

Herley, C. (2009), 'So long, and no thanks for the externalities: The rational rejection of security advice by users', in *Proceedings of the 2009 Workshop on New Security Paradigms Workshop (NSPW'09)*, 8–11 September, Oxford, UK, pp. 133–44.

Herley, C. (2012), 'Why do Nigerian scammers say they are from Nigeria?', in *Proceedings of the Eleventh Workshop on the Economics of Information Security (WEIS'12)*, 25–26 June, Berlin, accessed 15 July 2015 at http://weis2012.econinfosec.org/papers/Herley_WEIS2012.pdf.

Herley, C. and D. Florêncio (2010), 'Nobody sells gold for the price of silver: Dishonesty, uncertainty and the underground economy', in T. Moore, D.J. Pym and C. Ioannidis (eds), *Economics of Information Security and Privacy*, New York: Springer, pp. 33–53.

Hofmann, J. (2010), 'The libertarian origins of cybercrime: Unintended side-effects of a political utopia', *London School of Economics Discussion Paper, No. 62*, accessed 15 July 2015 at http://ssrn.com/ abstract=1710773.

Hofmeyr, S., T. Moore, S. Forrest, B. Edwards and G. Stelle (2013), 'Modeling Internet-scale policies for cleaning up malware', in B. Schneier (ed.), *Economics of Information Security and Privacy III*, New York and London: Springer, pp. 149–70.

Ioannidis, C., D. Pym and J. Williams (2013a), 'Fixed costs, investment rigidities, and risk aversion in information security: A utility-theoretic approach', in B. Schneier (ed.), *Economics of Information Security and Privacy III*, New York and London: Springer, pp. 171–91.

Ioannidis, C., D. Pym and J. Williams (2013b), 'Sustainability in information stewardship', in *Proceedings of the Twelfth Workshop on the Economics of Information Security (WEIS'13)*, 11–13 June, Georgetown University, Washington, DC, accessed 15 July 2015 at http://weis2013.econinfosec.org/papers/ IoannidisPymWilliamsWEIS2013.pdf.

Kanich, C., C. Kreibich and K. Levchenko et al. (2008), 'Spamalytics: An empirical analysis of spam marketing conversion', in *Proceedings of the 15th ACM Conference on Computer and Communications Security (CCS'08)*, 28–31 October, Alexandria, VA, pp. 3–14.

Kelley, T. and L.J. Camp (2012), 'Online promiscuity: Prophylactic patching and the spread of computer transmitted infections', in *Proceedings of the Eleventh Workshop on the Economics of Information Security (WEIS'12)*, 25–26 June, Berlin, accessed 15 July 2015 at http://weis2012.econinfosec.org/papers/Kelley_ WEIS2012.pdf.

Kramer, A.D.I., J.E. Guillory and J.T. Hancock (2014), 'Experimental evidence of massive-scale emotional contagion through social networks', in *Proceedings of the National Academy of Sciences*, **111** (24), 8788–90.

Krebs, B. (2011), '72M USD scareware ring used Conficker worm', 23 June, accessed 15 July 2015 at http:// krebsonsecurity.com/2011/06/72m-scareware-ring-used-conficker-worm/.

Kunreuther, H. and G. Heal (2003), 'Interdependent security', *Journal of Risk and Uncertainty*, **26** (2–3), 231–49.

Kwon, J. and M.E. Johnson (2011), 'An organizational learning perspective on proactive vs. reactive investment in information security', in *Proceedings of the Tenth Workshop on the Economics of Information Security (WEIS'11)*, 14–15 June, George Mason University, Fairfax, VA, accessed 15 July 2015 at http://weis2011. econinfosec.org/papers/An%20Organizational%20Learning%20Perspective%20on%20Proactive%20vs.%20 Rea.pdf.

Kwon, J. and M.E. Johnson (2013), 'Healthcare security strategies for regulatory compliance and data security', *46th Hawaii International Conference on System Sciences (HICSS)*, 7–10 January, Wailea, HI, pp. 3972–81.

Landau, S. and T. Moore (2012), 'Economic tussles in federated identity management', *First Monday*, **17** (10), accessed 15 July 2015 at http://uncommonculture.org/ojs/index.php/fm/article/view/4254.

Lessig, L. (1999), *Code and Other Laws of Cyberspace*, New York: Basic Books.

Levchenko, K., A. Pitsillidis and N. Chachra et al. (2011), 'Click trajectories: End-to-end analysis of the spam value chain', in *Proceedings of the IEEE Symposium on Security and Privacy*, 22–25 May, Berkeley, CA, pp. 431–46.

Lewis, J.A. (2005), 'Aux armes, citoyens: Cyber security and regulation in the United States', *Telecommunications Policy*, **29** (11), 82–30.

Liu, H., K. Levchenko and M. Félegyházi et al. (2011), 'On the effects of registrar level intervention', in *Proceedings of the 4th USENIX Workshop on Large-scale Exploits and Emergent Threats (LEET'11): Botnets, Spyware, Worms, and More*, 29 March, Boston, MA.

Miller, A.R. and C.E. Tucker (2011), 'Encryption and the loss of patient data', *Journal of Policy Analysis and Management*, **30** (3), 534–56.

Moore, T. and R. Anderson (2012), 'Internet security', in M. Peitz and J. Waldfogel (eds), *Oxford Handbook on the Digital Economy*, Oxford and New York: Oxford University Press, pp. 572–99.

Moore, T. and R. Clayton (2007), 'Examining the impact of website take-down on phishing', in *Proceedings of the Anti-Phishing Working Groups 2nd Annual eCrime Researchers Summit (eCrime'07)*, 4–5 October, Pittsburgh, PA, pp. 1–13.

Moore, T. and R. Clayton (2009), 'The impact of incentives on notice and take-down', in M.E. Johnson (ed.), *Managing Information Risk and the Economics of Security*, New York: Springer, pp. 199–223.

Musgrave, R.A. and P.B. Musgrave (1973), *Public Finance in Theory and Practice*, New York: McGraw-Hill.

Nieuwesteeg, B.F.H. (2013), 'The legal position and societal effects of security breach notification laws', MA thesis, Delft University of Technology, the Netherlands, accessed July 15 2015 at http://repository.tudelft.nl/ view/ir/uuid:38d4fa0e-8a3a-4216-9044-e8507a60ed66/.

Noam, E.M. (2009), *Media Ownership and Concentration in America*, New York: Oxford University Press.

OECD (2012), 'Proactive policy measures by Internet service providers against botnets', *OECD Digital Economy Papers No. 199*, Paris: OECD, accessed 15 July 2015 at http://dx.doi.org/10.1787/5k98 tq42t18w-en.

Perset, K. (2010), 'The economic and social role of internet intermediaries', *OECD Digital Economy Papers, No. 171*, Paris: OECD, accessed 15 July 2015 at http://dx.doi.org/10.1787/5kmh79zzs8vb-en.

Pfleeger, S.L. and R.K. Cunningham (2010), 'Why measuring security is hard', *IEEE Security & Privacy*, **8** (4), 46–54.

Ransbotham, S. and S. Mitra (2013), 'The impact of immediate disclosure on attack diffusion and volume', in B. Schneier (ed.), *Economics of Information Security and Privacy III*, New York and London: Springer, pp. 1–12.

Riccardi, M., R. di Pietro, M. Palanques and J. Aguilà Vila (2013), 'Titans' revenge: Detecting Zeus via its own flaws', *Computer Networks, Special Issue on Botnet Activity: Analysis, Detection and Shutdown*, **57** (2), 422–35.

Romanosky, S., R. Telang and A. Acquisti (2011), 'Do data breach disclosure laws reduce identity theft?', *Journal of Policy Analysis and Management*, **30** (2), 256–86.

Rosen, H.S. (2004), 'Public finance', in C.K. Rowley and F. Schneider (eds), *The Encyclopedia of Public Choice*, Dordrecht and Boston, MA: Kluwer Academic Publishers, pp. 252–61.

Rysman, M. (2009), 'The economics of two-sided markets', *The Journal of Economic Perspectives*, **23** (3), 125–43.

Schneier, B. (2004), 'Hacking the business climate for network security', *Computer*, **37** (4), 87–9.

Schneier, B. (2007), 'A security market for lemons', *Schneier on Security Blog*, accessed 15 July 2015 at https:// www.schneier.com/blog/archives/2007/04/a_security_mark.html.

Schneier, B. (2012), 'When it comes to security, we're back to Feudalism', *Schneier on Security Blog*, 26 November, accessed 15 July 2015 at https://www.schneier.com/essays/archives/2012/11/when_it_comes_ to_sec.html.

Shapiro, C. and H.R. Varian (1998), *Information Rules: A Strategic Guide to the Network Economy*, Boston, MA: Harvard Business School Press.

Shetty, N., G. Schwartz, M. Felegyhazi and J. Walrand (2010), 'Competitive cyber-insurance and Internet security', in T. Moore, D.J. Pym and C. Ioannidis (eds), *Economics of Information Security and Privacy*, New York: Springer, pp. 229–47.

Shim, W. (2006), 'Interdependent risk and cyber security: An analysis of security investment and cyber insurance', PhD dissertation, East Lansing, MI: Michigan State University.

Singer, P.W. and A. Friedman (2013), *Cybersecurity: What Everyone Needs to Know*, Oxford, UK: Oxford University Press.

Stajano, F. and P. Wilson (2011), 'Understanding scam victims: Seven principles for systems security', *Communications of the ACM*, **54** (3), 70–75.

Stone-Gross, B., C. Kruegel, K. Almeroth, A. Moser and E. Kirda (2009), 'Fire: Finding rogue networks', in *Proceedings of the Annual Computer Security Applications Conference 2009 (ACSAC'09)*, 7–11 December, Honolulu, HI, pp. 231–40.

Stone-Gross, B., R. Abman and R.A. Kemmerer et al. (2013), 'The underground economy of fake antivirus software', in B. Schneier (ed.), *Economics of Information Security and Privacy III*, New York and London: Springer, pp. 55–78.

Sullivan, K. (2012), *The Internet Health Model for Cybersecurity*, New York: East West Institute, accessed 15 July 2015 at http://issuu.com/ewipublications/docs/internethealth?e=0/5313787.

Sunshine, J., S. Egelman, H. Almuhimedi, N. Atri and L.F. Cranor (2009), 'Crying wolf: An empirical study of SSL warning effectiveness', in *Proceedings of the 18th USENIX Security Symposium (Security'09)*, 14–18 August, Montreal, Canada, pp. 399–416, accessed 15 July 2015 at http://static.usenix.org/legacy/events/sec09/tech/full_papers/sec09_browser.pdf.

Symantec (2015), *Internet Security Threat Report 2015*, accessed 15 July 2015 at http://www.symantec.com/security_response/publications/threatreport.jsp?themeid=threatreport.

Tang, Q., L. Linden, J.S. Quarterman and A.B. Whinston (2013), 'Improving Internet security through social information and social comparison: A field quasi-experiment', in *Proceedings of the Twelfth Workshop on the Economics of Information Security (WEIS'13)*, 11–13 June, Georgetown University, Washington, DC, accessed 15 July 2015 at http://weis2013.econinfosec.org/papers/TangWEIS2013.pdf.

Thomas, K., D.Y. Huang and D. Wang et al. (2015), 'Framing dependencies introduced by underground commoditization', in *Proceedings of the Fourteenth Workshop on the Economics of Information Security (WEIS'15)*, 22–23 June, Delft University of Technology, Delft, the Netherlands, accessed 15 July 2015 at http://weis2015.econinfosec.org/papers/WEIS_2015_thomas.pdf.

Thomas, R.C., M. Antkiewicz, P. Florer, S. Widup and M. Woodyard (2013), 'How bad is it? A branching activity model to estimate the impact of information security breaches', accessed 15 July 2015 at http://ssrn.com/abstract=2233075.

Van Eeten, M.J.G. and J.M. Bauer (2008), 'The economics of malware: Security decisions, incentives and externalities', Directorate for Science, Technology and Industry, Committee for Information, Computer and Communications Policy, DSTI/ICCP/REG(2007)27, Paris: Organisation for Economic Co-operation and Development.

Van Eeten, M.J.G. and J.M. Bauer (2009), 'Emerging threats to Internet security: Incentives, externalities and policy implications', *Journal of Contingencies and Crisis Management*, **17** (4), 221–32.

Van Eeten, M.J.G. and J.M. Bauer (2013), 'Enhancing incentives for Internet security', in I. Brown (ed.), *Research Handbook on Governance of the Internet*, Cheltenham, UK and Northampton, MA: Edward Elgar Publishing, pp. 445–84.

Van Eeten, M.J.G. and M.L. Mueller (2012), 'Where is the governance in Internet governance?', *New Media & Society*, **5** (5), 720–36.

Van Eeten, M.J.G., J.M. Bauer and S. Tabatabaie (2009), *Damages from Internet Security Incidents: A Framework and Toolkit for Assessing the Economic Costs of Security Breaches*, unpublished report for the Independent Post and Telecommunications Authority (OPTA), The Hague.

Van Eeten, M.J.G., J.M. Bauer, H. Asghari, S. Tabatabaie and D. Rand (2010), 'The role of Internet service providers in botnet mitigation: An empirical analysis based on spam data', accessed 14 July 2015 at http://ssrn.com/abstract=1989198.

Vasek, M. and T. Moore (2012), 'Do malware reports expedite cleanup? An experimental study', *CSET*, https://www.usenix.org/system/files/conference/cset12/cset12-final20.pdf.

Vratonjic, N., J. Freudiger, V. Bindschaedler and J.-P. Hubaux (2013), 'The inconvenient truth about web certificates', in B. Schneier (ed.), *Economics of Information Security and Privacy III*, New York and London: Springer, pp. 79–117.

Wash, R. (2010), 'Folk models of home computer security', in *Proceedings of the Sixth Symposium on Usable Privacy and Security (SOUPS'10)*, 14–16 July, Redmond, WA.

Wondracek, G., T. Holz, C. Platzer, E. Kirda and C. Kruegel (2010), 'Is the Internet for porn? An insight into the online adult industry', in *Proceedings of the Ninth Workshop on the Economics of Information Security (WEIS'10)*, Harvard University, 7–8 June, accessed 14 July 2015 at http://iseclab.org/papers/weis2010.pdf.

Wood, D. and B. Rowe (2011), 'Assessing home internet users' demand for security: Will they pay ISPs?', accessed 14 July 2015 at http://citeseerx.ist.psu.edu/viewdoc/download?doi=10.1.1.308.9669&rep=rep1&type=pdf.

Zhang, J., Z. Durumeric, M. Bailey, M. Liu and M. Karir (2014), 'On the mismanagement and maliciousness of networks', in *Proceedings of the Symposium on Network and Distributed System Security (NDSS'14)*, 23–26 February, San Diego, CA.

Zittrain, J. (2008), *The Future of the Internet – and How to Stop It*, New Haven, CT: Yale University Press.

14. Internet architecture and innovation in applications*
Barbara van Schewick†

14.1 INTRODUCTION AND OVERVIEW

The Internet's original architecture – its technical inner structure – was based on three design principles: the layering principle and two versions of the end-to-end arguments.[1] Over the past years, the Internet's architecture has been changing in ways that deviate from the Internet's original design principles. Some of these changes are driven by network providers' desire for more profit; some changes are the reaction to technical challenges the Internet is facing.

This chapter examines how deviations from the broad version of the end-to-end arguments affect the economic environment for innovation in Internet applications, content, and services and the overall amount and quality of application innovation that will occur.[2] The chapter's approach to the study of architecture and innovation is an example of a more general approach to studying the architecture of complex systems, an approach I call 'architecture and economics'.[3] The approach understands architecture as one of several constraints on human behavior and uses economic theory (broadly defined) to explore the effect of these constraints.

The chapter proceeds as follows. Section 14.2 sets out the theoretical framework for understanding how architectures relate to economic systems and, more specifically, how architectures affect innovation. Section 14.3 introduces the concepts necessary to understand network architectures – end hosts, the core of the network, layers, and protocols – and describes two of the design principles that were used to create the Internet's original architecture: the layering principle and the broad version of the end-to-end arguments. Section 14.4 explains how these design principles shaped the Internet's original architecture. Section 14.5 discusses how the Internet's original architecture affected the economic environment for innovation in applications, and how changes to this architecture will affect the amount and quality of application innovation that will occur. Section 14.6 concludes.

The effect of the Internet's architecture on innovation in other areas of the architecture (e.g., in the Internet layer or in physical network technologies) is outside the scope of this chapter.[4] Throughout the chapter, I use the term *network providers* to describe economic actors who provide Internet access or transport services and the term *applications* as shorthand for Internet applications, content, services, and uses.[5]

14.2 ARCHITECTURE AND INNOVATION

The architecture of a system denotes the fundamental structures of a complex system as defined during the early stages of product development. Similar to the way the architecture of a house is different from the house itself, the architecture of a system is not the final, working system, but is instead a description of the system's basic building blocks. In particular, the architecture describes the components of the system, what they do, and how they interact.[6] In networking, the architecture of a network describes the components of the network, what they do, and how they interact.

The relationship between architectures and the economic system can be understood within a broader framework that economists use to explain the evolution of the economy as a whole.[7] In this framework, the economic system evolves as economic actors pursue their own interests within a set of constraints, and as they act to change those constraints. Constraints delimit the options available to economic actors and influence the costs and benefits associated with these options. Well-known constraints include prices, laws, norms, and the natural and technical environments in which economic actors exist.

Like these other constraints, an architecture can affect human behavior by imposing constraints on those who interact with the architecture or are exposed to it.[8] Specifically, by imposing constraints on those who design, produce, and use a complex system, the architecture of the system (and the design principles that were used to create it) can influence the economic system in which the system is developed, produced, and used. Different architectures may impose different constraints, which may result in different decisions by economic actors, which in turn may result in different firm and market structures and different levels of economic activity. And by changing existing architectures or creating new ones, economic actors can change the constraints that architectures impose.[9]

Understanding that architecture may constrain potential innovators is only the first step toward explaining the relationship between architecture and innovation. An economic actor's reaction to a constraint depends on the characteristics of the economic actor, the other constraints on the actor, and the actor's existing relationships and anticipated interactions with other actors.[10]

First, the effect of architecture depends on the characteristics of the actors exposed to it.[11] Actors may have different resources, capabilities, cost structures, goals, motivations, and cost–benefit assessment practices; consequently, their perception of costs and benefits is idiosyncratic, and they may react differently to the same architectural constraint.[12] An actor who hopes to profit from selling their innovation may be disinclined to innovate if they are operating within an architecture that reduces their potential sales revenue. In contrast, an actor who innovates to use the innovation themselves may remain unaffected by the same architectural change (so long as the architecture lets them use the innovation).

Second, architecture is not the only constraint on potential innovators.[13] Laws, social norms, market conditions, and the natural and technical environments also influence innovators' actions. Like architecture, these constraints delimit the available choices and affect the corresponding costs and benefits. Intellectual property laws, for example, influence the expected benefits of an innovation by conferring a temporary monopoly on the innovator but impose costs on subsequent innovators who want to build on the original innovation. By striking different balances between the interests of the original innovator and those of subsequent innovators, alternative intellectual property regimes that differ in duration and scope facilitate different types and amounts of innovative activity.[14] The structures and operations of capital and labor markets (both heavily influenced by laws and norms) may affect the ease with which a potential innovator can acquire the financial and human capital necessary to realize his or her innovation. When operating simultaneously, different constraints interact and influence one another in complex ways.[15] For example, two constraints may support or contradict each other, ultimately reinforcing or weakening the other constraint's effect on an actor.[16]

Finally, a potential innovator's response to a constraint may be influenced by his or her extant relationships and anticipated interactions with other actors.[17] For example, if a market has only a few potential or anticipated innovators, each firm will base its level of investment on the level of investment it expects from the others. A firm that has long collaborated with another firm may be able to work with this firm on innovative projects that require constant interaction, because the trust and coordination mechanisms resulting from the long-term relationship may enable it to overcome the coordination problems that usually prevent firms from coordinating closely interdependent activities across firm boundaries.[18]

Thus, the same architecture, operating in environments with different actors and constraints, may enable very different types and levels of innovative activity. For example, consider an architecture that encourages entrepreneurial innovation, but that requires more capital than entrepreneurs are usually able to invest individually. In this case, we would expect to see more innovation from entrepreneurs in an environment in which funding from venture capitalists is available than in an environment in which similar financial actors do not exist.[19]

Within the framework just described, this chapter focuses on the effect of one constraint (network architecture) on one type of economic behavior (innovation). To focus on the specific effect of architecture, the analysis assumes that while the architecture changes, everything else (i.e., the group of actors exposed to the architecture and the other constraints under which they operate) stays the same, and that there are no legal rules that limit network providers' ability to take advantage of the capabilities provided by the architecture.[20]

14.3   NETWORK ARCHITECTURES AND DESIGN PRINCIPLES

14.3.1   Network Architecture

As explained above, the architecture of a system describes the components of the system, what they do, and how they interact.[21] In networking, the architecture of a network describes the components of the network, what they do, and how they interact.

14.3.2   Components of Computer Networks: End Hosts and Computers in the Core of the Network

At the highest level of a network architecture, designers distinguish two classes of components:[22] end hosts and computers in the core of the network. While end hosts are computers that use the network, computers in the core of the network form the network.

End hosts support users and run application programs; they use the services of the network to communicate with one another. The home computers many people use to surf the Internet, smartphones such as the iPhone that allow users to use the Internet wherever they are, the web servers that carry the content provided by Yahoo! or *The New York Times*, or the servers through which users access their Gmail accounts are all examples of end hosts.

Computers in the core of the network form or implement the network.[23,24] They establish connectivity among the computers attached to the network. They include the cable modem termination system operated by a cable provider (to which a subscriber's cable modem is connected to give them access to the Internet) and the routers that network providers use to forward Internet data from one physical network to another. Viewed from computers in the core of the network, end hosts are the sources and destinations of data.

Thus, the terms 'end hosts' and 'core of the network' denote a purely functional distinction between users and providers of communication services.[25] They do not refer to topological relationships or to administrative ownership and control. Thus, topologically, an end host may be co-located with routers belonging to the network's core. Similarly, a mail server is an end host regardless of whether it is owned and operated by an Internet access service provider.

14.3.3 Design Principles: Layering and the End-to-end Arguments

The original architecture of the Internet that governed the Internet from its inception to the early 1990s was based on three design principles: the layering principle,[26] the broad version of the end-to-end arguments, and the narrow version of the end-to-end arguments.

14.3.3.1 The layering principle

In networks designed according to the layering principle, each computer, whether it is an end host or a computer in the core of the network, is further subdivided into architectural components called layers.[27] Layers are thought of as being arranged in a vertical structure (Figure 14.1). Each layer has one or more architectural subcomponents called protocols.

Each protocol provides a well-defined set of services to the layer above, using the services of the layer below. To implement the services provided by the protocol, different instances of the same protocol located on different computers (protocol peers) cooperate by exchanging messages with one another. For example, web browsers like Firefox or

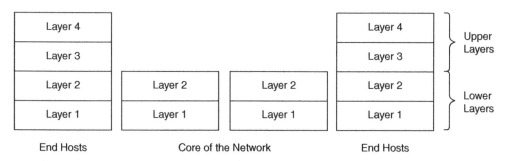

Figure 14.1   Architectural components of computer networks

Internet Explorer use the Hypertext Transfer Protocol (HTTP) to ask web servers such as the web server of *The New York Times* for a specific web page; the web server then uses the same protocol to send the desired web page back to the browser, which in turn displays it to the user.[28] While lower layers are implemented on end hosts and computers in the core of the network, higher layers only have to be implemented on end hosts.[29]

As in any layered approach to design, a protocol that is assigned to a layer can use any of the other protocols in the same layer or in a lower one, but it cannot use a protocol in a higher layer.[30] As a result, protocols in lower layers are independent from protocols in higher layers. This reduces complexity and insulates lower layers from changes in higher layers.[31]

In addition, the interaction between protocols is restricted by two additional constraints on the architecture that are specific to layering in the networking context. First, a protocol at a specific layer at a receiver must receive exactly the same object as sent by its protocol peer at the source.[32] This allows protocol designers to design protocols as if protocol peers (i.e., the instances of a specific protocol located on different computers) communicated directly. Designers do not have to worry about how the messages exchanged by protocol peers actually get from one protocol peer to the other, which greatly reduces the complexity of designing a protocol.

Second, a lower-layer protocol is not allowed to make any assumptions about the content or the meaning of the message (or, more technically, protocol data unit) passed to it by a higher-layer protocol for delivery to its higher-layer protocol peer.[33] The lower-layer protocol may neither access nor act on the information contained in a higher-layer protocol data unit. This constraint preserves the central feature of layering – the independence of higher layers from lower layers. Together with the broad version of the end-to-end arguments, it also results in a network that is application-blind, that is, unable to distinguish among the applications on the network.[34]

14.3.3.2   The broad version of the end-to-end arguments

The end-to-end arguments are design principles that help network architects decide how to allocate functions to the different layers of a network. The layering principle advises that the network's functionality should be organized in layers and imposes certain constraints on allowable interactions between layers. These constraints, however, do not necessarily determine in which layer specific functions should be placed. Thus, when designing a layered network, network architects still need to decide how exactly to divide the network's functionality among layers, and the end-to-end arguments help with these decisions.[35]

There are two versions of the end-to-end arguments that both shaped the original architecture of the Internet: the narrow version was first identified, named and described in a seminal paper by Saltzer et al. in 1981.[36] The broad version was the focus of later papers by the authors.[37] Although Saltzer et al. never explicitly drew attention to the change in definition, there are real differences between the two versions – differences in scope, in content, and in validity – that make it preferable to distinguish between the two.[38] Not surprisingly, the silent coexistence of two different design principles under the same name has created considerable confusion.[39]

While both versions shaped the Internet's original architecture, only the broad version affects the economic environment for innovation. Therefore, this chapter focuses on the broad version.[40] According to the broad version, 'specific application-level functions usually cannot, and preferably should not, be built into the lower levels of the system – the core of the network'.[41] Instead, 'a function or service should be carried out within a network layer only if it is needed by all clients of that layer, and it can be completely implemented in that layer'.[42] Lower layers of the system, the core of the network, should provide only general services that are of broad utility across applications in order to support as many higher-layer applications as possible. The network should not be optimized to better support specific higher-layer applications. All application-specific functionality should be concentrated in the higher layers of the system, at the end hosts.[43] The broad version does not prevent functions from being implemented in the network if they cannot be completely and correctly implemented at the end hosts only.[44]

Implementing application-specific functionality (i.e., functionality that is only needed by some applications) in lower layers of the network or optimizing the network for specific applications will usually improve the performance of these applications. The lower layers of the network, however, are used by all applications; functionality implemented at these layers therefore also affects current and future applications that do not need the application-specific functionality or have needs that differ from the needs of the applications for which the network was optimized. In the best case, these applications pay the price for a service they do not need. Beyond that, functionality that lets some applications work better may hurt applications with different needs. In the worst case, the functionality in the network may prevent these applications from being deployed at all.

Thus, the broad version prevents network architects from optimizing the network for specific applications in order to create a network that can support a larger, more diverse set of applications now and in the future.[45] The resulting reduction in the performance or efficiency of certain applications is the price for a system whose applications can evolve over time. In addition, the broad version supports application autonomy and is likely to increase the reliability of applications and the network.[46]

The broad version thus represents a trade-off between long-term system evolvability, application autonomy, and reliability on the one hand, over certain types of performance optimizations on the other.[47] Network architects should use the broad version only if the system's requirements imply that this trade-off is justified. If the system's requirements imply a different resolution of this trade-off, the broad version of the end-to-end arguments should not be applied.

The trade-off underlying the broad version is familiar from other areas. Consider a gaming console and a personal computer. A gaming console has been optimized for gaming applications, but as a result of this optimization, its ability to support other applications is limited. For example, the joysticks and buttons of gaming controllers have been developed to meet the needs of gamers; they are not well suited to entering large amounts of text. By contrast, a personal computer is a general purpose system that has been designed to support a wide variety of applications with different needs. It has not been optimized for specific applications. While games may run more efficiently or may perform better on a gaming console, a personal computer can support more and more diverse applications, including those that have not been foreseen at the time of design. Thus, gaming consoles and personal computers embody very different trade-offs between optimizing the performance of individual applications and increasing the number and diversity of applications that the device can support over time. Which trade-off is 'better' cannot be decided in general, but depends on the specific needs of the person considering buying a device.

Applying the layering principle and the broad version of the end-to-end arguments results in a network that is application-blind.[48] An application-blind network is unable to distinguish among the different applications running over it and, as a result, it is unable to make distinctions among data packets based on that information. This feature is often attributed to the layering principle or to the broad version of the end-to-end arguments directly; however, neither of these design principles deals explicitly with this question. Instead, the network's inability to distinguish among applications is a direct consequence of these design principles. In a network based on the broad version of the end-to-end arguments, all application-specific functionality is concentrated in and restricted to higher layers at the end hosts. As a result, only the messages sent by higher-layer protocols at the end hosts carry application-specific functionality or content. In such a network, lower layers in the core of the network can identify the applications on the network only by accessing or making assumptions about the messages of the higher-layer protocols carrying this information. This, however, would violate the second constraint of the layering principle, as applied to networking, which prescribes that a lower-layer protocol may not make any assumptions about the content or meaning of the message it is transporting on behalf of higher-layer protocols and may neither access nor act on the information contained in these messages.[49]

14.4   THE INTERNET'S ORIGINAL ARCHITECTURE

14.4.1   The Internet and the Layering Principle

The Internet's original architecture was based on a variant of the layering principle called 'relaxed layering with a portability layer'.[50]

The architecture of the Internet consists of four layers: the lowest layer is the link layer, followed by the Internet layer, the transport layer, and the application layer.[51] While the lower layers – the layers up to the Internet layer – are implemented on end hosts and on computers in the core of the network, the higher layers – the layers above the Internet layer – only have to be implemented on end hosts.[52]

The application of 'relaxed layering with a portability layer' imposes constraints on the interactions among protocols belonging to different layers and on the number of protocols that may populate a layer. The Internet layer is designated as the portability layer. Layers above the Internet layer are allowed to invoke the services of protocols in the same layer or in any layer below them, down to the Internet layer, but they are not allowed to directly invoke the services of protocols in a layer below the Internet layer. As in any layered architecture, lower-layer protocols are not allowed to invoke the services of higher-layer protocols. Whereas the Internet layer is restricted to a single protocol (the Internet Protocol), other layers may host a variety of different protocols. The resulting structure of protocol dependencies is often likened to an hourglass, with the Internet Protocol as the hourglass's waist (Figure 14.2).[53]

This design isolates the transport layer and the application layer from changes below

Layer	Structure	Protocols
Application		HTTP, SMTP
Transport		TCP, UDP
Internet		IP
Link		Ethernet, ATM

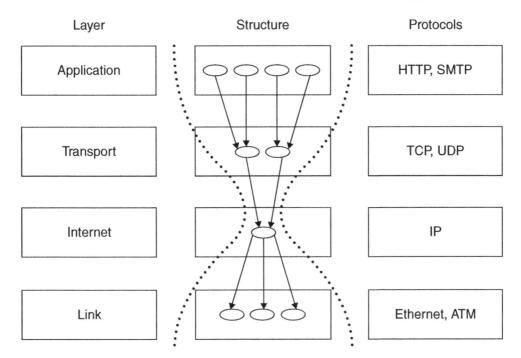

Note: ATM = Asynchronous Transfer Mode; IP = Internet Protocol; HTTP = Hypertext Transfer Protocol; SMTP = Simple Mail Transfer Protocol; TCP = Transmission Control Protocol; UDP = User Datagram Protocol.

Source: Reprinted from van Schewick (2010a, p. 89).

Figure 14.2   Layering in the Internet architecture

the Internet layer (and vice versa), and has allowed the lower layers of the Internet to take advantage of new physical network infrastructures and new transmission and link technologies without requiring changes in transport layer protocols or individual applications.

14.4.2   The Internet and the Broad Version of the End-to-end Arguments

During the initial design of the Internet's architecture, the broad version of the end-to-end arguments shaped the division of functionality between the Internet layer – the highest layer running on computers in the core of the network – and the layers above the Internet layer.[54]

In line with the guidelines established by the broad version, the Internet layer, the highest layer running on computers in the core of the network, provides a general functionality – transporting data packets from one end host to another – that is of broad utility across applications. All application-specific functionality (i.e., functionality that is only needed by some, but not all applications) is implemented in higher layers at the end hosts.

Originally, the Internet's architects considered implementing reliable, connection-oriented data transfer in the Internet layer.[55] Reliable data transfer and connection-oriented data transfer are application-specific functions that are needed only by some, but not all applications. Thus, implementing these functions in the Internet layer would have violated the broad version of the end-to-end arguments.

Different applications have different needs.[56] For example, e-mail and file transfer are very sensitive to packet loss, but can tolerate some delay. By contrast, applications that transmit uncompressed voice or video in real time can tolerate a certain amount of data loss, but suffer from increased delay (or variability of delay). Thus, reliable data transfer – ensuring that data does not get lost and arrives without errors, duplicates, and in the correct order – is an application-specific function. Similarly, while some applications such as remote log-in or file-sharing send streams of data back and forth between two end hosts, other applications send single packets in one direction. Thus, the provision of connection-oriented data transfer, which establishes a bi-directional virtual path ('virtual circuit') through the network over which all data packets travel, is an application-specific function as well.

Although performing error control in the Internet layer increases the performance of applications that need reliability (e.g., e-mail or file transfer), it also increases delay. Thus, implementing this function in the Internet layer optimizes the network for the needs of some applications (those that require reliability), but makes it more difficult or even impossible to support applications that do not need reliability but are sensitive to delay (e.g., applications that transmit uncompressed speech or other media streams in real time). Implementing reliable data transfer in the Internet layer therefore reduces the range of applications that the network can support.[57] A similar argument can be made for the provision of connection-oriented data transfer.

By contrast, a network offering unreliable, connectionless packet delivery can support applications that require connection orientation and reliability as well as applications that do not need these functions.[58] For applications that require connection orientation and reliability, transport-layer protocols at the end hosts can construct a virtual circuit based on an unreliable packet delivery service at the Internet layer. Applications that do not require these functions can avoid the associated delay and overhead by choosing a different transport-layer protocol that better meets their needs – for example, one that lets them send individual data packets without guaranteeing their delivery and without establishing a bi-directional connection first.

On the basis of these considerations and in line with the broad version of the end-to-end arguments, the Internet's architects decided to remove application-specific functions such as reliable data transfer and connection orientation from the Internet layer.[59] Instead, the Internet Protocol, the only protocol at the Internet layer, provides unreliable connectionless data delivery, a basic service that is of broad utility across applications.[60,61] Application-specific functionality is concentrated in higher layers at the end hosts. In particular, connection orientation and reliable data transfer are implemented at the transport layer – the highest layer that only has to be implemented at end hosts. Applications that need these services can use the Transmission Control Protocol (TCP), which provides connection oriented reliable data transfer, while others can use the User Datagram Protocol (UDP), which offers unreliable connectionless data delivery (Figure 14.3).[62]

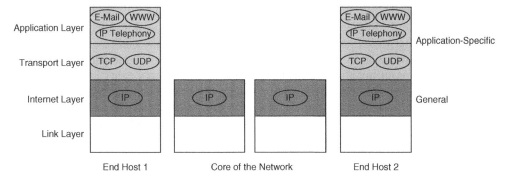

Figure 14.3   Distribution of functionality in the Internet's original architecture

Note: IP = Internet Protocol; TCP = Transmission Control Protocol; UDP = User Datagram Protocol.

Source: Reprinted from van Schewick (2010a, p. 100).

As a consequence of the use of the layering principle and the broad version of the end-to-end arguments, the Internet's original architecture was application-blind – it was unable to distinguish among the applications on the network – and, as a result, it was unable to make distinction among data packets based on that information.[63] Due to the application of the broad version, the Internet's architecture concentrates all application-specific functionality in protocols at or above the transport layer. The layering principle prevents protocols at the Internet layer or below from accessing the messages exchanged between protocol peers at or above the transport layer and from making assumptions about the content or meaning of these messages, making it impossible to identify the applications on the network without violating the layering principle.

14.5   THE IMPACT OF INTERNET ARCHITECTURE ON THE ECONOMIC ENVIRONMENT FOR APPLICATION INNOVATION

The economic environment for innovation in applications is shaped by two features of the Internet's original architecture.[64,65] First, the network is general and does not need to be changed to allow new applications to run on the network. Second, the network is application-blind. Both of these features directly result from the application of the broad version of the end-to-end arguments. They affect who can develop new applications, the costs and benefits of doing so, and who controls whether applications can be developed, deployed, and used.

14.5.1   Generality of the Network

In a network based on the broad version of the end-to-end arguments, the network does not have to be changed to allow new applications to run.[66] First, in such a network, the lower layers of the network – the core of the network[67] – have been designed to be as general as possible to support a wide variety of current and future applications with different needs, and will therefore be able to support new applications without requiring changes to the network first. Second, the broad version of the end-to-end arguments prohibits applications from implementing application-specific functionality in the core of the network, requiring applications to concentrate their functionality in higher layers at the end hosts instead. Third, since lower layers are independent of higher layers, an isolated change at a higher layer at the end hosts (here: the addition of a new application) will never require changes in the core of the network. In a network based on the broad version, developing a new application thus consists of writing a software program that runs on a computer attached to the Internet, or, more technically, that runs in a higher layer at an end host. All of this affects the economic environment for application innovation in a number of ways.

14.5.1.1   Control over application innovation
Since the network does not need to be changed before an application can run on the network, network providers do not have to do anything to enable new applications to run.[68] As a result, innovators can decide independently whether to realize their idea for an application; they do not need support or 'permission' from network providers in order to innovate. This characteristic of the economic environment for innovation is often called 'innovation without permission'.[69]

14.5.1.2   Cost of application innovation
As developing a new application consists of writing a program that runs on a computer attached to the Internet, innovators can develop new applications at very low cost.[70] A potential innovator needs access to an end host connected to the Internet, programming knowledge, programming tools, and access to the lower-layer protocols that let the application send data over the Internet. Like all software programs, the resulting application can be copied and distributed almost cost-free over the Internet.[71] Thus, developing a new application requires almost no physical capital.

14.5.1.3   Size and diversity of the innovator pool
Many of the resources required to develop a new application are often already available (e.g., many people have a computer or access to one) or can be acquired at relatively low cost. As a result, this cost structure lets a wide range of innovators with diverse motivations and funding models develop new applications.[72] In particular, an innovator does not have to be an employee of a firm or have outside funding to realize his or her idea for an application. Because the biggest investment often is the design and programming of the application itself, potential innovators can develop an application in their free time or as a 'side project', with the opportunity cost of the time spent the most important cost factor. Under these conditions, an application does not have to produce a profit in the future to cover the costs of developing it. Instead, a wide range of benefits may be sufficient to cover the development costs. For example, some innovators develop new applications because they love to program.[73] Others develop a new application to meet their own needs; after the fact, they may discover that others may want to use it, too.[74] Thus, the generality of the network's core allows innovators with a wide range of motivations and funding models to develop new applications.

14.5.1.4   Control over application deployment and use

Before a user can use a new application, he or she needs to install it on their computer. Due to the generality of the network's core, deploying or using a new application does not require any changes to the core.[75] Thus, network providers do not have to do anything before an application can run on the network. As a result, each user can decide independently which applications he or she wants to deploy and use.[76,77] This characteristic of the economic environment for innovation is often called 'user choice'.

14.5.2   Application Blindness of the Network

Like all networks that comply with the broad version of the end-to-end argument, the original Internet was application-blind, that is, it was unable to distinguish among the applications on the network. As a result, it was unable to make distinctions among data packets based on that information, for example, when transporting them across the network or when charging for them.

The application blindness of the network deprived network providers of three strategic options that would be available in an application-aware network.[78] First, a network provider in an application-aware network can block applications or discriminate against them. Second, it can charge an access fee to providers of applications and content who are not the network providers' Internet service customers. Third, it can charge different Internet transport prices for different applications, or it can exclude applications to price discriminate between customers of its Internet service. The difference in available strategies affects the economic environment for application innovation in a number of ways.

14.5.2.1   Blocking or discrimination

A network provider in an application-aware network can identify the applications on its network and can control their execution. This enables network providers to block applications or to discriminate against them. If a network provider blocks an application, the network provider's Internet service customers will be unable to use it. Discrimination is differential treatment that falls short of blocking, but makes an application or class of applications relatively less attractive.[79] For example, a network provider may slow down a specific application, or speed up competing applications. Blocking or discrimination allows network providers to distort competition among applications or classes of applications, and to interfere with the decisions of application innovators and users regarding application innovation, deployment, and use. Thus, an application-aware network shifts control over application innovation, deployment, and use to network providers.[80]

By contrast, since an application-blind network is unable to distinguish among applications, a network provider in such a network is unable to block applications or discriminate against them. If the network is application-blind and general, control over application innovation rests with application innovators, while users control application deployment and use.[81,82]

Blocking or discrimination enables network providers to distort competition among applications or classes of applications. An innovator whose application is blocked will be unable to benefit from the application. Discrimination puts an application at a competitive disadvantage relative to other applications that are not discriminated against, reducing the benefits an innovator can expect to realize. Thus, the threat of discrimination reduces the expected benefits of innovation, which reduces innovators' incentives to develop new applications and their ability to get funding.[83] As statements from entrepreneurs show, the threat of discrimination in the absence of network neutrality rules reduces innovators' ability to get funding today, so this is not just a theoretical concern.[84]

Network providers' ability to block or discriminate against applications can only affect application innovation, however, if network providers have an incentive to block or discriminate. A network provider in an application-aware network does not generally have an incentive to exclude applications. After all, more applications make the network provider's Internet service more attractive, allowing the network provider to attract more Internet service customers or charge a higher price to existing customers.[85] There are, however, situations in which a network provider nevertheless has an incentive to block specific applications or discriminate against them – to increase its profits (e.g., by blocking applications that compete with its own offering or that of a partner, or by excluding applications to price discriminate among its Internet service customers), to manage congestion on its network, or to exclude unwanted content that threatens the company's interests or does not comply with the network provider's chosen content policy.[86] In all of these cases, a network provider will only engage in exclusionary conduct if the benefits of exclusion exceed the costs in the market for Internet services.[87] Notably, the incentive to discriminate is often independent of whether the network provider participates in the market for the affected application and whether the exclusionary conduct is capable of monopolizing the market for that application. In other words, network providers often have an incentive to block or discriminate against an application even if they do not participate in the market for that application (e.g., when they block an application to manage congestion, block unwanted content, or price discriminate in the market for Internet services),[88] and discrimination will often be profitable even if it does not monopolize the market for the application in question.[89]

Over the past ten years, all of these types of discrimination have occurred in practice. For example, network providers in the USA, Europe, Saudi Arabia, United Arab Emirates and Mexico blocked Internet telephony applications such as Skype because the use of Internet telephony reduces network providers' revenue from traditional telephony service.[90] Cable providers in the USA have expressed their desire to interfere with over-the-top online video applications such as Netflix to protect their conventional television offerings.[91] Network providers in the USA prohibited the use of virtual private network applications on their basic Internet service offerings to price discriminate among their Internet service customers.[92] Network providers in the USA, Canada and Europe singled out specific applications or classes of applications to manage bandwidth on their networks.[93] A network provider in Canada blocked content that threatened its business interests, while network providers in the Middle East, China and other countries blocked content deemed politically, religiously, socially, or culturally inappropriate.[94] In many of these cases, the network provider did not participate in the market for the excluded application, and when it did participate, the exclusion did not allow the network provider to monopolize the market for the application in question.

Commentators often assume that competition in the market for Internet services will remove any incentives to engage in blocking or discrimination.[95,96] If there is competition and a network provider discriminates against an application that users would like to use, they argue, users can switch to another network provider that does not discriminate against the application, and this threat of switching will discipline providers.

These arguments fail to recognize that the market for Internet service is characterized by incomplete customer information, product differentiation in the market for Internet access and for wireless and wireline bundles, switching costs, and, in some countries, a concentrated market structure in the market for Internet services. These factors limit the effectiveness of competition, even in markets with several competing Internet service providers, and reduce consumers' willingness to switch Internet service providers in response to discriminatory conduct, giving network providers a degree of market power that enables them to impose restrictions on their Internet service customers that they would not be able to impose in a perfectly competitive market.[97]

In line with this theoretical argument, network providers in markets that are more competitive than the market for wireline, fixed Internet service in the USA have engaged in blocking or discrimination.[98] This evidence suggests that at least in the market for wireline Internet service in Europe and Canada and in the market for mobile Internet service in the USA, competition does not prevent Internet service providers from interfering with applications, content, or services on their networks, even if, as in the USA and in the European Union, network providers are required to disclose any discriminatory conduct that occurs.[99]

14.5.2.2   Access fees

A network provider in an application-aware network can charge an access fee to providers of applications and content who are not its Internet service customers.[100] By contrast, a network provider in a network based on the broad version is unable to do so, since it cannot distinguish among the applications on its network.

Access fees come in two variants.[101] In the first, a network provider charges application providers who are not its Internet service customers a fee for the right to access the network providers' Internet service customers. Applications whose providers do not pay the access fee cannot be used on the network provider's access network. In the second variant, a network provider charges application providers for prioritized or otherwise enhanced access to the network provider's Internet service customers. For example, if an application provider has paid such an access fee, the application's data packets may receive a better type of service (e.g., travel faster) on the network provider's access network or may not count against a user's monthly data cap.[102]

Access fees increase the costs of offering an application for all application providers subject to the fee, reducing the profits they can expect to make. The theory of two-sided markets even predicts that network providers would charge monopoly prices to application providers, which would reduce application providers' incentives to innovate even further.[103] In addition, access fees will disproportionately affect innovators with little or no outside funding: innovators with little or no outside funding may not be able to pay access fees, which would put them at a competitive disadvantage to those who can and do pay the fees.[104] Innovators who cannot pay the first type of access fees will be unable to compete at all. Those who cannot pay the second type of access fees will be able to reach end users, but their applications will perform worse or will cost users more (e.g., because the use of the application counts against the user's monthly data cap) than the applications of providers that pay the access fee. Thus, access fees will reduce the incentives of innovators with little or no outside funding to innovate and may remove (or at least impede) their ability to innovate in offerings subject to access fees, which in turn would reduce the size and diversity of the pool of potential innovators.[105] Finally, network providers can influence which applications are successful by allowing only selected application providers to pay for prioritized or otherwise enhanced treatment.[106]

14.5.2.3 Application-specific pricing and price discrimination

In an application-aware network, a network provider can identify which applications a user uses and can control their execution. This enables network providers to charge different Internet transport prices for different applications (e.g., charge higher Internet service fees for an e-mail packet than for a packet of web content of equal size), or to price discriminate among customers of its Internet service by excluding applications (e.g., allow the use of video conferencing only for users of its premium Internet service, not for users of its basic Internet service). By contrast, a network provider in an application-blind network can base Internet transport prices only on observable characteristics such as the total amount of bandwidth used by an Internet service customer, not on the application being used. Thus, network providers in an application-blind network have to charge the same quality- and bandwidth-adjusted Internet transport price to all applications.[107]

A network provider that can charge application-specific transport prices or price discriminate by excluding applications will be able to extract more of the consumer surplus associated with a specific application through the pricing of its Internet service than network providers in an application-blind network, leaving less consumer surplus and, therefore, less potential profits for the provider of that application and, in the case of price discrimination, for application providers in general.

14.5.3 Impact of Architectural Changes on the Amount and Quality of Application Innovation

In sum, the broad version of the end-to-end arguments created an economic environment for application innovation that is characterized by innovation without permission, user choice, application blindness, and low costs of application innovation (see Table 14.1). Together, these elements of the economic environment for innovation affect the amount and quality of application innovation that will occur under an architecture based on that design principle.

Architectures that deviate from the broad version of the end-to-end argument will result in different economic environments for application innovation. Architectures can deviate from the broad version along two dimensions, and, along each of these dimensions, to varying degrees: relative to an architecture based on the broad version, they can become more opaque, more controllable, or both.[108]

First, network providers can reduce the generality of the network by implementing, in the network's core, application-specific functionality that optimizes the network for the needs of existing applications. These changes make an architecture more opaque. Changes that make the network more opaque are often driven by the desire to increase performance or save costs.[109]

Second, network providers can remove the network's application blindness by adding, in the network's core, application-specific functionality that increases network providers' ability to monitor and control the applications on their networks. These changes make

Table 14.1   The economic environment for innovation under different network architectures

	Architecture Based on the Broad Version of the End-to-end Arguments	Architecture Deviating from the Broad Version of the End-to-end Arguments
Costs of application innovation	Low	Higher
Benefits of application innovation	Full	Lower
Size and diversity of the innovator pool	Large and diverse Anybody with programming knowledge and access to an end host	Smaller and less diverse In the extreme case, only network providers
Control over application innovation	Application developers	Network providers
Control over application deployment and use	Users	Network providers

an architecture more controllable. Network providers primarily move in this direction to increase their profits; however, changes that let network providers monitor what is happening on the network may also help them make the network more secure, manage traffic, or plan network upgrades.[110]

Over the past two decades, the Internet's architecture has become more opaque and more controllable. The past two decades have seen a proliferation of technical solutions that reduce the generality of the network by optimizing the network for the needs of a particular class of applications called client-server applications. For example, residential broadband networks provide asymmetric bandwidth for uploads and downloads, creating problems for applications that send and receive equal amounts of data.[111] To deal with the impeding shortage of Internet addresses, users and network providers deployed network-address translators that let several devices share the same Internet address. To protect their networks against attacks, organizations put firewalls that block potentially harmful applications at the borders of their private networks. Network-address translators and firewalls have made it increasingly difficult to deploy new transport-layer protocols or new applications whose behavior deviates from that of traditional client-server applications.[112] At the same time, technologies such as deep packet inspection have removed the application blindness of the network. They provide network providers with fine-grained awareness of and control over the applications on their networks, and allow them to implement the various pricing schemes (e.g., application-specific pricing or access fees) discussed throughout this chapter. These technologies have been widely deployed.[113]

How exactly deviations from the broad version of the end-to-end arguments affect the economic environment for application innovation depends on the exact nature of the architectural change.[114] Most generally, deviating from the broad version will increase the costs or reduce the benefits of application innovation, result in an innovator pool that is smaller or less diverse, or shift control over application development, deployment, and use to network providers. In the worst case, an architectural change has all of these effects (see Table 14.1).

Other things being equal (such as the group of actors exposed to the architecture or the other constraints operating on the actors) and assuming the absence of legal rules that limit network providers' ability to take advantage of the capabilities provided by the architecture, differences in these characteristics of the economic environment for innovation will affect the amount and quality of application innovation that will occur.

14.5.3.1　Costs and benefits of innovation

Some architectural changes may affect the benefits and costs of application innovation. An innovator decides to innovate if the expected benefits (broadly defined) are larger than the costs. If an architectural change increases the costs or reduces the expected benefits of an innovation relative to another architecture, some innovations that were justified under that other architecture may not be justified any more under the changed architecture.[115] For example, relative to an application-blind architecture, an application-aware architecture that allows network providers to block applications, charge access fees, or charge application-specific prices reduces the benefits an application developer can expect to reap.[116] Increasing the amount of application-specific functionality in the core of the network increases the costs of application innovation.[117] Thus, under these architectures, the same group of innovators will find less of their innovative ideas for applications worth pursuing than under an architecture based on the broad version.[118]

In addition to reducing the expected profitability of application innovation, an increase in the costs of application innovation or deployment may affect innovators' ability to serve niche markets or low-value markets, and may reduce their willingness to take risks.[119]

14.5.3.2　Size and diversity of the innovator pool

Architectural changes may also influence who can innovate, affecting the size and diversity of the pool of potential innovators.[120]

Under an architecture based on the broad version of the end-to-end arguments, almost anybody can be an innovator. Developing a new application requires only access to an end host connected to the Internet, programming knowledge, programming tools, and access to the lower-layer protocols that let the application send data over the Internet. This allows innovators with a wide range of motivations and funding models to develop new applications.[121]

By contrast, architectures that deviate from the broad version increase the requirements that potential innovators must meet, which reduces the size and diversity of the innovator pool.[122] For example, in an application-aware architecture that allows network providers to charge access fees, innovators with little or no outside funding will often be unable to pay access fees, which reduces or removes their ability to develop new applications.[123] Similarly, if the core of an architecture contains application-specific functionality, some applications may require changes to the network's core before they can run on the network.[124] As a result, the costs of developing and testing these applications will be significantly higher than in a network based on the broad version. They include not only the costs of developing and testing the application itself, but also the costs of developing and testing the changes to the network's core and the subsequent changes to applications that relied on the former version of the network's core. Because the application cannot run on the operational network, the innovator must have access to a test network. If the changes to the network's core include changes to hardware, the new hardware must be manufactured and physically distributed. Thus, the costs of production and distribution also may be higher under such architectures. Finally, the developer may incur considerable costs while trying to convince network providers of the usefulness and commercial viability of the new application and negotiate any necessary changes to the network's core and to other existing applications. Under such an architecture, many of the smaller or non-commercial innovators that would have been able to develop applications under an end-to-end architecture will lack the resources and capabilities necessary to overcome these technical, financial, or coordinational hurdles. Depending on the amount of application-specific functionality in the network's core, these obstacles may be so severe that independent innovators other than network providers lose the ability to innovate.[125]

If there is uncertainty (e.g., about technology or user needs) or if user needs are heterogeneous, differences in the size and diversity of the innovator pool will affect the amount and quality of application innovation under the different architectures.[126] If there is uncertainty, nobody really knows which applications will work, or which applications will be successful. Under these circumstances, evolutionary and neo-institutional theories of innovation predict that a larger, more diverse group of innovators will not only identify a larger, more diverse set of opportunities for innovation than a smaller, less diverse group; they will also realize a larger number of the opportunities that were discovered.[127] As I have shown in detail elsewhere, the history of application innovation on the Internet strongly supports these theories.[128]

Discovering opportunities for innovation is the first step in the innovative process.[129] Often it is not immediately apparent how a new technology could be used, or that customers have unmet needs that a new or improved product could fill. This problem is particularly pronounced for relatively general technologies, such as the Internet, that can be put to a wide variety of uses. For these technologies, identifying ways in which the technology could be used is an important kind of innovation. As history has shown again and again, it is usually impossible to decide in advance which new uses will become successful.[130] Most Internet applications that later became highly successful either were not envisaged by the designers of the network or were met by widespread skepticism when they first became available. This was true, for example, for e-mail, the World Wide Web, eBay, or search engines.[131]

Different actors have different motivations, backgrounds, and theories about the world. As a result, they will see different opportunities for innovation.[132] Even if different actors recognize the same opportunity, they may differ in their perception of the likelihood of success or of the likely costs and benefits. As a result, the same opportunity may appear profitable to some of the innovators, but not to others.[133] The impact of these differences among actors increases with uncertainty.[134] Beyond differences in perception, differences in actual cost structures may make a project profitable for some innovators but not for others.[135] For example, an innovator working from home in his or her free time incurs lower costs than a start-up that rents offices and pays its employees. That start-up, in turn, will often have lower costs than a large corporation with significant overhead. And even if the expected benefits of the application are larger than the costs for a number of innovators, the size of the potential benefits may be unattractive for some potential innovators, but not for others.[136] For example, large companies are interested in projects that have the potential to contribute significantly to their bottom line. Venture capitalists invest in projects that have the potential for extremely large rewards, because the profits from a few successful projects need to cover the venture capitalists' losses on their other projects. By contrast, entrepreneurs who finance a project themselves or through angel investors may be willing to invest in projects that large corporations or venture capital funds may not find attractive. Similarly, a user who wants to use the application themselves will not care about the size of the market at all, since he or she is motivated by the prospect of being able to use the application themselves.

For all these reasons, a larger, more diverse group of innovators will identify and realize a larger, more diverse set of potential projects than a smaller, less diverse group. Having a larger and more diverse set of innovation projects, in turn, guarantees a more complete search of the problem space, increasing the chance that beneficial uses (or approaches to specific problems) will be detected. If the various innovators pursue different technical approaches to the same problems or explore different business models, having a larger number of innovators increases the likelihood that at least one of them will be successful and increases the expected quality of the best results.[137] If users' needs are heterogeneous, a larger and more diverse group of potential innovators will also create a greater variety of products that better meet users' needs.[138] Thus, if there is uncertainty or user needs are heterogeneous, an increase in the size and diversity of the innovator pool will increase the amount and quality of application innovation.

Diversity is not without costs. Each approach incurs costs, and many projects will fail. Under fundamental uncertainty, successful projects cannot be identified in advance, so these costs seem to be unavoidable.[139]

14.5.3.3 Control over application innovation

Under an architecture based on the broad version of the end-to-end arguments, innovators independently choose which applications they want to pursue, without interference from network providers. Due to the generality of the network's core, they do not need support or 'permission' from network providers in order to realize their idea for an application ('innovation without permission'), and the application blindness of the network prevents network providers from interfering with these choices.[140]

By contrast, under architectures that deviate from the broad version, network providers may need to take action before an application can be realized. For example, if a network contains application-specific functionality in the network's core, the network may need to be changed before a new application can function on the network.[141] In an application-aware architecture, the network can be closed to new applications by default. In such a network, the network provider needs to enable an application before it can run on the network.[142] Depending on the architecture, contracting with a network provider may be the only way for potential innovators to realize their idea for an application. This may happen, for example, if the network's core contains a significant amount of application-specific functionality.[143]

The difference in control over application innovation affects the amount of innovation in various ways.[144] First, if there is uncertainty, increasing the number of decision-makers who need to approve an idea or take action before an idea can be realized reduces the chances that the idea will be realized. A network provider will see no need to support applications that it perceives as infeasible, as not viable, or as counter to its strategic interests. These projects would be realized under an end-to-end architecture, but not under an architecture in which network providers need to approve new applications.

Second, an innovator has to disclose its innovation when negotiating for the network provider's cooperation. If the innovation is not protected by intellectual property rights, there is a danger that the network provider may appropriate the innovation without paying for it, which may reduce the innovator's incentive to innovate in the first place.

Third, bargaining costs and strategic behavior may prevent the innovator and the network provider from reaching agreement.

Fourth, the incentives for independent innovators who can directly commercialize their innovation are higher owing to the possibility of exceptionally large gains. If innovators have to contract with a network provider in order to commercialize their innovation and cannot gain access to the market on their own, they do not have any bargaining power. In such a network, the network provider will be in a monopsony or oligopsony position, which leads to very low prices. In this case, the innovators will have to bear the risk of failure or bargaining breakdown, and will receive only modest compensation if they succeed. Such an incentive structure will probably not be sufficient to motivate innovators or their investors to put up with the risk.

Finally, if innovators have to contract or otherwise coordinate with network providers before they can innovate, they may be less able to react to new developments once they have started their project. Throughout the history of the Internet, successful innovators have often changed course repeatedly – for example, in response to feedback from consumers, or in response to an unexpected scarcity of funding. This happened, for example, in the cases of Blogger, Flickr, or PayPal. More generally, starting with one approach and then adapting it as events unfold may be the only way to successfully navigate fundamental uncertainty. In a network that requires innovators to coordinate their activities with the network provider, this may not be possible. According to transaction-cost and coordination-cost theories, deciding what to do in response to new developments is much more difficult and more time-consuming across firm boundaries than within a single firm. Firms have differing perspectives on how to react, and the lack of efficient mechanisms for inter-firm decision-making and dispute resolution may make the differences difficult to resolve.

Thus, relative to architectures in which innovators can innovate independently, architectures that require innovators to get approval from, contract with, or otherwise coordinate with a network provider before they can innovate constrain independent innovators' ability and incentives to start a project and reduce the chance that innovative ideas will be realized. They also limit innovators' ability to react to new developments during the lifetime of the project – a limitation that is particularly detrimental under uncertainty.

14.5.3.4 Control over application deployment and use
Under an architecture based on the broad version of the end-to-end arguments in which users control the end hosts,[145] users independently decide which applications they want to deploy and use. This characteristic has been called 'user choice'. Due to the generality of the network, network providers are not involved in the deployment and use of applications, and the application blindness of the network's core prevents them from interfering with users' choices regarding application deployment and use.[146]

By contrast, architectures that deviate from the broad version often shift control over application deployment or use to network providers. For example, if a network needs to be changed before an application can run on the network (e.g., because an application-aware network enables network providers to block new applications by default or because a network contains application-specific functionality that prevents the application from running), the network provider controls which applications can get deployed. If an application-aware network allows network providers to block applications or discriminate against them, network providers can control how the network is used.[147]

Allowing users to independently choose which applications to deploy and use increases the chance that a new application will be deployed and used. In a network based on the broad version, the only person who needs to be convinced that an application may be useful for the application to be deployed is the person who actually wants to use it. By contrast, increasing the number of decision-makers who need to take action or approve an application before it can be deployed reduces the chance that the application will be deployed.[148]

In addition, letting users choose which applications to deploy and use is an important part of the mechanism that produces innovation under uncertainty. If there is uncertainty, nobody knows in advance which applications will work, or which applications will be successful. Under these circumstances, neo-institutional and evolutionary theories of innovation suggest that it is best to try out many different ideas, and see what happens. Some applications may succeed, and some may fail, but trying is the only way to find out.[149] In a network that allows for this kind of experimentation, the actors that control application deployment and use effectively decide which applications will be successful.[150]

When choosing which applications will be successful, users and network providers will often make different decisions. Thus, differences in control over application deployment and use will result in different applications being successful.

First, network providers' interests may differ from users' interests, which can lead them to reject applications that users may find attractive.[151] Network providers and users use different criteria when choosing which application should be deployed and used. Users choose the applications that best meet their needs. By contrast, network providers will choose the applications that maximize their profits. As a result, they may, for example, reject applications that compete with their own applications or with a partner's application, block certain applications in order to price discriminate among their Internet service customers, exclude content that threatens their business interests or does not comply with their content policies, or single out applications or classes of applications to manage bandwidth on their network.[152] The market for Internet services is afflicted with a number of factors – incomplete customer information, product differentiation in the market for Internet access and for wireline and wireless bundles, and switching costs – that provide network providers with market power, even in markets with several competing Internet service providers. This market power allows them to impose restrictions on their users that they would not be able to impose in a perfectly competitive market, enabling them to exclude applications that users want.[153]

Second, even when network providers would like to deploy applications that users want, they do not necessarily know what these are. New applications are often afflicted with considerable uncertainty. No one knows which applications or features users will find attractive. Often users themselves do not know whether they like a specific application or find it useful until they have tried it or seen others using it. Thus, letting users choose applications replaces network providers' guesses about what users may like with a decision by users, who best know their current preferences and needs. It provides a chance to applications whose usefulness or attractiveness is not immediately apparent, and allows users' preferences and practices to evolve as a result of exposure to or experimentation with a new application. In addition, giving application developers direct access to users lets them experiment and change their product offerings in response to user feedback, which has been critical for applications like Flickr, Blogger, or PayPal. Finally, being able to choose which applications to deploy and use is important for users or user groups whose needs are idiosyncratic, since their needs may not be known to or may not be important to the network provider.[154]

Beyond innovation, letting users choose how they want to use the Internet enables them to use the Internet in a way that creates more value for them and for society than if network providers made this choice.[155]

In sum, the mechanism that produces application innovation under an architecture based on the broad version of the end-to-end arguments has two components: first, widespread experimentation by a large and diverse group of innovators who can innovate at low cost and who independently select whether to realize their innovative ideas, and second, user choice among the resulting applications. Under uncertainty or consumer heterogeneity, this mechanism will produce more and better applications than innovation in network architectures that reduce the size and diversity of the pool of potential innovators or concentrate control over innovation, deployment, or use in the hands of network providers.[156] If user needs are heterogeneous, this mechanism will also produce more diverse applications that better meet user needs.[157]

In the current Internet, technological uncertainty, market uncertainty, and user heterogeneity are high, so the conditions under which innovator diversity, user choice, and innovation without permission increase the amount and quality of application innovation are met.[158]

14.6 CONCLUSION

Network architectures (and the design principles that shape them) influence the economic system for application innovation, deployment, and use in different ways. In particular, they influence which actors can innovate, what incentives they have to do so, and who controls whether an application can be developed, deployed, and used.

The Internet's original architecture was based on the layering principle and the broad version of the end-to-end arguments. This design created an economic environment for application innovation that is more conducive to innovation in applications than architectures that deviate from this design principle.

In networks based on the broad version of the end-to-end arguments, the economic environment for application innovation is characterized by application blindness, innovation without permission, user choice, and low costs of application innovation. Architectures that deviate from the broad version will result in different economic environments for application innovation. How exactly deviations from the broad version of the end-to-end arguments affect the economic environment for application innovation depends on the exact nature of the architectural change. Most generally, deviating from the broad version will increase the costs or reduce the expected benefits of application innovation, reduce the size and diversity of the innovator pool, or shift control over application innovation, deployment, or use from application innovators and users to network providers. In the worst case, an architectural change has all of these effects. Other things such as the set of actors exposed to the architecture and the set of constraints under which they operate all being equal, these kinds of changes will reduce the overall amount, the type, and the quality of application innovation. If there is market uncertainty, technical uncertainty, or user heterogeneity, the effects of differences in the size and diversity of the innovator pool and of differences in control over application development, deployment, and use are particularly profound. In the current Internet, there is uncertainty and user needs are heterogeneous, so the conditions under which innovator diversity, innovator control over application innovation, and user control over application deployment and use increase the amount and quality of innovation are met.

To highlight the specific effect of architecture, this chapter assumed that while the architecture changes, everything else (i.e., the group of actors exposed to the architecture and the other constraints under which they operate) stays the same. In reality, the actual effect of a specific architecture or architectural change on innovation at a specific place and time cannot be determined without considering the characteristics of the actors exposed to the architecture, the other constraints (such as laws, norms, and the natural and technical environment) under which they operate, and the actors' existing or expected relationships with others.

For example, while the broad version of the end-to-end arguments allows anybody with access to an end host, programming tools, and programming knowledge to develop new applications, factors like an entrepreneurial culture that embraces the possibility of failure or the availability of sources of financing like angel investors and venture capitalists that specialize in early-stage, high-risk projects may make it more likely that a potential innovator with an idea for an application decides to realize it.

Similarly, an innovator's ability to leverage the opportunities provided by the architecture into a successful innovation may be influenced by the organizations, cultures, and networks in which he or she is embedded. For example, Yahoo! and Google started at Stanford University, a prestigious and well-connected institution with many formal and informal connections to Silicon Valley and with an infrastructure that encourages and supports student-led and faculty-led entrepreneurship. Other innovators with the same idea and similar personal resources who faced the same architectural constraints, but who were embedded in different organizations, cultures, or networks, may have been less successful in realizing the same innovation.[159]

Finally, the effect of architecture may be mediated by factors such as the amount of competition in the market for Internet services or the existence of laws and regulations that limit network providers' ability to the use the capabilities provided by an architecture ('network neutrality rules'). For example, a network non-discrimination rule that prevents network providers from discriminating among applications or classes of applications based on application-specific criteria, but allows application-agnostic discrimination, would recreate through law the same economic environment for application innovation and network use with respect to discrimination as an application-blind network, regardless of whether the underlying architecture is application-aware or not.[160,161] By contrast, in the absence of rules limiting discrimination, application-blind and application-aware architectures result in markedly different environments for application innovation and network use.

Thus, while the architecture of a network affects the economic environment for application innovation, deployment, and use in important ways, it is only one factor in a complex system that jointly influences the overall amount and quality of application innovation that will occur. Therefore, although the Internet's architecture in most countries has generally been the same, different countries have seen and will likely see different amounts of application innovation.

NOTES

* Parts of the chapter are adopted from van Schewick (2010a). Permission by MIT Press to reprint excerpts from the book is gratefully acknowledged. Due to space constraints, notes are reprinted only selectively. For a more detailed analysis of the questions discussed in this chapter and the full set of references, see van Schewick (2010a). For shorter summaries, see van Schewick (2010c; 2015a, pp. 19–23).

† Professor of Law and Helen L. Crocker Faculty Scholar, Stanford Law School; Director, Center for Internet and Society, Stanford Law School; Professor (by Courtesy) of Electrical Engineering, Stanford University. The author would like to thank Elaine Adolfo and Dolfin Leung for creating the figures and the librarians at Stanford Law School for their incredible work.

1. Throughout this chapter, the term *original architecture of the Internet* refers to the network architecture that was specified in the DARPA Internet Program protocol specifications for the Internet Protocol and the Transmission Control Protocol, RFC 791 (Postel, 1981a) and RFC 793 (Postel, 1981b). David Clark described this architecture in an important article on the design philosophy of the DARPA Internet Protocols (Clark, 1988).

2. Throughout this chapter, the term *innovation* refers to creating or improving goods, services, or methods of production (e.g., Hall, 1994, p. 2; Beije, 1998, pp. 1–2). As used here, the term innovation is not restricted to innovative activities that firms undertake to increase their profits (for this more restrictive use of the term, see, e.g., Hall, 1994, pp. 17–19), but denotes innovative activities by a wide range of actors – including individuals, groups, firms, and other organizations – whose actions and products may be motivated by various economic or non-economic concerns (van Schewick, 2010a, p. 28).

3. For a discussion of this term and more complete references to the literature exploring the economic effect of technical architectures, see van Schewick (2010a, pp. 13–14). Since the 1990s, scholars of management strategy have explored the economic effect of modular and integrated architectures. See, for example, Langlois and Robertson (1992); Garud and Kumaraswamy (1993); Ulrich (1995); Sanchez (1995); Baldwin and Clark (2000). The effect of the Internet's original architecture on innovation was first highlighted by Isenberg (1997); Isenberg (1998); Reed et al. (1998); Lemley and Lessig (1999); Lessig (2001).

4. See, for example, van Schewick (2010a, pp. 106–7, 151–4, 157–63, 366, 382–3 discussing the impact of Internet architecture on innovation in the Internet layer and pp. 88–90, 148–55 discussing the impact of Internet architecture on innovation in the link layer).

5. The analysis does not distinguish among Internet service providers that are vertically integrated into the operation of the network infrastructure and those that provide Internet access or transport services over another provider's physical infrastructure. See also van Schewick (2010a, p. 222).

6. van Schewick (2010a, pp. 20–21).

7. The framework described in the text is used by researchers in economics (North, 1990; Aoki, 2001; Furubotn and Richter, 2005; Greif, 2006), political science (Hall and Taylor, 1996; Thelen, 1999; Peters, 2005); law (Sunstein, 1996; Lessig, 1998; Benkler, 2006), and sociology (Powell and DiMaggio, 1991; DiMaggio, 1998; Scott, 2000). For a more detailed description of this framework with references to the literature, see van Schewick (2010a, pp. 23–8).

8. van Schewick (2010a, pp. 4, 28–30).

9. The effect of the economic system on the evolution of architectures is outside the scope of this chapter. On that topic, see, for example, van Schewick (2010a, pp. 3, 23–6, 28, 32, 151–63, 371–2, 389–402).

10. van Schewick (2010a, pp. 30–32).

11. van Schewick (2010a, p. 30).

12. van Schewick (2010a, p. 30). Economists usually treat resources and cost structures as constraints. Since they are specific to the individual actor, I mention them here. See also Ostrom (2005, pp. 828–9); Furubotn and Richter (2005, pp. 3, 308–9).

13. van Schewick (2010a, p. 31).
14. See, for example, Landes and Posner (2003).
15. Lessig (1998, pp. 663–4); van Schewick (2010a, pp. 26–8, 32).
16. For an example, see the Conclusion.
17. van Schewick (2010a, p. 30). This part of the framework also allows the integration of insights from sociology about the effect of existing social or economic relationships on economic behavior. See, for example, the research on embeddedness (e.g., Granovetter, 1985; Uzzi, 1996) or on the importance of organizational fields for firms' organizational choices (e.g., DiMaggio and Powell, 1983). On the relevance of embeddedness within organizations, cultures, or network connections for innovation, see, for example, Saxenian (1994); Castilla et al. (2000); Powell and Grodal (2005). See also the Conclusion.
18. See, for example, Dyer (1996, 1997); Takeishi (2001); van Schewick (2010a, pp. 178–9, 190).
19. van Schewick (2010a, pp. 32–3).
20. On the impact of such rules, see the Conclusion. See also van Schewick (2010a, pp. 218–21).
21. van Schewick (2010a, pp. 19–21).
22. van Schewick (2010a, pp. 50–52).
23. This description glosses over the fact that in some network architectures, the end hosts may not only use, but also offer network services. In the Internet, the end hosts (or computers 'on' the network) also participate in the operation of the network through the protocols at the Internet layer and below. Thus, one may say that in the Internet, end hosts form the network too. A more precise description of the Internet would focus on layers: the layers up to the Internet layer form or implement the network and are 'in' the network, while the layers above the Internet layer use the network and are 'on' the network. See, for example, Comer (2000, p. 186); Sterbenz and Touch (2001, p. 350).
24. Throughout this chapter, the term *the core of the network* will be used to denote the set of computers *in* the network, or, in the case of the Internet, the lower layers up to, and including, the Internet layer (see note 23). For a similar use, see Blumenthal and Clark (2001, pp. 71–2). Sometimes (but not in this chapter), the term *core network* is used to denote the part of a hierarchical telecommunications network that provides the highest level of aggregation, such as the backbone network, as opposed to the intermediate part of the entire network, which connects the core network with the access networks or edge networks.
25. van Schewick (2010a, pp. 50–51, 378, 107–10).
26. Layering, in turn, is a special form of modularity (e.g., van Schewick, 2010a, p. 46). On modularity, see van Schewick (2010a, pp. 38–44).
27. For a detailed discussion of the layering principle in the context of networking with references to the literature, see van Schewick (2010a, pp. 50–57). See also Tanenbaum and Wetherall (2011, pp. 29–33); Peterson and Davie (2012, pp. 24–31). On the layering principle in general, see van Schewick (2010a, pp. 46–50).
28. van Schewick (2010a, p. 88).
29. van Schewick (2010a, pp. 57–8). With respect to the International Organization for Standardization's Open Systems Interconnection reference model (the transport layer and higher layers are typically implemented on end hosts, not on the intermediate switches or routers), see, for example, Peterson and Davie (2012, pp. 32–3); Sterbenz and Touch (2001, pp. 41–2). With respect to the architecture of the Internet (end hosts implement all layers, while IP routers typically implement only lower layers, up to and including the Internet layer), see Kurose and Ross (2010, pp. 54–5). In practice, routers may implement higher layers to terminate routing protocols such as BGP or management protocols.
30. The text describes the 'relaxed' version of the layering principle. In the pure version of layering, a layer is allowed to use only the layer immediately below it. On the various versions of the layering principle, see van Schewick (2010a, pp. 46–7).
31. On the benefits and costs of layered architectures, see van Schewick (2010a, pp. 47–9).
32. See, for example, van Schewick (2010a, pp. 51–2, 54–6); Comer (2000, pp. 187–9); Sterbenz and Touch (2001, pp. 42–3).
33. See, for example, van Schewick (2010a, pp. 51–2, 56); Reed (2010); Peterson and Davie (2012, pp. 30–31).
34. See note 48 and accompanying text. In addition to being application-blind, the resulting network is also application-agnostic. While an application-agnostic network may have information about the applications on the network, it does not make distinctions among data packets based on that information. Thus, an application-blind network is necessarily application-agnostic: it does not make distinctions among data packets based on information about the applications on the network, because it does not have this information. By contrast, an application-agnostic network is not necessarily application-blind, because it may have information about the applications on the network. See van Schewick (2015a, pp. 24–6, Box 4).
35. van Schewick (2010a, pp. 57–8).
36. Saltzer et al. (1981). The 1981 paper was a conference paper. When referring to the original paper that

identified the end-to-end arguments, researchers usually refer to the revised version (Saltzer et al., 1984) that appeared in the *ACM Transactions on Computer Systems*.

37. See, for example, Reed et al. (1998); Reed (2000); Blumenthal and Clark (2001). See also Clark and Blumenthal (2011, pp. 383–8) (tracing the evolution of the end-to-end arguments and the existence of the two versions).

38. The difference was first noted and described in van Schewick (2004, Chapter 6); van Schewick (2010a, p. 59). The terminology – 'narrow' vs 'broad' – reflects the differences in scope between the two versions (van Schewick, 2004). For a comparison of the two versions and a discussion of the rationale for distinguishing between the two, see van Schewick (2010a, pp. 58–9, 75–81, 377–9, 408 fn. 67). In the literature, most older texts referring to 'the end-to-end arguments' simply quote either the narrow or the broad version (see, e.g., the references cited by van Schewick, 2010a, p. 59). For two exceptions, see Moors (2002); Kempf and Austein (2004).

39. van Schewick (2010a, pp. 5, 58–9, 79–80) (discussing examples).

40. For a detailed analysis of the broad version, see van Schewick (2010a, pp. 67–75, 378–9). For an analysis of the narrow version and its relationship to the Internet's original architecture, see van Schewick (2010a, pp. 60–67, 90–96, 103, 377–8, 380). On the two versions of the end-to-end arguments in the current Internet, see, for example, Saltzer (1999); Reed (2000); Blumenthal and Clark (2001); Clark and Blumenthal (2011); van Schewick (2010a, pp. 383–7, 388–9) (with references to the literature).

41. Blumenthal and Clark (2001, p. 71).

42. Reed et al. (1998, p. 69).

43. See, for example, Reed et al. (1998, pp. 69–70); Blumenthal and Clark (2001, pp. 71–2); Clark et al. (2005, p. 471); van Schewick (2010a, pp. 68–9).

44. Blumenthal and Clark (2001, p. 80) (citing personal communication with Jerome Saltzer).

45. See, for example, Reed et al. (1998, pp. 69–70); Reed (2000); Clark et al. (2005, p. 472); van Schewick (2010a, pp. 69–71).

46. Application autonomy is the idea that an application or higher layers close to it know best what services they need and should therefore be responsible for meeting these needs. On the broad version and application autonomy, see, for example, Reed et al. (1998, p. 70); van Schewick (2010a, pp. 71–2). On the broad version and reliability, see, for example, Blumenthal and Clark (2001, p. 71); Clark et al. (2005, p. 472); van Schewick (2010a, p. 72).

47. van Schewick (2010a, pp. 68–75, 355–71, 378–9) (discussing the trade-off underlying the broad version).

48. van Schewick (2010a, pp. 72–5, 217–18); van Schewick (2015a, pp. 128–30, Box 19 and fn. 455); van Schewick (2004). See also, for example, Lemley and Lessig (1999, para. 17); Cerf (2006, pp. 1–4, 7); Reed (2010). Like any application-blind network, the resulting network is also application-agnostic. See note 34.

49. See note 33 and accompanying text.

50. See van Schewick (2010a, pp. 88–90, 379). On the Internet layer as a portability layer or, in Clark's terminology, 'spanning layer', see also Clark (1997, pp. 134–5); Computer Science and Telecommunications Board and National Research Council (2001, pp. 126–30). On relaxed layering with a portability layer as a design principle, see van Schewick (2010a, pp. 47–8).

51. This terminology follows the terminology of the TCP/IP reference model used by the Internet Engineering Task Force (IETF). See, for example, Comer (2000, pp. 183–5); Tanenbaum and Wetherall (2011, pp. 45–8). For an overview of the different layers of the Internet's architecture and the main protocols at these layers, see van Schewick (2010a, pp. 83–8).

52. See note 29 and accompanying text.

53. See, for example, Computer Science and Telecommunications Board and National Research Council (2001, pp. 126–30); Peterson and Davie (2012, pp. 35–6).

54. See van Schewick (2010a, pp. 96–103, 110–12, 380–81). According to the networking literature, the end-to-end arguments are among the few design principles underlying the architecture of the Internet. See, for example, Carpenter (1996, section 2); Reed et al. (1998, p. 70); Computer Science and Telecommunications Board and National Research Council (2001, pp. 36–8); Braden et al. (2000, p. 15); Blumenthal and Clark (2001, p. 71); Clark et al. (2005, section VI.A). These texts effectively describe the broad version of the end-to-end arguments. See, for example, the citations in van Schewick (2010a, pp. 410–11 fn. 69). On the impact of the narrow version on the Internet's original architecture, see van Schewick (2010a, pp. 90–96, 380). On the impact of the two versions of the end-to-end arguments on application design, see van Schewick (2010a, pp. 103, 107–10).

55. For an overview of the initial proposal, see van Schewick (2010a, pp. 94–5). For technical descriptions of the initial monolithic protocol, see Cerf and Kahn (1974) (the first published description); Cerf (1977) and Cerf and Postel (1978).

56. See, for example, van Schewick (2010a, p. 97)

57. van Schewick (2010a, pp. 97–8, 102–3).

58. van Schewick (2010a, pp. 97–8).
59. The decision to split the initial monolithic protocol was made at a meeting of the researchers involved in the design of the Internet Transmission Control Protocol on 30–31 January 1978 at the Information Sciences Institute in Marina Del Rey. See, for example, Postel (1978) (describing the results of the meeting). See also Abbate (1999, pp. 129–30); van Schewick (2010a, Box 3.3, pp. 99–100). For a detailed discussion of the considerations that motivated this decision, for a description by David Reed (one of the authors of the papers describing the end-to-end arguments) of the events leading to the decision, and for references to the literature underlying the arguments in the text, see van Schewick (2010a, pp. 96–101 and Box 3.3, pp. 99–100).
60. In addition, the choice to offer only unreliable datagram service at the Internet layer was motivated by the designation of the Internet layer as the portability layer and the desire to enable applications to survive partial network failures. See, for example, Clark (1988, pp. 107–10); van Schewick (2010a, pp. 101–2).
61. For a short description of the Internet Protocol, see van Schewick (2010a, pp. 85–6).
62. For short descriptions of TCP and UDP, see van Schewick (2010a, pp. 86–7).
63. See also note 48 and accompanying text. Like any application-blind network, the Internet's original architecture was also application-agnostic. See note 34.
64. Again, I use the term *applications* as shorthand for applications, content, services, and uses.
65. The Internet's architecture also influences the environment for innovation in other layers of the Internet's architecture. See, for example, van Schewick (2010a, pp. 106–7, 151–4, 157–63, 366, 382–3) discussing the impact of Internet architecture on innovation in the Internet layer and pp. 88–90, 148–55 discussing the impact of Internet architecture on innovation in the link layer.
66. van Schewick (2010a, pp. 140–41).
67. On the term *core of the network*, see notes 23 to 24 and accompanying text.
68. I use the terms *network providers* to describe economic actors who provide Internet access or transport services, regardless of whether they are vertically integrated into the operation of the network infrastructure or not. See also note 5.
69. van Schewick (2010a, pp. 204, 211, 293); Cerf (2006, pp. 1–4). See also Balkin (2009) (focusing on the social, cultural, and political implications of innovation without permission).
70. See van Schewick (2010a, pp. 138–48, 204–5, 289–90). See also Benkler (2000, pp. 565–8); Balkin (2009) (both focusing on the social, cultural, and political implications).
71. The overall costs of developing an application and making it available to others on an ongoing basis differ depending on the type of application. While these costs will be lower for applications that run entirely on users' machines than for applications that need servers run by the developer or provider of the application, recent developments have drastically reduced the minimum level of investment needed to develop and operate server-based applications. See van Schewick (2010a, pp. 143–4).
72. van Schewick (2010a, pp. 204–13, 292–3). See generally van Schewick (2010a, pp. 115–18, 165–6) (discussing the relationship between architecture and who can innovate).
73. van Schewick (2010a, pp. 205, 206). This seems to be an important motivation of contributors to open-source projects. Lakhani and Wolf (2005, pp. 12–16). See also Benkler (2002).
74. van Schewick (2010a, pp. 205–6, 334–5).
75. The term *deploying* an application denotes all steps that a user and the operator of the network must perform before an application can be used for the first time. See van Schewick (2010a, pp. 137–8).
76. van Schewick (2010a, pp. 144, 152–5, 293–5, 362–4); Cerf (2006, pp. 1–3, 7). On the importance of user choice for the Internet's social, cultural, and political potential, see, for example, Balkin (2009); van Schewick (2010a, pp. 359–65).
77. Not every application of the broad version automatically results in decentralized control by users (instead of centralized control by a few network providers); it only results in decentralized control if end users control the end hosts. Thus, control over a network can be centralized even if the network is designed according to the broad version, if a central entity controls the end hosts. For example, an enterprise network based on the TCP/IP suite where applications can only be installed by system administrators is based on the broad version, but centrally controlled. See van Schewick (2010a, pp. 72, 414 fn. 118, 387). In the commercial Internet, users generally control the end hosts (ibid., pp. 152–5, 362–4). In the past, network providers and handset providers often controlled the handsets on mobile networks (ibid., pp. 390–91). On the impact of specialized appliances controlled by the manufacturer or the network provider on user choice and application innovation under an architecture based on the broad version, see ibid., p. 387; Gillett et al. (2001); Zittrain (2008).
78. van Schewick (2010a, pp. 217–18).
79. Discrimination not only encompasses differential handling of packets, but also other forms of conduct that make an application or class of application relatively more attractive to use than others, including, for example, application-specific pricing or differential counting of applications against

the monthly usage caps. See van Schewick (2015a, pp. 30–33); van Schewick (2015c, pp. 1–3); van Schewick (2016).

80. van Schewick (2010a, pp. 293–294). The effect of application-awareness on control over application innovation, deployment, and use is explained in more detail below. See subsections 14.5.3.3 Control over Application Innovation and 14.5.3.4 Control over Application Deployment and Use.

81. See the analysis in subsections 14.5.1.1 Control over Application Innovation and 14.5.1.4 Control over Application Deployment and Use.

82. In a network that is application-blind, but contains application-specific functionality in the network's core, the network may need to be changed before a new application can run on the network. Once the network is changed to enable an application, however, the network's application blindness prevents the network provider from interfering with the applications on its network. In such a network, network providers control application innovation and deployment, but users control which applications are used (van Schewick, 2010a, pp. 293–4) (discussing a purely opaque network, i.e., a network that is application-blind, but not general).

83. van Schewick (2010a, pp. 270–73). See also Lessig (2008, pp. 7–8).

84. For two publicly documented examples, see van Schewick (2008b, p. 2) and the letter from the founders of the online video company Zediva to the FCC (Srinivasan and Gupta, 2010, pp. 1–2).

85. van Schewick (2010a, pp. 222–5). See also Whinston (1990, pp. 840, 850–52); Farrell and Katz (2000); Farrell and Weiser (2003, pp. 89, 100–105).

86. For a detailed analysis of incentives to block, see, for example, van Schewick (2010a, pp. 222–64, 275–8) (increase profits), pp. 266–270 (block unwanted content), pp. 264–6 (manage congestion); van Schewick (2008a, pp. 5–6) (manage congestion).

87. van Schewick (2010a, p. 225). For a more detailed analysis of the costs of exclusionary conduct see van Schewick (2010a, p. 259–4); van Schewick (2015a, pp. 83–99) (discussing the factors affecting customers' ability to switch providers of Internet access service).

88. van Schewick (2010a, p. 273, 277); van Schewick (2015a, pp. 56–7) (discussing examples). The impact of blocking on application developers' incentives to innovate stems from the blocking as such and is independent of whether the network provider participates in the market for the application or not. By contrast, US antitrust law only condemns discriminatory conduct in the market for a specific application if the network provider participates in that market or is affiliated with a participant in that market. See van Schewick (2015a, p. 56).

89. See van Schewick (2010a, pp. 251–5, 264–70); Frischmann and van Schewick (2007, pp. 412–16). This chapter focuses on the impact of discrimination on application developers' incentives to innovate. To reduce application developers' incentives to innovate, the exclusionary conduct does not need to drive them from the market; it suffices if it reduces their profits. By contrast, scholars who evaluate discriminatory conduct within a framework based on US antitrust law will only be concerned about discriminatory conduct if the conduct is reasonably capable of monopolizing the market for the affected application or the market for Internet services. For a detailed analysis of this difference and references to the literature, see van Schewick (2015a, pp. 58–60). See also Frischmann and van Schewick (2007, pp. 414 fn. 119, 416 fn. 128).

90. AT&T (2009, pp. 6–7); van Schewick (2010a, pp. 241–2); BEREC (2012, p. 8).

91. See, for example, US Department of Justice (2011, pp. 11, 14–20, 37–9).

92. Wu (2003, pp. 151–2, 165); van Schewick (2010a, p. 471 fn. 237).

93. Comcast Corporation (2008); RCN Corporation (2010); Schatz (2008); Dischinger et al. (2008) (all US); Parsons (2009) (Canada); Cellan-Jones (2009); Cooper (2013) (all UK); BEREC (2012); Kroes (2012) (all Europe).

94. van Schewick (2010a, pp. 267–70) (describing the examples with references to the literature).

95. See, for example, Litan and Singer (2007, pp. 552–4); Yoo (2007, pp. 504, 506, 511–15); Becker et al. (2010, p. 505); Cave et al. (2009, pp. 1–2).

96. The following two paragraphs are adopted from van Schewick (2015a, pp. 83–99). For a full discussion with detailed references to the literature, see ibid., pp. 60–61, 83–9. For an earlier discussion, see van Schewick (2010a, pp. 259–64).

97. Relative to markets in which Internet service providers do not face any competitors, competition in the market for Internet services may even increase Internet service providers' incentives to block or discriminate. See generally van Schewick (2010a, pp. 255–9) and, regarding incentives to engage in discriminatory traffic management, Cooper (2013) (based on a case study of broadband traffic management in the UK).

98. See, for example, Cooper (2013) (wireline Internet services in the UK); BEREC (2012) (European wireline and mobile Internet services); Kroes (2012) (same); Parsons (2009) (wireline Internet services in Canada); van Schewick (2011b) (Verizon Wireless/tethering applications); van Schewick (2011a) (AT&T, Verizon Wireless, T-Mobile/Google Wallet); Ziegler (2012); Kang (2012) (AT&T/Apple Facetime). See

        also van Schewick (2015a, pp. 96–8) (summarizing the evidence). On the amount of competition in the market for Internet services in the USA and Europe, see van Schewick (2015a, pp. 88–9).

99.   For the EU, see Articles 20 and 21 Directive 2002/22/EC of the European Parliament and of the Council of 7 March 2002, as amended by Directive 2009/136/EC of the European Parliament and of the Council of 25 November 2009 (Universal Service Directive). For the USA, see 47 C.F.R. §8.3. On the effect of disclosure rules on network providers' incentives to discriminate, see van Schewick (2015a, pp. 83–99).

100. Any Internet service provider can charge fees to customers of its Internet access service, regardless of whether these customers are providers of applications or 'normal' end users. In the past, Internet users – both application providers and 'normal' end users – directly paid fees for Internet service only to their own Internet access provider.

101. A large body of literature discusses the different types of access fees and which, if any, regulatory intervention is needed. For a brief overview, see van Schewick (2010a, p. 4). For opponents of access fees, see, for example, Lee and Wu (2009); van Schewick (2010b); Economides and Tåg (2012); Economides and Hermalin (2012); van Schewick (2015b, pp. 11–17). For proponents, see, for example, Hemphill (2008) and Schuett (2010, pp. 2–4); Faulhaber (2011, pp. 62–8) (both reviewing the economic literature on access fees from the perspective of a proponent of access fees).

102. The practice of an ISP not counting selected applications against a user's monthly data cap is also called 'zero rating'. On the social costs and benefits of the different kinds of zero rating (including a discussion of real-world examples), see van Schewick (2015c); van Schewick (2016).

103. van Schewick (2010a, pp. 278–80, 290–92; 2010b, pp. 2–3).

104. van Schewick (2010a, pp. 207–10, 211–13, 292–3; 2010b, pp. 1–6; 2015b, pp. 11–14).

105. Reducing or impeding the ability of innovators with little or no outside funding to develop new applications may significantly reduce the amount and quality of application innovation. Throughout the history of the Internet, many important innovations (including eBay, Facebook, Yahoo!, Google, Apache Web Server, the World Wide Web, Flickr, and Blogger) have been developed by innovators of this type. See van Schewick (2010b, pp. 3–5); van Schewick (2010a, pp. 204–13, 310–14, 318–28, 334–45) (discussing the importance of different types of low-cost innovators, including many examples). As the comments by many start-ups in the FCC's Open Internet Proceeding in 2014–15 show, low-cost innovators continue to be important sources of innovation today. See van Schewick (2015b, pp. 12–13 and Appendix 'Internet Startups Need a Non-Discriminatory Internet').

106. van Schewick (2010b, p. 3; 2010c, pp. 4–5, 6). On the consequences of allowing network providers to influence which application will be successful, see section 14.5.3.4 Control over Application Deployment and Use.

107. van Schewick (2010a, pp. 217–18, 273) (discussing the impact of architecture on available pricing strategies). For a detailed analysis of network providers' incentives to engage in these strategies and of the impact on application developers and users, see van Schewick (2010a, pp. 273–5) (application-specific pricing), pp. 275–8 (price discrimination). Application-specific pricing may also be used to discriminate among applications or classes of applications (van Schewick, 2015a, pp. 32–3). For two real-world examples of these strategies, see Allot Communications and Openet (2010, p. 7) (application-specific pricing) and Wu (2003, pp. 151–2, 165); van Schewick (2010a, p. 471 fn. 237) (price discrimination).

108. van Schewick (2010a, pp. 286–7). For a description of four prototypical examples, see van Schewick (2010a, pp. 287–9).

109. van Schewick (2010a, pp. 286, 382, 385–6).

110. van Schewick (2010a, pp. 74–5, 286–7, 371–2).

111. van Schewick (2010a, pp. 70, 264–6, 286, 372).

112. van Schewick (2010a, pp. 286, 382, 385–6).

113. van Schewick (2010a, pp. 286–7, 371–2). On deep packet inspection (DPI) in general, see Anderson (2007); Cooper (2011). For specific examples, see, for example, Cisco Systems (2005); Free Press (2010a); Allot Communications and Openet (2010); Talbot (2014). On the state of DPI deployment, see Free Press (2010b, pp. 141–51).

114. For an analysis of the impact of four prototypical architectures (end-to-end, partially controllable, fully controllable, core-centered) on the economic environment for application innovation, see van Schewick (2010a, pp. 287–95, 351–3).

115. van Schewick (2010a, pp. 115–18, 215–16).

116. See section 14.5.2 Application Blindness of the Network and van Schewick (2010a, Chapter 6).

117. van Schewick (2010a, pp. 138–40, 144–8). See the section 14.5.3.2 Size and Diversity of the Innovator Pool.

118. van Schewick (2010a, pp. 144–7, 289–91). By contrast, deviating from the broad version of the end-to-end arguments may increase network providers' incentives to innovate at the application level. van Schewick (2010a, p. 291).

119. van Schewick (2010a, pp. 144–8, 152–5, 294–5, 352).

120. See generally van Schewick (2010a, pp. 115–18, 165–6).
121. See subsections 14.5.1.2 Cost of Application Innovation and 14.5.1.3 Size and Diversity of the Innovator Pool.
122. van Schewick (2010a, pp. 210–11, 292–3).
123. See notes 104 to 105 and accompanying text.
124. On the need for changes to the core of the network in an application-aware architecture and the impact on the costs of application innovation, see van Schewick (2010a, pp. 138–40, 144–8, 291).
125. van Schewick (2010a, pp. 210–13, 292–3).
126. For the full argument with references to the literature, see van Schewick (2010a, pp. 297–345).
127. van Schewick (2010a, pp. 298–301). Generally, see, for example, Nelson and Winter (1977, p. 47; 1982, pp. 389–90); North (1990, pp. 80–82); Merges and Nelson (1994, p. 6); Rosenberg (1994, pp. 87–108; 1996); Cohen and Malerba (2001). On the link between the end-to-end architecture of the Internet and evolutionary theories of innovation, see Wu and Lessig (2003, pp. 5–7); Wu (2003, pp. 145–6; 2004, section II.A).
128. van Schewick (2010a, pp. 297–345).
129. For example, Kirzner (1997); Shane (2000); Shane and Venkataraman (2000); Sarasvathy et al. (2003).
130. For example, Rosenberg (1996).
131. van Schewick (2010a, pp. 301–6).
132. For numerous examples from the history of the Internet, see van Schewick (2010a, pp. 301–10).
133. van Schewick (2010a, pp. 310–11).
134. van Schewick (2010a, pp. 300). The impact of differences among actors also increases with the complexity of the problem to be solved and with the heterogeneity of customers. Ibid.
135. van Schewick (2010a, pp. 116, 311–12).
136. van Schewick (2010a, pp. 312–14). For more on the differences among and specific value of different types of innovators with examples from the history of the Internet, see van Schewick (2010b, pp. 3–5); van Schewick (2010a, pp. 204–13, 310–14) (low-cost innovators), pp. 312–13, 319–28 (large companies), pp. 319–28 (new entrants), pp. 208–9, 312, 319, 328–34 (venture capitalists), pp. 206–7, 209, 319, 312–13 (self-funding or angel investors), pp. 205–6, 312–13, 319, 334–45 (users). See also note 105.
137. van Schewick (2010a, pp. 314–17).
138. van Schewick (2010a, pp. 318–19).
139. For a more nuanced analysis, see van Schewick (2010a, pp. 299–300, 349). See also Nelson and Winter (1982, pp. 389–90); Merges and Nelson (1994, p. 6); Rosenberg (1996, p. 353).
140. See section 14.5.1.1 Control over Application Innovation.
141. van Schewick (2010a, pp. 138–40, 293–4).
142. van Schewick (2010a, pp. 288–9, 293).
143. van Schewick (2010a, pp. 292–4, 345–6).
144. On the arguments in the text, see van Schewick (2010a, pp. 345–8) with references to the literature.
145. On this requirement, see note 77.
146. See section 14.5.1.4 Control over Application Deployment and Use.
147. van Schewick (2010a, pp. 152–5, 293–5, 362–4).
148. See van Schewick (2010a, p. 152–5, 294–5, 346, 349, 485 fn. 162).
149. van Schewick (2010a, pp. 299–300, 349).
150. In the terminology of evolutionary economics, different architectures create different selection environments.
151. van Schewick (2010a, pp. 350–51).
152. See van Schewick (2010a, p. 350–51) and section 14.5.2.1 Blocking or Discrimination.
153. See notes 89 to 99 and accompanying text.
154. van Schewick (2010a, p. 351).
155. See van Schewick (2010a, pp. 362–3); van Schewick (2008a, pp. 7–8). See also Cerf (2006, pp. 1–3, 7). On the importance of user choice for the Internet's social, cultural, and political potential, see, for example, Balkin (2009); van Schewick (2010a, pp. 359–5).
156. Increasing the costs or reducing the expected benefits of application innovation will always reduce the amount of application innovation, regardless of the degree of uncertainty or user heterogeneity.
157. van Schewick (2010a, p. 351).
158. van Schewick (2010a, p. 356).
159. van Schewick (2010a, pp. 212–13). See also note 17.
160. van Schewick (2015a, pp. 124–31). Alternative non-discrimination rules may provide network providers with more or less flexibility regarding discrimination than the Internet's original architecture. (In fact, the non-discrimination rule described in the text only requires the network to be application-agnostic; it does not require the network to be application-blind. See van Schewick, 2015a, pp. 24–5, Box 4, 130–31.) Thus, not all non-discrimination rules will necessarily recreate the economic environment created by an

architecture based on the broad version. In addition, different non-discrimination rules will impose different constraints on the evolution and operation of the network and will result in different costs of regulation. For an analysis of alternative proposals for non-discrimination rules, see van Schewick (2015a).

161. Application-specific criteria are criteria that depend on an application's characteristics. Application-specific criteria include application (i.e., the specific instance of an application a user is using, e.g., Vonage vs Skype), application type (e.g., e-mail vs Internet telephony), the application-layer protocol or transport-layer protocol the application is using (e.g., SIP vs Skype's proprietary protocol, or TCP vs UDP), or the application's technical requirements (e.g., latency-sensitive vs non-latency-sensitive applications). For a detailed description and analysis of the non-discrimination rule described in the text, see van Schewick (2015a, pp. 124–52).

REFERENCES

Abbate, J. (1999), *Inventing the Internet*, Cambridge, MA: MIT Press.

Allot Communications and Openet (2010), 'Managing the unmanageable: Monetizing and controlling OTT applications. FierceLive! Webinar presentation', attachment to the ex parte letter by Free Press In the Matter of Preserving the Open Internet, submitted 14 December, accessed 21 December 2015 at http://apps.fcc.gov/ecfs/document/view?id=7020923750.

Anderson, N. (2007), 'Deep packet inspection meets "net neutrality", CALEA', *Ars Technica*, 25 July, accessed 12 July 2015 at http://arstechnica.com/articles/culture/Deep-packet-inspection-meets-net-neutrality.ars.

Aoki, M. (2001), *Towards a Comparative Institutional Analysis*, Cambridge, MA: MIT Press.

AT&T (2009), 'AT&T response to Wireless Telecommunications Bureau letter, DA 09-1737 (31 July 2009), Letter to Federal Communications Commission, WT Dkt. No. RM-11361, August 21', accessed 21 December 2015 at http://www.wired.com/images_blogs/business/2009/08/att-response-to-fcc.pdf.

Baldwin, C.Y. and K.B. Clark (2000), *Design Rules: The Power of Modularity, Volume 1*, Cambridge, MA: MIT Press.

Balkin, J.M. (2009), *Testimony before the Federal Communications Commission at its Workshop on Speech, Democratic Engagement, and the Open Internet*, Washington, DC: Federal Communications Commission.

Becker, G.S., D.W. Carlton and H.S. Sider (2010), 'Net neutrality and consumer welfare', *Journal of Competition Law and Economics*, **6** (3), 497–519. Beije, P. (1998), *Technological Change in the Modern Economy. Basic Topics and New Developments*, Cheltenham, UK and Lyme, NH, USA: Edward Elgar Publishing.

Benkler, Y. (2000), 'From consumers to users: Shifting the deeper structures of regulation towards sustainable commons and user access', *Federal Communications Law Journal*, **52** (3), 561–79.

Benkler, Y. (2002), 'Coase's penguin, or, Linux and the nature of the firm', *Yale Law Journal*, **112** (3), 369–446.

Benkler, Y. (2006), *The Wealth of Networks: How Social Production Transforms Markets and Freedom*, New Haven, CT: Yale University Press.

BEREC (2012), 'BEREC findings on traffic management practices in Europe', Riga: Body of European Regulators for Electronic Communications, BoR (12) 30, accessed 19 July 2015 at http://berec.europa.eu/eng/document_register/subject_matter/berec/reports/45-berec-findings-on-traffic-management-practices-in-europe.

Blumenthal, M.S. and D.D. Clark (2001), 'Rethinking the design of the Internet: The end-to-end arguments vs. the brave new world', *ACM Transactions on Internet Technology*, **1** (1), 70–109.

Braden, R., D. Clark, S. Shenker and J. Wroclawski (2000), 'Developing a next-generation internet architecture', accessed 22 July at http://www.isi.edu/newarch/DOCUMENTS/WhitePaper.pdf.

Carpenter, B. (1996), 'Architectural principles of the Internet', *Request for Comments 1958*, Internet Engineering Task Force (IETF), accessed 22 July 2015 at http://www.rfc-editor.org/pdfrfc/rfc1958.txt.pdf.

Castilla, E.J., H. Hwang, E. Granovetter and M. Granovetter (2000), 'Social networks in Silicon Valley', in C.-M. Lee, W.F. Miller, M. Gong Hancock and H.S. Rowen (eds), *The Silicon Valley Edge: A Habitat for Innovation and Entrepreneurship*, Stanford, CA: Stanford University Press, pp. 218–47.

Cave, M., R. Collins and N. van Eijk et al. (2009), 'Statement by European academics on the inappropriateness of imposing increased Internet regulation in the EU', accessed 21 December 2015 at http://www.cerre.eu/sites/cerre/files/Statement_by_European_academics_on_the_inappropriateness_of_imposing.pdf.

Cellan-Jones, R. (2009), 'iPlayer: BBC v BT', *BBC News dot.life Blog*, 2 June, accessed 22 July 2015 at http://www.bbc.co.uk/blogs/technology/2009/06/iplayerbbc_v_bt.html.

Cerf, V.G. (1977), 'Specification of Internet Transmission Control Program TCP (Version 2)', IEN 5, accessed 22 July 2015 at http://www.rfc-editor.org/ien/ien5.pdf.

Cerf, V.G. (2006), 'Testimony before the United States Senate, Committee on Commerce, Science, and Transportation, at its hearing on: network neutrality', accessed 24 December 2015 at https://www.gpo.gov/fdsys/pkg/CHRG-109shrg30115/html/CHRG-109shrg30115.htm.

Cerf, V.G. and R.E. Kahn (1974), 'A protocol for packet network intercommunication', *IEEE Transactions on Communications*, **22** (5), 637–48.

Cerf, V.G. and J.B. Postel (1978), 'Specification of Internetwork Transmission Control Program, TCP Version 3', IEN 21, Information Sciences Institute, University of Southern California.

Cisco Systems (2005), 'Network-based application recognition and distributed network-based application recognition feature guide (Cisco IOS Release 12.4(4) T)', accessed 21 December 2015 at http://www.cisco.com/c/en/us/td/docs/ios/12_2s/feature/guide/fsnbarad.html.

Clark, D.D. (1988), 'The design philosophy of the DARPA Internet Protocols', *Computer Communication Review*, **18** (4), 106–14.

Clark, D.D. (1997), 'Interoperation, open interfaces, and protocol architecture', in NII 2000 Steering Committee Computer Science and Telecommunications Board and Mathematics Commission on Physical Sciences, and Applications and National Research Council (eds), *The Unpredictable Certainty: White Papers*, Washington, DC: The National Academies, pp. 133–44.

Clark, D.D. and M.S. Blumenthal (2011), 'The end-to-end argument and application design: The role of trust', *Federal Communications Commission Law Review*, **63** (2), 357–90.

Clark, D.D., J. Wroclawski, K.R. Sollins and R. Braden (2005), 'Tussle in cyberspace: Defining tomorrow's Internet', *IEEE/ACM Transactions on Networking*, **13** (3), 462–75.

Cohen, W.M. and F. Malerba (2001), 'Is the tendency to variation a chief cause of progress?', *Industrial and Corporate Change*, **10** (3), 587–608.

Comcast Corporation (2008), 'Comcast Corporation description of current network management practices, Attachment A to Comcast Corporation's Filing in the Matter of Formal Complaint of Free Press and Public Knowledge Against Comcast Corporation for Secretly Degrading Peer-to-Peer Applications submitted 19 September 2008, WC Dkt. No. 07-52', accessed 21 December 2015 at https://downloads.comcast.net/docs/Attachment_A_Current_Practices.pdf.

Comer, D.E. (2000), *Internetworking with TCP/IP: Principles, Protocols, and Architectures*, 4th edition, Upper Saddle River, NJ: Prentice Hall.

Computer Science and Telecommunications Board and National Research Council (2001), *The Internet's Coming of Age*, Washington, DC: National Academy Press.

Cooper, A. (2011), 'Doing the DPI dance', in W. Aspray and P. Doty (eds), *Privacy in America: Interdisciplinary Perspectives*, Lanham, MD: Scarecrow Press, Inc., pp. 139–65.

Cooper, A. (2013), 'How competition drives discrimination: An analysis of broadband traffic management in the UK', paper presented at the 41st Research Conference on Communication, Information and Internet Policy (TPRC'41), Arlington, VA.

DiMaggio, P.J. (1998), 'The New Institutionalism: Avenues of collaboration', *Journal of Institutional and Theoretical Economics*, **154** (4), 696–715.

DiMaggio, P.J. and W.W. Powell (1983), 'The iron cage revisited: Institutional isomorphism and collective rationality in organizational fields', *American Sociological Review*, **48** (2), 147–60.

Dischinger, M., A. Mislove, A. Haeberlen and K.P. Gummadi (2008), 'Detecting BitTorrent blocking', in *Proceedings of the 8th ACM SIGCOMM Conference on Internet Measurement Conference (IMC'08)*, pp. 3–8.

Dyer, J.H. (1996), 'Specialized supplier networks as a source of competitive advantage: Evidence from the auto industry', *Strategic Management Journal*, **17** (4), 271–91.

Dyer, J.H. (1997), 'Effective interfirm collaboration: How firms minimize transaction costs and maximize transaction value', *Strategic Management Journal*, **18** (7), 535–56.

Economides, N. and B.E. Hermalin (2012), 'The economics of network neutrality', *RAND Journal of Economics*, **43** (4), 602–29.

Economides, N. and J. Tåg (2012), 'Network neutrality on the Internet: A two-sided market analysis', *Information Economics and Policy*, **24** (2), 91–104.

Farrell, J. and M.L. Katz (2000), 'Innovation, rent extraction, and integration in systems markets', *Journal of Industrial Economics*, **48** (4), 413–32.

Farrell, J. and P.J. Weiser (2003), 'Modularity, vertical integration, and open access policies: Towards a convergence of antitrust and regulation in the Internet Age', *Harvard Journal of Law and Technology*, **17** (1), 85–134.

Faulhaber, G.R. (2011), 'Economics of net neutrality: A review', *Communications and Convergence Review*, **3** (1), 7–25.

Free Press (2010a), 'Ex parte letter to the Federal Communications Commission, GN Dkt. No. 09-191', 14 December.

Free Press (2010b), 'Comments to the Federal Communications Commission, GN Dkt. No. 09-191', 14 January.

Frischmann, B.M. and B. van Schewick (2007), 'Network neutrality and the economics of an information superhighway: A reply to Professor Yoo', *Jurimetrics Journal*, **47** (4), 383–428.

Furubotn, E.G. and R. Richter (2005), *Institutions and Economic Theory: The Contribution of the New Institutional Economics*, 2nd edition, Ann Arbor, MI: University of Michigan Press.

Garud, R. and A. Kumaraswamy (1993), 'Changing competitive dynamics in network industries: An exploration of Sun Microsystems' open systems strategy', *Strategic Management Journal*, **14** (5), 351–69.

Gillett, S.E., W.H. Lehr, J.T. Wroclawski and D.D. Clark (2001), 'Do appliances threaten Internet innovation?', *IEEE Communications Magazine*, **39** (10), 46–51.

Granovetter, M. (1985), 'Economic action and social structure: The problem of embeddedness', *American Journal of Sociology*, **91** (3), 481–510.

Greif, A. (2006), *Institutions and the Path to the Modern Economy: Lessons from Medieval Trade*, Cambridge, UK: Cambridge University Press.

Hall, P. (1994), *Innovation, Economics and Evolution. Theoretical Perspectives on Changing Technology in Economic Systems*, New York: Harvester Wheatsheaf.

Hall, P.A. and R.C.R. Taylor (1996), 'Political science and the three new institutionalisms', *Political Studies*, **44** (5), 936–57.

Hemphill, C.S. (2008), 'Network neutrality and the false promise of zero-price regulation', *Yale Journal on Regulation*, **25** (2), 135–80.

Isenberg, D. (1997), 'Rise of the stupid network: Why the intelligent network was once a good idea, but isn't anymore. One telephone company nerd's odd perspective on the changing value proposition', *Computer Telephony*, August, 16, 18, 20, 24, 26.

Isenberg, D.S. (1998), 'The dawn of the "stupid network"', *netWorker*, **2** (1), 24–31.

Kang, C. (2012), 'AT&T faces complaint over iPhone Facetime blocking', *Washington Post Technology Blog*, 18 September, accessed 24 July 2015 at http://www.washingtonpost.com/blogs/post-tech/post/at&t-faces-complaint-over-iphone-facetime-blocking/2012/09/18/799c8650-0183-11e2-b257-e1c2b3548a4a_blog.html.

Kempf, J. and R. Austein (2004), 'The rise of the middle and the future of end-to-end: Reflections on the evolution of the Internet architecture', *Request for Comments 3724*, IETF, accessed 19 July 2015 at http://www.ietf.org/mail-archive/web/ietf-announce/current/msg00031.html.

Kirzner, I.M. (1997), 'Entrepreneurial discovery and the competitive market process: An Austrian approach', *Journal of Economic Literature*, **35** (1), 60–85.

Kroes, N. (2012), 'Next steps on net neutrality – Making sure you get champagne service if that's what you're paying for', 29 May, European Commission blog archive, accessed 24 July 2015 at http://ec.europa.eu/archives/commission_2010-2014/kroes/en/blog/netneutrality.html.

Kurose, J.F. and K.W. Ross (2010), *Computer Networking: A Top-Down Approach*, 5th edition, Boston, MA: Pearson/Addison Wesley.

Lakhani, K.R. and R.G. Wolf (2005), 'Why hackers do what they do: Understanding motivation and effort in free/open source software projects', in J. Feller, B. Fitzgerald, S.A. Hissam and K.R. Lakhani (eds), *Perspectives on Free and Open Source Software*, Cambridge, MA: MIT Press, pp. 3–21.

Landes, W.M. and R.A. Posner (2003), *The Economic Structure of Intellectual Property Law*, Cambridge, MA: Belknap Press of Harvard University Press.

Langlois, R.N. and P.L. Robertson (1992), 'Networks and innovation in a modular system: Lessons from the microcomputer and stereo component industries', *Research Policy*, **21** (4), 297–313.

Lee, R.S. and T. Wu (2009), 'Subsidizing creativity through network design: Zero-pricing and net neutrality', *The Journal of Economic Perspectives*, **23** (3), 61–76.

Lemley, M.A. and L. Lessig (1999), 'Ex Parte to Federal Communications Commission, CS Dkt. No. 99-251', 10 November.

Lessig, L. (1998), 'The New Chicago School', *Journal of Legal Studies*, **27** (2), 661–91.

Lessig, L. (2001), *The Future of Ideas: The Fate of the Commons in a Connected World*, New York: Vintage Books.

Lessig, L. (2008), 'Testimony before the United States Senate, Committee on Commerce, Science, and Transportation, at its Hearing on the Future of the Internet', accessed 21 December 2015 at https://www.gpo.gov/fdsys/pkg/CHRG-110shrg74893/html/CHRG-110shrg74893.htm.

Litan, R.E. and H.J. Singer (2007), 'Unintended consequences of net neutrality regulation', *Journal on Telecommunications and High Technology Law*, **5** (3), 533–72.

Merges, R.P. and R.R. Nelson (1994), 'On limiting or encouraging rivalry in technical progress: The effect of patent scope decisions', *Journal of Economic Behavior and Organization*, **25** (1), 1–24.

Moors, T. (2002), 'A critical review of "end-to-end arguments in system design"', in *Proceedings of the IEEE International Conference on Communications (ICCC 2002)*, pp. 1214–19.

Nelson, R.R. and S.G. Winter (1977), 'In search of a useful theory of innovation', *Research Policy*, **6** (1), 37–76.

Nelson, R.R. and S.G. Winter (1982), *An Evolutionary Theory of Economic Change*, Cambridge, MA: The Belknap Press of Harvard University Press.

North, D.C. (1990), *Institutions, Institutional Change and Economic Performance*, Cambridge, UK: Cambridge University Press.

Ostrom, E. (2005), 'Doing institutional analysis: Digging deeper than markets and hierarchies', in C. Menard and M.M. Shirley (eds), *Handbook of New Institutional Economics*, Dordrecht: Springer, pp. 819–48.

Parsons, C. (2009), 'Summary of January 13, 2009 CRTC filings by major ISPs in response to interrogatory PN 2008-19 with February 9, 2009 updates', accessed August 4, 2015 at http://www.christopher-parsons.com/PublicUpload/Summary_of_January_13_2009_ISP_filings_with_February_9_2009_Updates_version_1.0(for_web).pdf.

Peters, B.G. (2005), *Institutional Theory in Political Science. The New Institutionalism*, 2nd edition, London: Continuum.

Peterson, L.L. and B.S. Davie (2012), *Computer Networks: A Systems Approach*, 5th edition, Burlington, MA: Morgan Kaufmann.

Postel, J. (1978), 'Meeting Notes, 1 February 1978', IEN 22.

Postel, J. (1981a), 'Internet Protocol. DARPA Internet program protocol specification', *Request for Comments 791*, IETF, accessed 24 July at http://www.rfc-editor.org/rfc/rfc791.txt.

Postel, J. (1981b), 'Transmission Control Protocol. DARPA Internet program protocol specification', *Request for Comments 793*, IETF, accessed 19 July 2015 at http://www.ietf.org/rfc/rfc0793.txt.

Powell, W.W. and P.J. DiMaggio (eds) (1991), *The New Institutionalism in Organizational Analysis*, Chicago, IL: University of Chicago Press.

Powell, W.W. and S. Grodal (2005), 'Networks of innovators', in J. Faberberg, D.C. Mowery and R.R. Nelson (eds), *The Oxford Handbook of Innovation*, Oxford, UK: Oxford University Press, pp. 56–85.

RCN Corporation (2010), 'Ex parte letter to Federal Communications Commission, GN Dkt. No. 09-191', 7 May, accessed 21 December 2015 at http://apps.fcc.gov/ecfs/document/view?id=7020916499.

Reed, D.P. (2000), 'The end of the end-to-end argument', accessed 19 July 2015 at http://www.reed.com/dpr/locus/Papers/endofendtoend.html.

Reed, D.P. (2010), 'A response to Barbara van Schewick: Code needs (only a little) help from the law', *dpr*, 15 December, accessed 19 July 2015 at http://www.reed.com/blog-dpr/?p=85.

Reed, D.P., J.H. Saltzer and D.D. Clark (1998), 'Commentaries on "active networking and end-to-end arguments"', *IEEE Network*, **12** (3), 69–71.

Rosenberg, N. (1994), *Exploring the Black Box. Technology, Economics and History*, Cambridge, MA: Cambridge University Press.

Rosenberg, N. (1996), 'Uncertainty and technological change', in R. Landau, T. Taylor and G. Wright (eds), *The Mosaic of Economic Growth*, Stanford, CA: Stanford University Press, pp. 334–56.

Saltzer, J.H. (1999), '"Open access" is just the tip of the iceberg', 22 October, accessed 19 July 2015 at http://web.mit.edu/Saltzer/www/publications/openaccess.html.

Saltzer, J.H., D.P. Reed and D.D. Clark (1981), 'End-to-end arguments in system design', *2nd International Conference on Distributed Computing Systems*, 8–10 April, Paris, pp. 509–12.

Saltzer, J.H., D.P. Reed and D.D. Clark (1984), 'End-to-end arguments in system design', *ACM Transactions on Computer Systems*, **2** (4), 277–88.

Sanchez, R. (1995), 'Strategic flexibility in product competition', *Strategic Management Journal*, **16** (Special Issue, Summer), 135–59.

Sarasvathy, S.D., N. Dew, S.R. Velamuri and S. Venkataraman (2003), 'Three views of entrepreneurial opportunity', in Z.J. Acs and D.B. Audretsch (eds), *Handbook of Entrepreneurship Research*, Boston, MA: Kluwer Academic Publishers, pp. 141–60.

Saxenian, A.L. (1994), *Regional Advantage: Culture and Competition in Silicon Valley and Route 128*, Cambridge, MA: Harvard University Press.

Schatz, A. (2008), 'Cox about to feel wrath of net neutrality activists', *WSJ Blogs: Washington Wire*, 15 May, accessed 19 July 2015 at http://blogs.wsj.com/washwire/2008/05/15/cox-about-to-feel-wrath-of-net-neutrality-activists/.

Schuett, F. (2010), 'Network neutrality: A survey of the economic literature', *Review of Network Economics*, **9** (2), 1–15.

Scott, W.R. (2000), *Institutions and Organizations*, 2nd edition, Thousand Oaks, CA: Sage Publications.

Shane, S. (2000), 'Prior knowledge and the discovery of entrepreneurial opportunities', *Organization Science*, **11** (4), 448–69.

Shane, S. and S. Venkataraman (2000), 'The promise of entrepreneurship as a field of research', *Academy of Management Review*, **25** (1), 217–26.

Srinivasan, V. and V. Gupta (2010), 'Ex parte letter to Federal Communications Commission, GN Dkt. No. 09-191', 10 December.

Sterbenz, J.P.G. and J.D. Touch (2001), *High-Speed Networking. A Systematic Approach to High-Bandwidth Low-Latency Communication*, New York: John Wiley and Sons, Inc.

Sunstein, C.R. (1996), 'On the expressive function of law', *University of Pennsylvania Law Review*, **144** (5), 2021–53.

Takeishi, A. (2001), 'Bridging inter- and intra-firm boundaries: Management of supplier involvement in automobile product development', *Strategic Management Journal*, **22** (5), 403–33.

Talbot, D. (2014), 'Net neutrality quashed: New pricing schemes, throttling, and business models to follow', *MIT Technology Review*, 14 January, accessed 19 July 2015 at http://www.technologyreview.com/news/523606/net-neutrality-quashed-new-pricing-schemes-throttling-and-business-models-to-follow/.

Tanenbaum, A.S. and D.J. Wetherall (2011), *Computer Networks*, 5th edition, Boston, MA: Prentice Hall.

Thelen, K. (1999), 'Historical institutionalism in comparative politics', *Annual Review of Political Science*, **2** (1), 369–404.

Ulrich, K. (1995), 'The role of product architecture in the manufacturing firm', *Research Policy*, **24** (3), 419–40.

US Department of Justice (2011), 'Competitive Impact Statement to United States District Court for the District of Columbia, United States of America, State of California, State of Florida, State of Missouri, State of Texas, and State of Washington v. Comcast Corp., General Electric Co. and NBC Universal, Inc., 18 January', accessed 21 December 2015 at http://www.justice.gov/atr/case-document/competitive-impact-statement-72.

Uzzi, B. (1996), 'The sources and consequences of embeddedness for the economic performance of organizations: The network effect', *American Sociological Review*, **61** (4), 674–98.

van Schewick, B. (2004), 'Architecture and innovation: The role of the end-to-end arguments in the original Internet', PhD dissertation, Technical University Berlin, Germany.

van Schewick, B. (2008a), 'Official testimony at the Federal Communications Commission's second en banc hearing on broadband management practices', Stanford, CA: Stanford University, accessed 21 December 2015 at https://transition.fcc.gov/broadband_network_management/041708/vanschewick-written.pdf.

van Schewick, B. (2008b), 'Oral testimony at the Federal Communications Commission's second en banc hearing on broadband management practices', Stanford, CA: Stanford University, accessed 21 December 2015 at http://cyberlaw.stanford.edu/publications/oral-testimony-federal-communications-commission%E2%80%99s-second-public-en-banc-hearing.

van Schewick, B. (2010a), *Internet Architecture and Innovation*, Cambridge, MA: MIT Press.

van Schewick, B. (2010b), 'Opening statement at the Federal Communications Commission's Workshop on Approaches to Preserving the Open Internet', Center for Internet and Society, accessed 21 December 2015 at http://cyberlaw.stanford.edu/publications/opening-statement-federal-communications-commission%E2%80%80%99s-workshop-approaches-preserving.

van Schewick, B. (2010c), 'Opening statement at the Federal Communications Commission's Workshop on Innovation, Investment and the Open Internet in Cambridge, MA, WC Dkt. No. 07-52, GN Dkt. No. 09-191', accessed 6 January 2016 at http://cyberlaw.stanford.edu/publications/opening-statement-federal-communications-commission%E2%80%99s-workshop-innovation-investment.

van Schewick, B. (2011a), 'Is Verizon Wireless illegally blocking Google Wallet? It's time for the FCC to investigate', *Internet Architecture and Innovation Blog*, 19 December, accessed 19 July 2015 at https://netarchitecture.org/2011/12/is-verizon-wireless-illegally-blocking-google-wallet-its-time-for-the-fcc-to-investigate/.

van Schewick, B. (2011b), 'Public interest requires public input: Verizon/Android tethering', *Internet Architecture and Innovation Blog*, 30 June, accessed 19 July 2015 at https://netarchitecture.org/2011/06/public-interest-requires-public-input-verizonandroid-tethering/.

van Schewick, B. (2015a), 'Network neutrality and quality of service: What a non-discrimination rule should look like', *Stanford Law Review*, **67** (1), 1–166.

van Schewick, B. (2015b), 'The case for meaningful network neutrality rules, submitted as an attachment to an ex parte letter to the Federal Communications Commission, GN Dkt. No. 14-28', 20 February.

van Schewick, B. (2015c), 'Zero-rating and network neutrality, submitted as an attachment to an ex parte letter to the Federal Communications Commission, GN Dkt. No. 14-28', 19 February.

van Schewick, B. (2016), 'T-Mobile's Binge On violates key net neutrality principles, submitted as an attachment to an ex parte letter to the Federal Communications Commission, GN Dkt. No. 14-28', 29 January.

Whinston, M.D. (1990), 'Tying, foreclosure, and exclusion', *American Economic Review*, **80** (4), 837–59.

Wu, T. (2003), 'Network neutrality and broadband discrimination', *Journal on Telecommunications and High Technology Law*, **2** (1), 141–75.

Wu, T. (2004), 'The broadband debate: A user's guide', *Journal on Telecommunications and High Technology Law*, **3** (1), 69–95.

Wu, T. and L. Lessig (2003), 'Ex parte submission to the Federal Communications Commission, CS Dkt. No. 02-52', 22 August.

Yoo, C. (2007), 'What can antitrust contribute to the network neutrality debate?', *International Journal of Communication*, **1**, 493–530.

Ziegler, C. (2012), 'AT&T only allowing Facetime over cellular on mobile share plans, no extra charge', *The Verge*, 17 August, accessed 19 July 2015 at http://www.theverge.com/2012/8/17/3250228/att-facetime-over-cellular-ios-6-mobile-share.

Zittrain, J. (2008), *The Future of the Internet and How to Stop It*, New Haven, CT: Yale University Press.

15. Organizational innovations, ICTs and knowledge governance: the case of platforms*

Cristiano Antonelli and Pier Paolo Patrucco†

15.1 INTRODUCTION

Platforms constitute a major organizational innovation that builds upon the new opportunities provided by information and communication technologies (ICTs) to improve efficiency in the generation and exploitation of technological knowledge. Platforms are organizational devices that support the integration of complementary knowledge in the generation of new technological knowledge and increase its scope of exploitation and appropriation. As such, platforms can be considered an organizational innovation induced and made possible by a technological innovation.

More specifically, platforms can be regarded as an innovative organizational mechanism that enhances the capability of its members to integrate externalities in the recombinant generation of technological knowledge and to increase their capabilities to appropriate the benefits of this knowledge. As is well known, technological knowledge as an economic good has several limits ranging from partial appropriability and divisibility, to non-excludability, non-exhaustibility and intrinsic tacitness. The generation of technological knowledge is a recombinant process in which knowledge is at the same time the output of a dedicated process and an indispensable input. Access to existing knowledge is crucial to effectively generating new knowledge as much as its appropriation is necessary to providing adequate incentives and guiding a correct allocation of resources for its generation. Because of the intrinsic complexity of this trade-off, perfect markets and pure hierarchies fail in the allocation and organization of resources to its generation and use.

Sophisticated knowledge governance mechanisms are necessary to organize its generation and exploitation (Arrow, 1969). Platforms constitute a major organizational innovation that makes it possible to improve the responsible participation and the dynamic identification of competent players in a collective and yet selective process of knowledge generation and exploitation that is based upon incentive and reward mechanisms. In this sense platforms enable and facilitate the division of labor among firms that possess complementary competencies and the internalization of knowledge externalities. Given the vast improvements in the capability to search, retrieve, store, process, share, command and monitor information, ICTs provide indispensable support for the recombinant generation of knowledge (van Schewick, 2010; Brynjolfsson, 2011).

Platforms are a key element of the emerging knowledge economy because they make it possible to 'industrialize' the generation of knowledge and to reduce the effects of the knowledge trade-offs that limit the working of both the markets for knowledge and hierarchies. Platforms allow the organization of the necessary division of scientific labor, identification of the incentives to specialize and improvement of the opportunities for the exchange of different knowledge items (Ostrom and Hess, 2006; Ostrom, 2010; Antonelli, 2015).

The notion of a 'knowledge economy'[1] emerged gradually in the 1990s to appreciate and describe the fundamental changes occurring in the structure and dynamics of economic systems, as well as in the competitive drivers utilized by firms to increase their economic gains and market power. The term 'knowledge economy' is meant to stress the shift in importance from traditional physical inputs in production processes, such as capital and labor, to immaterial inputs such as competencies, skills and knowledge (OECD, 1996).

Since the 1990s an array of factors have emerged that led to a rapid and radical transformation of the environment in which firms compete, raising questions about the applicability of the traditional capitalist model to the new innovation landscape. First, the increasing environmental turbulence (for instance, due to greater instability in prices, fluctuating cost of inputs, and variability of demand) and the intensification of global competition reduce the effectiveness of managerial planning and command. It is increasingly difficult for management to predict with a sufficient degree of confidence all factors relevant to decisions, and is therefore more complicated to organize activities in a coherent and rational way. Second, the increased complexity of the innovative dynamics, the acceleration in the process of obsolescence of technology and the significant increase in development costs required for innovation reduce the degree of autonomy of enterprises. No company is able to completely dominate all technological and organizational skills and has all the financial resources required to develop new knowledge on its own. Finally, and consequently, to explore new knowledge applicable to its innovative activity, a firm will need to search an increasing range of sources. As highlighted by Davenport and Prusak (1998), new and different players are emerging in the innovation system. In addition to public research laboratories and private, large R&D labs, other organizations are involved in the production of new knowledge, such as science parks, non-profit centers, university laboratories, start-ups, incubators, and supranational research networks (Foray, 2004).

New ICTs have played a major role in this context since they contributed to changing the innovation landscape, acting as centrifugal forces that support decentralization of activities, outsourcing, specialization and division of labor. In particular, the emergence of a bundle of intertwined and interdependent innovations in technologies (ICTs) and organizations (networks) introduced such a dramatic transformation in the structure and dynamics of economic coordination that Chris Freeman (2009) coined the term 'ICT paradigm'[2] to describe this pervasive change in the economic setting and in the way in which firms and organizations evolve, adapt and react to new emerging economic conditions. ICTs and networks developed in parallel and reinforced each other's diffusion, questioning the traditional, hierarchical way in which firms coordinated their productive and innovative capabilities.

Since the 1990s the rapidly expanding adoption of ICTs and the Internet as process innovations in the organization of productive activities has been associated with transformations in the conditions under which the production of goods and services takes place, and more precisely in the way in which economic agents interact with each other in order to coordinate such production. The pervasive diffusion of computer-based ICTs has exerted strong pressure on the governance mechanisms and the structure of formal organizations, fostering the adoption of administrative simplification, flatter hierarchical control and lean production processes. These transformations in both the technology and the organization of firms have been connected to the emergence of alternatives to traditional coordination structures like the well-known vertically integrated, hierarchical, and Fordist firm. Networks are increasingly viewed as structures that challenge formal organizations characterized by hierarchical control and well-defined boundaries.

The new gale of digital technologies has changed in depth not only the organization of corporations and the division of labor among firms, but also the organization of the generation of technological knowledge and of the introduction of new technological innovations. The introduction and diffusion of ICTs parallels the emergence of new models for the division of the innovative labor that is necessary to introduce new technologies. The generation of technological knowledge becomes a crucial activity where the borders of innovative firms need to be more and more porous so as to be able to access, absorb and use the distributed competence and the existing knowledge dispersed in the system. ICTs and the Internet are perceived as centrifugal forces that foster decentralization, boundary crossing and networking because they make available technological tools for the efficient development of subcontracting, outsourcing and modular strategies (Kallinikos, 2009).

This chapter focuses on innovation platforms that are emerging as new means to manage the recombinant generation of new technological knowledge and to coordinate the introduction of technological innovations exploiting the organizational opportunities opened up by technological innovation in ICTs and the Internet. At the same time, the innovation platform is itself an organizational innovation, widely diffused and adopted in the ICTs and Internet industries by platform leaders such as Cisco, Microsoft and Google.

However, despite this empirical relevance, the growth of innovation platforms across a range of industrial sectors, with new ICTs and the Internet at the forefront, has received only limited attention from innovation scholars. The nature of these structures and how they influence the evolution of industrial sectors and innovation processes remains a puzzle and few studies explore the impact of the emergence of platforms on industrial dynamics, the creation of new forms of competition and on new relations of inter-organizational cooperation in the framework of innovation processes (Gawer and Cusumano, 2002; Prencipe et al., 2003; Consoli and Patrucco, 2008; Patrucco, 2012).

In this context, this chapter defines platforms as hierarchical networks, that is, as networks in which the interactions do not emerge and evolve spontaneously, but in which key players (e.g., platform leaders and system integrators) exercise a guiding role in the behavior of the other actors, selecting the members of the platform itself and directing the behavior and the evolution of the system as a whole. A second distinctive element of these organizational forms is represented by the active search for knowledge complementarity and exploitation of variety (contrasted to mere agglomeration) between different activities. Hence platforms are institutional arrangements to internalize knowledge spillovers and externalities. They are structured and designed with precise and predetermined innovation objectives in mind (in contrast to spontaneous phenomena such as some types of networks such as innovation districts).

In this sense, with respect to both the coordination mechanisms and the assumptions about the characteristics of knowledge, platforms represent a significant organizational innovation, different from integrated companies, markets and the networks themselves.

Integrating a complexity approach to organizations into economics of innovation, this chapter traces the emergence of innovation platforms as both a result of technological innovation produced by the ICTs and as an organizational innovation widely adopted in the same sector to achieve and sustain competitive position and growth of the players.

The chapter is structured as follows. Section 15.2 briefly recalls the basic tenets of the economics of ICTs, of which the Internet is credibly the most evident and widespread subset of technologies and applications. Section 15.3 articulates the structures and dynamics that characterize the new innovation and knowledge landscape after the advent of the ICT paradigm, the rise of networked organizations and the demise of the traditional, Fordist mode of innovation based on large, vertically integrated corporations. Section 15.4 is dedicated to developing an understanding of the different features and processes that characterize platforms – a specific and nowadays pervasive type of networked organization – and the means by which platforms generate and manage innovation. Conclusions briefly summarize.

15.2   THE BASIC ELEMENTS OF ICTS

The distinctive element characterizing the transition to the new knowledge economy is the provision of new knowledge-based activities that rely heavily on the quality and variety of advanced digital communications. The advent of digital technologies changed the context in which knowledge-based activities were traditionally coordinated, organized and provided in many ways. Let us now briefly recall the main characteristics of new information and communication technologies.

New information and communication technologies provide clear evidence for the Schumpeterian notion of gales of innovation characterized by the increasing convergence between and integration of a variety of infrastructures, applications, tools and innovations each of which is generated in a wide range of industries and firms. In particular, technological convergence[3] is driven by the introduction of a number of innovations, such as ultra-broadband fiber optics, various generations of digital subscriber line (xDSL) and cable modem broadband, digital TV, mobile broadband (e.g., UMTS, LTE [universal mobile telecommunications system/long-term evolution]), and the Internet, which uses all these technologies. These technological advances open up the possibility of offering a variety of content, services, and applications over the same network infrastructure. Contemporary ICTs are inter-networked and evolving, ranging from complex and integrated enterprise-wide systems to distributed and ubiquitous technologies such as mobile email devices and weblogs (Fransman, 2002, 2006; Edquist, 2003; Jones and Orlikowski, 2009).

As a result, information and communication technologies, and the related technological knowledge, are both complex and fungible (Antonelli, 2003). On the one hand, new information and communication technologies are the outcome of the recombination of a variety of knowledge modules in electronics, telecommunications, software, microprocessors and television technologies, each of which cannot be fully controlled internally by one firm and thus requires the coordination of technological complementarities within the broader ICT technological system. On the other hand, new communication technologies can be applied to a large variety of manufacturing and service activities in both traditional and emergent sectors. The constant reduction in the price of ICT services, and especially telecommunications, in both nominal and hedonic terms, makes ICT-based products and services available at lower costs for a larger and larger range of users, with considerable effects in terms of improved productivity and profitability.

The integration of the array of interdependent, localized and sequential innovations, characterized by substantial indivisibility, has been shaped by the implementation of three factors: (1) economies of localized learning due to the increasing specialization in specific technological areas, the advantages of network externalities and the gains from knowledge externalities; (2) qualified user–producer and business–academic interactions; and (3) organizational innovations such as standardization committees, technological platforms, system integration, technological clubs and alliances to improve the dynamic coordination of the wide range of actors, products and technologies into a single working system and hence the complementarity, compatibility and interoperability of the variety of new localized technologies (David and Steinmueller, 1994; Shapiro and Varian, 1999; Antonelli, 2001).

Since the early 1990s the new ICT paradigm described above has thus led to a rapid and radical transformation of the context in which firms compete, produce and innovate. ICTs made possible the emergence of global networks based on distributed coordination processes that sell worldwide customized products, manufactured and assembled in a variety of regions through systematic outsourcing of lower-value activities, often to firms abroad, and retaining high-value and skill-intensive activities in home countries.

Firms can now rely heavily on ICTs to organize and coordinate their activity both locally and globally, with important effects on the economic organization of industries. On the one hand, flat and decentralized organizations, forming a net of manufacturing and service units, coordinate international flows of final and intermediary products by means of ICTs. Since the early 1990s decentralized and networked organizations paralleled the traditional hierarchical and vertical structures because of the advantages made possible by the adoption of ICTs. Work is often dispersed through temporary project teams that are cross-functional and distributed, spanning geographic, temporal and cultural boundaries, and involving decentralized decision-making. On the other hand, ICTs reinforce the power of a few global companies, now based on hybrid coordination processes that mix distributed and hierarchical coordination. This is, for instance, especially true and relevant in the new services industries and particularly in the new knowledge-intensive business service sectors (KIBS), such as software industries, and in high-tech industries more generally. The new knowledge-based industries are inherently global. They have direct access to international markets because of the footloose location of different branches and units across countries, and the rapid entry and exit in local markets through the adoption of outsourcing and networking strategies.

15.3 THE NEW ORGANIZATION OF THE GENERATION AND EXPLOITATION OF TECHNOLOGICAL KNOWLEDGE

Industrial economics and the economics of innovation during the last century considered the vertically integrated Fordist company as the most efficient organizational model for the production of technological innovation because it could realize economies of scale, economies of scope and take advantage of learning opportunities made possible by the vertical integration of R&D activities (Penrose, 1959; Chandler, 1990).

Following Chandler in *The Visible Hand* (Chandler, 1977) and subsequent works like *Scale and Scope* (Chandler, 1990), Langlois (2003, 2004) emphasized the discontinuities brought by the appearance, by the end of the nineteenth century, of the large, integrated corporation that replaced the previous fragmented and localized structure of production and distribution so vividly described in Adam Smith's *Wealth of Nations* and in the metaphor of the invisible hand (Smith, 1776). By the end of the twentieth century a new upsurge of Smithian forces (e.g., specialization, division of labor, outsourcing of production and the rise of distributed modes of organizing economic and innovative activities) again replaced the Chandlerian ones (vertical integration of production, scale economies, managerial control and the rise of the large corporation as the locus of production and innovation). Building upon this analysis, Langlois articulates the vanishing hand hypothesis, according to which population and income growth together with the accompanying technological changes (including improved coordination technology) have led to a new enhanced division of labor, based upon high levels of specialization by function and coordination via markets.

This stream of literature not only questions the model of the integrated corporation but also the traditional organization of innovation. It implies that the linear and closed model, which saw innovation as a direct and almost automatic effect of the investments in R&D and learning-by-doing processes, must be replaced. Not only must firms structure themselves so as to be able to draw advantage from the external knowledge available, integrating it effectively with the knowledge produced internally (Chesbrough et al., 2006), but industries and supply chains must reconfigure their boundaries and architectures to benefit from competencies and technologies developed in other sectors (Jacobides et al., 2006).

As a consequence, consensus has grown in recent times among innovation scholars around the idea that firms that are not able to develop sufficient innovation capacity on their own can implement a variety of alternative solutions. These range from the extreme of vertical integration to full reliance on the market, with a variety of hybrid strategies in between, including forms of strategic alliances and inter-organizational relations aimed at minimizing the costs of external coordination and the maximization of the creative contribution of the individual companies. This realization has opened the way to the analysis of various forms of decentralization, specialization and division of innovative labor and production that emerged following the crisis of the organizational model of the vertically integrated corporation.

On the one hand, a broad thread of studies on the organization of knowledge and technological innovation has directed its attention to modular systems, based on outsourcing and market transactions as the coordination mechanism of the division of labor in innovative activity (Baldwin and Clark, 1997; Arora et al., 1998; Langlois, 2002). When a system is extensive and complex so that the interdependencies between the elements and subsystems become particularly numerous, coordination through an integrated structure is almost impossible. Baldwin and Clark (1997) and Langlois (2002) have upheld that the organization of production and innovation through modular strategies is the most efficient way to organize and coordinate complex technologies and production systems.

According to this approach, companies can decide to adopt an integrated or modular organizational structure on the basis of the technologies and competencies that are the foundations for the introduction of innovation. The more the knowledge and technological competencies needed for innovation are varied and interconnected, the more efficient the adoption of a modular architecture and the recourse to formal contracts and market transactions will be. In contrast, the fewer the number of elements that have to interact to generate an innovation, the simpler their coordination through the vertical integration of R&D activities will be (Chesbrough and Teece, 1996).

In these models, innovative activities and production are not closely integrated and coordination between the two processes takes place through adherence to shared goals and common standards. In modular innovation, the adoption of mechanisms, such as standard interfaces, ensures the integration of several components designed and made by different and separated units, avoiding the need for specific and strict coordination mechanisms as the interface itself provides an implicit form of communication between all the different units involved in the innovation process (Schilling, 2009).

This so-called loose coupling strategy does, however, have some limits. In particular, activities that demand exchanges of complex technological knowledge, such as those in high-tech, knowledge-intensive and computer-mediated industries, require the presence of integration mechanisms that are much more rigid, frequent and long term than a modular organization usually manages to guarantee (ibid.). If the activity demands an intense form of coordination and continuity in time, the development process is conducted more efficiently within a more integrated and hierarchical organizational structure, which maintains closer integration between the partners involved. The empirical evidence also shows that, when dealing with decisions related to the organization of innovative activity, firms are not only swinging between purely modular or purely integrated models. Rather, firms are able to use a wide range of inter-organizational solutions in order to combine the advantages of spot, standardized market contracts and the benefits of long-term, collaborative interactions (Patrucco, 2012).

Moreover, it has been highlighted that innovation systems are complex in many ways and characterized by non-decomposability (Consoli and Patrucco, 2011), as opposed to the decomposability of pure modular systems. Innovation systems exhibit typical emerging properties. They are, first, inherently dynamic; indeed, the actions of individual agents and the evolution of the environment affect each other, therefore they can only be understood in historical perspective. Second, they are characterized by simultaneous changes and reconfigurations at different stages of production that make the existing know-how obsolete, requiring new skills and forcing organizations to acquire and develop new skills. Third, they are distributed, as their dynamics are based upon the integration and inclusion of a large variety of agents characterized by dedicated skills and specific competencies.

In this context, the dichotomy between markets and hierarchies needs to be bridged by the recognition and appreciation of the pervasive variety of hybrid forms of organization that impinge upon different combinations among markets and hierarchies. Two dimensions are relevant for this analysis: the appreciation of the distinction between interactions and transactions[4] and the identification and analysis of the variety of organizational forms that provide the coordination that is necessary to benefit from the division of labor. Coordination can be either ex ante or ex post. It can be obtained by means of managerial action ex ante, or by means of selective inclusion and exclusion, ex post.

Table 15.1   Crossing the borders between markets and hierarchies

	Pure, Personal Interactions with Ex Ante Coordination	Interactions-cum-Transactions and Ex Ante Coordination	Transactions-cum-Interactions and Ex Post Coordination	Pure, Impersonal and Spot Transactions with Ex Post Coordination
No hierarchy				*Perfect markets*
Weak hierarchy	Open source-based innovation	Centered networks	Long-term contracts; 'open' contracts; *venture capitalism*	
Flexible hierarchy		Internal markets within *Chandlerian corporations* Organized platforms	Joint venture company, in-house subcontracting; conglomerate groups; multinational corporations	
Strong hierarchy	*Perfect firm*			

Source: Authors' elaboration.

Pure interactions are organized by strong hierarchies. Pure impersonal transactions take place in perfect, impersonal, spot markets.

As Table 15.1 shows, we can identify a variety of hybrid forms based upon the mix between transactions and interactions that can be placed on a continuum between pure transactions and pure interactions. The overlap between interactions and transactions identifies an interesting area of complementarity where the two forms of organizing the division of labor complement each other. Here the type of coordination, whether ex ante or ex post, plays a central analytical role. When interactions prevail, coordination is typically ex ante. When transactions prevail, coordination takes place ex post. This overlap is relevant in a static context where technologies are given because of the pervasive role of information asymmetries. It is most relevant in a dynamic context where the generation of technological knowledge and the eventual introduction of technological innovations takes place and is endogenous to the system. Let us consider first the static context and the dynamic one in turn.

Within the perfect firm, characterized by strong hierarchies, coordination is achieved by means of pure interactions. Principals can trust agents if they have perfect information on the actual levels of their efforts and competence. When principals do not have access to perfect information on the matter, interactions are complemented by incentives and monitoring mechanisms based upon ex post assessment of the actual performance. Old traditional mechanisms, such as piecework and cottage industries, can be considered early forms of interactions-cum-transactions.

At the other extreme, we find transactions-cum-interactions when pure transactions in the market place are impeded by the lack of relevant information on the characteristics of the goods exchanged. Interactions complement transactions as they are the carriers of trust and loyalty. The parties can proceed with a transaction only if and when personal relations that entrust the actual quality and reliability of the goods complement it. Transactions-cum-interactions are typically found when transactions are reinforced by interactions, such as in the case of long-term contracts and 'open' contracts: transactions are no longer impersonal and no longer take place in spot markets. Partners in trade are personally identified and transactions are repeated over time. Here coordination, however, is left to the market place and the ensuing competitive forces: coordination is also achieved ex post by means of selection and exclusion. Partners that are no longer able to meet the requested levels of performances are sanctioned with failure and have to exit the market (Bonazzi and Antonelli, 2003).

This view is further reinforced once we note that, generally, most transactions that enable the division of labor both in product and factor markets are characterized by the idiosyncratic features of the good that are being exchanged and the complexity of their production processes. Perfect markets and perfect hierarchies are typically found when the goods are perfectly homogeneous with highly standardized characteristics and low levels of variance in their production processes. With increasing complexity, they are less and less undertaken in pure markets but take place only with the support of organization and interactions along a continuum of hybrid forms between the two extremes of pure transactions within perfect markets and pure interactions within perfect hierarchies.

When we move from a static to a dynamic context, one where technological knowledge matters, hybrid forms play an even larger role. The recent advances in the economics of knowledge have made it possible to better specify the intrinsic characteristics of the generation of technological knowledge as a recombinant and cumulative process characterized by high levels of uncertainty where existing bits of knowledge are indispensable yet sticky inputs together with competence based upon learning processes and research and development activities (Von Hippel, 1988, 2005; Weitzman, 1996, 1998).

This view has three major implications for the organization of the generation of technological knowledge:

- In order to be able to generate new knowledge, firms need to access existing bits of knowledge. Because of its irreducible tacit content, existing technological knowledge is sticky. High search, identification, and decodification costs are necessary in order to use it again as an input into the generation of new knowledge. Knowledge transactions are not sufficient to access, understand and reuse, as an input, the relevant bits of existing knowledge. It is necessary to rely upon knowledge transactions implemented with knowledge interactions. User–producer interactions are necessary to reduce absorption costs. Prospective users of existing knowledge need to interact with its inventor in a structured framework that favors bilateral cooperation and reciprocal participation.
- Because learning by doing and learning by using are at the origin of competence – a major input into the generation of new knowledge – principals need to stir the active participation and personal creativity of their agents. It is no longer sufficient to avoid shirking and other opportunistic behaviors of agents. It is necessary to activate the learning capabilities of employees. Interactions within hierarchical organizations must be implemented by incentive mechanisms – such as efficiency wages – based upon the actual contribution of employees to the increase of performances beyond their static levels. The members of an innovative organization

must be motivated to learn and accumulate competence so to feed the recombinant generation of new technological knowledge.

- Because of the high levels of serendipity and uncertainty that characterize the generation of technological knowledge not only with respect to the timing of the outcome, but also with respect to its actual content and the constraints caused by diseconomies of scope, firms have discovered the advantages of selective partnership to exploit new technological knowledge when its application exhibits high levels of variance with respect to the core business. The exploitation of such new technologies is implemented by the creation of joint ventures with other firms endowed with localized complementary competence that favor the introduction of innovations and their incremental variations so as to reduce coordination costs. Here, once more, ex post coordination mechanisms complement structured interactions.

Hybrid forms are necessary to generate new technological knowledge and introduce and exploit technological innovations, as interactions-cum-transactions are necessary within hierarchies to mobilize the learning capabilities of the agents and transactions-cum-interactions are necessary to access the existing bits of existing knowledge and appropriate the benefits of unexpected outcomes of the knowledge-generation process. A quote from Adam Smith is useful to grasp the vital role of interactions-cum-transactions within hierarchies:

> Whoever has been much accustomed to visit such manufactures, must frequently have been shewn very pretty machines, which were the inventions of such workmen, in order to facilitate and quicken their own particular part of the work. In the first fire engines – this was the current designation for steam engines – a boy was constantly employed to open and shut alternately the communication between the boiler and the cylinder, according as the piston either ascended or descended. One of those boys, who loved to play with his companions, observed that, by tying a string from the handle of the valve which opened this communication to another part of the machine, the valve would open and shut without his assistance, and leave him at liberty to divert himself with his play-fellows. One of the greatest improvements that has been made upon this machine, since it was first invented, was in this manner the discovery of a boy who wanted to save his own labor. (Smith, 1776, p. 6)

The accumulation and valorization of competence based upon learning by doing and learning by using within a firm is limited, if not inhibited, by the lack of appropriate incentive mechanisms that appreciate, stir up and support the active contribution of employees (Arrow, 1974). A clear example of the relevance of transactions-cum-interactions is provided by the new understanding of the central role of the interactions that follow a transaction where a vendor provides a customer with a new product. The benefits of learning by using are faster and larger when customers after the transaction – as users – can interact with competent producers that sold them the new product, so as to improve it and at the same time make its use easier and more effective. User–producer interactions that parallel and complement vertical transactions are a major source of technological knowledge for both parties (Von Hippel, 1988, 2005).

These hybrid forms take place in contexts that are characterized by weak hierarchies and organized markets. Particularly relevant for this chapter, interactions-cum-transactions and transactions-cum-interactions are typically found within hierarchical networks and especially structured platforms. In these hybrid forms, the coordination that is necessary to achieve and integrate an efficient division of labor is defined ex ante and implemented by managers that try to implement a hierarchical control of the recombinant knowledge-generation process and of its effective exploitation. This confirms the importance for the innovative firm to build and be embedded in networks and for economics to appreciate the systemic character of the structures into which the division of innovative labor takes place (Lane et al., 2009; Antonelli, 2011).

Platforms are characterized not only by transactions-cum-interactions and interactions-cum-transactions but also their dynamic membership within a changing architecture that makes it possible to implement and operationalize the mix between ex ante and ex post coordination. Membership in platforms is not permanent; inclusions and exclusions do take place at all times. The actual membership in the platform is in fact the object of continual assessment, monitoring and selective renewal. The division of labor within platforms is based upon stages at the end of which the actual contribution of each member is assessed and valued critically both in terms of results and efforts. The parties agree ex ante upon the procedures that will be applied in order to monitor the results and the efforts. Exclusion takes place ex post as a result of the assessment. The architecture of the platform, moreover, is intrinsically dynamic, also with respect to the role of each member that may shift in terms of degrees of centrality. Lazy or opportunistic members, or those that turn out to be less competent than expected, may gradually shift from high levels of centrality to marginal roles that lead to eventual exclusion. Competent members that are able to contribute more than expected may, on the contrary, move from peripheral roles into more central ones. Open contracts, where the parties agree upon the procedures rather than on actual contents, combining intellectual property rights with contractual law, enable the organization to change shape, structure and membership and play a central role in this context (Hagedoorn and Hesen, 2007).

The identification of the historic process that led to the introduction of platforms is most relevant to grasping their key features. Platforms can be regarded as the outcome of the evolution of the bilateral outsourcing of given inputs into the creation of a frame of multilateral cooperation for the generation and exploitation of new technologies, based upon the intensive use of ICTs and flexible, long-term contracts. One of the first platforms was introduced in the last decades of the twentieth century in the automobile industry where car manufacturers experimented with the integration of their component suppliers into the design of new models. This radically changed the traditional sequence in which suppliers manufactured components after the car company had completed the design of the model. The systematic use of large databases to which all the selected partners were granted access played a central role in the evolution of the new organizational procedure (Patrucco, 2014a).

According to our analysis and from an organizational viewpoint, platforms can be considered a new case of a dynamic hybrid form based upon interactions-cum-transactions and transactions-cum-interactions with changing architecture and membership (Consoli and Patrucco, 2008, 2011; Patrucco, 2014b). The next section is dedicated to understanding the different features and processes that characterize platforms and the means by which platforms generate and manage innovation.

15.4   VARIETY AND DYNAMICS OF PLATFORMS

Given the growing spread of the phenomenon in various industrial sectors, platforms are receiving attention across disciplines. Wheelwright and Clark (1992) first talked of platform products whose core design seeks to appeal to a large customer base while its openness to marginal modifications attempts to captivate peripheral users with more specific needs. A few years later Kim and Kogut (1996) talked about platform technologies, referring to models for the coordination of complementary components, such as computers. Rochet and Tirole (2003) first went beyond the physical features of artifacts, thinking of platforms as a way to organize economic relations. In general, management scholars connect platforms to the challenges and the strategic implications associated with the emergence of open systems for production, exchange and the governance of competencies (Gerstein, 1992; Ciborra, 1996; Garud and Kuramaswamy, 1996; Ethiraj and Levinthal, 2004; Jacobides and Billinger, 2006). In the policy realm, innovation platforms are looked at as a key reference model for the creation and management of mixed (i.e., public and private) coalitions (European Commission, 2004).

In this context, Cusumano and Gawer (2002) and Gawer (2009) successfully elaborate the concept of 'technology platforms' in order to account for ICT-based innovations, like virtual networks and modular structures, emphasizing the associated infrastructures, interfaces and standards. From this viewpoint, technology platforms facilitate interoperability of different firms and technologies in the context of, for instance, high-tech industries. Consoli and Patrucco (2008, 2011) and Patrucco (2012) stress instead the organizational implications of platforms, articulating the notion of 'innovation platforms' as hybrid coordination modes that combine both interactions and transactions with hierarchical coordination and management of the networks. Innovation platforms are strategic organizational vehicles for coordinating specialized and complementary actors.

Despite the differences that a comparison between different approaches and perspectives necessarily implies – an exercise that would be out of the scope of this chapter – common to both technology and innovation platforms is the notion of directed and coordinated organization as opposed to the spontaneous and anonymous organization typical of market processes. Innovation platforms, however, emphasize first the coexistence of both market transactions and collaborative interactions, and second that they produce an outcome – an innovation – that is the result of collective learning and alignment of investments.

In these structures a variety of agents participate in the production and supply of products and services; each unit exists independently according to own goals and capacity but, at the same time, responds to a collective goal through shared communication rules. The point, though, is that such differences across agents matter to a great degree. In turn, the architectures in which they operate are flexible and can be configured in different ways for different uses, very much akin to computer platforms. A central component of the rationale underpinning platforms is maximizing the variety of contributions stemming from a diverse knowledge base while maintaining coherence though a minimum level of hierarchy. As will be discussed further, innovation platforms are purposefully open to entry of new actors and, thereby, of new competencies. The extent of contribution by each additional unit depends endogenously on the relative value of internal competencies measured against the collective goal. At the core of the logic of a platform stand three powerful sources of increasing returns: economies of scale due to increased volumes of throughput; economies of scope due to lower costs of producing variations around the core product and services of the platform; and economies of system, that is, the creation of dedicated control procedures to improve utilization of the installed capacity. Another crucial characteristic of platforms is the functional relation in which services and manufacturing activities stand with one another (Suarez and Cusumano, 2009). The provision of some services, in fact, enables closer customer–producer interaction and opens up important feedback mechanisms useful to the effect of adapting the organization of the platform, or some of its components, to emerging features such as previously unmet customer needs, skill gaps, and future product developments.

Relevant dynamics within platforms span technological and organizational levels, and bear upon both the static and the dynamic coordination of knowledge. From a static viewpoint, platforms connect and integrate activities and capabilities of relevant agents within an industry, thus supporting specialization and favoring the accumulation of specific knowledge. From a dynamic viewpoint, platforms stimulate changes in both the structure of the network and the mechanisms for the governance of technological knowledge (Antonelli, 2015).

Let us now draw attention to the structural and dynamic properties that characterize innovation platforms (Table 15.2). The coupling of two distinctive characteristics of platforms: (1) their role, whether finalized, to support the generation of technological knowledge or its exploitation, and (2) the levels of exclusivity of membership make it possible to identify the basic elements of a typology. Closed platforms are characterized by substantial membership exclusivity. In closed platforms, the members belong to a single platform. In open platforms, members are active in many different platforms. Generative platforms are mainly finalized to support the generation of new technological knowledge, while exploitation platforms are implemented to support the exploitation of knowledge after its generation, and its incremental development.

This typology of platforms shows their performance and dynamics. Closed-generation platforms are likely to exhibit higher levels of stability and loyalty in partnership, lower risks of opportunistic behavior and hence higher overall levels of stability. Open-generation platforms are likely to perform better in terms of generating technological knowledge as they can draw from a wider variety of competencies that are fed by a larger diversity of interactions of the members that are able to transfer their tacit knowledge

Table 15.2   The dynamic variety of platforms

	Exclusive Membership	Non-exclusive Membership
	Closed platforms	Open platforms
Knowledge-generation platforms	Higher stability; lower risks of opportunistic behavior	High performance with substantial fragility
Knowledge-exploitation platforms	Stability with major asymmetries in dedicated knowledge appropriation	General purpose technologies Fragility

Source: Authors' elaboration.

from one platform to another. Open-generation platforms are characterized by higher fragility, as the members may have more opportunities to leave one platform and join one other or more platforms.

Open-exploitation platforms reduce asymmetries in the distribution of the rents stemming from knowledge as non-exclusivity increases the bargaining power of exploiters and reduces the monopolistic strength of 'inventors'. At the same time open-exploitation platforms may offer larger opportunities of knowledge exploitation if they have high levels of fungibility and thus can be applied to a variety of different fields. Typically, open-exploitation platforms are found when the scope of application of a technology is large. Closed-exploitation platforms are found with technologies that have a limited scope of application. Given these conditions open-exploitation platforms typically exhibit lower levels of stability. Closed-exploitation platforms favor the bargaining power of 'inventors' and are better suited to support the appropriation of technological innovations with a limited range of applications. Closed-exploitation platforms are more stable in time than open-exploitation platforms, which are far more fragile.

In this context, inclusion in collective structures for knowledge sharing does not diminish the uncertainty associated with competition in fast-changing contexts but rather changes the nature of such uncertainty. To be viable, infrastructures like innovation platforms require, on the one hand, a degree of stability that confers coherence to shared goals and, on the other hand, room for further novelty. From this, it follows that a necessary condition for the emergence of novelty is that a system maintains a degree of openness to be able to adapt to modified circumstances. The key point is that the implementation of major technical changes generates new opportunities for learning but in so doing also leads to skill shortages. For instance, empirical work, such as Brynolfsson and Hitt (2000), demonstrates that the large-scale diffusion of ICTs, often the backbone of innovation platforms, stimulates the emergence of new tasks and competencies. In turn, where new knowledge comes from and how it is to be absorbed, integrated and used by different members of the network depend on the degree of openness of the platform. Likewise, how the cost of this knowledge is borne by the participants also depends on the openness of the platform.

As anticipated by Richardson (1972), and reiterated by many others, when coordination between closely complementary activities and competencies is essential for the success of innovation, firms rely upon a variety of inter-organizational arrangements. Joint ventures, equity agreements, R&D partnerships, coalitions and consortia all allow blending market and contract-based with integral solutions, strong with weak relations, in order to acquire and coordinate the necessary productive and innovative knowledge. Complex and hierarchical governance forms emerge when the task is the coordination of knowledge – sourced both internally and externally – and the facilitation of multi-sided learning.

The view of platforms as collective structures bears important consequences for the management of platforms and centered networks in that it stresses the problem of inclusion and exclusion in the network and highlights the major role played by those firms that are the leaders of the network. Concepts like architectural knowledge (Henderson and Clark, 1990), platform leadership (Gawer and Cusumano, 2002), architectural capability (Jacobides, 2006), or that of system integrators (Prencipe et al., 2003) have been introduced recently to describe precisely that decisive capacity, possessed by the platform leaders, to coordinate and manage the work of complex organizations. More precisely they refer to the capability to combine elements typical of the integrated models (such as authority and control), with characteristics typical of networked structures (such as a sufficient degree of openness) in order to select the significant competencies and knowledge to include in the network.

As a matter of fact, the main object of the platform leader is to drive the innovation process in the industry. This cannot be achieved without loosening the collective structure and goal during the continuous adaptation to the fast-changing market conditions. In this regard, Iansiti and Levien (2004) talked of the three most important objectives that a network leader faces: (1) to maintain platform integrity and the compatibility between complementary products; (2) to manage technological innovation within the platform without losing backward compatibility with existing products and technologies; and (3) to preserve the leadership against other firms acquiring power within the platform. Iansiti and Levien labeled as 'keystone' those leaders able to benefit from and, at the same time, to generate significant externalities within the platform in order to sustain the collective performance of the network. While 'dominator' leaders behave mostly in a predatory way, integrate the network vertically and horizontally and seek to appropriate most of the value produced by the network, 'keystone' leaders achieve the mix between value appropriation and value sharing between the platform's partners.

Cusumano and Gawer (2002) argued that the main problem of platform leaders can be identified in two key features of contemporary platforms: (1) the increasing interdependency of products and services; and (2) the increasing ability to innovate through the participation of numerous partners, especially in the high-tech sectors. The combined effect of these two elements determines to what degree the development and improvement of one element in the product/service/organization of the platform is complementary and interdependent to the development of all others elements.

Platforms succeed only when the diverse incentives and capabilities of a variety of heterogeneous actors are organized so that they align and converge appropriately. In fact, only the convergence of a plurality of complementary actions aligned though sequential chains of user–producer relations can shape the actual direction and speed of the process. For instance, one of the problems faced by Intel in the 1990s was precisely to create the appropriate set of incentives for hardware and software producers to introduce innovations that parallel improvements in microchips.

The changing architecture of networks plays a key role here. The inclusion and exclusion of specific actors, characterized by idiosyncratic productive and innovative capabilities, as well as incentives, change the strategic behavior of the coalition, its objectives and the likely actions through which these can be achieved. The need for dynamic coordination (i.e., coordination at each point in time of the heterogeneous actors embedded in the network) is clear if the goal is to be the successful realization of a common innovation. In such a systemic context, dynamic coordination requires some forms of hierarchical organization and yet, for the complexity involved in the system, no single firm commands both the technological and managerial resources necessary to make such coordination effective technologically and efficiently in terms of the coordination costs. Some intermediate forms of organization are required and it is likely that the implementation of networks centered on key firms and their strategic action emerges as more appropriate than pure solutions such as market exchange and vertical integration. Innovation platforms as hybrid organizational forms emerge precisely as the appropriate strategy in order to allow bureaucratic organizations to react to improvements in product or services by acquiring externally the know-how necessary to innovate.

In a context of distributed capabilities and knowledge often sourced externally, the challenge for individual firms is to enlarge the range of external capabilities that can be accessed and integrated with internal ones, while guaranteeing efficiency and cohesion in access and integration of external knowledge, as well as the distinctiveness of capabilities. Also, empirical evidence about platforms shows that different firms developed different technologies as well as modeled their strategic decisions by fine-tuning their choices on the base of the characteristics of their environment and of internal and external resources available.

Intel and Microsoft are, for example, firms that largely benefited from both external collaboration and competition, making their innovations crucial elements of their platforms. Again, Intel and Cisco, despite their many differences, supported the acquisition of external knowledge in those technologies where internal competencies were less developed. This strategy enlarged the scope of their platforms and, especially in the case of Intel, resulted in a modular and open platform architecture. Microsoft, instead, can be described as a 'dominator' firm rather than a 'keystone' or a platform exploiting its innovation system. In many cases, Microsoft is fully appropriating value without supporting collective dynamics of knowledge, but, on the contrary, developing a closed and rather hierarchical network architecture (Bresnahan, 2002; Gawer and Cusumano, 2002; Casadesus-Masanell and Yoffie, 2007; Gawer and Henderson, 2007). Smaller firms, such as Palm (bought in 2010 by Hewlett Packard) and NTT DoCoMo, show further diversity and specificities. Finally, a special case such as Linux – although not a 'pure' company but a free operating system supported by a community of volunteering programmers and collaborators – demonstrates the power of collective dynamics based on collaboration, exchange of external knowledge, and the sharing of common goals and objectives in the development of platforms (Tee and Gawer, 2009; Eisenmann et al., 2011).

Table 15.3 summarizes the main elements of six different platforms in the ICTs sectors according to three main dimensions (Gawer and Cusumano, 2002) documenting the variety of their strategies and characteristics.

15.5   CONCLUSION

Platforms constitute a major organizational innovation in knowledge governance that exploit the advantages of ICTs in terms of improved flexibility, enhanced control and efficient networking. Platforms are becoming crucial tools for implementing and supporting knowledge governance, both at the firm and the system levels. At the firm level, the creation of and the inclusion in a platform is essential to manage the knowledge-generation process, thus widening the range of competencies that can be accessed and integrated by recombination. Platforms make it possible to increase the amount and the quality of external knowledge that can be used by each firm. As such, platforms enable a drastic reduction of the need to generate new technological knowledge and to introduce technological innovations within a single organization. Rather, firms can substitute cheaper external knowledge for internal more expensive research and development

Table 15.3 *Platform strategies and characteristics in the ICT sector*

	Key Platform Dimensions		
	Scope	Architecture	External network
Intel	Exploration of external resources Collaboration with external producers of complements	Modular structure Open interfaces Collaboration on standard setting	Long-term collaborations with complements producers Value sharing
Microsoft	Exploitation of internal core competencies	Closed structure Proprietary interfaces and standards	Horizontal and vertical competition Horizontal and vertical integration of producers Value appropriation
Cisco	External knowledge exploitation and acquisition	Mixed structure Open standards and interfaces Proprietary development of new technologies Proprietary software	Long-term collaborations with complements producers Horizontal and vertical integration of producers
Palm	Exploitation of internal core competencies on hardware and software Collaboration with external producers of applications	Modular structure that facilitate complements development Proprietary technologies on OS Open interfaces on applications	Long-term collaborations with complements producers Strong user–producer relations Collective learning
DoCoMo	Exploitation of internal resources External collaborations	Modular structure Open interfaces and standards	Long-term collaborations with producers
Linux	Strong exploration of external resources	Open standard	Collective learning

Sources: Authors' elaboration on information provided in Bresnahan (2002), Gawer and Cusumano (2002), Casadesus-Masanell and Yoffie (2007), Gawer and Henderson (2007), Tee and Gawer (2009) and Eisenmann et al. (2011).

activities. The advantages of knowledge cumulability and non-exhaustibility are better exploited. From this viewpoint, platforms are an emerging organizational innovation that is likely to replace the Chandlerian corporation in many areas.

Platforms make it possible to better organize the valorization of technological knowledge after its generation, reducing uncontrolled leakages and exploiting economies of scope with the systematic internalization of potential complementarities with a wide range of partners. At the firm level, platforms make it possible to command the endogenous creation of knowledge externalities and, in so doing, make it possible at the same time: (1) to shrink the absorption costs that stem from a variety of activities such as search, screening, identification, decodification and recodification that are necessary to actually using external knowledge as an input into the generation of new knowledge, and (2) to increase the command of the knowledge exploitation processes. This accelerates the rate of technological innovations and increases their market value.

Support for the diffusion of platforms at the system level may become a major tool of economic policies aimed at increasing the quality of knowledge governance. First, platforms can become a key element of national and regional innovation systems. In an evolutionary perspective, the notion of an innovation system stresses the role that the variety of actors and the connections among those actors play in the generation of new knowledge and innovations. The implementation of platforms within innovation systems emphasizes that both the active selection of the members of the innovation system and their structured coordination should become a major goal for policy-makers in order to support the creation and diffusion of new knowledge and the introduction of innovations (Patrucco, 2014a). The active selection of the members of the system should be centered on the exploitation of knowledge complementarities, minimizing redundancies of endowments, skills and competencies. In this regard, the active selection of the members and their structured and dynamic coordination enable overcoming the limits of the spontaneous coordination of innovative efforts within networks.

Furthermore, the identification of potential platforms and the intervention of public authorities to stir their implementation may help the economic system to hasten the rate of generating of new technological knowledge and of the introduction of technological innovations. Integrating public procurement with active support for the creation of platforms on the supply side can become an effective framework to improve the capability of the system to command the endogenous creation and exploitation of knowledge externalities, using public procurement as a powerful incentive. Because platforms, like a glass mirror, make it possible to multiply the light of knowledge candles, a system in which public policy has been able to facilitate the implementation of a variety of platforms is likely to experience better performance in the generation of new technological knowledge at lower unit costs than one with fewer or more homogeneous platforms.

NOTES

*   This project has received funding from the European Union's Seventh Framework Programme for research, technological development and demonstration under grant agreement no. 266959.
†   The authors acknowledge the institutional support of the Collegio Carlo Alberto and the University of Torino.
1.   The term 'knowledge society' is also used as a synonym for 'knowledge economy'.
2.   The emergence of the so-called 'ICT paradigm' has been paralleled by a broader set of changes introduced in the telecommunication industry itself. Impinging upon the centrifugal properties of new communication technologies and the diminishing importance of scale economies, regulators liberalized telecommunication markets worldwide. Moreover, in the EU especially, they supported the entry of new players, which often delivered their communication services (such as, broadband services, TV on demand, Internet Protocol TC [IPTV] and Voice-over-IP [VoIP]) exploiting new communication technologies, of which the Internet is just the epitome. In this regard, the emergence of the 'ICT paradigm' implies market changes both in the telecom market broadly speaking and in the industry that makes intensive use of ICTs. With regard to the former, ICTs and the Internet form both a product and a process innovation that radically change the way in which communication services are delivered (e.g., the shift from copper wires to fiber-optic cable and the introduction of wireless technologies) as well as the content of the services themselves (e.g., IPTV and VoIP). With regard to the latter, ICTs and the Internet are mainly used as process innovations that

change the way in which production is organized, products are manufactured and services are delivered (for instance, increasing delocalization and outsourcing). These changes have greatly improved efficiency and control over production, and have relaxed the requirement of physical proximity between producers and users to deliver a given service.

3. By 'technological convergence' we mean the growing direction that characterizes technologies originally belonging to different systems to progressively carry out similar tasks. In particular, this is the case for technologies such as voice (e.g., telephony features), media and video (e.g., music and television services), and data (e.g., productivity applications) that previously were delivered separately and now, exploiting digitalization, share network and other resources and interact with each other through single physical devices (e.g., tablets and smartphones). In this sense, technological convergence relies upon technological complementarities and network effects and implies a networked product architecture. The Internet is itself a driver and a product of technological convergence, and probably the most powerful and pervasive result of such a convergence between new information and communication technologies (Fransman, 2010).

4. We can define interactions as personal and socially based forms of coordination for economic activity that do not need formal agreements, such as contracts, and do not rely on a price system. On the other hand, transactions are defined as formalized and often standardized modes of coordination based on contracts and the price system. These two cases are clearly the two theoretical extremes of a continuum where intermediate combinations of interactions and transactions open the scope for empirical analysis of different forms of coordination.

REFERENCES

Antonelli, C. (2001), *The Microeconomics of Technological Systems*, Oxford, UK: Oxford University Press.

Antonelli, C. (2003), *The Economics of Innovation, New Technologies and Structural Change*, London: Routledge.

Antonelli, C. (2006), 'The governance of localized knowledge: An information economics approach to the economics of knowledge', *Industry and Innovation*, **13** (3), 227–61.

Antonelli, C. (ed.) (2011), *Handbook on the Economic Complexity of Technological Change*, Cheltenham, UK and Northampton, MA, USA: Edward Elgar Publishing.

Antonelli, C. (2015), 'The dynamics of knowledge governance', in C. Antonelli and A. Link (eds), *Handbook on the Economics of Knowledge*, London, Routledge, pp. 232–62.

Arora, A., A. Gambardella and E. Rullani (1998), 'Division of labour and the locus of inventive activity', *Journal of Management and Governance*, **1** (1), 123–40.

Arrow, K.J. (1969), 'Classificatory notes on the production and transmission of technical knowledge', *American Economic Review*, **59** (2), 29–35.

Arrow, K.J. (1974), *The Limits of Organization*, New York: W.W. Norton.

Baldwin, C.Y. and K.B. Clark (1997), 'Managing in an age of modularity', *Harvard Business Review*, **75** (5), 84–93.

Bonazzi, G. and C. Antonelli (2003), 'To make or to sell? The case of in-house outsourcing at Fiat Auto', *Organization Studies*, **24** (4), 575–94.

Bresnahan, T.F. (2002), 'The economy of the Microsoft case', *Stanford Law and Economics Olin Working Paper No. 232*, accessed 3 July 2014 at http://ssrn.com/abstract=304701.

Brynjolfsson, E. (2011), 'ICT, innovation and the e-economy', *EIB Papers No. 8/2011*, European Investment Bank, Economics Department.

Brynjolfsson, E. and L.M. Hitt (2000), 'Beyond computation: Information technology, organizational transformation and business performance', *Journal of Economic Perspectives*, **14** (4), 23–48.

Casadesus-Masanell, R. and R. Yoffie (2007), 'Wintel: Cooperation and conflict', *Management Science*, **53** (4), 584–98.

Chandler, A.D. (1977), *The Visible Hand*, Cambridge, MA: Harvard University Press.

Chandler, A.D. (1990), *Scale and Scope: The Dynamics of Industrial Capitalism*, Cambridge, MA: Belknap Press.

Chesbrough, H. and D. Teece (1996), 'Organizing for innovation: When is virtual virtuous?', *Harvard Business Review*, **74** (1), 65–74.

Chesbrough, H.W., W. Vanhaverbeke and J. West (eds) (2006), *Open Innovation: Researching a New Paradigm*, Oxford, UK: Oxford University Press.

Ciborra, C. (1996), 'The platform organization: Recombining strategies, structures and surprises', *Organizational Science*, **7** (2), 103–18.

Consoli, D. and P.P. Patrucco (2008), 'Innovation platforms and the governance of knowledge: Evidence from Italy and the UK', *Economics of Innovation and New Technology*, **17** (7), 701–18.

Consoli, D. and P.P. Patrucco (2011), 'Complexity and the coordination of technological knowledge: The case of innovation platforms', in C. Antonelli (ed.), *Handbook on the Economic Complexity of Technological Change*, Cheltenham, UK and Northampton, MA, USA: Edward Elgar Publishing, pp. 201–20.

Cusumano, M.A. and A. Gawer (2002), 'The elements of platform leadership', *MIT Sloan Management Review*, **43** (3), 51–8.

Davenport, T.H. and L. Prusak (1998), *Working Knowledge: Managing What Your Organization Knows*, Cambridge, MA: Harvard Business School Press.

David, P.A. and E. Steinmueller (1994), 'Economics of compatibility standards and competition in telecommunication networks', *Information Economics and Policy*, **6** (3–4), 217–42.

Edquist, C. (ed.) (2003), *The Internet and Mobile Telecommunications Systems of Innovation*, Cheltenham, UK and Northampton, MA, USA: Edward Elgar Publishing.

Eisenmann, T., G. Parker and M.W. van Alstyne (2011), 'Platform envelopment', *Strategic Management Journal*, **32** (12), 1270–85.

Ethiraj, S.K. and D. Levinthal (2004), 'Modularity and innovation in complex systems', *Management Science*, **50** (2), 159–73.

European Commission (2004), *Technology Platforms: From Definition to Implementation of a Common Research Agenda*, Director-General for Research.

Foray, D. (2004), *The Economics of Knowledge*, Cambridge, MA: MIT Press.

Fransman, M. (2002), *Telecoms in the Internet Age: From Boom to Bust to . . .?* Oxford, UK: Oxford University Press.

Fransman, M. (ed.) (2006), *Global Broadband Battles: Why the US and Europe Lag Behind While Asia Leads*, Stanford, CA: Stanford University Press.

Fransman, M. (2010), *The New ICT Ecosystem: Implications for Policy and Regulation*, Oxford, UK: Oxford University Press.

Freeman, C. (2009), 'The ICT paradigm', in R. Mansell, C. Avgerou, D. Quah and R. Silverstone (eds), *The Oxford Handbook of Information and Communication Technologies*, Oxford, UK: Oxford University Press, pp. 34–54.

Garud, R. and A. Kumaraswamy (1996), 'Technological designs for retention and reuse', *International Journal of Technology Management*, **11** (7/8), 883–91.

Gawer, A. (ed.) (2009), *Platforms, Markets and Innovation*, Cheltenham, UK and Northampton, MA, USA: Edward Elgar Publishing.

Gawer, A. and M.A. Cusumano (2002), *Platform Leadership: How Intel, Microsoft, and Cisco Drive Industry Innovation*, Boston, MA: Harvard Business School Press.

Gawer, A. and R. Henderson (2007), 'Platform owner entry and innovation in complementary markets: Evidence from Intel', *Journal of Economics & Management Strategy*, **16** (1), 1–34.

Gerstein, S. (1992), 'From machine bureaucracies to networked organizations: An architectural journey', in D.A. Nadler, M.A. Gerstein and R.B. Shaw (eds), *Organizational Architecture: Designs for Changing Organizations*, San Francisco, CA: Jossey-Bass, pp. 11–38.

Hagedoorn, J. and G. Hesen (2007), 'Contract law and the governance of inter-firm technology partnerships. An analysis of different modes of partnering and their contractual implications', *Journal of Management Studies*, **44** (3), 342–66.

Henderson R.M. and K.B. Clark (1990), 'Architectural innovation: The reconfiguration of existing systems and the failure of established firms', *Administrative Science Quarterly*, **35** (1), 9–30.

Iansiti, M. and R. Levien (2004), *The Keystone Advantage: What the New Dynamics of Business Ecosystems Mean for Strategy*, Cambridge, MA: Harvard University Press.

Jacobides, M.G. (2006), 'The architecture and design of organizational capabilities', *Industrial and Corporate Change*, **15** (1), 151–71.

Jacobides, M.G. and S. Billinger (2006), 'Designing the boundaries of the firm: From "make, buy, or ally" to the dynamic benefits of vertical architecture', *Organization Science*, **17** (2), 249–61.

Jacobides, M.G., T. Knudsen and M. Augier (2006), 'Benefiting from innovation: Value creation, value appropriation and the role of industry architectures', *Research Policy*, **35** (8), 1200–221.

Jones, M. and W.J. Orlikowski (2009), 'Information technology and the dynamics of organizational change', in R. Mansell, C. Avgerou, D. Quah and R. Silverstone (eds), *The Oxford Handbook of Information and Communication Technologies*, Oxford, UK: Oxford University Press, pp. 293–313.

Kallinikos, J. (2009), 'ICT, organizations, and networks', in R. Mansell, C. Avgerou, D. Quah and R. Silverstone (eds), *The Oxford Handbook of Information and Communication Technologies*, Oxford, UK: Oxford University Press, pp. 273–92.

Kim, D. and B. Kogut (1996), 'Technological platforms and diversification', *Organization Science*, **7** (2), 283–301.

Lane, D., D. Pumain, S. van der Leew and G. West (eds) (2009), *Complexity Perspectives on Innovation and Social Change*, Berlin: Springer.

Langlois, R.N. (2002), 'Modularity in technology and organization', *Journal of Economic Behavior & Organization*, **49** (1), 19–37.

Langlois, R.N. (2003), 'The vanishing hand: The changing dynamics of industrial capitalism', *Industrial and Corporate Change*, **12** (2), 351–85.

Langlois, R.N. (2004), 'Chandler in a larger frame: Markets, transaction costs, and organizational form in history', *Enterprise & Society*, **5** (3), 355–75.

OECD (1996), *The Knowledge-Based Economy*, Paris: Organisation for Economic Co-operation and Development.

Ostrom, E. (2010), 'Beyond markets and states: Polycentric governance of complex economic systems', *American Economic Review*, **100** (3), 641–72.

Ostrom, E. and C. Hess (eds) (2006), *Understanding Knowledge as a Commons: From Theory to Practice*, Cambridge, MA: MIT Press.

Patrucco, P.P. (2008), 'The economics of collective knowledge and technological communication', *Journal of Technology Transfer*, **33** (6), 579–99.

Patrucco, P.P. (2012), 'Innovation platforms and the knowledge-intensive firm', in M. Dietrich and J. Krafft (eds), *Handbook on the Economics and Theory of the Firm*, Cheltenham, UK and Northampton, MA, USA: Edward Elgar Publishing, pp. 354–78.

Patrucco, P.P. (2014a), 'The evolution of knowledge organization and the emergence of a platform for innovation in the car industry', *Industry and Innovation*, **21** (3), 243–66.

Patrucco, P.P. (ed.) (2014b), *The Economics of Knowledge Generation and Distribution: The Role of Interactions in the System Dynamics of Innovation and Growth*, London: Routledge.

Penrose, E. (1959), *The Theory of the Growth of the Firm*, Oxford, UK: Oxford University Press.

Prencipe, A., A. Davies and M. Hobday (eds) (2003), *The Business of System Integration*, Oxford, UK: Oxford University Press.

Richardson, G.B. (1972), 'The organisation of industry', *Economic Journal*, **82** (327), 883–96.

Rochet, J.C. and J. Tirole (2003), 'Platform competition in two-sided markets', *Journal of the European Economic Association*, **1** (4), 990–1029.

Schilling, M. (2009), *Strategic Management of Technological Innovation*, New York, McGraw-Hill.

Shapiro, C. and H.R. Varian (1999), *Information Rules*, Cambridge, MA: Harvard University Press.

Smith, A. (1776), *An Inquiry into the Nature and Causes of the Wealth of Nations*, London: W. Strahan and T. Cadell.

Suarez, F. and M.A. Cusumano (2009), 'The role of services in platform markets', in A. Gawer (ed.), *Platforms, Markets and Innovation*, Cheltenham, UK and Northampton, MA, USA: Edward Elgar Publishing, pp. 77–98.

Tee, R. and A. Gawer (2009), 'Industry architecture as determinant of successful platform strategies: A case study of the i-mode mobile Internet service', *European Management Review*, **6** (4), 217–32.

van Schewick, B. (2010), *Internet Architecture and Innovation*, Cambridge, MA: MIT Press.

Von Hippel, E. (1988), *The Sources of Innovation*, Oxford, UK: Oxford University Press.

Von Hippel, E. (2005), *Democratizing Innovation*, Cambridge, MA: MIT Press.

Weitzman, M.L. (1996), 'Hybridizing growth theory', *American Economic Review*, **86** (2), 207–12.

Weitzman, M.L. (1998), 'Recombinant growth', *Quarterly Journal of Economics*, **113** (2), 331–60.

Wheelwright, S.C. and K.B. Clark (1992), 'Creating project plans to focus product development', *Harvard Business Review*, **70** (2), 70–82.

16. Interconnection in the Internet: peering, interoperability and content delivery

*David D. Clark, William H. Lehr and Steven Bauer**

16.1 INTRODUCTION

The Internet is a network of networks that realizes its global reach by being able to route data from source nodes on one network to destination nodes that may be across town or on the other side of the globe, and in many cases, are on networks that are owned and operated by different Internet service providers (ISPs). Along the end-to-end path, the data may need to cross the networks of still other ISPs. Supporting the end-to-end, global connectivity, which is a hallmark of the Internet's value proposition, requires that the ISPs be interconnected both physically (i.e., there exists an electronic pathway for transporting packets) and via business relationships. These business relationships impact both the flow of traffic *and* the flow of money across the Internet value chain.

Historically, most traffic was exchanged between the largest ISPs on the basis of revenue-neutral peering agreements that routed traffic but not dollars across ISP interconnections. The explosive growth of video traffic, the increased socio-economic importance of the Internet, and the rise of business disputes over who should pay for the increased costs of traffic have raised questions about whether the time has now come for Internet interconnection to be regulated.

In this chapter, we focus on the growing challenge posed by the rise in traffic/usage-related costs for Internet interconnection – attributable today to the rise in entertainment video traffic from content delivery networks (CDNs) – and what this may mean for policy-makers. We conclude that the rising concern over a potential need to regulate interconnection is valid, but point to current structural features, costs, and usage data that suggest that strong regulatory intervention does not seem warranted at this time. While usage-related costs are significant, they are not so large as to require a major disruption in either retail or wholesale (interconnection) pricing. It is reasonable to expect that both upstream content delivery networks and end user subscribers may be called upon to contribute to recovering the growing traffic-related costs confronting access ISPs, which must continually invest in expanded capacity to meet the needs of exponential traffic growth. Nevertheless, we expect that the forces driving these changes imply that the potential need for regulation will continue and that interconnection will remain a focal issue for future broadband policy.

We organize the chapter into three major sections. First, we provide a review of the history of interconnection in the Internet and of some of the academic literature that has sought to make sense of it. Next, we provide our assessment of the current status of interconnection in the Internet and the basis for the preliminary conclusions summarized above. We are aware that our discussion is US-centric although it should be noted that many of the trends observed first in the USA are echoed by similar trends in many other markets. We conclude with some thoughts on the future of this important issue and some of the questions that need to be addressed.

16.2 UNDERSTANDING INTERCONNECTION IN THE INTERNET

Networks are a key component of much of our basic infrastructure, including the networks of roads, water, electricity, and telecommunications that are used ubiquitously in our daily lives. These networks connect supply (source) and demand (destination) nodes via a network of interconnected links (transport paths) and switching nodes. These networks allow us to flexibly route water, electricity, people, or telephone calls from their points of origination (reservoir, generator, town, or calling party) to their final destinations (home or business, another town, or called party). The links that connect the source and destination nodes may be referred to as the access connections.

To reduce total costs, it is usually desirable for access nodes to be connected via a hierarchy of network switching nodes, each of which is connected to multiple access or network nodes. Thus, a fabric of small local roads or local electric power distribution lines connects homes to highways or high-power distribution facilities to allow traffic to be aggregated and routed via shared facilities towards its final destinations. Similarly, telecommunications networks are comprised of local switches – or in packet networks, routers – that collect the traffic from access nodes and route it to tandem switches, which are in turn connected to other local or tandem switches in a hierarchy that allows traffic to be routed across town, across the state, or across the globe.

A common feature of such networks is that they allow a large number of source/destination nodes to share network resources economically to take advantage of the fact that demands are not perfectly correlated in time[1] and of the scale economies that are common with network technologies.[2] Also, larger networks that provide more options for routing traffic between a larger number of source and destination nodes are typically more valuable to each subscriber, or in economic terms, exhibit positive network externalities.[3] The presence of shared resources and benefits that characterizes networks poses a number of challenges for network economics. First, the network needs sufficient capacity to meet the traffic demands of the source/destination nodes. These change over time and across nodes and applications, thereby complicating the network capacity provisioning challenge. Second, for the network to be economically sensible, the value of the network services has to exceed the costs of sustaining the network. For economic viability, sufficient funds need to flow to network resource owners to allow them to recover the network investment and operating costs.

The cost recovery challenge is further complicated because much of the investment is long-lived and must be put in place in advance of the demand that it is intended to serve. In telecommunications networks like the Internet, the rapid pace of change introduces significant market, technical, and policy uncertainty and asymmetries that further complicate the capacity provisioning and cost recovery challenges. Furthermore, most big networks are actually networks of networks, comprised of multiple smaller networks that are interconnected and that are (at least partially) independently controlled. The focus of the discussion here is on the interconnection between these networks and how those are used to route both dollars (for cost recovery and value transfer) and traffic.[4]

Finally, in all of the examples cited above (roads, electricity, water, and telecommunications), the networks are viewed as basic infrastructure by society since they provide services that we use ubiquitously in the course of our social and economic lives. As a consequence, there is a government interest in ensuring that we have affordable and universal access to these basic infrastructures. In many cases, we rely on public utilities (water, electricity, roads) to provide the basic network infrastructure that is paid for by a mix of taxes (direct subsidies) and subscription fees. Moreover, because of the public interest in basic infrastructure, these networks are subject to significant regulatory oversight, and regulating interconnection is a key focus of network regulatory policy.

In telecommunications networks, there is a long history of interconnection regulations that established both the terms and prices for interconnection in ways that often embedded significant implicit and explicit subsidies. For example, in the USA, telecommunications network providers are required to provide interconnection services to each other to ensure connectivity. The terms and rates differ depending on the type of provider and by type of interconnection. As policy-makers have sought to transition toward competition, the legacy of asymmetric and above-cost interconnection charges has posed a significant obstacle to efficient competition, and efforts have been made to rationalize interconnection rules to leave more scope for market forces and to eliminate implicit subsidies and asymmetries. Collectively, these rules are sometimes referred to as 'intercarrier compensation' policies to highlight their role in managing cash flows between service providers as part of the interconnection challenge. The desire to cut the Gordian Knot of inefficient interconnection policies provided some of the motivation for proposals to adopt 'bill-and-keep' interconnection rules that would set intercarrier payments to zero.[5]

In contrast to legacy telephone networks, interconnection in the Internet has been unregulated. This is largely a consequence of the Internet's evolution as an application that ran on top of the regulated public switched telephone network (PSTN). From an economic perspective, this means that the decision of whether to interconnect, and if so, how to interconnect, was left to the ISPs.

From a technical perspective, the Internet is an end-to-end (e2e) packet delivery network that routes packets from source to destination Internet Protocol (IP) addresses. This often requires packets to traverse multiple networks. These networks, identified as autonomous systems (AS), control a range of IP addresses that they manage and that they are responsible for routing to.[6] Most AS are associated with ISPs. To route traffic between IP addresses on different AS or ISPs, the ISPs must be interconnected. These interconnections define both physical/technical and business relationships. The forms of these interconnection agreements impact how Internet traffic is routed, Internet connectivity, the services that may be supported, the quality of those services, and the cost and terms for how services are paid for at both wholesale and retail.

There are two basic ways in which ISPs may interconnect: at Internet exchanges where multiple ISPs interconnect, and directly via negotiated bilateral agreements. The focus of this chapter is on the bilateral interconnection agreements via which most traffic is exchanged.[7] In the early days of the commercialization of the Internet, two sorts of bilateral interconnection agreements among ISPs emerged. One was a traditional customer–supplier arrangement, in which one ISP purchased transit service from another, perhaps larger, ISP. An ISP that offers traditional transit service agrees to provide access to the entire Internet for its customers. The other arrangement was peering, in which two ISPs that each had traffic for the other agreed to interconnect to exchange that traffic directly. A peering arrangement between two ISPs does not give either ISP access to the entire Internet via the other; normally each ISP exchanges with the other ISP only traffic that is local to the region of that ISP and its customers. In other words, a peering agreement implies a routing restriction with respect to the traffic exchanged; the only traffic exchanged originates from the source ISP and its customers and terminates in the destination ISP and its customers.

In contrast to a transit arrangement, which is a commercial arrangement between a buyer and a seller in which monetary payments flow from the buyer to the seller as compensation for services rendered, peering (as the name might suggest) has been viewed as an interconnection among approximate equals, with value to both parties and no a priori obvious direction for monetary payments to flow. In early negotiations among potential peering partners, it became clear that it would be very difficult to determine if the balance of values favored one or the other ISP, and the convention emerged that peering was 'settlement free' or 'revenue neutral'. Given the perception that negotiation about relative value would be costly (i.e., incur potentially high transaction or bargaining costs) and under the assumption of approximately equal value accruing from the relationship on each side, this settlement-free approximation could be seen as economically efficient.

Earlier academic analyses of Internet interconnection focused on these two types of contractual arrangements based on a hierarchical identification of ISPs: transit, a vertical contract in which smaller ISPs serving end users purchased services from larger backbone ISPs; and peering, a horizontal contract between core or backbone ISPs to exchange traffic under a bill-and-keep or revenue-neutral arrangement.[8] A focus of this earlier literature was on investigating the incentives of backbone ISPs to peer and the implications for competition. For a number of years, these two options – transit and revenue-neutral peering – captured the set of expectations among parties that negotiated interconnections; they represented an informal norm or bargaining regime. But like many such informal norms, revenue-neutral peering has been breaking down slowly as the various parties to potential peering relationships no longer see the simplicity of the balanced-value approximation as serving their needs. It is being replaced (as has happened in other venues like the bargaining over international trade agreements) with a period of more unconstrained bilateral negotiation among the parties. There are a number of reasons why this seems to be happening:[9]

- In the past, many ISPs were more or less similar. There were small ISPs, and larger ISPs with larger footprints, of course, but many ISPs had the same mix of customers. When similar ISPs established peering interconnections, the similarity made the assumption of balanced value plausible. Today, ISPs are more specialized, with some serving broadband residential customers (sometimes called access or 'eyeball' networks), some serving enterprise customers, perhaps with a highly distributed footprint, some serving high-volume content providers and so on.
- Networks that serve different sorts of customers may have very different internal cost structures. A residential broadband provider, with an extensive 'outside plant' of fiber, HFC or copper pairs, may have a much higher cost (measured in dollars

per megabit) compared to an ISP that serves only business customers with typically much higher peak data rate connections.[10]

- Furthermore, with the continued evolution of the Internet (e.g., introduction of routing protocol enhancements[11]) and the rise of multi-homing, wherein end users and ISPs connect to multiple ISPs thereby expanding the range of routing options, it is increasingly feasible to implement more granular traffic treatments as part of interconnection agreements.

In light of these changes, it has become clear to many ISPs in the USA that they can reduce transit payments if they are able to negotiate peering arrangements to exchange traffic directly. However, in these new circumstances, it is possible that one party or the other regards the legacy approach of revenue-neutral peering as unacceptable, and thus other approaches to interconnection emerge, including the option of paid peering or partial transit. These latter models represent blends of the transitional pure transit or peering models that involve payments from one ISP to another and that restrict the range of addresses to which traffic may be delivered. In paid peering, one ISP pays the other ISP to accept the peering traffic, whereas in partial transit, the ISP that is paying for transit is only purchasing delivery to a subset of the rest of the Internet. These contracts are privately negotiated and are not standardized. The payment terms, the traffic (volume, address) restrictions, and other interconnection terms may be negotiated on a case-by-case basis.

16.2.1   High Volume Content and its Providers

A particular focus of policymakers' attention and for this chapter is the sub-case of interconnection between residential broadband ISPs such as Comcast and AT&T (access networks) and networks that deliver high-volume commercial content such as Level 3 and Cogent. During the first half of 2013, 62 percent of peak-time traffic was due to real-time entertainment, with Netflix accounting for 32 percent and YouTube from Google accounting for 17 percent.[12] In 2011, Netflix content was delivered by three commercial operators: Akamai, Limelight and Level 3.[13] So these three providers plus Google originate and control a significant majority of all real-time entertainment content and peak-time residential download traffic. Collectively, we will call these content delivery networks, in contrast to access networks. A cost-effective connection between a content delivery network and an access network will often be of advantage to both, because of the high volumes of data being transferred.

Negotiation between a content delivery network and an access network about direct connection is at heart a peering negotiation, because it would normally imply the same routing restriction as we described above. Specifically, the content delivery network is normally only trying to get access to the customers of the access network. But because of the high volumes of traffic potentially involved and the fact that the traffic is highly asymmetric (from content to access), negotiation about payment may be commonplace. The carriage of this high-volume traffic will generate costs for access networks, which they will naturally attempt to recover; at the same time one might argue that access to the content creates value for the access network's customers. Based on anecdotal evidence, it appears that the most common outcome is for content delivery networks to make payments to access networks. We are interested in understanding both the direction and magnitude of these sorts of payments.

Interconnection between content delivery and access networks has attracted significant attention in recent years. From a business point of view, these interconnection arrangements are of considerable interest because of the high volumes of data being exchanged, and the implications of this high volume for internal costs. Industry observers and regulators are also interested, because the high content-related value of this data raises questions as to whether any actor will have sufficient market power to benefit by extracting rents derived from the value of the content, not its delivery.

The desire to separate concerns about content and the delivery or 'conduit' of that content has a long regulatory history. Traditional telecommunications regulation focused on regulating 'conduits' and the need to ensure common-carriage access to basic telecommunications services, for which public utility regulation was long justified by the concern that telephone networks were a natural monopoly.[14] On the other hand, regulation of content was manifest in broadcast and programming regulation and media cross-ownership rules.[15] The regulation of cable television services, where investor interests in content and conduit services were conjoined, led to its own silo of regulation in the United States. With the rise of the Internet as the 'new PSTN', policy-makers are faced with the question of how much of the traditional regulatory model for telecommunications ought to be mapped over to the new world of the broadband Internet. In their efforts to craft a framework that is more technology-agnostic (i.e., less focused on whether the underlying infrastructure has evolved from a telephone or cable television network, or supports fixed or mobile services), policy-makers have opted for increased reliance on market forces and more light-handed regulatory approaches.[16] This debate continues in its current incarnation as the debate over network neutrality.[17]

One notable component of this debate is policy-makers' concerns that ISPs might engage in discriminatory network or traffic management practices that may interfere with competition, or worse, limit end users' access to content or applications of their choice. The implicit presumption is that access ISPs have market power[18] and may seek to use such market power to earn monopoly profits from over-charging end users or other participants in the value chain, such as application service providers or content providers. The focus of our concern here is on the potential for extracting excess payments from content providers and content delivery networks. To the extent that any discrimination might distort competition in content markets, the potential for discriminatory practices is especially worrisome to policy-makers for the reasons noted above.

In this chapter, we will maintain a clean distinction between two sorts of payments that flow among parties. Transport payments are payments among parties that cover the internal costs related to the delivery of flows of data. Content payments are payments that relate to the value and costs of the commercial content itself, not its transport.[19] While this distinction may not always be precise, we believe that it is an acceptable simplification for the purpose of this chapter.[20]

Traditionally, there has been no content-related component in residential customers' broadband access payments. If the consumer wants to receive fee-based commercial content, such as Netflix or *The Wall Street Journal*, the relevant content payments flow directly from the consumer to the content provider. However, this is starting to break down in small but suggestive ways. ESPN3, an online source of streaming sports content, has negotiated an arrangement with certain broadband providers in which they purchase bulk access to ESPN3 content for all their broadband customers, which implies that the cost of this is recovered by a part of the monthly bill that each customer pays. Right now, providers' per customer content payment related to ESPN3 is about $0.10 a month[21] but other content arrangements may follow.

Similarly, there has been no content-related component in the historical pricing of ISP interconnection. Transit is a service that provides access to any end point on the network, not specific high-value content; to date and for the most part, this seems to be a competitive, commodity business.[22] However, the special case of interconnection between content and access networks raises the possibility that there might be a content-related component to the negotiated payments. One of the goals of this chapter is to propose an approach for determining whether payments between parties are likely to include such a content-related component. But we stress that payment from a content delivery network to an access network (e.g., a form of paid peering) does not automatically imply that there is a content-related component in the payment. The payment may be only to cover the transport-related payment that the access network has successfully negotiated to recover some of its internal costs for delivering the content to end users.

16.3   A SIMPLE MODEL OF INTERCONNECTION AND COST

Let us consider a single access network A (e.g., Comcast, Verizon, Time Warner or AT&T) interconnecting with a content delivery network CD (e.g., Google/YouTube, Akamai or Limelight). Content providers or owners like the end users who produce and post YouTube videos, or Netflix that licenses and distributes premium content, rely on network CD to deliver the video traffic to the end users. The end users or consumer 'eyeballs' receive the content over their broadband connections provided by their access network, network A. Most of the traffic flows from network CD to network A, which adds usage-based costs to network A, designated as C_A. Network CD also incurs costs to deliver this traffic, which include the costs of servers and communication links, and we denote these as C_{CD}.

There is a slight asymmetry to the situation of CD and A, which is worth keeping in mind. Network A has a substantial base cost that existed prior to the growth of high-volume commercial content. For example, network A needs to have both the last-mile drops, distribution network and backbone network to support basic communication and other services, regardless of whether this same infrastructure is shared to deliver video. By assumption, C_A comprises only the incremental, usage-based component of the total cost of A. CD, on the other hand, exists only to deliver this content, and will tend to view their total network-related costs as associated with the delivery of content.

The sources of dollar flows (payments) in this model include the payments that content owners/producers make to network CD for content delivery services, and the payments that end users or 'eyeball' customers pay to their broadband access provider, network A, for their access and usage. (To keep things simple, we are ignoring other sources of third-party payments such as government subsidies or advertising.)[23] Finally, there is the potential of a payment flow, *P*, between networks CD and A, as follows:

- $P = 0$: Traditional revenue-neutral peering, where each network covers all its internal costs from its own customers.
- $P > 0$: Payment from CD to A to help cover some of the internal costs of A. Such a payment would be part of C_{CD} and presumably these costs are then passed through by CD to the content producers, who pay more to CD and thus indirectly cover the cost of transporting their content across A. This outcome is fairly common in today's content delivery network market.
- $P < 0$: Payment from A to CD. This payment arrangement seems uncommon, but makes sense in certain circumstances. Consider the case where A is a small, rural ISP. If there is no direct connection between CD and A, all of the content from the producers will come into A over a potentially very expensive transit link. Having CD make a direct connection to A may greatly reduce A's costs. However, if A is small, it may not be cost-effective for CD to connect to A; the connection might actually increase CCD, not reduce it. In this case, it might make sense for A to pay CD.

16.3.1   A Reality Check: The Size of CA

To better understand the current debate over usage costs, it is worth considering the potential magnitude of these costs. Unfortunately, the lack of publicly verifiable information about the terms and conditions for interconnection agreements makes it difficult to estimate C_A, but we believe it is possible to rely on anecdotal evidence to identify some reasonable bounds on estimates of what these costs may be. In an earlier paper, we estimated the cost at \$0.10 per gigabyte (GB) (Clark, 2008),[24] not including costs related to the access network. Other writers have suggested lower numbers, in the range of \$0.07 to \$0.10/GB.[25] Depending on the extent to which access network costs are allocated as fixed or usage related, the per GB costs may be considerably higher, perhaps \$0.20 to \$0.30/GB. These estimates are applicable for large urban/suburban broadband wireline access networks with low costs for their transit.[26] At one extreme, Netflix estimated that the costs were in the range of \$0.01/GB.[27] We believe such an estimate is unreasonably low. At the other extreme, some have pointed to the \$1.00/GB overage fees charged by some ISPs for subscribers' usage that exceeds their usage tier's monthly allotment. These average prices are not intended to reflect the incremental cost of additional usage, but to provide a strong inducement for subscribers to self-select into the appropriate usage tier. While these estimates cover a broad range, it is not so broad that we cannot reach some useful conclusions.

For example, Sandvine (2011) reported that average (mean) monthly download usage was 18.6 GB in the spring of 2011. If usage costs \$0.20/GB, it would mean that the per customer usage-related monthly costs are close to \$4. To watch a 90-minute movie in HD from Netflix (at about 5 megabits per second, or Mbps) would cost about \$0.65. By 2013, mean monthly usage had doubled to 38.6 GB.[28] Although not precise, these numbers imply that the emergence of high-volume content (video) has generated substantial new costs C_A.

16.3.2   Managing Access Costs CA

There are only four ways that access network A can manage usage-related costs C_A:

- Lower the total costs: by careful design of their network, specifically with attention to where the content delivery networks interconnect with them, they may be able to reduce the actual C_A incurred.[29]
- Payments from CD to A ($P > 0$): network A can negotiate to have the content network CD compensate them for some of these costs.
- Raise retail prices for consumers:
  - allocating an equal share of C_A to all customers;
  - creating mechanisms that will discriminate among users based on some proxy of usage, and increase the price of service for these users.
- Internally subsidize by accepting reduced margins: if the ISPs such as network A are competitive, however, then this is not a sustainable option.

16.3.3   Why Might CD Pay A (P > 0)?

When CD networks connect to large access networks A, payment seems to most commonly flow from CD to those access networks. Since both have costs, it is worth asking why payment should flow from CD to A instead of the other way.

One possible answer is that network A has a better bargaining position, because it holds a terminating monopoly with respect to its customers. However, this pattern of payment may be just as much the result of a persistent norm or common practice that is older than the emergence of high-value commercial content: the presumption that money flows and packet flows go in the same direction. That is, if X is delivering packets to Y, then (if there is payment) X pays Y and not the other way around. Of course, the difficulty of justifying this assumption is what led to revenue-neutral peering in the first place. One rule that ISPs use to determine if they will agree to revenue-neutral peering is whether the traffic in the two directions is roughly in balance. If it becomes unbalanced, one or the other party may employ it as a useful justification for renegotiating the agreement. Anecdotally, if there is complaint about the imbalance in costs associated with the asymmetric traffic, it is often the party receiving the excess traffic that complains. But increased traffic (say from X to Y) adds to the costs both for X and Y. So why would X pay Y?

There seems to be an unstated assumption that a transfer is of more benefit to the originator than the receiver, so the sender should be expected to cover more of the delivery costs. This assumption is not always true: for example, when a user downloads a large open-source software package (e.g., a Linux release) the benefit is essentially all to the receiver. However, these cases seem to be ignored as part of the current regime of bargaining.

So long as payment between the parties is an acceptable outcome, the parties will find it profitable to interconnect so long as the net benefit to all parties (including the payments) is positive. Paid peering can lead to more direct connections, which presumably reduces overall system cost and increases total surplus.[30]

This discussion concerns how costs of delivery are covered: they concern transport payments not content payments. However, the possibility of non-zero payments also raises the possibility that one actor (e.g., the access network A) might have enough market power (e.g., because it is a terminating monopoly with respect to its customers) to demand a payment from CD that exceeds its internal costs C_A. In this case, we should assume that the payment is not just a transport payment P_t, but includes a content payment, P_c as well. Regulators and industry observers have worried that access networks might have enough power to demand content payments, and this would signal the potential for unacceptable discrimination and manipulation in the business of content production. So the obvious question follows: if we allow non-zero values for P, how can we distinguish content payments from transport payments?

16.4 BOUNDING THE OUTCOME OF PEERING NEGOTIATIONS

One way to try to understand the context of negotiation between CD and A is to speculate about their relative market power. A has a terminating monopoly with respect to its customers, but CD may be hosting valuable content that the customers of A demand. So which network has the stronger bargaining position? Earlier we noted our assumption that content producers and content delivery networks are unlikely to possess significant market power, but even if one were to relax those assumptions (and we expect that some will argue for just such a case), we do not expect such speculation to be productive: one can likely find specific circumstances in which one or the other outcome seems to hold.[31] Ultimately, we believe that the determination of whether and on which side market power exists will depend on empirical facts that may vary case by case.

16.4.1 Finding Limits on Payment P

Rather than make assumptions about market power, we seek to identify constraints or bounds on the outcome of negotiation between CD and A that might allow policymakers to infer whether the result of the interconnection negotiation was about a reasonable allocation of delivery-related costs or about an unreasonable allocation of the surplus associated with end users' willingness to pay for content, above whatever it costs to efficiently deliver that content to the end users.

The model of traffic and payment flows described above is actually overly simplistic because ISPs and content delivery networks typically have multiple options for routing traffic from source to destination nodes. In reality, CD and A are typically embedded in a rich complex of interconnection agreements, and these agreements will limit the bargaining power of the two networks.

16.4.1.1 Transit as a bound on content delivery payments

Network CD may purchase transit from a third network T that subsequently either peers with network A directly or via its own transit agreements. Other peering agreements can affect the delivery of traffic from CD to the 'eyeball' customers of network A. Network A has multiple peering partners, and may have its own transit provider to enable it to sustain its connectivity to the rest of the Internet and provide diverse routing options to enhance reliability and facilitate load balancing.

In this case, if network A seeks to extract a large payment from network CD, then CD can choose to route the traffic to A indirectly via a transit connection to network T. Because the market for transit services appears relatively competitive, with prices consistently declining over time, the availability of this alternate routing choice provides a loose upper bound on what CD might be induced to pay A to deliver content to A's 'eyeball' customers. The reason it is a loose upper bound is because A might be able to offer valuable performance enhancements (e.g., caching services) or other quality assurances that CD desires, thereby making CD willing to pay a premium above the transit payment P_t.

While (as we noted above) it is difficult to get internal cost numbers for C_A, since most ISPs consider these proprietary, we can speculate that C_A (measured in dollars/GB transferred) is larger than current values of P_t, and in many cases substantially larger. Access networks have large outside plant or access networks, and to the extent that these have a usage-sensitive cost component, these are likely to be much larger than transit costs. We speculated above that C_A might be between \$0.10 and \$0.30/GB. Typical P_t for large volume agreements (e.g., with negotiated discounts) are currently as low as \$1/Mbps per month (peak rate). Assuming average link loading of 50 percent, 1 Mbps is about 151 GB/month. Put otherwise, \$1/Mbps is the same as \$.0066/GB – less than one cent. So as a practical matter, we speculate that even if CD is persuaded by A to pay a premium over P_t, they will by no means be able to recover all of their internal costs, which makes it unlikely that there will be a content-related payment that is part of the negotiated payment from network CD to network A.

There is anecdotal evidence that the relationship we predict here is true in practice. Bill Norton, who tracks peering and transit issues closely, reported in January 2011 that: 'The metered rate [of Comcast paid peering] is rumored to be in the \$2–\$4/Mbps price range, in the same ballpark as the market price of transit'.[32] Our intention in this chapter is to explain why this relationship might hold.

16.4.1.2 Single-hop access
The existence of 'single-hop interconnection services' provides another way by which potential paid-peering payments might be moderated. Under this model, another network O negotiates a peering agreement with network A, and then O solicits network CD to interconnect with network O at the same physical location where O interconnects with A. This 'single-hop' interconnection arrangement imposes very few costs on O so it will still find it profitable to offer this interconnection option to CD at a very low mark-up over O's cost of handing off traffic to network A.[33] Those costs may be zero if O and A exchange traffic under a revenue-neutral peering arrangement.

16.4.1.3 Changing the routing restriction
We described two sorts of traditional interconnection: transit, which gives one party access to the entire Internet via the other, and peering, which implies a routing restriction on each party that the traffic exchanged between them is local to them and their customers. Normally, a network would not agree to route traffic coming in from one peering partner out to another peering partner: it would be forwarding traffic without being paid

by either partner. However, once paid peering is an option, more variants open up for different sorts of routing restrictions.

For example, network CD might negotiate a partial transit agreement with network T, its transit provider, which guarantees delivery only to a subset of addresses. That subset might include network A's end customers. Structurally, this would be like a paid-peering arrangement in that it includes a routing restriction. Network CD would expect to pay less than P_t for a guarantee of delivery to only a portion of Internet addresses. Thus, the option of payment may facilitate more direct connections, and may also lead to greater diversity in the negotiated routing restrictions.

16.4.2 The Real Picture

In the real world a large access network such as A might have several tens of peers, and might purchase transit from several providers. A content delivery network CD might have thousands of servers, each able to serve the same content. So CD might have thousands of choices as to how to source content flowing into A and can use these in a very nuanced fashion to control overall flows. This enhances the bargaining power of network CD because this finer-grained control over traffic gives them some control over network A's costs.[34]

We noted above that traffic from networks of type CD into networks of type A now represents at least 40 percent of all traffic coming into A (Sandvine, 2011). Because content delivery networks control the routing of this traffic, control of routing has moved away from the low-level routing protocols, and into a space controlled by higher-level business agreements and subtle controls over the dynamics of how the large content delivery networks choose one source rather than another for content. This makes the management of interconnection agreements even more strategically important.

16.4.3 Norms of Negotiation

As we noted in the beginning of the chapter, as the old regime of revenue-neutral peering breaks down and is replaced by less constrained negotiation, we can expect to see the emergence of new norms and regimes of interconnection over time. The previous discussion hints at two sorts of norms. First are criteria by which one ISP would consider agreeing to revenue-neutral peering. One source[35] examines a number of existing peering policies, and identifies 25 criteria affecting these agreements, of which perhaps ten are commonly used. One such criterion is balance of flows, in which the data rates between the two parties are roughly in balance (perhaps no more than 2 to 1 in the peak direction).[36] Balance of flows is a rather rough approximation for balance of value, as we discussed above, but it can be used to impose limits on behavior such as single-hop access. If all parties understand up front the maximum amount of imbalance that A will tolerate, this can avoid the pain of after-the-fact attempts to renegotiate a peering agreement.

When revenue-neutral peering is not agreeable to both parties, we have speculated that a new norm might emerge to bound the price that might be charged for paid peering, which is that the rate for paid peering would be related to the price of transit. A proposal for a paid peering fee that greatly exceeds the customary price of bulk transit would be seen as evidence that the network proposing that fee does indeed have market power that allows it to distort the market. But a non-zero peering fee is not in itself a signal of such power.

Other norms might emerge, such as other proxies for cost (e.g., average route miles internal to an ISP), or industry average costs for outside plant. Average route miles could be used to bargain over the relative benefit of hot-potato vs cold-potato routing.

16.5   CHARGING THE CONSUMER

As we noted above, the only options for access network A to recover costs C_A are to impose fees on the interconnected content delivery networks or to impose additional fees on their own subscribers – the residential broadband consumers. (We ignore the final option of becoming less profitable in this analysis.) There are two obvious approaches for structuring the subscriber usage fees. Under flat-rate pricing, the total portion of the C_A to be recovered is apportioned equally on a per capita basis; alternatively, the fees may be proportional to subscriber usage. This latter option might be based on per GB pricing, or more probably price tiers, in which users pay for buckets with a fixed volume capacity. The ex ante price is fixed once a user has selected a usage tier, but the ex post effective average price/GB depends on actual usage, which provides a lumpy form of per GB pricing that seems to be more tolerable in the market since the consumers can self-select the right tier after which they see a fixed price.[37]

Price tiers seem like a reasonable way to allocate fees in rough proportion to costs, but a move to usage tier pricing can significantly alter the balance of power in negotiation about interconnection fees. For example, in countries where residential broadband access is sold with rather low monthly usage caps, some ISPs are offering a 'premium service' to their content network partners. With this premium service (sometimes referred to as 'zero rating'), the content delivery network CD pays a per GB fee to the access network A, in exchange for which the consumer can download the content without having it count against their monthly quota.[38] Setting a consumer-facing price for usage, in effect, allows network A to set a per GB price for interconnection.

For these reasons, access ISPs that move toward usage tiers and similar forms of usage-based pricing can expect to receive increased attention from consumer advocates and regulators, not just because of price tiers, but also because of the potential implications for interconnection agreements. Moreover, in the United States, where consumers have long been accustomed to flat-rate (non-usage-sensitive) pricing, any movement to usage-based pricing will attract significant attention.

One could ask whether usage-based pricing makes good sense, either from a business or 'fairness' point of view. In flat-rate pricing, the smaller users subsidize the larger users. However, the magnitude of the subsidy is important. If the average subsidy were a fraction of a dollar, we might expect few light users to argue for tiered pricing. The cost of implementation might swamp the benefit to the smaller users, and there is considerable evidence that flat-rate pricing has encouraged experimentation by users, and thus driven innovation and the creation of fresh value. On the other hand, if the cross-subsidy were (say) $10, it would be hard to imagine that flat-rate pricing could survive. If the cross-subsidy were substantial, there would be a strong temptation in a competitive market for one ISP to offer a cheaper price tier targeted to the large number of small users, leaving the other ISP only with the expensive larger users. That ISP would have to increase prices accordingly, and price tiers would emerge.

Again, it is hard to get exact values for costs, and somewhat challenging to get information about the distribution of usage by different broadband customers. The Sandvine data quoted above suggest that the mean usage is approximately 20 GB per month, but the medial usage is only around 5 GB per month. If usage costs $0.20/GB, this means the medial user is paying around $3/month to subsidize the heavy users. Reasonable people could disagree about what conclusion to draw from this $3/month number, but it seems large enough to pay attention to, but not so big that usage tiers will *necessarily* emerge. As evidence of this ambivalence, we see differences in approach in the USA and abroad. For example, in Australia there are relatively high per GB charges, presumably because a significant portion of the content is delivered via expensive inter-continental undersea cables.

16.5.1 What is Reasonable?

We have argued that negotiation to recover operating costs related to usage is reasonable. We called these transport payments. We observed that negotiations leading to fees that seem unrelated to transport costs would raise the concern that transport providers were using market power to extract a part of the content payments.

One way to mitigate this concern would be for the industry to provide additional information to make interconnection negotiations more transparent. First, better information about costs and how those relate to usage would support a more informed debate over what usage-based fees might be appropriate. Second, information about traffic trends and distributions (e.g., about how heavy and light users differ) would help verify cost claims.

Finally, information about actual interconnection agreements, which may include public commitments to interconnection or peering policies, may help in better understanding how interconnection markets are changing and what the emerging norms are. Because there are significant shared and non-traffic-sensitive costs that need to be recovered, and because the details of interconnection agreements may convey sensitive strategic information, we are not surprised that ISPs are reticent to share publicly the terms that are negotiated. If needed, the proprietary information might be shared with regulators with adequate disclosure restrictions to protect confidentiality.

In each case, we hope that industry and independent analysts will take the lead in expanding the information available to all stakeholders, since, ultimately, we think that the market may do a better job of ensuring transparency than regulatory interventions. However, we recognize that more activist interconnection policies may be needed in the future if clear evidence of market failures surfaces. Our policy recommendations focus on enhancing transparency because we are not convinced by the evidence we have seen to date that more activist policies (e.g., direct regulation of Internet interconnection) is warranted; and equally importantly, even if we were to see a need for such regulation, we are concerned any such regulation might cause more harm than good. The Internet ecosystem is evolving rapidly and the expansion in interconnection agreements seems consistent with the need to accommodate new types of business relationships and service requirements.

16.6   CONCLUSION

The norm of revenue-neutral peering has been breaking down for some time, and is being replaced by less constrained negotiation about paid peering, partial transit and other such variants. Paid peering may increase the number of direct peering connections and reduce transit costs, thus reducing ISP operating cost, but it also may increase transaction costs around peering agreements. The emergence of new norms for such contracts may help ameliorate such costs.

The emergence of networks that deliver high-volume commercial content (such as network CD in our discussion) raise potential concerns about the market power of both content delivery and access networks, given that there need to be payments for both content and transport flowing within the ecosystem. Interconnection between networks like our examples CD and A are a type of peering agreement insofar as routing is restricted (the traffic is destined for A's 'eyeball' subscribers), but with very asymmetric (one-way) traffic flows that contribute to significant traffic/usage-related costs (C_A) for the access network. The need to recover these costs provides a reasonable economic efficiency rationale for network CD paying network A. However, if network A has sufficient market (bargaining) power, there is a risk that network A might be able to extract excessive payments from network CD, potentially even extracting content-related payments and thus leveraging its market power beyond network services.

While this remains a valid concern, the current complex mesh of ISP interconnections that include multi-connected content delivery and ISP networks bound together with a mix of peering, transit, paid-peering and partial transit interconnection agreements constrains the ability of access ISPs to over-charge content delivery networks. For example, the price of competitive transit services provides a soft upper bound for what content delivery networks might be induced to pay access networks. Additionally, today's content delivery networks operate thousands of servers with multiple interconnection points that provide dynamic flexibility for how these networks inject their traffic into interconnection partner networks, and thereby provide them with bargaining leverage to influence costs incurred by interconnection partner networks.

To the extent access ISPs do not recover their incremental traffic costs (C_A) from upstream content delivery networks (or absorb those costs from their profits), the access ISPs may look to new usage-based pricing models to recover those costs. Anecdotal evidence on usage patterns and network costs suggests that there are significant costs that may need to be recovered, and could justifiably support the emergence of usage-based tiered pricing, but the costs are not so significant (yet) as to imply that such tiered pricing is necessary. Its emergence is likely to hinge, in part, on the implicit subsidy from light to heavy users that is implicit in flat-rate uniform pricing. However, any significant move to usage-based pricing will attract significant public attention in the USA (where consumers have become accustomed to flat-rate pricing) and will raise justifiable regulatory concern about the potential abuse of market power by access ISPs in both the retail and wholesale interconnection markets.

This poses a difficult challenge for regulatory policy-makers. Our analysis suggests that we ought to focus first on improving transparency into the workings of the Internet ecosystem in general, interconnection markets more specifically. We identified three categories of information that would contribute to improved transparency: (1) information about industry-wide cost models; (2) information about traffic trends and distributions; and (3) information about terms and conditions of interconnection agreements. Better data in these areas will contribute to the public debate, even if some categories of information are deemed too sensitive to be shared except under some restrictive confidentiality protections. This will help provide a foundation on which a better assessments of the need for further regulations might be made; should such a need be identified, this information will also be instrumental in helping to craft suitable rules.

NOTES

*   The authors would like to acknowledge support from NSF Awards 1040020 and 1040023, and the MIT Communications Futures Program (http://cfp.mit.edu). All opinions expressed herein are those of the authors alone.
1. Because not everyone needs to make telephone calls at the same time, source and destination nodes can share peak capacity that only needs to be large enough to meet the demand at the traffic peak. This resource sharing, which relies on the statistical multiplexing of supply and demand, is a key feature of the network planning.
2. Many transmission (link) technologies have a significant fixed cost component that does not vary significantly with link capacity or traffic. Thus transmission costs typically scale sublinearly with capacity (scale economies).
3. A positive network externality arises when the value of adding an additional subscriber to a network is greater than just the value realized by that subscriber from joining the network. A telephone network that allows a subscriber to call anyone anywhere is more valuable to each subscriber than would be a telephone network that only allowed each subscriber to call people in a single town.
4. For general discussions of network interconnection economics, see Armstrong (2002).
5. For a discussion of the need to rationalize intercarrier compensation by adopting bill-and-keep, see DeGraba (2000).
6. An AS is the unit of administrative policy in the Internet, comprised of one or more networks that are controlled by a common network administrator. An AS might be a university, a business enterprise, or a part of a division.
7. Internet exchanges where multiple providers interconnect to exchange traffic can be used for both peering and transit agreements. In the early days of the Internet, much of the traffic was exchanged at public interexchange points such as MAE-East and MAE-West where a large number of networks physically interconnected to exchange traffic without compensation. These early exchanges had relatively open interconnection policies and provided an inexpensive way for smaller ISPs to expand connectivity. However, they lacked mechanisms to provide incentives to provide capacity to deliver traffic from the public interexchange points. As a consequence, these public exchanges suffered from significant congestion. The bulk of Internet traffic subsequently shifted to bilateral interconnection agreements.
8. See, for example, Laffont et al. (2001, 2003), Greenstein (2004) and Besen et al. (2001).
9. For further discussion of how interconnection markets have been changing, see Farratin et al. (2007).
10. For example, the typical residential broadband service offers a peak data rate in the tens of Mbps, whereas many enterprise customers have access connections offering thousands of Mbps or higher data rates.
11. For example, the current version of the Border Gateway Protocol (BGP) used to route traffic between AS is Version 4, adopted in 2006, which updated and added functionality to earlier versions of BGP.
12. This estimate is for residential traffic on fixed access networks in North America during the first half of 2013 (see Sandvine, 2013).
13. Since the time of writing, Netflix appears to have changed its content delivery approach, but it is not clear precisely what it is doing. It is to be expected that such changes may occur.
14. Basic telecommunication services are regulated as common carrier services under Title II of the United States Communications Act of 1934 (as amended). Over time, the Federal Communications Commission (FCC) has grappled with defining the boundary between what services should or should not be regulated as basic telecommunication services (see, e.g., Brock, 1994). In a succession of decisions since 2002, the FCC sought to reclassify broadband services as 'information services' rather than basic telecommunication services. By so doing, they opened the possibility of shifting to a more light-handed form of regulation that could be more technology neutral, and evolve beyond the silo-based legacy regulatory models that characterized traditional telecommunications and cable television regulation. For a discussion

of evolving broadband policy, see 'Notice of Proposed Rulemaking, In the Matter of Preserving the Open Internet and Broadband Industry Practices', Federal Communications Commission, GN Docket No. 09-191 and WC Docket No. 07-52, released 22 October 2009 (hereafter, NPRM, 2009).

15. First Amendment 'free speech' concerns induce a special level of concern for content-based regulation in the USA, providing additional motivation for separating content and conduit regulation as much as possible. Traditional content regulation includes such things as program access rules (e.g., to ensure that incumbents make programming available to other distribution channels), public programming obligations (e.g., children and news programming), and censorship rules (e.g., pornography restrictions).

16. For example, a significant goal of the Telecommunications Act of 1996, which embodied significant reforms to the Communications Act of 1934, was to significantly expand the scope of competition in all telecommunication services and provide a roadmap for further deregulation. In the years that followed, talk turned to notions of layered regulation that would be more appropriate for the emerging world of facilities-based competition between multi-service platform networks offered by telephone, cable television, and potential new entrants (see, e.g., Werbach, 2002; Friedan, 2004; Sicker et al., 2007).

17. See, for example, Jordan (2007) who relates the layered regulation and network neutrality debates; or Lehr et al. (2007).

18. For example, some have argued that access ISPs have a terminating monopoly because subscribers face switching costs. This source of market power might exist even if the market for selecting a broadband service provider is competitive (see NPRM, 2009, note 15 *supra* at paragraph 73). For a critique of this view, see 'Testimony of Jeffrey Eisenach, PhD, Before the Subcommittee on Communications, Technology and the Internet, Committee on Energy and Commerce, United States House of Representatives, 21 April 2010'.

19. Content-specific costs include the costs of producing and promoting the content, and are logically separable from the costs of distributing the content via the Internet. One might also imagine there is a value to consumers in viewing the content, irrespective of the medium via which the content is viewed (in a movie theater vs at home).

20. The separation is not precise because the way in which content is delivered may impact its quality, and hence its value to the end user. For example, high-definition content may be down-coded for delivery to the small screen without deterioration in the user experience; alternatively, increased latency or congestion may severely adversely impact the user experience.

21. See 'ESPN charges broadband firms for access to ESPN3.com content', *Investors.com*, 24 August 2010, accessed 15 April 2015 at http://news.investors.com/technology/082410-544885-espn-charges-broadband-firms-for-access-to-espn3com-site.htm.

22. We see no evidence from their published annual reports that content delivery networks are earning significant supernormal profits. Moreover, anecdotal evidence suggests that the prices for content delivery networks have followed the downward trend in transit pricing, and are quite modest. See, for example, 'Internet transit pricing-historical and projected', accessed 15 April 2015 at http://drpeering.net/white-papers/Internet-Transit-Pricing-Historical-And-Projected.php, *DrPeering International*, 2010, and 'Data from Q1 shows video CDN pricing stabilizing, down 25% in 2010', *Streamingmedia.com*, 2010, accessed 15 April 2015 at http://blog.streamingmedia.com/the_business_of_online_vi/2010/06/data-from-q1-shows-video-cdn-pricing-stabilizing-should-be-down-25-for-the-year.html.

23. To the extent either may occur, we assume that these flow either via the content–producer/owner relationship to the content delivery networks or via the subscriber relationship to the access ISP.

24. This measurement in terms of cost/GB is perhaps confusing. As written, it is not a *rate* but a volume. That is, the implication is that it costs the ISP (say) $0.10 to deliver a GB of data, independent of rate. This characterization is obviously a simplification, but it implies that the cost to deliver a GB in one unit of time at one rate, or the cost to deliver that same GB at half the rate over twice the time is more or less the same. Another way of saying this is that $0.10/GB is a contraction of '$0.10/month for each GB/month'.

25. An estimate of CAD0.08/GB is given in 'What does a gig cost?', *Michael Geist*, 6 April, accessed 15 April 2015 at http://www.michaelgeist.ca/content/view/5727/125/ and 'What does a gigabyte cost, revisited', *Michael Geist*, 29 July, accessed 15 April 2015 at http://www.michaelgeist.ca/content/view/5952/125/.

26. In contrast, these numbers will not apply to rural ISPs that may be far from peering and transit interconnection points, or smaller networks, wherever they are located.

27. See 'Re: Ex parte, GN Docket No. 09-191, WC Docket No. 07-52', accessed 15 April 2015 at https://prodnet.www.neca.org/publicationsdocs/wwpdf/051211netflix.pdf.

28. Usage costs are expected to grow sublinearly with traffic. Also, median per customer usage has grown even faster, from 6.0 GB (2011) to 16.0 GB (2013). The high ratio of mean-to-median indicates a heavy-tailed distribution, with some users being very heavy indeed (see Sandvine, 2011, 2013).

29. See Sirbu and Agyapong (2011) for an alternate model of the relationship between content delivery networks and access ISPs that focuses on how routing/interconnection choices might influence total costs and potential payment flows.

30. See Dhamdhere et al. (2010) for an interesting alternative model for interconnection.
31. We noted the case above of ESPN3, which had content of sufficient popularity that it bargained with access networks such as Comcast to pay ESPN3 a per customer fee, which presumably is then passed on to the customers.
32. See 'Internet peering, paid peering and Internet transit', *DrPeering International*, 14 January, accessed 15 April2015athttp://drpeering.net/AskDrPeering/blog/articles/Ask_DrPeering/Entries/2011/1/14_Internet_Peering,_Paid_Peering_and_Internet_Transit.html.
33. The internal cost C_O of this service is low: only the load on the router backplane passing the traffic from one port to another. Hence the name 'single-hop'; this configuration has also been called 'backplane access'.
34. In the past, such control might have been limited to choosing between hot or cold potato routing. In hot (cold) potato routing the source ISP hands over the traffic sooner (later), thereby maximizing (minimizing) use of the destination ISP's resources. An Alcatel-Lucent white paper argues that the rise of large and increasingly complex content delivery networks may allow them to suck transit revenues out of the Internet ecosystem (see Alcatel-Lucent, 2011).
35. See 'A study of 28 peering policies', *DrPeering International*, accessed 15 April 2015 at http://drpeering.net/white-papers/Peering-Policies/A-Study-of-28-Peering-Policies.html.
36. Nine of the 28 peering agreements included a requirement for traffic ratios. ISPs with traffic ratio requirements include AboveNet, Comcast, Verizon, ATT, CableVision and Quest. Several of these are what we classify as access networks, which supports the hypothesis that these networks are especially concerned with how peering agreements with content delivery networks are negotiated.
37. Traffic that exceeds a tier's allotted volume may be priced at a pre-specified coverage rate, or the customer may be temporarily boosted into a higher-volume tier, or the traffic might be shaped (subject to reduced data rates) or even dropped.
38. Zero rating of select services is deemed contentious. Some promote it as a way to lower the price for broadband and expanding access, while others view it as a mechanism for access providers to extract revenues from content providers. For a discussion of the debate, see, for example, 'Zero rating: the FCC's war on affordable broadband', *TechPolicyDaily*, 26 May 2010, accessed 31 May 2015 at http://www.techpolicydaily.com/internet/fccs-war-on-zero-rating/ or 'Why "zero rating" is the new battleground in net neutrality debate', *CBC News*, 7 April 2015, accessed 31 May 2015 at http://www.cbc.ca/news/business/why-zero-rating-is-the-new-battleground-in-net-neutrality-debate-1.3015070.

REFERENCES

Alcatel-Lucent (2011), 'Analysis: Content peering and the Internet economy', Alcatel-Lucent white paper, 19 April 2011, accessed 15 April 2015 at http://www2.alcatel-lucent.com/blogs/techzine/2011/analysis-content-peering-and-the-internet-economy/.

Armstrong, M. (2002), 'The theory of access pricing and interconnection', in M. Cave, S.K. Majumdar and I. Vogelsang (eds), *Handbook of Telecommunications Economics, Volume I*, London and New York: Elsevier.

Besen, S., P. Milgrom, B. Mitchell and P. Srinagesh (2001), 'Advances in routing technologies and Internet peering agreements', *American Economic Review*, **91** (2), 292–6.

Brock, G. (1994), *Telecommunications Policy for the Information Age: From Monopoly to Competition*, Cambridge, MA: Harvard University Press.

Clark, D. (2008), 'A simple cost model for broadband access: What will video cost?', paper presented at the 36th Research Conference on Communication, Information, and Internet Policy, September, Arlington, VA: George Mason University.

DeGraba, P. (2000), 'Bill and keep at the central office as the efficient interconnection regime', *OPP Working Paper Series, No. 33*, Washington, DC: Federal Communications Commission, accessed 15 April 2015 at http://www.fcc.gov/working-papers/bill-and-keep-central-office-efficient-interconnection-regime.

Dhamdhere, A., C. Dovrolis and P. Francois (2010), 'A value-based framework for Internet peering agreements', in *Proceedings of 22nd International Teletraffic Congress (ITC 22)*, 7–9 September 2010, Amsterdam: IEEE, 1–8.

Faratin, P., D. Clark and P. Gilmore et al. (2007), 'Complexity of internet interconnections: Technology, incentives and implications for policy', paper presented at the 35th Research Conference on Communication, Information, and Internet Policy, September, Arlington, VA: George Mason University, accessed 15 April 2015 at http://ssrn.com/abstract=2115242.

Frieden, R. (2004), 'Adjusting the horizontal and vertical in telecommunications regulation: A comparison of the traditional and a new layered approach', *Federal Communication Law Journal*, **55** (207), 207–50.

Greenstein, S. (2004), 'The economic geography of Internet infrastructure in the United States', *CSIO Working Paper No. 0046*, Center for the Study of Industrial Organization, Northwestern University.

Jordan, S. (2007), 'A layered network approach to net neutrality', *International Journal of Communication*, **1**, 427–60.

Laffont, J.-J., S. Marcus, P. Rey and J. Tirole (2001), 'Internet peering', *The American Economic Review*, **91** (2), 287–91.

Laffont, J.-J., S. Marcus, P. Rey and J. Tirole (2003), 'Internet interconnection and the off-net pricing principle', *RAND Journal of Economics*, **34** (2), 370–90.

Lehr, W., J. Peha and S. Wilkie (eds) (2007), 'Special issue on network neutrality', *International Journal of Communication*, **1**, accessed 27 December 2015 at http://ijoc.org/ojs/index.php/ijoc/issue/view/1.

Sandvine (2011), *Global Internet Phenomena Report, Spring 2011*, accessed 15 April 2015 at: http://www.sandvine.com/news/global_broadband_trends.asp.

Sandvine (2013), *Global Internet Phenomena Report*, accessed 15 April 2015 at http://www.sandvine.com/news/global_broadband_trends.asp.

Sicker, D., J. Mindel and C. Cooper (2007), *The Internet Interconnection Conundrum: A Technology Policy Analysis of Service Provider Interconnection Issues*, Bloomington, IN: iUniverse.

Sirbu, M. and P. Agyapong (2011), 'Economic incentives in content-centric networking: A network operator's perspective', in *Proceedings of the 39th Research Conference on Communications, Information, and Internet Policy (TPRC)*, George Mason University, Arlington, VA, September 2011, accessed 15 April 2015 at http://ssrn.com/abstract=1979922.

Werbach, K. (2002), 'A layered model for Internet policy', *Journal of Telecommunications and High Technology Law*, **1**, 58–64.

PART IV

ECONOMICS AND MANAGEMENT OF APPLICATIONS AND SERVICES

17. Internet business strategies
Johann J. Kranz and Arnold Picot

17.1 INTRODUCTION

In business and beyond, the Internet has been a – if not *the* – most influential technological change within the last two decades. It has greatly affected traditional industries at the macro and micro levels. It has also created new markets such as online auctions, online gaming, search engines, social networks, online advertising, and digital marketplaces. In both new and old markets the Internet has changed traditional ways to gain competitive advantage. In particular, established firms struggle to adapt their business strategies and to reconfigure their value chains to embrace the opportunities offered by Internet-enabled information and communication technologies (ICTs). The fast and cost-efficient access to almost infinite amounts of data and information has affected almost every industrial sector, especially those business-to-business (B2B) and business-to-consumer (B2C) industries whose operations have been constrained by high transaction costs for gathering information, communicating, or controlling (Zerdick et al., 2000). Even stronger was the effect on markets whose goods can be digitally distributed. The Internet has not only emerged as an important distribution channel, it has also created new customer demands, made user-generated content globally accessible, and given rise to new forms of customer relationship and engagement.

Many established companies are challenged with the question of how to use the Internet as a complement to or even full transformation (Dosi and Galambos, 2013) of their offline business and capture appropriate value from their Internet activities. This has proven difficult for established firms as the Internet has usually intensified competition due to new rivals' entrance into formerly local or proprietary markets (Picot et al., 2008). Global communication networks enable companies to gain access to markets that were previously difficult to reach. Hence, customers have more choices and many markets have become more transparent (Teece, 2010). This is why today private and organizational customers possess more bargaining power. The shift from seller to buyer markets is reflected by customers who have more demanding expectations of product or service quality and less understanding for organization-related coordination problems such as long delivery times (Picot et al., 2008). Thus, higher levels of customer orientation and flexibility from suppliers are required. Given that the cost of ICT will further decline and their performance will continue to increase, the division of labor between organizations and within markets will intensify. Already today we can observe corporate boundaries to blur and in some cases even to dissolve (ibid.). The Internet and related ICTs are a trigger and enabler of co-opetitive inter-firm arrangements, meaning that firms simultaneously compete and collaborate with each other in different stages of the value chain (Bengtsson et al., 2010; Brandenburger and Nalebuff, 2011). Co-opetition is particularly prevalent in markets in which digitalization drives the convergence of multiple technologies and accelerates product life cycles (Gnyawali and Park, 2011). Competing and collaborating at the same time is a competitive option that helps firms to keep pace with rapidly changing customer needs and technological innovations by sharing intellectual property and resources (ibid.). Thereby, co-opetition reduces risks and uncertainty caused by the convergence of technologies and it can also serve as an instrument to set industry standards and to build platforms (Gomes-Casseres, 1994; Lei, 2003; Mione, 2009), both of which are powerful means to achieve market dominance.

'Platformization' is a new phenomenon especially widespread on the Internet (Economides and Katsamakas, 2006; Gawer and Cusumano, 2008; Ceccagnoli et al., 2012). Well-known examples of Internet platforms include trading platforms, auctions, web search, recruiting and dating services. Core elements of platforms are that (1) an intermediary links different groups of customers through a platform, creating a two- or multi-sided market, and (2) network externalities are present and decisive for a platform's success (Katz and Shapiro, 1994; Evans, 2003; Rochet and Tirole, 2003; Armstrong, 2006; Eisenmann et al., 2006, 2011). Another characteristic is complementary innovation by which a platform's functionality is extended (Gawer and Cusumano, 2008; Suarez and Kirtley, 2012). Facebook, for instance, opened its platform for third-party applications via an application programming interface (API) that allows others to offer a wide-range of new services based on the platform's core. As a result, a thriving ecosystem around Facebook's social network evolved that increased network effects and became a key differentiator.

The Internet also enables hybrid competitive strategies beyond cost and differentiation strategies. Using Internet technologies enables firms to reconfigure their value proposition and to differentiate themselves from competitors. While some companies may choose to use the Internet to offer an advanced and at the same time more efficient service (e.g., Cisco Systems; Tax and Brown, 1998) some may use it to 'mass customize' products (Salvador et al., 2009; Franke et al., 2010). Dell, for instance, revolutionized the computer industry by manufacturing individually configured PCs distributed solely over the Internet. Miadidas.com allows customers to create their own shoes and on Mymuesli.com, cereal aficionados can mix their individual muesli. Dell's example is especially worth a closer look. In contrast to Porter's (1985) perspective, Dell managed to gain a competitive edge by delivering differentiated and moderately priced products to customers. It did so by embracing opportunities enabled by the Internet, such as global sourcing, virtualization, or on-demand manufacturing at low transaction costs. Beyond these, Dell used the Internet as single distribution channel. Dell could do so as it did not have the constraints of upsetting existing distribution partners or resellers, which made it extremely hard for established competitors to imitate Dell's business model. Interacting directly with customers over the Internet gave Dell a further competitive advantage. Dell learned about changing consumer needs faster and was thus able to provide superior service and value.

Dell's case makes obvious that in the digital era choosing an appropriate business model is crucial. Together with many other examples this case shows that to a very large degree the strategic and market-oriented innovation potential of the Internet has not been exploited by incumbent companies but by newly founded firms. Driven by an open spirit, lower costs of market entry, as well as network effects, new players conquered new, so far unexplored business opportunities throughout different markets, including B2C, B2B, consumer-to-consumer (C2C) and government to business/consumer (G2B and G2C) relationships. Start-ups and innovative entrepreneurs were more suited to experimenting with the vast prospects provided by the new Internet technologies compared to most existing firms with their specific path dependency. In this way and in a short period of time, new industries and new large and leading companies emerged mainly in developed countries, above all the USA.

In this chapter, we particularly focus on the question of how established firms and dot-coms can leverage Internet technologies and do business on the Internet to gain competitive advantage. In the next section we elaborate on how the concepts of business strategy, business model, and business process modeling are theoretically and practically interrelated to each other and show why doing business on the Internet is different from doing business 'offline'. Section 17.3 looks at the strategic properties of the Internet. Section 17.4 outlines how Internet business models can be classified, and section 17.5 discusses the elements at the core of an Internet business strategy. The chapter concludes with a synopsis of critical success factors in the Internet business and provides an outlook on the future of doing business on the Internet.

17.2 DISENTANGLING BUSINESS STRATEGY FROM THE BUSINESS MODEL CONCEPT

Since its emergence, the business model concept has gained significant momentum in the domains of Internet economy and information systems (Al-Debei and Avison, 2010), strategic management (Zott et al., 2011) and innovation and technology management (Teece, 2010). Many works of scholars and business practitioners alike aim at defining the concept and integrating it within the extant literature. The question of how to relate the business model concept to business strategy and business process modeling has attracted considerable attention in particular. A business model typically provides answers to the following questions (Morris et al., 2005):

- Offering factors: how to create value?
- Market factors: who to create value for?
- Internal capability factors: what is the source of competence?
- Competitive strategy factors: how to position ourselves?
- Economic factors: how to make money?
- Personal/investor factors: what are the time, scope, and size ambitions?

Accordingly, Osterwalder and Pigneur (2009, p. 14) state that 'a business model describes the rationale of how an organization creates, delivers and captures value'. Based on this definition they developed a framework known as the business model canvas (Al-Debei, 2010 provides an overview of other definitions). This framework consists of nine elements covering the four key components: customer, offer, infrastructure, and finance (Figure 17.1).

As depicted in Figure 17.1, customers are attracted through a company's value proposition; that is, how a company's products or services create value for customers and satisfy their needs (e.g., cheap flights offered by no-frills airlines). The value proposition is conveyed to the customer through communication and distribution channels (e.g., booking

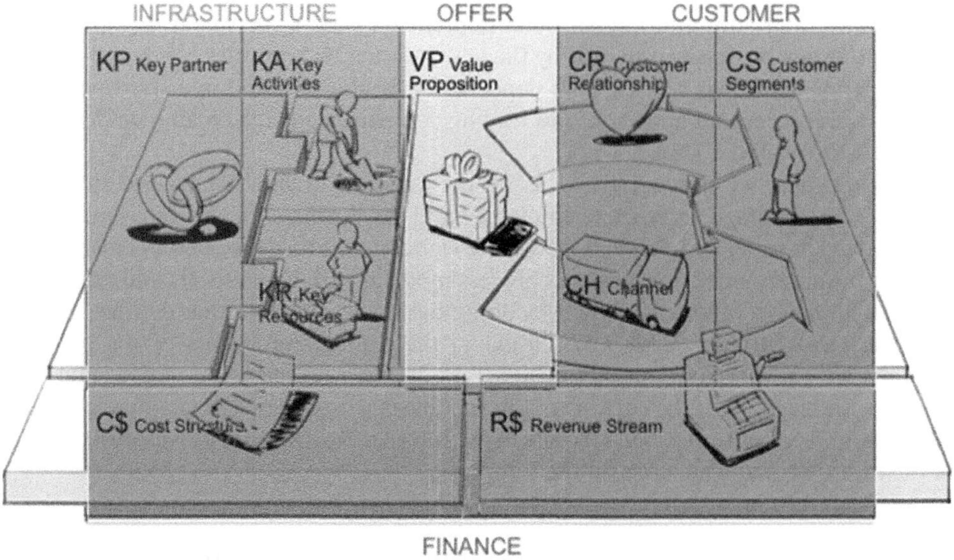

Source: Based on Osterwalder and Pigneur (2009).

Figure 17.1 The business model canvas

exclusively over the Internet) and based on the value proposition it is aimed to establish a long-term customer relationship with each customer segment (e.g., social media). Based on the value proposition revenue streams are generated (e.g., ticket sales, value-added services). Delivering customer value requires access to key resources (e.g., dynamic pricing including the necessary data) and the performance of a number of key activities (e.g., fleet maintenance). Through key partnerships some of these activities can be outsourced and some assets can be acquired externally (e.g., cash management). The costs associated with a business model are summarized in the cost structure component (Osterwalder and Pigneur, 2009).

After having established a common understanding of the business model concept and its components, we now shed light on its relation to corporate strategy and business process modeling. Business process models are used to analyze and improve organizational procedures by increasing process efficiency and quality (see Scheer and Nüttgens, 2000). Thus, the focus of modeling business processes is to support decision-making at the operational level ('how') while business models support strategic decision-making ('what') (Gordijn et al., 2000). The demarcation between business models on the one hand and corporate strategy on the other hand is more controversial. According to Porter (1985), a strategy depicts how a firm seeks to position itself in a given market by either implementing a cost leadership, differentiation, or focus strategy. Some scholars use the terms 'business strategy' and 'business model' synonymously (Leem et al., 2004; Kallio et al., 2006), while others regard business models as part of a business strategy (Chesbrough and Rosenbloom, 2002; Shafer et al., 2005). More specifically, they understand a business model as an abstraction of a firm's strategy that is applicable to more

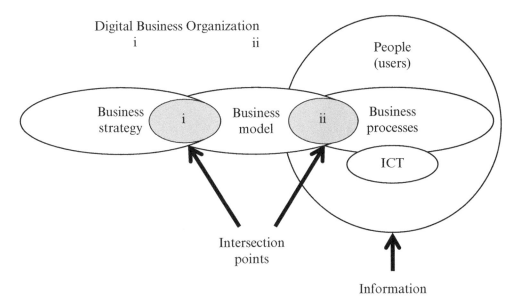

Digital Business Organization

Source: Based on Al-Debei (2010, p. 88).

Figure 17.2   Business model intersection points

than one company (e.g., Seddon, 2004). This means that two firms may have different strategies, but employ the same business model (Burkhart et al., 2011). Literature further proposes a third – integrative – perspective. According to this view, business models and corporate strategy are interrelated, however distinct from each other. While a business model addresses how a company creates value and revenues, strategy focuses on a company's competitive positioning in a given market (Magretta, 2002; Seddon et al., 2004). Correspondingly, business models are viewed as a theoretical layer between corporate strategy and business processes and their supportive information systems (Figure 17.2) (Morris et al., 2005; Osterwalder et al., 2005), which has become necessary because of 'the shift that the business world experienced from the traditional ways of doing business to the new ways of digital business, which feature a high level of complexity and rapid change' (Al-Debei, 2010, p. 87).

As depicted in Figure 17.2, there are two transitional points. In the first intersection point (i), the rather generic strategy is translated into a more concrete business logic defining how a firm aims to create value, generate revenues, finance its operations, and establish collaborations with other firms to achieve its strategic goals (Al-Debei and Avison, 2010). At the second intersection point (ii), a business process model is derived based on the business model. The process model specifies at the operational level the corporate activities necessary to perform in order to provide customers with a product or service. Further, it defines the requirements for how information systems can support these tasks. Although business models serve as bases for the configuration of business processes and information systems they do not specify processes and information systems in detail. Some degree of flexibility regarding their implementations remains.

17.3   STRATEGIC PROPERTIES OF THE INTERNET

Internet business strategies and derived business models need to consider that doing business on the Internet is distinct from offline business due to the heavy impact of particular properties of the Internet, which will be briefly outlined in the following (see Afuah and Tucci, 2007, pp. 32).

17.3.1   Distribution Channel

The Internet has become a powerful distribution channel for goods that can be digitized, such as music, video, information, software, tickets, brokerage, insurance, or vouchers. In case of tangible products that cannot be distributed through the Internet, information about their features can be made available on the Internet. For many industries, such as personal computers, media, and insurance, the Internet has emerged as a principal distribution channel that has heavily affected traditional distribution strategies.

17.3.2   Scalability

Many successful Internet business models are scalable in a business sense. This means that serving an additional customer or producing an additional unit of a product increases the associated revenues proportionally greater than its associated costs. For example, the expected value of an additional search engine request or an additional user of an online network outweighs the costs by far.

17.3.3   Ubiquity

In an informational sense ubiquity is 'access to information unconstrained by time and space' (Junglas and Watson, 2006, p. 578). Thanks to the global rise of mobile broadband and mobile access devices, using the Internet is no longer bound to wires. This enables a broad range of ubiquitous services in various sectors as diverse as manufacturing, media, healthcare, logistics, and commerce.

17.3.4   Universality

Universality refers to the Internet's ability to both enlarge and shrink the world. The Internet enlarges the world as no matter where a product is created and who creates it, the product can be offered worldwide. In another respect, the Internet also shrinks the world in that it enables global collaboration and exchange relationships.

17.3.5   Mediating Technology

The Internet is a mediating technology that facilitates exchange relationships between parties distributed in time and space. It either interconnects market actors or employees intra-organizationally, in which case it is called 'intranet'. Due to its universality and global accessibility, the Internet is also an important mediator in organizational exchange relationships leading to simultaneous re- and dis-intermediation. While the Internet makes it easier for sellers of goods to manage transactions with buyers independently (dis-intermediation), it also leads to the emergence of new forms of intermediaries (e.g., trust centers) and the lowering of coordination costs, which makes it more efficient to obtain intermediary services from the market (re-intermediation).

17.3.6 Network Externalities

A technology or product whose value increases with the number of users exhibits positive network externalities (Katz and Shapiro, 1994). This holds true for the Internet. The more people are using the Internet the greater the value of the network. This also applies for networks within the Internet. Besides these direct network effects, there are also indirect network effects in the sense that the more people join a network the more complementary products for these networks exist, which in turn makes the technology or product more attractive (Zerdick et al., 2000). However, network externalities can also be negative. Consider a job placement site, for instance, on which firms compete for the most qualified workers. The more firms use this site, the fiercer the competition among firms, resulting in negative (same-side) network externalities.

17.3.7 Customer Engagement

The Internet has changed the traditional role of customers. As customers' self-conception changes they are no longer pure recipients or beneficiaries, but become an active element in the value creation process. First, customers expect to communicate directly with firms to voice suggestions or criticism and to raise service requests. Many companies hence engage in communities or social networks to strengthen customer relationships and to obtain feedback and customer insights. However, because consumer expectations regarding authenticity are high, companies have to be careful not to provoke negative publicity. Second, the Internet enables consumers to easily create and make their own content globally available. User-generated content can be used by firms in many ways, including reviews, videos, question–answer databases, blogging, forums, or product wikis. Third, firms can tap into users' capabilities for innovation around their products or services. Widely applied approaches for involving customers in value creation processes are the lead-user approach (Von Hippel, 2005), the provision of application programming interfaces (APIs, e.g., Flickr API, Google Maps API), or crowdsourcing (Howe, 2006).

17.3.8 Information Asymmetry

In many markets the Internet reduces information asymmetries. These occur whenever one party in a transaction has more relevant information than the other party. As consumers share experiences (e.g., product prices or quality) globally over the Internet and product information can be accessed online, the information asymmetries between buyers and sellers have diminished. At the same time, however, large online service providers in particular can leverage individual 'digital trace data' on consumers to manipulate information in ways that are hidden to consumers. This information can be used to personalize offerings and to fine-tune actions based on individual customer preferences (Bharadwaj et al., 2013).

17.3.9 Transaction Cost Reducer

Transaction costs involve the costs for searching, negotiating, writing, monitoring, and enforcing contracts associated with a transaction (Williamson, 1985; Picot et al., 1996). Owing to the Internet's properties, such as universality, distribution channel, low-cost standard, and information asymmetry, the Internet decreases transaction costs substantially. The Internet makes finding information easier, which minimizes search costs and diminishes information asymmetries, which in turn reduces costs for negotiating, monitoring, and enforcement.

17.4 TAXONOMY OF INTERNET BUSINESS MODELS

A large variety of Internet business models have emerged since the mid-1990s. Most business activities on the Internet are covered by five categories: content, connection and communication, community, coordination, and commerce (Afuah and Tucci, 2007; Wirtz et al., 2010). As many business models rely on hybrid or integrated versions, these categories are not mutually exclusive (Wirtz et al., 2010). Although the value propositions and revenue models of these five activities differ, they are all based on the exchange of information via the Internet to some extent and are therefore influenced by the properties of the Internet. Concerning revenue models on the Internet, several common direct and indirect forms of generating revenue have emerged (Table 17.1).

17.4.1 Content

Content-oriented business models deliver information, games, movies or related products over the Internet. Companies offering entertainment heavily capitalize on the Internet's properties of universality, mediating technology, and ubiquity. Players of massively multiplayer online games (MMOGs) like *World of Warcraft*, for example, can interact simultaneously with thousands of other players worldwide. Media companies providing information depend on the Internet as a distribution channel and mediating technology. Their value proposition is to collect, select, compile, remix, distribute, and/or present content online in a user-friendly and convenient way. Digital technologies had a

Table 17.1 Typical Internet business revenue models

	Direct Revenues		Indirect Revenues
Usage-dependent	Usage-independent		
	Non-recurring	Recurring	
Transaction fees	Admission fees	Subscription fees	Advertising fees
Value-added service fees	Donations		Monetization of online behavioral data
License fees	Crowdfunding		

Sources: Mertens et al. (2007); Zerdick et al. (2000).

tremendous impact on how content providers create and capture value. New players have diminished the power of established gatekeepers and caused dis-intermediation finding new ways to create value. While many companies offering information still struggle to find a sustainable revenue model on the Internet beyond indirect, transaction-independent online advertising, entertainment-oriented business models have increasingly found such sustainable revenue streams such as subscription (e.g., Spotify, Netflix, *World of Warcraft*), individualized online advertising (e.g., Hulu.com), or pay-per-view services (e.g., Apple iTunes).

However, information providers could achieve success in the balance between subscription and advertising. Since March 2011 *The New York Times*, for instance, has adopted a paid-access model. This model allows reading a particular number of articles each month for free before readers have to pay. In October 2012, *The New York Times* had almost 600000 paid digital subscribers (*The Economist*, 2012). Although the Internet traffic dropped by around 20 percent, resulting in decreased online advertising revenues, the additional revenues from digital subscriptions could well make up for the losses in advertising.

17.4.2 Connection and Communication

Connection-based Internet business models provide physical network infrastructure and/or allow communication or participation in communities. Companies that provide consumers physical interconnections with the Internet or enable consumers to conveniently put content online are Internet service providers (ISPs), or providers of web hosting or 'infrastructure as a service'. These firms typically generate direct revenues on a subscription, time, or volume basis. While markets for physical Internet access are increasingly commoditized with shrinking profit margins, providers of virtual interconnections enabling users to connect to other people in online networks or to communicate by e-mail, text or video chats, or Voice-over-IP could capture much of the value added. These services capitalize on the Internet properties: time moderator, low-cost standard, infinite virtual capacity, and universality. The providers' business models of communication services and communities are primarily based on indirect revenue streams, predominantly online advertising, but direct revenues such as subscription fees are also increasingly common. Often providers combine indirect and direct revenue streams, employing a 'freemium' model that charges consumers for premium services while the basic service remains free (Anderson, 2009).

17.4.3 Context

As online information is growing fast, providers of context-oriented services help users to find individually relevant information rather than creating content themselves. The value proposition of these services is to reduce complexity and to structure the inevitably unstructured Internet. Prominent examples of these services are search engine providers like Google or Bing, which assist users in identifying websites that satisfy their particular needs. Their revenue streams are usually indirect, resting on (targeted) online advertising or commissions.

17.4.4 Commerce

Electronic commerce is defined as a digital trade transaction including the stages information, initiation, negotiation, clearing and delivery using computer networks; that is, the Internet (Bons et al., 1998). Buying and selling information, products and services over the Internet are globally increasing at an estimated rate of 19 percent per annum and sales are expected to reach about US$1 trillion in 2013 (Khan et al., 2011). The Internet's universality, ubiquity, and low access costs allow organizations and individuals to trade products and services worldwide with minimal transaction costs. The most common forms of e-commerce are B2C (e.g., Amazon, Groupon), B2B (e.g., Covisint), business-to-administration (B2A), or consumer-to-consumer (C2C; e.g., eBay). The value proposition of firms like Amazon or eBay is to offer a large variety of goods or services and handle transactions cost-efficiently for sellers and buyers. As price competition in e-commerce is fierce, logistics are complex, and handling of returns is expensive, online merchants increasingly seek to foster indirect revenue streams (commission based) replacing direct revenues from online sales.

17.5 CORE ELEMENTS OF AN INTERNET BUSINESS STRATEGY

In the quest for identifying an adequate Internet business strategy, both established and dot-com firms have to consider how the Internet's specific properties can be best leveraged for their business models and how the Internet affects a particular industry's structure. Many firms erroneously thought that defining a business model solely includes the question of how to provide customers value. However, it is important that firms also think of how to generate revenues and which core capabilities and resources are necessary and how they can be protected from imitation.

Therefore, defining an Internet business strategy that leverages the Internet to gain competitive advantage requires a thorough analysis of the Internet's effect on industry structures. While some industries are affected to a lesser extent, some sectors have been heavily shaken up. In the latter case, entire value chains were impacted and firms were forced to adapt their business models and strategies accordingly. Although the Internet affects each industry in particular ways, some general observations can be made. Employing Porter's (2008) five forces of competition, we outline the Internet's influence on industry structures in general.

17.5.1 Internet's Impact on Industry Structure

According to Porter (2001), industry structures are characterized by five competitive forces: the intensity of rivalry among existing competitors, the barriers to entry for new competitors, the threat of substitute products or services, the bargaining power of suppliers, and the bargaining power of buyers. It is suggested that these five forces determine the profitability of an average competitor.

While the Internet has created some new markets, its largest impact has been on old industries where it pushed the reconfiguration of value chains. In particular, industries that once were constrained by high costs for gathering information, communication, or bargaining have been affected. Take, for instance, the market for insurance. Hitherto, consumers had to gather information and obtain customized offers by contacting a local salesperson. Depending on the effort consumers were willing to make they had more or less offers from different insurance companies. However, gaining a complete market overview was almost impossible even with the help of brokers. Today, consumers have the opportunity to check and compare diverse offerings directly and obtain customized offers instantly over the Internet. As a result, buyers of insurance have more bargaining power as the Internet reduces information asymmetries and transaction costs. Established insurance companies have created extensive branch networks with mostly self-employed branch managers over the years. With the advent of direct insurance companies that exclusively offered insurance over the Internet, established firms had to adjust their strategies and business models by, for example, capitalizing on customer relationships, an asset that direct insurers did not have. Matching their business models with competitive strategies in an innovative way was a necessary response to the new industry structure resulting from amplified price competition and greater power of consumers.

No matter which industry, the five forces determine how the economic value of a product, technology, or service is shared between competitors in this market on the one hand, and buyers, suppliers, substitutes and potential new market entrants on the other hand. As mentioned, the Internet affects industries in different ways, but some trends are generalizable for several markets, as depicted in Figure 17.3.

Many established industries have been changed significantly by Internet technology and the unique properties of the Internet. Above all, the Internet decreased the overall profitability as Internet technology allowed more competitors to enter markets in a cost-efficient way. Such market entry is facilitated first because the Internet is a low-cost standard and second because once obligatory complementary capabilities or resources have become irrelevant or easier to replicate, they lose their entry-deterring effect. For instance, many businesses required a local sales force. With the Internet, new market entrants could easily offer products and services globally and interact with customers without having to rely on local channels. The competition further increased as once geographically confined markets were directly accessible for new competitors. Moreover, keeping offerings and business models proprietary is more complicated on the Internet, which reduces opportunities for differentiation. In addition to more competitors entering markets, the power of buyers has increased. Through the Internet, information asymmetries between vendors and consumers are reduced, which negatively affects the potential for price discrimination (Acquisti and Varian, 2005; Hinz et al., 2011). However, as ever more data on consumers' online behavior are collected and data analytical methods (e.g., in-memory computing, MapReduce algorithm) rapidly improve, both price and search discrimination may become more prevalent (Mikians et al., 2012).

However, the Internet also has some positive impacts on industries' profitability as it improves market efficiency in diverse ways. For example, by augmenting distribution areas and the overall markets' size, making value chains more efficient and enabling new opportunities in the competition with emerging substitutes. Moreover, the power of intermediaries has declined as the Internet facilitates direct customer access. As the Internet decreases transaction costs it also allows firms to outsource particular tasks to specialized service providers at lower prices and lower risk. Hence, the Internet has

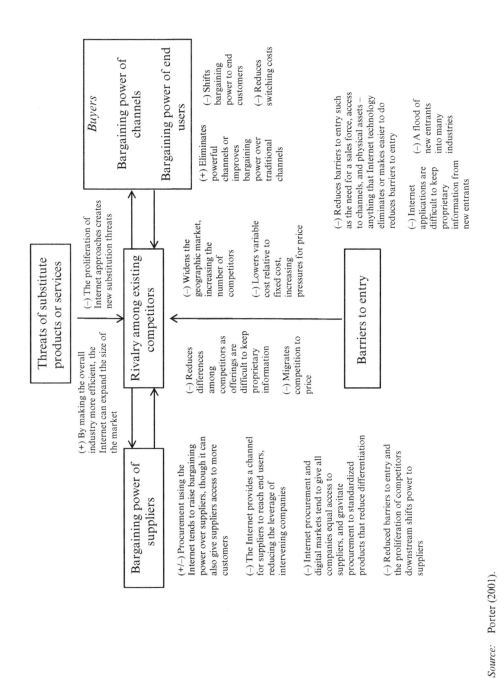

Source: Porter (2001).

Figure 17.3 Internet's influence on industry structure

facilitated firms to concentrate on their core competencies and to deliver value to consumers in a more cost-efficient way.

To summarize, in many established industries the Internet has increased consumers' power, meaning that they can capture many the Internet's benefits, such as lower transaction, marketing, distribution, and purchasing costs (Porter, 2001).

17.5.2   Sources of Competitive Advantage on the Internet

While the previous section focused on the Internet's impact on established industries' structures, we now examine how established and dot-com firms can create economically sustainable competitive advantages on the Internet.

Sustainable competitive advantage is referred to as a firm's capability to outperform the market, capitalizing on valuable and rare resources that facilitate creating value for consumers in a unique and superior fashion that is hard to imitate by current and future competitors (Simon, 1988). According to the resource-based view of the firm, the ability to protect special corporate resources from imitation is crucial in achieving and sustaining competitive advantage (Rumelt, 1984; Mahoney and Pandian, 1992). In general, firms can pursue three generic strategies: operating excellence, product leadership, and customer intimacy (Treacy and Wiersema, 1993). To achieve or maintain competitive advantage firms will have to outperform competitors in one or more of those areas.

The viability of each strategy depends on the extent to which a firm is able to protect its technology or business model from being replicated by rivals. Imitability refers to the ease of copying, substituting, or leapfrogging a technology or business model innovation (Teece, 1986). On the Internet, the risk of imitation is high as protecting intellectual property is intricate in most cases. When imitability is high, continuous innovations and improvements are requisite to keep ahead of competitors. By the time rivals equalize the advantage, a firm has to push its technology or innovation a step further. As this race is both risky and cost intensive, firms should seek to gain competitive advantage by leveraging other capabilities. These complementary assets are not directly associated to a particular technology or innovation but are required to profit from them (ibid.). These capabilities can include assets as diverse as company reputation, supply chain excellence, customer service, usability, installed user base, or access to distribution channels. Therefore, if the risk of being imitated is high, corporations need to identify complementary assets that are both mandatory for offering superior value to the targeted consumer segment and are hard to copy. Building assets of this kind strengthens a firm's position relative to competitors, consumers, and suppliers and allows it to claim a larger share of the generated value. For example, Groupon's offering of local discounted gift certificates requires a local sales force. As Groupon rolled out its local offering at a great pace all over the world to offer customers attractive deals, competitors were forced to set up similar organizational structures that were costly and time-consuming to develop.

If the development of complementary assets is not possible internally, firms have to ally with holders of those in partnerships ranging from strategic alliances to acquisitions. But how can firms identify complementary assets that are crucial sources for competitive advantage? First, the assets have to correspond to one of the generic strategies – operating excellence, product leadership, or customer intimacy – a firm wants to pursue. It is important to note that these specific capabilities can involve each stage of the value chain. The decisive criterion for a complementary asset is its ability to substantially enhance value from a customer's point of view. Second, investing in the deployment of complementary assets only makes sense if they cannot be replicated or substituted quickly and/or at modest costs. They should enable a lasting advantage with regard to competitors before they are able to develop similar or substituting capabilities.

To be successful the strategy of building complementary assets has to create substantial switching costs for consumers. Shapiro and Varian (1999, p. 133) state that 'you just cannot compete effectively . . . unless you know how to identify, measure, and understand switching costs and map strategy accordingly'. Creating or exploiting switching costs means lessening price competition and earning higher profits than rivals. Generally, at least three types of switching costs can be distinguished (Klemperer, 1987): transaction costs, learning costs, and artificial or contractual costs. Transaction costs occur when consumers engage in a new relationship with another firm potentially including termination costs for the existing relationship. Learning costs comprise the efforts necessary to make oneself familiar with a new product, service, or technology. Firms intentionally create artificial switching costs, such as bonus programs, proprietary standards, or repeat-purchase discounts. In the Internet business, switching costs related to direct or indirect network effects have proven to be highly effective, which is why many companies initially aim to grow quickly, no matter the cost – often not charging customers for their products or services at all – to create 'lock-in' effects (Anderson, 2009).

However, due to the enormous technological and competitive dynamics of the Internet, sustaining competitive advantage requires fast and continuous innovation. Often Internet technologies, applications, and business models are in a 'perpetual beta mode', meaning that they are continuously being further developed and adapted, never reaching a final status. Thus, companies need to have the 'sensing, seizing, and reconfiguring skills that the business enterprise needs if it is to stay in synch with changing markets and which enable it not just to stay alive, but to adapt to and itself shape' (Teece, 2010, p. 190), typically referred to as 'dynamic capabilities' (Teece, 2009). Having these capabilities is particularly important in an environment such as the Internet where competition is intense and fast moving. The key to preserving competitive advantage is to offer consumers a superior performance. As business models and technologies can often be imitated quickly on the Internet, competitive advantages are often not more than a snapshot. All the more important are dynamic capabilities that help sense emerging customer needs and the identification of future technological trends. Understanding the fundamentals of consumer demand and how these demands can be met using the potential of technological innovations and organizational arrangements requires in-depth knowledge about consumers, rivals, suppliers, technologies, and the industry as a whole. In markets like the Internet, which is especially affected by globalization, rapid technological changes and convergence, and new business models, companies tap into external sources of knowledge. Thereby they seek to accelerate internal innovation as internal research and development is no longer sufficient to keep pace with the rapid growth of global knowledge (Chesbrough, 2003; Gassmann, 2006; Chesbrough and Crowther, 2006).

However, many examples show that this is not enough. To find a viable business model comprising a compelling value proposition, dependable revenue sources, and key resources that are hard to duplicate, a firm needs to experiment. Business models are often provisional, meaning that they are permanently refined or superseded by new models that capitalize on new technological trends or complementary assets (Shirky, 2008). The prerequisite to innovate at high speed demands an organizational culture that encourages experimenting with new ideas and refining elements of their business model. This also requires the willingness of the entire organization to change established internal and external routines and to learn persistently. Knowing about consumer desires before the marketplace is an important asset. In this respect Web 2.0 technologies, like social networks, blogs, wikis, or media-sharing sites, play an essential role as they give both consumers and companies the chance to interact in new ways with each other. Embracing the dialogue with consumers gives firms the opportunity to build consumer intimacy, an asset that is hard to imitate. Moreover, it enables firms to react faster to changing demands and strengthen customer relations. Many firms also seek to leverage the collective intelligence of the Internet community by initiating crowdsourcing competitions (Howe, 2006). However, engaging in Web 2.0 also gives rise to challenges. The way firms communicate with customers has to be authentic in the sense that the conversations have to consider individual concerns and avoid giving 'prefabricated' statements. Furthermore, firms need to develop capabilities to exploit the information gathered from consumers strategically by 'translating' it into manageable change suggestions or requests. Thus, interacting with consumers is a prerequisite to gain or sustain competitive advantage, or as the manager of an Internet company puts it:

> It has never been more important [for Internet firms] to take user interests at heart and to be available for receiving and responding to customer feedback and inquiries 24/7. With customers getting used to significantly increasing service levels, firms not able to effectively manage the customer touch-points will ultimately fail. (Wirtz et al., 2010, p. 282)

17.6   THE FUTURE OF COMPETITION ON THE INTERNET

The aim of this chapter was to elaborate on essential factors impacting and constituting an Internet business strategy. We presented particular properties of the Internet that strongly influence corporate strategies and the business models derived from them. Internet business models can be categorized into five types dependent on their value proposition: context, connection and communication, commerce, coordination, and content. Based on these foundations we elaborated on the core elements of an Internet business strategy, which depends on the Internet's influence on competition in a particular industry. We further identified sources of competitive advantage on the Internet. Staying ahead of rivals in a high-velocity environment such as the Internet is challenging because the barriers to imitating or leapfrogging a technological or organizational innovation are usually low. A sustainable business model will therefore yield persuasive value propositions to customers, have beneficial cost and risk structures, and capture a significant proportion of the value generated in form of reliable revenue streams (Teece, 2010).

While business models are refined and changed regularly, the strategic focus of a firm's Internet venture should be well defined and stable over a longer period of time. By well defined, we mean that an Internet business strategy needs a clear focus with respect to which customer segments are addressed and how unique value can be created to satisfy the needs of a particular market segment. A robust strategic positioning avoids 'trying to be all things to all customers' (Porter, 2001, p. 71) but empowers firms to be perceived as distinct by consumers. This also requires that firms form a distinctive way of creating and delivering value. The strategy and each element of the value chain have to fit together to create a system of competing that is hard to come by for competing firms. Particularly for established companies, this implies that the strategy for doing business on the Internet has to match the 'offline strategy'. In the early ages of the Internet many established firms lost (some of) their competitive advantage because their online and offline features cannibalized each other, rather than complemented, leading to increased price competition.

Competing on the Internet, characterized by recurring and discontinuous changes in consumer needs, rivals, suppliers, technologies, and regulations, makes dynamic capabilities for old and new companies alike essential assets. Specifically, the ability to adapt business models to environmental changes quickly and frequently is crucial. Therefore, successful firms need extraordinary competencies in Internet technologies and in-depth knowledge about the industry to anticipate technological change, the development of costs, and future capabilities of rivals. While most dot-com firms have the necessary mindset in their 'corporate DNA', established firms in particular are often reluctant to adapt to environmental changes, especially disruptive innovations (Christensen and Raynor, 2003; Yu and Hang, 2010). Most firms have reacted to changes caused by the Internet in their respective markets. However, they have primarily addressed different aspects of digital changes in traditional domains, such as supply chain management, marketing, or manufacturing (Bharadwaj et al., 2013). Most firms fail to pursue the opportunities for value creation and capture arising from leveraging the company-wide opportunities of digital transformation.

The market turbulences of the last years have underlined that successful firms are those capable of quickly adjusting to changes in competitive and economic environments with regard to demand, costs, time, technology, or innovation. As research found that firm size is negatively correlated with the success of disruptive innovation (Tushman and O'Reilly, 2002; Christensen and Raynor, 2003), establishing smaller, flexible, and autonomous corporate units is regarded as key to solving the 'innovator's dilemma' (Christensen and Raynor, 2003). Consequently, ever more firms shift from a 'research and develop' to a 'connect and develop' approach (Arora et al., 2001; Huston and Sakkab, 2006). On the Internet, business value co-creation is more widespread than in traditional markets. Often, numerous companies are involved in complex and dynamic collaborations, which often rely on modularized business processes and 'plug-and-play capabilities for richly linking digital assets' (Bharadwaj et al., 2013, p. 476), for example, through APIs.

As combining and sharing services in ecosystems, alliances, and partnerships is common on the Internet, companies need to define and protect their unique sources of competitive advantage. As business models in these arrangements are highly dependent on each other, further research should focus on how these ecosystems are managed and evolve over time. Also, richer theorizing on business models, especially regarding dynamic aspects, value co-creation, and pricing, is needed. With the advent of the Internet of things and cyber physical systems that link computational with physical elements in areas like energy, transportation, healthcare, or education, an abundance of data will be generated. The key for firms will be to develop capabilities and processes to set up an appropriate corporate infrastructure to handle the data volume, velocity, variety, and veracity and to explore how to make use of the heterogeneous data. Scholars are also called upon to study the opportunities and threats of big data for organizations and society. To substantiate the current hype, research should also provide case studies on successful applications and further develop methods to store and analyze big data.

Internet business strategies heavily depend on national and international regulatory frameworks. For the time being, net neutrality and user privacy are important and controversial issues. As new sophisticated technology allows ISPs to block or degrade specific content, sites, platforms, applications, types of attached equipment, and modes of communication, net neutrality is essential for enabling – particularly smaller – companies to market innovations on the Internet (van Schewick and Farber, 2009; Bauer, 2010; van Schewick, 2010; Picot and Krcmar, 2011). Further, many established and future data-driven Internet business models (e.g., big data, Internet of Things, online advertising) may be affected by stricter laws regarding privacy depending on national regulations and culture. Regulation may also be needed if the trend towards platformization results in a few powerful platforms dominating the Internet. Already today Internet business resembles a flat inverted pyramid with a few platforms at the bottom and a multitude of contributors of complementary services and products at the top (*The Economist*, 2014), giving platform operators considerable market power.

Competing on the Internet requires firms to permanently reflect on how to adapt to the rapidly changing environment and how to leverage the Internet to gain or sustain competitive advantage. For established firms this is not necessarily a blessing since the offline business may be cannibalized and the firms' profitability may drop. However, the digital era has generated many examples of struggling firms in media, digital imaging, commerce, or even manufacturing, showing that adhering to conventional business strategies, models, and practices for too long can be an unpleasant experience (e.g., Tripsas and Gavetti, 2000; Agarwal and Helfat, 2009; Lucas and Goh, 2009; Dosi and Galambos, 2013).

REFERENCES

Acquisti, A. and H.R. Varian (2005), 'Conditioning prices on purchase history', *Marketing Science*, **24** (3), 367–81.

Afuah, A. and C.L. Tucci (2007), *Internet Business Models and Strategies: Text and Cases*, 2nd edition, New York: McGraw-Hill Higher Education.

Agarwal, R. and C.E. Helfat (2009), 'Strategic renewal of organizations', *Organization Science*, **20** (2), 281–93.

Al-Debei, M.M. (2010), 'The design and engineering of innovative mobile data services: An ontological framework founded on business model thinking', thesis, School of Information Systems, Computing and Mathematics, Brunel University, UK.

Al-Debei, M.M. and D. Avison (2010), 'Developing a unified framework of the business model concept', *European Journal of Information Systems*, **19** (3), 359–76.

Anderson, C. (2009), *Free: The Future of a Radical Price*, New York: Hyperion.

Armstrong, M. (2006), 'Competition in two-sided markets', *RAND Journal of Economics*, **37** (3), 668–91.

Arora, A, A. Fosfuri and A. Gambardella (2001), 'Markets for technology and their implications for corporate strategy', *Industrial & Corporate Change*, **10** (2), 419–51.

Bauer, J.M. (2010), 'Regulation, public policy, and investment in communications infrastructure', *Telecommunications Policy*, **34** (1), 65–79.

Bengtsson, M., J. Eriksson and J. Wincent (eds) (2010), *Coopetition: New Ideas for a New Paradigm*, Cheltenham, UK and Northampton, MA, USA: Edward Elgar Publishing.

Bharadwaj, A., O.A. El Sawy, P.A. Pavlou and N. Venkatraman (2013), 'Digital business strategy: Toward a next generation of insights', *MIS Quarterly*, **37** (2), 471–82.

Bons, R.W.H., R.M. Lee and R.W. Wagenaar (1998), 'Designing trustworthy interorganizational trade procedures for open electronic commerce', *International Journal of Electronic Commerce*, **2** (3), 61–83.

Brandenburger, A.M. and B.J. Nalebuff (2011), *Co-Opetition*, New York: Random House Digital, Inc.

Burkhart, T., J. Krumeich, D. Werth and P. Loos (2011), 'Analyzing the business model concept – A comprehensive classification of literature', in *ICIS 2011 Proceedings*, accessed 28 January 2015 at http://aisel.aisnet.org/icis2011/proceedings/generaltopics/12.

Ceccagnoli, M., C. Forman, P. Huang and D. Wu (2012), 'Co-creation of value in a platform ecosystem: The case of enterprise software', *MIS Quarterly*, **36** (1), 263–90.

Chesbrough, H.W. (2003), *Open Innovation: The New Imperative for Creating and Profiting from Technology*, Boston, MA: Harvard Business School Press.

Chesbrough, H. and A.K. Crowther (2006), 'Beyond high tech: Early adopters of open innovation in other industries', *R&D Management*, **36** (3), 229–36.

Chesbrough, H. and R.S. Rosenbloom (2002), 'The role of the business model in capturing value from innovation: Evidence from Xerox Corporation's technology spin-off companies', *Industrial & Corporate Change*, **11** (3), 529–55.

Christensen, C.M. and M.E. Raynor (2003), *The Innovator's Solution: Creating and Sustaining Successful Growth*, Boston, MA: Harvard Business School Press.

Dosi, G. and Galambos (eds) (2013), *The Third Industrial Revolution in Global Business*, Cambridge, UK: Cambridge University Press.

Economides, N. and E. Katsamakas (2006), 'Two-sided competition of proprietary vs. open source technology platforms and the implications for the software industry', *Management Science*, **52** (7), 1057–71.

Eisenmann, T., G. Parker and M.W. van Alstyne (2006), 'Strategies for two-sided markets', *Harvard Business Review*, **84** (10), 92–101.

Eisenmann, T., G. Parker and M. van Alstyne (2011), 'Platform envelopment', *Strategic Management Journal*, **32** (12), 1270–85.

Evans, D.S. (2003), 'Some empirical aspects of multi-sided platform industries', *Review of Network Economics*, **2** (3), 191–209.

Franke, N., M. Schreier and U. Kaiser (2010), 'The "I designed it myself" effect in mass customization', *Management Science*, **56** (1), 125–40.

Gassmann, O. (2006), 'Opening up the innovation process: Towards an agenda', *R&D Management*, **36** (3), 223–8.

Gawer, A. and M. Cusumano (2008), 'How companies become platform leaders', *MIT Sloan Management Review*, **49** (2), 28–35.

Gnyawali, D.R. and B.J. Park (2011), 'Co-opetition between giants: Collaboration with competitors for technological innovation', *Research Policy*, **40** (5), 650–63.

Gomes-Casseres, B. (1994), 'Group vs. group: How alliance networks compete', *Harvard Business Review*, **72** (4), 62–76.

Gordijn, J., H. Akkermans and H. Vliet (2000), 'Business modelling is not process modelling', in S. Liddle, H. Mayr and B. Thalheim (eds), *Conceptual Modeling for E-Business and the Web*, Berlin and Heidelberg: Springer, pp. 40–51.

Hinz, O., I.-H. Hann and M. Spann (2011), 'Price discrimination in e-commerce? An examination of dynamic pricing in name-your-own price markets', *MIS Quarterly*, **35** (1), 81–98.

Howe, J. (2006), 'The rise of crowdsourcing', *Wired*, 1 June, accessed 19 June 2014 at http://www.wired.com/wired/archive/14.06/crowds.html.

Huston, L. and N. Sakkab (2006), 'Connect and develop', *Harvard Business Review*, **84** (3), 58–66.

Junglas, I. and R.T. Watson (2006), 'The u-constructs: Four information drives', *Communications of the Association for Information Systems*, **17**, Article 26, accessed 28 January 2015 http://aisel.aisnet.org/cais/vol17/iss1/26.

Kallio, J., M. Tinnilä and A. Tseng (2006), 'An international comparison of operator-driven business models', *Business Process Management Journal*, **12** (3), 281–98.

Katz, M. and C. Shapiro (1994), 'Systems competition and network effects', *The Journal of Economic Perspectives*, **8** (2), 93–115.

Khan, I., B. Weishaar and L. Polinsky et al. (2011), *Nothing But Net: 2011 Internet Investment Guide*, New York: J.P. Morgan, accessed 23 December 2015 at http://documents.tips/documents/asia-pacific-equity-research-06-january-2011-nothing-but-net-asia-2011-internet-investment-guide.html.

Klemperer, P. (1987), 'Markets with consumer switching costs', *The Quarterly Journal of Economics*, **102** (2), 375–94.

Leem, C.S., H.S. Suh and D.S. Kim (2004), 'A classification of mobile business models and its applications', *Industrial Management & Data Systems*, **104** (1), 78–87.

Lei, D. (2003), 'Competition, cooperation and learning: The new dynamics of strategy and organisation design for the innovation net', *International Journal of Technology Management*, **26** (7), 694–716.

Lucas Jr., H.C. and J.M. Goh (2009), 'Disruptive technology: How Kodak missed the digital photography revolution', *The Journal of Strategic Information Systems*, **18** (1), 46–55.

Magretta, J. (2002), 'Why business models matter', *Harvard Business Review*, **80** (5), 86–92.

Mahoney, J.T. and J.R. Pandian (1992), 'The resource-based view within the conversation of strategic management', *Strategic Management Journal*, **13** (5), 363–80.

Mikians, J., L. Gyarmati, V. Erramilli and N. Laoutaris (2012), 'Detecting price and search discrimination on the Internet', in *Proceedings of the 11th ACM Workshop on Hot Topics in Networks*, ACM, pp. 79–84.

Mione, A. (2009), 'When entrepreneurship requires co-opetition: The need of norms to create a market', *Journal of Entrepreneurship and Small Business*, **8** (1), 92–109.

Morris, M., M. Schindehutte and J. Allen (2005), 'The entrepreneur's business model: Toward a unified perspective', *Journal of Business Research*, **58** (6), 726–35.

Osterwalder, A. and Y. Pigneur (2009), *Business Model Generation, A Handbook for Visionaries, Game Changers, and Challengers*, Amsterdam: Moddermann Druckwerk.

Osterwalder, A., Y. Pigneur and C.L. Tucci (2005), 'Clarifying business models: Origins, present, and future of the concept', *Communications of the Association for Information Systems*, **16**, 1–25.

Picot, A. and H. Krcmar (2011), 'Interview with Marvin Ammori and Christof Weinhardt on network neutrality and the future of telecommunication', *Business & Information Systems Engineering*, **3** (5), 327–38.

Picot, A., R. Reichwald and R. Wigand (2008), *Information, Organization and Management*, Berlin and Heidelberg: Springer.

Picot, A., T. Ripperger and B. Wolff (1996), 'The fading boundaries of the firm: The role of information and communication technology', *Journal of Institutional and Theoretical Economics*, **152** (1), 65–79.

Porter, M.E. (1985), *Competitive Advantage: Creating and Sustaining Superior Performance*, New York: Free Press.

Porter, M.E. (2001), 'Strategy and the Internet', *Harvard Business Review*, **79** (3), 62–79.

Porter, M.E. (2008), *On Competition*, Boston, MA: Harvard Business School Publications.

Rochet, J.C. and J. Tirole (2003), 'Platform competition in two-sided markets', *Journal of the European Economic Association*, **1** (4), 990–1029.

Rumelt, R.P. (1984), 'Toward a strategic theory of the firm', in R.B. Lamb (ed.), *Competitive Strategic Management*, Englewood Cliffs, NJ: Prentice-Hall, pp. 556–70.

Salvador, F., P.M. de Holan and F. Piller (2009), 'Cracking the code of mass customization', *MIT Sloan Management Review*, **50** (3), 71–8.

Scheer, A.-W. and M. Nüttgens (2000), 'ARIS architecture and reference models for business process management', in W. van der Aalst, J. Desel and A. Oberweis (eds), *Business Process Management, Lecture Notes in Computer Science Volume 1806*, Berlin and Heidelberg: Springer, pp. 376–89.

Seddon, P.B.L., P. Geoffrey, P. Freeman and G. Shanks (2004), 'The case for viewing business models as abstractions of strategy', *Communications of the Association for Information Systems*, **13** (1), 427–42.

Shafer, S.M., H.J. Smith and J.C. Linder (2005), 'The power of business models', *Business Horizons*, **48** (3), 199–207.

Shapiro, C. and H. Varian (1999), *Information Rules, A Strategic Guide to the Network Economy*, Boston, MA: Harvard Business School Press.

Shirky, C. (2008), *Here Comes Everybody: The Power of Organizing Without Organizations*, New York: Penguin.

Simon, H. (1988), 'Management strategischer Wettbewerbsvorteile' [Management of strategic competitive advantages], *Zeitschrift für Betriebswirtschaft*, **58** (4), 461–80.

Suarez, F.F. and J. Kirtley (2012), 'Dethroning an established platform', *MIT Sloan Management Review*, **53** (4), 35–41.

Tax, S.S. and S.W. Brown (1998), 'Recovering and learning from service failures', *Sloan Management Review*, **40** (1), 75–89.

Teece, D.J. (1986), 'Profiting from technological innovation: Implications for integration, collaboration, licensing and public policy', *Research Policy*, **15** (6), 285–305.

Teece, D.J. (2009), *Dynamic Capabilities and Strategic Management: Organizing for Innovation and Growth*, Oxford, UK and New York: Oxford University Press.

Teece, D.J. (2010), 'Business models, business strategy and innovation', *Long Range Planning*, **43** (2), 172–94.

The Economist (2012), 'News adventures: After years of bad headlines the industry finally has some good news', *The Economist*, 8 December, accessed 19 June 2014 at http://www.economist.com/news/business/21567934-after-years-bad-headlines-industry-finally-has-some-good-news-news-adventures.

The Economist (2014), 'Something to stand on: Proliferating digital platforms will be at the heart of tomorrow's economy, and even government', *The Economist*, 18 January, accessed 23 December 2015 at http://www.economist.com/news/special-report/21593583-proliferating-digital-platforms-will-be-heart-tomorrows-economy-and-even.

Treacy, M. and F. Wiersema (1993), 'Customer intimacy and other value disciplines', *Harvard Business Review*, **71** (1), 84–94.

Tripsas, M. and G. Gavetti (2000), 'Capabilities, cognition, and inertia: Evidence from digital imaging', *Strategic Management Journal*, **21** (10–11), 1147–61.

Tushman, M.L. and C.A. O'Reilly (2002), *Winning through Innovation: A Practical Guide to Leading Organizational Change and Renewal*, Cambridge, MA: Harvard Business Press.

van Schewick, B. (2010), *Internet Architecture and Innovation*, Cambridge, MA: The MIT Press.

van Schewick, B. and D. Farber (2009), 'Network neutrality nuances', *Communications of the ACM*, **52** (2), 31–7.

Von Hippel, E. (2005), 'Democratizing innovation', *Journal für Betriebswirtschaftslehre*, **55** (1), 63–78.

Williamson, O.E. (1985), *The Economic Institutions of Capitalism*, New York: Free Press.

Wirtz, B.W., O. Schilke and S. Ullrich (2010), 'Strategic development of business models: Implications of the Web 2.0 for creating value on the Internet', *Long Range Planning*, **43** (2–3), 272–90.

Yu, D. and C.C. Hang (2010), 'A reflective review of disruptive innovation theory', *International Journal of Management Reviews*, **12** (4), 435–42.

Zerdick, A., A. Picot and K. Schrape et al. (2000), *E-conomics: Strategies for the Digital Marketplace*, Berlin and Heidelberg: Springer.

Zott, C., R. Amit and L. Massa (2011), 'The business model: Recent developments and future research', *Journal of Management*, **37** (4), 1019–42.

18. The economics of Internet search*

Hal R. Varian

18.1 INTRODUCTION

Search engines are one of the most widely used Internet applications. According to Purcell et al. (2012) '91% of online adults use search engines to find information on the web . . . On any given day online 56% of those using the internet use search engines'. Not only are search engines widely used, they are also highly profitable. Their primary source of revenue comes from selling advertisements that are related to the search queries. Since users tend to find these ads to be highly relevant to their interests, advertisers will pay well to place them. Furthermore, the marginal cost of an addition query is very low for search engines, so profit margins tend to be high.

Advertising is, in general, a low-yield business. Ad rates are typically measured in cost-per-thousand (CPM) impressions. A typical CPM for a prime-time TV ad would be US$10, which translates to 1 cent per impression per user. Online display ads might sell for US$1 or US$2 CPM, which is an order of magnitude less than TV ads. Search engine ads, by contrast, could easily have CPMs in the range of US$100. Why? Because the ads are much more relevant to users' interests since they are tied to user queries. Even though the yield of search engine ads is high by comparison to other forms of advertising, it is low in absolute terms. A good ad click-through rate might be 3 percent and a typical conversion (purchase) rate might also be around 3 percent. This implies that fewer than one out of a 1000 people who see the ad are actually induced to buy the product being advertised.

The fixed costs of entering and running a search engine were at one time substantial since the entrant was required to build or lease a data center. Nowadays, those fixed costs have become variable costs due to the availability of cloud computing services such as Amazon Web Services. This has enabled the proliferation of special purpose search engines that focus on particular types of searches such as travel and shopping.

However, it must be acknowledged that *general* purpose search engines tend to build and operate their own data centers and so incur significant fixed costs. Companies that already operate such data centers are in a good position to offer general purpose search services. Examples would include IBM (Watson is, in fact, to large degree a search engine), Facebook and Apple. The latter two companies already have a substantial user base for services that they may choose to offer in the future.

On the demand side, user switching costs for search engine users are very low: the competition is just a click away. Fallows (2005) indicates that 56 percent of search engine users use more than one search engine. Hence, we can expect to see robust competition for users among incumbent search engines.

Not only are users not exclusively tied to a single search engine, neither are advertisers. Typically advertisers will 'multi-home' and advertise wherever there are enough potential customers to warrant the relatively small costs to port ad campaigns. These characteristics of the search engine business – low marginal costs, low switching costs, and an advertiser-supported business model – means that the likely market structure for general purpose search engines will be one with a few large competitors in a given country or language group.

On the other hand, there could be a multitude of special purpose search engines. There are special purpose search engines for travel, shopping, local services, academic articles, and so on. The equilibrium industry structure might be similar to that of national newspapers or news magazines: a few large providers, supported mainly by advertising with ongoing competition for new readers. There are no significant network effects or demand-side economies of scale that would drive the market to a single supplier in either the search engine industry or the magazine industry.

Another analogy would be to think of department stores as general purpose shopping venues with shoe stores, men's stores, cosmetic stores, furniture stores, and so on, offering special purpose shopping services. Even if there are only a couple of department stores in a given mall, there will generally be many special purpose stores that compete for customers, just as general purpose search engines compete with special purpose engines.

I will argue later that the most important economic factor determining search engine success is learning-by-doing (Arrow, 1962). Because of the low user switching costs, search engines have to continually invest in improving both their search and their monetization. Though this could be said to be true of virtually any product, continuous improvement is particularly important in online products since pace of experimentation and implementation is particularly rapid. Though there are dozens of search engines available, the big three in the USA are Google, Yahoo! and MSN. I will mostly discuss Google, since I am most familiar with its practices, but the other search engines tend to use similar business models.

18.2   TWO-SIDED MATCHING

First, what does Google do? The answer, I claim, is that Google is a 'matchmaker'. On the search side, it matches people who are seeking information to people who provide information. On the ad side, it matches people who want to buy things to those who want to sell things. Ads are themselves a form of search, namely sellers searching for buyers.

From an economics perspective, Google runs a 'two-sided matching' mechanism. This subject has a long history in economics, starting with the classical linear assignment problem, which seeks to find a matching of partners that maximizes some value function. Not surprisingly, the mathematical theory of the assignment problem turns out to be closely related to the Google ad auction.

The need for efficient matching of users and content is apparent: the growth of content on the Internet has been phenomenal. According to Netcraft.com there were about 650 million web servers as of 2012. Obviously, the more content that is on the web, the more important it is to have good search engines. The web without search engines would be like Borges's universal library with no card catalog.

In this chapter I will briefly discuss the history of information retrieval, emphasizing some of the points of interest to economics. I will then describe the evolution of the business model to support online search engines, and conclude by sketching some of economic aspects of the Google ad auction.

18.3   A BRIEF HISTORY OF INFORMATION RETRIEVAL

Almost as soon as textual information was stored on computers researchers began to investigate how it could be easily retrieved. Significant progress was made in the 1960s and operational systems were widely available by the 1970s. The field was reasonably mature by the 1990s, with the primary users being professional librarians and researchers (see Lesk, 1995). By the early 1990s most of the low-hanging fruit had been harvested and intensive users of information retrieval technology were worried that technological progress was grinding to a halt. This concern led to the creation in 1992 of the TREC (Text Retrieval and Extraction Conference) by DARPA.

DARPA compiled training data consisting of many queries and many documents along with a 0–1 indicator of whether or not the document was relevant to the query. Human judges determined the relevance of these indicators. Research teams then trained their systems on the TREC data. Subsequently, TREC provided a second set of data for which the research teams tried to forecast relevance using their trained systems. Hence TREC provided a test collection and forum for exchange of ideas and most groups working in information retrieval participated in TREC (see Vorhees, 1999). Having a standard base for comparing different algorithms was very helpful in evaluating different approaches to the task.

Though search engines use a variety of techniques, one that will be very familiar to economists is logistic regression. One chooses characteristics of the document and the query and then tries to predict the probability of relevance using simple logistic regression. As an example of this approach, Cooper et al. (1993, 1994) used the following variables:

- the number of terms in common between the document and the query;
- log of the absolute frequency of occurrence of a query term in the document averaged over all terms that co-occur in the query and document;
- square root of the query length;
- frequency of occurrence of a query term in the collection;
- square root of the collection size;
- the inverse collection frequency, which is a measure of how rare the term is in the collection.

Other systems use different variables and different forms for predicting relevance, but this list is representative for the time.

By the mid-1990s it was widely felt that search had become commoditized. There were several algorithms that had roughly similar performance and improvements tended to be incremental. When the web came along in 1995, the need for better Internet search engines became apparent and many of the algorithms developed by the TREC community were used to address this need. However, the challenge of indexing the web wasn't as compelling to the information retrieval community as one might have thought. The problem was that the web was not TREC. TREC had become so successful in defining the information retrieval problem that most attention was focused on that particular research challenge, to the exclusion of other applications.

The computer scientists, on the other hand, saw the web as the problem *du jour*. The NSF Digital Library project and other similar initiatives provided funding for research on wide-scale information retrieval. The Stanford computer science department received one of these Digital Library grants and two graduate students there, Larry Page and Sergey Brin, became interested in the web search problem. They developed the PageRank algorithm – an approach to information retrieval that used the link structure of the web. The basic idea (to oversimplify somewhat) was that sites that had a lot of links from important sites pointing to them were likely to contain relevant information.[1] PageRank was a big improvement on existing algorithms and Page and Brin dropped out of school in 1998 to build a commercial search engine: Google. The algorithm that Google now uses for search is proprietary, of course. It is also very complex. The basic design combines PageRank score with an information retrieval score. The real secret to Google's success is that it is constantly experimenting with the algorithm, adjusting, tuning and tweaking virtually continuously.

One of the tenets of the Japanese approach to quality control is *kaizen*, which is commonly translated as 'continuous improvement'. One reason for the rapid pace of technological progress on the web is that it is very easy to experiment – to use a new search algorithm for one query out of 1000. If the new algorithm outperforms the old one, it can quickly be deployed. Using this sort of simple experimentation, Google has refined its search engine over the years to offer a highly refined product with many specialized features. Google is hardly the only online business that engages in *kaizen*; Amazon, eBay, Yahoo! and others are constantly refining their websites. Such refinements are typically based on systematic experimentation and statistical analysis, as in the traditional quality control practice.

18.4   DEVELOPMENT OF A BUSINESS MODEL

When Brin and Page started Google they did not have a business model in mind. At one point they offered to sell the PageRank algorithm they used to Yahoo! for US$1 million. When Yahoo! turned them down, they thought about selling intranet search services to companies. Meanwhile, a company in Pasadena named GoTo.com was starting to auction off search results. In 1999 they filed US Patent 6 296 361 (granted 31 July 2001), which described the idea of auctioning search results.[2]

Auctioning search results didn't work very well, since willingness to pay for placement is not a very good indication of relevance to users, so GoTo eventually adopted a new business model in which they auctioned off advertisements to accompany what they referred to as the 'algorithmic' search results. At about the same time they changed their name to Overture. Two Google employees, Salar Kamangar and Eric Veach, watched what Overture was doing and decided they could improve upon it. During the fall of 2001 they developed the Google Ad Auction.[3]

In their model ads were ranked by the product of bids and estimated click-through rate. Since bids are expressed in units of cost/click and the click-through rate is clicks/

impressions, this means that ads are ranked by cost per impression. The idea was to put the ads that have the highest expected revenue in the best positions – that is, the positions where they would be most likely to receive clicks. Just as a firm cares about price *times* quantity sold, a search engine should care about the price per click *times* the number of clicks expected to be received since that is the total revenue from showing the ad. Of course, this requires a way to estimate the probability of a click – a non-trivial task. I will discuss how this is done below.

During the project development Google realized that a first-price auction (where advertisers paid their bid amount) was not attractive since advertisers would want reduce their bid to the lowest amount that would retain their position. This constant monitoring of the system would put a significant load on the servers, so Google decided to automatically set the price paid to be equal to the second highest bid – since that is what the advertisers would want to do anyway. This choice had nothing to do with Vickrey auctions[4] – it was primarily an engineering design decision.[5]

Initially the Google ad auction only applied to the ads appearing on the right-hand side of the page, with the top ads (the best-performing area) reserved for negotiated pricing by a sales force. Eventually it became clear that the prices generated by the auction were more appropriate than those generated by negotiation, so Google switched to using an auction for all ads displayed.

18.5   THE GOOGLE AD AUCTION

The Google ad auction is probably the largest auction in the world, with billions of auctions being run per week. It turns out also to have a very nice theoretical structure as described in Edelman et al. (2007) and Varian (2006). There are several slots where advertisements can go, but higher slots tend to receive more clicks than others. In equilibrium, each bidder must prefer the slot it is in to any other slot. This leads to a series of 'revealed preference' relations that can be solved for equilibrium bidding rules. Conversely, given some observed bids, one can invert the bidding rules to find out what values the advertisers place on clicks.

To see how this works, consider a bidder who is contemplating entering a keyword auction. The current participants are each bidding some amounts. Hence the new bidder thus faces a 'supply curve of clicks'. As it bids higher it will displace more of the incumbent bidders, leading to a higher position and more clicks. In choosing its bid, the advertiser should consider the incremental cost per click: how much more money it will have to spend to get additional clicks. If the incremental cost per click is less than the value per click, the advertiser should increase its bid; if the incremental cost per click is less than the value per click, it should decrease its bid. In equilibrium the incremental cost of moving up one position should exceed the bidder's value per click, but the incremental savings from moving down one position should be less than the bidder's value per click.

This has the implication that in equilibrium the incremental cost per click should be increasing in the click-through rate. Why? Suppose it decreased in moving from one position to the next. Then there was some bidder who purchased expensive clicks but passed up cheap ones, contradicting the assumption of equilibrium. Furthermore, since the value per click should be bounded by the incremental cost per click in equilibrium, the observed incremental costs allow us to infer valuable information about the bidders' values. In practice, incremental cost per click seems to give a plausible estimate of click value. However, it is important to note that there is still a certain indeterminacy of equilibrium. The requirement that each agent prefers its position to other possible positions does not pin down a unique outcome. Rather it determines a range of equilibrium bids. Two particularly interesting equilibria are the ones that yield the maximum and the minimum revenue for the search engine.

18.6   COST CURVES

From the viewpoint of the individual advertiser, the fact that prices are determined by an auction is not particularly relevant. In practice an advertiser sets a single bid that applies over many different auctions. We could think of a reduced form model where the advertiser faced a 'click cost curve' which showed the relationship between clicks, x, and the cost of achieving those clicks, $c(x)$. If we assume that the advertiser has a value per click of v, then profit can be written as $vx - c(x)$. The first-order condition for profit maximization is $v = c'(x)$, which simply says the advertiser should operate where value per click equals marginal cost per click. Google's Bid Simulator service actually depicts an estimated cost curve of this sort, which allows advertisers to rationally choose operating positions.

Since $v = c'(x)$ at the optimal position, profit can be expressed as $c'(x)x - c(x)$ and profit/cost can be written as $c'(x)/(c(x)/x) - 1 = MC/AC^6 - 1$. Note the somewhat surprising appearance of the Lerner ratio in this expression. This calculation is outlined in Varian (2006) using a somewhat more robust revealed preference approach. Varian (2006) also reports an attempt to estimate bounds on the value/cost ratio using proprietary Google data. It turns that that value/cost is about 2, indicating a return on investment (ROI) of 100 percent. This is a remarkably large number; I will describe why it makes sense in section 18.8 on the importance of competition.

18.7   VCG PRICING

The Google ad auction is one way to auction off ad positions, but there are other ways that can be considered. One defect of the current auction is that each advertiser has to compare its incremental costs to its value, and those incremental costs depend on other bidders' choices. As it happens there is another auction-like mechanism that does not have this defect: the Vickrey-Clarke-Groves (VCG) mechanism (Varian, 2009). In the VCG mechanism: (1) each agent reports a value; (2) the search engine assigns agents to slots to maximize total value of the assignment; (3) each agent a then pays a charge equal to the total value accruing to the other agents if a is present minus the total value accruing to the other agents if a is absent. Thus each agent pays an amount equal to the cost that it imposes on the other agents.

It can be shown that for this mechanism, each agent should report its true value, regardless of the reports of the other agents. Leonard (1983) was the first to apply this mechanism to the classic assignment problem. A few years later Demange and Gale

(1985) showed that this mechanism results in the same payments as the minimum-revenue Nash equilibrium of a market equivalent to the second-price ad auction.[7]

There are other nice properties of the VCG auction. For example, Krishna and Perry (1998) show that the VCG mechanism maximizes the search engine's revenue across all efficient mechanisms. Despite the apparent advantages of VCG, it has not as yet been deployed by any of the major search engines, though it is apparently being used for ad pricing by Facebook and Business.com.

18.8   THE IMPORTANCE OF COMPETITION

It is widely recognized that revenue realized in an auction depends critically on how much competition there is in that auction. Klemperer (2002) describes the case of the June 2000 auctions for mobile phone licenses in the Netherlands where there were five licenses and six bidders. One bidder threatened another with legal action if it continued bidding, inducing it to drop out, thus leaving only five bidders for five licenses – not much competition! In fact the auction raised less than 30 percent of what the Dutch government had forecast.

The same principle holds true for the position auction: revenue doesn't really take off until there is competition. In the Google auction there are eight slots for ads on the right-hand side of the page and up to three slots on the top of the page. As mentioned earlier, the ordering of ads is determined by bids and click-through rates, but the ads that are 'promoted' (moved to the top of the page) have to satisfy some additional criteria involving ad quality.

To simplify a bit, if an auction has fewer bidders than available slots, or just enough bidders to fill the available slots, we say it is 'undersold'. If it has more bidders than slots we say it is 'oversold'. If an auction is undersold, the price paid by the last bidder on the page is the reservation price, which we will take to be five cents.[8] If the page is oversold, the price paid by the last bidder on the page is determined by the bid of the first excluded agent, which can easily be at least ten times higher than the reserve price.

Consider a simple example where all bidders have the same value v and the reserve price is r. Let p_s be the price paid for slot s and let x_s be the number of clicks that slot s receives. If the page is undersold, each bidder has to be indifferent between paying p_s and receiving x_s clicks versus paying r and receiving x_m clicks, where m is the last ad shown on the page. This implies:

$$(v - p_s)x_s = (v - r)x_m \tag{18.1}$$

or:

$$p_s x_s = v(x_s - x_m) + r\, x_m \tag{18.2}$$

Equation (18.2) says that the expenditure on slot s has to be the expenditure on the last slot plus the *incremental* value of the clicks in position s.

On the other hand, suppose the page is oversold so that there is at least one excluded bidder with value v. Then each bidder has to be indifferent between what it is paying and the profit from being excluded – which is zero. This gives us $(v - p_s)x_s = 0$, which implies $p_s = v$.

Note the big leap in revenue in going from a partially sold page to an oversold page. In the first case, everybody is indifferent between being in the slot they are in and being in the worst slot. In the second case, everybody is indifferent between being shown and not shown at all, which means prices are competed up to the equal value. To drive this point home, consider a simple example.

Suppose that there are two slots. The top one gets 100 clicks per day, the second one 80 clicks per day. There are two advertisers, each of whom values a click at 50 cents. In this model, one advertiser occupies slot two and gets 80 clicks per day, for which he or she pays five cents per click = $4.00 in total spend. The second advertiser occupies the top slot getting 20 additional clicks per day. Competition forces him or her to pay $10 more for those clicks than the advertiser in slot two. Thus he or she spends $14 = $4 + $10 in total. Total revenue from the two advertisers is $18.

Now suppose there are three advertisers who value clicks at 50 cents each, but there are still only two slots. The equilibrium bid is now 50 cents per click, there are 180 clicks in total, so the total revenue from the two advertisers is $90. The addition of one more advertiser increases revenue from $18 to $90!

This example illustrates the important point that oversold pages are far more profitable than partially sold pages not just because there are more bidders, but also because the forces of competition are much stronger. It is this insight that explains the rather remarkable 100 percent ROI described in the previous section. Most auctions only have a few participants, so the reserve price is important in determining revenue. However, the reserve price tends to be set quite low. Hence advertisers in these auctions end up with a tremendous deal. On the other hand, some auctions are highly competitive. That competition translates into higher prices and hence more revenue. In net, search engine advertising turns out to be exceptionally attractive on average.

This point also illustrates the importance of the matching algorithm used for displaying ads. The user enters a 'query' and the advertiser buys 'keywords'. The advertiser can specify 'exact match', which means that the ad is only shown if the user's query exactly matches the advertiser's keywords. But it is more common for advertisers to specify 'broad match', which means that the query will match various expansions of the keyword such as synonyms and substrings. The additional ads due to broad match benefit the user and the advertiser, since they make it more likely that the user will click. But they also increase the competition in the auction, raising prices.

18.9 AD QUALITY

I have indicated earlier that the ranking used by both Google and Yahoo! is based not only on bids, but also on a measure of ad quality. In the simplest case, we can think of ad quality as the predicted click-through rate. Google ranks ads by bid times expected click-through rate, but where does the estimate of expected click-through come from?

Think of a model where the actual click-through rate that an ad receives depends on both a position-specific effect (x_p) and an ad-specific effect (e_a). The simplest specification that the click-through rate for ad a in position p is given by $e_a x_p$.

Given this multiplicative form, it is relatively easy to estimate the relevant values: simply put random ads in position p to estimate the position-specific effect. Once this is known, you can use the history of clicks on a given ad to estimate the ad-specific effect. One can also use various other predictors to supplement the historical data. In practice this is done using a kind of huge logistic regression utilizing nearly a trillion observations.

The ranking of ads is based on bids times ad-specific effects: $b_a e_a$. The bid is dollars per click and the ad-specific effect is clicks per impression. Hence $b_a e_a$ is bids per impression: how much the advertiser is willing to pay for its ad to be shown to a user. The advertiser with the highest value for an impression is given the best position: the position most likely to receive a click. The advertiser with the second highest value per impression gets the next best position, and so on. Hence an ad with a high bid per click could be displaced by an ad with a lower bid if the high-bid ad had a low click-through rate. Assigning ads on the basis on $b_a e_a$ maximizes the value of the impressions on the page, leading (potentially) to an increase in expected revenue.[9]

Just as it is important to determine which ads to show, it is equally important to determine which ads *not* to show. The reason is that the likelihood of a user clicking on an ad depends on how relevant he or she expects that ad to be. And this expectation depends, at least in part, on what the user's previous experience has been. Thus showing a 'bad ad' can affect users' future propensity to click. Offering a bad ad in a particularly prominent position can be especially costly.

The decision of whether and where to show an ad should depend not just on current ad revenue, but on an estimate of how the ad's relevance will affect future propensities to click. It is possible to model these choices analytically. Showing an ad today brings in a known amount of revenue but also has a probabilistic effect on future revenue by influencing the propensity to click in the future. Modeling these effects leads to a stochastic dynamic programming problem that offers a rationale for current practices and a guide to how they might be refined.

18.10   CONCLUSION

Search engines are an example of a two-sided matching model supported by advertising. Not only are they interesting in their own right, but they also offer a fertile ground for economic analysis. During the 1960s and 1970s the scientific study of financial markets flourished due to the availability of massive amounts of data and the application of quantitative methods. I think that marketing is at the same position finance was in the early 1960s. Large amounts of computer readable data on marketing performance are just now becoming available via search engines, supermarket scanners, and other sorts of information technology. Such data provide the raw material for scientific studies of consumer behavior and I expect that there will much progress in this area in the coming decade.

NOTES

*   This chapter is an updated and extended revision to the author's 2007 Angelo Costa Lecture presented Rome, which was published in the *Rivista di Politica Economica*, November–December 2006.

1. See Langville and Meyer (2006) for a detailed description of the mathematics behind PageRank.
2. I am told that this idea may have been stimulated by a student who took Charlie Plott's course in experimental economics at Cal Tech. So economists seemed to have played a role in this auction design from an early stage!
3. A detailed and reasonably accurate history of the development of the Google ad auction model is available in Levy (2009).
4. A type of sealed-bid auction.
5. GoTo.com experimented with a first-price auction for some time and found it to lead to unstable behavior. Zhang and Feng (2005) and Zhang (2005) document and model this phenomenon. I am told that GoTo's decision to move to a second-price auction was motivated by some experiments run by a group of Cal Tech auction specialists.
6. Marginal cost/average cost.
7. I am simplifying the actual result for ease of exposition; see Varian (2006) for the details.
8. The reservation price actually depends on ad quality as well.
9. In theory the revenue impact of ranking by bids per click or bids per impression is ambiguous. In practice, ranking by bids per impression is better.

REFERENCES

Arrow, K.J. (1962), 'The economic implications of learning by doing', *Review of Economic Studies*, **29** (3), 155–73.

Cooper, W., A. Chen and F.C. Gey (1993), 'Full text retrieval based on probabilistic equations with coefficients fitted by logistic regression', in D. Harman (ed.), *The Second Text REtrieval Conference (TREC-2)*, National Institute of Standards and Technology Special Publication No. 500-215, Gaithersburg, MD.

Cooper, W., A. Chen and F.C. Gey (1994), 'Experiments in the probabilistic retrieval of full text documents', paper at the Third Text REtrieval Conference (TREC-3), accessed 9 April 2015 at http://citeseerx.ist.psu.edu/viewdoc/summary?doi=10.1.1.17.8927.

Demange, G. and D. Gale (1985), 'The strategy structure of two-sided matching markets', *Econometrica*, **53** (4), 873–8.

Edelman, B., M. Ostrovsky and M. Schwartz (2007), 'Internet advertising and the generalized second price auction', *American Economic Review*, **97** (1), 242–59.

Fallows. D. (2005), *Search Engine Users*, Washington, DC: Pew Internet & American Life Project, accessed 23 June 2014 at http://www.pewinternet.org/files/old-media/Files/Reports/2005/PIP_Searchengine_users.pdf.pdf.

Klemperer, P. (2002), 'What really matters in auction design', *Journal of Economic Perspectives*, **16** (1), 169–89.

Krishna, V. and M. Perry (1998), 'Efficient mechanism design', accessed 23 June 2014 at http://papers.ssrn.com/sol3/papers.cfm?abstract_id=64934.

Langville, A.N. and C.D. Meyer (2006), *Google's PageRank and Beyond: The Science of Search Engine Rankings*, Princeton, NJ: Princeton University Press.

Leonard, H.B. (1983), 'Elicitation of honest preferences for the assignment of individuals to positions', *Journal of Political Economy*, **91** (3), 461–79.

Lesk, M. (1995), 'The seven ages of information retrieval', *UDT Occasional Paper No. 5*, International Federation of Library Associations and Institutions, accessed 23 June 2014 at http://www.ifla.org/VI/5/op/udtop5/udtop5.htm.

Levy, S. (2009), 'Secret of Googlenomics: Data-fueled recipe brews profitability', *Wired*, **17** (6), accessed 23 June 2014 at http://archive.wired.com/culture/culturereviews/magazine/17-06/nep_googlenomics?currentPage=all.

Purcell, K.J., J. Brenner and L. Rainie (2012), *Search Engine Use 2012*, Washington, DC: Pew Internet & American Life Project, accessed 23 June 2014 at http://www.pewinternet.org/files/old-media//Files/Reports/2012/PIP_Search_Engine_Use_2012.pdf.

Varian, H.R. (2006), 'Position auctions', *International Journal of Industrial Organization*, **24** (7), 1–10.

Varian, H.R. (2009), 'Online ad auctions', *American Economic Review*, **99** (2), 430–34.

Vorhees, E. (1999), 'The TREC conferences: An introduction' [slides], 16–19 November, Gaithersburg, MD, accessed 23 June 2014 at http://trec.nist.gov/presentations/TREC8/intro/sld001.htm.

Zhang, X.M. (2005), 'Finding Edgeworth cycles in online advertising', MIT Sloan School of Management, accessed 23 June 2014 at http://web.mit.edu/zxq/www/mit/15575/keyword.pdf.

Zhang, X.M. and J. Feng (2005), 'Price cycles in online advertising auctions', in *Proceedings of the 26th International Conference on Information Systems*, Las Vegas, NV.

19. The economics of algorithmic selection on the Internet

Michael Latzer, Katharina Hollnbuchner, Natascha Just and Florian Saurwein

19.1 INTRODUCTION

Algorithms have come to shape our daily lives and realities. They change the perception of the world, affect our behavior by influencing our choices, and are an important source of social order. Algorithms on the Internet have significant economic implications in newly emerging markets and for existing markets in various sectors. A wide range of our daily activities in general and our media consumption in particular are increasingly shaped by algorithms operating behind the scenes: the selection of online news via search engines and news aggregators, the consumption of music and video entertainment via recommender systems, the choice of services and products in online shops and the selection of status messages displayed on social online networks are the most prominent examples of this omnipresent trend. Algorithms suggest friends, news, songs and travel routes. Moreover, they automatically produce news articles and messages, they calculate scorings of content and people, and are employed to observe our behavior and interests as well as to predict our future needs and actions. By assigning relevance to certain pieces of information they keep consumers, companies and authorities from drowning in a growing flood of information and online data. At the same time, they mine and construct realities, guide our actions and thereby determine the economic success of products and services. Algorithms form the techno-functional basis of new services and business models that economically challenge traditional industries and business strategies. These economic changes and challenges are accompanied by and interact with significant social risks such as manipulation and bias, threats to privacy and violations of intellectual property rights that compromise the economic and social welfare effects of algorithmic selection applications.

This rapidly growing Internet phenomenon is here called 'algorithmic selection'. It is a central and structuring bundle of Internet innovations in digital economies. Algorithmic selection is embedded in a variety of Internet-based services and is applied for numerous purposes. Although their modes of operation differ in detail, all of these applications are characterized by a common basic functionality: they automatically select information elements and assign relevance to them. This common feature defines the properties of algorithmic selection and allows a formal distinction from other Internet phenomena such as Web 2.0 (O'Reilly, 2007), the Internet of Things (Ashton, 2009; Mattern and Flörkemeier, 2010) and big data (Feijóo et al., Chapter 25 this volume).

The development of algorithmic selection is closely related to a number of techno-economic and social trends in information societies, including computerization, big data, personalization, automation and economic optimization. In essence, its diffusion and growing importance is fueled by the combination of ubiquitous computerization and the proliferation of an increasingly mobile Internet. In a growing number of economic and social domains, the spread of algorithmic selection is driven by the diffusion of online information, communication and transactions. Computers and the Internet serve as enabling technologies that provide the infrastructure – the technological and functional precondition for a wide range of applications. At the same time, ubiquitous computerization and Internet use generate additional demand for algorithmic selection, because they result in a massive proliferation of data volumes and a growing need for orientation by selection. This (big) data forms the raw material (World Economic Forum, 2011a) for algorithmic selection, creates economic opportunities and calls for data/reality-mining tools in order to harness the economic opportunities. Altogether, the combination of technological, data-based opportunities and economic demand for selection is a major driver for the establishment of new industries, applications and business models, where automation of data processing plays a central role, and algorithmic selection perfectly supports business strategies, especially in terms of process optimizations. Automated algorithmic selection advances optimizations in various ways: faster processing of larger amounts of data by automation; cost reductions in production and transmission by automation of data processing; strategic enhancements by increased data-driven, evidence-based decision-making (McAfee and Brynjolfsson, 2012); and personalization by mass customization of products and services that are tailored to meet diverse consumer needs.

With a high potential for economic improvement, algorithmic selection services are spreading fast in a wide range of industries. As illustrated by the Organisation for Economic Co-operation and Development (OECD, 2013) for big data, their diffusion is especially high in sectors characterized by a high degree of digitization and high data intensity. Accordingly, it already plays a major role in industries that rely heavily on digital production and online transmission such as Internet search, news, advertising, entertainment and social online networks. Further, algorithmic selection has gained importance in areas such as retail, trade, the stock exchange, banking, insurance, politics, security, intelligence, transportation, logistics, science, education, health and employment (Latzer et al., 2014). Given the combination of ubiquitous computerization, rapidly growing amounts of available data, and economic pressure for optimizations, the trend towards increased algorithmic selection in a rising number of domains seems to be irreversible. This provides the starting point and the rationale for more in-depth analyses on the characteristics, role and consequences of algorithmic selection for markets and societies.

Most social science research on algorithms has focused on search engines (Varian, 2006; Machill and Beiler, 2007; Lewandowski, 2012; König and Rasch, 2014) and recommendation systems (Resnick and Varian, 1997; Senecal and Nantel, 2004; Klahold, 2009; Jannach et al., 2011; Ricci et al., 2011; Robillard et al., 2014). This chapter extends the scope of analysis and provides a comprehensive overview, with a special focus on how to think economically about algorithmic selection. It explores the characteristics and implications of an increasingly adopted technology on the Internet that automates nothing less than the commercialization of reality mining and reality construction in information societies. The following questions are tackled: How can the plethora of algorithmic selection applications on the Internet be analytically grasped and categorized? How does algorithmic selection operate and where is it applied? What market structures and business models are evolving and how do they affect existing media markets? What are the major social and economic benefits and risks of algorithmic selection, and what governance choices are available to minimize risks and thus maximize economic and social welfare?

The chapter is organized as follows. The next section offers a typology of applications based on algorithmic selection and provides a basic input-throughput-output model in order to show the functioning and economic purposes of the different types of algorithmic selection. Section 19.3 explains the theoretical perspective applied for its analysis. Section 19.4 presents results from market analyses and shows the different phases of markets for applications using algorithmic selection, explores their structures and explains concentration tendencies. Section 19.5 provides insights into business models of algorithmic selection with an emphasis on value proposition, value creation and revenue streams. Section 19.6 examines selected implications of algorithmic selection for traditional media markets and the incumbents' profitability. Section 19.7 identifies areas of risk, such as possible violations of basic rights, the effects of algorithmic selection on perceptions of the world and potential impacts of algorithmic selection on human development. Finally, section 19.8 summarizes regulatory challenges and discusses opportunities and limitations of available governance choices such as market solutions, self-regulation and state intervention. Section 19.9 draws conclusions about the economics of algorithmic selection.

19.2   THE OPERATION MODEL AND FUNCTIONAL TYPOLOGY

Algorithmic selection is applied for a number of purposes. It is the technological basis or functional feature of many of the most popular and economically successful Internet services, among others, by Google, Facebook, Amazon, Netflix or Spotify. Applications and groups of services based on algorithmic selection often contain prefixes such as 'algorithmic' or simply 'algo' (e.g., algo trading), 'computerized' or 'computational' (e.g., computational advertising), 'smart' or 'intelligent' (e.g., intelligent filtering). This plurality of applications, services and terms constitutes a challenge for research. In order to explore algorithmic selection it has to be defined and distinguished from other phenomena. Moreover, it is helpful to differentiate certain groups of applications in order to compare and contrast functions, markets and risks associated with certain types of application.

Although there are numerous definitions of algorithm, it can generally be described as a finite series of precisely described rules or processes to solve a problem. It is a sequence of stages that transforms input through specified computational procedures (throughput) into output (Cormen et al., 2009; Mössenböck, 2014). Generally, all algorithmic selection applications can be described with the help of a basic input-throughput-output model (ITO), depicted in Figure 19.1.

The centerpiece of this process model is the throughput stage at which the algorithms operate that define the input–output relationship. Starting from a user request and available user characteristics they apply statistical operations to select elements from a basic data set (DS1) and assign relevance to them. Accordingly, algorithmic selection on the Internet is defined as a process that assigns relevance to information elements of a data set by an automated, statistical assessment of decentrally generated data signals. Input, throughput and output vary for different applications and services. In many cases, big data serves as input, but there is a wide spectrum of input sources, depending on the field of

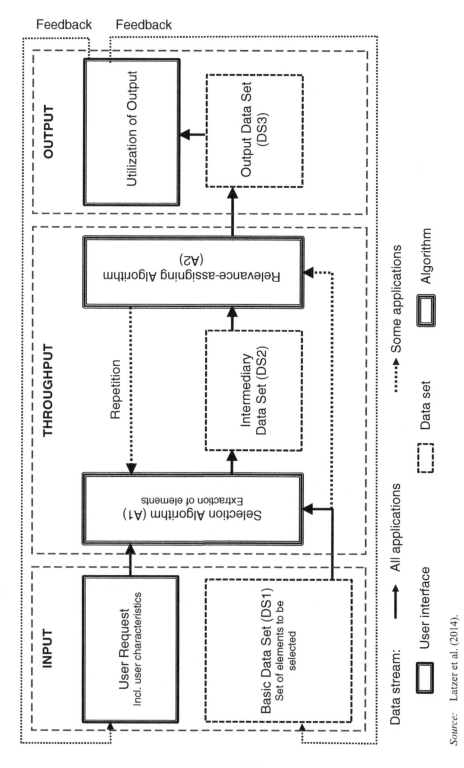

Source: Latzer et al. (2014).

Figure 19.1 Input-throughput-output model of algorithmic selection on the Internet

Table 19.1   Functional typology of applications using algorithmic selection

Types	Examples
Search	General search engines (e.g., Google search, Bing, Baidu) Special search engines (e.g., Mocavo, Shutterstock, Social Mention) Meta search engines (e.g., Dogpile, Info.com) Semantic search engines (e.g., Yummly) Questions & answers services (e.g., Ask.com)
Aggregation	News aggregators (e.g., Google News, nachrichten.de)
Observation/ surveillance	Surveillance (e.g., Raytheon's RIOT) Employee monitoring (e.g., Spector, Sonar, Spytec) General monitoring software (e.g., Webwatcher)
Prognosis/forecast	Predictive policing (e.g., PredPol), Predicting developments: success, diffusion etc. (e.g., Google Flu Trends, ScoreAHit)
Filtering	Spam filter (e.g., Norton) Child protection filter (e.g., Net Nanny)
Recommendation	Recommender systems (e.g., Spotify, Netflix)
Scoring	Reputation systems: music, film, etc. (e.g., eBay's reputation system) News scoring (e.g., reddit, Digg) Credit scoring (e.g., Kreditech) Social scoring (e.g., Klout)
Content production	Algorithmic journalism (e.g., Quill, Quakebot)
Allocation	Computational advertising (e.g., Google AdSense, Yahoo! Bing Network) Algorithmic trading (e.g., Quantopian)

Source: Latzer et al. (2014).

application. The throughput process is characterized by the assignment of relevance (A2) and respective selections (A1), and there is a multitude of different codes based on different operating modes (e.g., matching, sorting or filtering algorithms). Finally, the output (DS3) also takes on different forms (e.g., rankings, recommendations, biddings, text, and music). In many cases, it serves as an input to subsequent algorithmic selection processes.

Applications can be differentiated according to their central function, that is, the general purpose that these applications serve. Here, a functional typology is proposed that covers nine categories (Table 19.1). It should be kept in mind, though, that these categories are neither meant to be all embracing nor mutually exclusive.

Search applications have become indispensable tools for exploring the Internet and are the most widespread algorithmic services with great economic significance. Relevance is assigned to elements according to the best fit with users' queries. Alongside general purpose algorithmic search engines such as Google and Bing, there are a vast number of applications for special (vertical) searching in particular domains or regarding particular issues (e.g., Mocavo, a genealogy search engine). General search engines play an important role in the growing e-commerce sector, which has led to the development of connected industries of web content production and website optimization (known as search engine optimization, SEO, agencies) as well as search engine marketing (SEM) specialists. The gatekeeping role of general search engines and especially the dominant market position of Google (Haucap and Stühmeier, Chapter 9 this volume) are highly contested issues in the public debate.

Aggregation applications, most prominently news aggregators such as Google News, collect, categorize and regroup information from multiple sources into one single point of access (Zhu et al., 2001; Águila-Obra et al., 2007; Calin et al., 2013). Unlike syndicators, aggregators often acquire the data they offer (e.g., news) without paying. This business model has attracted severe criticism and debate, especially regarding the impact on the profitability of other media industries (in particular, newspapers) and alleged intellectual property rights violations (Isbell, 2010; Weaver, 2013).

Observation/surveillance applications such as Raytheon's Rapid Information Overlay Technology (RIOT) have gained prominence lately and were heavily criticized in the context of the National Security Agency scandal (Greenwald and MacAskill, 2013). Not only do secret service agencies make use of algorithmic surveillance, but companies also employ surveillance technologies, for example for social sorting (Lyon, 2003), to control their networks, employees (Ciocchetti, 2011) and customers (Pridmore and Zwick, 2011). Many applications monitor online behavior in order to detect abnormalities associated with certain risks (e.g., credit card fraud, cyber attacks). Moreover, for several other algorithmic applications, such as forecasting services or computational advertising, observation and surveillance are a basic function.

Prognosis/forecast applications aim at predicting future behavior or scenarios (Küsters et al., 2006; Issenberg, 2012; Silver, 2012), for instance, in areas such as consumption, natural disasters, entertainment hits and crime. Respective applications, such as the predictive policing technology PredPol, are of particular importance in the context of big data analyses. The distinction between surveillance applications and forecast applications is often not clear-cut, as both employ similar data/reality mining methods, or are applied in combination. To distinguish them, surveillance applications are sometimes called 'now-casting' applications (Banbura et al., 2010; Faigle, 2010), which points to time as the differentiating factor. Surveillance refers to the present (real time), while forecasting relates to future occurrences.

Filtering applications such as the Norton spam filter often work behind the scenes as passive or active information filters (Hanani et al., 2001). Passive filters select certain elements, but instead of displaying these to the user, they prevent access to them. Algorithmic or intelligent filtering is applied, for instance, to counter spam or malware. However, filtering is also used to block political information, especially in authoritarian regimes (Deibert et al., 2008, 2010).

Recommendation applications such as music recommendations by Spotify are among the most widely known services. These online applications are intended to replace traditional recommendations by shop assistants or friends. To provide the most fitting recommendations they apply various filtering methods relying on data concerning the item, the user, or the artificial group a user is assigned to (Klahold, 2009). Recommender systems are very common in e-commerce and play an important role for increasing sales by reducing search costs and building e-trust (Pathak et al., 2010).

Scoring applications such as eBay's reputation system gather and process feedback about participants' behavior and derive ratings and scores relating to behavior from this (Resnick and Zeckhauser, 2002). A central purpose of these services is to build trust in an anonymous online environment and reduce transaction costs. Applications include sensitive areas such as credit scoring (Rothmann et al., 2014) or social scoring (measuring a person's creditworthiness or social resources). Accordingly, these systems involve considerable risks of social discrimination on the grounds of a person's race, age or religion and may infringe personal privacy (Bostic and Calem, 2003; Pavlov et al., 2004; Steinbrecher, 2006).

Furthermore, algorithms can be used to create content automatically, for example with applications such as Quill, developed by Narrative Science. These developments have recently been discussed under terms such as algorithmic, automated or robotic journalism (Levy, 2012; Steiner, 2012; Anderson, 2013; Dörr, 2015). Automated production is not limited to text (e.g., tweets, news articles, business reports) but music production is affected as well. It allows for massive content production and contains the potential for the further rationalization and commercialization of media production. These applications touch deeply upon human areas of creativity and expression, leading to a revival of discussions about artificial intelligence software.

Allocation applications independently and automatically conduct transactions (e.g., placement of ads) and allocate resources (Lee, 2007; Varian, 2009; Leinweber, 2009). Algorithmic trading software or computational advertising services such as Google AdSense are good examples of such applications. Computational advertising especially is the core revenue source for many online platforms such as search and social online networks (Evans, 2008).

19.3   THE INNOVATION–CO-EVOLUTION–COMPLEXITY PERSPECTIVE

The Internet is a multi-purpose infrastructure for innumerable and highly diverse applications. This considerably limits the prospects of deriving generalized economic consequences. The identification of and focus on one distinct set of Internet-based innovations – algorithmic selection – is an effort to take a more differentiated look at its economic and social implications. Other analytical challenges are the great significance of technological change and its interplay with economic, political and social transformations.

This chapter adopts an integrated innovation–co-evolution–complexity perspective (Latzer, 2013a), an evolutionary economics of innovation (Frenken, 2006), which conceives media change as an innovation-driven, co-evolutionary process in a complex environment, marked by adaptive, non-linear system behavior (Schultze and Whitt, Chapter 3 this volume). Algorithmic selection by search engines and recommendation systems on the micro level, for example, result in unpredictable, unintended emergent effects on the link structure of the WWW at the macro level. Accordingly, the Internet is understood as an open adaptive system, an 'innovation machine' because of its specific (end-to-end) architectural design (Whitt and Schultze, 2009; van Schewick, 2010). Co-evolution – sometimes addressed as co-construction or confluence (Benkler, 2006) – is a durable relation between agents that influence each other's evolutionary paths. Hence, according to a complexity economics perspective (Beinhocker, 2006), processes in economics, politics, technology and society are driven by mutually selective pressure or adaption. This explains the reciprocal interplay – more precisely the pressure and adaptive behavior of technology, organizations and business models that nurture each other. The advantages of such a co-evolutionary perspective include its contribution to better understanding and integrating evolutionary technological change (Ziman, 2000) – where technology is not only output but also input into the economy; to overcome the antagonism of technological and social determinism (Rip, 2007); and to direct the focus from static assessments to dynamic approaches. Finally, such a co-evolutionary perspective results in other (adaptive) strategies for media management and governance than traditional approaches alone, due to an acknowledgment of the limited predictability and steerability of dynamic co-evolutionary developments. Strategies seek less to dictate developments, avoiding attempts to pick winners from technological alternatives and different business models, and are more oriented to enabling and fostering co-evolutionary processes by creating favorable frameworks, for example by strengthening adaptive policies and feedback mechanisms (Latzer, 2013b, 2014).

Selecting and relevance-assigning algorithms on the Internet can be understood, with reference to Bresnahan (2010), as micro general purpose technologies, as widely used clusters of (radical) innovations that enable and trigger innovations in many other economic sectors, because they offer not one specific solution but various new opportunities. The co-evolution with political, economic and cultural factors determines what opportunities will ultimately be used and what the consequences will be for socio-economic welfare. Governance activities to minimize risks – discussed below – are closely interlinked with economic factors and also interact with technological characteristics.

Algorithmic selection can lead to creative destruction, and even has the potential to be a disruptive technology (Christensen, 1997), a special form of creative destruction marked by inferior technology and the replacement of incumbents (low-end disruption, e.g., credit scoring, and new market disruptions, e.g., computational advertising). Innovations are co-evolutionary, adaptive processes of renewal, marked by variation, selection and adaptive reactions. Corporations play a crucial role in selection processes of technologies and of appropriate business models. This will be described in the following sections of this chapter, together with other characteristics of markets of services using algorithmic selection and their market phases.

Starting from an innovation–co-evolution–complexity perspective, several other approaches help to better understand algorithmic selection. The *power* of technology and the ability of algorithms to shape realities and societies have been variously discussed by researchers and journalists who focus, among other things, on the role of algorithms as agents (Machill and Beiler, 2007), institutions (Napoli, 2013), ideologies (Mager, 2012) and gatekeepers (Jürgens et al., 2011; Wallace, 2016). An institutional point of view, for example, highlights the enabling and restricting role of technologies in general and of algorithms in particular.

Further, algorithmic selection can be conceived as a mode of intermediation (Águila-Obra et al., 2007), which is central, for example, to understanding platforms and multi-sided markets. It connects supply and demand, that is, providers and consumers of products and content. Algorithms are involved in the allocation of resources, and often have the role of market makers in the value creation system – discussed below. Additionally, the intermediation perspective highlights the role as gatekeeper and its effects on the public sphere and public opinion formation as well as its role in the algorithmic construction of realities that differs considerably from realities constructed by traditional mass media (Just and Latzer, 2016).

19.4 MARKETS, MARKET PHASES AND STRUCTURES

Algorithmic selection is creating new Internet-based markets and changing existing ones on a large scale. It can constitute the (economic) core function of Internet-based services, for example in the case of the general search services of Google or Microsoft, and/or it is applied as an ancillary function, for example in e-commerce applications for filtering/recommendation purposes by Amazon, or for the automated selection of status messages displayed in online social media applications by Facebook. Core function basically means that the result of algorithmic selections is the demanded product; ancillary functions are used to support the core service of a company in order to gain competitive advantage.

Altogether, almost all of the most popular and economically successful Internet-based services rely heavily on algorithmic selection in one form or another. Table 19.2 shows the ten most visited websites worldwide in 2014 and their applications based on algorithmic selection as a core and/or ancillary service. Seven of these rely heavily on computational advertising, and four on general search engines. Three websites use algorithmic selection as an ancillary service only (Wikipedia and two online shopping platforms). Further, the dominance of US (seven) and Chinese (three) companies is striking.

Despite variations between different categories, market sizes tend to be high (e.g., search, computational advertising) and growth rates impressive (e.g., music and film streaming) for services and products based on algorithmic selection.

Markets pass through different phases in their life cycles: from experimental and expansion phases to maturity, stagnation and decline. Accordingly, they show different market structures, sizes and growth rates, and call for different business strategies and public policies. Based on a review of available market data, a rough appraisal of various types of algorithmic selection by market phases can be given. Most types are still in an experimental (e.g., algorithmic prognosis of the future success of films and music) or an early expansion phase (e.g., automated content production, scoring, surveillance) with comparatively low market sizes as yet but considerable future growth potential. Examples of the expansion/growth phase are recommender systems for music and films (e.g., Spotify, Netflix) with high annual growth rates. Computational advertising markets can roughly be classified within the maturity phase, and general search markets are already tending toward stagnation, with decreasing growth rates but impressive market sizes. These latter two categories show high concentration rates. Search markets are highly concentrated on a global scale with regional market shares of Google Search up to 97 percent (Table 19.3). The major display ad selling companies are Google and Facebook, which in 2013 possessed net US digital display ad revenue shares of 14.4 percent and 18.6 percent respectively. These shares are estimated to grow to 26.9 percent for Facebook in 2017, resulting in the top two companies capturing 38 percent of the market (eMarketer, 2015). Concentration is not only evident for search and computational advertising. The leading US dating platform, for example, is Match.com (Statista, June 2014), a brand belonging to InterActiveCorp (IAC), which in 2012 had a 41 percent US market share in online

Table 19.2   Algorithmic selection in top ten websites worldwide

Ranking	Website	Company and Country of Origin	Algorithmic Selection as Core Service	Algorithmic Selection as Ancillary Service
1	Google.com	Google (USA)	General search engine Computational advertising	Autocomplete
2	Facebook.com	Facebook (USA)	Computational advertising	Filtering (EdgeRank) Social search (GraphSearch) Recommendations (contacts)
3	Youtube.com	Google (USA)	Computational advertising	Variety of recommendations Special search engine
4	Yahoo.com	Yahoo! (USA)	General search engine Computational advertising	Autocomplete
5	Baidu.com	Baidu (CHN)	General search engine Computational advertising	Autocomplete
6	Wikipedia.org	Wikimedia Foundation (USA)		Special search engine
7	Twitter.com	Twitter (USA)	Computational advertising	Aggregations/ recommendations (Twitter Trends, Who to Follow)
8	QQ.com	Tencent (CHN)	General search engine Computational advertising	Autocomplete
9	Taobao.com	Alibaba Group (CHN)		Special search (products) Recommendations (products) Reputation (marketplace sellers)
10	Amazon.com	Amazon (USA)		Special search (products) Recommendations (products) Reputation (marketplace sellers)

Source: Latzer et al. (2014), ranking based on Alexa.com, 15 July 2014.

Table 19.3   *Concentration of search engine markets in selected countries, Europe and worldwide (end of 2013)*

	Google (USA) (%)	Yahoo! (USA) (%)	Bing (USA) (%)	Baidu (CHN) (%)	Yandex (RUS) (%)
Thailand	97.0				
Spain	96.3	0.9	1.1		
Vietnam	96.0				
United Kingdom	94.2	1.8	2.7		
Germany	94.1	0.8	1.6		
France	92.8	1.7	2.6		
India	90.0				
Indonesia	88.0				
Malaysia	87.0				
Philippines	84.0				
Singapore	84.0				
USA	67.3	10.8	18.2		
China	1.7	0.3	0.6	63.6	
Russia	26.5				61.9
Japan[a]	36	51.4			
Europe[a] (18 countries incl. RU)	86.0		1.0		10.0
Worldwide[a]	65.2	4.9	2.5	8.2	2.8

Note: a. 2012 data.

Sources: ComScore (2013a, 2013b, 2013c, 2014) (Europe, ID, IN, MY, PH, SG, TH, US, VN), Pavliva (2013) (RU), CNZZ (2013) (CN), Schautzer (2013) (JP), AT Internet (2014) (DE, ES, FR, UK), Sullivan (2013) (worldwide).

dating. Altogether, the shares of the top two online dating companies amounted to 64 percent (VanderMey, 2013).

Concentration tendencies are a constituent feature of many of the Internet businesses that offer products and services that operate on algorithmic selection. Many of these can be described as two- or multi-sided platforms, operating on two- or multi-sided markets (Rochet and Tirole, 2003) – a characteristic that has important interrelated economic, business and policy implications. In such cases, for example, the platform acts as an intermediary, as a market maker, between (at least) two demand sides that are interlinked by indirect network effects, which may be one reason for concentration in these markets.

These concentration tendencies can be explained by various industrial economic characteristics such as cost structures, scale and scope economies, direct and indirect network effects. As with traditional media markets, cost structures for markets of services using algorithmic selection are characterized by considerable economies of scale, resulting from high fixed and sunk costs (e.g., R&D, hardware and software maintenance), and extremely low marginal cost of additional selection processes (e.g., an additional music recommendation). Hence dominant players enjoy cost advantages, resulting in high market entry barriers due to cost disadvantages of new entrants. A large market size is often necessary to operate efficiently, an issue that is also evident when considering indirect network effects that arise when the number of participants on one side (positively or negatively) affects the number of participants on the other. Usually the participation of one group raises the value of participating for the other group. For example, the more users a search engine has, the greater the positive indirect effects on advertisers. Although advertising might be a nuisance for users, both sides need to join the platform for success – a task usually accomplished through the pricing structure, where a higher price is typically paid on the side that generates less positive network effects.

This leads to another important characteristic: markets that rely on algorithmic selection are predominantly characterized by quality and innovation competition and less by price competition. Many applications are free of charge for end customers. Hence the perceived quality of a service is particularly important for gaining competitive advantage. The quality of service depends, inter alia, on the quality of algorithms, hardware (e.g., server farms) and (input) data (Argenton and Prüfer, 2012). Exclusive access to data by service suppliers who create data (e.g., social media companies) results in a strong competitive advantage. These data form an essential input for selection processes, and might lead to exclusive quality improvements on the input side, thus contributing to concentration tendencies.

Moreover, exclusive access to user and usage data of one's own service results in a competitive advantage for established players and forms a market-entry barrier for newcomers, because they will not be able to offer services of a comparable quality. In contrast to traditional media markets, the quality of services – in essence, the quality of selections – increases with the growing use of a service. The reason is that the results of earlier selections feed back into future selection processes and thus increase their quality. The quality of selections depends, inter alia, on the number of earlier selections, which is why more users and usage result in quality improvements of services. This is true for individual users (by improved personalization/customization of products that also increases users' switching costs) and all other users as well. There are network effects, in other words demand-side scale effects. In addition, there is a positive feedback loop between network effects on the demand side and scale effects on the supply side. This again results in concentration tendencies, even in winner-takes-all markets with widening disparities.

Finally, concentration and market entry barriers are facilitated by considerable economies of scope, resulting from the use of central resources for multiple purposes, in particular of technological know-how – especially on algorithms, of hardware infrastructures and databases. Accordingly, many big players such as Google, Microsoft and Amazon are diversifying and offering a range of different types of algorithmic selection services, thus exploiting economies of scope. Among other things, Google offers search, advertising, aggregation and recommendation, Microsoft is active in search, advertising, surveillance, prognosis and aggregation, IBM in prognosis and surveillance.

Moreover, there is a connection between market phases and market structures. Many algorithmic selection applications are still in the experimental phase or an early expansion phase. These phases are, in general, characterized by high concentration, by temporary monopolies of innovators and early movers. In these early phases, innovators (often US companies in the case of algorithmic selection) also find favorable conditions to export and dominate markets abroad (e.g., Netflix, which uses algorithmic selection as a key part of its business).

19.5 BUSINESS MODELS OF ALGORITHMIC SELECTION

Innovation theory suggests that potential benefits of technical innovations can best be exploited in combination with appropriate social/organizational innovations. Among such social innovations are business models that have long 'been given short shrift in the innovation literature' (Teece, 2006, p. 1142), however. Awareness of the importance of business models has increased recently, not least because of the growth of the Internet, which both challenged and destroyed traditional business models and opened up debates about how to make money in an online environment that is characterized by expectations that services should be free (Teece, 2010). Business models systematically describe the value proposition, the value creation as well as the revenue streams and cost structures (Osterwalder et al., 2005; Jaeggi, 2010). They not only focus on companies' products and services, but also on core resources and activities that are needed to create value, and on the channels of delivery to customers.

Comparative business model analyses of services using algorithmic selection show common patterns. Similarities are mostly found in services offered to end users, resulting in part from market characteristics (e.g., pricing in two- or multi-sided markets) or from imitation strategies in business models of similar services, whereas services for business and public service customers (e.g., the police) vary more widely, as they are frequently custom-made for specific purposes (Latzer et al., 2014).

19.5.1 Value Proposition

Value propositions of suppliers of services using algorithmic selection reveal economic and social benefits for individuals, corporations, administrations and society. Among the economic benefits are reductions in transaction costs, cost and performance advantages, and customized problem-solving solutions (Klingenberg, 2000; Zollenkop, 2006). Predominantly, algorithmic selection promises to reduce various kinds of transaction costs, such as search and information costs – mostly in the case of search, filter, aggregation, and recommender applications – or information asymmetries, for example through reputation systems. A reduction of transaction costs is also realized with allocation services (e.g., computational advertising and advertising networks, algorithmic trading) by mass-customized process automation and by replacing human labor by algorithms. The last of these is also evident in certain areas of content production (e.g., algorithmic journalism). In such cases, companies may use efficiency gains differently: to save costs or to increase the quality of other segments of content production, as in the case of algorithmic journalism (Van Dalen, 2012). Various studies show that the reduction of search costs results in increased consumption and sales, like increased news consumption because of news aggregators (Athey and Mobius, 2012; Chiou and Tucker, 2013), increased TV consumption due to recommender systems (Pronk et al., 2009), or increased sales because of search and recommender systems in online stores (Hinz and Eckert, 2010).

Cost and performance advantages are especially manifest for business and public service customers. In particular, for services in categories like surveillance and prognosis, as well as allocation and content production, algorithmic processing of big data offers advantages to corporate customers and public authorities. For example, computational advertising reduces scatter losses due to personalization and improves performance-based remuneration by exploiting pay-per-click possibilities, algorithmic trading services enter huge amounts of orders at a faster pace than humans, or predictive policing applications are useful in coordinating processes (e.g., stationing of police officers in crime-prone areas). The possibilities of enhanced personalization and customization in particular are the basis of many customized solutions provided to customers by algorithmic selection services.

Potential social benefits of algorithmic selection services include their contribution to social orientation, information gathering and public opinion formation. News aggregators (e.g., Google News, nachrichten.de), general search engines (e.g., Google, Bing), news-scoring applications (e.g., Reddit, Digg), automated content production and social online networks are expected to contribute to these social benefits.

19.5.2   Value Creation

Various resources, skills and activities are needed to deliver value to consumers. Within the value creation system of algorithmic selection services there are core resources that are of particular relevance regarding the quality and thus competitive advantage of automated selection processes: technical expertise, especially regarding software/algorithms, the hardware infrastructure (e.g., server farms, computer networks) and access to and quality of data (information elements and externally produced data signals – see Figure 19.1). These influence the value production chain, including R&D, data collection (input), selection processes (throughput) and the use, placement and distribution of selection results (output).

Providers of algorithmic selection applications fulfill different roles within the external value creation system (Heuskel, 1999). Analyses indicate that they are most frequently active as market makers (intermediaries) or layer players (specialists). They are less active as orchestrators that outsource various stages of the value chain, yet occupy strategic positions (e.g., Yahoo!), or as integrators that integrate nearly all stages of the value chain in their companies (e.g., Google).

As platforms, in particular as market makers between suppliers and consumers (e.g., search engines, news aggregators, advertising networks, music and film streaming), they create new activities within the value chain and bring together products of different companies and offer those, or a selection, to potential customers. Based on this platformization of markets (Kranz and Picot, Chapter 17 this volume), these services increase transparency (e.g., comparability) and influence customer choice (decisions). Most of the algorithmic selection services directed at end users are active as market makers within the value creation chain.

Another group of algorithmic selection services, the layer players, specialize in one particular stage of the value chain, which often results in superior knowledge and scale effects. They fulfill this stage for individual companies, for a specific sector or across various sectors. Examples include surveillance, security, prognosis and content production services.

For algorithmic selection applications, not only the various undisclosed algorithms but also the supply and the quality of selection elements and data signals are crucial for competitive advantages and economic success. There are different types of suppliers of selection elements: suppliers based on contracts who are financially compensated (e.g., music labels that license music for streaming services); customers who provide the data to service suppliers (e.g., police for predictive policing applications); and suppliers whose content is mostly used, some would say appropriated, without approval and compensation (e.g., websites of newspapers). Such appropriation of content has raised serious concerns by competitors as it directly affects their profitability (see below). Finally, value creation by algorithmic selection is based, among other things, on the assessment of decentralized data signals in order to assign relevance to information elements (see Figure 19.1). Suppliers of decentralized data signals are, for example, Internet-based services that deliver user data with the consent of users, customers of services that provide data either by consent or unintentionally because they are unwittingly being tracked, and data companies that collect and sell different kinds of data (e.g., sports statistics, historic weather data).

19.5.3 Revenue Models

Revenue models focus on the sources of revenue and on price setting. They are strongly influenced by the fact that algorithmic selection applications often serve different, inter-dependent customer segments in two- or multi-sided platform markets, where prices have to be weighted accordingly. As a consequence, in many cases advertising revenues typically indirectly finance the basic algorithmic selection services for end users. Most search and social online networks, for example, offer their services for free to end users and charge the other side of the market, for example the advertisers, for access to what is often considered the actual product, that is, the audience. Computational advertising has now developed into a very sophisticated way to reach target groups, among other things with the help of auctions (Varian, Chapter 18 this volume). In contrast, most applications directed only at business and public service customers (e.g., security, prognosis) serve independent customer segments, and are therefore not usually constrained by price-setting strategies required in multi-sided markets.

Indirect forms of revenue, both transaction dependent and independent, predominate in markets of services relying on algorithmic selection, and direct transaction-dependent forms are rare. There are many indirect transaction-dependent forms of revenue generation, such as pay per click or impression ads, Powerplay campaigns (e.g., LastFM) or Promoted Tweets. In many cases revenue is generated from a combination of different sources, however. This can be exemplified with various freemium services like Spotify or LinkedIn. Often a basic service – with limited features, usage restrictions, or offered in exchange for advertising – is free to the user, who is charged a premium, however, for services with added functionality, quality and no restrictions. Premium profiles are then a form of direct transaction-independent source of revenue, as are various subscription-only services like Netflix.

19.6   SELECTED IMPLICATIONS OF ALGORITHMIC SELECTION FOR TRADITIONAL MEDIA MARKETS

The economic implications of algorithmic selection services are as wide as their fields of application in various sectors of the economy. This section focuses on media markets only, in particular on media incumbents' profitability. For decades traditional news companies have dominated the construction of public spheres. They were unchallenged and made high profits in advertising markets. Now both core businesses of news companies – the audience and advertising markets – are increasingly coming under pressure from activities of IT companies like Microsoft or dot-coms like Google and Yahoo!. As market makers, they squeeze themselves between traditional news companies and their two customer segments, the audience and the advertisers (Águila-Obra et al., 2007). Their competitive advantages result from the generation of huge amounts of data and the automated algorithmic selection and placement of news, on the one hand, and from the automated selection and placement of advertisements on the other. News aggregators (e.g., Google News or Bing News) and online advertising networks (e.g., Google AdSense) are examples of such intermediaries.

Thus far, the majority of research on the impact of algorithmic selection on media industries predominantly focuses on news aggregators and online advertising, revealing that they increase both the reading consumptions and the quality of news (e.g., Athey and Mobius, 2012; Chiou and Tucker, 2013; Dellarocas et al., 2013) and have impacts on price strategies and targeting methods in online and offline advertising markets (Edelmann et al., 2005; Evans 2009; Bergmann and Bonatti, 2011). Many other questions remain unanswered and call for further research, especially those regarding the combined economic impact of various algorithmic selection applications that affect both the audience and the advertising market. Moreover, the impact of algorithmic selection on other media industries such as music or film has not yet been examined.

A basis for such analysis is Porter's (1979, 2008) concept of five forces that shape industry competition, which has been applied, for example, by Maass et al. (2009) to assess the robustness of concentration in search markets. Coupled with comparative analyses of business models and market structures, Porter's approach also makes it possible to assess the impact of algorithmic selection applications such as news aggregators, algorithmic content production, computational advertising, music streaming or subscription video-on-demand services on the news, music, film and TV industries. Changes to the five competitive forces – the threat of new entrants and of substitute products and services, the bargaining power of both suppliers and buyers, and the rivalry among existing competitors – affect the average profitability of media incumbents.

Theoretical considerations suggest that algorithmic selection services predominantly come into effect as intermediaries or suppliers in media industries, and tend to change their profitability. In his early assessment of the Internet in general, Porter (2001) argues that the Internet tends to decrease profitability. Theoretical analyses of algorithmic selection applications indicate that the impact on incumbents' profitability seems to vary from media industry to media industry (Latzer et al., 2014). For example, in the news industry, algorithmic selection tends to decrease average profitability overall. Although incumbents benefit from added traffic streams (Chiou and Tucker, 2013; Dellarocas et al., 2013) and from integrating algorithmic selection (e.g., news created by algorithms) as an ancillary function, intermediaries such as news aggregators or advertising networks change the competitive forces of the industry (Porter, 1979) to the disadvantage of incumbents. Increasingly high concentration in these markets is shifting the bargaining power to these intermediary platforms and allowing them to amplify their market power. This is especially the case if they are able to establish themselves as bottleneck monopolists that control the access to products of others (Shelanski, 2013), as in the case of news publishers' content or as evident in the struggles between book publishers or sellers, and lately Disney and Amazon. Some have turned to opt-out options, for example by blocking their sites from search engines (e.g., News Corp. blocked Google services by using robot.txt files). Opting out of search services has not been a feasible solution for publishers, however. Search engines, for example, are responsible for high visitor rates to news websites, with widely differing figures up to 35 percent (SimilarWeb.com, 2013). Further, aggregation of news in single access points also results in lower transaction and switching costs for news customers and tends to increase their bargaining power. As new entrants, online advertising networks in particular are straining incumbents' profitability.

For the music industry, in contrast, it can be argued that the adoption of algorithmic selection as key part of their services tends to increase incumbents' profitability overall, as music-streaming services (e.g., Last.FM, Spotify) strongly stimulate (legal) music consumption and have been revenue drivers in recent years. Although they also established themselves as intermediaries they are faced with a highly concentrated music industry with great bargaining power.

The differences in impact on various media industries can be explained by different business models of algorithmic selection services (market makers, layer players) and by the different stages of market development (market phases) of the relevant algorithmic selection services as well as business models and market structures of traditional industries (Latzer et al., 2014).

These first rough estimates and theoretical considerations of the possible impact of algorithmic selection on media industries are still in need of further research, and in particular need to be combined and weighed with current market data in order to receive an accurate picture of the full economic implications for media industries.

19.7 SOCIAL RISKS

Algorithmic selection and attendant personal data collection have become objects of public concern and have raised questions about their impact on society as well as the need for public policy. Generally, the assessment of risks is an appropriate method to relate estimated economic and social benefits to risks, for example the benefits gained by search engines in managing information overflow versus the risk to user privacy. A first step in such analysis is generally to identify possible risks and benefits and assess the probability of their occurrence and the number of people affected. For example, how many people or institutions use an algorithmic application, do these people or institutions have a multiplying effect, and how often and how intensively do people/institutions use the application?

The various risks of algorithmic selection applications found in the literature are here grouped in three overlapping categories, which in particular indicate that such analysis not only touches upon cost–benefit calculations but also extends into ethical/moral value judgments: (1) threats to basic rights and liberties, (2) impacts on the mediation of reality, and (3) challenges to the future development of the human species. Overall, eight specific risks can be distinguished that accompany the diffusion of algorithmic selection: (1) manipulation, (2) diminishing variety, the creation of biases and distortions of reality, (3) constraints on the freedom of communication and expression, (4) threats to data protection and privacy, (5) social discrimination, (6) violation of intellectual property rights, (7) possible transformations and adaptations of the human brain, and (8) uncertain effects of the power of algorithms on humans, for example growing independence of human control and growing human dependence on algorithms.

Empirical examples of manipulation are 'Google bombs' (e.g., Bar-Ilan, 2007), described as planned massive influence on search results, or the improvement of websites through search engine optimization that improperly tries to increase the attention achieved. Manipulations have also been identified for recommender and reputation systems for goods and services such as hotel or product recommendations (e.g., Rietjens, 2006; Schormann, 2012). Algorithmic selection is furthermore associated with bias inasmuch as it is presumed to develop an algorithmic reality where content is only visible when it is produced and shaped according to the rules that algorithmic selection prescribes (Zhang and Dimitroff, 2005; Cushing Weigle, 2013). The rules themselves leave out certain aspects of reality and have incorporated specific values that unknowingly discriminate against particular content. Qualified empirical evidence for this phenomenon is rare, but various authors have discussed the self-enforcing mechanisms of algorithms and their biasing effects (e.g., filter bubble; Pariser, 2011), or the creation of a digital divide on a content and usage level (Segev, 2010). Accordingly, the much-discussed media realities that are being formed by the gatekeeping function of traditional mass media reach a new level, leading to discussions about algorithmic realities that follow different, increasingly automated, personalized and commercialized rules (Just and Latzer, 2016).

Constraints on the freedom of communication are also identified as a possible risk of algorithmic selection – an argument derived largely from its technological design. As the name implies, it has a selective element that can be shaped, with differing effects, however. On the one hand it can be used to gain access to relevant content or to protect IP rights (Wunsch-Vincent, Chapter 11 this volume) or to keep children from accessing harmful content (Hinman, 2005). On the other hand, algorithmic selection may be adopted to diminish the democratic potential of digital media by being used for censorship (Zittrain and Palfrey, 2008).

To fulfill their role as information intermediaries and information brokers, algorithmic selection applications have to rely on content produced by third parties and on data produced by consumers. Both sources of information involve certain risks. It is argued that, without infringing the intellectual property rights of content producers and distributors, many applications such as search engines, information aggregators or recommender systems would have no data basis on which to build their services (Stühmeier, 2011). This kind of use of third-party content has led to disputes over copyright and other intellectual property rights, and publishers all over the world have sued Google for infringing such laws (Clark, 2010, 2012; Chiou and Tucker, 2013; Quinn, 2014). Moreover, many algorithmic selection applications are personalized/customized applications, that is, applications that use data collected from the users to personalize results. This incorporates great risks concerning users' privacy and data protection (Brown, Chapter 12 this volume). Today, personal data has become the new oil for the economy (World Economic Forum, 2011b) and operators of algorithmic selection applications are major collectors of such data online. They use these data to customize services and monetize them (as an exchange for other/more data or by selling them directly) – activities that have resulted in various data privacy challenges (Chaleppa and Sin, 2005; Zimmer, 2008; Xu et al., 2011; Toch et al., 2012). Algorithmic applications also raise debates concerning their influence on human cognitive abilities – a pressing object for future research. Current discussions range between questions of whether these applications result in the loss of abilities (Carr, 2010; Henig and Henig, 2012) or whether they are simply helping in allocating cognitive resources more efficiently, like other technologies in history (Sparrow et al., 2011). Finally, there is a general discussion on how the relationship between humans and algorithms can be described and how this human–machine relationship will develop or should be shaped in the near future (Bunz, 2012; Schirrmacher, 2013). This includes questions about the power of algorithms, about whether humans are still able to control them or to what extent they control human behavior and development.

There are economic motives that promote major risks such as manipulation, threats to privacy or the infringement of IP laws. These motives are mainly predicated on efforts to maintain and amplify market power, for example by prioritizing one's own services in search results and excluding others – a concern that has raised discussions of whether search results should be subject to a search neutrality principle (Lao, 2013), for example. Systematic manipulation is said to be mainly applied where goods, services and information are sold, or where trust in transactions needs to be built (e.g., deceptive recommendations). Major groups affected are search engines and recommender systems. New markets of manipulation evolved around algorithmic applications, provided, among other things, by search engine optimization and marketing agencies as well as web content production agencies. In the meantime, they have become a vital and essential branch of the rapidly growing e-commerce sector.

Altogether, the production of economic wealth by algorithmic selection co-evolves with the emergence of social risks. Algorithmic selection leads to a commercialization/economization of automated reality mining and construction. The construction of realities – well known from research on traditional media – is not only automated by algorithmic selection and extended to further aspects of life but at the same time increasingly oriented on economic and less on social rationales (Just and Latzer, 2015). As a consequence of these increasingly automated and commercialized mining and formations of realities on the Internet, certain forms of governance seem to be necessary and are being discussed in order to realize the economic and social welfare goals anticipated by algorithmic selection.

19.8 RISK REDUCTION BY MARKET SOLUTIONS AND GOVERNANCE CHOICE: OPPORTUNITIES AND LIMITATIONS

There are two perspectives on governance and algorithms: governance *by* algorithms refers to the above-mentioned power of technology and the ability of algorithms to shape society (Just and Latzer, 2015); governance *of* algorithms refers to the practices to control, shape and regulate algorithms (Saurwein et al., 2015). In connection with the increasing awareness of risks, the opportunities for a social shaping of algorithmic selection by means of governance have attracted increased attention, most prominently the governance of search applications (e.g., Moffat, 2009; Langford, 2013; Lewandowski, 2014). Further, disputes on certain practices and implications of news aggregation, search and algorithmic trading have resulted in regulatory provisions such as the German ancillary copyright law (*Bundesgesetzblatt Jahrgang*, 2013), the right to be forgotten for search engines in the EU (European Court of Justice, 2014), and measures to prevent stock market crashes caused by algo trading, for example the European Markets in Financial Instruments Directive (MiFID 2, 2014/65/EU).

This section discusses justifications, opportunities and limitations for the governance of algorithmic selection. From a public interest point of view, governance should reinforce benefits and minimize risks. Benefits and risks are tightly interlinked, because risks are central barriers for the exploitation of potential benefits. Accordingly, a 'risk-based approach' (Black, 2010) examines the risks and explores the opportunities and limitations to reduce them. There are various arrangements to reduce risks and increase the benefits of algorithmic selection, ranging from market mechanisms at one end, to command and control regulation by state authorities at the other (Latzer et al., 2002, 2003). In between there are several additional governance options: self-organization by individual companies; (collective) industry self-regulation; and co-regulation – regulatory cooperation between state authorities and the industry. The subsequent analyses of opportunities and limitations of governance options reveal that there are no one-size-fits-all solutions for the governance of algorithms. Moreover, they show that governance of algorithms does not just mean regulating the actual code, the technology itself (Brown and Marsden, 2013). More often, the primary targets of governance interventions are organizational settings, for example the business models in the case of the ancillary copyright, with direct ramifications for the economics of the markets concerned. And finally, the analyses indicate that adequate governance strategies do not solely rely on one type of actor (e.g., the state, an industry association or companies), but often call for an interplay between the various levels and actors involved.

19.8.1   Market Solutions: Risk Reduction Strategies by Consumers, Content Providers and Suppliers

Not all risks of algorithmic selection necessarily call for regulation. Risks may also be reduced by (voluntary) changes in the market conduct of consumers, suppliers of algorithmic services and by providers of the content that is processed by algorithms.

Consumers and providers of content may refrain from using problematic services, switch to other service providers or make use of technologies to protect themselves against risks. There are, for instance, technical self-help solutions for consumers in the case of censorship, bias and privacy violations, for example tools for anonymization and de-personalization of services. Content providers could avoid violations of copyright by using robots.txt files. In areas like search, recommendation and filtering, a digital arms race is observable, where market participants are trying to avoid disadvantages by using content optimization strategies (Wittel and Wu, 2004; Jansen, 2007). Insights from behavioral economics applied to the Internet of Things might help in understanding the motivations and practice of market participants for using technological design for self-help (Fleisch, 2010). Moreover, public awareness campaigns regarding the risks of algorithmic selection (governance by information) might support market conduct that is more aware of risks.

However, there are also several limitations to self-help for consumers and content providers. Algorithmic applications often work without explicit consent and opt-out possibilities, for example from state and company surveillance programs. Switching service providers requires the existence of alternative services, but several markets are highly concentrated. If there are hardly any alternative suppliers, the switching opportunities are limited. For consumers, information asymmetries often make the risks of algorithmic selection barely visible, hence a direct motivation for consumer reaction is missing. Moreover, the usage of algorithmic services is mostly a low-cost situation for users, because advertising revenues finance services. The absence of costs decreases the incentives to switch to lower-risk alternatives. Finally, behavioral economics points out that even if costs and risks are detectable, consumers often do not carefully calculate the precise costs and benefits of their decisions (bounded rationality). Instead they rely on cognitive biases, which do not always increase their long-term benefits, for example regarding the self-protection of privacy (Acquisti and Grossklags, 2005; Brown, Chapter 12 this volume).

Suppliers of algorithmic selection services may counter risks by product innovations, that is, with new services or technological modifications of established ones. In such a case, the reduction of risks is part of the business strategy. There are, for example, services that aim at avoiding bias and violations of privacy and copyright in the first place. Some news aggregators' business models integrate content providers, who receive compensation (e.g., nachrichten.de). Other algorithmic services do not collect user data (e.g., the search engine DuckDuckGo). Services such as ConsiderIt, Reflect and OpinionSpace are designed to avoid filter bubbles and bias and integrate elements of serendipity (Munson and Resnick, 2010; Schedl et al., 2012; Resnick et al., 2013). To increase privacy standards, services may apply privacy by default and privacy by design on the technological level (Schaar, 2010; Cavoukia, 2012). But there are also several limitations on the reduction of risks by market strategies of service suppliers. There are high entry barriers in some market segments, and the conditions for newcomers and product innovations are difficult. Low-risk alternatives are mostly niche products with a very limited number of users and the reduction of risks may be accompanied by a quality reduction. Moreover, a low number of users and reduced quality may mutually reinforce each other and further decrease the attractiveness of niche services. Altogether, for the reduction of risks it is not advisable to rely on market forces only.

19.8.2 Self-organization by Individual Companies

Individual suppliers of algorithmic services may reduce risks or strengthen their accountability by means of 'self-organization'. Typical measures are principles and standards, which reflect the public interest, internal quality assessment and ombudsmen at the corporate level. The commitment to self-organization is often part of a broader corporate social responsibility (CSR) strategy. From an economic point of view the purpose is to increase a company's reputation or to avoid reputation losses.

Suppliers of algorithmic services can commit themselves to certain 'values' (Introna and Nissenbaum, 2000), such as search neutrality or the minimum principle for data collection, for instance (Langheinrich, 2001; Cavoukia, 2009). Ethics boards may be an option for issues with ethical implications such as software development or interferences with user experience. For risks such as censorship, discrimination, bias and manipulation, companies may further adopt principles and internal quality control. Qualified personnel are essential for quality assessment and conflict resolution. For big data, in-house algorithmists have been suggested to oversee big-data operations, and who would be the first points of contact for people who feel harmed by an organization's big-data predictions (Mayer-Schönberger and Cukier, 2013). Additionally, more transparency is one of the strategies to better inform consumers and facilitate the market mechanism, because the lack of transparency is one of the reasons for market failure in the area of algorithmic selection.

However, several potential barriers may inhibit voluntary measures at company level. Self-organization depends on incentives, that is, benefits and costs for the company. However, the benefits of high standards of data protection (Hustinx, 2010; London Economics, 2010) and of the disclosure of the codes/algorithms may be limited. Disclosure would increase transparency, but also the danger of manipulation and imitation, resulting in the 'transparency dilemma' (Rieder, 2005; Bracha and Pasquale, 2008; Granka, 2010). The willingness for self-restrictions also depends on reputational factors. High levels of public attention on well-known companies in B2C markets may promote self-organization in the public interest. Google, for instance, runs an ethics board at the company level (Lin and Selinger, 2014). Low public awareness of companies in B2B markets, such as data brokers (e.g., Acxiom, Corelogic and Datalogix; see FTC, 2014) reduces the reputational sensitivity and therefore also the preconditions for voluntary self-organization. Finally, the suitability of self-organization depends on the type of risk. It is not suitable, for example, for reducing problems like market concentration and transformations of cognitive capabilities.

19.8.3   Self-regulation by the Industry

Self-regulation refers to collective self-restrictions of an industry in order to pursue public objectives. Typical instruments are codes of conduct, industry standards, quality seals and certification bodies, ombudsman schemes and ethics committees.

There are sectoral initiatives of self-regulation in the advertising industry (e.g., USA, Europe), the search engine market (e.g., Germany), social online networks (e.g., Europe) and in the domain of algo trading. These initiatives deal with risks such as violations of privacy and copyright, manipulation and controllability. In the advertising industry there are initiatives for the technical standardization of do-not-track (DNT) and for better data protection in the area of online behavioral advertising (OBA). Additionally, there are organizational and technical industry standards for the protection of copyright, for example the creative commons licensing system and digital rights management (DRM) systems. Moreover, certification schemes, ombudsmen and ethics commissions seem to be appropriate instruments for dealing with controversial issues such as bias, manipulation, restrictions on communications and controllability of applications. However, these options have hardly been taken up by the industry so far.

At the same time, there are reasons why self-regulation for algorithmic selection has not yet been comprehensively applied and suggestions as to how the conditions could be improved. Algorithmic selection is applied in a wide range of sectors. Due to the large number and the heterogeneity of the branches involved a common overall self-regulatory initiative is unlikely. In order to get a grip on fragmentation the establishment of a profession of 'algorithmists' and special professional rules and ethics have been suggested (Meyer-Schönberger and Cukier, 2013). However, there are additional factors that inhibit self-regulation. For instance, self-regulation is more likely to occur in mature industries with like-minded market players. But some of the markets are rather new (e.g., algorithmic content production) and often the developers of algorithmic solutions want to challenge established players and do not voluntarily comply with older industry schemes. Minimum standards that apply to all market participants would then have to be introduced by statutory regulation. In particular, self-regulation is not suitable in cases where there is a sharp divergence between public and private interests, and where damage in the case of regulatory failure would be high (Latzer, 2007; Saurwein, 2011).

19.8.4 Co-regulation and State Regulation

The limitations of market mechanisms and self-regulation in reducing the risks can provide reasons and justifications for state intervention in algorithmic selection. Typical instruments of state intervention are: command and control regulation, incentives by subsidies/funding and taxes/fees, soft law and information measures.

In practice there are several examples of state influence in the domain of algorithmic selection, and regulations are related to particular risks rather than to a certain sector or a special technology. There are command and control regulations for violations of privacy and copyright, freedom of expression and fair competition. For example, in Europe, the Privacy Protection Directive (95/46/EC, Art. 15) protects people against automated individual decisions on certain personal aspects such as performance at work, creditworthiness, reliability and conduct. In the area of privacy protection the development of privacy-enhancing technologies (PETs) is funded by the EU, and some have even suggested introducing a data fee/tax in order to decrease the economic incentives for data collection (Lanier, 2013; Collin and Colin, 2013). Co-regulation has been established with the safe harbor principles and with data protection certification schemes and seals of quality. Another area of ongoing regulatory debate is search. Due to concerns regarding fair competition, Google was the subject of investigations by US and European competition authorities, because competitors claimed that a Google search gives undue preference to the company's other services. Some regulatory suggestions for the search engine market aim at increased transparency and controllability by public authorities (e.g., algorithm disclosure requirements), while others propose cutting the barriers to market entry (Schulz et al., 2005). A publicly funded 'index of the web' (Lewandowski, 2014) or user data sets (Argenton and Prüfer, 2012) are suggested as common resources in order to enhance market contestability, facilitate market entry and promote competition. Altogether, state intervention is multi-faceted in the area of data protection, and there are many suggestions for regulating searches. But state intervention does not apply to all the problems of algorithmic selection. As for risks such as bias, uncontrollability and effects on cognitive capabilities, for instance, there are hardly any measures or suggestions for state intervention via regulation. In some of these areas it might be helpful to promote consumer awareness (governance by information), enhance user media literacy and stimulate conscious usage and self-protection abilities. Since algorithmic selection also involves ethical concerns, political actors may consider the appointment of ethical committees with broad stakeholder involvement to deal with conflicting values. It is evident that not all types of risk are suited to state intervention and when it comes to regulatory choice one also has to bear in mind the disadvantages of state regulation as compared to self-regulation, for example higher regulatory costs to the state, lower regulatory flexibility, and lower industry commitment to comply with regulations (Latzer et al., 2002; Bartle and Vass, 2005).

19.9   CONCLUSION

This chapter offers an innovation–co-evolution–complexity perspective, that is, an evolutionary innovation economics approach, on algorithmic selection on the Internet, a rapidly growing phenomenon, characterized by automated selection of information elements and the assignment of relevance to them. The advantages of this approach are its contribution to a better understanding and conceptual integration of evolutionary technological change. It overcomes the antagonism of technological and social determinism, focuses on dynamic approaches and thereby challenges strong rationality assumptions, and highlights selection processes of companies (technology, business models) and selection/search processes through user choice. Altogether, this approach leads to different business and governance strategies. Algorithmic selection automates the commercialization of reality mining and reality construction in a fast-growing number of fields of life in information societies. This radical and potentially disruptive bundle of innovations has far-reaching economic implications for existing and emerging markets. It challenges traditional business strategies, guides our actions and thereby influences economic success or failure. The production of economic wealth by algorithmic selection co-evolves with the production of social risks and with governance efforts that try to curb risks and thereby boost socio-economic welfare gains. This chapter proposes a typology that covers nine categories including search, aggregation, recommendation, surveillance, allocation and scoring applications and describes their operation with a basic input-throughput-output model. Although these services share a common basic functionality, their modes of operation as well as their economic and social implications differ in detail.

Applications are in different market phases. Many services are still in an experimental phase; others are in the expansion or stagnation phase and show impressive growth rates or high market sizes, respectively. A combination of various industrial economic characteristics (e.g., cost structures, scale and scope economies, direct and indirect network effects) and the availability of essential core resources (e.g., technical expertise, hardware infrastructure, access to and quality of data) facilitate concentration tendencies and the subsequent preservation and amplification of market power.

Comparative business model analyses of algorithmic selection applications reveal similarities in services offered to end users, resulting in part from market characteristics (e.g., pricing in two- or multi-sided markets) or from imitation strategies. Services for business and public service customers, on the other hand, vary more widely, because they are frequently custom-made for specific purposes.

Algorithmic selection promises to reduce information asymmetries and various kinds of transaction costs (e.g., search and information costs) and as a result increases consumption and sales, and facilitates social orientation. Providers of algorithmic selection are mostly active as market makers (intermediaries) or layer players (specialists), and less as orchestrators or integrators. Revenue strategies in these markets depend on the fact that algorithmic selection applications often serve different, interdependent customer segments in two- or multi-sided markets, where prices have to be weighted accordingly and cross-financing is indispensible. As a result, indirect forms of revenue predominate.

The effects on traditional media incumbents' profitability vary from industry to industry. Theoretical considerations indicate a tendency to decrease profitability for incumbents of the news industry and a tendency towards a profitability increase in the music industry, as music-streaming services have been pushing revenues of the traditional music industry and have enhanced legal music consumption.

Products and services based on algorithmic selection have become vital and essential for the generation of economic wealth but are also compromised by the production of social risks, among other things, threats to basic rights and liberties as well as impacts on the mediation of realities and people's future development. The emergence of social risks is coupled with discussions of whether and what governance approaches are appropriate to remedy such risks. Analyses indicate that there are no one-size-fits-all solutions, and that there is the need for a governance mix consistent with the respective risks and applications in question. Adequate governance strategies often call for an interplay between the various levels and actors involved (e.g., self-help of consumers depends, among other things, on organizational or technical dispositions). Finally, governance measures are not only directed towards the algorithms (technical design) alone, but predominantly target organizational settings, for example, the business models and strategies, with far-reaching effects for the economics of the markets concerned.

REFERENCES

Acquisti, A. and J. Grossklags (2005), 'Privacy and rationality in individual decision making', *IEEE Security & Privacy*, **3** (1), 26–33.

Águila-Obra, A.R., A. Pandillo-Meléndez and C. Serarols-Tarrés (2007), 'Value creation and new intermediaries on Internet. An exploratory analysis of the online news industry and the web content aggregators', *International Journal of Information Management*, **27** (3), 187–99.

Anderson, C.W. (2013), 'Towards a sociology of computational and algorithmic journalism', *New Media & Society*, **15** (7), 1005–21.

Argenton, C. and J. Prüfer (2012), 'Search engine competition with network externalities', *Journal of Competition Law & Economics*, **8** (1), 73–105.

Ashton, K. (2009), 'The 'Internet of Things' thing', *RFID Journal*, accessed 23 July 2014 at http://www.itrco.jp/libraries/RFIDjournal-That%20Internet%20of%20Things%20Thing.pdf.

AT Internet (2013), 'Search engine barometer December 2013', accessed 7 September 2014 at http://www.atinternet.com/en/documedoc/search-engine-barometer-december-2013.

Athey, S. and M. Mobius (2012), 'The impact of news aggregators on internet news consumption: The case of localization', accessed 12 August 2014 at http://www.markusmobius.org/sites/default/files/localnews.pdf.

Banbura, M., D. Giannone and L. Reichlin (2010), 'Nowcasting', *European Central Bank Working Paper Series No. 1275*, December, accessed 12 August 2014 at http://www.ecb.europa.eu/pub/pdf/scpwps/ecbwp1275.pdf.

Bar-Ilan, J. (2007), 'Google bombing from a time perspective', *Journal of Computer-Mediated Communication*, **12** (3), 910–38.

Bartle, I. and P. Vass (2005), *Self-regulation and the Regulatory State. A Survey of Policy and Practice*, Research Report No. 17, Bath, UK: University of Bath School of Management.

Beinhocker, E.D. (2006), *The Origin of Wealth: Evolution, Complexity, and the Radical Remaking of Economics*, Boston, MA: Harvard Business School Press.

Benkler, Y. (2006), *The Wealth of Networks: How Social Production Transforms Markets and Freedom*, New Haven, CT: Yale University Press.

Bergmann, D. and A. Bonatti (2011), 'Targeting in advertising markets: Implications for online versus offline media', *RAND Journal of Economics*, **42** (3), 417–43.

Bundesgesetzblatt Jahrgang (2013), 'Eighth Law Amending the Copyright Act', *Bundesgesetzblatt Jahrgang*, Part 1, No. 23, p. 1161, accessed 12 August 2014 at http://www.bgbl.de/banzxaver/bgbl/start. xav?startbk=Bundesanzeiger_BGBl&jumpTo=bgbl113s1161.pdf.

Black, J. (2010), 'Risk-based regulation: Choices, practices and lessons learnt', in OECD (ed.), *Risk and Regulatory Policy: Improving the Governance of Risk*, Paris: Organisation for Economic Co-operation and Development, pp. 185–224.

Bostic, R.W. and P.S. Calem (2003), 'Privacy restrictions and the use of data at credit registries', in M.J. Miller (ed.), *Credit Reporting Systems and the International Economy*, Boston, MA: MIT Press.

Bracha, O. and F. Pasquale (2008), 'Federal Search Commission? Access, fairness and accountability in the law of search', *Cornell Law Review*, **93** (6), 1149–210.

Bresnahan, T. (2010), 'General purpose technologies', in B. Hall and N. Rosenberg (eds), *Handbook on the Economics of Innovation, Volume 2*, Amsterdam: Elsevier, pp. 761–91.

Brown, I. and C.T. Marsden (2013), *Regulating Code: Good Governance and Better Regulation in the Information Age*, Cambridge, MA: MIT Press.

Bunz, M. (2012), *Die stille Revolution* [The Silent Revolution], Berlin: Suhrkamp.

Calin, M., C. Dellarocas, E. Palme and J. Sutanto (2013), 'Attention allocation in information-rich environments: The case of news aggregators', *Boston University School of Management Research Paper No. 2013-4*, accessed 12 August 2014 at http://papers.ssrn.com/sol3/papers.cfm?abstract_id=2225359.

Carr, N. (2010), *The Shallows: What the Internet is Doing to Our Brains*, New York: W.W. Norton.

Cavoukia, A. (2009), 'Privacy by design', lecture at the Trust Economics Workshop, London, 23 June 2009, accessed 12 August 2014 at http://www.ipc.on.ca/images/Resources/2009-06-23-TrustEconomics.pdf.

Cavoukia, A. (2012), 'Privacy by design: Origins, meaning, and prospects for ensuring privacy and trust in the information era', accessed 12 August 2014 at http://www.privacybydesign.ca/content/uploads/2010/03/PrivacybyDesignBook.pdf.

Chaleppa, R.K. and R.G. Sin (2005), 'Personalization versus privacy: An empirical examination of online consumer's dilemma', *Information, Technology and Management*, **6** (2–3), 181–202.

Chiou, L. and C. Tucker (2013), 'Digitization and aggregation', accessed 12 August 2014 at http://bellarmine.lmu.edu/media/lmubellarminesite/bcladepartments/economics/economicsdocuments/Digitization%20 and%20Aggregation.pdf.

Christensen, C.M. (1997), *The Innovator's Dilemma: When Technologies Cause Great Firms to Fail*, Boston, MA: Harvard Business Review Press.

Ciocchetti, C.A. (2011), 'The eavesdropping employer: A twenty-first century framework for employee monitoring', *American Business Law Journal*, **48** (2), 285–369.

Clark, B. (2010), 'Google Image Search does not infringe copyright, says Bundesgerichtshof', *Journal of Intellectual Property Law & Practice*, **5** (8), 553–5.

Clark, B. (2012), 'Google Image Search still does not infringe copyright, reaffirms Bundesgerichtshof', *Journal of Intellectual Property Law & Practice*, **7** (11), 788–9.

CNZZ (2013), 'Search engine data', accessed 7 September 2014 at http://engine.data.cnzz.com/main. php?s=engine&uv=&st=2013-11-01&et=2013-11-30.

Collin, P. and N. Colin (2013), *Mission d'expertise sur la fiscalité de l'économie numérique* [Expert Mission Report on the Taxation of the Digital Economy], accessed 28 December 2015 at http://www.economie.gouv. fr/files/rapport-fiscalite-du-numerique_2013.pdf.

ComScore (2013a), '2013 India digital future in focus', accessed 7 September 2014 at https://www.comscore. com/Insights/Presentations-and-Whitepapers/2013/2013-India-Digital-Future-in-Focus.

ComScore (2013b), '2013 Southeast Asia digital future in focus', accessed 7 September 2014 at https:// www.comscore.com/Insights/Presentations-and-Whitepapers/2013/2013-Southeast-Asia-Digital-Future-in-Focus.

ComScore (2013c), '2013 Europe digital future in focus', accessed 7 September 2014 at https://www.comscore. com/ger/Insights/Presentations-and-Whitepapers/2013/2013-Europe-Digital-Future-in-Focus.

ComScore (2014), '2014 U.S. digital future in focus', accessed 7 September 2014 at https://www.com score.com/Insights/Presentations-and-Whitepapers/2014/2014-US-Digital-Future-in-FocusCormen,   T.H.,

C.E. Leiserson, R.L. Rivest and C. Stein (2009), *Introduction to Algorithms*, 3rd edition, Cambridge, MA: MIT Press.

Cushing Weigle, S. (2013), 'English language learners and automated scoring of essays: Critical considerations', *Assessing Writing*, **18** (1), 85–99.

Deibert, R., J. Palfrey, R. Rohozinski and J. Zittrain (eds) (2008), *Access Denied: The Practice and Policy of Global Internet Filtering*, Cambridge, MA: MIT Press.

Deibert, R., J. Palfrey, R. Rohozinski and J. Zittrain (eds) (2010), *Access Controlled: The Shaping of Power, Rights, and Rule in Cyberspace*, Cambridge, MA: MIT Press.

Dellarocas, C., Z. Katona and W.M. Rand (2013), 'Media, aggregators and the link economy', *Management Science*, **59** (10), 2360–79.

Dörr, K.N. (2015), 'Mapping the field of Algorithmic Journalism', *Digital Journalism*, published online ahead of print: DOI: 10.1080/21670811.2015.1096748.

Edelmann, B., M. Ostrovsky and M. Schwarz (2005), 'Internet advertising and the generalized second price auction: Selling billions of dollars worth of keywords', *NBER Working Paper Series No. 11765*, accessed 12 August 2014 at http://www.nber.org/papers/w11765.pdf.

eMarketer (2015), 'Facebook and Twitter Will Take 33% Share of US Digital Display Market by 2017', *eMarketer*, 26 March, accessed 29 February 2016 at http://www.emarketer.com/Article/Facebook-Twitter-Will-Take-33-Share-of-US-Digital-Display-Market-by-2017/1012274.

European Court of Justice (2014), 'Judgment in Case C-131/12 Google Spain v AEPD and Mario Costeja Gonzalez' [press release], accessed 12 August 2014 at http://curia.europa.eu/jcms/upload/docs/application/pdf/2014-05/cp140070en.pdf.

Evans, D. (2008), 'The economics of the online advertising industry', *Review of Network Economics*, **7** (3), 359–91.

Evans, D. (2009), 'The online advertising industry: Economics, evolution and privacy', *Journal of Economic Perspectives*, **23** (3), 37–60.

Faigle, P. (2010), 'Googeln einmal anders' [Googling with a difference], *Zeit Online*, accessed 24 July 2014 at http://www.zeit.de/2010/43/Google-Oekonomie-Indikator.

Fleisch, E. (2010), 'What is the Internet of Things? An economic perspective', *Auto-ID Labs White Paper No. WP-BIZAPP-053*, accessed 18 August 2014 at http://cocoa.ethz.ch/media/documents/2014/06/archive/AUTOIDLABS-WP-BIZAPP-53.pdf.

Frenken, K. (2006), *Innovation, Evolution and Complexity Theory*, Cheltenham, UK and Northampton, MA, USA: Edward Elgar Publishing.

FTC (2014), 'Data brokers: A call for transparency and accountability', Washington, DC: Federal Trade Commission, accessed 12 August 2014 at http://www.ftc.gov/system/files/documents/reports/data-brokers-call-transparency-accountability-report-federal-trade-commission-may-2014/140527databrokerreport.pdf.

Granka, L.A. (2010), 'The politics of search: A decade retrospective', *The Information Society*, **26** (5), 364–74.

Greenwald, G. and E. MacAskill (2013), 'NSA prism program taps in to user data of Apple, Google and others', *The Guardian*, 6 June, accessed 23 July 2014 at http://www.theguardian.com/world/2013/jun/06/us-tech-giants-nsa-data.

Hanani, U., B. Shapira and P. Shoval (2001), 'Information filtering: Overview of issues, research and systems', *User Modeling and User-Adapted Interaction*, **11** (3), 203–59.

Henig, R.M. and S. Henig (2012), *Twentysomething: Why Do Young Adults Seem Stuck?*, New York: Hudson Street Press.

Heuskel, D. (1999), *Wettbewerb jenseits von Industriegrenzen: Aufbruch zu neuen Wachstumsstrategien* [Competition Beyond Industry Boundaries: Setting Out New Growth Strategies], Frankfurt: Campus Verlag.

Hinman, L.M. (2005), 'Esse est indicato in Google: Ethical and political issues in search engines', *International Review of Information Ethics*, **3** (6), 19–25.

Hinz, O. and J. Eckert (2010), 'The impact of search and recommendation systems on sales in electronic commerce', *Business & Information Systems Engineering*, **2** (2), 67–77.

Hustinx, P. (2010), 'Privacy by design: Delivering the promises', *Identity in the Information Society*, **3** (2), 253–5.

Introna, L.D. and H. Nissenbaum (2000), 'Shaping the web: Why the politics of search engines matters', *The Information Society*, **16** (3), 169–85.

Isbell, K. (2010), 'The rise of the news aggregator: Legal implications and best practices', *Berkman Center for Internet & Society Research Publication 2010-10*, accessed 12 August 2014 at http://papers.ssrn.com/sol3/papers.cfm?abstract_id=1670339.

Issenberg, S. (2012), *The Victory Lab: The Secret Science of Winning Campaigns*, New York: Crown Publishers.

Jaeggi, M. (2010), 'Business model innovation in wealth management', dissertation, St. Gallen, Switzerland: St. Gallen University.

Jannach, D., M. Zanker, A. Felfernig and G. Friedrich (2011), *Recommender Systems: An Introduction*, New York: Cambridge University Press.

Jansen, B.J. (2007), 'Click fraud', *Computer*, **40** (7), 85–6.

Jürgens, P., A. Jungherr and H. Schoen (2011), 'Small worlds with a difference: New gatekeepers and the filtering of political information on Twitter', in *Proceedings of the 3rd International Web Science Conference (WebSci'11)*, accessed 12 August 2014 at http://dl.acm.org/citation.cfm?id=2527034.

Just, N. and M. Latzer (2016), 'Governance by algorithms: Reality construction by algorithmic selection on the Internet', *Media, Culture & Society*, forthcoming.

Klahold, A. (2009), *Empfehlungssysteme. Recommender Systems – Grundlagen, Konzepte, Lösungen* [Recommender Systems: Basics, Concepts, Solutions], Wiesbaden: Vieweg + Teubner.

Klingenberg, B. (2000), 'Kundennutzen und Kundentreue. Eine Untersuchung zum Treue-Nutzen aus Konsumentensicht' [Customer value and customer loyalty. An investigation into loyalty value from the consumer's perspective], dissertation, University of Munich.

König, R. and M. Rasch (eds) (2014), *Society of the Query Reader: Reflections on Web Search*, Amsterdam: Institute of Network Cultures, accessed 20 August 2014 at http://networkcultures.org/blog/publication/society-of-the-query-reader-reflections-on-web-search/.

Küsters, U., B.D. McCullough and M. Bell (2006), 'Forecasting software: Past, present and future', *International Journal of Forecasting*, **22** (3), 599–615.

Langford, A. (2013), 'gMonopoly: Does search bias warrant antitrust or regulatory intervention?', *Indiana Law Journal*, **88** (4), 1559–92.

Langheinrich, M. (2001), 'Privacy by design: Principles of privacy-aware ubiquitous systems', in G.D. Abowd, B. Brumitt and S.A. Shafer (eds), in *Proceedings of the Third International Conference on Ubiquitous Computing (UbiComp 2001)*, pp. 273–91.

Lanier, J. (2013), *Who Owns the Future?*, New York: Simon & Schuster.

Lao, M. (2013), '"Neutral" search as a basis for antitrust action?', *Harvard Journal of Law & Technology*, **26** (2), 1–12.

Latzer, M. (2007), 'Regulatory choice in communications governance', *Communications – The European Journal of Communication Research*, **32** (3), 399–405.

Latzer, M. (2013a), 'Medienwandel durch Innovation, Ko-Evolution und Komplexität. Ein Aufriss' [Media change through innovation, co-evolution and complexity. A perspective], *Medien und Kommunikationswissenschaft*, **61** (2), 235–52.

Latzer, M. (2013b), 'Towards an innovation–co-evolution–complexity perspective on communications policy', in M. Löblich and S. Pfaff-Rüdiger (eds), *Communication and Media Policy in the Era of Digitization and the Internet*, Baden-Baden: Nomos, pp. 15–27.

Latzer, M. (2014), 'Convergence, co-evolution and complexity in European communications policy', in K. Donders, C. Pauwels and J. Loisen (eds), *The Palgrave Handbook of European Media Policy*, Houndmills, UK: Palgrave Macmillan, pp. 36–53.

Latzer, M., N. Just, F. Saurwein and P. Slominski (2002), *Selbst- und Ko-Regulierung im Mediamatiksektor. Alternative Regulierungsformen zwischen Markt und Staat* [Self- and Co-regulation in Mediamatics. Alternative Forms of Regulation Between Market and State], Wiesbaden: Westdeutscher Verlag.

Latzer, M., N. Just, F. Saurwein and P. Slominski (2003), 'Regulation remixed: Institutional change through self- and co-regulation in the mediamatics sector', *Communications & Strategies*, **50** (2), 127–57.

Latzer, M., J. Gewinner, K. Hollnbuchner, N. Just and F. Saurwein (2014), *Algorithmische Selektion im Internet. Ökonomie und Politik automatisierter Relevanzzuweisung in der Informationsgesellschaft* [Algorithmic Selection on the Internet. Economics and Politics Automated Relevance Allocation in the Information Society], research report, Zurich, University of Zurich, IPMZ, Media Change and Innovation Division.

Lee, J. (ed.) (2007), *Algorithmic Trading: A Buy-side Handbook*, London: The Trade.

Leinweber, D. (2009), *Nerds on Wall Street. Math, Machines and Wired Markets*, Hoboken, NJ: John Wiley & Sons.

Levy, S. (2012), 'Can an algorithm write a better news story than a human reporter?', *Wired*, 24 April, accessed 20 August 2014 at http://www.wired.com/2012/04/can-an-algorithm-write-a-better-news-story-than-a-human-reporter/.

Lewandowski, D. (ed.) (2012), *Web Search Engine Research*, Bingley, UK: Emerald.

Lewandowski, D. (2014), 'Why we need an independent index of the web', in R. König and M. Rasch (eds), *Society of the Query Reader: Reflections on Web Search*, Amsterdam: Institute of Network Cultures.

Lin, P. and E. Selinger (2014), 'Inside Google's mysterious ethics board', *Forbes*, 3 February, accessed 15 September 2014 at http://www.forbes.com/sites/privacynotice/2014/02/03/inside-googles-mysterious-ethics-board/.

London Economics (2010), *Study on the Economic Benefits of Privacy Enhancing Technologies (PETs)*, Final Report to the European Commission DG Justice, Freedom and Security, accessed 12 August 2014 at http://ec.europa.eu/justice/policies/privacy/docs/studies/final_report_pets_16_07_10_en.pdf.

Lyon, D. (2003), 'Surveillance as social sorting: Computer codes and mobile bodies', in D. Lyon (ed.), *Surveillance as Social Sorting. Privacy, Risk, and Social Discrimination*, London and New York: Routledge, pp. 13–30.

Maass, C., A. Skussa, A. Hess and G. Pietsch (2009), 'Der Markt für Internet-Suchmaschinen' [The market for

Internet search engines], in D. Lewandowski (ed.), *Handbuch Internet-Suchmaschinen. Nutzerorientierung in Wissenschaft und Praxis*, Heidelberg: Akademische Verlagsgesellschaft, pp. 3–17.

Machill, M. and M. Beiler (2007), *Die Macht der Suchmaschinen/The Power of Search Engines*, Cologne: Herbert von Halem Verlag.

Mager, A. (2012), 'Algorithmic ideology: How capitalist society shapes search engines', *Information, Communication & Society*, **15** (5), 769–87.

Mattern, F. and C. Flörkemeier (2010), 'From the Internet of computers to the Internet of Things', in K. Sachs, I. Petrov and P. Guerrero (eds), *From Active Data Management to Event-Based Systems and More*, Berlin and Heidelberg: Springer, pp. 242–59.

Mayer-Schönberger, V. and K. Cukier (2013), *Big Data. Die Revolution, die unser Leben verändern wird* [Big Data. The Revolution that Will Change Our Lives], Munich: Redline Verlag.

McAfee, A. and E. Brynjolfsson (2012), 'Big data: The management revolution', *Harvard Business Review*, **90** (10), 60–68.

Moffat, V.R. (2009), 'Regulating search', *Harvard Journal of Law & Technology*, **22** (2), 475–513.

Mössenböck, H. (2014), *Sprechen Sie Java? Eine Einführung in das systematische Programmieren* [Do You Speak Java? An Introduction to Systematic Programming], 5th revised edition, Linz: dpunkt Verlag.

Munson, S.A. and P. Resnick (2010), 'Presenting diverse political opinions: How and how much', in *Proceedings of the SIGCHI Conference on Human Factors in Computing Systems (CHI'10)*, New York, pp. 1457–66.

Napoli, P.M. (2013), 'The algorithm as institution: Toward a theoretical framework for automated media production and consumption', *Fordham University Schools of Business Research Papers*, accessed 23 August 2015 at http://ssrn.com/abstract=2260923.

OECD (2013), 'Exploring data-driven innovation as a new source of growth. Mapping the policy issues raised by "big data"', *OECD Digital Economy Papers, No. 222*, Paris: OECD, accessed 23 July 2014 at http://www.oecd-ilibrary.org/science-and-technology/exploring-data-driven-innovation-as-a-new-source-of-growth_5k47zw3fcp43-en.

O'Reilly, T. (2007), 'What is Web 2.0: Design patterns and business models for the next generation of software', *Communications & Strategies*, **65** (1), 17–37.

Osterwalder, A., Y. Pigneur and C.L. Tucci (2005), 'Clarifying business models. Origins, present, and future of the concept', *Communications of the Association for Information Systems*, **16** (1), 1–25.

Pariser, E. (2011), *The Filter Bubble: What the Internet is Hiding from You*, London: Penguin Books.

Pathak, B.K., R. Garfinkel, R.D. Gopal, R. Venkathesan and F. Yin (2010), 'Empirical analysis of the business value of recommender systems', *Journal of Management Information Systems*, **27** (2), 159–88.

Pavliva, H. (2013), 'Yandex Russia web search share flat, LiveInternet reports', accessed 7 September 2014 at http://www.bloomberg.com/news/articles/2013-11-18/yandex-russia-web-search-share-flat-liveinternet-reports.

Pavlov, E., J.S. Rosenschein and Z. Topol (2004), 'Supporting privacy in decentralized additive reputation systems', in C. Jensen, S. Poslad and T. Dimitrakos (eds), *Trust Management, Proceedings of the Second International Conference, iTrust, Oxford, UK, 29 March–1 April*, Berlin: Springer, pp. 108–19.

Porter, M.E. (1979), 'How competitive forces shape strategy', *Harvard Business Review*, **57** (2), 137–45.

Porter, M.E. (2001), 'Strategy and the Internet', *Harvard Business Review*, **79** (3), 1–20.

Porter, M.E. (2008), 'The five competitive forces that shape strategy', *Harvard Business Review*, **86** (1), 78–93.

Pridmore, J. and D. Zwick (2011), 'Editorial: Marketing and the rise of commercial consumer surveillance', *Surveillance & Society*, **8** (3), 269–77.

Pronk, S.P.P., J.H.M. Korst, M. Barbieri and A.J. Proidl (2009), 'Personal television channels: Simply zapping through your PVR content', *Philips Research Papers*, accessed 21 August 2014 at http://repository.tudelft.nl/view/philips/uuid:293926ed-4562-48c0-bae3-1baa5939cdb7/.

Quinn, D.J. (2014), '*Associated Press* v. *Meltwater*: Are courts being fair to news aggregators?', *Minnesota Journal of Law, Science and Technology*, **15** (2), 1189–219.

Resnick, P. and H.R. Varian (1997), 'Recommender systems', *Communications of the ACM*, **40** (3), 56–8.

Resnick, P. and R. Zeckhauser (2002), 'Trust among strangers in Internet transactions: An empirical analysis of eBay's reputation system', in M.R. Baye (ed.), *The Economics of the Internet and E-commerce (Advances in Applied Microeconomics, Volume 11)*, Bingley, UK: Emerald, pp. 127–57.

Resnick, P., R.K. Garrett, T. Kriplean, S.A. Munson and N.J. Stroud (2013), 'Bursting your (filter) bubble: Strategies for promoting diverse exposure', in *Proceedings of the 2013 Conference on Computer Supported Cooperative Work Companion (CSCW'13)*, San Antonio, Texas, 23–27 February, pp. 95–100.

Ricci, F., L. Rokach, B. Shapira and P.B. Kantor (eds) (2011), *Recommender Systems Handbook*, Heidelberg: Springer.

Rieder, B. (2005), 'Networked control: Search engines and the symmetry of confidence', *International Review of Information Ethics*, **3** (1), 26–32.

Rietjens, B. (2006), 'Trust and reputation on eBay: Towards a legal framework for feedback intermediaries', *Information & Communications Technology Law*, **15** (1), 55–78.

Rip, A. (2007), 'Die Verzahnung von technologischen und sozialen Determinismen und die Ambivalenz von

Handlungsträgerschaft im "Constructive Technology Assessment"' [The integration of technological and social determinism and the ambivalence of action sponsorship in 'Constructive Technology Assessment'], in U. Dolata and R. Werle (eds), *Gesellschaft und die Macht der Technik*, Frankfurt: Campus, pp. 83–106.

Robillard, M.P., W. Maalej, R.J. Walker and T. Zimmermann (eds) (2014), *Recommendation Systems in Software Engineering*, Heidelberg: Springer.

Rochet, J.-C. and J. Tirole (2003), 'Platform competition in two-sided markets', *Journal of the European Economic Association*, **1** (4), 990–1029.

Rothmann, R., J. Sterbik-Lamina and W. Peissl (2014), *Credit Scoring in Österreich*, Report No. ITA-PB A66, Vienna: Institut für Technikfolgen-Abschätzung (ITA), accessed 25 September 2014 at http://epub.oeaw.ac.at/ita/ita-projektberichte/a66.pdf.

Saurwein, F. (2011), 'Regulatory choice for alternative modes of regulation. How context matters', *Law & Policy*, **33** (3), 334–66.

Saurwein, F., N. Just and M. Latzer (2015), 'Governance of algorithms: Options and limitations', *Info*, **17** (6), 35–49.

Schaar, P. (2010), 'Privacy by design', *Identity in the Information Society*, **3** (2), 267–74.

Schautzer, K. (2013), 'Japan search engine market share 2012', accessed 7 September 2014 at http://www.theegg.com/blog/seo/japan-search-engine-market-share-2012.

Schedl, M., D. Hauger and D. Schnitzer (2012), 'A model for serendipitous music retrieval', in *Proceedings of the 2nd Workshop on Context-Awareness in Retrieval and Recommendation (CaRR'12)*, New York, pp. 10–13.

Schirrmacher, F. (2013), *Ego. Das Spiel des Lebens* [Ego. The Game of Life], Munich: Blessing.

Schormann, T. (2012), 'Online-Portale: Grosser Teil der Hotelbewertungen ist manipuliert' [Online portals: Many of the reviews are manipulated], *Spiegel Online*, 9 March, accessed 12 August 2014 at http://www.spiegel.de/reise/aktuell/online-portale-grosser-teil-der-hotelbewertungen-ist-manipuliert-a-820383.html.

Schulz, W., T. Held and A. Laudien (2005), 'Search engines as gatekeepers of public communication: Analysis of the German framework applicable to Internet search engines including media law and anti-trust law', *German Law Journal*, **6** (10), 1418–33.

Segev, E. (2010), *Google and the Digital Divide. The Bias of Online Knowledge*, Oxford, UK: Chandos Publishing.

Senecal, S. and J. Nantel (2004), 'The influence of online product recommendation on consumers' online choice', *Journal of Retailing*, **80** (2), 159–69.

Shelanski, H.A. (2013), 'Information, innovation, and competition policy for the Internet', *University of Pennsylvania Law Review*, **161** (6), 1663–705.

Silver, N. (2012), *The Signal and the Noise: Why So Many Predictions Fail – But Some Don't*, New York: Penguin.

SimilarWeb (2013) [website], accessed 12 August 2014 at http://www.similarweb.com/.

Sparrow, B., J. Liu and D.M. Wegner (2011), 'Google effects on memory: Cognitive consequences of having information at our fingertips', *Science*, **333** (6043), 776–8.

Statista (2014), 'Leading dating websites in the United States in June 2014, based on visitor numbers (in millions)', *Statista, The Statistics Portal*, accessed 12 August 2014 at http://www.statista.com/statistics/274144/most-popular-us-dating-websites-ranked-by-monthly-visitors/.

Steinbrecher, S. (2006), 'Design options for privacy-respecting reputation systems within centralised Internet communities', in S. Fischer-Hübner, K. Rannenberg, L. Yngström and S. Lindskog (eds), *Security and Privacy in Dynamic Environments, Proceedings of the IFIP TC-11 21st International Information Security Conference (SEC 2006), 22–24 May, Karlstad, Sweden*, New York: Springer, pp. 123–34.

Steiner, C. (2012), *Automate This: How Algorithms Came to Rule Our World*, New York: Penguin.

Stühmeier, T. (2011), 'Das Leistungsschutzrecht für Presseverleger: Eine ordnungspolitische Analyse' [Ancillary copyright for publishers: A regulatory analysis], *Ordnungspolitische Perspektiven*, **12**, 1–20.

Sullivan, D. (2013), 'Google still world's most popular search engine by far, but share of unique searchers dips slightly', accessed 7 September 2014 at http://searchengineland.com/google-worlds-most-popular-search-engine-148089.

Teece, D.J. (2006), 'Reflections on "Profiting from Innovation"', *Research Policy*, **35** (8), 1131–46.

Teece, D.J. (2010), 'Business models, business strategy and innovation', *Long Range Planning*, **43** (2–3), 172–94.

Toch, E., Y. Wang and L.F. Cranor (2012), 'Personalization and privacy: A survey of privacy risks and remedies in personalization-based systems', *User Modeling and User-Adapted Interaction*, **22** (1–2), 203–20.

Van Dalen, A. (2012), 'The algorithm behind the headlines: How machine-written news redefines the core skills of human journalists', *Journalism Practice*, **5** (5–6), 648–58.

van Schewick, B. (2010), *Internet Architecture and Innovation*, Cambridge, MA: MIT Press.

VanderMey, A. (2013), 'Outsourcing the algorithm of love to online dating', *Fortune*, 14 February, accessed 12 August 2014 at http://fortune.com/2013/02/14/outsourcing-the-algorithm-of-love-to-online-dating/.

Varian, H.R. (2006), 'Position auctions: A theoretical and empirical analysis of the ad auction used by Google and Yahoo', *International Journal of Industrial Organization*, **25** (6), 1163–78.

Varian, H.R. (2009), 'Online ad auctions', *American Economic Review*, **99** (2), 430–34.

Wallace, J. (2016), 'Digital gatekeeping. New roles of gatekeepers, gates and gatekeeping mechanisms in digital news diffusion', IPMZ-Working Paper, Zurich.

Weaver, A.B. (2013), 'Aggravated with aggregators: Can international copyright law help save the newsroom?', *Emory International Law Review*, **26** (4), 1159–98.

Whitt, R.S. and S.J. Schultze (2009), 'The new "emergence economics" of innovation and growth, and what it means for communications policy', *Journal on Telecommunications and High Technology Law*, **7** (2), 217–316.

Wittel, G.L. and S.F. Wu (2004), 'On attacking statistical spam filters', in *Proceedings of the First Conference on Email and Anti-spam (CEAS)*, accessed 12 August 2014 at http://pdf.aminer.org/000/085/123/on_attacking_statistical_spam_filters.pdf.

World Economic Forum (2011a), *Personal Data: The Emergence of a New Asset Class*, accessed 23 July 2014 at http://www3.weforum.org/docs/WEF_ITTC_PersonalDataNewAsset_Report_2011.pdf.

World Economic Forum (2011b), 'Personal data: The "new oil" of the 21st century', *World Economic Forum*, 9 June, accessed 12 August 2014 at http://www.weforum.org/sessions/summary/personal-data-new-oil-21st-century.

Xu, H., X.R. Luo, J.M. Carroll and M.B. Rosson (2011), 'The personalization privacy paradox: An exploratory study of decision making process for location-aware marketing', *Decision Support Systems*, **51** (1), 42–52.

Zhang, J. and A. Dimitroff (2005), 'The impact of webpage content characteristics on webpage visibility in search engine results (Part I)', *Information Processing and Management*, **41** (3), 665–90.

Zhu, H., M.D. Siegel and S.E. Madnick (2001), 'Information aggregation: A value-added e-service', *E-Business@MIT Paper No. 106*, accessed 23 July 2014 at http://ebusiness.mit.edu/research/papers/106%20SMadnick,%20Siegel%20Information%20Aggregation.pdf.

Ziman, J. (ed.) (2000), *Technological Innovation as an Evolutionary Process*, Cambridge, UK: Cambridge University Press.

Zimmer, M. (2008), 'The externalities of Search 2.0: The emerging privacy threats when the drive for the perfect search engine meets Web 2.0', *First Monday*, **13** (3), accessed 12 August 2014 at http://www.firstmonday.dk/ojs/index.php/fm/article/view/2136/1944.

Zittrain, J. and J. Palfrey (2008), 'Internet filtering: The politics and mechanisms of control', in R. Deibert, J.G. Palfrey, R. Rohozinski and J. Zittrain (eds), *Access Denied: The Practice and Policy of Global Internet Filtering*, Cambridge, MA: MIT Press, pp. 29–56.

Zollenkopp, M. (2006), *Geschäftsmodellinnovation* [Business Model Innovation], Wiesbaden: Deutscher Universitätsverlag.

20. Online advertising economics
Wenjuan Ma and Steven S. Wildman

20.1 INTRODUCTION

While the Internet was used to deliver advertising messages earlier, it was only after it was turned over to largely commercial funding in 1995 that Internet advertising began a still continuing period of rapid revenue growth. In the USA it was propelled to second place behind television among paid advertising media after surpassing print (newspapers plus magazines) in 2012 (eMarketer, 2013). While slightly lagging behind developments in the USA, the trend has been similar for other economically advanced nations. Research focused on online advertising has grown apace and, while this interest did not develop entirely overnight, recent years have seen an unprecedented flurry of research on the economics of online advertising. Like Internet advertising itself, the volume of research on economic aspects of Internet advertising has grown dramatically in recent years.

For the most part, this research has focused on advancing our still very incomplete understanding of the economic logic underlying services, features and practices that visibly, and, in many cases, quite dramatically, distinguish online ads from their offline counterparts. At the same time, less visible aspects of the organization of online advertising markets and the institutional infrastructure that supports them have yet to be subjected to rigorous economic study. One of our aims for this chapter is to identify topics in need of serious investigation if we are to develop a thorough understanding of the economics of this still evolving segment of the larger advertising industry.

The chapter is organized as follows. The next section provides a brief overview of the historical development of online advertising and highlights the diversity of the types of advertising services that are counted as part of the online advertising sector. The two sections that follow provide, respectively, an overview of the economics research on ad targeting and search advertising, the two topics that comprise most of the economics literature on Internet advertising. A final section presents our assessment of the current state of research on Internet advertising and thoughts on future research that would help further advance our understanding of this subject.

20.2 A BRIEF HISTORY AND OVERVIEW OF THE ONLINE ADVERTISING SECTOR

20.2.1 Key Technological and Institutional Developments

ARPANET and NSFNet, the government-funded predecessors to today's Internet, had acceptable use policies that banned their use for advertising. Nevertheless, what may have been the first use of the Internet for advertising occurred in 1978 when American West Coast ARPANET users received emailed ads for personal computers (Seabrook, 2008).

Display advertising began in the 1980s when the subscription-based online service provider, Prodigy, which was jointly owned by IBM and Sears, displayed banner-like ads for Sears. The date for the first clickable online ad is a matter of dispute. Tim O'Reilly, the founder of Global Network Navigator (GNN), claimed that the first clickable ad appeared on his website in 1993 (Bourn, 2013), but Kaye and Medoff (2001) date the first clickable ad to 1994 when Hotwire sold its first banner advertisement. By today's standards, when the average click-through rate is reported to be about 0.1 percent (Interactive Advertising Bureau, 2012), these early clickable ads were very effective. According to Morrissey (2013), AT&T's first clickable ad had a 44 percent click-through rate.

As is detailed by Hal Varian in Chapter 18 in this volume, search advertising services tried out a variety of mechanisms for ordering search results before Google's introduction of the page ranking mechanism for ordering organic listings established a standard that, while it has evolved, still rules today. The first search advertising auction was created by GoTo.com in 1998, which changed its name to Overture in 2001 and was acquired by Yahoo! in 2003. Google launched its 'AdWords' search advertising program in 2000. In 2002, Google introduced the generalized second-price (GSP) auction, which, with modifications, is the pricing mechanism used for most search ad sales today.

Display ads and the ways they are sold have also changed considerably as the online ad industry has grown and evolved. The massive online data storage and computational capabilities that made possible the profusion of interactive Web 2.0 services since 2000 have also been employed to create the targeting capabilities that are now routinely used to match an advertiser's online ads to Internet users with web-generated profiles that mark them as more likely to be receptive to the advertiser's messages. While untargeted display ads have not disappeared, targeted ads have accounted for much of the growth of this segment.

In the 1990s, almost all display advertising inventory was sold through salespeople, but by the end of the 2008–09 recession real-time bidding for audiences defined by preset descriptive parameters had emerged as an important alternative for selling and buying online inventory. The use of pre-set parameters made it possible to computerize and automate the purchase process so that ads targeted to users that matched the specified parameters could be loaded automatically when users matching those parameters loaded websites to which an advertiser had purchased access. The process by which such ads are purchased is known as pre-set bidding and is commonly managed by ad networks, which are described below. Automation of the process has also made it possible to bid on ads in real time, with the option to purchase remaining inventory available up to the time an ad is placed before a user with the requested pre-set parameters (Reynolds, 2011).

20.2.2   Growth and Proliferation of Online Advertising Services

According to the Interactive Advertising Bureau (IAB) (2007), total online advertising was a fairly modest $55 million in 1995, the first year the Internet was commercialized. While in percentage terms, growth in its early years was quite rapid, through the 1990s this was accounted for largely by growth in display ads, which in 2000 accounted for over three-quarters of online ad sales of $8.2 billion. This was also the first year that search advertising shows up (at $0.1 billion) in IAB's time series. By 2004 the search share of total online ad sales had passed that of display. In 2013, search accounted

Table 20.1   USA online advertising spending by formats in 2013 ($ billions)

Ad Format:[a]	Search	Display	Classifieds	Lead Generation	Mobile	Email	Total
	18.4	12.8	2.6	1.8	7.1	NA	42.8

Note: Four of the format labels for this table are self-explanatory, but two are not. Lead generation refers to the use of any of several online vehicles, including email, display ads and online forums, to place before consumers news of product deals they can learn more about by contacting a vendor directly using an identifier provided. The vendor then compensates the lead generator when contacted by 'leads' that provide the corresponding identifier. Email ads are messages customized for delivery through mobile devices, such as smartphones, feature phones and tablets. Mobile ads can include static or rich media display ads, text messages, search ads and audio or video ads in mobile apps.

Source: Interactive Advertising Bureau (2013).

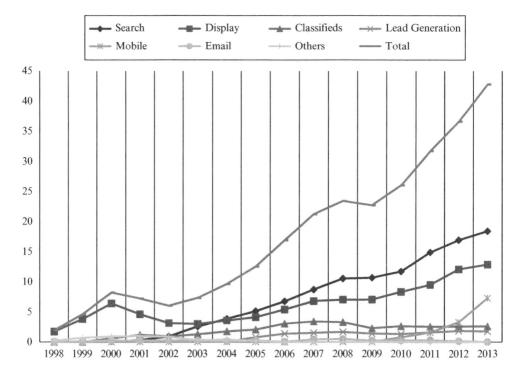

Sources: Interactive Advertising Bureau (1999–2014).

Figure 20.1   US online advertising spending by formats, 1998–2013 ($ billions)

for $18.4 billion, 43 percent of all online ad sales, which is about double the share for display. Other categories of online advertising have emerged since 1999 to account for noticeable, though much smaller shares of online ad sales, with mobile ads the most recent category to emerge. The IAB's 2013 revenue totals for the six major categories of online advertising are presented in Table 20.1. Figure 20.1 shows the levels and trends for the six major categories plus the minor categories that are combined under 'others' from 1998 on.[1] Table 20.1 and Figure 20.1 both illustrate the diversity of services that contribute to the online advertising total, and even these figures mask diversity within the six categories, such as the distinction between the targeted ads and run-of-site ads that contribute to the display total. Run-of-site advertisements are displayed to anyone who visits a webpage where they are placed. Advertisers who want to reach broader audiences, such as those selling fast-moving consumer goods (FMCG), often choose this type of advertisement. A targeted ad appears only in front of visitors identified as matching the profiles of individuals deemed most likely to respond to the ad's appeal.

20.2.3 Supporting Services

Advertising in online media is supported by a large collection of intermediaries, facilitators and suppliers of various complementary services that collectively, and sometimes individually, are substantial businesses in their own right. While some have close counterparts in offline advertising, many do not. Major categories of support services for the online advertising industry include advertising networks, advertising exchanges, demand-side platforms (DSPs), search management platforms (SMPs), audience measurement services, and advertising agencies.

The fact that the Internet audience is dispersed across millions of webpages and services (such as RSS [really simple syndication] feeds and email advertising services) makes it highly desirable, if not necessary, to aggregate audiences across multiple outlets to achieve meaningful scale. Advertising networks perform this aggregation service in exchange for a portion of the fees advertisers pay for placements with online publishers and other online services that affiliate with them. They also provide the targeting services, described in more detail below, that allow an advertiser to place its ads before specified subsets of the web users accessing a network's affiliates who, by various metrics, are judged to be particularly attractive recipients of the advertiser's message. In some cases fees paid by advertisers are set by the affiliated outlets, while in other cases networks set these prices and remit a predetermined fraction of revenues generated to the participating sites and services.

In the USA the market for ad networking services is highly fragmented and has no clearly dominant providers. For example, for June 2012 comScore listed the Google Ad Network as the largest in the USA with nearly 206 million unique visitors while crediting Undertone, the twentieth ranked network, with close to 124 million unique visitors, approximately 60 percent of Google's total (comScore Media Metrix, 2012).

Not all online advertising inventory is sold through networks. Some web services sell some or all of their ad inventory directly and some is sold through advertising exchanges, which, like ad networks, help reduce the transaction costs associated with connecting online inventory suppliers to buyers of ad availabilities. Exchanges are totally automated with prices set through online auctions. Exchanges also help advertisers evaluate suppliers of online inventory by providing data on the audiences they attract.

Demand-side platforms (DSPs) help advertisers and agencies perform many of the tasks associated with managing the display component of an online advertising campaign. Search management platforms (SMPs) provide analogous services for the search components of such ad campaigns. Services include budget allocation and management and development and implementation of bidding strategies.

Audience measurement services play the same roles for online advertising that they have played for offline media for many decades, providing third-party estimates of the sizes and characteristics of the audiences attracted by media vehicles. Unlike offline media, where one or occasionally a couple of audience measurement services typically dominate the supply of audience measurements for a given medium,[2] currently measurement of Internet audiences is a more competitive affair. comScore, which is indigenous to the Internet, and Nielsen, the primary supplier of television audience measurements in the USA, are the largest players, but face competition from ad networks and DSPs and from some publishers, like Google, Facebook and Yahoo!, all of whom provide information on their audiences that includes much more than mere counts.

Whether in the long run online advertising markets will also settle on a very small number of audience measurement services whose measures are accepted universally by both publishers and advertisers remains to be seen. Auditing print circulation is a time- and people-intensive operation and the small but supposedly statistically representative panels of television viewers and radio listeners that have traditionally been the foundation for measuring television and radio audiences are also expensive to administer. Economies of scale and near homogeneous services may have dictated monopoly or duopoly structures for the markets for these services. On the other hand, the basic count data used to estimate the sizes of Internet audiences is both comprehensive and relatively easy and inexpensive to produce and the costs of the analytics services offered by ad networks and exchanges has yet to produce significant concentration in the provision of these services.

20.3   TARGETING

20.3.1   Why it is Different Online

Even though the methods, indices and technologies employed to measure media audiences have advanced considerably over the years, advertisers still find it difficult to assess the value delivered by the audiences they purchase. The audience measurement uncertainties with which advertisers contend are often illustrated with the famous quip commonly attributed in the USA to early department store magnate John Wanamaker (1838–1922): 'Half the money I spend on advertising is wasted; the trouble is I don't know which half'. The universality of advertisers' frustration with the uncertainties associated with audience assessment are illustrated by the fact that in Europe nearly identical variants of this expression are attributed to William Hesketh Lever (1851–1925), First Viscount Leverhulme and founder of Lever Brothers (which became Unilever). To avoid dubious attributions of authorship of our own, we will simply refer to the 'half is wasted' (HIW) dilemma.

The HIW dilemma has two sides, reflected separately in the 'half is wasted' and the 'I don't know which half' components of the Wanamaker quote. On the 'I don't know' side is advertisers' uncertainty concerning the value of the audiences they purchase. This is a measurement problem and, because risky products typically sell for less than their risk-free counterparts, advertisers and media firms alike thus have a vested interest in reducing the uncertainty in measures of media audiences. Not surprisingly, there is a sizeable industry devoted to reducing the measurement uncertainties that make ad purchases risky. The 'half is wasted' side of the dilemma is the fact that the audience delivered by a media service to an advertiser always includes some individuals for whom the likelihood of purchasing the advertiser's product is slim or none along with the prospective customers the advertiser really wants to reach. Because the price an advertiser negotiates reflects only how much it is willing to pay to present its ads to the prospective customers it believes are members of an audience, it is not paying for some 'wasted' portion of the audience. The waste here is the unsold portion of the audience whose members could be sold to other advertisers if only different ads could be delivered simultaneously to different members of the audience. These are the teetotalers watching beer commercials during televised sports events who might be receptive to commercials promoting soft drinks or iced tea. Obviously media services have a strong financial interest in finding solutions to this side of the HIW dilemma.

For online audiences, Internet 2.0 interactivity and cloud computing have made possible new tools for measuring, segmenting, and delivering audiences to advertisers that can be used to address both sides of the HIW dilemma. Because an online publisher has a direct connection to every Internet user that accesses its content, various measures of audience can be collected at the level of the individual audience member, which mitigates long-standing concerns over the representativeness of the audience members sampled to create measures of offline audiences. Further, cookies and other tools can be used to track users' online activities over time and create behavioral indices of individual audience members' interests in various products and services for which there are no close offline counterparts. This information can then be used to deliver an advertiser's message directly to a constructed online audience composed of individuals selected (targeted) for their predicted receptivity to the advertiser's message. This process, called behavioral targeting,[3] addresses both the measurement uncertainty and the unsold audience sides of the HIW dilemma. It also raises a variety of privacy-related policy concerns (Goldfarb and Tucker, 2011).

With tracking a publisher can also keep track of the number of times individuals attracted to its content have been exposed to its advertiser clients' ads during previous visits to its website, or, if the publisher belongs to an ad network, the network's records can be used to determine how often members of the publisher's audience have been exposed to specific advertisers' ads when visiting the websites of other network members. Tracking can thus provide advertisers with a degree of control over frequency of exposure that is unattainable with offline media.

An additional advantage of audience measurements for online ads is that user activities, such as clicks on links in online ads and consummated sales following clicks, can also be recorded as more direct measures of an audience member's attention to and engagement with an ad. Most Internet advertising is now sold on a pay-per-action basis.

To summarize, three notable features distinguish the targeting capabilities of online media from those of their offline counterparts. (1) With offline media, all members of a publisher's audience are delivered the same ads whether they are likely to be customers for the products advertised or not. By contrast, the members of the online audience attracted by a publisher may be shown entirely different sets of ads, based on individualized assessments of their consumption interests. (2) Rather than accepting that members of an audience differ in the number of times they have been exposed to its ads, an online advertiser, working through an online publisher or an ad network, can select recipients for its ads based on the number of times they have been exposed to its ads in the past. (3) Activity-based assessments of Internet users' consumption interests can be used to match ads with individual Internet users. Offline media have no comparable mechanism for matching ads to ad recipients. It is not surprising then that Goldfarb (2014) sees 'the substantial reduction in the cost of targeting' as the fundamental difference between online and offline media.

20.3.2   The Economics of Online Targeting

The earliest work on economic aspects of targeted advertising appeared first in management and marketing journals, where the focus was primarily on ways sellers of consumer goods might use targeted ads to increase profits, often as a vehicle for implementing price discrimination strategies or segmenting markets (see, e.g., Iyer et al., 2005). This contrasts with the dominant approach in the media economics literature, where advertising has been examined in the contexts of strategies employed by media firms and the organization and performance of media markets. In this review, we focus primarily on the still quite small body of research that explores the implications of targeted advertising from this perspective; research that has been inspired largely by what has been happening online, but also by the development of more advanced targeting capabilities by other electronic media, such as cable TV.

Gal-Or and Gal-Or's (2005) article in *Marketing Science* was the earliest article on targeting we found that based its analysis on a model of a media firm. Gal-Or and Gal-Or develop a model where consumers are distributed uniformly along a Hotelling line describing the range of variation for a differentiated product. The market is served by two firms, one at each end of the product line. A firm can advertise to increase consumers' awareness of its product and, holding awareness of the other firm's product constant, sales increase with the level of consumer awareness. Gal-Or and Gal-Or show that the media firm can profit by offering firms the opportunity to have their ads delivered primarily to those consumers located closer to their end of the product line than their competitor's end. Firms choose this option because differential awareness created through targeted ads softens price competition and allows them to raise prices and profits.

Kim and Wildman (2006) were also early contributors to the targeted advertising literature with a model of competing cable TV networks that, in addition to earnings on their ad sales, collected license fees from the cable systems that carried them. Because viewers disliked ads, a network's audience size and its license fee earnings varied inversely with the amount of commercial time in its programs. Consumers in television programs' audiences differed in the sets of products they consumed and advertisers paid only for access to the audience subsets that comprised their potential customers. Kim and Wildman showed that without targeting, sellers whose products were consumed by the most viewers also purchased the majority of the advertising time, but this disparity disappeared with targeted ads. Depending on the elasticities of advertisers' demands for commercial time, the number of ads to which individual viewers were exposed could increase or fall following a switch to targeted ads. If viewers' program tastes were correlated with their product preferences, a shift to targeting could also change the equilibrium mix of program types offered viewers.

Targeting fully entered the mainstream of the economics literature on advertising with *AER Papers and Proceedings* articles by Athey and Gans (AG) (2010) and Levin and Milgrom (2010). AG in particular have served as a point of reference for subsequent work. AG model a situation in which every consumer belongs to one of a fixed number (say *n*) of mutually exclusive sets of consumers. For each set of consumers there is a corresponding set of products that only they consume. In the story motivating the model, a consumer's set membership is determined by the local area in which he or she resides and each local area is served by a publication distributed only to local residents. In addition, there is a single general publication that draws its audience from all local areas. Consumers only buy products for which they have seen ads. Consumers are media single-homers and choose either the general publication or their local publication, so an advertiser would have to advertise in both its local publication and the general interest publication to reach all of its potential customers. Because the audience for each publication is assumed fixed, the general publication and the local publications do not compete for audience members. This means that the effects on all publishers of a switch to geographically targeted ads from ads delivered to its entire audience by the general publisher are manifest only on the advertising sides of their two-sided platforms.

Even with its rather severe restrictions, the AG analysis generates several insights that should apply in more realistic settings. One is that targeting can increase the general publication's profits only if it lowers costs or increases advertising revenue relative what would be observed with untargeted ads. While this observation is trivially true, it also forces us to think carefully about what might make targeting the more profitable strategy. Suppose, for example, that ad clutter doesn't divert audience members' attention from their local merchants' ads and that the publication's delivery costs do not increase with the number of ads packaged with its content. Then the same ads that might have been delivered to subsets of its audience through targeting could be presented to all members of its audience and advertisers would value the total impressions delivered the same in either case, leaving profits the same whether ads were targeted or not. AG also show that when advertisers are constrained in their media buys, perhaps due to fixed marketing budgets, the general publisher and local publishers compete for the marginal impression purchased by each advertiser and this competition depresses per impression prices to the detriment of the local publishers.

While it may seem obvious that subdividing an audience into more homogeneous subgroups of consumers for delivery to advertisers would cause price per impression to rise, Bergemann and Bonatti (2011) use a model with single-homing media consumers to show that this is not necessarily the case. The reason is that when the audience offered to advertisers contains a mix of consumers who differ in the products they consume, sellers of all the products consumed by audience members will want to reach this audience. However, as the mix of consumers in a targeted audience becomes less diverse, the number of advertisers bidding for access to that audience declines. Bergemann and Bonatti (2011) find that while price per impression increases initially as targeting becomes more precise, eventually thinning of the advertiser side of the market reduces the intensity of competition for impressions and price per impression can fall, potentially quite dramatically, a possibility first noted by Gal-Or and Gal-Or (2005). This possibility is also highlighted in Levin and Milgrom's (2010) broader discussion of the pricing implications of targeting, where they further point out that some advertisers may prefer audiences with fairly diverse mixes of consumers over ones that are narrowly targeted.

The models of targeted advertising just reviewed are all single-period models that assume publishers know enough about their audience members' preferences over consumer goods to implement a targeting strategy. However, the tracking technologies employed to develop that knowledge can also be used to record individuals' exposures to online ads and then dynamically adjust the mix of ads delivered to individual Internet users over time. Athey et al. (ACG) (2013) represent the first significant effort to model this process and explore its implications for advertising market equilibria.

ACG present a two-period model of an advertising market that contains two publishers and many advertisers and consumers. Each consumer visits one of the two publishers each period, with the choice determined stochastically. As a consequence, the two-period audience for each publisher consists of a mix of 'loyals' who are in the audience both periods and 'switchers' who visited a different publisher each period. The full effect of an ad on a prospective consumer is realized after a single exposure and, while any individual advertiser assigns the same value to a first impression regardless of the consumer who is impressed, advertisers differ in their valuations of first impressions. So the market demand for first impressions is downward sloping. Publishers set per impression ad prices and advertisers choose the number of periods they purchase ads from each publisher. ACG identify publishers' profit-maximizing pricing strategies when tracking can only be used to ensure that a member of its audience is not presented with the same ad twice within a period, when tracking makes it possible for a publisher to guarantee advertisers that their ads will not be presented to its loyals twice over the two periods, and when it is possible to track exposures within the publishers' combined audience and the same no duplication guarantee is offered for switchers as well.

ACG's results provide some theoretical support for the conventional wisdom that ability to use tracking to sell advertisers audiences with fewer duplicated exposures should increase publisher profits and, depending on how this influences per impression prices, benefit advertisers as well. But they also show that there are conditions under which publisher profits are lower for a tracking equilibrium than for an equilibrium with no tracking. This is due to higher-value advertisers being willing to pay considerably more for a first impression than low-value advertisers. When all advertisers are charged the same per impression price, high-value advertisers will purchase ads for both periods to pick up the added first exposures, even though the audience purchased will include some individuals who have seen their ads before. Low-value advertisers will purchase ads for only one period to avoid paying for 'wasted' impressions. High-value advertisers are thus paying a higher effective price for first impressions and there are distributions of advertisers' first impression valuations for which profits from this implicit form of price discrimination can be higher than what can be achieved through tracking. This could be at least part of the explanation for why a considerable portion of Internet display ads are still sold on an untargeted basis.

20.4   SEARCH ADVERTISING

If, as Goldfarb (2014) says, dramatically improved targeting capabilities are the most important feature distinguishing Internet advertising from advertising in other media, then search engines' pairings of ads with consumers who have self-identified as interested in related products or services should represent the pinnacle of what can be accomplished through targeting with Internet ads. Because paid ads are placed around the unpaid listings that dominate the center of a search page and presumably are there to help build audience, it would be too strong to say that consumers use search engines for access to the paid ads alone. However, Fu et al. (2015) provide evidence that paid search ads contribute substantially to the sizes of the audiences generated by search terms. Because search ads are by nature targeted, the questions concerning the implications of targeting for Internet display ads that were discussed in the previous section simply do not arise.

Reflecting Hal Varian's observation in Chapter 18 in this volume that search engines 'offer a fertile ground for economic analysis', a very large literature on search engine economics has developed during the relatively short time that search engines have existed in something approximating their current form. Because the questions that must be answered to improve our understanding of search engines are many, this literature is also quite diverse. In this section, we focus on key findings and unresolved questions for the most prominent lines of research.

20.4.1   Background

A search engine faces the challenge of simultaneously setting prices for each of the multiple paid ad positions on a search page. As a general rule, paid ads positioned immediately above the unpaid listings on a search page are expected to generate more clicks for a search ad than positions to the right of the unpaid listings and the contribution to an ad's click count increases with the height of its position on the page. Search engines experimented with a variety of pricing mechanisms in the early days of search advertising, but the major search engines all adopted generalized second-price (GSP) auctions within a fairly short period of time after Google introduced it in 2002. A search engine employing a GSP auction ranks advertisers' bids and each advertiser is charged the lowest per click price required to retain its position above the bid ranked immediately below its own bid.

There is still debate over the reasons GSP auctions have become the de facto standard for setting prices for search ad positions. One of the ostensible reasons offered for the switch from first-price auctions to GSP auctions was that equilibria for GSP auctions are more stable. However, recent empirical studies (Zhang and Feng, 2011; Yuan, 2012) do not support this claim. Yuan (2012) used data from before and after Yahoo! switched from a generalized first-price (GFP) auction to an unweighted GSP auction and found that after the switch advertisers changed their bids more often and the magnitudes of price changes were greater. Zhang and Feng (2011) observed sawtooth-like price cycles for both GFP and GSP auctions. On the other hand, Yuan's (2011) study of comparative efficiency for the two auction mechanisms found that efficiency (measured by the frequency with which higher value advertisers were assigned better positions) was 4 percent higher for the GSP.

The literature on search engine economics that has developed since the introduction of the GSP auction has focused largely on GSP auction properties and the implications of its use for market outcomes, including market efficiency and the relative payoffs to the various participants in search markets. GSP auctions have a number of features that search engines can adjust to change the character of the auctions they run and these choices have implications for market performance. Bid ranking formulas and reserve prices are two that have received considerable attention in the literature.

20.4.1.1   Bid ranking

An advertiser's bid is the amount it offers to pay for each click generated by its ad and when search engines first started using GSP auctions advertisers were ranked by their bids alone. A GSP auction that ranks bids in this manner is referred to as an unweighted auction. But the major search engines fairly quickly switched to 'rank-by-revenue' formulas (also called click-weighted formulas) that assign ads positions based on what can roughly be described as (search engines') predictions of their revenue-generating potential calculated as price per click times predicted number of clicks. Because an ad's content and its position on a search page both influence the number of clicks it receives, it is common to think of the number of clicks received by an ad as the product of a position effect and an ad-specific effect that is commonly referred to as an ad's relevance. The 'rank-by-revenue' rule employs bid weights proportional to predicted relevance and assigns each bid a rank based on the product of its bid and predicted relevance.

Of course search engines are free to employ bid weights that differ from those used for unweighted auctions and rank-by-revenue auctions and the effects of different bid weights on market performance and search engine revenue have been a matter of considerable interest. A family of ranking rules introduced by Lahaie and Pennock (2007) has probably received the most attention by researchers examining alternative ranking rules, possibly because its functional form is easily incorporated in economic models of search markets. For b_i the bid submitted by advertiser i, q_i the relevance of i's ad and 'squashing factor' s, i's bid is given a score of $b_i q_i^s$. All other bids are similarly scored and ranks determined accordingly. In theory there are no bounds on the values s might take, but it is often assumed that $s \in [0, 1]$. Squashing factors of 0 and 1 correspond, respectively, to unweighted bids and rank-by-revenue bids.

20.4.1.2   Reserve prices

Although they did not at the beginning, GSP auctions now typically include as a restriction a minimum price that must be paid by an advertiser to secure a position on a search page. Reserve prices can be either weighted or unweighted. An unweighted reserve price is simply a minimum nominal price per click that the advertiser occupying the lowest paid ad position on a search page must pay. If the reserve price is weighted, advertiser-specific relevance weights are applied to a nominal reserve price. Reserve prices can increase a search engine's revenue by increasing the bid required to secure the lowest position, which in turn can raise the bids and prices paid for higher positions. In fact, Lucier et al. (2012) show that for a Bayesian model of GSP auctions a positive reserve price may be required to eliminate zero revenue equilibria and Thompson and Leyton-Brown (2013) show that reserve prices can be combined with a squashing factor of less than one to further increase search engine revenue. They also find that unweighted reserve prices outperform weighted reserve prices if enhancing search engine revenue is the objective.

20.4.2 Search Market Equilibria

The economics literature on search advertising markets has focused primarily on the nature of search market equilibria, with efficiency, comparative payoffs to search engines and advertisers and market stability the primary topics of investigation. The majority of the work to date has focused on formal models of search market equilibria, although the analyses based on these models are often helpfully informed by data and empirical studies of search markets.

GSP auctions present a number of challenges to model builders. For one thing, GSP auctions do not compel truthful bids (bids that reveal bidders true valuations for ad positions). Given a range of bids and a limited number of bidders, within a finite range a representative bidder will be able to change its bid without affecting the position it secures or its payment. As a consequence, there may be situations where truthful bids cannot be sustained in a Nash equilibrium because at least one advertiser would find it profitable to undercut the bid of the advertiser with the next lower position to reduce its advertising costs even though its sales would also be reduced by shifting its ad to a less productive position (Aggarwal et al., 2006). In this case, the allocation of positions would be inefficient because advertisers' positions would not correspond to their relative valuations of the positions.

The fact an advertiser's bid determines the price paid by the advertiser occupying the next higher position also means that an advertiser so inclined could set its own bid near the top of the range that leaves its own position and price unchanged just to increase a rival bidder's costs, a strategy known as malicious bidding. Liang and Qi (2007) show that search markets may not always converge when bidding is malicious. As a general matter, the fact that advertisers' best response bids can be selected from a range of values leaves open the possibility that bidding strategies selected will not support convergence to stable equilibria (Cary et al., 2007; Zhou and Lukose, 2007).

20.4.2.1 Full information models

Similar simultaneous-move, full-information models developed by Edelman et al. (2007) and Varian (2007) constituted a breakthrough in the modeling of search market equilibria and have served as touchstones for subsequent analysis. The breakthrough was a refinement to the Nash auction equilibrium that restricts the equilibria considered to those for which, given the prices associated with the positions, each advertiser prefers the position he or she has acquired to all other positions. The resulting set of equilibria, called 'envy free' by Edelman et al. (2007) and 'symmetric Nash' by Varian (2007), is still an infinite set, but all members of this set have attractive stability properties and the envy-free restriction substantially simplifies the derivation of equilibrium properties. Furthermore, because agents that value clicks more are always assigned better positions, allocations are efficient and the efficient equilibrium that would be produced by a VCG auction is contained within the set of envy-free equilibria (Varian, 2007; Lucier et al., 2012).

Lahaie and Pennock (2007) elaborate on the Varian (2007) and Edelman et al. (2007) models by adding the squashing factors described above to the bid ranking formula and show that when relevance and bids are positively correlated, a search engine can increase its revenue relative to what would be generated by a pure rank-by-revenue rule by selecting a squashing factor of less than 1. However, market efficiency is reduced when this strategy is employed. Athey and Nekipelov (2011) show that this finding holds for a model with less than fully informed bidders.

20.4.2.2 Incomplete information models

The fully informed bidders assumption has been criticized as unrealistic. Even for an unweighted GSP auction, a bidder would acquire direct knowledge of only the per click price paid by the bidder claiming the position immediately above his or hers, because it is his or her bid, and the bid of the advertiser occupying the position immediately below his or hers, which is the per click price he or she pays. The ad-specific weights applied to bids in weighted GSP auctions are not revealed by search engines. The standard argument justifying use of full information bidding models is that advertisers engage in repeated rounds of bidding against the same competitors and this gives them opportunities to vary their bids and observe the resulting allocation of positions. With the information gained through this process they can form relatively accurate estimates of their competitors' bids and bid weights. Full information critics respond that a number of factors make this information difficult to acquire in real search markets where advertisers adjust their bids less frequently than auctions occur, advertisers with different ad budgets participate in auctions with different frequencies, and the mix of competing bidders changes from auction to auction. Edelman and Ostrovsky (2007) and Athey and Nekipelov (2011) provide evidence that search ads' positions vary across auctions and Edelman and Ostrovsky (2007) report that bids fluctuate as well.

For agents with less than full information, Varian (2007) showed how GSP auctions could be modeled as Bayes-Nash equilibria and Thompson and Leyton-Brown (2013) employed such a model to examine the effects of squashing and reserve prices on search engine revenues, as described above. Gomes and Sweeney (2014) have probably provided the most thorough exploration of the properties of Bayes-Nash search equilibria. The critical simplifying assumptions underlying their model are that advertisers' valuations for clicks are known only to themselves, these valuations are drawn from independent but identical distributions that are common knowledge to all advertisers, the value of a click to an advertiser is independent of the position of the advertiser's ad, and the likelihood that exposure to an ad will elicit a click is the same for all advertisers. It is worth noting that the assumption regarding the distributions from which bids are drawn might be susceptible to some of the same criticisms levied against the full information models and the assumption that exposure to its ad has the same probability of being followed by a click for all advertisers rules out advertiser-specific relevance weights.

Gomes and Sweeney's primary result identifies a necessary and sufficient condition for an efficient Bayes-Nash equilibrium to exist for a multi-position auction. Expressed in terms of positions' click-through rates, the click-through rate associated with each position must exceed the click-through rate of the next lower position by at least the non-negligible amount required to ensure an advertiser with a higher valuation does not find it profitable to shift to the next lower position by undercutting the bid of the lower-valuation advertiser occupying that spot. Because nothing guarantees that this condition will be satisfied in search markets, there is no guarantee that an efficient Bayes-Nash equilibrium will exist. Gomes and Sweeney (2014) point out that their model is a static model of a single-shot game and suggest that further advances may be made by developing dynamic models of search market equilibria.

20.4.2.3   A closer look at consumers' influence on equilibria

The research discussed so far has focused primarily on interactions between advertisers and search engines. In a notable departure, Athey and Ellison (2011) assume that search users incur a positive cost each time they click on an ad and show that positive search costs can change the character of a search equilibrium considerably. Modeling search auctions as common value auctions, the authors find that in equilibrium advertisers are allocated positions according to their relevance, that this allows users to infer ads' relevance rankings from their positions, and that advertisers submit bids that are monotone in relevance. Athey and Ellison also find that a positive reserve price can increase search engine profits and social welfare by keeping low-relevance ads off search pages and that an unweighted reserve price works better than a weighted reserve price in this regard.

20.4.3   There is Still Much to Do

From the literature reviewed in this section, it should be clear that we have come a long way in developing a better understanding of how search advertising markets operate, but that we also have a long way to go before we can claim with confidence that the models of search markets we work with provide reasonably accurate depictions of the way search markets really work, how efficiently they operate, or whether they are inherently stable. Work to develop upper-bound estimates on the extent to which the efficiency of search market equilibria might depart from the efficient market outcome is helpful when assessing the efficiency with which search markets operate (see, e.g., Caragiannis et al., 2012; Paes Leme and Tardos, 2010), but it is important to recognize that these estimates vary with the theoretical model that is employed to describe how search advertising markets operate. Better empirical grounding is needed to help with the assessment of how closely the assumptions of various search market models approximate conditions in real search markets.

Athey and Ellison's (2011) model of search advertising markets in which clicks are costly to consumers highlights the importance of looking more closely at how consumers use and experience search engines and more work of this nature is needed. It is also important that we do not lose sight of the fact that the suppliers of the unpaid listings in the center of search pages are not passive participants in search advertising markets. Many of these listings are also ads and it is not unusual for an advertiser to have a paid ad and an unpaid listing on the same search page. Suppliers of unpaid listings work actively to improve their positions on search pages and strategies for doing so are actively discussed in trade press articles on 'search engine optimization' (SEO). The Huffington Post's success in rapidly establishing a position as a major online media player has been attributed by some to its SEO skills (Shafer, 2007). There is also a tiny academic literature on SEO strategy (see, e.g., Parikh and Deshmukh, 2013). How can we know how efficiently search advertising markets operate if we don't know whether advertisers consider paid and unpaid listings to be substitutes or complements or whether efforts by suppliers of unpaid listings to improve their positions on search pages serve consumers' interests or not?

20.5   CONCLUSION

Growth in Internet advertising has paralleled that of the Internet overall. In a little over two decades Internet advertising has grown from near invisibility to the second largest advertising category by revenue in the USA and its growth has been nearly as impressive in most other advanced economies. It almost certainly will occupy the top spot for many countries within the next several years. An economic phenomenon of this magnitude merits attention from economists, but what makes Internet advertising an especially interesting topic for economic research is that we are not just witnessing the application of old business models to a new medium.

Point-to-point delivery of messages combined with advanced data collection and data analytics capabilities have made it possible for advertisers to connect with consumers in entirely new ways. Researchers have focused on what this means for search advertising and display advertising, the two categories of Internet advertising that overwhelmingly dominate expenditures on Internet ads. Search advertising is unique to the Internet and Internet display ads can take advantage of advanced targeting capabilities that other media simply cannot provide. For both types of Internet advertising, it is clear that our understanding of the fundamental questions that need to be addressed has advanced considerably; but it is also clear that much work remains to be done before we can claim a deep and empirically grounded understanding of these phenomena.

NOTES

1. In 2013, 'other' included interstitial, slotting fees, and referrals. The list of minor categories has varied over time as new categories have been introduced and others have disappeared.
2. For example, in the USA, Nielsen dominates in the supply of standardized television ratings and the Audit Bureau of Circulation (ABC) has long been the principal audience measurement service for newspapers and magazines.
3. Contextual targeting, where an advertiser selects a media outlet because the advertiser expects its content will attract an audience with a high percentage of prospective customers, is another common form of targeting. Contextual targeting is employed with both online and offline media services. It is not covered in this review because no compelling case has been made that that this strategy works better or differently in an online environment.

REFERENCES

Aggarwal, G., A. Goel and R. Motwani (2006), 'Truthful auctions for pricing search keywords', in *Proceedings of the 7th ACM Conference on Electronic Commerce (EC'06)*, pp. 1–7.
Athey, S. and J.S. Gans (2010), 'The impact of targeting on advertising markets and media competition', *American Economic Review*, **100** (2), 608–13.
Athey, S. and G. Ellison (2011), 'Position auctions with consumer search', *The Quarterly Journal of Economics*, **126** (3), 1213–70.
Athey, S. and D. Nekipelov (2011), 'A structural model of sponsored search advertising auctions', unpublished paper, accessed 9 August 2015 at http://eml.berkeley.edu/~nekipelov/pdf_papers/paper16.pdf.
Athey, S., E. Calvano and J.S. Gans (2013), 'The impact of the Internet on advertising markets for news media', *NBER Working Paper No. 19419*, accessed 8 August 2015 at http://ssrn.com/abstract=2325793.
Bergemann, D. and A. Bonatti (2011), 'Targeting in advertising markets: Implications for offline vs. online media', *RAND Journal of Economics*, **42** (3), 417–43.
Bourn, J. (2013), 'Online advertising: A history from 1993 to the present day', *MarketingTech*, 11 September,

accessed 8 August 2015 at http://www.marketingtechnews.net/news/2013/sep/11/online-advertising-history-1993-present-day-infographic/.

Caragiannis, I., C. Kaklamanis and P. Kanellopoulous et al. (2011), 'On the efficiency of equilibria in second price auctions', in *Proceedings of the 12th ACM Conference on Electronic Commerce (EC'11)*, pp. 81–90.

Cary, M., A. Das and B. Edelman et al. (2007), 'Greedy bidding strategies for keyword auctions', in *Proceedings of the 8th ACM conference on Electronic commerce (EC'07)*, pp. 262–71.

comScore Media Metrix (2012), 'comScore Media Metrix ranks top 50 US web properties for June 2012' [press release], accessed 8 August 2015 at http://www.comscore.com/Insights/Press_Releases/2012/7/comScore_Media_Metrix_Ranks_Top_50_US_Web_Properties_for_June_2012.

Edelman, B. and M. Ostrovsky (2007), 'Strategic bidder behavior in sponsored search auctions', *Decision Support Systems*, **43** (1), 192–8.

Edelman, B., M. Ostrovsky and M. Schwarz (2007), 'Internet advertising and the generalized second-price auction: Selling billions of dollars worth of keywords', *American Economic Review*, **97** (1), 242–59.

eMarketer(2013),'UStotalmediaadspendinchesup,pushedbydigital',*eMarketer*,22August,accessed9August2015 at http://www.emarketer.com/Article/US-Total-Media-Ad-Spend-Inches-Up-Pushed-by-Digital/1010154.

Fu, W., W. Ma, C. Ting and S.S. Wildman (2015), 'Feedback effects in search advertising', accessed 9 August 2015 http://ssrn.com/abstract=2588245.

Gal-Or, E. and M. Gal-Or (2005), 'Customized advertising via a common media distributor', *Marketing Science*, **24** (2), 241–53.

Goldfarb, A. (2014), 'What is different about online advertising?', *Review of Industrial Organization*, **44** (2), 115–29.

Goldfarb, A. and C. Tucker (2011), 'Privacy regulation and online advertising', *Management Science*, **57** (1), 57–71.

Gomes, R. and K. Sweeney (2014), 'Bayes-Nash equilibria of the generalized second-price auction', *Games and Economic Behavior*, **86**, 421–37.

Interactive Advertising Bureau (1999), 'First quarter 1999 Internet advertising revenues double over first quarter 1998' [press release], accessed 28 December 2015 at http://www.iab.com/about_the_iab/recent_press_releases/press_release_archive/press_release/4337.

Interactive Advertising Bureau (2000), *IAB Internet Advertising Revenue Report*, accessed 15 December 2013 at http://www.iab.net/media/file/IAB_PWC_1999Q4.pdf.

Interactive Advertising Bureau (2001), *IAB Internet Advertising Revenue Report*, accessed 15 December 2013 at http://www.iab.net/media/file/IAB_PwC_004_2000.pdf.

Interactive Advertising Bureau (2002), *IAB Internet Advertising Revenue Report*, accessed 15 December 2013 at http://www.iab.net/media/file/resources_adrevenue_pdf_IAB_PWC_2001Q4.pdf.

Interactive Advertising Bureau (2003), *IAB Internet Advertising Revenue Report*, accessed 15 December 2013 at http://www.iab.net/media/file/resources_adrevenue_pdf_IAB_PwC_2002final.pdf.

Interactive Advertising Bureau (2004), *IAB Internet Advertising Revenue Report*, accessed 15 December 2013 at http://www.iab.net/media/file/resources_adrevenue_pdf_IAB_PwC_2003.pdf.

Interactive Advertising Bureau (2005), *IAB Internet Advertising Revenue Report*, accessed 15 December 2013 at http://www.iab.net/media/file/resources_adrevenue_pdf_IAB_PwC_2004full.pdf.

Interactive Advertising Bureau (2006), *IAB Internet Advertising Revenue Report*, accessed 15 December 2013 at http://www.iab.net/media/file/resources_adrevenue_pdf_IAB_PwC_2005.pdf.

Interactive Advertising Bureau (2007), *IAB Internet Advertising Revenue Report*, accessed 15 December 2013 at http://www.iab.net/media/file/resources_adrevenue_pdf_IAB_PwC_2006_Final.pdf.

Interactive Advertising Bureau (2008), *IAB Internet Advertising Revenue Report*, accessed 15 December 2013 at http://www.iab.net/media/file/IAB_PwC_2007_full_year.pdf.

Interactive Advertising Bureau (2009), *IAB Internet Advertising Revenue Report*, accessed 15 December 2013 at http://www.iab.net/media/file/IAB_PwC_2008_full_year.pdf.

Interactive Advertising Bureau (2010), *IAB Internet Advertising Revenue Report*, accessed 15 December 2013 at http://www.iab.net/media/file/IAB-Ad-Revenue-Full-Year-2009.pdf.

Interactive Advertising Bureau (2011), *IAB Internet Advertising Revenue Report*, accessed 15 December 2013 at http://www.iab.net/media/file/IAB_Full_year_2010_0413_Final.pdf.

Interactive Advertising Bureau (2012), *IAB Internet Advertising Revenue Report*, accessed 15 December 2013 at http://www.iab.net/media/file/IAB_Internet_Advertising_Revenue_Report_FY_2011.pdf.

Interactive Advertising Bureau (2013), *IAB Internet Advertising Revenue Report*, accessed 15 December 2013 at http://www.iab.net/media/file/IABInternetAdvertisingRevenueReportFY2012POSTED.pdf.

Interactive Advertising Bureau (2014), *IAB Internet Advertising Revenue Report*, http://www.iab.net/media/file/IAB_Internet_Advertising_Revenue_Report_FY_2013.pdf.

Iyer, G., D. Soberman and J.M. Villas-Boas (2005), 'The targeting of advertising', *Marketing Science*, **24** (3), 461–76.

Kaye, B.K. and N.J. Medoff (2001), *Just a Click Away: Advertising on the Internet*, Boston, MA: Allyn and Bacon.

Kim, E. and S.S. Wildman (2006), 'A deeper look at the economics of advertiser support for television: The implications of consumption-differentiated viewers and ad addressability', *Journal of Media Economics*, **19** (1), 55–79.

Lahaie, S. and D.M. Pennock (2007), 'Revenue analysis of a family of ranking rules for keyword auctions', in *Proceedings of the 8th ACM conference on Electronic Commerce (EC'07)*, pp. 50–56.

Levin, J. and P. Milgrom (2010), 'Heterogeneity and conflation in market design', *American Economic Review*, **100** (2), 603–7.

Liang, L. and Q. Qi (2007), 'Cooperative or vindictive: Bidding strategies in sponsored search auction', in X. Deng and F.C. Graham (eds), *Internet and Network Economics: Third International Workshop, WINE 2007, San Diego, CA, USA, December 12–14, 2007*, Berlin and Heidelberg: Springer, pp. 167–78.

Lucier, B., R. Paes Leme and E. Tardos (2012), 'On revenue in the generalized second price auction', in *Proceedings of the 21st International Conference on World Wide Web (WWW'12)*, pp. 361–70.

Morrissey, B. (2013), 'How the banner ad was born', *Digiday*, 12 April, accessed 15 July 2014 at http://digiday.com/agencies/how-the-banner-ad-was-born/.

Paes Leme, R. and E. Tardos (2010), 'Pure and Bayes-Nash price of anarchy for generalized second price auction', paper at the 1st Annual IEEE Symposium on Foundations of Computer Science (FOCS), 23–26 October, Las Vegas, NV.

Parikh, A. and S. Deshmukh (2013), 'Search engine optimization', *International Journal of Engineering Research & Technology*, **2** (11), 3146–53.

Reynolds, K. (2011), 'Are ad exchanges and real time bidding the next big thing?', *Advertising Perspectives*, accessed 15 July 2014 at http://www.advertisingperspectives.com/adblog/media-technology/are-ad-exchanges-and-real-time-bidding-the-next-big-thing/.

Seabrook, A. (2008), 'At 30, spam going nowhere soon', *NPR*, 3 May, accessed 12 December at 2013 http://www.npr.org/templates/story/story.php?storyId=90160617.

Shafer, J. (2011), 'SEO speedwagon: The rapid rise and sale of Arianna Huffington's Post', *Slate*, 7 February, accessed 11 January 2015 at http://www.slate.com/articles/news_and_politics/press_box/2011/02/seo_speedwagon.html.

Thompson, D.R.M. and K. Leyton-Brown (2013), 'Revenue optimization in the generalized second-price auction', in *Proceedings of the Fourteenth ACM Conference on Electronic Commerce (EC'13)*, pp. 837–52.

Varian, H.R. (2007), 'Position auctions', *International Journal of Industrial Organization*, **25** (6), 1163–78.

Yuan, J. (2011), 'Estimating the efficiency improvement of the resource allocation in the Yahoo! keyword auction', *International Journal of Humanities and Social Science*, **1** (18), 272–84.

Yuan, J. (2012), 'Examining the Yahoo! sponsored search auctions: A regression discontinuity design approach', *International Journal of Economics and Finance*, **4** (3), 139–51.

Zhang, X. and J. Feng (2011), 'Cyclical bid adjustments in search-engine advertising', *Management Science*, **57** (9), 1703–19.

Zhou, Y. and R. Lukose (2007), 'Vindictive bidding in keyword auctions', in *Proceedings of the Ninth International Conference on Electronic Commerce (ICEC'07)*, pp. 41–46.

21. Online news
Lucy Küng, Nic Newman and Robert G. Picard

21.1 INTRODUCTION

Online news is an extremely complex and fast-changing field. What began as the simple provision of news using websites on the Internet has morphed into an environment of multiple digital platforms and products and numerous ways of accessing news content. The online news sector was born with the Internet, and its development has been both furious and messy. Like the Internet it is still an adolescent, and has a number of growth challenges it needs to master, not least finding a sustainable business model. Although online platforms offer exciting new ways to reach and connect with audiences, news providers are continuing to struggle to create effective and self-sustaining businesses on them.

This means that creating a single theoretical architecture that accommodates and analyses recent developments in online news is not possible, or at least not without ignoring anomalies or over-simplifying categorizations. There is much excellent analysis of sector developments – but that excellence is grounded more often than not in a nuanced appreciation of the context dependency of any particular conclusions that have been drawn.

Strategists on the ground in media organizations use the term 'VUCA' to describe their organizations' strategic environments – volatile, uncertain, complex and ambiguous. It is these VUCA characteristics that preclude the precise definition and clear definitions that are necessary for academic analysis of an industry sector: industry boundaries are indistinct, corporate structures in a state of flux, competitors and sources of competitive advantage fast-changing. Journalism is melding with technology. In the news field disrupters become part of the established eco-system and themselves subject to disruption surprisingly fast. BuzzFeed, a native of the social era, has pioneered a high value but labor-intensive social advertising model that bypasses much of the Google universe. Non-media, or non-classic media, organizations have moved into news provision perhaps on a temporary basis simply as a means of achieving other strategic goals. Legacy news providers have added online to their existing operations, but just as paywalls are put up, taken down, and put up again, so too can online divisions be created as skunkworks, integrated into newsrooms, and then separated off again.

This chapter has therefore necessarily adopted a narrative approach. However, a clear development path in online news can be discerned only in retrospect, and even today its trajectory is relatively murky. At this stage, two eras in the development of online news are apparent. First is the 'era of digital publishing', roughly corresponding with the Web 1.0 era. It begins in approximately 1993 with the emergence of the Internet as we know it today – a mass-market global medium for the use of the general public, offering content, communication and community services. It extends through the dot-com bubble to close around 1999. From a media content perspective, text-based, traditional publishing–style content, accessed via portals, dominated during this period.

Table 21.1   Eras in the development of online news, the technological inflection points that triggered them, and incumbent responses

Era (and Key Events)	Technology Inflection Points	Internet Media Developments	Incumbent Developments/ Reactions
Digital publishing (1993–99) Web 1.0	CompuServe Internet connectivity (1989) Mosaic (1993) Yahoo! (1994) Netscape (1994) Microsoft Windows 98 with integrated web browser DoubleClick (1995) Google (1998) RSS (1999) Blogger.com (1999)	Salon.com (1995) CNN.com (1995) FT.com (1995) New York Times Online (1995) MSNBC (1996) Craigslist (1996) Drudge Report (1996) Slate.com (1996) BBC News Online (1997)	Newspapers: by 1999 one-third of all newspapers have online edition. Much shovelware and churnware. Business model: content free, revenues from advertising and e-commerce Broadcasters: web portals, focus on news, sport and weather. Business model: cross-financed via existing income streams, plus ad revenues where possible
Digital participation and multimedia (2000–2014) Dot-com boom and crash Web 2.0	Napster (2000) Wikipedia (2001) Google AdWords/ AdSense (2003) YouTube (2005) iPhone (2007) Apple App Store (2008) iPad (2010)	Wikipedia (2001) Google News (2002) OhMyNews.com (2002) Gawker Media (2002) Facebook (2004) Huffington Post (2005) Mashable (2005) Twitter (2006)	Newspapers: shift towards unique digital content and then towards digital first strategies. Business model: increase in pay-per-use and subscription, paid-for apps Broadcasters: online sites established as reference medium for breaking news. Sites become more complex, with increased use of blogs, social media, and user-generated content. Increasing desire to generate advertising revenue, generating conflict with newspapers

The second era extends from 2000 to 2014 and is termed here the 'era of participation and multimedia' (essentially Web 2.0). It starts with the bursting of the dot-com bubble. From a media content perspective, this era sees the growing importance of social media and multimedia storytelling.

Table 21.1 provides a visual summary of these eras. For each era it highlights the technology inflection points (the key technological advances that triggered new developments in online media), the Internet media products and services that emerged as a result, and developments or reactions on the part of incumbent news providers in response.

Discussion of online news and the business models underlying it in each of these eras addresses three sectors of the media: print (primarily newspapers and magazines), broadcasting (chiefly television organizations), and 'pure plays' (new players whose businesses include news that started with the Internet and developed in step with it). Coverage of the sectors is inevitably unequal, reflecting the fact that online news is a core business for newspapers and new Internet media companies dedicated to news coverage, but one (albeit central) element of a larger and more complex content palette for traditional broadcasters.

After discussing developments in these three sectors during these two eras, the chapter moves on to discuss the strategic, organizational and editorial implications of online news. It closes by drawing conclusions about the development of online news for the media industry, suggesting how the field may develop in the future, and highlighting likely future challenges and controversies.

21.2 1993–99: ERA OF DIGITAL PUBLISHING (WEB 1.0)

Despite widely articulated fears of cannibalization, the print media, particularly newspapers, began to experiment with the Internet relatively early on (e.g., FT.com was launched in 1995, NYTimes.com in 1996). Evolution has continued ever since, with different organizational and market contexts resulting in a variety of editorial offerings and business models (Boczkowski, 2004).[1]

By 1999, nearly one-third of all daily newspapers (5212 newspapers worldwide) had online editions (*Editor & Publisher*, 1999). In comparison to newspapers' current online services, these early online news offerings were unsophisticated. They reflected an assumption on the part of the newspapers that the Internet would function as a reuse platform for their existing content. Online editions were viewed as line extensions, in much the same way as new geographic editions.

Investment in dedicated online news content was correspondingly modest. In the words of Clay Shirky (2009), 'the core assumption . . . was that the organizational form of the newspaper, as a general-purpose vehicle for publishing a variety of news and opinion, was basically sound, and only needed a digital facelift'. 'Shovelware' (print articles that were simply transferred to the Internet by software without adaptation) was common, meaning online news sites that were often little more than copies of their text-heavy, non-interactive print editions (Van der Wurff, 2008). 'Churnalism' was also widespread – online content derived from uploading little-altered items from sources outside the organization, particularly press releases from PR agencies.

Publishers initially hoped to finance their online editions by subscription; however, apart from a few celebrated examples from the financial press (e.g., *The Wall Street Journal*, which implemented a paywall in 1997 and has retained it ever since), in the main subscription funding models failed. It was not surprising that financial news providers would be more successful online: their readers were already accustomed to consuming and paying for information online (in the form of financial information services from Bloomberg or Reuters, for example). Furthermore, these online newspapers offered additional content, tools and services tailored for their readers, plus the readers' employers often paid the subscriptions.

Faced with the failure of subscription models, newspapers began to experiment with variants of free content models. Here, online content was provided free to readers, in the hope that income from advertisers seeking to reach these online consumers would cover the costs of the online editions. At this point it was still widely expected that e-commerce would create a significant additional income stream for newspapers. This also failed to materialize. Although e-commerce did develop very substantially, newspapers never managed to gain a foothold in this fast-growing field for a variety of reasons: newspaper brands were not associated with shopping, large online retailers like Amazon.com and eBay emerged as dominant e-commerce destinations, major offline retailers grabbed large parts of the online market, and search engines sent customers directly to specialty and local retailers.

Legacy broadcasters' move into online was more organic and less dramatic than their print media peers'. As it became clear that the Internet would develop into a third broadcasting medium, after radio and television, broadcasters gradually added Internet activities to their portfolio, with news one of the first online genres. CNN.com was launched in 1995, and BBC.com in 1997.

Most broadcasters began with some kind of portal combining news, weather and sports content. Not only did the broadcasters have these content genres to hand, but it also reflected the fact that news, weather and sports are all excellently suited to the functionalities of the Internet in that it allows frequent updating, is perfect for short-form text-based stories, and has an addictive appeal to audiences. Relatively quickly they learned to enhance this content with localization and personalization features.

Because the Internet was then primarily a text-based medium, these news portals required broadcast news organizations to acquire a new competence – that of text journalism. Cable television news channels in the USA tended to handle this in-house or in partnership with digital firms. European broadcasters also produced online content by setting up their own digital newsrooms. In the USA, news broadcasters began to cooperate with their network affiliates and with newspapers within their media group in order to reduce the costs of online news and to increase the amount of content available.

In terms of business models, for radio and television broadcasters that have offered content that is free at the point of consumption, online news content initially represented an extension of their existing way of doing business. For public service broadcasters in particular there was a strong intrinsic match between the public service funding model, the news genre, and the Internet (Küng, 2005), and this fit will grow stronger as video comes to dominate Internet content.[2] The extent to which news provision will be dominated by video is uncertain because even broadcasters are increasing the supply of text-based news. Chan-Olmsted and Ha (2003) found that television broadcasters focused their online activities primarily on building audience relationships, rather than generating online advertising sales. Thus the Internet was used mostly to complement stations' offline core products.

Initially, for free-to-air broadcasters at least, the fact that they operated under indirect financing models (i.e., via license fee or advertising income) meant that they were free to concentrate on their content proposition, unlike their print media peers who had to devote time and energy to solving the problem of missing revenues. More fundamentally they were more at home with the underlying Internet content proposition that content should be free, or at least, not directly charged for. More recently, as media systems become both more fragmented and complex, legacy broadcasters' and newspapers' positions have moved closer together as both face the challenge of funding the addition of an entirely new dimension of media activities against a backdrop of falling revenues.

Digitalization and the Internet made it easy and cheap to produce and distribute content to virtually unlimited audiences at minimal cost, and as a result many new media organizations moved into online news. These developed rapidly into a complex field with a range of organizations that can be roughly grouped into search engines; technology players and ISPs; and online-only start-ups (pure players), blogs and social media.

In the early days of the Internet, building a scalable publishing platform capable of supporting a news service was challenging for all but the largest companies, and as a result the early movers were largely Internet access providers like AOL and CompuServe and search engines such as Yahoo!, Lycos, Infoseek and Excite. They recognized that frequently updated free news could lure users to their portals – users who would hopefully move on from there to other, premium, services. Their early sites combined news, weather, sports and business with services such as search and email in a single easy-to-use consumer proposition. The news provision was typically the top stories obtained from news agencies and local newspapers or broadcasters.

For these ISPs and search engines, news was an important part of the editorial formula. For the most part they were not only curating other people's news and paying content providers for access to stories, but also taking a cut of the advertising revenues; they also ran limited newsroom operations. Portals like MSN, AOL and Yahoo! still have prominent news services on their home pages and these remain an important part of the online news landscape.

Technology companies like Microsoft also saw the Internet's potential to disrupt traditional print and broadcast news models and began to develop online news services, although even Microsoft's deep pockets were unequal to the costs of establishing a global newsgathering operation. In 1996 Microsoft formed an online partnership with the US broadcaster NBC to create MSNBC, which for a time was the largest news site in the world.

In 1998 Google was founded. Its basic idea was that the relevance and value of a webpage could be measured by the number of other pages linked to it; the quality of its search results meant it quickly established itself as market leader in search. Google struggled to monetize its service until it introduced text-based advertisements based on users' keyword searches. This transformed Google into one of the world's most powerful companies, and undermined newspapers' ability to translate their advertising finance models online.

'Pure play' (online only) news providers have relatively straightforward profit-based business models. They have low cost bases and the advantages conferred by freedom from traditional media's legacy asset investments. These providers also focus on specialist areas with strong audience appeal that had not been covered rigorously or in depth by traditional media, such as technology and entertainment news, which can deliver advertising revenue.

One of the early notable pure plays is the Drudge Report. Founded in 1996, this was initially a weekly subscriber-based email that made its name with the sex and political scandals surrounding the Clinton administration. Today it is a low-cost news aggregation website – the front page is a simple list of news headlines and links from mainstream news providers, supplemented from time to time by tips and exclusives unearthed by proprietor Matt Drudge or his colleagues. By 2012, it was reported to have over a billion page views and 14.4 million US readers per month. Estimated revenues were $15–20 million a year, yielding after-tax profits of $10–15 million (Blodget, 2012).

Other new players sought to redefine feature or long-form journalism. Salon.com, founded in 1995 by a group of disaffected San Francisco journalists, created a forum for cultural and political commentary and allowed readers to offer their own thoughts via electronic discussion groups. But despite bringing in more than three million regular visitors, Salon.com struggled financially, burning over $83 million of investment by 2003. *Slate* is an online magazine publishing on news, politics and culture that was created in 1996 by Michael Kinsley and was initially owned by Microsoft as part of MSN. In 2004 the Washington Post Company purchased Salon.com. Salon.com, *Slate* and similar web pioneers experimented with subscriptions but found that readers wouldn't pay – and were forced to slash costs and output to survive. Recently, experimentations with subscription have resurfaced. A common solution involves making some content available for free (but with registration) with additional content and bonuses available to subscribers.

These new players were squarely focused on the news and journalism area. Other new online organizations during this period were focused on other niches, but had important implications for legacy media organizations. Craigslist, founded in 1996, is a classified advertising website with sections devoted to jobs, housing, personal advertisements, and so on. This demonstrated and exploited the effectiveness of the Internet as a forum to match buyers and sellers. Craigslist spread to cover hundreds of categories of products and services in cities around the world, a development mirroring a wider shift whereby an ever-greater percentage of classified advertising moved from newspapers to online sites.

This first era thus created the basic ecosystem of online news, influenced expectations of news providers and audiences about how news would be provided, and brought new communication intermediaries into play that altered the nature of online markets and the business opportunities for news providers.

21.3   2000–2014: ERA OF PARTICIPATION AND MULTIMEDIA (WEB 2.0)

By 2002 the World Association of Newspapers had recognized that 'the Internet is proving to be neither the threat nor the opportunity that we all once expected' (WAN-IFRA, 2002). The bursting of the dot-com bubble in 2000 removed any hope of recovering investments in online businesses via IPOs or spinoffs. As Internet sites became more sophisticated, publishers realized that print content could not simply be transferred online. It needed to be presented differently and the content itself needed to be adapted for online consumption styles – more depth was often required, and immediacy was critical. The realization also dawned that digital editions needed primacy over print ones. Newsrooms were not simply going to need a stronger digital component, but ultimately would have to become digital news operations with a print component. Breaking news needed to appear online first.

And just as content did not transfer happily online, neither did their traditional advertising pricing models. In print newspapers, the amount of space for advertising is limited. This scarcity increases its economic value and price. In the digital world the amount of advertising space is nearly unlimited and supply outstrips demand. As a result, online advertising prices are lower than in print and falling constantly – 'print dollars have been replaced by digital dimes', as the adage goes.

So although the volume of online advertising increased during this period, and indeed grew faster than all other forms of advertising, overall revenue levels remained low. Moreover, not only were prices lower online, but there were more competitors. Even by 2014, print media still account for about two-thirds of all advertising expenditures world-wide.[3] Despite the migration of classified advertising to the Internet – and an overall decline in advertising expenditures – print newspapers are still producing profits.

One of the most disruptive elements of the Internet has been the way it has enabled the unbundling of the various component parts of traditional newspapers. Search engines and aggregators allow Internet users to find a range of articles on any subject without having to visit publishers' online sites. A large percentage of classified advertising has moved online. And contextual search advertising has reduced the appeal of publishers' display markets.

Even so, publishers were reluctant to switch to digital-only distribution, even though this would allow news to be produced and distributed far more cheaply – three-quarters of their costs derive from printing, distribution, property and facilities management (Picard and Brody, 1997). This dilemma has led an increasing number of publishers to look again at pay models. Strategies vary, according to local market conditions, the size and role of the news provider, and the competing services. A more subtle factor affecting the strategy is the fundamental trade-off publishers must make between maximizing the income paid by subscribers versus maximizing the greater advertising revenue that will result from a larger number of unique visitors: generally the higher the subscription fee, the lower the overall visitor number and by extension the lower the advertising revenue.

Publishers must also make a basic choice between a pay-per-use or subscription-based models. Pay-per-use provides access to a single article or a single issue, or one-day access to all content. Payment can be by currency transfers, credit cards, or e-money held in an account with the media company. These systems involve high numbers of micropayments and carry high transaction costs for managing transactions, accounting and auditing, and conveying payments. To be viable they must be highly efficient and used by a large number of people. News providers are starting to establish joint systems, as with the Project Piano payment system that provides paid access to parts of publishers' sites in Slovakia, Slovenia and Poland, or the industry-wide user management and payment system introduced in 2013 by 11 Belgian newspapers.

Subscription models allow access over a fixed period of time (say one, three or 12 months). Some provide access to all content, and some to basic content with additional charges for premium content. Payments for subscriptions can typically be made both online and offline.

All these models involve a 'paywall' that prevents users from accessing the content without payment. Paywall strategies differ. They can be 'hard' and block access to all or most content without payment, or 'soft' or 'metered', where there is limited free access, after which users must pay. The *Financial Times*, for example, instituted such a model in 2007 when it set up a system allowing users to view five articles per month for free, required registration to obtain 6–30 free articles per month, and required users to pay for a subscription after viewing more than 30 articles. *The New York Times* also introduced a metered model in 2011 and has a complex range of payment options including print + digital access, all digital access from any device, or access restricted to various combinations of computers, smartphones and tablets.

Another option pursued by some websites is the 'freemium' approach in which some basic content is free (usually breaking news, blogs and some other current content) but payment is required to access more in-depth or premium content. A further revenue source for newspapers and news magazine is charging for app-based delivery of news to tablets and smartphones, while online content consumed on a computer remains free. Newspapers are typically sold by subscription or short-term trial subscriptions, but many weekly news magazines, such as the Canadian news and public affairs magazine *Macleans*, offer single-issue app-based purchases as well as subscriptions.

By 2013, payment for digital content and online advertising was providing 15–25 percent of the total income for many large news providers, but the progress has been modest.[4] In order to make online news provision viable they, along with smaller news organizations and many digital-only start-ups, are exploring a 'long tail' of new revenue sources. These include e-commerce, the digital agency concept (where they act as online marketers and provide training and consulting), 'people media' (public events such as conferences and festivals), training courses, and grants and subsidies.

Broadcasters' news portals or sites became more sophisticated, complex and interactive during the second web era. There was increased use of user-generated still picture and video content, blogs, personalization features, and RSS feeds,[5] and social media such as Facebook, YouTube and Twitter were added to their existing services.

In addition, the distribution of broadcast programming over broadband networks became standard, via streaming, on-demand services or via smartphone and tablet apps. This rapidly became an accepted dimension of television distribution and consumption, but unlike the stand-alone news websites that were a new activity for broadcasters, the online (re)distribution of news broadcasts involved minimal changes to the content. Rather, it was a new means of distributing traditional types of content, including news content.

Second- and third-screen consumption also became standard during this period. Here, audiences can be consuming broadcast news on one screen, looking at an Internet site in parallel on another, and using social media to communicate about that content on a third. In this context social media are functioning as a means of promoting content, drawing audiences back to the broadcast content, and increasing audience engagement.

During the second Internet era, the greatest disruption for legacy news providers came from new Internet-based news organizations (the pure plays) and aggregators. They were successful in attracting significant audiences (although this differs around the world, as shown in Figure 21.1), and created new market demand by engaging new audiences. They also contributed to the commoditization of breaking news, a key element of newspapers' product packages.

The arrival of powerful self-publishing software led to the phenomenon known as the 'blogosphere', and a dimension of this comprised blogs dealing with news and politics. The concepts of the blog, the Web 2.0 movement, and social media were all driven in part by the idea that every citizen can create news, and brought a new wave of disruption to the field.

Blogs written by individuals widened the range of news perspectives available but had limited appeal to advertisers. It has been estimated that 60 percent of bloggers do so for fun, that only 18 percent aim to make a full- or part-time living from it, and that the average earnings for bloggers who run ads is around $5000 per year with the top 10 percent

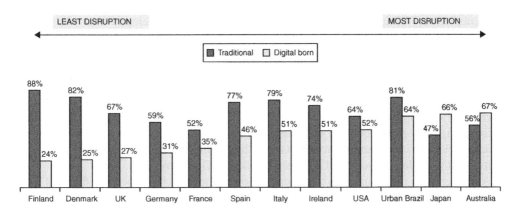

LEAST DISRUPTION   MOST DISRUPTION

▣ Traditional ☐ Digital born

| | | | | | | | | | | | |
Finland Denmark UK Germany France Spain Italy Ireland USA Urban Brazil Japan Australia

Source: Reuters Institute (2015).

Figure 21.1   Strength of traditional news brands by country

of bloggers earning an average of $19 000.[6] The rise of social media sites like Twitter and Facebook has further undermined the prospects of blogging, and many 'A-list' bloggers have quit, cut down their commitments, or returned to mainstream media.

Cheap blogging technology has, however, proved to be the inspiration for a small number of successful new online news businesses. Entrepreneur Nick Denton established Gawker Media in 2002 in New York City, which after a troubled start emerged with eight blogs focusing on specific content niches (e.g., Gizmodo, which deals with technology). These new players did not have the financial cushion of still-profitable (just) print businesses to subsidize growth until they had revenue streams in place. Those that have succeeded combined low-cost models with previously unserved niche audiences (the so-called boutique aggregators), or are able to access large audiences with an innovative news offer. Two such examples are Mashable and TNZ. Mashable.com, which was founded in 2005 by 19-year-old Pete Cashmore in his bedroom in Scotland, developed into a social media and technology blog that was at one stage valued at $200 million. TNZ is a celebrity news website founded in 2005 as a collaboration between AOL and a division of Warner Bros. that is focused on breaking celebrity stories such as the death of Michael Jackson.

Crowdsourced journalism has been another important aspect of this second phase. The Korean website OhMyNews.com, launched in 2002, attracted international attention as the first news site in the world to be written by its (paid) contributors. It had a major impact on the South Korean media scene by opening up a new type of news stories, but struggled with the costs of managing and editing the contributions. Its international version closed in 2010 and today relies on some big advertisers and public appeals for cash for its domestic edition.

Another significant new content player was Wikipedia, founded in 2001, a free encyclopedia written almost entirely by volunteers. The basic idea is that collaborators initiate entries on subjects they find interesting, and other collaborators add to these entries – in the process cleaning up errors or misleading elements. While it is still primarily a reference work, Wikipedia has somewhat surprisingly also developed into important reference point for information about news.

During this second Internet era some new players have matured into significant and powerful forces in the news establishment. The Huffington Post, a US website, content aggregator and blog founded by Arianna Huffington in 2005, has become the most heavily trafficked political news site in the United States. It aggregates content from various news sources, including blogs, has its own columnists, and has won a Pulitzer Prize. Bought by AOL for $315 million in 2011, it has since developed into more of a general news site, hired more journalists, and has branched out into video. It now has editions in Canada, France, the UK, Italy, Spain and Germany.

A further wave of change in online news followed the launch of social media sites like Facebook (2004) and Twitter (2006). These networks do not create content themselves, but act as fora where links to both user-generated content and professional journalism can be quickly and efficiently shared. In this sense they have become an important source of news as well as a powerful new distribution mechanism, helping drive traffic to traditional news sites. By 2012 it was estimated that one in five people (20 percent) in the UK find news stories each week via news streams on social networks and social news aggregators (Reuters Institute, 2012).

From a business perspective, however, social networks have made it even harder for news sites to make money, by providing extra competition for the limited amount of online advertising expenditure. And like Google, they bring additional disruption because they have created new types of advertising by drawing on the extremely rich data they have collected from, and about, their users. Online news players, particularly legacy players, do not have access to comparable aggregated data, potentially further undermining their competitive position in the delicate advertising ecosystem.

Smartphones, tablets and other mobile media devices are also disrupting online news provision. Many news providers have created apps for mobile devices that function as 'destination news brands' that can be accessed directly from the home screen. Although it is early days, it appears that strong news brands tend to do better in a mobile environment than on a PC where the browser acts as the gateway to the Internet and where portals and ISPs have traditionally acted as homepages for large numbers of users.[7]

New mobile gateways are also emerging for online news. Apple's Newsstand is an app that simulates a real newsstand with virtual shelves offering digital versions of newspapers and magazines. Amazon's version is a folder that allows access to publications users have subscribed to. But while apps represent a welcome new income source, publishers are unhappy about the terms offered by Apple, Google, and Amazon. In 2011 the *Financial Times* removed its iPad and iPhone apps from Apple's App Store after losing a battle to keep the consumer data generated through purchase process, and because it was unhappy with Apple's policy of taking a 30 percent share of revenues.

This second online era is marked by the appearance of start-up news and information providers using emerging software and applications, and by increased use of visual and audiovisual content. It also produced significant changes in publishers' views of how news should be provided online, growing understanding of differences among digital platforms, and a search for new revenue models. Online news provision became more competitive because of the significant inroads made by broadcast news organizations and new 'born digital' news providers.

21.4   ORGANIZATIONAL IMPLICATIONS

In the early days of the Internet, legacy players tended to compartmentalize their new online businesses in standalone units. But as digital technologies spread into all processes of media organizations, the organizational forms that had been developed for the industrial production of mass media products proved increasingly inappropriate. Once content creation, production and distribution systems are digitized, distinctions between old and new media and between different media platforms and products begin to evaporate, and structures need to be optimized for digital data: the route is clear for bi-media, tri-media and cross-media working and converged newsrooms.

Integrated newsrooms have been described as the dominant discourse on the future of news production (Garcia Avilés et al., 2009). These take the form of a single newsroom with a single planning and newsgathering operation that replaces the individual production systems for radio, TV, print and online that had existed before, and with technical specialists and designers integrated right the heart of the newsroom, rather than located in an 'IT support function' (Westlund, 2011).

Integrated newsrooms not only bring online and offline journalism closer together, but are also altering the practice of journalism. Journalists need to be able to produce content for different platforms, and to adapt that content in response to feedback from audiences and the information on users' needs, interests and preferences that are intrinsic to the online environment. Such newsrooms have also led to the emergence of high-profile multimedia journalists who are 24-hour news brands in their own right, both generating income for the parent brand and building their own individual economic value. New players in comparison are not burdened with the legacy systems and assets of legacy media firms, and can therefore focus investments on what is essential to the fast-developing online news industry (Christensen et al., 2012).[8]

Ironically, although online news operations and new workflows create synergies and allow simpler organizational structures, they have increased investment costs. Digital production and distribution systems must be bought, installed and continuously upgraded in order to remain competitive. Software engineers and digital designers need to be employed, and buildings must be bought or renovated.

The immediacy and volume of news available for free on the Internet undermined the value of newspapers, and transformed the strategic assets that once acted as barriers to industry entry, notably non-digital production and distribution infrastructures, into liabilities. As Warren Buffet told attendees at Berkshire Hathaway's 2009 annual meeting: 'Imagine that someone came along saying, "I have a great idea: Let's chop trees down, buy expensive printing presses, and buy a fleet of delivery trucks, all to get pieces of paper to people to read about what happened yesterday".'

Amidst mounting losses publishers are implementing a range of cost-cutting measures, including reducing the extent of their publications, cutting special supplements, introducing pay freezes, reducing their use of freelancers, and cutting jobs. Financial pressures are accelerating the shift towards integrated newsrooms. Synergies can be achieved by combining content, staff and resources. This degree of organizational change, combined with cost cutting, provokes high levels of stress and limits the ability to respond innovatively to the new environment.

21.5   OUTLOOK

Prospects for legacy news organizations   Although the Internet has brought agile new competitors into the news field, traditional news providers look likely to remain dominant in online news provision in most, if not all, markets. In the words of Ken Doctor (2012) 'most of the reporting power, much of the brand power, and the political power still resides in the big companies and their leadership'. However, they will also need to get used to profit levels that are much lower than they were previously, when there were high barriers to entry and in many cases a monopoly of distribution. In the future, publishers will have to learn how to capitalize on and build their existing presence and traffic to secure future opportunities online.

Role of brands   Brand strength and total reach will likely become the key performance metrics, replacing circulation. News providers will focus on building brand awareness and trust and be agnostic concerning the channel by which this is done. They will seek to maximize involvement with users, build a relationship with them, and shape them into a community, as well as capture their data, and use all of this to generate advertising income. This strategy will be backed by 'one brand, many platforms' business models that are multi-product, multi-platform and multi-revenue stream.

Long tail of revenue-generating activities   Legacy news businesses will continue to develop their long tails of activities designed to generate revenues from existing assets and capabilities, in the hope that these will eventually support their online businesses and compensate for the loss of print advertising. In addition to news products, the skills and expertise that go into the creation of news products will also be sold to other business, and to members of the public who would like to acquire them. The number of public events – festivals, conferences, seminars, and so on – will increase further. Attempts to boost revenues by designing e-commerce offers targeted at their audiences will continue as well.

Good prospects for mobile   There are grounds for optimism concerning online news services on mobile devices, which have now become a primary gateway for accessing online news in many countries. While the Internet grew up with a free-content ethos, consumers are accustomed to paying for mobile services, and robust payment systems are in place that will potentially allow seamless micropayment. Further, consumers that own mobile devices, particularly tablets, tend to come from more affluent socioeconomic groups. A survey found that 87 percent of newspaper and magazine publishers in the USA have an iPad app (AAM, 2012).

Pursuit of legal remedies   In some countries publishers will also continue their efforts to improve their financial situation via legal channels. Aggregators' practice of 'scraping' may drive traffic to news sites, but is regarded by publishers in a number of European markets as copyright infringement. Legislation has been proposed in Germany, France and Belgium that would require aggregators to pay for linking to and taking excerpts from publishers' websites. Some publishers have also sought legal redress for such activities that they felt were illegal. For example, in 2005 Agence France-Presse (AFP) sued

Google, claiming it had infringed AFP's copyright by reproducing its pictures and articles.

Online news has also brought public service broadcasters and newspapers into direct competition. In Germany and Switzerland there have been heated debates over whether Internet portals and online products fall into the public service broadcasting (PSB) remit, and whether PSBs should be allowed to advertise online. Germany's legislation, the RStV Interstate Treaty on Broadcast and Telemedia, initiated in April 2011, introduced strict limits on public broadcasters' online activities.

Continued scaling back of print activities   The outlook for print newspapers will not improve. The size of print editions will continue to shrink, staff will continue to be laid off, and editorial energies will become more and more focused on the areas with the greatest appeal to advertisers. Many can now envisage ceasing print operations at some point, but only a few – those with print operations that are currently losing money – are seriously considering making the change now. Nevertheless, many are beginning to understand there is some benefit creating some original content outside their legacy operation or in forms not used by their original news organization.

Investigative journalism under threat   Integrated newsrooms – and the reduction in overall staffing levels – have implications for the future of investigative and other forms of serious long-form journalism. The majority of such reporting has traditionally been done by legacy media, particularly print media and news agencies, and the vast majority of journalists overall remain employed by print media. It would be very hard for social media or a blog to challenge large vested interests in the way *The Guardian* did by exposing phone hacking in the UK or the Associated Press did in revealing the extent of the New York City Police Department's spying on Muslim communities.

21.6   CONCLUSION

The Internet has brought growth and dynamism to the news industry. There are new products and new markets. The rate of consumption of news and the size of the news market are increasing. Yet the financial outlook for online news providers, old or new, is bleak. Even for those providers that are not hobbled by the hurdles of legacy assets and heavy overheads online news is a highly unstable arena where revenues are uncertain and investments in journalism are increasingly under pressure.

The online environment has created unique opportunities for both established and new enterprises to gather and distribute news, as well as an unprecedented flow of news to all types of audiences on all types of platforms. But despite these positive developments, a business model that will provide solid revenues necessary for sustaining these businesses in the online world has thus far proved elusive. Both legacy and born-digital news organizations are struggling to find value configurations that will bring not only survival but also perhaps even financial success, and news journalism is under threat as a result.

Online operations allow cost savings, and create economies of scale and scope as well as the potential for synergies and integration. Taken together, these change the traditional economics of news production and distribution and allow costs to be significantly reduced. These changes lower barriers to entry for news providers from afar and completely new competitors. As online news operations shift the economic base of news provision from variable to fixed costs, the economic focus shifts also from achieving economies of scale with large audiences toward niche news provision. Issues of quality, service, and brand strength come to the fore as a result.

The fundamental challenge that has been created by the advent of online news is that the supply of news is dramatically increased because economic, geographic, and regulatory limits have been removed or reduced. This has heightened competition, which, combined with the pick and choose nature of online consumption and challenges in excluding those not prepared to pay, makes it difficult to create an effective consumer market for news in the online environment today. Emerging technologies and software are beginning to provide possible solutions for some of these issues, but the complications created by the need for increased control of the platforms and services necessary for effective online operation continue to present fresh challenges to news providers.

NOTES

1. For an overview see the 2010 OECD report *The Evolution of News and the Internet*, accessed 23 August 2015 at http://www.oecd.org/sti/ieconomy/45559596.pdf.
2. Video exceeded half of global consumer Internet traffic by year-end 2011. The sum of all forms of video (TV, video on demand [VoD], Internet, and P2P) will be approximately 86 percent of global consumer traffic by 2016 (Cisco.com, 2014).
3. See the World Advertising Research Center's Ad Spend Database, accessed 23 August 2015 at http://www.warc.com/Topics/ForecastsandData.topic.
4. Part of the reason for the growth of the digital share is the continuing decline in print advertising, sale of access through apps, and increasing use of paywalls on websites (Hagey, 2012; Lee, 2012; Reynolds, 2012).
5. Google closed Google Reader in July 2013, citing declining usage (Ha, 2013).
6. The *State of the Blogosphere* report (Technorati.com, 2010).
7. A number of news brands (e.g., *The Guardian*, BBC, and *The New York Times*) had a higher market share on smartphones and tablets than on computers.
8. Clayton Christensen's theories of incumbent failure in the face of what he terms 'disruptive innovation' (see Christensen and Bower, 1996; Christensen, 1997; Christensen and Overdorf, 2000) have found great resonance since their first publication. His thesis is that leading companies' search for profitability and growth, reinforced by adherence to best practice, causes them to miss out on new markets that result from disruptive technologies. The core problem is a maladaptive resource allocation process that concentrates resource commitments on markets and products that match existing priorities and ignore initially 'downmarket' products and markets based on emerging technologies. For further discussion see Küng (2005).

REFERENCES

Alliance for Audited Media (AAM) (2012), *How Media Companies Are Innovating and Investing in Cross-Platform Opportunities: Results from AAM's 2012 Digital Publishing Survey*, Arlington Heights, IL, New York and Toronto, ON: Alliance for Audited Media, accessed 17 July 2014 at http://www.auditedmedia.com/media/182933/aam2012survey.pdf.
Blodget, H. (2012), 'It's time people realized that the Drudge Report is a major media property worth hundreds of millions of dollars', *Business Insider*, 10 October, accessed 17 July 2014 at http://www.businessinsider.com/drudge-report-is-worth-2012-10.
Boczkowski, P. (2004), *Digitizing the News: Innovation in Online Newspapers*, Cambridge, MA: MIT Press.
Bruno, N. and R.K. Neilsen (2012), *Survival is Success: Journalistic Online Startups in Western Europe*, Oxford, UK: Reuters Institute for the Study of Journalism, University of Oxford.

Chan-Olmsted, C. and L.S. Ha (2003), 'Internet business models for broadcasters: How television stations perceive and integrate the Internet', *Journal of Broadcasting & Electronic Media*, **47** (4), 597–616.

Christensen, C.M. (1997), *The Innovator's Dilemma: When New Technologies Cause Great Firms to Fail*, Boston, MA: Harvard Business School Press.

Christensen, C.M. and J. Bower (1996), 'Customer power, strategic investment, and the failure of leading firms', *Strategic Management Journal*, **17** (3), 197–218.

Christensen, C.M. and M. Overdorf (2000), 'Meeting the challenge of disruptive innovation', *Harvard Business Review*, **78** (2), 66–76.

Christensen, C.M., D. Skok and J. Allworth (2012), 'Breaking news: Mastering the art of disruptive innovation in journalism', *Nieman Reports*, **66** (3), 6, accessed 17 July 2014 at http://www.nieman.harvard.edu/assets/ebook/niemanreports/fall2012/NiemanReports-Fall2012CoverStory.pdf.

Cisco.com (2014), 'Cisco visual networking index: Forecast and methodology, 2013–2018', *2014–2019 White Papers*, accessed 17 July 2014 at http://www.cisco.com/c/en/us/solutions/collateral/service-provider/ip-ngn-ip-next-generation-network/white_paper_c11-481360.html.

Doctor, K. (2012), 'The newsonomics of 2013 wizardry: Tribune, Buffet, Murdoch, Paton, Bloomberg, and more', *NiemanLab*, 20 December, accessed 17 July 2014 at http://www.niemanlab.org/2012/12/the-newsonomics-of-2013-wizardry-tribune-buffett-murdoch-paton-bloomberg-and-more/.

Editor & Publisher (1999), *Editor & Publisher International Yearbook*, New York: Editor & Publisher Co.

Garcia Avilés, J.A., K. Meier, A. Kaltenbrunner, M. Carvajal and D. Krauss (2009), 'Newsroom integration in Austria, Spain and Germany – Models of media convergence', *Journalism Practice*, **3** (3), 285–303.

Ha, A. (2013), 'Google closes the book on Google Reader on July 1, seven other products also get the chop', *TC*, 13 March, accessed 17 July 2014 at http://techcrunch.com/2013/03/13/rip-google-reader/.

Hagey, K. (2012), 'Paywalls giving newspapers chance at a comeback', *The Wall Street Journal*, 14 October, accessed 17 July 2014 at http://online.wsj.com/article/SB10000872396390444657804578052984268608600.html.

Küng, L. (2005), 'When innovation fails to disrupt: A multi-lens investigation of successful incumbent response to technological discontinuity: The launch of BBC news online', Jönköping: Jönköping International Business School.

Lee, E. (2012), 'The New York Times paywall is working better than anyone had guessed', *Bloomberg Business*, accessed 17 July 2014 at http://go.bloomberg.com/tech-blog/2012-12-20-the-new-york-times-paywall-is-working-better-than-anyone-had-guessed/.

Lyons, D. (2009), 'Time to hang up the pajamas: I learned the hard way – while blogs can do many wonderful things, making huge amounts of money isn't one of them', *Newsweek*, **153** (7), 19.

Newman, N. (2011), *Mainstream Media and the Distribution of News in the Age of Social Discovery: How Social Media are Changing the Production, Distribution And Discovery of News and Further Disrupting the Business Models of Mainstream Media Companies*, Oxford, UK: Reuters Institute for the Study of Journalism, University of Oxford, accessed 17 July 2014 at https://reutersinstitute.politics.ox.ac.uk/sites/default/files/Mainstream%20media%20and%20the%20distribution%20of%20news%20in%20the%20age%20of%20social%20discovery.pdf.

Picard, R.G. (2003), 'Cash cows or entrecôte: Publishing companies and new technologies', *Trends in Communication*, **11** (2), 127–36.

Picard, R.G. and J.H. Brody (1997), *The Newspaper Publishing Industry*, Boston, MA: Allyn and Bacon.

Reuters Institute (2012), *Reuters Institute Digital News Report 2012*, Oxford, UK: Reuters Institute for the Study of Journalism, University of Oxford, accessed 17 July 2014 at http://media.digitalnewsreport.org/wp-content/uploads/2012/05/Reuters-Institute-Digital-News-Report-2012.pdf.

Reynolds, J. (2012), 'MailOnline revenue surges 74% to £48m', *MediaWeek*, 22 November, accessed 29 July 2014 at http://www.mediaweek.co.uk/News/MostRead/1161068/MailOnline-revenue-surges-74-28m/.

Shirky, C. (2009), 'Newspapers and thinking the unthinkable', *Clay Shirky* [blog], accessed 19 July 2014 at http://www.shirky.com/weblog/2009/03/newspapers-and-thinking-the-unthinkable/.

Technorati.com (2010), *State of the Blogosphere 2010*, *Technorati.com*, 3 November, accessed 19 July 2014 at http://technorati.com/state-of-the-blogosphere/.

Van der Wurff, R. (2008), 'The impact of the internet on media content', in L. Küng, R. Picard and R. Towse (eds), *The Internet and the Mass Media*, London and Los Angeles: Sage.

WAN-IFRA (2002), *Internet Strategies for Newspapers Revisited*, Shaping the Future of the Newspaper Strategy Report, World Association of Newspapers and News Publishers.

Westlund, O. (2011), 'Cross-media news work: Sensemaking of the mobile media (r)evolution', PhD dissertation, Department of Journalism, Media and Communication, University of Gothenburg.

22. The economics of online video entertainment
Ryland Sherman and David Waterman

22.1 INTRODUCTION

Although online video entertainment dates back to the mid-1990s, its revenue models, market structure, and programming content continue to evolve. Driving these changes have been dramatic technological advances, accompanied by rapid broadband Internet adoption, from about 3 percent of households in 2000, to about two-thirds of households only a decade later (Pew Research Center, 2011), and by a growing migration of consumers from offline to online media delivery systems.

In this chapter we address some broad questions about this industry to provide a framework for thinking about its economic future. Has Internet distribution of video entertainment created real economic value for consumers, relative to established 'offline' media? How are its market structure and revenue models evolving? How does Internet entertainment programming differ from offline media? While our answers are necessarily incomplete, patterns of market organization, income sources, programming content, and other characteristics of this industry have now emerged.

For our purposes, we consider online video entertainment to be the streaming or downloading of videos to a personal computer or other Internet-connected media device. Our main focus is on professionally produced content, but user-generated video is a remarkable part of the online video entertainment landscape, and is also part of this study. Video games and music videos are an important part of online commercial entertainment as well, but their online business patterns are distinct from those of online video. We thus focus on television, movies, and similar forms of video entertainment, or what has been widely regarded as the 'over-the-top' (OTT) video industry. Finally, our geographic focus is on the United States, although we recognize that Internet technology fells international boundaries, and that parallel changes to those in the USA are occurring in many other countries (Fontaine et al., 2010; Simon, 2012).

A number of scholarly works on the economics of online media provide a foundation for this chapter. Among earlier works, Owen (1999) addressed the economic and technological potential of the Internet for television delivery. Shapiro and Varian (1999) discussed how firms could utilize economic and technological advantages of digital technologies, including the Internet. Several authors contributing to a volume edited by Kahin and Varian (2000) discussed economic and legal aspects of Internet media delivery. A Harvard Business Case (Eisenmann and Brown, 2000) identified basic economic characteristics of online content providers and how they could potentially create value for consumers. A National Research Council (2000) report, *The Digital Dilemma*, analyzed the economics and technology of the Internet from the standpoint of copyright and other government policy questions. Among more recent works, several edited books, notably Noam et al. (2004),[1] Gerbarg (2009), Noam (2008) and Gannes (2009) have addressed the emerging technologies, economics, and content of Internet television and video, including the economics of peer-to-peer (P2P) file sharing. Several recent Harvard Business Cases (e.g., Yao et al., 2008; Elberse and Gupta, 2010a, 2010b; Brochet et al., 2012), as well as Screen Digest and publications by SNL Kagan Media Research and the Federal Communications Commission provide extensive data and insightful discussion of economic and technological features of Internet television in a business or regulatory context.

We begin in section 22.2 with a review of the US-oriented history and current state of the online video industry. In section 22.3 we turn to the subject of value creation by comparing the economics and technology of online and offline media delivery systems. Then in sections 22.4 and 22.5 we explore empirical development of online video, first in relation to content aggregation and market structure, then revenue models and programming. In sections 22.6 and 22.7 we briefly discuss the industry's economic future and some directions for research.

22.2 INDUSTRY DEVELOPMENT

The history of online video entertainment reflects vibrant industry responses to continuously unfolding opportunities that developing technologies, especially in transmission speeds, have made possible.[2]

In the mid- to late 1990s, before the broadband era, a flurry of now mostly defunct Internet content providers (e.g., Icebox.com, Entertaindom.com, Ifilms.com, Atomfilms. com) began experimenting with online video entertainment. Many were Internet-original productions, but the majority were brief in length, such as TV-mimicking 'webisodes', and short films, and they tended toward bandwidth-lean animation to permit streaming or to shorten tedious download times. Many were professionally produced, with the hope of future profit, but others were user-posted amateur productions. At the other end of the spectrum were some theatrical features; most were old and time-worn, but in one 2000 experiment, Sightsound.com offered recent films from a major Hollywood producer, Miramax. Other providers, including NBCi.com, offered promotional clips of current TV series. These early online activities were characterized by experimentation. Sony's Screenblast.com, for example, allowed viewers to determine future plot direction interactively or to piece together their own stories from ready-made clips of popular TV series.

The dot-com bust in 2000–2001 swept away most of the early experimenters. The subsequent recovery in the early 2000s and the promising dawn of mainstream household broadband adoption marked a new phase in online video entertainment. In 2002, a consortium of five major Hollywood studios started Movielink.com,[3] which offered a selection of recent movies for download or rental. With less fanfare, iTunes began offering recent TV series episodes in 2005 and, soon after, movies for direct sale. The development of secure digital rights management (DRM) encryption systems for Internet Protocol (IP)-delivered commercial video enabled the debuts of Movielink, iTunes's video library, and other later entrants. Outside of the industry's control, however, was another landmark event: the introduction of BitTorrent technology in 2003. Its robustness and decentralized coordination of distribution greatly facilitated illegal P2P file sharing of movies pirated from DVDs or theater prints.

A phenomenal and enduring response to YouTube's launch in 2005 marked another major technological breakthrough: the seamless uploading of user-generated video. Amid a growing ocean of amateur content on YouTube, users were soon posting full episodes of recent major network series illegally. After an initial period of tolerance, the networks and program suppliers issued 'takedown' orders under the 1998 Digital Millennium Copyright Act (DMCA) (see 17 USC. § 512(c)), and were largely successful. With accelerating broadband diffusion and network speed advances enabling seamless video streaming, professionally produced online video distribution began to take off. Netflix launched its 'instant streaming' subscription video service in 2007, relying mostly on older movies and TV programs. In 2008, NBC and Fox (later joined by ABC) launched Hulu.com, and in 2009, CBS started TV.com (later CBS Interactive), primarily as outlets for time-delayed, ad-supported exhibition of regular prime time series programs.

Since 2009, entry into online video entertainment has proliferated, with subscription or video on demand (VOD) services developed by Amazon, Sony, and others, or purchased and relaunched, like Wal-Mart's 2010 acquisition of VUDU.com. Several cable operators and other multi-channel video program distributors (MVPDs) also launched 'TV Everywhere,' an umbrella concept for services that give offline subscribers free access to a menu of online programming they already receive with their monthly subscription. YouTube made a move toward the top-down professional production model with the financing of 100 'channels' of niche programming in late 2011 (Bond and Szalai, 2011). Though begun experimentally at an early date, multi-cast streaming of live television programming over the Internet has also become increasingly viable as network capacity has expanded, as evidenced by the ESPN3's streaming of specialized sports events after 2007, and the first streaming of the Super Bowl by NBC in 2012.

By the 2010s, the online video industry had transitioned from experimentation to a more stable group of players. The state of the industry as of 2014 is summarized in Table 22.1. The list of providers is not intended to be comprehensive. Rather, it is a snapshot of a specific point in 'Internet time' intended to illustrate the variety of revenue and content models offered by leading industry players.[4]

Notable from the 'launch date' column of Table 22.1 is how new the online video entertainment industry is at the time of writing; no significant players in the current market were present before 2005. Sobering comparisons between the usage and the economic resources of online video and offline television also reflect its novelty. According to Nielsen (2012), the average individual in 2011 watched almost 34 hours of television per week, compared to 30 minutes of 'watching video on the Internet' and eight minutes 'watching video on a mobile phone', a ratio of offline to online viewing of about 53 to 1.[5] One industry analyst estimated that about 5 percent of all prime time TV program viewing in the USA in 2010 was online (Convergence Consulting Group, 2012), and another that 8 percent of all US TV viewing was online in that year (Screen Digest, 2011a, p. 210), but these percentages have surely risen since these estimates, and will continue rising in the future.

Online video entertainment revenues are also low but growing. Waterman et al. (2012, p. 15) estimated that online television program revenues from advertising, subscriptions, and VOD accounted for less than 2 percent of television industry revenues in 2010. Though still exceeded by theaters, DVD/Blu-ray, and license fees from offline television, revenue from online distribution of movies has grown steadily since the mid-2000s,

Table 22.1　Some major players in the US online video entertainment industry, 2014

Service	Launch Date	Primary Content	Primary Revenue Model(s)
Hulu	2008	NBC, ABC, Fox TV shows; limited movies, cable network shows, original content	Advertising/subscription
CBS	2008	CBS TV shows	Advertising
iTunes	2005	Broadcast/cable programs; movies	Pay to download/rent
Viacom Digital	2007	Viacom-owned cable network programs	Advertising
Netflix	2007	Broadcast/cable programs; movies; limited original content	Subscription
Crackle	2007–08	Sony-owned movie and TV content	Advertising
Amazon	2006	Broadcast/cable programs; movies	Subscription/pay to download/rent
VUDU	2007	Broadcast/cable programs; movies	Pay to download/rent
Comcast Xfinity	2010	Broadcast/cable programs; movies	Free to offline subscribers[a]
Verizon FiOS	2009–10	Broadcast/cable programs	Free to offline subscribers[a]
Dish Network	2012	Broadcast/cable programs	Free to offline subscribers[a]
HBO Go	2010	HBO series and licensed movies	Free to HBO subscribers of most MVPDs
YouTube	2005	User-generated content; limited 'channels' of professionally produced original content, movies	Advertising, experimenting with pay to rent and subscription

Note:　a. By package level that the subscriber buys for offline service from the MVPD.

reportedly accounting for over 7 percent of studio domestic market revenues in 2011 (SNL Kagan Research, 2012a, p. 2).

Table 22.1 also highlights the development of five basic online video business models: à la carte rentals and purchases, or VOD; subscription; ad-supported professional content; ad-supported user-generated content; and MVPD subscription-dependent, bundled content.

In the first four of these segments, a leading or dominant firm has emerged. With 63 percent of the total online movie downloads in the first half of 2011 (Screen Digest, 2011b, p. 294), iTunes is the leader in the VOD category. In the monthly subscription category, Netflix dominates. The bandwidth demands of its 25 million subscribers as of July of 2012 were 18 times greater than those of Amazon, its main apparent competitor (Sandvine, 2012, pp. 20–21). In the ad-supported professional content category, Hulu.com is the leading firm, earning the fourth highest comScore ranking for 'total ad minutes viewed' during December 2012 (comScore, 2013).[6] In the ad-supported user-generated segment, YouTube has dominated since its launch, accounting for 33.7 percent of all video 'minutes per viewer' recorded by comScore in December 2012, with its competitors (e.g., Vimeo and the French website Dailymotion) struggling to achieve even consumer awareness.

In the MVPD subscription-dependent offline/online bundling category, competition is at the local market level, and except for direct broadcast satellite (DBS)-based services, the mix of competitors varies by market. No information about the performance of these nascent services was available, but it is notable that the websites of many major cable networks, such as HBO GO, also require users to authenticate an offline subscription to a participating MVPD. An emerging new category, however, is subscription services based on individual cable or broadcast networks, or aggregations of such networks, independently of an MVPD subscription. HBO, for example, made its streaming package of movies and exclusive series programming available as a standalone service in April, 2015, labelling it HBO Now. Around the same time, Sling TV began offering an aggregation of over 20 cable channels, including ESPN, without any MVPD authentication requirement.

In the following sections, we explore the economic basis for the industry as it has developed thus far. Unsurprisingly, there has been relatively little economic research about the online video entertainment industry itself. We rely primarily on descriptive information we have assembled for this chapter.

22.3   COMPARISONS TO OFFLINE MEDIA

A first step to understanding the economic prospects of the online video entertainment industry is to ask how online video either creates or reduces value for consumers in terms of costs or product attributes, including interface characteristics and the quality and variety of the programming itself, relative to offline media. Clear-cut comparisons are often difficult, in part because established media delivery systems – notably cable TV and other MVPDs[7] – are themselves undergoing rapid technological development. We can, however, identify several basic ways in which online video technology may improve upon, or fall short of, offline media:

- *Reduced capacity constraints:* The basic architectural advantage of the Internet is the virtual elimination of product carriage constraints, thus enabling the famous 'long tail' of product variety (see Anderson, 2006). In the video media context, DVD retailers, MVPDs, and other offline media systems face significant marginal costs in adding another DVD or cable channel to their product lines. Online content providers also face marginal costs of capacity to support servers on which videos are stored, but for most suppliers, these are surely very minor.

  The most remarkable illustration of the long tail in Internet video is the billions of user-created videos hosted by YouTube, few of which could conceivably generate sufficient demand to be supported by offline media. The long tail is less obvious for online video distributors offering professionally produced content, although Netflix, iTunes, and others offer large selections of lower-demand offerings such as obscure foreign films, for example. YouTube's limited foray into professionally produced content is an apparent milestone in top-down creation of long tail programs that are ostensibly narrow in appeal (e.g., Tony Hawk's professional skateboarder channel, Machinima; The Onion; *InStyle* magazine) and also very inexpensively produced.[8]

- *Cost-effective video delivery:* It is difficult to make cost comparisons among media because they involve fixed capital infrastructures and home premises equipment costs, and thus depend on usage rates. In the case of online video transmission, the Internet also serves many other uses. Several early authors (e.g., Owen, 1999) argued that as a switched network, the Internet is relatively inefficient for live multi-casting of high-quality video. The slow development of live television transmission via the Internet seems to bear out that assessment. The Internet is well designed for asynchronous video transmission, however, and it is heavily utilized for that purpose. In 2011 video and music transfer accounted for 60 percent of peak period downstream Internet traffic (Bazilian, 2011). Netflix alone accounted for 33 percent of peak period North American downstream bandwidth use (Sandvine, 2012, p. 7). Judging from the profusion of video traffic, low prices for video transport, and low consumer prices for broadband access, it is apparent that on-demand video transmission is relatively cost-efficient.[9]

  To the consumer's benefit, cost-efficient delivery implies low consumer prices for video programming as well as broadband access, and thus competitiveness with offline media. As the Internet's bandwidth capacity has risen, delivery costs have also fallen rapidly.

- *Interactivity and computer functionality:* For video distribution, perhaps the most remarkable advantage of Internet architecture over offline media is its sophisticated computer-to-computer communications. Consumers have direct control over program selection and time of viewing. MVPDs have long used limited two-way interactivity for VOD systems, which have become progressively more efficient. DVRs have also enabled time-shifting control, but computer-to-computer Internet communication is much more flexible. For example, content providers, rather than the MVPDs alone, can create their own user interfaces and innovative advertising systems.

  Interactivity and search are also essential to asynchronous management of the 'long tail' of content proliferation on YouTube and other online video services listed in Table 22.1. Search engines and video sites' search functions trump offline media in several ways. They enable viewers to search on a variety of dimensions, and tie massive amounts of meta-data to their content, including previous consumers' ratings and correlations of viewer habits. Through the use of user IDs or cookies, they also record consumers' previous choices and can then build suggestion profiles customized to each user.[10]

  Online interactivity also enables cheap user participation in content creation and distribution. The closest offline substitutes for YouTube and other video sharing sites are clumsy and little-used cable TV local access channels.

- *Portability:* Laptops computers have been available since the launch of the first online video providers and have become increasingly light and efficient. Developments in the late 2000s of portable media players, smartphones, and tablets have increased the convenience of access to online video entertainment. Together with interactivity, portability has brought to practical fruition the 'anytime, anywhere' mantra of online video entertainment. Simultaneously, the development of apps and browser-based video platforms used by portable devices for video reception has accelerated.

- *More efficient advertising:* The ability of Internet content providers to target ads to individuals based on their past browsing, viewing, or purchasing behavior derives from interactivity and has generated a large economic literature that is beyond the scope of this chapter (for recent surveys, see Evans, 2009 and Anderson, 2012).

  Advertiser-supported video providers such as Hulu and YouTube take advantage of targeted advertising, including strategic placement of in-program video commercials. DRM controls also make in-program commercials harder to evade. Reportedly, however, user tolerance of video commercials has been lower on the Internet, and other forms of Internet advertising, such as display ads, have proven less effective than offline display ads. The difficulties experienced by YouTube in monetizing user-generated content with ads have been widely reported and are likely responsible for its segue into offering professionally produced content. Internet advertising is evolving rapidly, but it remains uncertain whether video entertainment providers have to date experienced a net benefit from Internet video ad targeting.

- *More efficient pricing and bundling:* Interactivity and secure payment systems have made direct pricing of online entertainment products very efficient to manage. A great variety of alternative bundles are offered, and cookies potentially enable sellers to practice 'dynamic' pricing and product matching to individuals based on browsing and previous purchasing behavior. These features are common to the sale of other products marketed on the Internet, but there are particular advantages for the efficient sale of online video products.

  First, efficient Internet pricing and bundling help to enable efficient VOD systems with virtually unlimited product variety. Second, the essentially zero marginal capacity costs of carrying information products have particular implications for efficient bundling and price discrimination on the Internet. Bakos and Brynjolfsson (1999, 2000) showed that due to the essentially zero marginal costs of carrying information products, large bundles of information products (such as those now offered by Netflix, Hulu Plus, and other subscription services) facilitate efficient price discrimination via large-scale value averaging. (See Choi, 2012, for a survey of the economic literature on information product bundling.)

  Meanwhile, cable television and other MVPDs have developed efficient systems for direct pricing of the bundles of programming channels they offer, and they maintain increasingly large VOD systems. However, Internet video providers appear to have an advantage over MVPDs in their ability to bundle large quantities of video products, instantaneously change prices, and price their products dynamically.

- *More efficient copying and sharing:* The basic technology by which a computer file can be downloaded and shared with other users electronically, such as by email or via P2P file sharing, is obviously far cheaper than the alternative of buying a DVD and physically distributing it to friends, or of burning a copy to a blank DVD and sharing it. To the benefit of copyright holders, electronic sharing or DVD burning of legally distributed online videos has been greatly limited by sophisticated DRM controls, which are applied to virtually every product of significant commercial value. 17 USC. § 1201-03 of the DMCA 1998 also makes any action used to defeat DRM encryption into a crime.[11]

P2P video file sharing, however, has proven far less easy to control, at least in the case of movies; even a single copy of a DVD that is decrypted and illegally posted can end up spreading the movie worldwide. There is some limited statistical evidence that movie file sharing reduces legitimate sales (Waldfogel, 2012). Engineering studies also document high volumes of illegal movie file transfers worldwide (e.g., Mateus and Peha, 2011), and it seems likely that this activity has contributed to a steady decline in DVD sales and rentals that began in about 2005.

Television, on the other hand, does not appear much affected by file sharing. Incentives to pirate most popular TV shows are probably limited because they are already 'free' on broadcast, basic cable, or online video streaming, or they are priced cheaply by iTunes and other à la carte program sellers.

In summary, Internet technology for video distribution offers some remarkable improvements upon offline media, but also creates threats to copyright owners and potential bandwidth-capacity challenges. The rapid growth of the industry since about 2005 is testimony to its consumer value, but it has a long way to travel to play as significant a role in the market as offline video distribution.

22.4   CONTENT AGGREGATION AND MARKET STRUCTURE

We take content aggregation to mean the supply of large amounts of content via a single website, app, or platform, typically comprising content from multiple creators or copyright owners. Aggregation is important because of its implications for the evolution of market structure in the online video entertainment industry.

The firms listed in Table 22.1 have a range of aggregation levels. At least in economic terms, however, large-scale aggregation from multiple copyright owners appears to be a dominant model in online video entertainment. iTunes, the leading VOD supplier, aggregates TV programs and movies from all the major studios and broadcast networks, as well many more minor players. Netflix offers a large menu of movies, TV programs, and other content from many different owners, including films from a number of foreign countries, to its monthly subscribers. Hulu aggregates mainly TV programs from the three major broadcast networks that co-own the site, and also offers programs from The CW broadcast network and hundreds of other 'content partners.' Viacom's strategy is an intermediate case, offering programming content that has appeared on numerous cable networks through each of their own portals and often Hulu, but most of those programs are owned or licensed by Viacom, a major content provider. Similarly, CBS Interactive offers content from a number of other suppliers in addition to the CBS broadcast network. The major MVPDs' 'TV Everywhere' services typically aggregate programming from a number of different basic and premium cable networks, in addition to other suppliers.

Whether or not content aggregation is prevalent in the online video entertainment industry is simply an empirical matter. The efficiency of both aggregating and disaggregating media content is enhanced by Internet architecture. Enabled by efficient search, and by the lack of physical economies of scale in IP delivery of more than one program at a time, a provider can set up a website to market even a single video program. At the other end of the spectrum, a provider can take advantage of low-capacity costs to assemble a virtually unlimited amount of content under the umbrella of one website, and utilize within-site search.

There are some compelling economic advantages of the aggregation model. Content aggregation in the 1990s by portals that charged flat rates per month (such as America Online) was the basis for the bundling theory of Internet content aggregation developed by Bakos and Brynjolfsson (1999, 2000). The 'one-stop shop' marketing model is probably more relevant to the current online video market – especially to advertiser-supported sites such as Hulu, and to VOD sellers such as Amazon and iTunes that also offer digital music and other non-video products. These sellers apparently attempt to build brand identity among consumers (said to be a major consideration in the development of Hulu, for example) (Yao et al., 2008), or to capitalize on established names, as in the case of iTunes and Amazon. It is notable, however, that leading online video distributors that rely less upon content aggregation, such as CBS.com (which was the only one of the four major broadcast networks that decided to go it alone in 2007), HBO GO, and ESPN, appear to already have well-established offline name identities. Another force driving aggregation is that website operators undoubtedly experience certain economies of scale due to fixed costs, like website design, maintenance, and administrative overhead. Other Internet developments also seem to display the economic advantages of content aggregation. Google TV and Apple TV, for example, partially serve as aggregators of program suppliers who are willing to be sold as part of an online package that can be watched on a TV set. Microsoft's Xbox 360 and One, Sony's PlayStation 3 and 4, and a variety of set-top boxes, tablets, and Internet-connection programs for smart TVs essentially function as content aggregators in a similar way.

Although the marketing and efficiency advantages of online content aggregation seem to favor larger firms, there are no compelling indications that they will lead online video distribution, at least that of professionally produced programming, to become a concentrated industry in the long term. The prototype model of online content aggregation's competitive advantages is YouTube, which has obviously benefited from network effects by offering consumers access to the largest possible collection of user-generated video and offering users who desire to upload content the largest possible collection of potential viewers (see comScore, 2012). Presumably, YouTube's expansion into a top-down commercial programming model will benefit from traffic generated by user-created content. However, top-down online video providers of professionally produced programming do not appear to be subject to network effects, and consumer switching costs are evidently minor. Considered more broadly, reasons for the apparently high concentration within the individual industry segments of VOD, subscription, ad-supported professional production and user-generated content are speculative. In each case, the leaders are the first movers. In the case of Hulu, this consortium of three out of the four major broadcast networks simply holds the rights to the most popular programming. In the subscription category, recent exclusive programming contracts, especially by the market leader, Netflix, are a potential concern that could limit competition. Nevertheless, industry participants (e.g., Amazon and Hulu) have been actively seeking to enter each other's business model segments. In any case, they all compete with each other for consumer attention as well as with other online and offline media.

A related issue affecting market structure is the *disaggregation* of existing MVPD packages that Internet architecture makes possible. Individual content suppliers can potentially bypass MVPDs and offer their programming directly to consumers, much as a variety of Internet information providers have disaggregated print newspapers. At least to date, however, few individual networks other than HBO have attempted to step outside of the 'TV Everywhere' packages requiring MVPD subscription authentication from users. Even in the absence of exclusive contracts, there are strong disincentives for single program suppliers to take this step on their own. The history of both the MVPD and the online video entertainment industries to date suggests that the competitive battles are likely to be fought among large-scale content aggregators, with even new entrants like Sling TV's online video subscription service able to obtain valuable networks like ESPN only in the context of an aggregated bundle.

22.5   PROGRAMMING CONTENT AND THE MULTI-MEDIA WINDOWING MODEL

By any account, online content providers have brought forth a tremendous volume of available programming, both Internet-original and 'aftermarket' or 'windowed' (by which we mean movies and TV programs that originally appeared in theaters, on standard television, or on other video media). Undoubtedly much of online video entertainment of either type fits into the 'long tail' of programs too narrow in appeal or too low in quality to be profitably supported offline. Economically viable online entertainment content is overwhelmingly dominated by windowed programming. Virtually all the content offered by iTunes, Amazon, and other VOD suppliers consists of such programming, as does content available on Hulu.com, CBS.com, Viacom-affiliated sites, and other ad-supported content providers whose parent companies are major offline content suppliers. Netflix and other online video subscriptions services rely heavily on theatrical movies and broadcast network or cable TV programs that have already appeared on those offline media.

There are compelling economic advantages to the multi-media windowing model of video media release, because it allows production investments to be spread over more than one medium (Owen and Wildman, 1992; Wildman, 2008). The windowing model of theatrical movie release is by far the most refined and complex. In outline, major Hollywood features are typically offered on Internet VOD for sale or rental a few months after their theatrical releases, at about the same time as they appear on VOD/PPV (pay-per-view) systems of MVPDs and are released to DVD and Blu-ray. Then several months later, they become available to monthly subscription cable networks and occasionally Netflix or other Internet subscription services. When that window ends, they are typically licensed to ad-supported cable networks, or sometimes broadcast networks or local stations. Many of the movies available on Internet VOD or online subscription services are older or niche films that are not currently in active rotation through the sequence of media, or that have never been licensed to offline TV networks or stations.

The movie windowing model has been widely recognized as a method of intertemporal price discrimination by which high- and low-value consumers are segmented by waiting time and transmission quality of the media (Waterman, 1985, 2005; Owen and Wildman, 1992).

Table 22.2   Total online content provider revenues for digital movies and TV programs, 2011

	Revenue (billion US$)	Price ($)
Subscription	2.08	n.a.
Movie sales	0.33	14.00
Movie rentals	0.46	4.05
TV sales	0.26	1.73
TV rentals	0.01	1.23
Total VOD	1.04	
Total online direct payment	3.12	

Source: SNL Kagan Research (2012b, p. 3).

Table 22.2 shows 2011 pricing and revenue estimates for online VOD and subscription sales published by SNL Kagan Research, a leading consultant in the field. As reflected by their VOD sales and rental prices, movies are relatively high-value products. They have online sale and rental prices in the same range as DVDs and the VOD systems of MVPDs with which they share the window – thus suggesting that they appeal to consumers within comparable willingness-to-pay categories.[12]

Bundled services such as monthly subscription premium cable networks and Netflix are less efficient for extracting money from high-value consumers with intense demand for particular programs, and thus usually have assigned time slots after VOD release. MVPD and online subscription services differ in that the online versions rely heavily on both movies and TV programs. Internet and MVPD consumers of bundled subscription services appear to hold similar valuations for movies, and although the online subscription window remains unsettled, it appears to be moving toward simultaneous release with HBO, Showtime and other premium cable networks as broadband Internet subscribers grow in number. At under US$10 per month, prices for online subscription services such as Netflix and Hulu Plus are generally comparable to or less than those of premium cable TV packages, although the gateway price of broadband Internet access is far lower than the gateway price of a basic MVPD subscription that is usually required before monthly subscription premium service can be added.

A similar windowing model, though it involves fewer different media, has evolved for advertiser-supported, prime-time television programming (see Wildman, 2008 for an early analysis). Most of these programs are made available on advertiser-supported Internet services such as Hulu and CBS.com, but only after a delay of one day or more. For subscribers to Hulu Plus, this delay window is generally shorter, and the duration of availability is also much longer, often providing access to previous seasons of some shows. After a significant delay, many of these programs are then made available to Netflix or other online subscription services, often to hype a subsequent season of series programs and enable new fans to catch up on plot developments.

The series programming of the four major broadcast networks, which generally still attract the largest TV audiences offline, account for the majority of the direct TV program sales and rentals shown in Table 22.2. As suggested by their prices, TV programs are relatively low-value products. Though not shown in Table 22.2, the broadcast networks' income from online distribution apparently comes mostly from advertising on Hulu and CBS Interactive.

It is difficult to tell how the television windowing system may evolve. A plausible general explanation for its current state is that advertisers pay higher net prices per viewer for standard television audiences, and the networks choose an array of delay times that maximize total revenues from these interdependent media. Some settling from the current period of experimentation is also likely. After a sufficient portion of viewers have migrated to online viewing as smart TVs and set-top boxes continue to diffuse, the special demographic targeting opportunities of online advertising may steadily increase their relative value, which could change the windowing patterns altogether.

The disproportionate share of total online video revenues held by subscription services (Table 22.2) reflects a rapid growth of this component since these data were first reported in 2008, when they accounted for only 15 percent of direct payments (SNL Kagan Research, 2012b). Rapid advances in streaming technology and bandwidth capacity since the late 2000s have enabled the growth of subscription. Meanwhile, program sales are still limited by lengthy download times, especially for theatrical films.

Though still evolving, the emerging pattern of higher revenues from subscription than à la carte transactions parallels a long-established historical pattern for cable television. Although PPV service began to be offered by cable in the mid-1980s, available data show that by 2006, when online video revenues were still negligible, cable subscribers spent approximately four times more money in total for monthly subscription channels (primarily movie-based services like HBO) than they did for all PPV or VOD (also primarily theatrical movie) purchases.[13] PPV/VOD delivered by cable includes only 'rentals' (since download-to-own is not practical with cable technology), which handicaps comparison with the online market. However, consumer preference for monthly flat fee rates over à la carte transactions has a long history in other industries (Fishburn et al., 2000). A well-known media example is the monthly DVD rental plans pioneered in 1999 by Netflix, which proved a highly popular alternative to à la carte VHS and DVD rentals at brick and mortar stores.

Online video content suppliers have also brought forth a vast supply of Internet-original programming, most of which is very cheaply produced and which surely accounts for much of the 'long tail'. These programs include animation, short subjects and content similar to that introduced in the mid-1990s, and of course the billions of user-generated videos on YouTube, Vimeo, and similar. Most of Internet-original video entertainment programming could thus not be classified as professionally produced. Well-established sites including Netflix and Hulu have, however, more recently begun offering higher-quality original series programs.

Parallels can be made between the developing mix of online video entertainment programming and the early years of cable television. A 1986 content analysis of basic cable networks found 3 percent of dramatic format programming hours to be cable-original, and 97 percent to acquired broadcast programs or theatrical films (Waterman and Grant, 1991). Because of its architecture and low delivery costs, the Internet has greater potential than cable to reach niche audiences. It is already apparent, however, that online entertainment faces some of the same fundamental demand constraints that niche cable networks have faced. Other things being equal, a given video program that is focused toward a potential audience only half as large as that of another program must have double the willingness-to-pay among those viewers (or among advertisers who want to reach those viewers) in order to support the same production quality. The graveyards of audio-visual entertainment are littered with suppliers of original programming who underestimated this constraint.

22.6 THE FUTURE OF ONLINE ENTERTAINMENT

As the speed and quality of IP video transmission continue to rise, broadband diffusion grows, more efficient and portable media players continue to proliferate, and interaction between consumers and video content providers becomes more seamless, the economic viability of the online video entertainment industry seems bound to improve.

At some time in the future, the online and offline television and video industries are likely to become indistinguishable as television sets become more seamlessly integrated with computer-controlled media devices. Even as technological constraints fall away, however, the online video entertainment industry faces significant uncertainties and constraints in the reasonably near future.

Among these uncertainties are technological advances in competing media, the viability of illegal file sharing (especially for movies), and the continuing viability of Internet business models (especially for advertising). Another complex issue is how video delivery costs, content provider prices, and Internet service provider (ISP) pricing structures will evolve as consumer bandwidth demands for online video accelerate. For example, more widespread adoption by ISPs of data caps or other bandwidth usage–sensitive pricing may result in heavy video entertainment users paying effectively higher prices per movie or TV program, reducing demand for online video.

Perhaps the greatest economic constraint on the online video entertainment industry in the reasonably near future may be limits on the availability of recent movies and television programming from content providers. As we have seen, the owners of these programs maximize their profits by releasing their products to a variety of different media over time. At least in the short term, MVPDs and ISPs are unlikely to unbundle their 'TV Everywhere' portals from their offline services or distribute them beyond geographic connection service constraints. The Internet is adopting an increasingly important role in intertemporal content-release strategies, but as long as higher returns per viewer can be realized by earlier release of movies to theaters, and earlier release of television programs on broadcast and cable networks distributed by MVPDs, the ultimate 'Virtual Video Store' in which any program is available at any time online will itself be delayed.

22.7 A NOTE ON RESEARCH NEEDS

One of the central questions about video over the Internet is how much benefit, if any, it will eventually have to media consumers. Will it substantially increase the quality and variety of video entertainment products, and reduce prices to consumers? The evidence so far suggests so, but online video entertainment is a still a new industry. In music and in news, for example, the weakening of intellectual property protections and the trading of established media revenue models for apparently much less lucrative online models has raised questions about whether the transitions to digital music and online news are positive or negative sum games overall.[14] While it is challenging to study new and unsettled industries productively, progress can be made to inform these questions. For example, can the sharp decline in DVD sales and rentals since 2005 be attributed to movie piracy, or to consumer substitutions of cheaper online video alternatives? Does the more efficient targeting of online video ads actually result in higher cost-per-thousand ad prices? How valuable to consumers is the 'long tail' of online content? More generally, one could attempt to measure consumer surplus generated by online video. Or focusing on segments of the audience, how successful is online video in serving the needs of racial and ethnic minorities?

It will also be important for informing policy decisions, such as reviews of proposed mergers, whether MVPDs or ISPs should be constrained by regulation or antitrust from attempting to monopolize online video distribution. For this purpose, establishing a strong economic foundation and clear explanations of the market structure of the industry, or explaining the motives behind business practices, can often be the best support for good policy. Are levels of concentration in online video distribution, for example, reasonably attributable to the natural forces of economies of scale, network effects, or similar economic factors? Are the prices that online content aggregators pay for programming plausibly attributable to monopsony bargaining power? Can the offline-to-online program windowing practices of the major television networks be explained by the standard inter-temporal price discrimination model? Or, can the offline/online video bundling practices of MVPDs be explained by straightforward marketing objectives?

Finally, we mention the value of developing historical analogies by studying policy or market outcomes in other media industries. For example, what have been the results of competitive battles between premium cable television networks that have attempted to gain competitive advantage through exclusive programming contracts? Or, what has resulted from historical attempts by established media industry players to slow the development of new media industries that threaten competition? How have policy initiatives in these situations affected the outcomes? Such studies can often give us better insight into the likely path of a new industry like online video entertainment, than can study of the new industry itself.

NOTES

1. The chapter by Waterman (2004), published in Noam et al. (2004), provides a basis for the present work.
2. See Greenstein (2012) for economic development and analysis of the Internet infrastructure.
3. After spending US$100–150 million to develop video-on-demand (VOD) services, these five studios sold Movielink to Blockbuster in 2007 for US$6.6 million (Ali, 2007).
4. The Federal Communications Commission (FCC) reports on the status of competition in the video industries provide detailed descriptions of events in the online video industry and discuss the wide variety of revenue models, content, and levels of aggregation used or employed in this industry (e.g., FCC, 2012, 2015).
5. Online viewing is relatively concentrated among a small group, but offline TV viewing is pervasive among a broad majority of the population. Nielsen reported that 12.4 percent of all individuals (the highest quintile among the 61.9 percent of individuals who stream at least some video) watched an average of 20.7 minutes of video per day, which accounted for 84.1 percent of all video streaming minutes, but this group also watched roughly ten times as much offline TV per day (241.2 minutes), nearly as much as the

average US individual (264.7 minutes) (Nielsen, 2012, Table 8a). See also Liebowitz and Zentner (2012), who found the impact of Internet use more generally on television viewing to be relatively low, but higher among younger Americans.

6.   comScore (2013) ranks the top ten sites by the number of video ads viewed. The fourth ranking in terms of ad minutes viewed is the authors' inference.
7.   Telecommunications companies such as Verizon and AT&T use Internet Protocol TV (IPTV) delivery, but for our purposes they are grouped with other MVPDs because they basically offer a linear multi-channel service over private networks. The FCC's annual reports on video competition include excellent commentary on and analysis of industry development of MVPDs and online video distributors. The sixteenth report, the latest at the time of writing, was published 2 April 2015.
8.   YouTube's total announced budget for all of the 100 channels together was US$100–150 million. YouTube has invested another US$200 million into the programming and added 60 more channels (Efrati, 2012).
9.   For a survey article on the cost-efficiency of Internet vs offline video transfer, see Screen Digest (2012).
10.   In 2006, Netflix offered US$1 million to the first team that could improve its movie search and recommendation engine by 10 percent, a competition that was eventually won by a consortium of teams in September 2009. The collective knowledge produced by this crowdsourcing contest pushed the boundaries of how machine learning and statistical techniques could handle big datasets, and Netflix immediately created another, more open-ended contest, suggesting that the organization believed the competitive advantage offered from improved search efficiency was worth the investment (Lohr, 2009).
11.   The DMCA 1998 imposes statutory damages penalties of between US$200 and US$2500 per act of circumvention or actual damages, and does not preclude the application of copyright violation remedies.
12.   SNL Kagan Research (2012b, pp. 3, 5) reported average retail prices of DVD sales and DVD rentals to be US$14.23 and US$2.71, respectively.
13.   SNL Kagan Research (2008) reported consumer spending for monthly subscription networks in 2006 to be US$6.5 billion vs US$1.6 billion for spending on PPV movies. 'Digital video' (online) spending, first reported by SNL Kagan in 2006, amounted to US$46 million (SNL Kagan, 2012b).
14.   For discussion of the news case, see Pew Research Center (2011). An empirical study by Waldfogel (2012) finds that the precipitous decline in recorded music revenues since Napster has not significantly reduced the supply of music.

REFERENCES

Ali, R. (2007), 'Movielink-Blockbuster deal: $6.6M; BB paid Netflix $7M for patent dispute', 14 August, *Forbes*, accessed 3 April 2015 at http://www.forbes.com/2007/08/14/movielink-blockbuster-netflix-tech-cx_pco_0814paidcontent.html.
Anderson, C. (2006), *The Long Tail: Why the Future of Business is Selling Less of More*, 1st edition, New York: Hyperion.
Anderson, S. (2012), 'Advertising on the Internet', in M. Peitz and J. Waldfogel (eds), *The Oxford Handbook of the Digital Economy*, New York: Oxford University Press, pp. 355–96.
Bakos, Y. and E. Brynjolfsson (1999), 'Bundling information goods: Pricing, profits and efficiency', *Management Science*, **45** (12), 1613–30.
Bakos, Y. and E. Brynjolfsson (2000), 'Bundling and competition on the Internet', *Marketing Science*, **19** (1), 63–82.
Bazilian, E. (2011), 'Netflix takes up a third of Internet bandwidth traffic shifting from computers to connected devices', *Adweek*, 27 October, accessed 3 April 2015 at http://www.adweek.com/news/technology/netflix-takes-third-internet-bandwidth-136115.
Bond, P. and G. Szalai (2011), 'YouTube announces TV initiative with 100 niche channels', *The Hollywood Reporter*, 28 October, accessed 3 April 2015 at http://www.hollywoodreporter.com/news/youtube-tv-channels-kutcher-poehler-254370.
Brochet, F., S. Srinivasan and M. Norris (2012), 'Netflix: Valuing a new business model', *Harvard Business School Case No. 9-223-018*.
Choi, J.P. (2012), 'Bundling information goods', in M. Peitz and J. Waldfogel (eds), *The Oxford Handbook of the Digital Economy*, New York: Oxford University Press, pp. 273–305.
comScore (2012), 'comScore study finds professionally-produced video content and user-generated product videos exhibit strong synergy in driving sales effectiveness', accessed 3 April 2015 at http://www.comscore.com/Insights/Press-Releases/2012/3/comScore-Study-Finds-Professionally-Produced-Video-Content-And-User-Generated-Product-Videos-Exhibit-Strong-Synergy-in-Driving-Sales-Effectiveness.
comScore (2013), 'comScore releases December 2012 US online video rankings', accessed 3 April 2015 at

https://www.comscore.com/Insights/Press-Releases/2013/1/comScore-Releases-December-2012-U.S.-Online-Video-Rankings.

Convergence Consulting Group (2012), 'The battle for the American couch potato: Online & traditional TV and movie distribution', Convergence Consulting Group White Paper.

Efrati, A. (2012), 'YouTube to double down on its "channel" experiment', *The Wall Street Journal*, 30 July, accessed 3 April 2015 at http://online.wsj.com/article/SB10000872396390444840104577549632241258356.html.

Eisenmann, T.R. and A. Brown (2000), 'Online content providers', *Harvard Business School Background Note No. 9-801-261*.

Elberse, A. and S. Gupta (2010a), 'Hulu: Evil plot to destroy the world?', *Harvard Business School Case No. 510-005*.

Elberse, A. and S. Gupta (2010b), 'YouTube: Time to start charging users?', *Harvard Business School Case No. 510-053*.

Evans, D.S. (2009), 'The online advertising industry: Economics, evolution, and privacy', *Journal of Economic Perspectives*, **23** (3), 37–60.

FCC (2012), *Annual Assessment of the Status of Competition in the Market for the Delivery of Video Programming*, Fourteenth Report by the Federal Communications Commission, FCC 12-81, MB Docket No. 07-269, released 20 July 2012, Washington, DC, accessed 3 April 2015 at https://apps.fcc.gov/edocs_public/attachmatch/FCC-12-81A1.pdf.

FCC (2015), *Annual Assessment of the Status of Competition in the Market for the Delivery of Video Programming*, Sixteenth Report by the Federal Communications Commission, FCC 15-41, MB Docket No. 14-16, released 2 April 2015, Washington, DC, accessed 3 April 2015 at http://transition.fcc.gov/Daily_Releases/Daily_Business/2015/db0402/FCC-15-41A1.pdf.

Fishburn, P.C., A. Odlyzko and R. Siders (2000), 'Fixed-fee versus unit pricing for information goods: Competition, equilibria, and price wars', in B. Kahin and H. Varian (eds), *Internet Publishing and Beyond: The Economics of Information and Intellectual Property*, Cambridge, MA: MIT Press, pp. 167–89.

Fontaine, G., F. Le Borgne-Bachschmidt and M. Leiba (2010), 'Scenarios for the Internet migration of the television industry', *Communications & Strategies*, **1** (77), 21–34.

Gannes, L. (2009), 'YouTube changes everything: The online video revolution', in D. Gerbarg (ed.), *Television Goes Digital*, New York: Springer, pp. 147–55.

Gerbarg, D. (ed.) (2009), *Television Goes Digital*, New York: Springer.

Greenstein, S. (2012), 'Internet infrastructure', in M. Peitz and J. Waldfogel (eds), *The Oxford Handbook of the Digital Economy*, Oxford, UK: Oxford University Press, pp. 3–33.

Kahin, B. and H.R. Varian (eds) (2000), *Internet Publishing and Beyond: The Economics of Digital Information and Intellectual Property*, Cambridge, MA: MIT Press.

Liebowitz, S.J. and A. Zentner (2012), 'Clash of the Titans: Does Internet use reduce television viewing?', *The Review of Economics and Statistics*, **94** (1), 234–45.

Lohr, S. (2009), 'Netflix awards $1 million prize and starts a new contest', *The New York Times* [blog], accessed 3 April 2015 at http://bits.blogs.nytimes.com/2009/09/21/netflix-awards-1-million-prize-and-starts-a-new-contest/.

Mateus, A. and J.M. Peha (2011), 'Quantifying global transfers of copyrighted content using BitTorrent', paper presented at the 39th Research Conference on Communications, Information and Internet Policy (TPRC), Arlington, VA, 24 September, accessed 3 April 2015 at http://ssrn.com/abstract=1985737.

National Research Council (2000), *The Digital Dilemma: Intellectual Property in the Information Age*, Committee on Intellectual Property Rights and the Emerging Information Infrastructure, Washington, DC: National Academies Press, accessed 3 April 2015 at http://www.nap.edu/openbook.php?record_id=9601.

Nielsen (2012), *The Nielsen Cross-Platform Report Q4 2012*, accessed 3 April 2015 at http://www.nielsen.com/content/corporate/us/en/insights/reports/2013/the-nielsen-march-2013-cross-platform-report--free-to-move-betwe.html.

Noam, E.M. (2004), 'Will Internet TV be American?', in E.M. Noam, J. Groebel and D. Gerbarg (eds), *Internet Television*, Mahwah, NJ: Lawrence Erlbaum, pp. 235–42.

Noam, E.M. (2008), 'If fiber is the medium, what is the message? Next-generation content for next-generation networks', *Communications and Strategies*, Special Issue on Ultrabroadband: The Next Stage in Communications, November, 19–34.

Noam, E.M., J. Groebel and D. Gerbarg (eds) (2004), *Internet Television*, Mahwah, NJ: Lawrence Erlbaum.

Owen, B.M. (1999), *The Internet Challenge to Television*, Boston, MA: Harvard University Press.

Owen, B.M. and S. Wildman (1992), *Video Economics*, Boston, MA: Harvard University Press.

Pew Research Center (2011), *The State of the News Media 2011 – Overview*, accessed 3 April 2015 at http://www.stateofthemedia.org/overview-2011/.

Sandvine Intelligent Broadband Networks (2012), *Global Internet Phenomena Report: 2H 2012*, accessed 3 April 2015 at http://www.electronics.dit.ie/staff/dclarke/Otherpercent20Files/Sandvine_Global_Internet_Phenomena_Report_2H_2012.pdf.

Screen Digest (2011a), 'Timeshifted TV viewing increases: However, traditional scheduled viewing continues to dominate', *Screen Digest*, May, 209–19.

Screen Digest (2011b), 'US online movie market up 25 per cent: In the first half of 2011, transactions were worth $229m', *Screen Digest*, October, 294.

Screen Digest (2012), 'The economics of over-the-top', *Screen Digest*, October, 119.

Shapiro, C. and H.R. Varian (1999), *Information Rules: A Strategic Guide to the Network Economy*, Boston, MA: Harvard Business Press.

Simon, J.P. (2012), *The Dynamics of the Media and Content Industries: A Synthesis*, Seville: JRC-IPTS, accessed 3 April 2015 at http://ftp.jrc.es/EURdoc/JRC76471.pdf.

SNL Kagan Research (2008), 'US consumer entertainment spending patterns', *Media Trends*.

SNL Kagan Research (2012a), *Motion Picture Investor*, 26 September.

SNL Kagan Research (2012b), *Motion Picture Investor*, 30 November.

Waldfogel, J. (2012), 'Copyright protection, technological change, and the quality of new products: Evidence from recorded music since Napster', *Journal of Law & Economics*, **55** (4), 715–40.

Waterman, D. (1985), 'Prerecorded home video and the distribution of theatrical feature films', in E.M. Noam (ed.), *Video Media Competition: Regulation, Economics and Technology*, New York: Columbia University Press, pp. 221–43.

Waterman, D. (2004), 'Business models and program content', in E.M. Noam, J. Groebel and D. Gerbarg (eds), *Internet Television*, Mahwah, NJ: Lawrence Erlbaum, pp. 61–80.

Waterman, D. (2005), *Hollywood's Road to Riches*, Boston, MA: Harvard University Press.

Waterman, D. and A. Grant (1991), 'Cable television as an aftermarket', *Journal of Broadcasting and Electronic Media*, **35** (2), 179–88.

Waterman, D., R. Sherman and S.W. Ji (2012), 'The economics of online television: Revenue models, aggregation, and "TV everywhere"', paper presented at the 40th Research Conference on Communications, Information and Internet Policy (TPRC), Arlington, VA, 21–23 September, accessed 3 April 2015 at http://ssrn.com/abstract=2032828.

Wildman, S.S. (2008), 'Interactive channels and the challenge of content budgeting', *The International Journal on Media Management*, **10** (3), 91–101.

Yao, D.A., J. Rozovsky and F.P.B. Rodrigues-Quiero (2008), 'CBS and online video', *Harvard Business School Case No. 709-447*.

23. Business strategies and revenue models for converged video services
Yu-li Liu

23.1 INTRODUCTION

Convergence has been identified since the 1970s as a force that would reshape media and telecommunications industries (Baldwin et al., 1996). The notion is often used in ambiguous ways, confounding technological, economic, social, cultural, and global aspects (Jenkins, 2001, 2006). Moreover, the focus is often on the homogenizing and integrative aspects whereas the equally present diversifying and differentiating aspects are often overlooked (Greenstein and Khanna, 1997; Bauer et al., 2003). A first wave of technological convergence in the 1960s and 1970s (often referred to as 'telematics') contributed to an integration of computing and telecommunications. A second wave starting in the 1990s was intricately related to the emergence of the Internet. Sometimes referred to as 'mediamatics' it muddled the boundaries between telecommunications, broadcasting, and media in general (Latzer, 1998, 2009). Krattenmaker (1996, p. 6) stressed the unfolding of 'a convergence of devices and a plethora of transmission paths'. Convergence and divergence are the outcome of technological developments, policy and regulatory developments, corporate strategies, and consumer preferences.

A main effect in the media industries is the blurring of lines between formerly separate media platforms such as over-the-air broadcasting, cable TV, and streamed media. Consequently, content that previously was only available on television can be delivered seamlessly to consumers via personal computers, smartphones, tablets and other mobile devices. Moreover, content that was once delivered via different, specialized technologies (e.g., broadcasting, cable TV) can now be distributed through multiple platforms, allowing easier viewer access independently of time and space. Convergence also provides consumers with new means of accessing entertainment and audiovisual content. Many converged video services such as Internet Protocol TV (IPTV) and mobile TV have appeared in the market. The most recent development is over-the-top (OTT) video services. The newly converged services have created new markets and have had wide-ranging displacement and complementary effects on traditional media. In response to the emergence of converged video services, media firms have developed new business strategies and revenue models for both new and traditional services. While convergence creates significant challenges and threats it also opens remarkable opportunities for new and innovative business strategies that are often designed to alleviate the competitive impact of intensified competition in converged video services markets.

Picard (2000) pointed out that the success or failure of a new communications technology is not only dependent upon its innovativeness, usefulness or desirability but also on whether a business model can be found that generates a sustainable revenue stream while satisfying users and investors. A 'business model' refers to how an organization creates and distributes value in a profitable manner (Baden-Fuller and Morgan, 2010). It is also described as a mechanism for turning ideas into revenue at reasonable cost (Gambardella and McGahan, 2010, p. 263). As used in the modern communications sector, the notion of a business model looks at the entire value chain by taking into account the resources of production and distribution technologies, content creation, acquisition and aggregation (Picard, 2000).

In contrast, 'business strategies' are often described as the art of formulating and implementing decisions that allow pursuing the goals and objectives of an organization. Therefore, the analysis of business strategies needs to be linked to the organization and its external environment. Business models can then be defined as abstract representations or blueprints of an organization's strategies. While a firm's strategies may be specific to its particular nature, business models can be generally applied to many different organizations (Seddon and Lewis, 2003; Osterwalder and Pigneur, 2010; Mustafa and Werthner, 2011).

Most of the converged services offered by firms utilize multiple revenue streams. Advertisements and subscriptions are the most frequently used funding models (Huang, 2012; Waterman et al., 2013). With the broader adoption of video-on-demand (VOD) services, pay-per-view (PPV) and pay-to-download models are also gaining. Converged video platforms may also employ a freemium approach, where users enjoy a basic service for free and pay for premium services that offer additional value (Anderson, 2009; Kotliar, 2011) and revenue sharing (Bouwman et al., 2008).

This chapter analyzes business strategies for converged video services, with a focus on IPTV, mobile TV, and OTT video services. It starts with a look at the development of converged video services followed by a discussion of the ecosystem of converged video services. From there, the chapter will proceed to explore the new media value chain. Business strategies and revenue models of converged video services will be addressed in sections 23.4 and 23.5. Section 23.6 provides succinct case studies before conclusions are drawn in the last section.

23.2 THE DEVELOPMENT OF CONVERGED VIDEO SERVICES

In the early 2000s, telecommunications companies in Europe, Asia and the United States started to introduce IPTV. The service was frequently offered as part of triple-play packages. In countries where broadband development was already advanced, considerable growth in both linear and non-linear online video content was deemed suitable for the launch of IPTV.[1] By 2006, IPTV services had been started or offered on a trial basis in at least seven of 13 Asia-Pacific economies (Kim, 2009; Shin, 2009). In Taiwan, for example, the incumbent telephone company Chunghwa Telecom (CHT) launched the first IPTV service, named multimedia-on-demand (MOD), in 2004. In South Korea, which has been a leader in broadband and new media development since the 1990s, Korea Telecom (KT) and Hanaro Telecom initially scheduled the launch of IPTV for 2006. However, due to regulatory setbacks the introduction was delayed until 2008 (Shin, 2009). In recent years, the IPTV market in South Korea has shown rapid service innovation and an impressive increase in the number of subscribers. As of March 2014, the total worldwide number of IPTV subscribers was around 92.7 million. With 45.6 million subscribers, the Asia-Pacific region comprised 49.2 percent of the global market. Subscribers in Western Europe reached 27.3 million (29.4 percent) while North America accounted for 11.7 million or 12.6 percent of the global market (PRWEB, 2014).

A second platform is offered by mobile television. In this chapter, mobile TV refers to 'the transmission of TV programs or video for a range of wireless devices ranging from mobile TV-capable phones to PDAs and wireless multimedia devices' (Kumar, 2007, p. 5). There are two main kinds of mobile TV. One is broadcast over a terrestrial network or via satellites to mobile devices, utilizing a separate frequency from the one used for mobile voice and data and hence requiring handsets that are equipped to receive such signals. The other is transmitted 'in-band' over a 3G or 4G network (ITU, 2013) and hence does not require additional hardware functionality. This chapter focuses on the former service and only briefly touches on the latter. Although mobile TV was initially developed in Japan, SK Telecom launched the first mobile TV service based on satellite digital mobile broadcasting (S-DMB) in South Korea in May of 2005 (Lee and Kwak, 2005). In the following year, S-DMB managed to provide 15 video channels and 19 audio channels. When the service was inaugurated, some called it a new technology that would change people's lifestyles. Yet in August 2012 S-DMB was shut off. A main reason was that terrestrial stations supported free terrestrial digital mobile broadcasting (T-DMB), diluting the willingness of consumers to pay for content on S-DMB that was seen by many as less appealing (Seo, 2012).

In China, although the government adopted China Mobile Multimedia Broadcasting (CMMB) as a standard, mobile TV was also not successful. For one, the service initially also relied on a for-pay model. Moreover, China Mobile received an exclusive three-year contract, excluding subscribers of other mobile phone companies from receiving mobile TV programs.[2]

In European countries several mobile operators adopted digital video broadcasting-handheld (DVB-H) as the standard for mobile TV. However, only Nokia supported the standard in its devices and thus consumer uptake was limited. All European countries have now stopped DVB-H broadcasts (OECD, 2013). In the United States, Dyle, a joint-venture of 12 broadcast groups including ABC, NBC, Fox and Telemundo, is the major example of broadcast mobile TV offering its services since August 2012 (ITU, 2013).

Since its introduction to the market in 2005, broadcast mobile TV has encountered many challenges, including a lack of appealing content and sustainable business models. Its quality of service also varies depending on the technology and the mobile handsets. With the increasing bandwidth and download speeds in terrestrial long-term evolution (LTE) networks, in-band transmission has become increasingly used for mobile video. It can be provided as streamed mobile video and multicast mobile video, which utilizes the available bandwidth more efficiently (see Bauer et al., 2007 for an early analysis).

In addition to IPTV and mobile TV, OTT video now allows content creators, aggregators and new or existing content distributors to provide consumers with content via broadband (Frieden, 2012). IPTV and OTT differ in several ways. For one, IPTV is often provided by incumbent telecom providers in a 'walled-garden' format, which may narrow the technological options of users but allows guaranteeing quality of service. In contrast, OTT video services are typically provided via any broadband connection. Consequently, the market for OTT service is highly fragmented and composed of many different devices and solutions. A second distinctive difference is the need for a set-top box, which is often mandatory for IPTV but not necessary for OTT services. In terms of geographical reach, IPTV is mainly offered at a national level while many OTT services are, at least technically, available internationally. In most countries, IPTV service providers need to obtain a license from the (tele)communications authority whereas OTT video service providers usually do not require a license (China and Singapore are among exceptions).

Netflix, YouTube, and Hulu are the most vivid examples of OTT video service providers. Netflix was delivering content through video rental services as early as 1997. Digital distribution was introduced in 1999. YouTube launched at the beginning of 2005 and quickly became a household name before it was sold to Google for US$1.65 billion in October 2006 (White, 2006). In 2008 Hulu joined these competitors as an over-the-top service for content streaming and storage. Although these services have emerged only recently, they have grown rapidly. Recent data indicate that video constitutes the largest type of Internet traffic in most countries and regions, and exceeds 60 percent of peak traffic in some cases (Mocerino, 2011).

23.3   THE ECOSYSTEM AND VALUE CHAIN OF CONVERGED VIDEO SERVICES

The relationship between different players in the converged media ecosystem is depicted in Figure 23.1. In this system, consumers can access video content via terrestrial TV, cable TV, direct broadcast satellite (DBS), IPTV, mobile TV or OTT TV platforms. Four dimensions are needed to understand the converged media ecosystem. A first necessary component is innovative technology. Digital convergence, interactivity, sufficient bandwidth and the use of the Internet Protocol (IP) all have expanded the scope of feasible technological innovation. A second component is public policy. Technology and policy co-evolve, each shaping and constraining the other (Bauer, 2014). The development of new media platforms and services is influenced by government policies and regulations affecting convergence such as measures encouraging new services, allowing cross-media ownership, promoting competition, and the design of light touch regulation.

A third component comprises corporate strategies, which are contingent on the potential added value that can be generated, cost efficiencies achievable by convergence services, the availability and cost of content sources and expected economic benefits. The fourth component consists of consumer preferences and choices, which are affected by attributes such as the convenience of services, their price and quality, as well as their adaptability across various platforms. In the long run, stakeholders in the market will interact both competitively and cooperatively with one another in the ecosystem (Brandenburger and Nalebuff, 1996). In Figure 23.1 OTT video is the most recent service to compete or cooperate with the incumbent media. TV media such as terrestrial TV, DBS, IPTV and cable TV might offer OTT TV service as well. Mobile TV, which is transmitted via broadcasting or satellite, has technical limitations in terms of providing OTT video service, because OTT needs to be accessed via broadband.

As an effect of convergence, value generation in the media market also has changed. The new value chain can be broken down into several segments (Figure 23.2). Each of them, from creation, content aggregation, distribution to consumption, is populated

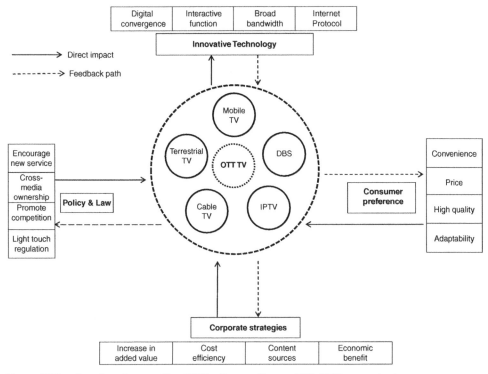

Note: DBS = direct broadcast satellite; IPTV = Internet Protocol TV; OTT = over-the-top.

Source: Adapted from Bauer et al. (2003).

Figure 23.1 Converged media ecosystem

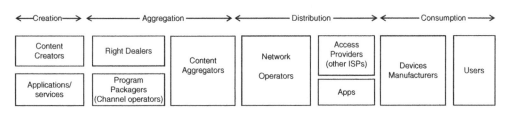

Source: Adapted from Venturini (2011).

Figure 23.2 Converged video service value chain

with key actors. Content creators, application and service providers mainly take part in creation; rights dealers, program packagers and content aggregators provide content aggregation. Network operators and access providers as well as apps are involved in the distribution of content to consumers. Furthermore, device manufacturers and users contribute to the consumption of content from the converged media platforms. In fact, in a digital economy, value is co-created when various players in the market join forces and engage in cooperative activities to innovate or increase their competitive advantage (Evens, 2010).

23.4   BUSINESS STRATEGIES FOR CONVERGED VIDEO SERVICES

23.4.1   Bundling

From the beginning in the early 2000s telecommunication operators have provided IPTV services as part of a bundling strategy, often carried out as 'triple play', packaging voice (phone), video (IPTV) and data (broadband) services. Bundles are typically offered at a lower price than the sum of the prices of the individual services. Telecommunication companies that also offer mobile services (or are able to contract them from other operators) may adopt a 'quadruple play' strategy by adding mobile phone service to the package. Most telecommunication companies pursue mixed bundling strategies, selling services as part of bundles and on a stand-alone basis. A successful example of bundled service is U-verse offered by AT&T in the USA. The company offers an integrated mobile and tablet app to allow consumers to download and watch TV episodes from anywhere. Recently, it also offers access to Amazon Prime on a trial basis as part of one of its bundles. Price bundling is not always a revenue-enhancing strategy but it typically works if consumer preferences and demand for the individual services are heterogeneous (Stremersch and Tellis, 2002). The profitability of bundling will be enhanced if marketing costs are only incremental and if churn can be reduced by bundling (Huang, 2012). This is illustrated in the cases of three Internet service providers in France (Free, Orange and Neuf Cegetel), which were able to increase the average revenue per user (ARPU) by offering bundled IPTV and broadband access services (Park et al., 2009).

23.4.2   Compelling, Original and Exclusive Content

While branded content is available on traditional platforms such as terrestrial and cable television, compelling, original, and exclusive content helps attract viewers to OTT services. Although the strength of converged video services may not be original content, suppliers provide some original content in order to attract more viewers. For instance, in Hong Kong, PCCW's Now TV (an IPTV service) provides its own news and sports channels in addition to carrying other news channels and sports channels on its platform. It also competed with i-Cable for the right to broadcast the Barclays Premier League (one of the most prestigious soccer leagues in the world) live, which is considered to be compelling content for people in Hong Kong.

   In the USA and abroad Netflix is positioned as an OTT service. It is not anchored to any facility-based infrastructure. The production of original content helps distinguish Netflix in the competitive video market. For example, the original series *House of Cards* and *Orange is the New Black* are only available on Netflix. In terms of creating original content, Netflix's main concern is to appeal to the audience. One of the key features of Netflix is that subscribers can view the video content any time they want and as many times as they like. As of September 2013, with 40.4 million subscribers each paying

$7.99 per month, Netflix had invested about $100 million in the first two seasons (a total of 26 episodes) of the original series *House of Cards*. The show is an example of a successful business strategy since it was produced with a fairly low investment but with a massive return. This original series not only increased the popularity of Netflix, but it was also the first production by an online video distributor to ever receive an Emmy award, for Best Director (Sharma and Cheney, 2013).

23.4.3   Complete Release

Serial watching of one TV show or DVD after another over a weekend has been known for a long time and used to be called 'marathon viewing'. Today, viewing multiple episodes of a TV show in one session online has been given a new name: 'binge viewing'. On OTT platforms, binge viewing was first catered to by Netflix when it released all 15 episodes of *Arrested Development*, allowing viewers to watch the entire season at once if desired. The strategy of complete release further reinforces the behavior of binge viewing. In a recent survey by Harris Interactive on behalf of Netflix, the results showed that, of those who stream at least one episode per week online, 61 percent reportedly binge view regularly. Described as 'viewing 2–6 episodes of the same TV show in one sitting' in the survey, Netflix has also declared that binge viewing has become a prevalent and normal behavior (PR Newswire, 2013).

In the same survey, it was also revealed that binge viewing nowadays carries a different meaning. While negative connotations such as guilt are often associated with the traditional concept of binging, close to 73 percent of TV streamers reported positive feelings after binge watching. Over three-quarters claimed that viewing the episodes all at once in their own preferred time made the shows more enjoyable (ibid.). Online video distributors such as Hulu and Netflix offer the choice of binge viewing to attract more viewers and subscribes to the premium services (Fixmer, 2013).

23.4.4   Multi-screen Service

Technically speaking, multi-screen service can be provided by IPTV, cable TV, and OTT TV. It is a strategic decision contingent on holding all the relevant audiovisual broadcast rights. Multi-screen service emphasizes a seamless service, which allows users to view content on multiple devices such as TVs, mobile devices, and personal computers, preferably via just one account. The multi-screen feature allows great convenience for users to access content anytime, anywhere (Berman et al., 2011). According to estimates by the US research firm Parks Associates, in 2012 multi-screen services reached 66 percent of pay-TV subscribers in Western Europe, 21 percent in Eastern Europe, and 9 percent in Asia, compared to 90 percent in North America (Beach, 2012b).

In the UK, cable company Virgin Media launched its Virgin TV Anywhere platform in November 2012, offering 30 live channels and over 2000 hours of on-demand content to its subscribers on tablets, mobile devices and computers at no extra charge. It offers OTT services via adaptive streaming for multi-screen purposes. By doing so, it can better accommodate a viewer's circumstances and ensure a smoother transition from screen to screen (Wright, 2013).

Netflix claimed that its content can be accessed via up to 900 different devices. For instance, smartphones with either iOS or Android systems, tablets, gaming consoles, digital television and Smart TV are all devices through which users can gain access to Netflix's content. Dailymotion, the world's second largest video-sharing website, also pursues a multi-device approach.

24.4.5 Strategic Co-opetition

In the highly interconnected Internet ecosystem, players in different segments in the value network are often in ambiguous competitive relationships. Whereas they may be competitors in one geographic market or one point in time they may offer complementary services in others and might benefit from cooperating (Brandenburger and Nalebuff, 1996). Companies will need to choose when and where to compete and when and where to cooperate. If the elements of cooperation and competition are both visible, then the relationship between the competitors is referred to as co-opetition (Bengtsson and Kock, 2000).

For instance, Verizon cooperates with DirecTV (DBS service) in areas where its FiOS video service is not available by splitting revenue with it. Another example of co-opetition can be found in the case of YouView in the UK. Formed by four broadcasters and three telecommunication carriers, YouView provides free access to a total of 70 channels offered by digital terrestrial television (DTT) and TV on-demand ('catch-up TV') channels as well as access to pay channels.[3] Although the service providers involved are also competing with each other, they have agreed to make their content available on the same YouView platform since it is a way of reaching a larger audience base. A third example is the co-opetitive relationship between KT and Samsung in South Korea. KT laments that Samsung's Smart TV takes up bandwidth without any compensatory payment. However, despite this dispute, the two companies also cooperate in some areas, such as the incorporation of KT's set-top box in Samsung's Smart TV.

24.4.6 Differentiation

Where convergence leads to an intensification of competition (e.g., by making available new platforms for the delivery of content), firms will seek to reduce that pressure by differentiating their offerings (Greenstein and Khanna, 1997). Differentiation strategies may be implemented by varying prices, service quality, by adding features, and so on. Not surprisingly, differentiation is a strategy often used by converged video services, especially for content aimed at different platforms, such as mobile devices or personal computers. For example, for mobile devices, short-form content (such as news updates) would probably be more appealing, since users are often on the go with a mobile device. This suggests that it is advantageous to create and design content specifically for the intended device. There are many examples of differentiation strategies employed by players offering converged services, especially OTT video services. For instance, in terms of the revenue models, YouTube and Dailymotion adopted an advertisement model, Netflix adopted a subscription model, and YouView adopted a freemium model. Speaking of content, YouTube and Dailymotion focus on user-generated content, Netflix focuses on original content, and Lovefilm focuses on premium content. With regard to programming, three OTT players in Taiwan emphasize different genres, with Elta focusing on sports, UDN TV on news, and Catchplay on movies.

23.4.7   Disruptive Innovation

According to Christensen (1997), disruptive innovation occurs when the design of new products or services takes place at a lower price, and only marginal customer segments are attracted at first. However, as time goes by, the new product or service has the potential to displace the incumbent service or product providers. Examples of market disruptors can be found in OTT video services as well. For instance, in China, many online video services have started to provide all content for free.[4] There is no requirement for a password or monthly subscription. Service quality was not stable in the very beginning and there was also pirated content. In the course of time, the online video platforms improved download quality, avoided pirated content, and provided some premium content at a cheaper rate than IPTV and cable TV. Online video services have consequently had an impact on both cable TV and IPTV.

The complete release of all programs and providing users with the opportunity to view all content without limitation is also a means of disruptive innovation. It is different from traditional TV, which usually airs the program based on a schedule, often only once a day or once a week. In addition, the way in which the OTT video services carry the advertisements also disrupts the TV market. In many OTT video services, the advertisement can be skipped by the users after it is shown for a few seconds. This disruptive strategy is widely welcomed by the users.

23.4.8   Flexible Pricing

A flexible pricing strategy allows consumers to choose and select what is suitable for them. According to Cryan (2012), video streaming online exceeded physical video sales such as DVD and Blu-ray discs beginning in 2012. Although a direct comparison is difficult, US audiences watched 3.4 billion movies online and spent US$2.4 billion to purchase physical hardcopies. Market intelligence firm ABI Research (2013) reported that companies like Netflix and Hulu helped expand the global OTT video market past the $8 billion mark in 2012 and revenues are predicted to exceed $20 billion by 2015. Two likely reasons why online video services have become so popular are their convenience and the flexible pricing strategies adopted by providers. For instance, subscribers of Netflix and Amazon Prime may opt to pay a monthly flat fee to enjoy 'all-you-can-watch' services and video content (Oppenheim, 2012). On the other hand, consumers may also choose to pay à la carte according to their usage and downloads. In addition to gaining unlimited access to content available on the newly converged platforms, consumers can also pay for the particular movie or episode they watch. On mobile platforms, some network operators have begun to collaborate with content providers to offer sponsored data ('zero rating'), a model in which data related to content from partners or certain applications is not deducted from a user's data allowance.

23.4.9   SoLoMo, O2O, and SoMoCloGlo

Several other models – including SoLoMo (social, local, and mobile), O2O (online to offline), and SoMoCloGlo (social, mobile, cloud, and global) – are emerging and promise interesting innovation opportunities in OTT. SoLoMo, a term coined by John Doerr in

2011, is a useful strategy for converged services. Examples of SoLoMo can be found in popular social networking apps like WeChat and Line. The apps exemplify its sociability, locality and mobility by connecting users in proximate locations through the 'shake' function on their mobile handsets. Users can also use the 'look around' function to search for their friends and acquaintances. Once connected, users can send texts, voice messages and images to communicate and socialize.

By utilizing the features of SoLoMo, service providers can bring more interactivity to the users. For instance, *iPartment* (Love Apartment) is a popular sitcom on Mainland China. It was first aired by Jiangxi TV in August 2009. Later, it was adopted by other TV channels and two online video websites (iQIYI and PPS). In the beginning, *iPartment* was only a social network focusing on dating and chatting. The founders borrowed the theme of the social network and made dramas based on love stories they collected on the Internet. They utilized SoLoMo features and became well received by the audience.

SoLoMo also enables key concepts such as O2O activities to be prevalent. O2O refers to how online activities of users can lead to offline activities at the store front (Xia and Zhu, 2014). For instance, viewers who watch OTT video content may watch the same program again offline. Online viewing can sometimes boost the rating of offline media, because it can increase the visibility of the program and the awareness of the audience.

SoMoCloGlo is another strategy coined by Fred Wilson, a venture capitalist and co-founder of Union Square Ventures. SoMoCloGlo evolved from SoLoMo. In the acronym, Clo stands for the cloud, and Glo for global. Global OTT players such as Netflix, YouTube, and Dailymotion are good examples of companies utilizing the SoMoCloGlo strategy.

23.4.10   Big Data Analysis and Applications

With the growth of connected devices such as smartphones, tablets, and smart TV, media platforms can use the detailed data collected to analyze viewers' use of their services. Over time, the collection will amount to a tremendous volume of data, often referred to somewhat sloppily as 'big data'. What is most significant about big data is not the quantity of data, the storage capacity, or processing capability of computers. It is the fact that statistical and computational methods are improved with better algorithms, in which specialists are now able to link the datasets and see patterns in the data.

Unlocking the value of big data has become an efficient way to optimize the media platforms' position and investments. By analyzing the rich data in the service and spotting the patterns of user behavior, media platforms will be able to drive profitability, meet customer needs, and grow market share. For instance, companies such as Netflix and Amazon have 'recommendation engines' to make purchase suggestions to the users. They are doing so based on the prior interests of not just one individual, but of large numbers, often millions, of customers (Shaw, 2014), enabling them to leverage rich information to their competitive advantage.

Big data analysis is now being frequently used by Internet service providers (ISPs) and Internet content providers (ICPs) to refine their customer service and new platform strategies (Gao, 2013, p. 26). Thanks to big data, *House of Cards* produced by

Netflix was a huge success. Netflix can track when viewers pause, rewind, and fast forward. It also tracks the day, time, and location of viewing and the used devices. Furthermore, it collects information about ratings, searches, browsing and scrolling behavior and even looks at data within movies (Bulygo, 2013). Viewer data helps the company to learn about viewer preferences and behavior including the appeal of directors, stars, and genres. *House of Cards* successfully demonstrates how Netflix uses data and analytics to select movies, create content, and make investment decisions to produce attractive original content and thus offers exactly what viewers want (Carr, 2013).

23.5   REVENUE MODELS FOR CONVERGED VIDEO SERVICES

A broad range of revenue models for converged services is employed by service providers. The following section offers an overview of main approaches, including advertisements, subscriptions, pay-per-view or pay-to-download, freemium, retail, shopping program, and revenue sharing (Bouwman et al., 2008; Kotliar, 2011; Huang, 2012; Waterman et al., 2013).

23.5.1   Advertisements

The world's leading OTT players YouTube and Dailymotion mainly rely upon an advertisement-funded model. Likewise OTT players such as Viacom Digital and Crackle rely on advertising revenue for their primary business models (Waterman et al., 2013). Many online video platforms in China such as Youkou Toudou (historically the two largest providers, integrated by a merger in 2012) also rely on the advertisement model. Advertisements on OTT platforms can be shown in different ways. Some ads appear on the main page of the website. Some are shown before a program is aired. Some ads can also be skipped, improving user satisfaction with OTT. According to US firm IMS Research's forecast, the rate of growth in OTT advertising revenues will increase over the next five years. With the increasing popularity and consumption of OTT content, OTT advertising revenues are forecast to rise to US$13.4 billion by 2017 (Beach, 2012a).

23.5.2   Subscriptions

Cable TV, DBS, and IPTV all employ subscriptions as their main revenue models. Some mobile TV and OTT services also adopt the subscription model. Monthly subscriptions can guarantee a certain amount of revenue for the service providers as long as users see sufficient value in the available content to be willing to pay the subscription price. The subscription model works for Netflix, which has a large high-quality library, but it may not work for other OTT services such as YouTube, which offers a broader quality spectrum. Mobile TV such as NOTTV in Japan also adopted the subscription model. However, S-DMB (mobile TV) could not survive in South Korea because an insufficient number of users were willing to pay for the content, presumably because they had free access to appealing content on T-DMB.

23.5.3   Pay per View and Pay to Download

Many online video platforms use the pay-per-view or pay-to-download models that are also employed by VOD service on cable TV and IPTV. Both Amazon and iTunes allow users to pay according to what they choose to download. The advantage of this revenue model is that users do not have the expense of purchasing a monthly subscription. It also allows the providers to price differentiate by introducing premium content initially in one of these models. From a consumer perspective, a disadvantage is that they could end up paying more if they pay separately and without discount.

23.5.4   Freemium

Freemium is a term first coined by venture capitalist Fred Wilson in a blog post in 2006. As described by Anderson (2009), freemium refers to a business model that works by offering core services or products for free, while charging a premium for advanced or special features. It is a hybrid model of 'free to use' and 'pay for premium content' and is described as 'get the basics for free, pay for more' (Osterwalder and Pigneur, 2010). The free service constitutes an incentive to promote the premium services that generate revenue (Kotliar, 2011). For example, Flickr offers a free photo storing service but charges users for additional storage. OTT providers such as Hulu use free content to attract subscribers to premium services on Hulu Plus.

23.5.5   Retail and Revenue Sharing

Some manufacturers try to sell set-top boxes or smart TVs by providing free content to watch or download on their devices. Some may pay the content providers a one-time fee whereas others may share revenues with content providers if users pay for viewing on these devices. Suppliers could also require that users pay a low monthly fee in order to receive updated programs. Another option is to connect users to other content providers and share revenues with those content providers. For instance, Samsung TV may help users to connect to content providers who share revenues with Samsung TV. Another example is Apple TV, which can be connected to a smart TV. Users can pay to view the movies on the iTunes server. Samsung and Apple seem to have similar revenue sharing ratios with their app developers. For example, Samsung's terms state that any revenue collected by Samsung shall be shared by Samsung and the app developers at the rate of 30 percent for Samsung and 70 percent for the app developers. However, Samsung, Apple and other platform providers may agree to alternative revenue sharing arrangements if both parties incorporate such terms in the respective contracts.

23.5.6   Shopping Programs or Channels

Cable TV has had some experience in running shopping channels. Some IPTV providers also try to run shopping channels. Japan's NOTTV tried to offer shopping programs when it started its service, but the approach did not operate very well because of low subscriptions. Other IPTV or OTT service providers try to provide shopping programs on demand. The users can choose to watch the ads of different categories from the on-demand service at their convenience. Customer service and quality of product are both important for this revenue model.

23.6　MINI CASE STUDIES

23.6.1　BT TV (United Kingdom)

As mentioned, telephone companies often provide IPTV services as a part of their bundling packages to attract consumers. British Telecom (BT) in the UK employs a similar strategy. BT launched its IPTV service BT Vision in December 2006. With a set-top box, subscribers of BT could access video-on-demand services through BT Vision (later rebranded as BT TV). In addition, BT has decided to take part in YouView, a partnership forming a new digital distribution platform. The YouView set-top box provides access to and allows recording of the free-to-air digital terrestrial TV services in the UK. Six players including the BBC iPlayer, ITV Player, and BT Vision Player (for BT customers only) are available and provide access to free and selected premium channels.

In an interview conducted on 2 July 2013 by the author with the executive in charge of TV strategy, BT emphasized that allowing viewers to 'get access to the whole world of content' is a way to increase its competitive edge in a world of highly converged content delivery:

> It's actually a potential opportunity for us [to join YouView] because it makes the YouView platform a strong platform. That [being] said, it could disrupt the market for SkyTV, since they have over 10 million subscribers now and we have less than 1 million subscribers. It will drive the users to YouView. And that's a good thing [for us].

Although YouView and BT TV originally had two separate set-top-boxes, they eventually decided to integrate them to allow BT subscribers to access to content available on YouView. BT TV subscribers can now watch programs provided by YouView on BT TV.

23.6.2　KT (South Korea)

According to the OECD (2014), as of June 2013, South Korea's fixed (wired) broadband subscriptions per 100 inhabitants ranked number four in the world, behind Switzerland, the Netherlands, and Denmark. Telcos such as KT, Hanaro Telecom and Dacom all provide IPTV services. KT's IPTV has the largest share in the IPTV market. KT offers three IPTV options: HomeN service, TV portal and IP media (ROA Holdings, 2010). In December 2012, KT launched the Olleh TV smart pack. In essence, the smart pack utilizes a hybrid set-top box that allows viewers to receive content from both IPTV (Olleh TV) and DBS (Skylife). With the smart pack, subscribers no longer need a satellite dish to receive content for DBS. As of January 2013, Olleh TV dominated the South Korean market with roughly 61 percent of the market.

According to a 4 April 2013 interview by the author with KT's IPTV manager, '[although] cable currently offers more programs than ours, we jointly with the satellite company, Skylife, offer high-quality channels. The HD quality we provide is better than cable TV. And we have the most HD channels among all the pay-TV providers in Korea'.

The new service provided by the Olleh TV smart pack offers up to 87 interactive services and 138 channels, of which 22 are of foreign origin. Although cable TV currently has more channels than IPTV, the latter makes up for content via satellite broadcasting. The major difference between IPTV and cable TV is not the content available on these platforms, but the available interactive services such as karaoke. In November 2013, KT's broadband subscribers reached 8.1 million and its IPTV subscribers grew to 4.9 million.

23.6.3   NOTTV (Japan)

Multimedia Broadcasting Inc. (mmbi, Inc.) is a multimedia broadcaster based in Tokyo, Japan. Established in 2009, mmbi, Inc. is also a subsidiary of NTT Docomo of Japan (Bloomberg Business, 2014). A mobile TV service, NOTTV was launched in April 2012. As the parent company of this new mobile service provider, mmbi facilitates NOTTV in providing original content for its channels. NTT Docomo is a major investor of NOTTV and the service is currently only available on NTT Docomo's cell phones. NOTTV offers three real-time channels, where one of the channels offers news from Nippon Television (NTV) and TBS. Meanwhile, the fourth channel serves as a database for videos downloaded by users. This particular channel also emphasizes the time-shifting feature of NOTTV.[5]

Since the launch of its services, NOTTV has attracted approximately 1.5 million paid subscribers. These subscribers contribute 99 percent of the revenue generated by NOTTV. At the beginning of the launch, NOTTV included shopping programs. It also offered additional discounts in subscription fees with purchases from the shopping programs. However, NOTTV explained in an interview on 29 August 2013 that 'there were not enough subscribers to support the shopping programs'. The insufficient number of subscribers eventually led to the cancellation of shopping programs due to the lack of profits.

In terms of content, 50–60 percent of original content acquired by NOTTV is produced by mmbi. It also purchases broadcasting rights for major sporting events. In addition to that, NOTTV also has access to soap operas since mmbi co-produces with Fuji TV to increase its competitiveness. In brief, most of the content broadcast by NOTTV is original, while a limited amount of content is exclusive. Another mobile TV service available to consumers is One Seg, which solely provides programs from terrestrial broadcasters. According to the author's interview with NOTTV, '[we] are not competing [with One Seg] . . . One Seg does not have any strategies because it only broadcasts programs. Instead, YouTube is more like our competitor and [our strategy is that] we want to keep the quality of our content'. Interestingly NOTTV sees YouTube rather than One Seg as its main competitor.

23.6.4   T-DMB vs S-DMB (South Korea)

Between 2005 and 2006 South Korea launched its mobile broadcasting service via digital mobile broadcasting (DMB). It was deployed in two types – terrestrial (T-DMB) and satellite (S-DMB). SK Telecom introduced S-DMB via its subsidiary telecommunications operator, which was the majority owner of TU Media ('TV for you'). Only a few months later in 2005, TU Media, together with other broadcasters such as Korean Broadcasting, started to offer T-DMB. Companies such as Samsung Electronics and LG Electronics had been introducing handsets that supported mobile broadcasting (Paulson, 2006). However, despite the fact that these two types of mobile broadcasting were launched around the same time, observers predicted that T-DMB would become more popular since it was free and its content from terrestrial television included the nation's most popular TV programs (Galbraith, 2005). Due to lack of profitability the S-DMB service was shut down in August 2012.

In an interview conducted by the author with SK Telecom on 5 April 2013, it was explained that S-DMB started in 2005 but only lasted for seven years:

> S-DMB only survived because of the support from SK Telecom. The first reason is the incompatibility with the mobile handsets. Most of the feature phones in Korea are only compatible with T-DMB. And there was not enough incentive for manufacturers to produce devices to match S-DMB since the number of subscribers for S-DMB is too small. The second reason is that most consumers prefer T-DMB over S-DMB, since T-DMB offers five major terrestrial channels for free.

In addition to viewer preferences, the high license fee also played a role in SK Telecom's decision to terminate S-DMB. Furthermore, S-DMB was unable to compete with attractive content from the free channels provided by T-DMB. While SK Telecom sought government intervention to get access to terrestrial content, the regulator did not support this request. Consequently, SK Telecom decided to shut down S-DMB due to its weak performance.

23.6.5   Hulu and Netflix (USA)

Hulu and Netflix are two major OTT video service providers in the USA. As of 2011, Netflix already had more than 20 million subscribers. In 2012, Hulu and Netflix both premiered their own original series within an eight-day period. Netflix started to provide more original content in 2013 with award-winning series such as *House of Cards* and *Orange is the New Black* (Morabito, 2013). Hulu has also released exclusive and original pieces of content in the same year (Fixmer, 2013). The number of subscribers for both services increased rapidly. Founded only in 2010, Hulu already had 3 million subscribers by the end of 2012, reached 4 million by March 2013 (Perez, 2013), and by 2014 claimed 6 million paying 'Hulu Plus' subscribers. Netflix reached a total number of 29 million domestic streaming subscribers and over 1 billion in revenue by the first quarter in 2013 (Cooper, 2013). After rapid growth in the US market, Netflix started to expand internationally and by 2015 claimed more than 60 million streaming customers worldwide.

Taking Hulu as an example, users may view free content on the site, or subscribe to paid, premium content via Hulu Plus. The user-friendly interface and quality content have won Hulu much support from its viewers. Essentially, paid subscribers on Hulu Plus can now enjoy the original and exclusive content at a cost of $8 per month. The same strategy also applied to the original production *House of Cards* on Netflix, where Netflix released all episodes in the series at once. Netflix has kept a strong stance in favor of an advertising-free experience, as emphasized in a 7 August 2013 interview with the author:

It distinguishes us from the advertising supported channels . . . that we do not have to have a million people sit down on Thursday at 8 pm to show that there is value and to get advertisers to support us. For us, it is more about how our members enjoy [the content] over the entire licensed period.

23.6.6   Dailymotion (France)

Dailymotion is a video-sharing website owned by the French telecommunications company Orange. Similar to YouTube, it was launched in 2005. The site now has about 120 million unique monthly visitors and 2.5 billion viewers on a monthly basis (Abboud, 2013). Dailymotion invested in a 600 m³ studio in the middle of Paris in 2013. Since December 2013, people have been able to book appointments at no charge from up to one hour to a day to use the studio for their own content production. While the users assume the property right of these videos produced inside the studio, they must provide the content to Dailymotion in exchange for using the facility. Moreover, Dailymotion also employs the co-production approach. In an interview with Dailymotion conducted by the author on 9 July 2013, Dailymotion explained its role in production: '[Sometimes] we can be sponsors and co-producers, but we do not do that solely for the TV rights. The reason why we co-produce is because we want to let the media environment know that we are able to promote their content by providing the platform'. Although Dailymotion is a French company, only 15 percent of its web traffic comes from France, with its biggest source of traffic being the USA. It therefore also plans to launch production studios in the USA (Digital TV Europe.net, 2013).[6] By doing so, Dailymotion can attract more quality content and provide that to the viewers.

In addition to establishing a studio and co-producing original content, Dailymotion also takes actions against the issue of piracy. According to Giuseppe de Martino (interviewed 9 July 2013), users do not feel safe to upload original content if it is susceptible to Internet piracy. Therefore, Dailymotion takes the initiative to implement a safeguard mechanism by 'fingerprinting' the original content. Although it is not a legal obligation, Dailymotion is willing to invest to protect the content. As of 2015, content was available in 18 languages and 35 localized versions.

23.7   CONCLUSION

This chapter summarized ten business strategies and six revenue models for converged video services such as IPTV, mobile TV and OTT services. The strategies and models used are related to the external environment and the internal resources of the providers. Among them, bundling, flexible pricing and strategic co-opetition are the most common strategies. With regard to exclusive and original content strategies, all but the largest of the converged services face financial limitations when it comes to adopting the strategy. Their economic scale and number of subscribers need to be taken into consideration. If the newly emerging media platform is unable to pay for copyrighted content, there is very little chance that the content will be sold or made available to the new media platform. In order to reach larger audiences, the new media platforms need to re-package their content to attract viewers. For instance, Netflix deliberately uses complete release (binge viewing) but Amazon prefers to provide the new content weekly in order to stimulate discussion among viewers and prevent the subscribers from terminating the service (Sharma, 2013).

Multi-screen strategies are contingent on the cost of obtaining copyrights and applicable license fees. Some IPTV operators are afraid of the high fees for the programs, since they do not see the extra revenue generated by multi-screen services. So they hesitate to provide all the content via multi-screen services. Disruptive innovation does not work for all the converged video services. Usually, the new entrants will consider adopting disruptive innovation tactics first. The incumbent tends to be a follower of the disruptive innovation in order to maintain its advantage in the market. SoLoMo also works for some converged services, but it does not fit very well for global players such as Netflix. In recent years, big data analytics has been widely employed by converged services to help the converged video services target the right users and provide the right content and services.

With regard to the revenue models, advertisements and subscriptions are sometimes used as alternative options although they can also be employed jointly in a hybrid revenue model. Most of the users do not want to pay for online content. For mobile TV, since more and more users have access to the free content via apps, it is very difficult to adopt a pay model. Therefore, the ads-funded model is very common for some OTT video services. For a big player like Netflix, large subscriber numbers can provide support in buying or producing compelling or original content. Therefore, Netflix can rely on the subscription model only and market the absence of advertising to its competitive advantage. For new services, freemium is a good model for attracting users who might only want to watch the basic content for free. Once they find the premium content interesting, they might be willing to pay for some content that is really appealing to them. Revenue sharing is a common model for many converged video services. However, since the media ecosystem is dynamic, the outcome of a business strategy applied in relation to the converged video services needs to be evaluated regularly. There is no perfect business strategy, and any strategy adopted has to be used at the right time, under the right conditions and in a smart way.

NOTES

1. According to the Audiovisual Media Services Directive (AVMSD) of the European Union, linear video content refers to television broadcasts while non-linear content refers to the on-demand services. More specifically, linear service means that the service is for simultaneous viewing on the basis of a program schedule. Non-linear service means that programs are viewed 'at the moment chosen by the user and at his individual request on the basis of a catalogue of programs selected by the media service provider' (EU, 2010).
2. Personal communication with X.J. Wang, 12 September 2013.
3. See YouView, accessed 3 May 2015 at http://www.youview.com/.
4. The Chinese government only granted seven OTT TV licenses to seven big TV groups. Other OTT TV-like players that do not have OTT TV licenses are referred to as video websites (or online video services). In fact, they are more flexible and dynamic than the seven OTT TV license holders.
5. Time shifting is the recording of programming to a server to be viewed or listened to at a time more convenient to the user. It has the ability to play back recorded programming by skipping commercials (*Online Interactive Television Dictionary*, accessed 11 June 2015 at http://www.itvdictionary.com/personal_tv.html).
6. Google did the same in Los Angeles to assist in the creation of YouTube content. See 'Google opens LA YouTube studio free to content creators', *Deadline*, 12 July 2013, accessed 9 May 2015 at http://www.deadline.com/2013/07/google-youtube-space-la/.

REFERENCES

Abboud, L. (2013), 'Video site Dailymotion working on partnerships in U.S. and Asia', *Reuters*, 11 December, accessed 2 May 2015 at http://www.reuters.com/article/2013/12/11/us-orange-dailymotion-idUSBRE9BA0Q620131211.

ABI Research (2013), 'Over 60 percent growth in worldwide over-the-top video revenue in 2012', *ABIresearch*, 10 April, accessed 2 May 2015 at https://www.abiresearch.com/press/over-60-growth-in-worldwide-over-the-top-video-rev.

Anderson, C. (2009), *Free: The Future of a Radical Price*, New York: Hyperion.

Baden-Fuller, C and M.S. Morgan (2010), 'Business models as models', *Long Range Planning*, **43** (2–3), 156–71.

Baldwin, T.F., D.S. McVoy and C. Steinfield (1996), *Convergence: Integrating Media, Information and Communication*, Thousand Oaks, CA: Sage Publications.

Bauer, J.M. (2014), 'Platforms, systems competition, and innovation: Reassessing the foundations of communications policy', *Telecommunications Policy*, **38** (8–9), 662–73.

Bauer, J.M., I.S. Ha and D. Saugstrup (2007), 'Mobile television: Challenges of advanced service design', *Communications of the Association for Information Systems*, **20** (39), 621–31.

Bauer, J.M., M.P.C. Weijnen, A.L. Turk and P.M. Herder (2003), 'Delineating the scope of convergence in infrastructures', in W.A.H. Thissen and P.M. Herder (eds), *Critical Infrastructures: State of the Art in Research and Application*, Boston, Dordrecht and London: Kluwer, pp. 209–31.

Beach, J. (2012a), 'OTT video ads market to reach US$ 13bn by 2017', *IP&TV News*, 12 October, accessed 2 May 2015 at http://www.iptv-news.com/2012/10/ott-video-ads-market-to-reach-us-13bn-by-2017/.

Beach, J. (2012b), 'Multiscreen offerings "dramatically increasing" in Europe and Asia', *IP&TV News*, 7 December, accessed 2 May 2015 at http://www.iptv-news.com/2012/12/multiscreen-offerings-dramatically-increasing-in-europe-and-asia/.

Bengtsson, M. and S. Kock (2000), '"Coopetition" in business networks – to cooperate and compete simultaneously', *Industrial Marketing Management*, **29** (5), 411–26.

Berman, S.J., B. Battino and K. Feldman (2011), 'New business models for emerging media and entertainment revenue opportunities', *Strategy & Leadership*, **39** (3), 44–53.

Bloomberg Business (2014), 'Company overview of mmbi, Inc.', *Bloomberg Businessweek*, 21 December, accessed 28 June 2014 at http://investing.businessweek.com/research/stocks/private/snapshot.asp?privcapId=143764941.

Bouwman, H., Z. Meng, P. van der Duin and S. Limonard (2008), 'A business model for IPTV service: A dynamic framework', *Info*, **10** (3), 2–38.

Brandenburger, A.M. and B.J. Nalebuff (1996), *Co-opetition*, New York: Currency Doubleday.

Bulygo, A. (2013), 'How Netflix uses analytics to select movies, create content, and make multimillion dollar decisions', *Kissmetrics*, accessed 2 May 2015 at http://blog.kissmetrics.com/how-netflix-uses-analytics/.

Carr, D. (2013), 'Giving viewers what they want', *The New York Times*, 24 February, accessed 2 May 2015 at http://www.nytimes.com/2013/02/25/business/media/for-house-of-cards-using-big-data-to-guarantee-its-popularity.html?_r=0.

Christensen, C.M. (1997), *The Innovator's Dilemma: When New Technologies Cause Great Firms to Fail*, Boston, MA: Harvard Business School Press.

Cooper, C. (2013), 'Netflix shares explode as revenue tops $1 billion', *CNET*, 22 April, accessed 2 June 2014 at http://news.cnet.com/8301-1023_3-57580785-93/netflix-shares-explode-asarevenue-tops-$1-billion/.

Cryan, D. (2012), 'US audiences to pay for more online movies in 2012 than for physical videos', *IHS iSuppli* [press release], 22 March, accessed 2 June 2014 at http://www.isuppli.com/media-research/news/pages/us-audiences-to-pay-more-for-online-movies-in-2012-than-for-physical-videos.aspx.

Digital TV Europe.net (2013), 'Dailymotion plans studio expansion', *Digital TV Europe*, 12 December, accessed 29 May 2014 at http://www.digitaltveurope.net/131231/dailymotion-plans-studio-expansion/.

European Union (EU) (2010), *Audiovisual Media Services Directive*, accessed 29 December 2015 at http://eur-lex.europa.eu/legal-content/EN/ALL/?uri=CELEX:32010L0013.

Evens, T. (2010), 'Value networks and changing business models for the digital television industry', *Journal of Media Business Studies*, **7** (4), 41–58.

Fixmer, A. (2013), 'Hulu targets binge viewers with full original series', *Bloomberg Business*, 1 August, accessed 28 June 2014 at http://www.bloomberg.com/news/2013-07-31/hulu-targets-binge-viewers-with-full-release-of-original-series.html.

Frieden, R. (2012), 'Threats and opportunities from next generation television', *Intermedia*, **40** (1), 18–25.

Galbraith, M. (2005), 'T-DMB takes on S-DMB in Korea', *Telecom Asia*, 15 April.

Gambardella, A. and A.M. McGahan (2010), 'Business-model innovation: General purpose technologies and their implications for industry architecture', *Long Range Planning*, **43** (2–3), 262–71.

Gao, Q. (2013), 'Big data and how to use it', *Winwin*, 25–26 April, accessed 11 June 2015 at http://www.huawei.com/en/static/HW-259980.pdf.

Greenstein, S. and T. Khanna (1997), 'What does industry convergence mean?', in D.B. Yoffie (ed.), *Competition in the Age of Digital Convergence*, Boston, MA: Harvard Business School Press, pp. 201–26.

Huang, R. (2012), 'Pay TV operators need multiscreen offering to survive', *ZDNet*, 21 June, accessed 28 June 2014 at http://www.zdnet.com/pay-tv-operators-need-multi-screen-offering-to-survive-2062305198/.

ITU (2013), *Measuring the Information Society 2013*, accessed 2 June 2014 at http://www.itu.int/en/ITU-D/Statistics/Documents/publications/mis2013/MIS2013_without_Annex_4.pdf.

Jenkins, H. (2001), 'Convergence? I diverge', *MIT Technology Review*, accessed 5 May 2015 at http://www.technologyreview.com/article/401042/convergence-i-diverge/.

Jenkins, H. (2006), *Convergence Culture: Where Old and New Media Collide*, New York and London: New York University Press.

Kim, P. (2009), 'Internet Protocol TV in perspective: A matrix of continuity and innovation', *Television & New Media*, **10** (6), 536–45.

Kotliar, S. (2011), *Freemium as a Business Model for Mobile Video*, unpublished Master of Science thesis, Royal Institute of Technology, Sweden.

Krattenmaker, T.G. (1996), 'The Telecommunications Act of 1996', *Federal Communications Law Journal*, **49** (1), 1–49.

Kumar, A. (2007), *Mobile TV: DVB-H, DMB, 3G Systems and Rich Media Applications*, Oxford, UK: Focal Press.

Latzer, M. (1998), 'European mediamatics policies: Coping with convergence and globalization', *Telecommunications Policy*, **22** (6), 457–66.

Latzer, M. (2009), 'Convergence revisited: Toward a modified pattern of communications governance', *Convergence: The International Journal of Research into New Media Technologies Online*, **15** (4), 411–26.

Lee, S. and D.K. Kwak (2005), 'TV in your cell phone: The introduction of Digital Multimedia Broadcasting (DMB) in Korea', paper presented at the Research Conference on Communications, Information and Internet Policy (TPRC), Arlington, VA, accessed 23 August 2015 at http://konkuk.ac.kr/~cyim/dtv/DMBintroduction.pdf.

Mocerino, J. (2011), 'One last thing: Bandwidth goes over the top on 4G LTE networks', *Communications Technology*, **28** (12), 5.

Morabito, A. (2013), 'Netflix content chief plays cards in bid to broaden reach', *Broadcasting & Cable*, **143** (4), 30.

Mustafa, R. and H. Werthner (2011), 'Business models and business strategy: Phenomenon of explicitness', *International Journal of Global Business and Competitiveness*, **6** (1), 14–29.

OECD (2013), *OECD Communication Outlook*, accessed 28 June 2014 at http://www.oecd.org/sti/broadband/communications-outlook.htm.

OECD (2014), 'OECD broadband statistics update', accessed 2 June 2014 at http://www.oecd.org/internet/broadband-statistics-update.htm.

Oppenheim, R. (2012), 'The video stream rises', *Searcher*, **20** (8), 16–19.

Osterwalder, A. and Y. Pigneur (2010), *Business Model Generation: A Handbook for Visionaries, Game Changers and Challengers*, Hoboken, NJ: John Wiley & Sons, Inc.

Park, Y., Y. Chen and M. Ueda (2009), 'Business models for IPTV service; integrated or platform?', in *Proceedings of the IEEE Ninth Annual International Symposium on Applications and the Internet (SAINT'09)*, 20–24 July, Bellevue, WA, pp. 216–19.

Paulson, L.D. (2006), 'TV comes to the mobile phone', *Computer*, **39** (4), 13–16.

Perez, S. (2013), 'Hulu announces adding 1 million paid subscribers in Q1 2013; streamed over 1 billion videos', *Techcrunch*, 30 April, accessed 2 June 2014 at http://techcrunch.com/2013/04/30/hulu-announces-adding-1-million-subscribers-in-q1-2013-streamed-over-1-billion-videos/.

Picard, R.G. (2000), 'Changing business models of online content services: Their implications for multimedia and other content producers', *The International Journal on Media Management*, **2** (2), 60–68.

PR Newswire (2013), 'Netflix declares binge watching is the new normal', *PRNewswire*, 13 December, accessed 2 June 2014 at http://www.prnewswire.com/news-releases/netflix-declares-binge-watching-is-the-new-normal-235713431.html.

PRWEB (2014), 'Worldwide IPTV subscriber market, 1Q 2014 new research report available at Sandlerresearch.org' [press release], *PRWEB*, 29 March, accessed 28 June 2014 at http://www.prweb.com/releases/worldwide-iptv-subscriber/market-1q-2014/prweb11713871.htm.

ROA Holdings (2010), *Challenges for Korean IPTV Industry*, accessed 2 June 2014 at http://global.roaholdings.com/report/research_view.html?type=country&num=61.

Seddon, P. and G. Lewis (2003), 'Strategy and business models: What's the difference?', in *Proceedings from the 7th Pacific Asia Conference on Information Systems*, Adelaide, South Australia.

Seo, J. (2012), 'Free video-to-mobile goes into the black', *Korea Joongang Daily*, 1 August, accessed 2 June 2014 at http://koreajoongangdaily.joins.com/news/article/Article.aspx?aid=2957174.

Sharma, A. (2013), 'Comparing the online TV pioneers: Netflix v. Amazon', *The Wall Street Journal*, 4 November, accessed 2 June 2014 at http://blogs.wsj.com/corporate-intelligence/2013/11/04/comparing-the-online-tv-pioneers-netflix-v-amazon/?KEYWORDS=netflix.

Sharma, A. and A. Cheney (2013), 'Netflix makes some history with showing at Emmys', *The Wall Street Journal*, 23 September, accessed 2 June 2014 at http://online.wsj.com/news/articles/SB10001424052702303759604579092061505560526.

Shaw, J. (2014), 'Why "big data" is a big deal', *Harvard Magazine*, March–April, accessed 28 June 2014 at http://harvardmagazine.com/2014/03/why-big-data-is-a-big-deal.

Shin, D.H. (2009), 'An empirical investigation of a modified technology acceptance model of IPTV', *Behaviour & Information Technology*, **28** (4), 361–72.

Stremersch, S. and G.J. Tellis (2002), 'Strategic bundling of products and prices: A new synthesis for marketing', *Journal of Marketing*, **66** (1), 55–72.

Venturini, F. (2011), *Bringing TV to Life, Issue II: The Race to Dominate the Future of TV*, New York: Accenture.

Waterman, D., R. Sherman and S.W. Ji (2013), 'The economics of online television: Industry development, aggregation, and "TV Everywhere"', *Telecommunications Policy*, **37** (9), 725–36.

White, R. (2006), 'Treasure tube', *Film Quarterly*, **60** (2), 3.

Wright, D. (2013), 'Virgin Media bridges to OTT TV Anywhere', *TVB Europe*, 37.

Xia, X. and J. Zhu (2014), 'The study of O2O business model development strategy in SMEs', *International Journal of Business and Social Science*, **5** (9).

24. The economics of virtual worlds
Isaac Knowles and Edward Castronova

24.1 INTRODUCTION

Virtual economies refer to the systems of production, distribution, and trade that have emerged in online spaces, especially virtual worlds. Their origins can be traced to the 1970s, when videogame developers first gave players the ability to play and trade with one another in the same virtual world. As the number of people with Internet connections increased, and as computer power advanced, the populations of virtual worlds rose along with the size and complexity of the economies in those worlds (Figure 24.1).

Virtual economies began to receive substantial academic and media attention in the early 2000s after Castronova (2001) valued the economy of Norrath in the game *EverQuest* at $135 million. In the last five years, the proliferation of free-to-play games on mobile, Facebook, and other platforms has vastly increased the number of environments in which players purchase and trade virtual goods and services.[1] Trade in virtual assets like virtual currencies and items has become a commonplace activity in games, as has the exchange of these assets for real-world currency.

In this chapter we review the development of and the research surrounding these economies. We examine how the real and virtual economies interact with one another and the issues such interactions create for virtual world operators. We discuss why the industry has evolved new business models in order to deal with the 'real money trade', that is, the market in which players trade real money with each other and with third parties in exchange for virtual goods and services. We also look at the economic research resulting from the study of virtual economies.

Academic work in the area of virtual economies began in the early 2000s. The key takeaway from this work is not that virtual economies and real economies behave in the same way – for that is debatable (Williams, 2010). Instead, what economic research in virtual worlds has taught us is that economic agents behave similarly, whether the economy they act in is real or virtual. That said, the economics of games and virtual worlds remains a niche area of study. Scholars have not had an easy time drawing the links between real and virtual economic behavior in a way that makes the phenomenon of virtual economies interesting to the broader economics profession. However, as production begins to move out of the real world and into the virtual one, it seems inevitable to us that economists and policy-makers will need to have a better understanding of the economic motivations for entering and exiting virtual economies and their associated virtual worlds.

The line between work and play can become rather fuzzy inside of virtual words, and this highlights the complexity of their motivations for production and consumption. Other interesting, more practical questions remain unanswered as well. For example, how might virtual world and video game operators compete with one another by setting

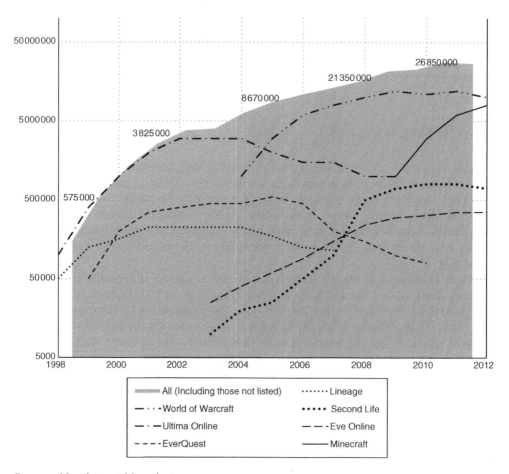

Sources: Mmodata.net, Mmo-sheet.com.

Figure 24.1   Number of residents in selected virtual worlds, 1998–2012

policies inside their virtual economies? What makes virtual assets attractive to players, beyond their real-world value? Untangling those knotty issues remains a preoccupation of so-called 'virtual economists'.

The phrase 'virtual economy' has become an overloaded term in a world where goods, services, and the means to trade them are increasingly virtual. One particularly important development has been the rise of virtual currencies such as Bitcoin and Litecoin – so-called 'crypto-currencies', which are not backed by any government. Users trade crypto-currencies on peer-to-peer networks in exchange for goods and services. Although this is an important development in its own right, in this chapter we will focus exclusively on economies inside and surrounding video games and virtual worlds (for more information on the proliferation of non-state-controlled currencies see Castronova, 2014).

This chapter is organized as follows. In the next section, we review the origins of virtual economies, the development of which eventually led to the fundamental edifice of virtual economic design: the faucet-drain system. In section 24.3, we look at how virtual economies and real economies interact with one another. We describe the real money trade and discuss how it led to the creation of the free-to-play business model. We also discuss the issue of virtual property. Section 24.4 discusses the available research on virtual economies, and section 24.5 concludes.

24.2   THE ORIGINS OF MODERN VIRTUAL ECONOMIES

For about 30 years, virtual economies were exclusively the province of video games, and it is important to understand the changing role that economies have played in games. In a sense, a great number of video games are some form of economy: Mario must obtain mushrooms and flowers to grow stronger and hedge against the risk of death, Sonic the Hedgehog must collect rings to survive any damaging encounters, and the Master Chief (of the popular *Halo* franchise) must gather and expend weapons and ammo to cull the alien hordes. Some single-player games even have simulated markets, where players can use the currency they gather from the game world to buy items from a game's non-player characters (NPCs).[2] But when we speak of a virtual economy, we are particularly speaking of the systems of trade, production, and distribution that arise when players can exchange items and currency with one another within the same virtual world.

What, then, are virtual worlds? While definitions can differ in small details, we use the term 'virtual world' to signify any persistent online space in which two or more people can interact to some extent with one another and with that space. Key terms here are 'space' and 'persistent'. By *space*, we mean anything that players treat as if it were a physical environment. So worlds can be 2D or 3D, but they can also be text based, where the program describes the world to the user and the user issues typed commands to the program to move through the world. By *persistent*, we mean that the world exists on a server regardless of whether any players are logged into it, and that the changes that players make to the world are not reset when they log out or quit the game entirely. Finally, as in many video games, players are represented by avatars – objects that are usually humanoid in form – by which they interact with the virtual world (see Bartle, 2003, pp. 1–3).

The first virtual economies existed in so-called multi-user dungeons, or MUDs, which appeared in the late 1970s (ibid., pp. 4–7; Castronova, 2003). MUDs were a kind of role-playing game in which players explored, fought in, and learned about a magical, fantasy world. These games were frequently modeled after board games like *Dungeons & Dragons*. Early MUDs were text-based virtual worlds, and were usually hosted by a server on a university campus. The developers were students at the university, as were the players. MUDs could host a limited number of concurrent users, and were also limited in the overall number of players; nevertheless, they were persistent virtual worlds. As in single-player role-playing games, MUD players are rewarded treasure, or 'loot', for their exploration and for winning battles against monsters and other ne'er-do-wells inside the game. The loot might be a more powerful sword, or a magic potion that temporarily improves the avatar's ability to slay monsters. The player might also receive a sum of virtual currency, which he or she can use to buy items from NPCs.

Early MUD developers introduced trade into their games as a way to make the fantasy worlds more immersive, but it had unexpected consequences. When a new MUD was released to the playing public, the first players would enter the game and begin slaying dragons and acquiring currency. They would then exchange their rewards from questing with one another. Later, new players would join the game, and because the first generation of players had created so much virtual wealth, they could sell some of their older equipment to these new players. The prices were low enough that some new players preferred to buy from older players rather than doing the work necessary to get the equipment on their own. The old players would pass on their knowledge about the game to the new players as well. New players used this human capital and 'virtual physical' capital to improve the rate at which they moved through the virtual world. They experienced greater overall productivity compared to the earlier generation of players. By the time the third or fourth generation of new users joined, the game was trivial, because the most powerful items were available in large quantities for very low prices to new players.

MUD developers, intending only to introduce an engaging game mechanic – trade – had unwittingly introduced economic growth! But while economic growth is always appreciated in real life, it can mean disaster in a video game as it trivializes the game, leading players to quit. The only solution MUD developers had for the problem at the time was to completely reset the game and wipe all player inventories, so that everyone had to start over again from square one.[3]

Another issue that could arise, either because of unforeseen imbalances or bugs in the game code, was that players could sometimes generate enormous amounts of in-game currency quickly. These exploits, if not quickly detected and remedied, could result in extreme levels of inflation. In many cases, the only solution was, again, to completely reset the game.

Though technology progressed, these basic problems of virtual economies were not remedied until 1997 with the release of Origin's *Ultima Online* (*UO*), the first widely popular, massively multi-player online role-playing game, or MMO. Since it was developed by a major gaming studio and took advantage of the latest technologies, the world of *UO* was much larger than that of any of its predecessors (Bartle, 2003, pp. 21–3), as was the size of the player population, which was in the thousands per server. To solve the problem of economic growth and inflation, the developers introduced a variety of item and currency sinks into the game. For example, the equipment that players used would depreciate over time, requiring repairs that could only be made by NPCs and only in exchange for some of the player's virtual currency. NPCs would also offer players fixed sums of virtual currency in exchange for any quantity of a given good. The game company also introduced the idea of big-ticket money sinks. Players were granted an item that conferred an important advantage (such as a horse that greatly increased their avatar's speed), at the expense of large amounts of virtual currency (Simpson, 2000).

UO developers learned to take advantage of the fact that they could control the sources of items and currency as well as the sinks. They were able to finely tune the rate at which items and currency flowed in and out of the system at any time, given the overall patterns of player behavior. If that behavior changed in a way that caused the amount of currency or items of a particular type to begin to rise above a certain threshold, they need merely dial down the rate at which players received items and currency, or dial up the rate at which those assets exited. This system of management became known as the faucet-drain system. While the manner in which the drains and faucets are manifested may differ between virtual worlds, that paradigm underlies the management of every single virtual economy that exists (Simpson, 2000; Bartle, 2003, p. 310).[4]

24.3 THE REAL MONEY TRADE – HOW THE REAL AND VIRTUAL ECONOMY INTERACT

There is a curious tension in the goals of every video game player. On the one hand, players enter a game in order to be challenged. They are apparently willing to pay money for developers to place obstacles in their way as they work toward some final goal – saving the princess, slaying the demon, building a city, and so forth. On the other hand, those same players are willing to use any means necessary to 'game the game' – to skirt rules and exploit coding flaws for an advantage that makes finishing game tasks easier. In games where players can trade, this tension often manifests in the phenomenon known as the 'real money trade', or RMT (Castronova, 2003, and 2005, Chapter 7).

RMT refers to any activity in which players exchange real world currency for virtual assets and services (Heeks, 2009). Players may also sell entire game accounts for money. Players typically agree on a price for the assets either by chatting inside the game or by meeting on a third-party site, such as eBay. After the money changes hands in the real world, the two players log in to the game and exchange the associated virtual assets. Depending on the game, the size of large transactions can be remarkable. One hundred gold pieces might sell for $20, a legendary sword for $200, and an entire game account – including currency, sword, and one or more high-level characters – could go for $2000 or more.[5]

The RMT can take place in a primary market or a secondary market. Primary RMT refers to any RMT in which a virtual world company sells virtual assets directly to players. Secondary RMT refers to any RMT that takes place between players (Lehtiniemi, 2007). Whatever the form, firms either sanction RMT or they do not. This is summarized in Table 24.1.

Table 24.1   Sanctions and virtual trade

	Sanctioned	Unsanctioned
Primary	Virtual world owner sells virtual assets directly to player. Modern examples: *Farmville, World of Warcraft, Habbo*	No known instances where items were sold by a virtual world owner (or its employees) directly to players against game world policy
Secondary	Virtual world owner does not oppose RMT between players and/or third parties. Rare. Notable virtual worlds: *Second Life, Entropia Universe*	RMT between players and third parties that is officially forbidden by the associated virtual world owner. Modern examples: *World of Warcraft, EVE Online*, most Facebook games

24.3.1   The Problem with RMT

During the 2000s, RMT was an important issue for virtual worlds. There are several reasons for this. First, when large-scale virtual worlds were first released in the late 1990s, the end user licensing agreements (EULAs) – to which all consumers had to give assent before entering the world – usually stipulated that the game publisher was the sole owner of any virtual goods that players produced or used in the game.[6] RMT was considered a violation of property rights by the game publisher because people who did not own virtual property were making money from its sale. In the case of services like speed-leveling, sharing account information was also against the EULA.

Second, because game publishers did not usually sanction RMT, exchange of goods required money to change hands first in the real world before it could change hands in the virtual one. Thus, buyers of virtual assets were at the mercy of sellers to follow through on their side of the bargain. Players would often hand out credit card information to pay for virtual assets or services, and then later find that they were victims of identity theft. In other cases, players would pay for a good or service and the seller would keep the money but never deliver. If the player handed over their account for character-improvement services like speed-leveling, they might never get the account back.

Players who were victims of fraud often took their complaints to game companies. Usually, the companies could not prove that the player had not simply been a victim of an unprovoked hacking, and so representatives had to spend time recovering accounts for players. RMT thus substantially increased customer service costs (Castronova, 2005, Chapter 7). Fraud due to RMT remains an especially salient issue.[7]

A third reason for the issue's salience was that many players could not afford RMT, or were otherwise unhappy with its existence. RMT was thought by many players and developers to impinge upon the so-called 'magic circle', a barrier between the real and the virtual worlds in which players are supposedly ensconced when logged into the game. This violation of the wall between fantasy and reality reduced the value of the game for many players (Castronova, 2006a). Detractors also saw RMT buyers as cheaters because they paid outside contractors either for virtual goods or for other services that granted 'unearned' advantages. Allowed to run rampant, RMT gave many players an excuse to quit the game. At that time, the industry made most of its revenues through subscriptions, so early cancellation was a major concern.

Fourth, unchecked RMT made virtual economies difficult or impossible to manage using the faucet-drain system. RMT encourages sellers to specialize in gathering currency as quickly as possible. The influx of additional currency from these sellers can lead to an increase in the amount of money in the virtual economy relative to the number of goods and services. This leads to inflation, and only the incomes of RMT buyers can keep up with that inflation. Under normal circumstances, a game company facing inflation would simply widen the sinks so that more money would exit the virtual economy. However, in the case of RMT such a policy response adversely affects players who are not supplementing their virtual incomes. Thus, operators who combat inflation in the normal fashion face the ire of their players, while operators who do not act face the possibility of hyperinflation and economic collapse (Simpson, 2000). In either case, RMT can lead to player unhappiness and mass exodus.

Despite these issues, however, the total effect of RMT on a game and its profits are unclear for several reasons. First, the presence of RMT may cause non-buyers to leave, but it may also cause buyers to stay longer. On the other hand, the accelerated advancement of RMT buyers might cause them to leave sooner. Second, RMT may cause the number of goods and services in a game economy to rise faster than they otherwise would; that is, it may cause players to gain virtual wealth at an undesirable rate. As we discussed before, this can decrease the player's effective lifetime in a game because they can get through the content more quickly. Third, although players who feel that RMT is cheating may quit, other players may be attracted to a game because of the availability of RMT (Huhh, 2009). Fourth, to the extent that online games depend on social network externalities for success, the existence and extent of RMT will affect the value of the game for all players. Finally, if a game is so challenging that it turns players off or causes them to quit, RMT may reduce that challenge and attract more players, without requiring more expensive work by the game operator in an effort to rebalance the game.

Needless to say, these are highly complex and dynamic variables to consider and balance, and it is unclear how deeply game operators analyze the issue when forming policy responses to deal with RMT.[8] One thing is certain: the difficulties and intrigue of fighting RMT (or not) gave many virtual world developers pause to consider other approaches to the phenomenon, and to their revenue model.

24.3.2   Gold Farming

Early RMT was supplied by a domestic, cottage industry: Western sellers serviced Western buyers in the EU and the USA, and Chinese and Korean sellers serviced their Eastern counterparts (Dibbell, 2007). The situation in the West changed radically with the release of Blizzard-Activision's *World of Warcraft* (*WoW*) in 2004. With total sub-scribing players peaking at over 12 million, *WoW* players represent a significant demand for RMT. Meeting this demand became the business goal of so-called 'gold farms' (Ahmed et al., 2009).

Predominantly based in China, gold farms are businesses that industrialized the process of producing virtual assets for sale on the RMT market. Employees work in shifts, producing assets, ferrying them to buyers, advertising wares, and so forth. Gold farms sell virtual assets directly to players or through intermediaries (ibid.; Heeks, 2009).

The rise of gold farming is notable for two reasons. First, it greatly exacerbated many of the problems RMT created for virtual world operators. By industrializing it, gold farmers drove down the price of virtual currency, making it affordable to far more players than the cottage industry could have achieved. This brought the problem of RMT to a head, and forced the industry to evolve to deal with it in new ways. Second, gold farming represents an important new source of employment for many developing nations. As outlined by Lehdonvirta and Ernkvist (2011), gold farming and similar services represent an important new industry whose cost structure is well suited for poor and developing nations. Gold farming operations require a small initial technology investment, but the main element of the business is cheap labor. By having low-wage workers conduct resource-extraction tasks in the game for eight-hour shifts, the gold farming business can rapidly acquire a large stock of in-game resources. Those resources can then be sold via the Internet at considerable profit to players from high-wage countries.

24.3.3 Modern Approaches to RMT

As early as 2000, there were some virtual world operators that tried to integrate RMT into their virtual economies. These attempts met with mixed success. *Habbo*, formerly *Habbo Hotel*, run by Finnish firm Sulake, is one of the few early, successful virtual worlds that integrated primary RMT. *Habbo* is not a game world, like *UO* or Sony's *Star Wars: Galaxies*. Rather, it is a virtual world built for socialization and chat. Residents buy items from the game developers and trade with one another in order to furnish their rooms in a large, virtual motel. They can then invite others to view their room and socialize. Because Sulake does not need to maintain a balance between a game's economy and the challenges that the game provides, RMT is not as much of an issue for them. Nevertheless, the company has had to develop unique ways to maintain the value of virtual assets and currency, and is a benchmark of success for modern non-game virtual worlds.[9]

Linden Lab's *Second Life* allows RMT on both primary and secondary markets. The company sells the virtual world's currency, the Linden, at a fixed rate of exchange to create a price floor, but residents and other third parties can trade with one another at prices above that floor. Linden Lab guarantees the transaction and takes a small cut. Linden Lab also sells and leases virtual land to residents. The remainder of the economy of *Second Life* is entirely player driven. Residents must create objects using the toolset provided by Linden Lab. Those items can then be bought and sold through Linden Lab or via another third-party broker. Since Linden dollars are only created when players buy them from the company, RMT does not create major problems for *Second Life*. Despite early hype, however, *Second Life* and similar worlds like MindArk's *Entropia Universe* did not enjoy the success of contemporary, game-based virtual worlds.

More recently, game companies have begun to experiment with market-based solutions to the RMT problem. In CCP's *EVE Online*, players may purchase a virtual item called a Pilot License Extension (PLEX) using real money. One PLEX grants its user a one-month extension to his or her subscription ($14.99 as of June 2014). The player who purchases the PLEX may, if he or she chooses, sell it to another player in exchange for *EVE Online*'s virtual currency, the ISK. This allows players who have extra cash a way to obtain additional ISK from players who have a surfeit of that currency, and who may wish to use it to purchase a month of access to the game.[10]

24.3.4 Free-to-play Games

One particularly important response to the RMT was the rise of the video game revenue model known as free-to-play, or F2P. F2P publishers give away some or all of the game content to players. The players may then purchase additional virtual goods and services from the publisher. Some publishers sell these goods and services directly in exchange for cash, while others prefer to sell so-called 'hard currency' for cash. Players then use this hard currency to buy items and services from the company (see Lehdonvirta, 2009; Hamari and Lehdonvirta, 2010).

There are a few early, game-based virtual worlds that sold virtual assets directly to players. Korean firm Nexon's *MapleStory* was released in 2003 and remains quite successful. Korean and other Chinese game companies in general demonstrate much less hostility toward RMT than their Western counterparts, and embraced the phenomenon early on. Though invented by Western game developers, the F2P business model for games exploded in countries like China and South Korea (Wang et al., 2012). This model makes sense in countries where a $40 upfront cost for a game client and a $10 to $15 monthly subscription – common in the EU and USA in the late 1990s and early 2000s – represent a substantial chunk of the average disposable personal income.

In the West, and with notable exceptions, F2P was a very small part of the video game industry until 2007, when Apple released the iPhone and Facebook released its Facebook platform. These two application development platforms aided the rise of the F2P industry in wealthier countries. Both platforms made it possible to market a game to a large number of people across a broad range of tastes, gaming experience, and skill levels. At the time of this writing, common F2P platforms like tablets and mobile phones are the only areas of the video game industry that are currently projected to experience substantial growth in revenues.[11] While there are many factors contributing to this growth, including the age of the last console generation and the growth in the number of people owning mobile devices, it is clear that F2P is an important innovation.

What has this to do with virtual economies? As mentioned, F2P often depends for revenues on players purchasing a hard currency directly from the developer. This business model is a response to the RMT issue, and it has led to a proliferation in the number of virtual economies and associated virtual currencies. The real consequences of this substantial shift of real currency into virtual scrip – already a hallmark of more traditional industries like airlines and their miles programs – are as yet poorly understood (Castronova, 2014). Especially in games where trade remains possible between players, the realization of gains from trade may mean that there is a large amount of important economic activity that is going unnoticed and unaccounted for in games.

24.3.5 Virtual Property

Although it is clear that goods and services in virtual economies have economic value, the question of 'whose value?' remains open. From the earliest legal writing on virtual economies, the question of property rights has remained central (Lastowka and Hunter, 2004). As we will see in a moment, courts have not been especially helpful in clarifying these issues. As a result, the legal status of virtual property remains fuzzy.

Virtual property is an intangible property, much like a URL or a brand name. Virtual property physically exists in the form of sequences of bits in databases on hard drives. Yet it is manifested to people, and used by them, in ways that are completely analogous to tangible property. As a result, virtual property evokes several legal metaphors whose implications conflict.

A game can be viewed as a document authored by the designer, in which case the virtual property within it is the intellectual property of the designer. Copyright issues are evoked. But a game can also be viewed as a forest. The designer plants the trees and allows ordinary people to go among them, for a fee. According to a labor theory of property, a man who gathers wood there owns the wood. It would follow that goods in games belong to the people who make them, that is, the people who use the software to create virtual items. Finally, a game can be viewed through the lens of its contract. Most virtual economies operate under an EULA between the game owner and the player. The EULA generally declares that everything in the game is merely licensed to the player; there is no 'property' in a legal sense. Thus under contract law, virtual property is not property; what looks, acts, and smells like a duck is declared not to be a duck (Fairfield, 2009).

Courts have not spoken uniformly on the issue of virtual property. In some countries (Korea), the legal system clearly recognizes the property status of virtual goods. In others (the USA), judgments tend to rely on contract law and intellectual property arguments (see Lastowka, 2011 for an overview).

Much of the discussion of virtual property treats that property as individual and potentially private, when in fact a great deal of property in games and social media is common. Thus an unfortunate side-effect of the legal respect now accorded to developer-to-individual contracts, is that player community legal agreements are impossible (Fairfield, 2008). If switching costs were low, this would not present a problem. Developers would make games and rule them, but sorting among the players would allow each player to find the ideal game. Unfortunately, switching costs in these environments can be high, meaning that generally there would exist a reallocation of policies and players that would raise welfare. A system of covenants among players (much like neighborhood associations) could relieve some of these inefficiencies. Virtual property certainly exists and certainly has value, but disputes over ownership of the value will continue.

24.4   RESEARCH IN VIRTUAL ECONOMIES

Beginning with Bradley and Froomkin (2004) and Castronova (2006b), the argument has been made that virtual worlds would be interesting research tools. A virtual world contains a small human society, in the same way that a beehive contains a colony of bees. Just as one could make targeted changes in the structure and location of a beehive, and track the results, one could make targeted changes in a virtual world. This would allow a type of controlled experimentation at a social scale that has heretofore been impossible for social scientists.

The main advantage of controlled experiments with virtual worlds is the power of such a method to identify causation. Causation is the great bugbear of social science at the macro scale. Historical studies can only reveal the order in which effects occurred, not whether a prior effect made a posterior effect happen. Comparative studies can only reveal that two countries or provinces or villages had different experiences, not that characteristic X caused those differences. Cross-sectional data can only reveal patterns of correlation; ethnography reveals narratives and symbols. None of these methods show in a clear, replicable way that the presence or absence of factor X resulted in a change in factor Y. This is precisely what a controlled virtual experiment does: it takes two societies that are alike in every way, and changes one factor in one of the societies. By comparing the experimental society to the controlled one, the researcher can observe the causal effect of the change.

Great questions of social science can be directly addressed by such a method. To what extent does taxation inhibit growth? How does inequality alter labor supply? Do the media affect culture? How does money affect political outcomes?

While virtual worlds would allow causal conclusions on such questions, the results are of questionable generality. A virtual world is at best a small abstraction from the real world. It may not reach the necessary scale in terms of population and time to enable social processes similar to those in the real world. Moreover, it is not at all clear that behavior of people in game worlds is an exact replica of their behavior in real life. Most evidence to date suggests a remarkable consistency between real and virtual behavior (Yee and Bailenson, 2007; Castronova et al., 2009a, 2009b). But, there are also instances where virtual world patterns likely have little to do with real world patterns. As an example, the analogy between death of a game character and death of a player is very weak, but it has been suggested that one might use virtual worlds to test how societies react to epidemics (Lofgren and Fefferman, 2007). But, as Williams (2010) has pointed out, not everything we do in the virtual world maps well into what we do in the real world. In the case of epidemiology, the absence of a real threat of sickness or death likely means that virtual simulations of a plague means that results of such a study would not be generalizable to the real world.

Like any test tube or petri dish, virtual worlds can shed light on some questions but not on others. As software for building virtual worlds becomes more accessible, there will be more reports of controlled experiments with populated artifact environments. In the course of this research, the best and worst properties of virtual worlds as research tools will come to light.

For now, researchers must usually rely on existing virtual worlds to perform research. Most published work in 'pure' economics of virtual worlds has come from Edward Castronova. Castronova (2001) explored the nature and magnitude of the virtual goods trade in the *EverQuest* online game. The more theoretical article 'On virtual economies' (Castronova, 2003) considers the consequences of a simple model of choice between time spent 'in the real world' and time spent playing a game. The primary conclusion of the model is that when player preferences for a game depend on the game's challenge relative to the player's skill, players are willing to pay to be constrained (i.e., willing to pay for a 'harder' game). We will return to this conclusion in a moment.

Castronova (2004) examined the market for game accounts, one kind of RMT. Hedonic models of game account value showed that accounts with female avatars sell for 9 to 10 percent less than game accounts with male avatars, even though avatar gender is a purely cosmetic feature. Castronova (2006a) considers the problem of RMT, discussed above, and shows that the negative consequences of unsanctioned RMT mean that participants in that market create a negative externality that is born by non-participants. Depending on the assumptions made about the parameters in Castronova's model, the externality can be quite substantial, on the order of several million dollars per 100 000 game subscribers per year.

Wang et al. (2013) investigate the sources of value of virtual goods from a number of online games, with a focus on the effect of social networks. Interestingly, and quite unexpectedly, the authors find that social network intensity is negatively associated with the value of virtual goods. This might be because productive resources created by stronger social ties act as a partial substitute for virtual goods. The effect is mitigated, however, by the fact that the stronger social ties create greater demand for game time, which is a complement of virtual goods.

A curious feature of virtual economy research is the substantial number of insightful but unpublished manuscripts on the matter. Marks (2009) looks at auctions of virtual goods in the game *World of Warcraft* and finds that the so-called in-game auction house is a misnomer – in fact, some 98 percent of items posted sell at buy out prices, rather than being bid up in the style of a traditional auction. This finding suggests players' discount rates in games might be extremely high, given how much more players are willing to pay to receive desired goods immediately.

The model produced in the working paper (Huhh, 2009) served as an important precursor of Wang et al. (2013). Huhh showed that the availability of RMT, even if unsanctioned, may create positive network externalities enjoyed by both the users and the game producers. It is even possible that these externalities may overcome those discussed in Castronova (2006a).

One unpublished manuscript that we find particularly important is Jung, Lee, Yoo, and Brynjolfsson (2011) (hereafter JLYB). In an effort to understand the RMT market and its relationship with the game whose goods are being sold, JLYB model a player's decision to spend time in a game primarily as a function of their productivity in the game. That is, they explicitly deal with the fact that game companies can set the rate at which virtual resources are rewarded to players, given their skill levels. This rate of reward, in turn, drives the player's decision of time commitment to a game. JLYB show that players who commit substantial time (that is, who are higher skilled or who have a lower opportunity cost of playtime) become sellers in the RMT market, while those who have lower skill or higher opportunity cost become buyers. JLYB then derive the conditions of the RMT market as a derivatives market. Because this derivatives market affects the value of the game to both low and high-opportunity cost players, profit maximization of the game firm demands that they consider effects of in-game reward rates on both the value of the game and the value of the items in the derivatives market.

JLYB is important in that it is the first paper to reject the idea that a user's preference for a game depends directly on the game's challenge relative to the player's skill. Instead, challenge only affects game demand indirectly, by regulating the rate at which the game's content can be consumed. We think this is an important innovation, and its consequences for the structure of the game industry – especially the F2P sector – deserve renewed scrutiny from virtual world economists. An industrial organizational analysis of the videogame industry using the JLYB framework seems a natural next step. Currently, models of duopoly using this framework are in development.

24.5   CONCLUSION

This chapter has reviewed the history and development of virtual economies, as well as the small subfield of economic research that has grown up around them. Virtual economies have existed in various video games since the late 1970s, but they grew in size and scope substantially, beginning with the 1997 release of the MMO *Ultima Online*. The developers of that game developed the now standard method of managing virtual economies – the faucet-drain system. By manipulating the flows of items and currencies in and out of the economy, virtual economy managers can exert a great deal of control over what assets players can acquire in the game and how rare or plentiful those assets are.

This system is susceptible to interference from the real-money trade, where players trade real money in exchange for virtual assets. In extreme cases, this can lead to virtual economic collapse or hyperinflation. Much of the last five years of development in virtual worlds and games that have virtual economies has been spent trying to find ways to get RMT under control so that revenues from it are directed back to the virtual world operator. Many different strategies have been deployed to combat RMT, and the free-to-play revenue model is probably the most important development that resulted from the phenomenon.

The academic interest in virtual economies began with the recognition that, under certain conditions, the worlds could be used to perform policy experiments that would be either unethical or too expensive to run in the real world. Though there have been some developments in this area, most research is retrospective in nature, and deals with the effect that a game's structure has on the value of RMT in the secondary market.

The exigencies of virtual economies are perhaps obscure issues, but we are reticent to dismiss them out of hand because virtual worlds contain a substantial and increasing amount of economic value. Moreover, the population of virtual worlds is rising, as is the amount of time spent within them. At some point, virtual economies must show up on the radars of policy-makers. When that happens, good policy will depend on experts having a deep knowledge of what drives the production of value in virtual worlds. We strongly recommend further research in this field.

NOTES

1. In 2012, some 251 million people on Facebook played games on that platform, including free-to-play games with virtual economies. See '1/4 of Facebook users play games, up 11% to 251m this year as it fights spam and genres diversify', *TC*, 25 October, accessed 18 June 2014 at http://techcrunch.com/2012/10/25/facebook-games/.
2. That is, characters controlled by the computer that the player interacts with using his or her 'player character'.
3. Much of our knowledge about this issue comes from reports by industry insiders. For an example see Koster (2007).
4. Actually, the developers of *UO* had originally established a much more intricate game economy that recycled currency and materials. That this system was an abject failure is a very interesting story in itself, and readers are encouraged to see Simpson (2000) for details.
5. Readers interested in a much more in-depth discussion of early RMT may wish to read Dibbell (2007).
6. These stipulations remain in all modern EULAs. See, for example, http://us.blizzard.com/en-us/company/legal/wow_eula.html (accessed 18 June 2014), which is the EULA for Blizzard-Activision's *World of Warcraft*: 'All title, ownership rights and intellectual property rights in and to the Game and all copies thereof (including without limitation any titles, computer code, themes, *objects*, *characters*, character names, stories, dialog, catch phrases, locations, concepts, artwork, *character inventories*, structural or landscape designs, animations, sounds, musical compositions and recordings, audio-visual effects, storylines, character likenesses, methods of operation, moral rights, and any related documentation) are owned or licensed by Blizzard' (emphasis added).
7. See 'The grey economy: MMOs, RMT and credit card fraud', accessed 18 June 2014 at http://www.mmorpg.com/blogs/UnSub/022008/1233_The-Grey-Economy-MMOs-RMT-and-Credit-Card-Fraud.
8. We are also ignoring the options game operators have to change other mechanics of the game to balance the RMT problem. For example, making the game easier to play could reduce demand for RMT, but it will also affect how attractive the game is to current and prospective players.

9. See 'The evolution of Habbo Hotel's virtual economy', accessed 18 June 2014 at http://sulka.net/2010/03/the-evolution-of-habbo-hotels-virtual-economy/.
10. See https://secure.eveonline.com/plex/, accessed 18 June 2014, for more information.
11. See 'Global games market report infographics 2013', accessed 18 June 2014 at http://www.newzoo.com/infographics/global-games-market-report-infographics/.

REFERENCES

Ahmad, M., B. Keegan, J. Srivastava, D. Williams and N. Contractor (2009), 'Mining for gold farmers: Automatic detection of deviant players in MMOGs', in *Proceedings of the IEEE International Conference on Computational Science and Engineering (CSE'09), vancouver, BC, 29–31 August 2009*, pp. 340–45.

Bartle, R. (2003), *Designing Virtual Worlds*, Indianapolis, IN: New Riders Publishers.

Bradley, C. and A.M. Froomkin (2004), 'Virtual worlds, real rules', *New York Law School Law Review*, **49** (1), 103–46.

Castronova, E. (2001), 'Virtual worlds: A first-hand account of market and society on the Cyberian frontier', *CESifo Working Paper No. 618*, accessed 1 February 2015 at http://ssrn.com/abstract=294828.

Castronova, E. (2003), 'On virtual economies', *Game Studies*, **3** (2), accessed 18 June 2014 at http://www.gamestudies.org/0302/castronova/.

Castronova, E. (2004), 'The price of bodies: A hedonic pricing model of avatar attributes in a synthetic world', *Kyklos*, **57** (2), 173–96.

Castronova, E. (2005), *Synthetic Worlds: The Business and Culture of Online Games*, Chicago, IL: The University of Chicago Press.

Castronova, E. (2006a), 'A cost–benefit analysis of real-money trade in the products of synthetic economies', *Info*, **8** (6), 56–68.

Castronova, E. (2006b), 'On the research value of large games: Natural experiments in Norrath and Camelot', *Games and Culture*, **1** (2), 163–86.

Castronova, E., T.L. Ross and M.W. Bell et al. (2009a), 'A test of the law of demand in a virtual world: Exploring the petri dish approach to social science', *International Journal of Gaming and Computer-Mediated Simulations*, **1** (2), 1–16.

Castronova, E., D. Williams and C. Shen et al. (2009b), 'As real as real? Macroeconomic behaviour in a large-scale virtual world', *New Media and Society*, **11** (5), 685–707.

Castronova, E. (2014), *Wildcat Currencies*, New Haven, CT: Yale University Press.

Dibbell, J. (2007), *Play Money: Or, How I Quit My Day Job and Made Millions Trading Virtual Loot*, New York: Basic Books.

Fairfield, J.A.T. (2008), 'Anti-social contracts: The contractual governance of virtual worlds', *McGill Law Journal*, **53** (3), 427–76.

Fairfield, J.A.T. (2009), 'The God paradox', *Boston University Law Review*, **89** (3), 1017–68.

Hamari, J. and V. Lehdonvirta (2010), 'Game design as marketing: How game mechanics create demand for virtual goods', *International Journal of Business Science and Applied Management*, **5** (1), 14–29.

Heeks, R. (2009), 'Understanding "gold farming" and real-money trading as the intersection of real and virtual economies', *Journal of Virtual Worlds Research*, **2** (4), accessed 18 June 2014 at http://journals.tdl.org/jvwr/index.php/jvwr/article/view/868.

Huhh, J.-S. (2009), 'An economic analysis on online game service', unpublished manuscript, accessed 18 June 2014 at http://ssrn.com/abstract=1335120.

Jung, G., B. Lee, B. Yoo and E. Brynjolfsson (2011), 'Analysis of the relationship between virtual goods trading and performance of virtual worlds', accessed 8 January 2016 at http://ssrn.com/abstract=1938313.

Koster, R. (2007), 'Flation', accessed 18 June 2014 at http://www.raphkoster.com/2007/01/17/flation/.

Lastowka, G. (2011), *Virtual Justice*, New Haven, CT: Yale University Press.

Lastowka, G. and D. Hunter (2004), 'The laws of the virtual worlds', *California Law Review*, **92** (1), 1–74.

Lehdonvirta, V. (2009), 'Virtual item sales as a revenue model: Identifying attributes that drive purchase decisions', *Electronic Commerce Research*, **9** (1–2), 97–113.

Lehdonvirta, V. and M. Ernkvist (2011), *Knowledge Map of the Virtual Economy*, Washington, DC: The World Bank.

Lehtiniemi, T. (2007), 'How big is the RMT market anyway?' *Virtual Economy Research Network*, accessed 18 June 2014 at http://virtualeconomyresearchnetwork.wordpress.com/2007/03/02/how_big_is_the_rmt_market_anyw/.

Lofgren, E. and N. Fefferman (2007), 'The untapped potential of virtual game worlds to shed light on real world epidemics', *The Lancet Infectious Diseases*, **7** (9), 625–29.

Marks, E. (2009), 'Price dynamics in virtual world auctions', unpublished manuscript, accessed 31 December 2015 at https://economics.stanford.edu/sites/default/files/publications/marks_e._2009_honors_thesis.pdf.

Simpson, Z.B. (2000), 'The in-game economics of Ultima Online', presented at the Computer Game Developers Conference, San José, CA, accessed 18 June 2014 at http://www.mine-control.com/zack/uoecon/uoecon.html.

Wang, Q.-H., V. Mayer-Schönberger and X. Yang (2013), 'The determinants of monetary value of virtual goods: An empirical study for a c-section of MMORPGs', *Information Systems Frontiers*, **15** (3), 481–95.

Williams, D. (2010), 'The mapping principle, and a research framework for virtual worlds', *Communication Theory*, **20** (4), 451–70.

Yee, N. and J. Bailenson (2007), 'The Proteus effect: The effect of transformed self-representation on behavior', *Human Communication Research*, **33** (3), 279–90.

25. Economics of big data
Claudio Feijóo, José-Luis Gómez-Barroso and
Shivom Aggarwal

25.1 BACKGROUND AND DEFINITIONS

As a general concept, big data loosely refers to datasets exceeding a certain size, although there is no widely agreed formal or informal threshold above which a dataset shall be considered 'big'. As of 2014 there seems to be tacit agreement that this value is at least in the terabyte range and that it is increasing rapidly. The term big data is also invoked in reference to the huge amounts of varied data stored by the public and private sectors in the course of their regular activities. Both ideas – size and/or heterogeneity – hint at the challenges of managing the data as well as the promises embedded in it. Alluding to new economic and social opportunities the term is frequently invoked in policy declarations, initiatives and scientific as well as non-scientific documents.

A more technical approach defines big data as 'data whose size forces us to look beyond the tried-and true methods for data analysis that are prevalent at that time' (Jacobs, 2009). In other words, 'big data refers to datasets whose size is beyond the ability of typical database software tools to capture, store, manage, and analyze' (Manyika et al., 2011). Obviously this definition is a moving target and will change along with the evolution of 'typical database software'. Furthermore, size is just one parameter when pronouncing a dataset as big data. Another important dimension to define big data relates to the structural construct of the dataset. Traditional relational database management systems have in-built capabilities to store, manage and analyze quite large datasets subject to one important attribute: that the datasets are sufficiently structured. Significant amounts of data created nowadays via social media, devices and sensors in smart cities, public agencies, and so on, are highly unstructured, thus requiring different technologies to store, manage, and analyze them. A more eloquent definition for big data therefore is 'a large dataset combining structured and unstructured data, which cannot be managed and/or analyzed by legacy – conventional – database management methodologies'.

These technical approaches are complemented by a strand of definitions adopting an economic perspective. For instance the **BBVA** banking corporation defines big data as 'a set of processes, technologies and business models that are based on data and on capturing the value hidden in the data itself'.[1] From such a value and business point of view, big data could then be considered as a new class of economic asset (World Economic Forum, 2012) and the basis of 'a drift toward data-driven discovery and decision-making' (Lohr, 2012).

Summarizing and restating what has been discussed, big data can be characterized by specific properties or 'dimensions', most importantly:[2]

- *Volume:* The threshold above which a dataset could be considered big data. Some experts suggest the idea that every database surpassing the capacity of one single – contemporary – ordinary computer can be considered as big data.[3]
- *Variety:* The different types of data involved in big data, including non-structured data.
- *Velocity:* The need to manage and analyze big data as much as possible in real time or near-real time.[4]
- *Veracity and/or validity:* In contrast to the traditional statistical inference, implications of data sampling are not the origin of the relevant issues in big data analytics, because there is no scarcity of data; rather, the opposite.

Around the term big data other concepts such as data science, data mining and data visualization have arisen. Probably 'data science' should be highlighted as the global term encompassing all the others including big data. Data science is different from statistics and other similar disciplines because of the increasingly heterogeneous and unstructured nature of the data and the new processes required to analyze it (Dhar, 2013). Big data needs to be acquired, ingested, processed, persisted, integrated, analyzed and exposed (Akred et al., 2013) to produce results. Thus, 'the real issue is not that you are acquiring large amounts of data. It's what you do with the data that counts'.[5] In Hal Varian's words: 'the complimentary [sic] scarce factor is the ability to understand that data and extract value from it' (Varian, 2009). In any case, the technologies that have made possible the emergence of big data are different from conventional techniques and maybe this is the ultimate reason why the term has prevailed. Other similar terms such as business intelligence and analytics (Chen et al., 2012) are losing momentum compared to big data. Moreover, it is worth mentioning that big data is intricately linked with the 'app economy'. It may even be considered as part of it (Mulligan and Card, 2014). Many applications and the business models that support them are based on the exploitation of data about users and related to users.

Big data has been also heralded as contributing to a major transformation in the methodology of scientific work. Traditional notions of causality may be (at least, partially) replaced by a focus on correlation, a shift from knowing 'why' to only knowing 'what' (Mayer-Schönberger and Cukier, 2013). Others speak of a fourth paradigm in science, based on data-intensive computing where data would be stored in some archival media – like libraries for paper-based storage – and be publicly accessible in the cloud to humans and machines to extract knowledge out of it (e.g., Hey et al., 2009).

Big data is also linked to concepts such as the 'Internet of Things' (IoT) and 'open data', which are becoming increasingly popular on their own. The IoT is essentially a network of sensors and devices that is fully compatible and accessible from the Internet. A network of 'countless digital sensors worldwide in industrial equipment, automobiles, electrical meters and shipping crates' that 'can measure and communicate location, movement, vibration, temperature, humidity, even chemical changes in the air' (Lohr, 2012) is an obvious source of big data. Open data makes reference, according to the Open Data Institute,[6] to 'data that is available and can be reused by anyone at no cost, subjected to a pre-defined license under which, the user/distributor of the data has to provide appropriate credit to the primary owner of the data'. Murray-Rust (2008) contends that open data in science is published data that should be available to the scientific community for reuse with proper crediting to the primary owner, but should not include any copyright or monetary value associated with its reuse.

A number of non-profit foundations and organizations define open data, or sometimes 'open access to data', with different terminologies, but mostly revolve around the two constructs of open standards/interoperability and freedom to use/reuse. Many governments around world are providing open data through different agencies such as the European Union Open Data Portal,[7] the US Government General Service Administration's Open Government Initiative,[8] the UK Government,[9] and international organizations that study its impact such as the Organisation for Economic Co-operation and Development (OECD).[10] It is worth noting that this data displays in different types, formats, structures, file systems, and so on, that are not necessarily compatible with each other. The combination of open with big data, that is massive open data along with varied levels of complexity, results in 'open big data' (Marton et al., 2013). Last but not least, in parallel with this relatively new discipline 'a new kind of professional has emerged, the data scientist, who combines the skills of software programmer, statistician and storyteller/artist to extract the nuggets of gold hidden under mountains of data'.[11]

Aware of the considerable hype about the big data concept, available figures from research institutions and market analysts nonetheless talk about its huge potential. There is some evidence indicating that data-driven decision-makers are better off (McAfee and Brynjolfsson, 2012). To provide perspective, industry analysts estimate that a typical corporation of 1000 employees has about 200 TB of stored data and that the total amount of data stored in companies amounts to some tens of exabytes (Manyika et al., 2011). Industry forecasts (Cisco, Gartner, or McKinsey) put this figure at hundreds of exabytes by 2016. The same sources suggest that banking will take the largest share of big data (about 25 percent). It will be followed by services (15 percent), manufacturing (15 percent) and government (12 percent). At a macroeconomic level, the Warsaw Institute for Economic Studies estimates that big and open data will contribute 1.9 percent of EU-28 GDP by 2020 (Buchholtz et al., 2014). The forecast anticipates that trade will contribute 23 percent of this total, manufacturing 22 percent, finance and insurance 13 percent, public administration 13 percent, and health and social care 5 percent.

Given the emergent nature of the big data domain, it is no wonder that from an economic perspective it is still a field with more questions than answers. Main topics that slowly start to appear in the scientific literature and the research roadmaps are, among others, issues related to the economic value of data[12] and their impact on growth, jobs and the quality of life, the analysis of the structure of this emerging industry and its implications for innovation and competition, and the application of new and existing economic theories to explain its dynamic behavior (see, among others, Feijóo et al., 2013 on personal data). Beyond the narrower economic aspects, considerable uncertainties prevail over the overall effects of the intensive usage of big data on society. boyd and Crawford (2012) rightly state that it is time to start critically interrogating the phenomenon of big data as well as its assumptions and its biases.

Within the framework described in this introductory section this chapter explores the emerging domain of big data economics. The next section describes the features of the big data ecosystem, the main players, and their relationships. From there different economic approaches are used to explore the big data market, its dynamics and the value of data within it. Opportunities and challenges for both researchers and marketers are presented in section 25.4. Conclusions with a policy view close the chapter.

25.2   THE BIG DATA ECOSYSTEM

25.2.1   Basic Processes

Figure 25.1 shows the basic operations in big data. From different possible sources, data are first extracted[13] and consolidated as each source may have a different structure, organization and format. During the transform stage a set of rules is applied to the data, including parsing to ensure its validity and completeness, modifying values, as well as merging and disaggregating data. The results from this stage are then loaded into the data warehouse. Data are also loaded to a number of data marts, subsets of the database prepared or adapted to some business process or user need. Big data is different from conventional database systems in the amount of data that is extracted, transformed and loaded and, in particular, in the strategies for storage and management in the data

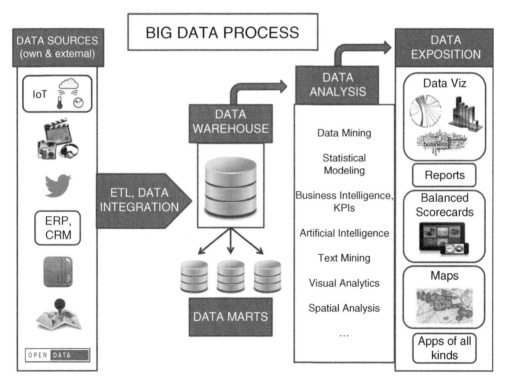

Note: CRM = customer relationship management; Data Viz = data visualization; ERP = enterprise resource planning; ETL = extract transform load; IoT = Internet of Things; KPIs = key performance indicators.

Figure 25.1   The stages of big data processing

warehouse, often spread across different servers and locations. Data curation refers to all the processes described above once data are acquired.

Data analysis is the core process in big data. It comprises techniques derived from statistical analysis (all types of statistical models and regressions), computer science (data mining, machine learning, artificial intelligence), managerial and business administration (business intelligence, key performance indicators), visualization (visual analytics, spatial analytics), and an increasing number of new techniques developed specifically in the big data context (text mining, sentiment analysis, behavioral patterns) and/or derived from other scientific disciplines (network theory, agent-based modeling, complexity theory, game theory).

The last stage is most difficult to precisely define and categorize. It basically refers to the applications that can be built from the analysis. Among others it includes data queries and results as those in a search engine, visualization of results as in a map, and all types of reports from a model or simulation.

25.2.2   Players

In conventional data management, the data collected according specific rules were fed into the enterprise integration tool that transferred them into data warehouses or operational units. Then different analytical capabilities were used to extract information from the data. The process was conducted in-house or with standard database software packages and hardware. However, the volume and variety of requirements in big data has brought a considerable range of players into the sector, which can broadly be classified into four categories (see Figure 25.2):

- *Technology providers (TP):* Provide the core technologies upon which the whole data infrastructure is built. Given the unstructured nature of data, unlike relational database management systems (RDBMS), these technologies support nodal structures, massive parallel processing, NoSQL queries, and so on. Some key players in this category are Hadoop, MapReduce, and Cassandra.
- *Infrastructure providers (IP):* Provide back-end architecture for storage, analyses and retrieving of structured as well as unstructured data. IP range from individual offerings such as massive data warehouses for storage or analytics for querying to combo solutions for operational activities and storage. They can further be sub-classified as analytics infrastructure (AI), operational infrastructure (OI) and databases & warehouses (D&W) (Feinleib, 2012). Key players include Oracle, Sybase, MySQL, Cloudera, TeraData, and InfoChimps.
- *Analytics & visualization tools (A&VT):* Provide specialized services and methodologies for analyzing big data and generating business intelligence (BI) insights for decision-making. Most of these tools have viable graphical user interface (GUI) and client-server architectures. Important players include SAP, Hyperion, Microsoft, DataSpora, TIBCO, Ayata, Platfora, Cognos, and Autonomy.
- *Big data applications (BDA):* Develop niches in terms of particular uses of big data, such as media applications for real-time consumer targeting, studying consumer trends, vertical applications for interpreting consumer demand and delivering relevant user experiences, log data applications for log management services or

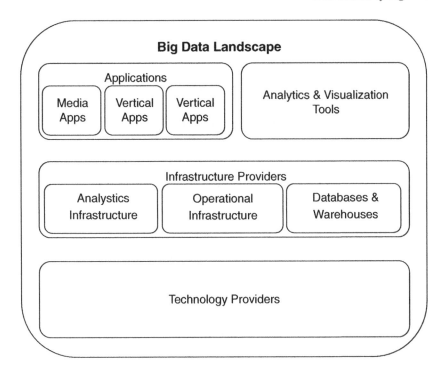

Figure 25.2   Players in big data

'data-as-a-service' through cloud infrastructure. Among the key players are Loggly, Media Science, Bloomreach, INRIX, and Gnip.

In more general terms, it can be said that the big data market is composed of three supply-side areas: hardware, software and services. According to industrial sources vendor revenue in the big data market reached $18.6 billion in 2013 with a growth rate of 58 percent over the previous year (Kelly, 2014). Services revenues made up 40 percent of the total market, followed by hardware at 38 percent and software at 22 percent. This breakdown is due in part to the open source nature of much big data software as well as the need for professional services to help organizations build successful use cases.

The big data ecosystem is deeply connected with cloud computing, as data are typically stored in an infrastructure consisting of a set of remote servers and the solutions to technologically manage the data as well as providing analytics and applications use this data remotely. Ignoring the acquisition part of the big data process, big data could be considered a particular sub-set of the general cloud computing paradigm.

25.2.3   Business Models and Innovations

According to Hemerly (2013) the innovations brought by big data to companies can be grouped in two broad categories: improvements in decision-making and improvements in efficiency. Data-driven decision-making would facilitate increased objectivity, decision-making in real time, and the discovery of hidden patterns. Improved efficiency can be achieved with better and more personalized products and services. From another perspective, Buchholtz et al. (2014) talk about three ways in which data can be turned into value for a company or organization: data-to-information where data are mined for information and value is created the moment the search succeeds; data-to-product/service where insights from data analysis are implemented in practice; and data-to-management where evidence-based information feeds into the decision-making process. Finally, the OECD (2013) identifies five types of benefits from the exploitation of data in data-intensive sectors such as online advertisement, health care, utilities, logistics and transport, and public administration: enhancing research and development (data-driven R&D); developing new products (data products and services); optimizing production or delivery processes (data-driven processes); improving marketing by providing targeted advertisements and personalized recommendations (data-driven marketing); and developing new organizational and management approaches or significantly improving existing practices (data-driven organization).

All in all, it can be said that big data business models are based on the achievable improvements of service quality and/or marketing capabilities of firms and organizations. With big data analytical methods, firms are supposed to be able to predict aggregate trends as well as individual preferences. This allows optimizing the returns on marketing investment and, equally important, the lowering of advertising costs and of service provision costs. Firms may also be able to increase revenues through recommendations to consumers and targeted offers (Acquisti and Varian, 2005) – the so-called behavioral advertising – as well as innovative marketing strategies (coupons, consumer loyalty enhancement, CRM techniques, etc.). Moreover, the use of big data enables firms and organizations to improve their ability to price discriminate. Furthermore, by observing individual behavior, firms can learn how to improve their services and redesign them in response to observed customer behavior (ibid.).

25.3　THE ECONOMIC VALUE OF DATA IN BIG DATA

Attaching an economic value to the data in big data is a difficult task, as this data is used in many situations and contexts for many different purposes as discussed above. Arguably, approximating the specific value of big data is only possible in specific cases. There are at least two potentially differing ways to define value in big data: from a provider perspective (supply) and from a user perspective (demand).

25.3.1　Value for Providers

In the case of providers three different approaches for approximating monetary values of data exist: valuation based on company reports, valuation according to observed market prices, and 'production cost' (i.e., the cost of obtaining and/or preparing data) (Feijóo et al., 2013). These monetary transactions and market valuations can serve as an initial base for further understanding the economics of data, although each of the methods has strengths and weaknesses.

Provided that datasets are capitalized and thus appear on the balance sheet as assets, a direct way of approaching the value of data would be to rely on companies' own accounts. Unfortunately, this is rarely the case and most companies that ground their businesses on the commercial use of data opt not to disclose this type of information.

The valuation of data assets based on financial figures such as market capitalization and revenues is easier and more straightforward given that most companies, whether publicly traded or not, report such figures. However, several challenges related to the use of financial company information for approximating the value of data exist. First, a wealth of other company (internal) components beyond data influence the firm's financial results, such as its human and physical capital stock, volume of other intangibles, expertise/know-how, and so on. The same holds for approximations relying on the measures of intangible assets and/or derived from the goodwill of a company. Moreover, the financial results of a company are also influenced by external factors, such as market trends, random shocks, and speculation. This means that measures of data value will be imprecise and fluctuate over time in response to general market sentiments or speculative activity rather than according to the intrinsic value of the data. Overall, the revenue per data record has been recently suggested as the most appropriate approximation of economic returns to data. Where future earnings attributed to the data can be considered and appropriately discounted a net present value may be determined. Feijóo et al. (2014) applied this approach to the largest collectors of personal data. According to their results, figures for the value of personal profiles ranged from US$8 to US$43, although these figures vary considerably from region to region.

Several data brokers publish their retail prices for various types of data records. These prices reflect at least partially the real market price for obtaining specific data in a given market. The observed retail price of a record incorporates several economic components. These include the (marginal) value of the data (which might be different from the average price of an individual record if purchased as part of a comprehensive database), the costs incurred in generating the data, as well as current and future revenues achievable utilizing the data. The price will also be influenced by considerations concerning the competitive use of the information and how the corresponding business activity may evolve in future. Moreover, the price at which data are exchanged in an open market relates to a specific context. The quality of data provided by data brokers cannot be verified ex ante and can be flawed or inaccurate. Data are also exchanged on illegal markets but these are difficult to collect. Given the illegal nature of the goods and services offered, the prices of offers and deals will never be fully transparent and thus they are difficult to measure. As a result, estimations based on such transactions are subject to biases due to unrepresentative samples.

From the perspective of producing big data, that is, from a cost perspective and given the current stage in the evolution of data markets, big data requires considerable investment in the infrastructure for acquisition and storage, as well as in tools for management and analytics. It is, therefore, similar to typical ICT industries characterized by high fixed costs and low incremental costs. The cost structure, however, could be different if infrastructure and tools are shared in some way and/or the prices for such infrastructure and tools drop significantly in the future.

25.3.2   Value for Users

Particular types of data are – supposedly – controlled by their owners that have to – should – grant access to it. In those cases, assuming that markets are not fully developed, a completely different way of associating an economic value to data is to attempt to approximate the price a firm would need to pay in exchange for obtaining them.

This is particularly the case for personal data. In recent years, several experimental studies attempting to quantify individual valuations of personal data in diverse contexts have been conducted. Even though this research remains at a preliminary stage, two general messages can already be extracted. First, people differ with respect to their individual valuation of personal data (measured by the monetary compensation sufficient for them to divulge personal information) and with respect to their individual valuation of privacy (i.e., the amount of money they are prepared to spend in order to protect their personal data from disclosure) (Grossklags et al., 2007). Second, theoretical and empirical studies point out that both the valuation of privacy and the valuation of personal data are extremely sensitive to contextual effects (Nissenbaum, 2010).

To deepen the understanding of data value from the demand side several additional methods have been proposed. One is the application of a method widely used in areas such as transport or health, known as the stated preference discrete choice experiment (SPDCE) approach, which can be used to estimate the value of personal data in real-life contexts and situations (Potoglou et al., 2013). Another is to conduct laboratory experiments (Jentzsch et al., 2012). In the case of individuals, the SPCDE approach reveals users' latent utility function, allowing for the gauging of respondents' welfare over a range of circumstances in relation to a range of services that imply the disclosure and/or collection of personal information. These methods, although promising, include two potential sources of bias: the data may lack market verification – hence the need for a realistic setting of the experiment – and they may capture the individually perceived cost of damage caused by data breaches rather than value of the data themselves.

25.4   INNOVATION AND COMPETITION IN BIG DATA: FROM SILOS TO PLATFORMS AND MULTI-SIDED MARKETS

A silo model is perhaps the initial approach to any big data value network model, where all the processes described in section 25.2 on the bid data ecosystem – acquisition, consolidation, storage, analysis and applications – are carried out by the same entity. This is the situation when the owner of the data is the same entity as the analyzer of the data and, more important, it is also the provider of solutions – applications – on these data.

However, specialization in some of these processes or legal or strategic decisions – such as publicly funded open data, open innovation schemes – calls for a different approach where some of the above processes are externalized and performed by other players or, even more interesting, carried out with synergies and common goals between different players. In these cases, probably indications of a more mature stage in the evolution of the big data ecosystem, it would be possible to talk about a 'platformization' (Ballon, 2009) of big data. Data gathered about players and their roles as presented in the ecosystem section point in this direction.

In the techno-economic literature, the notion of a platform refers to a combination of technologies with product and services originated in different firms to provide a solution as complete as possible to users (e.g., Gawer and Cusumano, 2002). They are an increasingly popular strategic approach in the ICT ecosystem with examples in devices, operating systems, networks operation, services, applications and even content. Platforms are established as a means to combine the advantages of enjoying as much control as possible on the value network while taking advantage of the power of open innovation and different types of network externalities. There is an increasing number of platform-based companies that have become leaders in their domains, including the examples of Amazon, eBay, Apple, Google and Facebook. However, the academic literature on the economics of platforms is still relatively immature and mainly devoted to strategic issues (Hidding et al., 2011). Nonetheless, it highlights relevant facts, worthy to be considered in the big data domain, especially in connection with the market positioning of the platform provider.

From an economic perspective, data-based platforms can be seen as cases of multi-sided or simply two-sided markets. In the big data market the sides involved are users, developers of apps, providers of analytics and visualization tools, and – if the business model is linked with personalized or targeted services – marketing and advertising companies. Of these participants, users and developers are the two most prominent sides. The key stakeholder, however, is the platform owner, the provider of technology and infra-structures (servers, databases), user interfaces, development kits, business model systems and possibly some analysis and visualization tools. The owner decides on appropriate technology, sets the rules for the interaction with other players on the platform, establishes a pricing strategy, and cares about the integrity and quality of the user experience. The owner acts as a gatekeeper: controls the software and hardware evolution of the platform, encourages developers, provides a storefront for users, manages the business model, and retains (some form of) intellectual property. It is this gatekeeping position that allows the owner to extract value from the transactions taking place on the platform.

Gawer and Henderson (2007) have characterized the strategies of firms operating in the context of modular ICT systems – as has been shown is the case when describing the big data ecosystem – as the quest for 'platform leadership'. This refers to the strategic objective to control a central system module around which other companies may develop a range of complementary technologies and products. This involves fostering a thriving ecosystem of internal and external complementary innovations and innovators; influencing architectural design through open interfaces combined with core intellectual property assets; balancing consensus and control strategies towards contributors of complementary innovations; and reflecting this in the internal organization, for example by adopting a systemic and neutral mindset that extends to the whole industry.

This results in a range of possible market-positioning schemes for platforms. Adapting the classification of Belleflamme and Peitz (2010) to the big data market, four basic strategies (not mutually incompatible) can be distinguished: resellers of data, marketplaces for data, facilitators of data analysis, and trusted third parties for data. Each of these options has specific advantages and difficulties from a technical, economic and legal perspective, an interesting avenue for further research. These strategies are also combined with the degree of openness in the platform: from closed models à la Apple, where tight control is exerted on each element of the platform, to open innovation schemes akin to open source development. In addition, platforms can range from integrated – meaning that all required hardware and software is provided through the platform – to just hardware, software or infrastructure, or even be reduced to some particular application or tool.

From a developer's perspective the choice of the appropriate platforms is crucial as, at least in the current emerging stage of the big data market, there are a number of competing platforms and big data applications do not operate on all platforms. Choice criteria could be the size of the platform in terms of number of customers, revenues per application, or any combination of techno-economic features (amount of data, openness, data quality, availability of development tools, etc.).

25.5   SOME CONCLUSIONS ON OPPORTUNITIES AND CHALLENGES WITH A POLICY VIEW

The past two decades have witnessed extraordinary developments related to data storage capacity, high-speed networks to move and acquire data, and rapid growth in computational power. Significant changes in the volume and uses of data have been enabled by improvements in the ability to collect, transfer, store, aggregate, link and analyze this data. Therefore, data are nowadays processed, redeployed, shared and transferred around the clock and across the globe. Whether this data creates economic and social value at an increasingly greater pace is no longer in question. However, measuring the value generated remains a complex task, as data are used in so many situations and contexts for many purposes. In addition, it is clear that the Internet is not simply an excellent tool for acquiring and assembling data of all types, but also a key platform for many emerging innovative applications that transform this data into valuable services for consumers and businesses. Throughout this chapter the context for our analysis has been the increasing importance of understanding developments in the Internet economy that are drivers of innovation and growth.

Big data economics appears as a challenging field of research with considerable opportunities to provide value to the academic community and to practitioners. In the following paragraphs, ideas, extracted and summarized from the analysis of previous sections, many of them in incipient stages, are presented as potential avenues for further research.

25.5.1   Knowledge Discovery

Deriving knowledge from very large amounts of data – knowledge discovery – needs tools other than data-based traditional models, in particular when considering unstructured information (Dhar, 2013). Unlike conventional database querying that asks 'What data satisfy this pattern?' or econometric modeling that follows hypothesis-driven research, knowledge discovery asks 'What patterns satisfy this data?', taking advantage of observations that would not have been made under controlled circumstances. In general, statistical and econometric models need to be augmented by theoretical arguments and additional tests to overcome difficulties with causality or when scaling conclusions to a different situation.

Therefore, there is considerable room for developments combining statistics, econometrics and computer science. For instance, the usual approach in machine learning detects structure in data without strong assumptions about linearity or the parameters of underlying distributions. Apart from the need for high quantities of data, a disadvantage of this approach is that it could also pick up spurious relations in data, thus arriving at meaningless conclusions. Therefore, big data analytical techniques will typically benefit from combining them with more traditional (modeling) approaches.

Another area of interest is forecasting. In conventional statistics and econometrics, errors in prediction are derived from three main sources: the mis-specification of the model (too many variables, too few variables, wrong assumptions about the relationships between variables or about their distribution), use of a limited number of observations for the estimation of parameters, and the random disturbances and measurements errors. Using big data allows reducing the first two types of challenges significantly as the need to specify the model in detail decreases and as availability of large numbers of observations and finely grained data mitigates the problems of sampling. The use of big data hence allows the introduction of new forms and methods of forecasting.

25.5.2 Data-based Platforms

From a narrower economic perspective more research is needed on the value of data and the contribution of data to economic growth and jobs. Several areas look promising including the increasing relevance of metadata and context, the implications of open (big) data and data portability across platforms and applications, data formats and types, and the capabilities of users to control their data (i.e., privacy-enhancing technologies).

Another area of interest is research on data platforms and multi-sided markets. From the brief analysis in the section above several issues can be identified as promising avenues for further research. They include the creation and sustainability of both direct and indirect network effects, as well as the design and structure of the platform business. Moreover, the technological and business relationships, the pricing of – and subsidies to – sides belonging to the platform, as well as strategic decisions on quality, degree of openness and differentiation raise challenging research problems.

25.5.3 Data Governance

From an economic policy perspective 'data governance' is also an increasingly relevant subject. According to OECD (2014) data governance is the overall management of the availability, accessibility, usability, integrity and security of the data collected and stored. In addition, data governance includes policies and regulations that form a consistent and effective framework for such data management.

We suggest, additionally, that data governance should not be construed merely as an economic matter but that it should also encompass a social perspective. The issue at stake is an emerging mythology of big data (boyd and Crawford, 2012) that could lead to a blind acceptance of this new paradigm. Areas for careful consideration include acknowledging that conclusions based on data are always subject to a process of interpretation, that bigger data does not necessarily equate to better data, the relevance of the context of data, the ethical consequences of the intensive usage of data, and the new digital divides because of lacking access to data.

Governance is particularly important for data from public sources or in open data schemes. In this regard, the health and security domains are paramount examples, particularly if multiple stakeholders and different countries are required to cooperate. Additional challenging areas to those already mentioned appear to be: financial sustainability of initiatives, framework and incentives for exchange and access to data, coordination and complementarity of initiatives, quality and efficiency of collected data, and capacity building and training. Deficits in existing skills in the big data domain are particularly relevant as main decisions on acquisition, storage, and analysis of data are being taken today and will condition upcoming developments. These skills are transversal in nature and include prominently knowledge on state-of-the art technology (sensors, networks, and databases), analysis (from econometrics to machine learning as discussed previously), and legal aspects (privacy, ownership, and regulation).

25.5.4   Policy and Regulatory Framework

As an emerging area, still rather immature and full of innovation promises, many stakeholders including big companies assert that big data should not be regulated (Hemerly, 2013). However, there are some areas affected by big data where public policies and regulation do exist and that can have a deep impact on the evolution of the field. The most prominent of these areas are (1) the domain of privacy and use of – mostly personal – data by service providers; (2) data ownership; and (3) the extent of open data.

Starting with privacy, regulation of service providers' usage of personal information represents a true challenge for policy-makers, as difficult trade-offs between innovation and user rights may need to be resolved (Gómez-Barroso and Feijóo, 2013). On the one hand, excessively restrictive access to data can inhibit the growth of potentially valuable services or applications. On the other hand, risks associated with privacy intrusions must be carefully inspected because they affect not only economic interests but also people's lives.

Several approaches are possible from a very general policy perspective ranging from the use of market forces in a laissez faire framework to reliance on some regulation 'by design' or 'by law' (or any combination of both). Considering the pure market approach, existing evidence as described in the chapter suggests that interested companies are still in a very early phase in their learning curve on big data, basically gathering all available information on every aspect of their businesses. Most of them are also trying rather basic approaches as business models on this data: deducting behavioral patterns of users and adjusting whatever is the business model – advertising, subscription, sales, other – to these observed patterns, or even simpler: just selling data to interested third parties, which in turn include the user profiling in their business models. Is the market responding rapidly to concerns of users about the (mis)use of their personal information – supposing they are aware? Most evidence today suggests that this is not the case. Unclear terms in service agreements, significant market position of leader providers – and absence of respectful providers – unbounded usage of information gathered in a particular transaction and, above all, prominent examples of data gathering without users knowing all point toward slow market reaction by its own means, if any.

Regulation by design is linked with the fact that the amount of information that users reveal to providers increases with the ability of technology to provide better and more personalized services. In this regard, users – or rather, consumers – lack information and tools concerning the amount of data that it is collected and about the preservation of contextual integrity during the flow of information. On the supply side of the market, privacy-enhancing technologies may make it possible to reach equilibria where data holders can still analyze aggregate and anonymized data while subjects' individual information stays protected. Open big data or data portability could help to increase transparency in the domain and avoid users' lock-in effects.

Data portability is obviously linked with data ownership. In this area, two issues appear attract increasing attention in current discussions. The first is the application of intellectual property rights (IPRs) on data. There are different positions on how and to what apply IPRs. The traditional position suggests distinguishing between raw data without IPRs and findings and facts on data – structured datasets included – that would have some form of IPR. It is unclear if this 'legacy' solution will contribute to innovation or deter it.

The second issue, related to the previous one, refers to data obtained through public funds. There is an increasing pressure to release in an open manner all publicly funded data. For instance, the National Science Foundation in the USA and the Horizon 2020 framework program in Europe contain provisions for open data management in research projects. The provision of open data by all types of government requires technical resources to ensure that data are readily available in adequate formats or even in some standardized version. It is not just a matter of publishing data in whatever circumstances. The availability of this data – often in the context of cities and/or the Internet of things – could give rise to opportunities for innovation and improvement of public services within so-called 'data civics' (Hemerly, 2013) (or 'data governance' as discussed in this chapter).

In sum, the big data domain is full of opportunities and challenges for economic research and a more robust understanding of the economics of (big) data is needed. The brief introductory review presented in this chapter is a modest first step in that direction.

NOTES

1. See BBVA, 'Big data: En qué punto estamos?' [Big data: where are we?] *Innovation Edge*, June 2013, accessed 6 January 2015 at http://www.centrodeinnovacionbbva.com/en/innovation-edge/big-data/big-data-where-we. Translation from the original Spanish document by the authors.
2. Sometimes referred to as the four (or sometimes three) Vs of big data. See IBM (2014), 'The four V's of big data', accessed 23 March 2015 at http://www.ibmbigdatahub.com/infographic/four-vs-big-data.
3. Attempts to define big data by means of size are a daunting task. A few numbers suffice to illustrate the challenges: in 2013 30 billion pieces of content were shared on Facebook every month, 2.9 million emails were sent every second, 72.9 products were ordered on Amazon per second, and so on, reaching 2.5 quintillion bytes of data exchanged every day. See IBM (n.d.), 'What is big data?', accessed 22 January 2015 at http://www.ibm.com/big-data/us/en/.
4. See *Glossary of Telecommunications Terms* from US National Communication Systems (Federal Standard), accessed 6 January 2015 at http://www.its.bldrdoc.gov/fs-1037/fs-1037c.htm.
5. See SAS (n.d.), 'What is big data?', *SAS.com*, accessed 24 January 2015 at http://www.sas.com/en_us/insights/big-data/what-is-big-data.html.
6. Open Data Institute accessed 23 March 2015 at http://theodi.org/.
7. European Union Open Data Portal accessed 23 March 2015 at http://open-data.europa.eu/.
8. See Data.Gov: The Home of the US Government's Open Data, accessed 23 March 2015 at http://www.data.gov/.
9. See Data.Gov.UK: Opening Up Government, accessed 23 March 2015 at http://data.gov.uk/.

10. See OECD, Data-driven Innovation for Growth and Well-being, accessed 23 March 2015 at http://oe.cd/bigdata.
11. 'Data, data everywhere', *The Economist*, 25 February 2010, accessed 22 January 2015 at http://www.economist.com/node/15557443.
12. See the work of the Institute for Prospective Technology Studies (IPTS) of the European Commission (EC), the EC research program on big data within Horizon 2020, and the OECD work program mentioned above.
13. From a very abstract perspective it would be possible to distinguish between data that exist prior to any measurement from data that only exist they have been obtained. The former are sometimes termed 'raw data', although in essence all data are raw, as stated by Gitelman (2013). In this chapter the term is largely avoided except in the last section where differences in intellectual property rights (IPR) before and after data acquisition are discussed.

REFERENCES

Acquisti, A. and H. Varian (2005), 'Conditioning prices on purchase history', *Marketing Science*, **24** (3), 1–15.

Akred, J., R. Williamson and S. O'Sullivan (2013), 'Building a data platform', paper presented at the Strata Conference + Hadoop World, New York, 28 October 2013, accessed 1 January 2016 at http://conferences.oreilly.com/strata/stratany2014/public/schedule/detail/36512.

Ballon, P. (2009), 'The platformisation of the European mobile industry', *Communications & Strategies*, **3** (75), 15–34.

Belleflamme, P. and M. Peitz (2010), *Industrial Organization: Markets and Strategies*, Cambridge, UK: Cambridge University Press.

boyd, d. and K. Crawford (2012), 'Critical questions for big data', *Information, Communication & Society*, **15** (5), 662–79.

Buchholtz, S., M. Bukowski and A. Śniegocki (2014), *Big and Open Data in Europe: A Growth Engine or a Missed Opportunity*, report commissioned by demosEUROPA – Centre for European Strategy Foundation, Warsaw Institute for Economic Studies, accessed 12 January 2015 at http://www.bigopendata.eu/wp-content/uploads/2014/01/bod_europe_2020_full_report_singlepage.pdf.

Chen, H., R.H.L. Chiang and V.C. Storey (2012), 'Business intelligence and analytics: From big data to big impact', *MIS Quarterly*, **36** (4), 1165–88.

Dhar, V. (2013), 'Data science and prediction', *Communications of the ACM*, **56** (12), 64–73.

Feijóo, C., J.L. Gómez-Barroso and P. Voigt (2014), 'Exploring the economic value of personal information from firms' financial statements', *International Journal on Information Management*, **34** (2), 248–56.

Feijóo, C., J.L. Gómez-Barroso and D. Potoglou et al. (2013), 'Analysis of the economic value of personal information', Seville: Institute for Prospective Technological Studies–European Commission.

Feinleib, D. (2012), 'Big data landscape', *Forbes*, 19 June, accessed 22 January 2015 at http://www.forbes.com/sites/davefeinleib/2012/06/19/the-big-data-landscape/.

Gawer A. and M.A. Cusumano (2002), *Platform Leadership: How Intel, Microsoft, and Cisco Drive Industry Innovation*, Boston, MA: Harvard Business School Press.

Gawer, A. and R. Henderson (2007), 'Platform owner entry and innovation in complementary markets: Evidence from Intel', *Journal of Economics & Management Strategy*, **16** (1), 1–34.

Gitelman, L. (ed.) (2013), *'Raw Data' is an Oxymoron*, Cambridge, MA: MIT Press.

Gómez-Barroso, J.L. and C. Feijóo (2013), 'Información personal: la nueva moneda de la economía digital' [Personal information: the new currency of the digital economy], *El Profesional de la Informacion*, **22** (4), 290–97.

Grossklags, J., S. Hall and A. Acquisti (2007), 'When 25 cents is too much: An experiment on willingness-to-sell and willingness-to-protect personal information', in *Proceedings of Sixth Workshop on the Economics of Information Security (WEIS 2007)*, Pittsburgh, PA, 7–8 June.

Hemerly, J. (2013), 'Public policy considerations for data-driven innovation', *Computer*, **46** (6), 25–31.

Hey, T., S. Tansley and K. Tolle (eds) (2009), *Fourth Paradigm. Data Intensive Science Discovery*, Redmond, WA: Microsoft Research, accessed 22 January 2015 at http://research.microsoft.com/en-us/collaboration/fourthparadigm/.

Hidding, G., J. Williams and J. Svlokla (2011), 'How platforms leaders win', *Journal of Business Strategy*, **32** (2), 29–37.

Jacobs, A. (2009), 'The pathologies of big data', *Communications of the ACM*, **52** (8), 36–44.

Jentzsch, N., S. Preibusch and A. Harasser (2012), 'Study on monetising privacy. An economic model for pricing personal information', *European Union Agency for Network and Information Security*, 28 February, accessed 22 January 2015 at http://www.enisa.europa.eu/activities/identity-and-trust/library/deliverables/monetising-privacy.

Kelly, K. (2014), 'Big data vendor revenue and market forecast 2013–2017', *Wikibon*, 12 February, accessed 23 January 2015 at http://wikibon.org/wiki/v/Big_Data_Vendor_Revenue_and_Market_Forecast_2013-2017.

Lohr, S. (2012), 'The age of big data', *The New York Times*, 11 February, accessed 23 January 2015 at http://www.nytimes.com/2012/02/12/sunday-review/big-datas-impact-in-the-world.html?pagewanted=all/&_r=0.

Manyika, J.M. Chui and B. Brown et al. (2011), 'Big data: The next frontier for innovation, competition, and productivity', *McKinsey.com*, May, accessed 23 January 2015 at http://www.mckinsey.com/insights/business_technology/big_data_the_next_frontier_for_innovation.

Marton, A., M. Avital and T.B. Jensen (2013), 'Reframing open big data', paper presented at the 21st European Conference on Information Systems, Utrecht, 5–8 June 2013.

Mayer-Schönberger, V. and K. Cukier (2013), *Big Data: A Revolution That Will Transform How We Live, Work, and Think*, New York: Houghton, Mifflin Harcourt.

McAfee, A. and E. Brynjolfsson (2012), 'Big data: The management revolution', *Harvard Business Review*, **90** (10), 3–9.

Mulligan, M. and D. Card (2014), *Sizing the EU App Economy*, European Commission Digital Agenda for Europe, accessed 23 January 2015 at https://ec.europa.eu/digital-agenda/en/news/sizing-eu-app-economy.

Murray-Rust, P. (2008), 'Open data in science', *Serials Review*, **34** (1), 52–64.

Nissenbaum, H. (2010), *Privacy in Context. Technology, Policy and the Integrity of Social Life*, Stanford, CA: Stanford University Press.

OECD (2013), 'Exploring data-driven innovation as a new source of growth: Mapping the policy issues raised by big data', *OECD Digital Economy Papers, No. 222*, OECD Publishing, accessed 23 January 2015 at http://dx.doi.org/10.1787/5k47zw3fcp43-en.

OECD (2014), 'Unleashing the power of big data for Alzheimer's disease and dementia research: Main points of the OECD expert consultation on unlocking global collaboration to accelerate innovation for Alzheimer's disease and dementia', *OECD Digital Economy Papers, No. 233*, OECD Publishing, accessed 23 January 2015 at http://dx.doi.org/10.1787/5jz73kvmvbwb-en.

Potoglou, D., S. Patil, C. Gijón-Tascón, J. Palacios and C. Feijóo (2013), 'The value of personal information online: Results from three stated preference discrete choice experiments in the UK', in *Proceedings of the 21st European Conference on Information Systems (ECIS)*, Utrecht, accessed 23 January 2015 at http://www.staff.science.uu.nl/~Vlaan107/ecis/files/ECIS2013-0899-paper.pdf.

Varian, H. (2009), 'Hal Varian on how the web challenges managers', *McKinsey & Company Insights and Publications*, January 2009, accessed 6 January 2015 at http://www.mckinsey.com/insights/innovation/hal_varian_on_how_the_web_challenges_managers.

World Economic Forum (2012), *Big Data, Big Impact: New Possibilities for International Development*, Geneva, accessed 23 January 2015 at http://www3.weforum.org/docs/WEF_TC_MFS_BigDataBigImpact_Briefing_2012.pdf.

PART V

PAST AND FUTURE TRAJECTORIES

26. The evolution of the Internet: a socioeconomic account

D. Linda Garcia

26.1 INTRODUCTION: THE NEED FOR A HISTORICAL ANALYSIS

The US Internet emerged more or less *sui generis* amidst the technological advances that sparked a revolution in the field of communications. In contrast to the old conception of the communication infrastructure as a regulated natural monopoly, these rapid advances allowed for its unbundling and modularization (OTA, 1990, pp. 50–51), thereby giving rise to a radically new paradigm, one that called for deregulation and greater market competition (Noam, 1988, 1995; Stone, 1991; Drake, 1995; Geller, 1995). And just as in the case of the Internet itself, each new phase of its development, and the policy puzzles each posed, arose *de novo* (Abbate, 1994; Blumenthal and Clark, 2001; Clark et al., 2002). Hence, from a historical perspective, we cannot speak of an 'economics of the Internet' per se. To the contrary, our understanding of the history of Internet economics has coevolved with each phase of the Internet's development, together with each policy framework that has been associated with it (Abbate, 1994; Bailey and McKnight, 1995; Tapscott, 1996; Beinhocker, 2006; Benkler, 2006).

As a result, although the technological architecture of the Internet has remained much the same in terms of its modularity, openness, and generativity, each phase of the Internet's evolution can be differentiated based on aspects such as its political economy, the economic motivations and incentives fostering its development, and the socioeconomic organization of the Internet space. The development of the Internet must also be analyzed with respect to how each episode relates to past and future periods. As Paul Pierson (2004, p. 20) argues, only by linking historical events can we address the 'causal power of temporal connections among events', including path dependency, critical junctures, sequencing, and unintended consequences.

Even then, to make theoretical statements based on historical material, a single, linear narrative will not do. To capture the complexity of the Internet's evolution and interactions among players, technologies and events over time requires a comparative methodology (Braudel, 1980, p. 67). Although comparative history is wide ranging, its core concern is causal analysis using systematic contextual comparisons (Mahoney and Rueschemeyer, 2003, p. 7). Skocpol and Somers (1980, p. 179) identify three different approaches. The first, macro-causal analysis, resembles multivariate hypothesis testing. A second, parallel demonstration of theory, identifies similarities across cases that support a particular theoretical proposition. The third approach, the contrast of contexts, challenges general theories by identifying features associated with each case, and by examining how these features differentially impact socio-economic processes (Skocpol and

Somers, 1980). Given the dynamic evolution of the Internet, it is this latter approach that will be employed in this historical analysis.

To address the problem of historical specificity, as well as to allow for the incorporation of social and political forces in the analysis, the economy is defined in accordance with Karl Polanyi's 'substantive' definition. Polanyi defines the economy as an empirically instituted process by which individuals engage with each other and their environments to meet their material needs (Polanyi, 2011, p. 4). Conceived as such, the economy can be organized in a variety of ways. So defined, the economy is embedded and enmeshed not solely in what we typically think of as economic institutions, but also in society at large (Braudel, 1980; Granovetter, 1985). This definition is especially useful for studying the Internet's economic history insofar as market relations have governed interactions only during certain periods and aspects of the Internet's development.

For the purpose of comparison, this chapter frames four historical periods in the context of organizational fields (Powell and DiMaggio, 1991; Schwartz, 1997; Fligstein, 2001; Fligstein and McAdam, 2012). The following section describes organization fields and their modi operandi. Section 26.3 examines the period of AT&T's rise and fall. Section 26.4 lays out the history of the ARPANET era and the emergence of TCP/IP. Section 26.5 describes the National Science Foundation's role as the 'midwife' of the Internet, followed by a section characterizing the emergence of the Internet market-place. The final section compares and contrasts the four historical periods. It divides the Internet's history into four distinct periods: AT&T – the unified telephone regime; the ARPANET era and the emergence of TCP/IP; NSF – the midwife of the Internet; and to market to market – history in the making. To frame these periods, it draws on the literature on organizational fields (Powell and DiMaggio, 1991; Schwartz, 1997; Fligstein, 2001; Fligstein and McAdam, 2012).

26.2   ORGANIZATIONS AND ORGANIZATIONAL FIELDS

An organizational field refers to the entire network of interdependent actors and organizations that comprise a recognized area of institutional life (Powell and DiMaggio, 1991; Scott, 2001; Fligstein and McAdam, 2012). Although organizations have much in common, they differ depending on their specific purposes and the circumstances in which they operate. Organizations, moreover, are in a continuous state of flux. Constituted through human interactions, organizational goals and relationships are constantly being reinterpreted and renegotiated by diverse organizational actors, each with their own values, interests, and agendas (Powell and DiMaggio, 1991, p. 9). Thus, over time, an organization takes on a life of its own (Weick, 1995). To survive, an organization must be responsive not only to its own internal dynamics but also to external developments and events. Hence, its effectiveness and ability to survive depends on how well it can manage the multiple, and at times competing, demands of those upon whom it depends for resources and support (Pfeffer and Salancik, 2003). Thus, much of an organization's structure and behavior can be explained in terms of how the organization is situated and networked to meet these needs (Powell and DiMaggio, 1991; Amin and Hausner, 1997; Gulati and Gargiulo, 1999; Scott, 2001).

Needless to say, given the complexity involved, organizations can hardly attend to all surrounding occurrences and events. Rather, organizations are loosely coupled to their environments. Thus, they typically attune themselves to a limited number of other like-minded organizations – those upon which they are most dependent. In effect, organizations construct their own 'relevant' relationships and environments (White, 1992; Pfeffer and Salancik, 2003). This networked environment, which is situated at the level between the organization and its overarching institutional environment, constitutes an 'organizational field'.

Organizational fields emerge over time, as interdependent organizations act together to create stability within their domains. In the process, they develop a set of structured practices and patterns of interactions, as well as a common meaning system unique to their institutional space. Once taken for granted, these practices recreate and reconstruct the existing order of things (White, 1992; Fligstein, 2001). It is this structuration of the field that allows for its governance. Typically, the most powerful incumbents dominate the field, defining the boundaries and meaning of the space as well as the roles and relationships of its occupants (Fligstein, 2001; Fligstein and McAdam, 2012). Weaker parties generally accept their inferior status, given their dependence and the benefits that accrue from participation in the field. Incumbents can, moreover, strengthen their positions if they can link their claims to general societal understandings about how things ought to be done (Schwartz, 1997, p. 236). Note, however, that increased structuration cannot only generate consensus, but also dissent (Fligstein and McAdam, 2012). Hence, although organizational fields are relatively stable, they are subject to effective challenges and transformations over the long term.

This conceptualization provides a common framework for analyzing each episode of the Internet's evolution. For each case, the chapter identifies the specific technologies involved; the resource requirements necessary to put these technologies in place; and the costs of developing and deploying the technologies, as well as how these costs are allocated across the field. Also, for each case the chapter characterizes the structure of the field, how decisions are made, the culture and internal practices associated with the field, and the field's relationship to its institutional surroundings. In addition, each case describes the dynamics of the field and the forces that drive its evolution. The conclusion relates each episode to the others, identifying more general patterns in the evolution of the Internet (Beinhocker, 2006; Hodgson and Knudson, 2010; Padgett and Powell, 2012).

26.3   AT&T: THE UNIFIED TELEPHONE REGIME

If ever there were an organizational field that approximated unity and stability, it would be the US telecommunications sector in the years following the Kingsbury Commitment. This 1913 agreement between the Bell System and the US government legitimated the company's monopoly status while subjecting it at one and the same time to government regulation. The operational goal was 'one system, one policy, universal service'. Comprised of AT&T and its subsidiaries and affiliates, the regulated Bell System offered a complete range of telecommunication services. Having a total of $150 billion in assets in 1983, it constituted the world's largest corporation (Gilroy, 1984).

Even prior to the agreement the organization of the field was crafted to meet the needs of a rapidly expanding industrial society. Like many other industrial firms of the period,

AT&T, the predominant telephone provider, sought to reduce complexity and uncertainty by vertically integrating all aspects of its business into one bureaucratic hierarchy (Chandler, 1977; Beniger, 1986; Lazonick, 1991). To do so, it had to subdue its rivals in the field, which it did relentlessly by denying interconnection to competitors unwilling to join the Bell System on its terms (Stone, 1991; Ryan, 2010, p. 67; Wu, 2011). AT&T's successful dominance of the field had unintended consequences. As the value of the telephone industry's monopoly grew, so did the threat from competitors. Under challenge, Theodore Vail, the president of AT&T sought to head off the opposition by asking the US government to regulate the company. Acknowledging the benefits of monopoly, the government restructured the field, allowing AT&T to operate as a near monopoly, subject to government scrutiny (Galambos and Pratt, 1989; Stone, 1991; Wu, 2011). AT&T was required to provide services as a common carrier with the government assuring compliance. Taking the form of a monopoly, the Bell System provided guaranteed interoperability, thereby enjoying the advantage of economies of scale and scope (Brock, 1981). Having waged a nationwide public relations campaign, AT&T convinced the public that a regulated monopoly was the only way to reduce 'wasteful competition' (Kolko, 1963). Under this arrangement, the System was considered legitimate.

Given its popularity, what accounted for the Bell System's demise? It might be characterized as a phase transition, which is to say a gradual build up over time followed by a sudden and total restructuring of the field (Perez, 2010; Padgett and Powell, 2012). As its environment changed, AT&T was no longer fit to operate successfully (Kauffman, 1995). As described below, four interdependent factors accounted for this shift: technological developments, economic developments, changes in approaches to regulation, and the opening of the long-distance market to competition (Coll, 1986; Tunstall, 1986; Temin, 1988; Noam, 1988, 1995; Crandall, 1989; Geller, 1995).

Technological developments had a major impact, bringing about the convergence of the telecommunications and information technology fields. This convergence led to the unbundling of the network, allowing customers to purchase technologies and services as single units (OTA, 1990, pp. 50–51). In addition, as new technologies both increased in capabilities while costs declined, barriers to entry into telecommunications were greatly reduced. Hence, many newcomers made significant inroads into AT&T's traditional markets. The entry of these competitors put pressure on the system of subsidized pricing that had been so elaborately constructed over the years (OTA, 1990).

Economic developments also greatly increased others' incentives to enter the market. In particular, as information began to play a more strategic role in business, larger users began to seek more efficient ways of purchasing telecommunications services (Schiller, 1982; Noam, 1995). Thus, they established their own internal telecommunications networks, bypassing the Bell System and purchasing services and equipment in the unregulated market. Recognizing the high stakes, they joined forces with the burgeoning new service providers to press for greater competition (OTA, 1990).

Changes were also taking place in the way regulators and economists thought about regulation. As early as the 1940s, some began to challenge the public utility concept (Gray, 1940; Stigler and Friedland, 1962; Kahn, 1983; Coll, 1986). In the field of telephony, this attitude was reflected in the radical changes in the nature of the relationship between the Federal Communications Commission (FCC) and AT&T (Temin, 1988). Impressed by the innovative potential of new technology, the FCC issued a number of decisions leading to the divestiture of the Bell System. In 1959 the FCC promulgated its 'Above 890' decision, liberalizing the licensing of private microwave systems and allowing the newly created Microwave Communications, Inc. (MCI) to offer private line service. With the subsequent Carterfone decision in 1969, the FCC opened the customer-premises market to entry. And finally, with the 1976 and 1978 decisions on ExecuNet requiring AT&T to provide connections to MCI, the FCC struck a final blow to the 100-year-old AT&T monopoly by opening the long-distance market to competition (Brock, 1981). Effective as of January 1984, after the approval of the Modification of Final Judgment (MFJ) by the United States District Court for the District of Columbia, settling the anti-trust law suit *United States* v. *AT&T*, the Bell System came to an end.

Organizational fields serve to coordinate actors' efforts to accomplish a common goal. In the field of telephony, AT&T maintained the dominant role for 100 years, defining the narrative that legitimated its monopoly, incorporating all other players in its verti-cally integrated bureaucracy, and spawning a new regulatory framework that served to perpetuate its predominance. AT&T's regulated monopoly was fitting for the times, and legitimate in the eyes of the public. Its elaborate structure of internal subsidies allowed it to cover its costs while meeting its goals of universal service. But AT&T's fate was ulti-mately determined by new technologies that generated changes in its fitness landscape, leading to new competitors and more differentiated users, as well as new perspectives about the role of communications in society.

26.4   THE ARPANET ERA AND THE EMERGENCE OF TCP/IP

Whereas creating a stable, integrated field of telephony required a top-down strategic approach, the task of creating a unified data communication field was altogether dif-ferent. In contrast to AT&T, which subdued its competitors by 'carrying a big stick', the creators of the ARPANET sought to attract adherents with positive inducements (Ryan, 2010, p. 43). In addition, while telephone service was a commercialized private good, packet-switched data services were at best an inchoate public good. Thus, whereas US government regulation often constrained AT&T's economic ambitions, in the case of ARPANET, the government sponsored and actively promoted the Internet's success. Not surprisingly, the economics of the ARPANET unfolded in very different ways. The result was a non-commercial, user-oriented organizational field, which was based on the principles of sharing and reciprocity rather than on profit-oriented calculations.

ARPANET was one of the most successful instances of sustainable government invest-ment in infrastructure (Leiner et al., 1997). Unlike the privately funded public switched telephone network, the ARPANET was publicly financed through the Advanced Research Project Agency (ARPA) to the amount of $833 million over four years (Pelkey, 2014, Chapter 6). The government's willingness to back such an untried venture reflected the Cold War climate of the time. In October 1957 the Soviet Union launched Sputnik, raising US fears that the US prowess in science and defense technology was at risk (Abbate, 1994, p. 8). In response, President Eisenhower prioritized research and devel-opment, resulting in the 1958 establishment of ARPA within the US Department of Defense (ibid.; Hafner and Lyon, 1996). Tasked with testing innovative technologies such as packet switching, distributed computing, and the interconnection of heterogeneous computer systems, the aim was to enhance productivity and innovation by allowing for greater resource sharing (Bolt, Beranek and Newman, Inc., 1981, pp. 11–12).

Despite the magnitude of the effort, ARPA was not organized from the top down, with a strict hierarchy and standardized roles and practices. Instead, seeking to capture the benefits of diversity, ARPA was organized in an open, loosely coupled, decentralized fashion, so that roles and relationships were not set a priori but rather negotiated in an ongoing practice (Hauben, 1997; Ryan, 2010). Thus, ARPA did not conduct research on its own. Instead, it established a distributed division of labor, funding major computer research centers with grants of $500 000 to $3 million to work on various aspects of inter-related computer research (Hafner and Lyon, 1996, p. 46). The first four centers were at the University of California, Los Angeles, Stanford Research Institute, the University of California, Santa Barbara, and the University of Utah. In addition, ARPA contracted with the firm Bolt, Beranek and Newman (BBN) to build the communications layer and administer the system. By addressing different, but related, aspects of research, each center complemented the others (Hauben, 1997).

With the research centers in place, ARPA coordinated its efforts through informal working groups comprised of representatives from each center. These centers pooled their diverse resources, and developed a framework for building a network of heterogeneous computers and researchers that could work together and share resources. Their goal was to create a low-level communication platform, upon which higher communication functions might be built (Abbate, 1994; Hafner and Lyon, 1996; Hauben, 1997).

The principal investigators (PIs) from the computer centers were at first reluctant to engage in collaboration (Abbate, 1994, p. 53). Nonetheless, a core group of PIs committed to pursuing the ARPANET vision. Together they formed the Network Working Group (NWG), which assembled periodically 'to develop software for host computers and discuss early experiences with the network' (ibid., p. 48). From this group, a plan emerged to create an autonomous sub-network of computers within the network designed to provide a common, mediating interface, or instant message processor (IMP), that could link to all computers as well as route traffic throughout the network. An autonomous sub-network allowed researchers to concentrate on developing their own, specialized content, rather than being responsible for interconnection and traffic routing (ibid., p. 37).

A new technology – packet switching – was adopted to carry out the functions of the sub-network. This technology allowed messages to be routed through the sub-network via a common 'message' protocol, where they were broken up into packets that could then be transmitted separately through the network, taking different paths depending on which were free at the moment. On reception at the host computer, the packets would be recombined in the correct sequence. Packet switching was well suited to handling the 'bursty' traffic associated with data transmission. Moreover, it was faster, cheaper, and more accurate than circuit-switched telephony, and as such it was ideal for real-time interactive communication (ibid., p. 44). This was evermore true as the cost of switching in relationship to transmission significantly declined (MacKie-Mason and Varian, 1994, pp. 4–5).

ARPA's network – the ARPANET – evolved into three layers: a sub-network, or communication layer that comprised the packet-switching IMPs; a host layer, labeled the Network Control Center, which provided end-to-end communication between host computers as well as a universal interface for user service; and an applications layer that fed data to the Network Control Program (NCP) where it was packaged and sent to the local IMP (Abbate, 1994, pp. 45, 58). Once this architecture was established, building the network was relatively straightforward: by 1969, the sub-network was put into place, while the host and application protocols followed in the next two years (ibid., p. 68).

Creating a social network linking researchers at the computer research centers was somewhat more difficult. Despite the potential network benefits, a culture of sharing was slow to take hold. Given the limited resources at each computer center, researchers were hesitant to expend their efforts collectively. Moreover, demand was low because available applications were limited, a problem that the NWG sought to rectify by developing new software (ibid., p. 63). Over time, however, ARPA's informal, decentralized, consensus-based management style and participatory organizational culture promoted a collective approach to problem solving (ibid.; Passy, 2003). The researchers' common background in computer science played an important role in this regard (Hauben, 1997). Because this new field was so small, many of its top researchers were acquainted with, if they did not personally know, one another (Abbate, 1994, p. 77; Hafner and Lyon, 1996). Moreover, engaging in many of the same problems, they shared much in common (Abbate, 1994, p. 80; Hauben, 1997). Equally important, their 'hacker' culture emphasized openness, experimentation, and freewheeling, interactive engagement, as exhibited in the reiterative 'Request for Comment Process' (Hauben, 1997; Hauben and Hauben, 1997; Ryan, 2010, p. 35). This shared culture not only fostered participation, it also generated the social capital required for collaboration and knowledge sharing to take place (Coleman, 1988; Tsai and Ghoshal, 1998; Inkpen and Tsang, 2005, p. 151). Hence, it was only as a last resort that the ARPA directors had to use their financial leverage to gain compliance (Abbate, 1994, p. 79).

Such synergies and positive externalities continued to expand the ARPANET as experimental applications, such as remote interactive login, file transfer protocol, and electronic mail were developed by users, refined by the NWG, and put into place. In 1971, ARPANET ran at only 2 percent of its capacity (Rosenzweig, 1998, p. 6). However, a turning point came when ARPA rallied the members of the NWG and software experts to develop network applications to be showcased on the ARPANET at an International Conference on Computer Communications (ICCC) held in October 1972. The demonstration was a great success (Hauben, 1997). Witnessing the actual working ARPANET, observers became 'early adopters', moving it up the diffusion curve (Rogers, 1993). For example, in August 1972 the Internet consisted of only 29 IMP nodes. By September 1973 there were 30; by June 1974 there were 40; and by July 1975 they totaled 65. This rapid growth continued, and by 1981 there were 213 host computers, with another host added about every 20 days.[1]

Efforts were also underway to port ARPANET to packet radio and satellite technology. However, to transfer data packets across these diverse networks required redesigning the NCP protocol (Russell, 2006, p. 50). Between 1973 and 1978, four reiterations took place. The final version, designed to accommodate voice transmission, divided the original NCP protocol into two layers, TCP (Transmission Control Protocol) and IP (Internet Protocol) (Cerf, 2004, pp. 2–5). Accordingly, the TCP breaks messages into streams of packets at the source, and reconfigures them when they reach their destination. In turn, the IP addresses the messages, ensuring that the packets are routed across multiple nodes and even across multiple networks with different standards (Sterling, 1993).

TCP/IP's open, non-proprietary protocol engendered numerous externalities that moved the ARPANET up the diffusion curve. This growth was propelled by externalities that stemmed not only from the extension of the TCP/IP across networks of all types, but also from the growing availability of low-cost computers, and the creation of an extended user base that was engaged in network applications development (Rosenzweig, 1998; Ryan, 2010). In fact, so great was the ARPANET's growth it soon overwhelmed ARPA's ability to take it forward (Russell, 2006, p. 50).

Thus, in 1972, ARPA sought out private-sector actors to assume responsibility for the network. There were no bidders, however (Rosenzweig, 1998). Skeptical of ARPA's venture from the start, and fearing that data networking might undermine its own telephone monopoly, AT&T had emphatically shied away from any offers of collaboration (Abbate, 1994; Hafner and Lyon, 1996, pp. 65–6; Ryan, 2010, p. 18). And the computer industry, although by now realizing the market for data communication, was threatened by open standards (Ryan, 2010, p. 44). To maintain the industry's integrated businesses intact, IBM and DEC (the Digital Equipment Corporation) sought to develop proprietary data communication standards of their own. With no alternatives in sight, the ARPANET was turned over to the Defense Communication Agency (DCA) in 1975 (Abbate, 1994). This transfer did not tighten the reigns on the ARPANET, as one might have expected; instead, the DCA made the open standard, TCP/IP, mandatory for all ARPANET users (Russell, 2006). In 1983, access was extended further, when the military cordoned off its segment, MILNET, but maintained TCP/IP as the ultimate, connecting link.

By all measures, the ARPANET was a remarkable, innovative feat. Its success stemmed not only from having public funding in its initial stage, but also from its unique institutional milieu, which engendered a community of practice (Wenger, 1998) that encouraged trial and error, learning by doing, and participatory feedback (Brown and Duguid, 2001). The architecture of the development process was itself exceptionally important. As characterized in social network theory, both the ARPA process and the ARPANET took the form of a small world network (Watts and Strogatz, 1998; Watts, 1999; Buchanan, 2002; Uzzi et al., 2007; Borgatti et al., 2009), which is optimal for innovation to take place (Burt, 1992; Uzzi, 1997; Burt, 2005; Fleming and Marx, 2006). As Uzzi and others have described it, a small world network is characterized by cohesive clusters composed of strong ties that provide the trust and social capital required for collective action, and weak ties emanating from these clusters that assure that new and diverse information is made available. In ARPA's case the research centers constituted the cluster of strong ties, whereas the NWG allowed for interconnection based on weak ties.

The broader institutional environment also favored ARPANET. Government investment, sparked by international crises, allowed ARPA to experiment as well as operate on a trial and error basis without having to preoccupy itself with profit-making and other market criteria. Similarly, cordoned off in the Department of Defense, ARPA researchers could operate without external stakeholders and rivals, thereby establishing a community with a common narrative and script, which fostered innovation and knowledge sharing. At the same time, ARPA benefited from external system-wide advances, such as those in computer technology and computer science, which generated many of the externalities that fueled the diffusion of ARPANET.

ARPA, which spanned the worlds of academics, computer scientists, defense specialists, and industry practitioners, constituted an organizational field, with its own internal modes of operation. However, unlike the field of telephony, which was highly structured and deeply embedded in society, the ARPA field was both loosely coupled as well as lightly embedded in its surroundings. As a result, in contrast to AT&T, which was unable to adapt to its changing environment, ARPA's flexible structure allowed it to coevolve when its very success brought about major changes in the landscape. Moreover, the open, interactive culture developed during this period generated the modus operandi for the period that followed (Ryan, 2010, p. 33).

26.5 THE NSF: 'MIDWIFE' TO THE INTERNET

When it comes to networks, success breeds transitions. For, just as the growing value of the telephone network gave rise to a diversified competitive market, so too did the increasing externalities and added value associated with ARPANET generate private-sector interest in developing for-profit data communication services (Cave and Mason, 2001; Rohlfs, 2001). However, this transition was not unaided. As described below, the National Science Foundation (NSF) helped in the birth of a new organizational field, comprised of a more inclusive and diverse group of players, all of whom had special interests of their own. By building and subsidizing the high-speed NSFNET, the NSF helped overcome problems of collective action that typically inhibit collaboration. At the same time, the NSF not only generated a public good that induced cooperation and participation among heterogeneous players, it also provided an economic platform upon which participants could coordinate their interactions and create a market for Internet services (Kazumori, 2003). Additionally, by creating demand through its advanced computing research centers and business sites, the NSF helped engender a critical mass of users, paving the way for sustainable private investments. Its science-oriented practices and policies also contributed to a narrative that distinguished the Internet field from other commodity markets (Rogers, 1993; Abbate, 1994; CSTB, 1996; Rohlfs, 2001).

In January 1981 NSF approved a proposal from Professor Lawrence Landweber of the University of Wisconsin to provide five years of funding to develop a computer science network linking university campuses across the United States. This proposal reflected growing demands by university computer scientists to gain ARPANET access, which was then only open to defense-related researchers (Rogers, 1993, p. 214; Ryan, 2010, p. 93). The ARPANET's restricted access policy had created a two-tiered field of computer science, such that those without access saw themselves, as did others, as second-class citizens. Coming at a time when ARPA had partitioned its military network (MILNET) from the ARPANET, Landweber's proposal was feasible for the first time (Abbate, 1994).

In spite of the proposal's merits, the NSF had some serious concerns, which led to the rejection of Landweber's first request made in 1979. Not the least of these was the issue of management. Focusing on peer-reviewed basic research, the NSF was ill equipped to manage a large-scale infrastructure project (Rogers, 1993, p. 215). Continued interest in the burgeoning field of computer science led to a second look, however. With the encouragement of the computer science staff within the NSF, Landweber's second proposal was approved in January 1981. Accordingly, the NSF pledged to create a Computer Science

Network (CSNET) with support for five years, after which it would be self-supporting. Backbone users were required to conform to NSF's 'Acceptable Use Policy' restricting traffic to open research and education and prohibiting commercial activity. Usage fees ranged from $5000 annually for universities to $30 000 for industry facilities (Ryan, 2010, p. 94).

Moving from CSNET to the NSFNET required more than financing; it required buy-in from government agencies and academic science programs. Over the next three years, NSF's effort gained increasing support due in part to a changed environment. Just as ARPANET had been inspired by Sputnik, the NSFNET gained traction after the Japanese launch of its fifth-generation supercomputing program. Concerned lest the USA lose its pre-eminence in microelectronics and computing, Congress asked the NSF to create a supercomputing program so as to make high-performance computing available to all fields of science (Rogers, 1993, p. 216; Abbate, 1994).

Coordinating and integrating the diverse players needed to carry out the NSF's mission posed significant challenges. Congress had emphasized that the NSF's program should not lead to redundant capabilities, but to new opportunities for collaboration among government, industry, and academia (Rogers, 1993, p. 318). To achieve these goals, the NSF had to assure that each participant played its own unique, but interdependent, role. By establishing the NSFNET, the National Science Foundation brought together a critical mass of players, and gave them each a stake in the future of the NSFNET (ibid., p. 214; Abbate, 1994, p. 175).

As a first step, the NSF set out to support supercomputing research at all US universities. To this end, it developed a multi-tiered system, much like the network itself, whereby each level was both independent of, but also interdependent on, the others. Accordingly, each university center was to build its own network with seed money from the NSF. These research centers were then connected at the regional level, using leased lines from local and regional network providers. These networks, of which there were seven by early 1988, constituted the mid-level network. To get them up and running, the NSF initially subsidized them, but they were expected to become self-supporting. The regional networks were then connected to the high-speed national 'backbone' network, CSNET (Rogers, 1993).

CSNET, however, was poorly equipped to handle the subsequent increase in traffic, or to manage a network of such rapidly growing size (Kazumori, 2003; Ryan, 2010, p. 96). Cost was one issue. In 1992, the NSF spent approximately $11 million annually on NSFNET, and an additional $7 million to support the regional networks. Close to 80 percent of these costs went to leasing lines and routers (MacKie-Mason and Varian, 1994, pp. 5–6). Management costs were also high, as NSF had only 14 staff members to oversee the network (Kazumori, 2003). Hence in 1987, the NSF turned over the construction and management of the backbone network, subsequently renamed the NSFNET, to the Michigan Educational Research Information Triad (MERIT) in collaboration with MCI and IBM at the cost of $14 million (Hart et al., 1992, p. 671). Under the terms of the contract, MERIT was to manage and administer the NSFNET; MCI to maintain it; while IBM was to provide its management software and packet switches.

Under MERIT's tenure, the NSFNET backbone network underwent a major transformation. Employing many of the same concepts and participants as the ARPANET, the NSFNET was deliberately designed to ensure widespread access, interoperability and long-term sustainability (CSTB, 1996, p. 29). To accommodate increased traffic and high-speed users, MERIT upgraded transmission lines from 54 Kbps to speeds ranging from 1.5 to 45 Mbps. Importantly, the NSFNET also employed the TCP/IP rather than the more formal but underdeveloped International Standard Organization's Open Systems Interconnection (OSI) suite (Rogers, 1993, p. 220).

TCP/IP gave the NSFNET its decentralized, modular, 'end-to-end' architecture, whereby application-specific functions were located on the end users' hosts at the 'edges' of the network (Saltzer et al., 1984; Blumenthal and Clark, 2001). This allowed all participants to manage their own portion of the network, while still being able to connect to the network as a whole. Given this modular design, the NSFNET was very flexible in handling new service providers, innovations, applications, and so on (CSTB, 1996). Changes to the system could be made on a piecemeal basis rather than in a costly system-wide overhaul. In this way, several new protocols were added to TCP/IP to accommodate new services (Hart et al., 1992, p. 673).

This design fostered a critical mass of users, generating a 'bandwagon effect'. As Jeffrey Rohlfs (2001) has pointed out, interconnection leads to benefits for virtually everyone. A major source of NSFNET's externalities was the expanding user base. Individuals benefited from greater interconnections and the increased applications that additional users inspired (Cave and Mason, 2001, p. 198). There were also a number of complementary externalities, resulting from the advent of personal computers, the declining cost of computing, the development of a Domain Name System, as well as the addition of new search applications such as Gopher, Veronica, and Archie (Abbate, 1994; Rohlfs, 2001; Ryan, 2010). Characterizing these network effects, Rohlfs points out that the NSF, by providing open interconnection at a subsidized cost, 'internalized the externalities for the greater public good' (Rohlfs, 2001, p. 189).

The result was precipitous growth in NSFNET traffic. In the fall of 1985, only 2000 computers could access the network. Two years later there were 30 000, increasing to 159 000 over the following two years (Abbate, 1994, p. 180). Internet traffic kept pace. Between May 1989 and May 1991, Internet traffic expanded from 1 billion packets per month to 7.65 billion packets. Two years later it was almost twice as high, at 14.9 billion packets (Hart et al., 1992, p. 671).

These externalities did not go unnoticed. Anticipating the potential profits, MERIT spun off a non-profit corporation in 1990 called Advanced Network Services (ANS). By subcontracting the backbone network's operations to ANS, MERIT was free to create a for-profit subsidiary – CO+RE – to offer services to the growing number of businesses users of TCP/IP (Ryan, 2010, p. 190). Other organizations, including the recently divested regional Bell operating companies, joined partnerships to realize similar opportunities (Rogers, 1993, p. 220; Hart, 1992, p. 676; Frischmann, 2001). Because commercial networks could not run over NSFNET, these providers had to build their own backbone networks, assuring that the capacity and reach of the backbone was greatly expanded. By the mid-1990s, the regional companies had become national, commercial Internet providers with commercial networks paralleling the NSFNET. Importantly, given the low cost of entry, new players entered the market, bringing with them adaptations of technology for new uses, locations, market settings and applications (Greenstein, 2001, p. 153–4). As a result, a competitive market for high-speed national computer networking services emerged (Frischmann, 2001, p. 18; Ryan, 2010, p. 191).

Signaling a changing narrative and a new kind of rhetoric, the Internet community welcomed commercialization (Rosenzweig, 1998; Ryan, 2010, p. 191). NSF managers also favored these developments, given their limited management capacity and financial resources. They believed commercialization would allow the NSFNET to incorporate new technologies and industrial partners upon whom the future Internet would depend (Frischmann, 2001). NSF managers also thought that, without commercial constraints, private-sector networks would greatly expand their networks' capacities and usage.

Congress confirmed this approach on 11 September 1991 with the passage of the High-Performance Computing and National Research and Education Network Act of 1991. This Act cancelled the NSF Acceptable Use Policy. At the same time, it reiterated the government's support for science and for the expansion of the Internet to the public at large though the development of a National Research Education Network (NREN), which, as Rogers points out, became 'the vehicle for discussing the information infrastructure of the future' (Rogers, 1993, pp. 223–4).

The NSF encouraged and supported the development of the mid-level regional networks by fostering network synergies through partnerships of universities, network providers, and businesses, such as BARNET, SURNET, and NYSERNET (ibid., p. 222). These partnerships not only brought diverse providers together, they also helped to aggregate user demand (Bailey, 1995). Notable in this regard was the development by the NSF and MCI of very high-performance Backbone Network Service (vBNS) to provide university communities with broadband capabilities. This effort was continued under the auspices of EDUCAUSE in the post-NSF period in the form of the Internet2 Project, which spawned the Abilene Network.[2]

Commercial arrangements for interconnection also helped to determine the structure of the emerging Internet field. Acting through its proprietary company CO+RE, MERIT asserted its dominance based on its exclusive ability to move commercial traffic over the NSFNET. Its leverage was significant, given that at the time approximately 35 percent of all network sites could only be reached by travelling on the NSFNET backbone network (Kazumori, 2003). In February 1991, three commercial ISPs, PSINET, UUNET, and CERFnet of California sought to offset this advantage by forming the Commercial Internet Exchange (CIX) with a router in Santa Clara, California (Wheeler and O'Kelly, 1999, p. 328). CIX aimed to interconnect its members on a peering basis, for an initial one-time fee of $10 000.

Concerns about unfair competition led to a Congressional hearing in March 1992. The House Subcommittee on Science called on the NSF to establish four network access points (NAPs), where providers could work out their interconnection agreements, either bilaterally or multilaterally. In June 1992, ANS and CIX agreed to interconnect. The NAPs, each operated by a different telecommunications company, were subsequently created in 1994, located in San Francisco, Chicago, New York and Washington, DC. At each of these ISPs could interconnect and share data in a peering fashion. Generally speaking, the large national ISPs established bilateral peering agreements and negotiated payment schemes with smaller providers. Smaller providers, which might serve only a few thousand customers, established a number of multilateral agreements, allowing them to send traffic on others' communication lines (ibid.).

While the transition to the commercial Internet went relatively smoothly (Greenstein, 2001), its success was by no means preordained. Building a market not only entails tremendous coordination problems and transaction costs, it also requires building trust, overcoming problems of collective action, establishing interoperability of human practices as well as technology, and creating – either through shared norms or legal requirements – an institutional framework, or as Douglass North (1990) calls it, 'the rules of the game'. In this regard, the NSF served as a midwife, providing the essential conditions to pave the way for the commercial birth of the Internet. In the years during which the NSF oversaw the NSFNET, it provided an institutional platform to match the Internet architecture, which attracted an ever-increasing number of diverse entities to create a dynamic common-pool resource rife with positive externalities. Just as importantly, the NSF provided a safe, and relatively cost-free site where all the divergent participants could converge to negotiate the Internet field and work out a governance system to preserve the commons (Ostrom, 1990).

Most notable was the development of Internet norms and governance institutions that sustained themselves even in the context of commercialization (Brown, 2013). These include, for example, the Internet Activities Board (IAB), which was established in 1984 to manage and guide the development of the network and its protocols. (In 1992 it took the name Internet Architecture Board to reflect its increasingly global composition.) Under its purview were two additional organizations: the Internet Engineering Task Force (IETF), formed in 1986, which was charged with addressing short-term, practical issues; and the Internet Research Task Force (IRTF), which was set up in 1989 to examine long-term issues. In addition, the Internet Society (ISOC) was founded in 1992 to serve as an umbrella organization that would provide leadership for the IETF and the IAB (Ryan, 2010, pp. 101–2). Finally, the Internet Corporation for Assigned Names and Numbers (ICANN) was established in 1988 as a non-profit global organization responsible for coordinating the Internet system of unique identifiers.[3]

26.6   TO MARKET, TO MARKET: HISTORY IN THE MAKING

On 30 April 1995, the commercial backbone networks formally replaced the NSFNET (Frischmann, 2001). Private network providers, eager to get into the game, subsequently invested enormous resources in further developing the Internet. With the advent of the World Wide Web, the field exploded as externalities multiplied. When new participants, with new ideas and business models, joined the fray, the relationship among them became increasingly complex. Everything was up for grabs. Hence, in contrast to the NSF period, where players were brought together in a relatively orderly fashion, in the post-NSF period, the market had to sort it all out.

Carlotta Perez describes the period as a technological revolution in the Schumpeterian sense of the word. According to her, 'a technological revolution is a set of interrelated radical breakthroughs, forming a major constellation of interdependent technologies' (Perez, 2010). Such revolutions occur when a radically new technology, such as the Internet, or the World Wide Web, sets off a chain reaction whereby interdependent innovators and entrepreneurs, benefiting from the positive externalities associated with a common pool of knowledge and resources, as well as dense feedback loops, generate new breakthroughs and spaces for profitable opportunities (ibid.).

Such periods are characterized by dramatic ups and downs, as investors overreact to

financial signals; regulators add complexity and uncertainty to the process; users struggle to interpret their choices in the new environment; and newcomers try out risky ideas,
all the while jockeying for position in the restructuring of the field. Such technological
revolutions are unique not simply because of the tremendous synergies between entrepreneurs, technologists and markets; equally important is the transformative power of the
technology to change the economy and society as a whole (ibid.; Mokyr, 1990; Freeman
and Louca, 2001; Beinhocker, 2006; Benkler, 2006; Arthur, 2009).

A revolutionary perspective such as Perez's helps make sense of the market's seemingly haphazard evolution following the commercialization of the Internet, as well as the
structural changes in the economy and society and the communication field in particular.
While this chapter cannot detail all the events and business strategies that have been
played out, it depicts a number of well-chosen examples that suggest the direction in
which things are headed.

Booms and busts are, perhaps, the best place to start. As one might expect, exuberant
investment in the Internet followed in the wake of its commercialization. Thus, between
1996 and 2001, AT&T, MCI and Sprint increased the amount of fiber cable deployed
sevenfold, enough to circle the equator 750 times (Shampine and Sider, 2007). At the
same time, between the first quarter of 1996 and the fourth quarter of 2000, investment in communications equipment grew at a rate of nearly 18 percent, increasing from
approximately $62 billion to more than $125 billion (Couper et al., 2003). Hence from
April 1997 to March 2000, the NASDAQ index of telecommunications shot up from 198
to 1230, that is to say, by an average annual gain of 84 percent (Couper et al., 2003, p. 5).

This telecom investment was stimulated by a number of factors. For one, the commercialization of the Internet coincided with the advent of the World Wide Web and
the first major commercial browser, Netscape Navigator. Telecom providers anticipated
that both of these technologies would greatly stimulate bandwidth demand, while greater
bandwidth would generate higher bandwidth applications. The Telecommunications Act
of 1996 also provided a strong incentive for expansion. Opening up local service markets
to competition, the Act induced many participants to become full service providers. So to
beat out the others, each built out their capacity as fast as they could (ibid., p. 3).

But the bubble was unsustainable. From late 2000, investment in communications was
negative for seven quarters in a row, reaching a nadir in the fourth quarter of 2001, when
investment totaled less than $93 billion, a drop of approximately 30 percent from the
previous year. By the end of 2002, investment in communication equipment, as a percentage of total private investment, had dropped from 7 percent in 2000 to 4.8 percent. The
NASDAQ index of telecommunication stocks declined from 1230 in 2000 to around 200
in 2002. By May 2003, it was only 136 (ibid., p. 4). What followed was a rash of bankrupt-
cies, large devaluations of company equity, declines in prices, and industry consolidation
(Shampine and Sider, 2007, p. 4).

While many have attributed the crash to over-exuberance, leading to excess capacity,
there was more to it than that. Legal battles stemming from the Telecommunications Act
of 1996 created a general atmosphere of uncertainty, making it difficult for companies
to correctly assess the economic landscape and model their business plans accordingly
(ibid., pp. 8–9). The downward swing of the whole economy magnified the uncertainty.
By June 2001 the end of the boom became starkly apparent when the tried-and-true
Canadian equipment manufacturer, Nortel, took a $19 million loss (ibid., p. 19).

Paralleling the boom in telephony was the inflation of the dot-coms, companies who do most of their business on the Internet. With the commercialization of the Internet and the development of the World Wide Web, investors rushed to enter e-commerce (Ryan, 2010, p. 127). The success of online companies such as eBay demonstrated the gains to be made. Having set up shop in September 1995, the eBay site had 41000 users within a year, and trades were valued at $7.2 million. Growth continued steadily, so that by the end of 2000 the site had 22 million users trading $5.4 billion worth of goods (ibid.). Seeking to replicate such success, a flood of dot-com companies jumped on the bandwagon (Greenstein, 2001, p. 162). By the late 1990s somewhere between 7000 and 10000 dot-coms had been established (Wang, 2006). These companies had little trouble finding financial backers. Investors, fearing that others would pre-empt them and enter the market faster, made a number of hasty and rash decisions (Ryan, 2010, p. 128). By 1999, venture capital investments in dot-coms reached $48.3 billion, at which point Warren Buffet noted that: 'Rationality had been given its sedative dose' (ibid.).

The dot-com bubble burst in the spring of 2000, as companies began to fold precipitously (Wang, 2006). In the two-year period between spring 2000 and 2003, approximately 5000 dot-com companies went under. Reflecting these developments, the Dow Jones Internet stock index plunged 93 percent, while the NASDAQ composite index lost 78 percent of its value (ibid., p. 2).

As in the case of telephony, uncertainty played a role in the dot-com crash. The Internet was a new phenomenon, and both investors and users were unsure what to make of it. No one could predict the changes it would bring, and hence what strategies to employ. Assuming new business paradigms, many greenhorn and imprudent investors overrated the prospects, and underrated the pitfalls. Like fools rushing in, they were unprepared as well as unwilling to learn the ropes along the way. Consider Netscape, for example. Within a year of its founding, the company increased its workforce from five employees to 2000. Growing at this pace the company was unable to develop a corporate culture that allowed for feedback and learning by doing (Ryan, 2010, p. 130).

Despite the collapse, e-commerce survived, and the proportion of US retail conducted over the Internet remained steady as entrepreneurs caught up with the technology and retrofitted their business plans accordingly. Users also became more comfortable with and trusting of Internet technology and online relationships during this period (Ryan, 2010). In addition, the competitive relationship between online and brick-and-mortar players changed, as traditional firms – building on their strong assets, and having incorporated many of the lessons of the dot-com era – increased their share of the market while many of the pure dot-coms exited it (Wang, 2006, p. 20).

Likewise, the telecom sector made a comeback, and many of the large media conglomerates remained in place, such that concentration levels approximated those of the 1950s (Wu, 2011, p. 274). Faithful to their well-entrenched industrial-era paradigm, they aimed to turn the Internet to their advantage. Many were concerned lest the Internet, having become a universal network capable of handling all types of data, undermine their modi operandi. Seeking to retain audiences numbering in the billions, and combined revenues totaling trillions, these conglomerates sought to tame the Internet by incorporating it into their vertically integrated model (Lemley and Lessig, 2001; Wu, 2011, p. 274). They envisioned a time when a few consolidated firms would absorb the prime Internet players, much as they had absorbed other new, and potentially threatening, media companies in the past (Ryan, 2010, p. 265).

Time Warner provides a prime example of such an approach, mirroring that of many others. In January 2000 it merged with AOL, the largest Internet firm, with the intent of becoming a major content platform. This turned out to be a great miscalculation. The merger was premised on the notion that customers, using dial-up Internet connections, would only be able to access content through AOL. However, with the advent of web technology and broadband capacity offered through phone and cable companies, ISPs like AOL could be circumvented. Within a year of the merger, AOL's share value declined dramatically from its lifetime high of $240 billion. AOL's founder, Steve Case, was forced out, and Carl Levin, from Time Warner, retired. In the end, it was AOL that was modeled after an online service provider, not the other way around (Ryan, 2010, pp. 265–6).

Other incumbent companies had greater success. The early 'browser wars' provide a case in point (Sebenius, 2002). In 1995, Netscape controlled the browser market, with a 90 percent installed user base for Netscape Navigator (Windrum, 2000, p. 1). Netscape Navigator's great lead in the market notwithstanding, the Goliath Microsoft was able to demolish its rival with a browser of its own, Internet Explorer. Because Netscape Navigator could be employed across multiple network platforms, and be used by software designers to create software for any operating system, it was a major threat to Microsoft's dominance in the operating systems market (Sebenius, 2002, p. 44; Ryan, 2010). Determined to squash the competition, Microsoft made its browser free to all, bundled it together with its operating system, thereby loading it on the desktops of 50 million new computers each year; and then used its market power to make it the ISPs' browser of choice (Windrum, 2000, p. 8; Sebenius, 2002, p. 43). As a result, Internet Explorer became the Internet's default browser, and Netscape went into decline. Despite Netscape's first-mover advantage, it could not compete without the financial resources and industry alliances available to Microsoft.

Even as the conglomerates were prospering, a new, user-oriented, participatory business model was emerging under the radar. It was based in the sharing culture and ideology that had been nurtured within the ARPANET community (Agre, 2003). Epitomized by open-source undertakings such as Linux, Apache, and Wikipedia, this model reflected the notion that individuals were naturally creative and eager to be so, given the opportunity and resources to collaborate around a joint interest or goal (Lerner and Tirole, 2002; Weber, 2004). To facilitate and promote such participation, open-source advocates wanted property rights systems to ensure free access to the tools necessary for user participation. Open-source advocates – and even rivals – contended that a production system structured around collaborative user interaction could be an extremely efficient and effective way of organizing economic activities, especially when complex systems were involved (Weber, 2004).

Most notable, in this regard, was a secret Microsoft memo made public – the so-called 'Halloween Memo' – claiming that Microsoft believed open source to be competitive with their top-down software development approach, so much so that the company needed to either borrow from it, or otherwise undermine it (ibid.). However, Microsoft's efforts to diminish open source were to no avail. In fact, open-source methodology and culture were legitimated when formal institutions (such as variations on the General Public

License [GPL] for free software) and organizations (such as Red Hat) were established to promote and support it, while major corporations, such as Hewlett Packard, IBM, and Sun Microsystems, built open source into their business plans (ibid.).

As end users became directly engaged in online activities, the participatory culture spread from the technology arena to the realm of cultural production (Benkler, 2006; Shirky, 2008, 2010; Schafer, 2011). Yochai Benkler (2006) attributes this development, in part, to the affordances of digital technologies, which allowed individuals to follow their inclinations to be creative and engage collectively with one another (Lessig, 2004; Benkler, 2006). Clay Shirky (2010) points out, moreover, that a significant increase in leisure time gave rise to a 'cognitive surplus', resulting in more and more individuals contributing to the public sphere. The enhanced role of information in the economy also helps to explain the growth of peer-based activities. As Benkler notes, because information exhibits properties of public goods, non-profit, collaborative efforts centering on the production of information content are – given appropriate institutional underpinnings – not only sustainable, but, more importantly, competitive with pure market-based efforts (Benkler, 2006, p. 3; Shirky, 2008). Evidencing these trends is the accelerating rate of collaborative peer-to-peer sites ranging from social networks, such as Facebook and YouTube, to game platforms such as *Minecraft* and *Second Life*, to fan sites and crowdsourcing (Benkler, 2006; Shirky, 2010; Schafer, 2011).

As Perez (2010) points out, technological revolutions take time to be absorbed into the social fabric. They only do so when all of the interdependent social, economic, and political processes and subsystems are in place, and a new, shared techno-economic paradigm has been constructed. Achieving such an outcome can be problematic, however, because these subsystems do not necessarily evolve at the same pace (Freeman and Louca, 2001). Accordingly, the structuration of today's media field is still in the making. Two alternative modes of production – the vertically integrated system and the decentralized, peer-to-peer system – are each operating successfully, but more often than not in competition with one another. The competition, however, is not just about the most appropriate mode(s) of production; equally, if not more, important, it is about the social and political relationships structured around them.

The tensions between these two modalities can best be seen in the recent debates over net neutrality – that is, non-discriminatory access to network services. At stake is the Internet end-to-end principle (Lemley and Lessig, 2001; Wu, 2011). The conglomerate network providers want to provide a tiered access system, which would allow them to reduce network congestion by giving preference to some Internet services – perhaps even their own – over others. They argue that having discretion over provisioning is essential for generating sufficient revenues to build out their systems and meet growing demand, an argument that the cable companies successfully made several years ago. In contrast, those in favor of preserving the Internet's end-to-end architecture, including big content players, such as Netflix and Google, as well as smaller content providers, non-profits, and general users, are concerned lest network providers use such discretion to recreate the top-down vertically integrated media industries of the past (Ganley and Allgrove, 2006). The outcome, they argue, would not only be higher costs, but also the loss of collaborative social benefits that would otherwise be gained via greater externalities.

That such conflicts may be difficult to resolve is clearly evidenced by the recent battles between content providers and Internet service providers, which have ended up in the US

Court of Appeals for the District of Columbia. Because the FCC had classified Internet services as information services, which can only be regulated with a light hand, the Court ruled that the FCC does not have the authority to bar Internet service providers from discriminating among their customers, thereby allowing them to strike deals in their favor. The FCC is currently developing a new approach to safeguard an open Internet, possibly by reclassifying broadband access providers as common carriers.

Although the ultimate configuration of the communication field is highly unpredictable, convergence around a new techno-economic paradigm seems likely, due to market discipline in sorting winners from losers and the tendency of organizations and institutions to exhibit isomorphism over time (Meyer and Rowan, 1977). Already we have seen some convergence, as in the case of open-source communities collaborating with the corporate world. Likewise, as Schafer points out, businesses are not only engaging more directly with users; users are also collaborating with businesses, as, for example, when they contribute content to online business sites (Schafer, 2011). Failing to come to some private-sector agreement, contenders in the field – now much more broadly conceived than in the past – will likely call on government to establish new rules of the game. When decided at this level, public interest goals will more likely be taken into account.

26.7   CONCLUSION

Although the evolution of organizational fields is characterized by uncertainty and non-linearity, the process by which it takes place is by no means random or incoherent (Perez, 2010; Padgett and Powell, 2012). Rather, it is held together by path-dependent motifs that are interwoven in new and different ways, much as the strands of colored wool are woven together to create a pattern in a fine cloth. In similar fashion, organizational fields do not emerge in a vacuum. Rather, as Padgett and Powell (2012, p. 2) attest: 'All organizational forms, no matter how radically new, are combinations and mutations of what was there before ... Evolution, therefore, is not a teleological progress toward some ahistorical ideal. It is a thick and tangled bush of branches, re-combinations, transformations, and sequential path-dependent trajectories'.

Viewing the social order as a system of layered social networks, constituting, for example, economic activities, cultural activities, kinship activities, religious activities, military activities, and so on, Padgett and Powell posit that new organizational forms (in this case organizational fields) emerge as a result of autocatalytic processes that occur when spillovers take place not only within a given domain but also across diverse societal realms (Padgett and Powell, 2012). Hence, we might posit that, as more users from different domains become part of the Internet environment, a new transformation will take place.

What might it look like? One way to anticipate the long-term socioeconomic evolution of the Internet is to pursue the metaphor of weaving. Starting from today's organizational field we can follow the different threads, backwards as in an elaborate fabric, to see where they were picked up, dropped, and added along the way. Moreover, we can identify the junctures in the process, where critical choices led to major variations in the original design. Employing this approach, we can see that transformations in the organizational field resulted, in part, from the continued extension of network externalities. As more and more users from diverse realms of life became part of the Internet bandwagon, spillovers occurred more frequently and across more domains. There were many more design choices as a result.

Today's communication/media field is characterized by two major threads, which constitute competing techno-economic paradigms – the closed, top-down, profit-oriented, vertically integrated model, and the open, decentralized, peer-to-peer, sharing model. Significantly, both can trace their present modi operandi back to their precursors in the communication field.

The vertically integrated model draws its inspiration from the industrial age. It is best epitomized by the Bell Telephone system, which, although serving a semi-public function, was financed with private capital and propelled by the profit motive. Given its integrated monopoly, AT&T benefited not only from economies of scale and scope; it also cross-subsidized its services so as to provide universal service to all. Allying itself with the federal government by maintaining a unified network that served the country's needs, AT&T was able to monopolize the field and be assured of a generous 'rate of return'. At the same time, AT&T maintained its legitimacy by wooing the public with a highly successful public relations campaign. Equally important, while it maintained central control, it shared the network benefits and resources so as to satisfy all stakeholders In fact, so fixed was AT&T on its way of doing business, it lacked the incentive to push forward with innovative products, as, for example, in areas such as data communications.

The peer-to-peer model, as first developed by ARPA, is the antithesis of the vertically integrated model. Funded by government and focused on problem solving rather than profit making, the ARPANET was mostly user-driven. The computer scientists who took part in ARPANET's development not only created packet switching, TCP/IP standards, and an end-to-end open architecture based on them, they also developed a community of practice based on sharing, user participation and user feedback. The rewards for contributing were inherent in the collaborative process.

When DARPA turned ARPANET over to the NSF, a TCP/IP platform served to aggregate users from multiple realms, including academics, businesses and non-profits. In the process, the NSF drew the telecommunication providers back into the fold, even subsidizing them, to build the mid-level network. However, even as the communication incumbents re-emerged, many much stronger than before, the TCP/IP-based end-to-end architecture, as well as much of the sharing, collaborative culture, has survived, providing a viable model for non-proprietary economic ventures such as open source.

Capitalizing on the broadband networks and data services market spawned by NSF, as well as the development of radical new application technologies such as the World Wide Web and the browser, traditional telephone incumbents and the growing number of new Internet service providers competed fiercely for their share of the newly deregulated market. Nevertheless, the TCP/IP-based end-to-end architecture, as well as much of the reciprocal collaborative culture, has survived. More importantly, this architecture, and the Internet governing institutions that helped to sustain it, has extended the Internet, and its modus operandi, to new communities and new users, allowing them to be producers as well as users, all the while bringing their own unique creativity and perspectives to the fore. Today, as the field is increasingly contested, a much broader group of participants will have their say.

What can this history tell us? Where does the future of the organizational field lie?

While we cannot predict the future, we can – building on our analysis – identify some key variables:

- *Governance structure:* The field has yet to develop a stable governance structure. Typically, the largest, most powerful players assume this leadership role. Given recent mergers and acquisitions, we might anticipate that significant consolidation of the market will take place. However, given the tendency towards isomorphism and the fact that newcomers in the field are essential for innovation and growth, accommodations will likely take place, as participants in the field come to some agreement about how it should be divided up. If they are unable to, the government will likely intervene.
- *Market structure:* A competitive market will depend on the continued ability of firms to employ innovative technology to generate externalities and increase market size. Absent innovation and growth, there will be fewer economies of scale and scope to sustain a large number of vertically integrated providers. Those operating in the peer-to-peer tradition might survive – if not thrive – in this environment by continually generating externalities and greater demand. To do so, they must continue to attract talent and maintain their user orientation, flexibility and penchant for innovation. Whether they will be able to do so will depend in part on the level of consolidation in the field.
- *Legitimacy:* Today's users are far more active and vocal than those in the past. Hence, leading firms will require a convincing narrative that serves not only to motivate and drive their operations, but also to garner public support. The need for such a narrative will be all the greater given intense competition between providers in general, and especially between companies pursuing competing modes of production. The less-traditional providers may hold an advantage in this regard, insofar as their origins are linked to a positive social as well as techno-economic narrative.
- *The role of government:* Organizational fields are relatively autonomous. Typically governments only step in when the market creates, or cannot solve, a major public problem, or when members of an organizational field cannot govern themselves. When governments do intervene, a broader range of interests and issues are taken into account. In the case of the Internet, the government has held back from regulation, treating Internet service like any other commodity. Whether it will continue to do so will depend on a much more active and highly invested public and the ability of industry to meet its needs.

In concluding, we should recall Douglass North's proposition – history matters. But in terms of the future of the Internet, history is still in the making. This analysis suggests, however, that the future will depend on how, and by whom, the restructuring of the communication field is undertaken, as much as on the more or less definitive economic determinants.

NOTES

1. See http://en.wikipedia.org/wiki/ARPANET#Growth_and_evolution; accessed 10 July 2014.
2. EDUCAUSE is a 'nonprofit association whose mission is to advance higher education through the use of information technology'. See http://www.educause.edu/; accessed 11 July 2014.
3. See http://en.wikipedia.org/wiki/Internet_Corporation_for_Assigned_Names_and_Numbers; accessed 10 July 2014.

REFERENCES

Abbate, J.E. (1994), 'From ARPANET to Internet: A history of ARPA-sponsored computer networks, 1966–1988', PhD dissertation, University of Pennsylvania.

Abbate, J.E. (2000), *Inventing the Internet*, Cambridge, MA: MIT Press.

Agre, P. (2003), 'Peer to peer and the promise of internet equality', *Communications of the ACM*, **46** (2), 39–42.

Amin, A. and J. Hausner (1997), *Beyond Hierarchy: Interactive Governance and Social Complexity*, Cheltenham, UK and Lyme, NH, USA: Edward Elgar Publishing.

Arthur, W.B. (2009), *The Nature of Technology: What It Is and How It Evolves*, New York: Free Press.

Bailey, J.P. (1995), 'Economics of internet interconnection agreements', *Journal of Electronic Publishing*, **1** (1&2), accessed 7 July 2014 at http://dx.doi.org/10.3998/3336451.0001.109.

Bailey, J.P. and L.W. McKnight (1995), 'Internet economics: What happens when constituencies collide', paper presented at INET'95, Honolulu, accessed 7 July 2014 at http://18.7.29.232/bitstream/handle/1721.1/1531/final_paper2.pdf?sequence=2.

Beinhocker, E.D. (2006), *The Origins of Wealth: Complexity and the Radical Remaking of Economics*, Boston, MA: Harvard University Business School Press.

Beniger, J.R. (1986), *The Control Revolution: Technological and Economic Origins of the Information Society*, Cambridge, MA: Harvard University Press.

Benkler, Y. (2006), *The Wealth of Networks: How Social Production Transforms Markets and Freedom*, New Haven, CT: Yale University Press.

Blumenthal, M.S. and D.D. Clark (2001), 'Rethinking the design of the Internet: The end-to-end arguments vs. the brave new world', *ACM Transactions on Internet Technology*, **1** (1), 70–109.

Bolt, Beranek and Newman, Inc. (1981), *A History of the ARPANET: The First Decade*, Report No. 4799, Arlington, VA: DARPA.

Borgatti, S.P., A. Mehtra, D.J. Brass and G. Labianca (2009), 'Network analysis in the social sciences', *Science*, **323** (892), 1–5.

Braudel, F. (1980), *On History*, Chicago, IL: University of Chicago Press.

Brock, G.W. (1981), *The Telecommunications Industry: The Dynamics of Market Structure*, Cambridge, MA: Harvard University Press.

Brown, I. (ed.) (2013), *Research Handbook on the Governance of the Internet*, Cheltenham, UK and Northampton, MA: Edward Elgar Publishing.

Brown, J.S. and P. Duguid (2001), 'Knowledge and organization: A social practice perspective', *Organizational Science*, **12** (2), 198–213.

Buchanan, M. (2002), *Small World Networks and the Groundbreaking Science of Networks*, New York: W.W. Norton & Company.

Burt, R.S. (1992), *Structural Holes: The Social Structure of Competition*, Cambridge, MA: Harvard University Press.

Burt, R. (2005), *Brokerage and Closure: An Introduction to Social Capital*, New York: Oxford University Press.

Cave, M. and R. Mason (2001), 'The economics of the Internet: Infrastructure and regulation', *Oxford Review of Economic Policy*, **17** (2), 188–201.

Cerf, V. (2004), 'The Internet phenomenon', *Computer Networking: Global Infrastructure for the 21st Century*, accessed 9 February 2015 at http://homes.cs.washington.edu/~lazowska/cra/networks.html.

Chandler, A.D. (1977), *The Visible Hand: The Managerial Revolution in American Business*, Cambridge, MA: Harvard University Press.

Clark, D.D., J. Wroclawski, K.R. Sollins and R. Braden (2002), 'Tussle in cyberspace: Defining tomorrow's Internet', in *Proceedings of the 2002 ACM SIGCOMM Conference*, Pittsburg, PA, pp. 347–56.

Coleman, J.S. (1988), 'Social capital and the creation of human capital', *American Journal of Sociology*, **94** (Supplement), S95–S120.

Coll, S. (1986), *The Deal of a Century*, New York: Atheneum Press.

Computer Science and Telecommunications Board (CSTB) (1996), *Realizing the Information Future: The Internet and Beyond*, National Research Council, Computer Science and Telecommunications Board, Washington, DC: National Academy Press.

Couper, E.A., J.P. Hejkal and A.L. Wolman (2003), 'Boom and bust in telecommunications', *Economic Quarterly – Federal Reserve Bank of Richmond*, **89** (4), 1–24.

Crandall, R.W. (1989), 'Fragmentation of the telephone network: New directions in telecommunications policy', in P.R. Newberg (ed.), *Regulatory Policy: Telephony and Mass Media*, Durham, NC: Duke University Press, pp. 49–65.

Drake, W.J. (1995), *The New Information Infrastructure: Strategies For US Policies*, New York: The Twentieth Century Fund.

Fleming, L. and M. Marx (2006), 'Managing creativity in small worlds', *California Management Review*, **48** (4), 6–27.

Fligstein, N. (2001), *The Architecture of Markets: An Economic Sociology of Twenty-First Century Capitalist Societies*, Princeton, NJ: Princeton University Press.

Fligstein, N. and D. McAdam (2012), *A Theory of Fields*, New York: Oxford University Press.

Freeman, C. and F. Louca (2001), *As Time Goes By: From the Industrial Revolution to the Information Revolution*, New York: Oxford University Press.

Frischmann, B. (2001), 'Privatization and commercialization of the Internet infrastructure: Rethinking market intervention into government and government intervention into the market', *Columbia Science and Technology Law Review*, **2** (1), 1–37.

Galambos, L. and J. Pratt (1989), *The Rise of the Corporate Commonwealth: US Business and Public Policy in the Twentieth Century*, New York: Basic Books.

Ganley, P. and B. Allgrove (2006), 'Net neutrality: A user's guide', *Computer Law and Security Report*, **22** (6), 454–63.

Geller, H. (1995), 'Reforming the US telecommunications policymaking process', in W.J. Drake (ed.), *The New Information Infrastructure: Strategies for U.S. Policy*, New York: The Twentieth Century Fund, pp. 115–35.

Gilroy, A.A. (1984), *The American Telephone and Telegraph Company Divestiture: Background, Provisions, and Restructuring*, Report No. 84-58E, Washington, DC: Congressional Research Service.

Granovetter, M. (1985), 'Economic action and social structure: The problem of embeddedness', *American Journal of Sociology*, **91** (3), 481–510.

Granovetter, M. and R. Swedberg (eds) (2011), *The Sociology of Economic Life*, 3rd edition, New York: Westview Press.

Gray, H.M. (1940), 'The passing of the public utility concept', *Journal of Land and Public Utility Economics*, **16** (1), 8–20.

Greenstein, S. (2001), 'Commercialization of the Internet: The interaction of public policy and private choices or why introducing the market worked so well', in A.B. Jaffe, J. Lerner and S. Stern (eds), *Innovation Policy and the Economy, Volume 1*, Cambridge, MA: MIT Press, pp. 151–86.

Gulati, R. and M. Gargiulo (1999), 'Where do interorganizational networks come from?', *American Journal of Sociology*, **104** (5), 1439–93.

Hafner, K. and M. Lyon (1996), *Where Wizards Stay up Late: The Origins of the Internet*, New York: Simon & Schuster.

Hart, J.A., R.R. Reed and F. Bar (1992), 'The building of the Internet: Implications for the future of broadband networks', *Telecommunications Policy*, **16** (8), 666–89.

Hauben, M. (1997), 'Behind the Net: The untold history of the Internet', in M. Hauben and R. Hauben, *Netizens*, Los Alamitos, CA: IEEE Computer Society Press, accessed 9 February 2015 at http://www.colum bia.edu/~hauben/book-pdf/CHAPTER%207.pdf.

Hauben, M. and R. Hauben (1997), *Netizens: On the History of Usenet and the Internet*, Los Alamitos, CA: IEEE Computer Society Press.

Hodgson, G.M. and T. Knudson (2010), *Darwin's Conjecture: The Search for General Principles of Social and Economic Evolution*, Chicago, IL: Chicago University Press.

Inkpen, A.C. and E.W.K. Tsang (2005), 'Social capital, networks and knowledge transfer', *Academy of Management Review*, **30** (1), 146–65.

Kahn, A.E. (1983), 'The passing of the public utility concept, a reprise', in E.M. Noam (ed.), *Telecommunications Regulation Today and Tomorrow*, New York: Harcourt Brace Jovanovich, pp. 3–37.

Kauffman, S.S. (1995), *At Home in the Universe: The Search for Laws of Self Organization*, New York: Oxford University Press.

Kazumori, E. (2003), 'Coordination and decommissioning: NSFNET and the evolution of the Internet in the United States 1985–95', *SIEPR Discussion Paper No. 02-07*, Stanford, CA: Stanford University, Stanford Institute for Economic Policy Research, accessed 7 July 2014 at http://www-siepr.stanford.edu/papers/pdf/02-07.pdf.

Kolko, G. (1963), *The Triumph of Conservatism: a Reinterpretation of American History, 1900–1916*, New York: Free Press.

Lazonick, W. (1991), *Business Organization and the Myth of the Market Economy*, Cambridge, UK: Cambridge University Press.

Leiner, B.M., V.G. Cerf and D.D. et al. (1997), 'The past and future history of the Internet', *Communications of the ACM*, **40** (2), 102–8.

Lemley, M.A. and L. Lessig (2001), 'The end of end-to-end: Preserving the architecture of the Internet in the broadband era', *UCLA Law Review*, **48** (4), 925–72.

Lerner, J. and J. Tirole (2002), 'Some simple economics of open source', *The Journal of Industrial Economics*, **1** (2), 197–223.

Lessig, L. (2004), *Free Culture: The Nature and Future of Creativity*, New York: Penguin Press.

MacKie-Mason, J.K. and H.R. Varian (1994), 'Some economics of the Internet', in W. Sichel (ed.), *Networks, Infrastructure and the New Task for Regulation*, Ann Arbor, MI: University of Michigan Press.

Mahoney, J. and D. Rueschemeyer (2003), 'Comparative historical analysis: Achievements and agendas', in J. Mahoney and D. Rueschemeyer (eds), *Comparative Historical Analysis in the Social Sciences*, Cambridge, UK and New York: Cambridge University Press, pp. 3–38.

Meyer, J.Q. and B. Rowan (1977), 'Institutionalized organizations: Formal structures as myth and ceremony', *American Journal of Sociology*, **83** (2), 340–63.

Mokyr, J. (1990), *The Lever of Riches: Technological Creativity and Economic Progress*, New York: Oxford University Press.

Noam, E.M. (1988), 'The future of the public network: From the star to the matrix', *Telecommunications*, **22** (3), 58–59, 65, 90.

Noam, E.M. (1995), *Interconnecting the Network of Networks*, Cambridge, MA; MIT Press.

North, D.C. (1990), *Institutions, Institutional Change and Economic Performance*, Cambridge, MA: Cambridge University Press.

Office of Technology Assessment (OTA) (1990), *Critical Connections: Communications for the Future*, OTA-CIT-407, Washington, DC: US Government Printing Office.

Ostrom, E. (1990), *Governing the Commons: The Evolution of Institutions for Collective Action*, New York: Cambridge University Press.

Padgett, J. and W. Powell (2012), *The Emergence of Organizations and Markets*, Princeton, NJ: Princeton University Press.

Passy, F. (2003), 'Social networks matter. But how?', in M. Diani and D. McAdam (eds), *Social Movements and Networks Relational Approaches to Collective Action*, New York: Oxford University Press.

Pelkey, J. (2014), *Entrepreneurial Capitalism and Innovation: A History of Computer Communications 1968–1988*, accessed 9 February 2015 at http://www.historyofcomputercommunications.info/.

Perez, C. (2010), 'Technological revolutions and techno-economic paradigms', *Cambridge Journal of Economics*, **34** (1), 185–202.

Pfeffer, J.A. and N.G. Salancik (2003), *The External Control of Organizations: A Resource Dependence Perspective*, Stanford, CA: Stanford University Press.

Pierson, P. (2004), *Politics in Time: History, Institutions and Social Analysis*, Princeton, NJ: Princeton University Press.

Polanyi, K. (2011), 'The economy as an instituted process', in M. Granovetter and R. Swedberg (eds), *The Sociology of Economic Life*, 3rd edition, New York: Westview Press.

Powell, W. and P. DiMaggio (1991), *The New Institutionalism in Organizational Analysis*, Chicago, IL: University of Chicago Press.

Rogers, E. (1993), *The Diffusion of Innovations*, New York: The Free Press.

Rohlfs, J. (2001), *Bandwagon Effects in High-Technology Industries*, Cambridge, MA: MIT Press.

Rosenzweig, R. (1998), 'Wizards, bureaucrats, warriors, and hackers: Writing the history of the Internet', *The American Historical Review*, **103** (5), 1530–52.

Russell, A.L. (2006), '"Rough consensus and running code" and the Internet-OSI standards war', *IEEE Annals of the History of Computing*, **28** (3), 48–61.

Ryan, J. (2010), *A History of the Internet and the Digital Future*, London: Reaktion Books.

Saltzer, J.H., D.P. Reed and D.D. Clark (1984), 'End-to-end arguments in systems design', *ACM Transactions on Computer Systems*, **2** (4), 277–88.

Schafer, M.T. (2011), *Bastard Culture! How User Participation Transforms Cultural Production*, Amsterdam: Amsterdam University Press.

Schiller, D. (1982), 'Business users and the telecommunications network', *Journal of Communications*, **32** (4), 84–96.

Schwartz, D. (1997), *Culture and Power: The Sociology of Pierre Bourdieu*, Chicago, IL: The University of Chicago Press.

Scott, R. (2001), *Institutions and Organizations*, Thousand Oaks, CA: Sage Publications.

Sebenius, J.K. (2002), 'Negotiating lessons from the browser wars', *MIT Sloan Management Review*, **43** (4), 43–51.

Shampine, A. and H. Sider (2007), 'The telecom boom and bust: Their losses, our gain?', *Milken Institute Review*, accessed 9 February 2015 at http://www.milken-inst.org/publications/review/2007_10/54-60mr36. pdf.

Shirky, C. (2008), *Here Comes Everybody: The Power of Organizing Without Organizations*, New York: Penguin Books.

Shirky, C. (2010), *Cognitive Surplus: Creativity and Generosity in a Connected World*, New York: Penguin Books.

Skocpol, T. and M. Somers (1980), 'The uses of comparative history in macrosocial inquiry', *Comparative Studies in Society and History*, **22** (2), 174–97.

Sterling, B. (1993), 'A short history of the Internet', accessed 9 February 2015 at http://www.internetsociety.org/ internet/what-internet/history-internet/short-history-internet.

Stigler, G.J. and C. Friedland (1962), 'What can regulators regulate: The case of electricity', *The Journal of Law and Economics*, **5** (1), 1–16.

Stone, A. (1991), *Public Service Liberalism: Telecommunication and Transitions in Public Policy*, Princeton, NJ: Princeton University Press.

Tapscott, D. (1996), *The Digital Economy: Promise and Peril in the Age of Network Intelligence*, New York: McGraw-Hill.

Temin, P. (1988), *The Fall of the Bell System*, New York: Cambridge University Press.

Tsai, W. and S. Ghoshal (1998), 'Social capital and value creation: The role of interfirm networks', *Academy of Management Journal*, **41** (4), 464–76.

Tunstall, J. (1986), *Communications Deregulation: The Unleashing of America's Communication Industry*, Oxford, UK: Basil Blackwell.

Uzzi, B. (1997), 'Social structure and competition in interfirm networks: The paradox of embeddedness', *Administrative Science Quarterly*, **42** (1), 35–67.

Uzzi, B., L.A.N. Amaral and F. Reed-Tsochas (2007), 'Small world networks and management science research: A review', *European Management Review*, **4** (2), 74–91.

Wang, Z. (2006), 'Technological innovation and market turbulence: The dot-com experience', *Review of Economic Dynamics*, **10** (1), 78–105.

Watts, D. (1999), 'Networks, dynamics, and the small world phenomenon', *American Journal of Sociology*, **105** (2), 493–527.

Watts, D. and S. Strogatz (1998), 'Collective dynamics of "small-world" networks', *Nature*, **393** (6684), 440–42.

Weber, S. (2004), *The Success of Open Source*, Cambridge, MA: Harvard University Press.

Weick, K.E. (1995), *Sensemaking in Organizations*, Thousand Oaks, CA: Sage Publications.

Wenger, E. (1998), *Communities of Practice: Learning, Meaning, and Identity*, New York: Cambridge University Press.

Wheeler, D.C. and M.E. O'Kelly (1999), 'Network topology and city accessibility of the commercial backbone', *Professional Geographer*, **52** (3), 327–39.

White, H. (1992), *Identity and Control*, Princeton, NJ: Princeton University Press.

Windrum, P. (2000), 'Back from the brink: Microsoft and the strategic use of standards in the browser wars', Maastricht: MERIT, Maastricht Economic Research Institute on Innovation and Technology, accessed 9 February 2015 at http://arnop.unimaas.nl/show.cgi?fid=292.

Wu, T. (2011), *The Master Switch*, New York: Knopf.

27. From the Internet of Science to the Internet of Entertainment
Eli M. Noam

27.1 INTRODUCTION

Revolutions are said to devour their children, as well as their parents. The Internet is no exception. Its success and impact have been overwhelming. But in the process it is also undermining its own technological, organizational, and economic foundations. If its origin was cutting-edge science and engineering, then its present is that of commerce and its future is that of entertainment. Yet that descent from lofty aspirations to popular diversions should not be seen as negative. It will enable major upgrades of infrastructure, encourage diverse advances in technology and generate cultural innovation. But it will not be the same good old Internet. On the content side, too, we can be certain that the next generation of video will not simply be the same good old TV over yet another platform.

This chapter analyzes these changes and will take several steps ahead. Here is how it proceeds. First, we will discuss the drivers of the emergence of an Internet of Entertainment and the major media industry approaches to it (section 27.2). We then explain the implications, focusing on three fundamental changes: impacts on the infrastructure (section 27.3); on the Internet system (section 27.4); and on the TV system (section 27.5). The key players of the new system, the media clouds, are analyzed in section 27.6. Emerging policy issues are identified in section 27.7 and questions for further research in section 27.8 before conclusions are offered in section 27.9.

27.2 THE MOVE TO THE INTERNET OF ENTERTAINMENT

The technology drivers of media change are the rapid advances in microelectronics and photonics. They raise performance and lower the cost of creating, processing and storing information, and distributing it to and among users. The price decline and greater distribution capacity make it possible to move away from the system of shared and synchronous mass media that existed before and whose economic basis had been the lowering of costs. With technological advances it becomes increasingly feasible to individualize the previous mass media into specialized and personalized media streams. The move to encode all types of information in the binary code that is favored by the electronic processes ('digitalization') leads to the emergence of multi-media devices, content, and content providers ('convergence'). The low marginal cost with respect to distance of distributing content makes these media systems widespread ('globalization'). And the economic characteristics of high fixed costs, low marginal costs, and strong network effects create major economies of scale that lead to market concentration.

The Internet is both the result and the accelerator of these technology trends, becoming the central institution of the new media environment. It changes many aspects of society and the economy. And it is subject to change itself. Originally, it was a text-based system serving the needs of engineers and scientists. As it became cheaper and more convenient to transmit and store information, the Internet became a consumer-based platform for communications and transactions. Prices kept dropping while performance rose, with the result that media uses beyond text became possible and affordable, first for photos and music and then for video. In this phase of the evolution of the Internet, entertainment is the demand driver.

Entertainment includes music, games, and text-based media. But by far the main presence on the Internet is video, an application that is rapidly taking over the Internet in terms of bandwidth usage. Today, during the early evening hours, 71 percent of Internet download traffic in the USA is entertainment and 67 percent is video (Sandvine, 2013). Soon, entertainment is expected to make up over 90 percent of peak download traffic. This growth is extraordinarily rapid – only a few years ago, the Internet was mostly text-based.

Early dial-up Internet speeds started at a few hundred bits per second and eventually rose to about 56 thousand (kilo) bits per second. At that speed one could download a film for subsequent viewing but it would have taken several years to download an uncompressed HD quality film of 90 minutes duration. This was impractical for a mass medium.

The constraints were whittled away in several ways:

- By reducing the required data stream with compression algorithms that eliminate unneeded bits. This cut the speed requirements by a factor of up to 100 (currently H.265/MPEG-4).
- By building more powerful transmission networks reaching the user. Consumer-affordable broadband data communications connectivity rose in speed from kilobits to megabits and even reached gigabits. The main approaches were digital subscriber lines (DSL) on telecom copper networks, coax cable, fiber-optical lines, and combinations of all. These technologies enabled speeds a thousand times faster than dial-up. Another transmission medium that increased in speed and reach were wireless mobile networks. The fourth generation of mobile services (LTE – long-term evolution) enables megabit speeds, and added geographic ubiquity to user connectivity.
- Viewers' acceptance of a picture quality that is lower in resolution than the high-definition video of cable TV.
- Faster signal processing at the user end of incoming video transmission and its transformation into moving images on various devices, including TV sets, PCs, tablets, and smartphones.
- Cheaper storage of video bits on the consumer end, enabling user-based buffering and archiving, as well as the placement of servers closer to users.

Taking these factors together, video could be transmitted about 200 000 times "faster" than in the days of dial-up. This meant that the downloading of video became readily possible. It was accomplished in four ways:

- File-sharing of users with each other, facilitated after the year 2000 by sites such as Kazaa, Gnutella, and BitTorrent, which enabled peer-to-peer video transfers without license from the copyright holder.
- Licensed transactions through direct sales by retailers such as Apple's iTunes Store after 2005.
- More interesting, perhaps, were two other approaches. The first was streaming. The higher video transfer rate made it possible to move to a low-latency (live or near-live) system. This enabled convenient and spontaneous use of on-demand libraries on distant servers, without time-consuming advance downloads. It also enabled lower transaction prices since the owner of the content could grant a one-time viewing license rather than a permanent one. And it also made possible the transmission of live content. In 1993, the garage band Severe Tire Damage – whose drummer happened to be the Chief Scientist of Xerox PARC – claimed to have been the first live video performance on the Internet. The first sports transmission was reputedly the New York Yankees playing the Seattle Mariners, in 1995. Similarly, websites offering independent films, music videos, and events emerged during the dot-com bubble years. AtomFilm, DEN, and Pseudo.com drew users and created buzz but mostly went under in the 'Black September' of 2000, because the number of users with fast enough broadband connectivity was insufficient at the time.
- The second innovation was the emergence of user-based video content storage sites. Of these, YouTube, founded by three former PayPal employees in 2005 and taken over by Google in 2006, became dominant.

As the streaming model emerged, a period of intense rivalry followed among the developers of the required video player software – Microsoft, Apple, RealNetworks, and Macromedia/Adobe whose Flash developed into the leading platform.

Another rivalry involved devices enabling users to connect their TV sets and other video devices to the Internet in order to access content. This included Echostar Slingbox (after 2005), Apple TV (2007), Roku (2008), Boxee (2010) and Amazon FireTV (2014) – all of which offer a controlled ('walled garden') set of reachable content originations. In contrast, Google Chromecast (2013) has a browser and allows accessing most sites. Boxee incorporated social media connectivity, but was phased out after 2015.

By 2005, the elements for consumer-friendly video over the Internet had started to come together. Commercial applications took off, using several models that coexist and contend with each other. They are listed below. Many of the providers mentioned actually operate with a mixed system that incorporates several of the approaches:

1. *Video hosts:* Google YouTube (2005) is the prime example, with over 6 billion hours of video consumed each month and 1.2 billion monthly visits. Other providers are Vimeo; Dailymotion (France); Youku Toudu (China, 2005); and Yahoo Flickr.
2. *Video stores:* Examples are Apple iTunes; Amazon Instant Video; Google Play; Sony Crackle; Walmart VUDU. Some of these players also store the buyers' films. This reduces, in practice, the difference between downloading/owning and streaming. The difference becomes mostly one of a pricing arrangement.
3. *Video subscription services:* Examples are Netflix; Amazon Instant Video (including

LoveFilm in the UK and in Germany, since renamed Amazon Instant Video in the UK); Zattoo (Switzerland and Germany); Redbox Instant; EverywhereTV (subscriptions for re-transmissions of foreign TV broadcasters); and Alibaba Tmall Box Office (China).

4. *Advertising-based content sites:* Examples are Veoh and Viacom CC Studios.
5. *Online sites of traditional broadcasters and channel providers:* Examples are BBC iPlayer; ITV Player; Now TV (21st BSkyB); Hulu (21st Century Fox, NBC, Disney); Time Warner HBO Go/HBO Now; and Viacom Showtime Anytime.
6. *Program sites of specialized content providers:* Examples are the servers of professional sports such as the World Wrestling Entertainment (WWE) Network and the National Basketball Association (NBA).
7. *Internet distributors of broadcast TV channels:* The provider Aereo supplied over-the-air TV to subscribers by way of the Internet, for a fee. While the approach was fought by broadcasters and stopped by the US Supreme Court, the technical model is sound and returned in a different licensing configuration. Examples are Sling TV and Sony PlayStation Vue.

These seven categories can be loosely described as 'over-the-top' (OTT) content providers, in reference to being delivered over the networks of facilities-based Internet service providers (ISPs) but independent of them and hence 'on top' of their channel bundles. The ISPs, however, can also provide their own Internet content services, typically as an extension of their video-on-demand offerings, and this comprises an eighth category of video services:

8. *Online on-demand content provision of cable channels by cable or telecom providers:* Examples are Comcast Xfinity; Verizon FiOS; and AT&T U-verse. Most cable operators offer their subscribers access to cable channels.

All of these providers are jostling each other on numerous fronts – for users, subscribers, advertisers, content providers, network partners, consumer electronics platforms, cloud hosts, software applications developers, marketing buzz, regulatory benevolence, and court approval. They arose first in those countries most active in Internet and video or that possess a large user base, but they are now spreading everywhere. Even greater disruptions are likely from the globalization of content distribution that is inherent to the fairly distance-insensitive Internet and its huge economies of scale. Whereas in the past video distribution was mostly a national matter through geographically defined and regulated TV broadcasters and cable providers, online video is characterized by worldwide footprints, at least on a technological/economic basis, though not necessarily on a legal/regulatory one.

In the process, the Internet is increasingly becoming a distribution pipe for entertainment content. Already at the end of 2012 during evening peak hours, entertainment video usage in the USA accounted for 67 percent of all download traffic. With 31 percent, Netflix accounted for about half of that total (Sandvine, 2013). YouTube took up another 18.7 percent. Together with other video use on the Internet, video constituted over two-thirds of all peak hour Internet traffic in 2013, up from near zero in 2005. Real-time entertainment has accelerated enormously and will likely continue on this trajectory. In terms of video usage, US viewers consume about 1.16 hours per day of video over the Internet. Since Americans watch, on average, 40.7 hours of video per week (Nielsen, 2013), this suggests a very high growth potential.

Thus, based on traffic flows, the Internet is moving away from a system primarily used for transactions, information, data, and person-to-person communication, and is becoming a global mass entertainment medium. This is in contrast to the perspective that has gained much currency, that of the 'Internet of Things', where machines exchange data with each other in a near autonomous fashion. Although such traffic is also growing rapidly, in terms of bits transmitted it pales in comparison to entertainment.

27.3   VIDEO ENTERTAINMENT AS THE DRIVER FOR NETWORK INFRASTRUCTURE

The upgrade of networks to faster Internet connectivity speeds has been expensive (Atkinson and Schultz, 2009). Much of it piggybacked on existing cable and telecom networks, adding some tweaks rather than massive investments. Fiber upgrades were driven by telecom companies' move into cable-like Internet Protocol TV (IPTV) service, not by their desire for higher speeds for the public Internet. For rural areas and poor countries, the prospects for fast (or any) connectivity were relegated to mobile wireless (FCC, 2010; Noam, 2011, 2013). On the telecom side this reluctance to upgrade ahead of demand ('supply push') was partly due to an expectation of low interest by users in high-speed connectivity beyond their basic needs for email, web browsing, and music. Governments were cheerleading Internet deployment with an emphasis on do-good goals such as fostering e-education, e-health, e-government, and other worthy causes (OECD, 2012; Broadband Commission, 2013; LaRose et al., 2013). Upgrading networks for online entertainment, in contrast, was seen as frivolous. Yet this view is short-sighted. Instead of wringing hands one should in fact embrace this evolution as a great opportunity for development (O'Neill et al., 2014). Entertainment use will become a driver for network upgrades in both rich and particularly in poor countries. People need a 'killer app' to justify paying for high speed Internet. And entertainment, is such a killer app. For access to entertainment, people will save and invest. They are willing to pay for it directly, through a user tax, or through advertising that ends up in their product prices. Such a demand will generate the business incentives to upgrade the telecom and mobile infrastructure and to reallocate cable bandwidth to Internet usage.

Thus, a demand for entertainment creates the economic foundation for network upgrades, and other applications can then piggyback on it. By unleashing the demand for Internet-based entertainment, media policy becomes economic development policy. Instead of supplying investment funds or seeking foreign assistance for upgrading the basic Internet infrastructure, governments can focus on residual problems of equality, gaps, and openness.

27.4   VIDEO ENTERTAINMENT AS THE AGENT OF CHANGE FOR THE ENTIRE INTERNET SYSTEM

The past Internet was a system of interconnection and interoperability arrangements created to a large extent by computer scientists, most of them in US universities and affiliated research labs. It enabled the linkage of individual networks and thereby the easy flow of information across such networks. It was based on a common set of values, a non-profit, sharing ideology, and a libertarian philosophy of minimal government. The decision process was one of rough consensus. This mechanism was so successful that it enabled the emergence of the key communications system around the world.

At some point, as is often the case when a revolution succeeds, it becomes orthodoxy and even theology. The Internet morphed from a technological system of data communications into a belief system.

It is true that many elements of this belief system were right at a certain point (Benkler, 2006). The Internet has been an awesome and splendid force for change. But just because it was so at its dawn does not mean that it is now or will be so in its maturity. There is always dynamism – much of it unleashed by the Internet. Why should it not affect the Internet itself? Internet advocates see clearly and correctly that the Internet is a force that disrupts everything. The same logic of disruption applies to the Internet itself.

Major drivers of centrifugalism for the Internet are the numerous approaches to video that were described above, and which are proceeding to take over the Internet in terms of traffic. Many of them are pushed by large, influential, innovative, and well-funded companies. Various governments support different companies and approaches. They also promote different, greatly varying regulatory approaches. National media policies are deeply intertwined with domestic politics.

Many network operators now use the Internet Protocol for their operations. One needs to differentiate networks running on IP from the public Internet. Companies run IP networks for their own internal uses and in order to supply services to customers. By using IP they can use widely available hardware and software. Similarly, telecom and cable TV companies create IP-based networks that are outside the public Internet. They have control over performance and quality. They can do things that they cannot do over the public Internet system. They can charge for usage, differentiate, discriminate, and block. In fact, the more the public Internet becomes regulated as 'neutral', the more likely it is that for their own use, network providers will migrate their core traffic to private arrangements.

The next stage then is that these private IP platforms interconnect with each other, through commercial peering arrangements. This is not the public Internet as the network of networks. It's the private Internet of private Internets (Noam, 2014). In a way, this is not new. The Internet was not born as a public and open system but as a private system of non-profit and research-oriented networks from which commercial networks and users – that is, almost everyone without a STEM PhD – was at first excluded.

The emergence of such a system of interconnected private Internet arrangements does not negate a public Internet. To the contrary, the two arrangements supplement each other. If private Internet arrangements are too restrictive, costly, or discriminatory, the public system provides a safety valve and vice versa (Yoo, 2012). This will prevent such a system from becoming a walled garden of walled gardens, which would be unacceptable.

It is therefore inevitable that there will be a divergence of technical specifications. Company A will do things differently than company B; industry coalition C will do it differently than industry coalition D. A technical centrifugalism is unavoidable. It is especially inevitable if it becomes readily possible to interoperate among the approaches. Such interoperability across non-uniform protocols can be provided by intermediaries that supply bridging as a service. These intermediaries are likely to be the 'cloud providers' that are emerging. We must therefore get used to the idea that the standardized Internet is the past but not the future. And that the future is a *federated* Internet, not a uniform one. Even though these dynamics are often denigrated as a 'splinternet', it is actually a good development. The single Internet was a good system in the past but not in the future.

One of the basic tenets of the belief system is that the Internet, the fundamental system that guides the interconnectivity and interoperability of individual data networks, needs to be uniform. Without such uniformity, it would break apart and become either useless or inefficient, and all users and uses would suffer. But this position is not tenable going forward.

First, it is *inevitable* for different variations of Internets to emerge. As the Internet became an essential part of business and society, the interests of the different governments became too big to stay out of it. And since governments around the world diverge widely, their Internet perspectives are very different.

There are earnest and well-meaning efforts to bridge these divergences (for a discussion, see Brown, 2013; Mueller, 2013; Van Eeten, 2013; DeNardis, 2014; Dutton, 2014). They may succeed for a while but the reality is that the world is a multi-faceted place, and the Internet is part of the world. The divergence will grow further as the Internet system of interconnected networks becomes the platform for mass video media, where the discrepancy of interests and values of different countries and societies is substantial.

So far, this discussion has been why it is inevitable that the Internet is fragmenting, and how to create bridging arrangements. But now we move on and argue that such a diversification is actually beneficial.

Of course, uniformity and standardization is helpful in some ways. There are operational reasons of technology, as well as scale and network effects of economics. But standardization also reduces competition among technologies. Such competition creates innovation, even if it might be messy. In a highly competitive world, where standards and protocols such as those of mobile or operating systems are upgraded in dizzying speed, the Internet system is slow-moving. No Moore's Law rate of change governs here. The technical specifications are set by the Steering Group of the Internet Engineering Task Force (IETF), a small group of 15 engineers, almost all employees of big companies around the world. It is not a system of openness and discovery through competition. It is a system of a group of essentially internally self-appointed wise men and women. A brilliant new idea must be approved in an administrative system that might have to balance the perspectives of the various major companies that sponsor their delegates.

We can see some of the positive dynamics of competitive innovation in the mobile industry. There are standards coalitions but no mandated uniformity. Without such divergence, the technically superior CDMA (code division multiple access, developed by Qualcomm) technology would not have emerged. When it comes to smartphones, corporate strategies go in different directions and come up with competing products with rival operating systems. Yet they inter-operate fairly readily through intermediate connection providers. Where problems exist, regulators are a safety net.

Here, we have different coalitions emerging centered around rival products, operating systems, and proprietary app stores. Mobile operators, device makers, and app stores operate with varying degrees of openness and interoperability. Voice can operate across platforms but apps often cannot. There is much more control, segmentation, and incompatibility than for the classic Internet. There is a loss of some openness, for sure, but also a gain of innovation and accelerated connectivity. Smartphones and tablets are in the process of adding billions of people to the Internet, broadly defined, and these people connect through proprietary apps and servers and less through the classic web.

As more online video activities take place on tablets and other mobile devices, why should it stop there? The same commercial logic of convenience, quality control, and end-to-end responsibility could apply also to proprietary 'Internets' that are not mobile but fixed.

And thus, what is now a uniform system would evolve into a more diverse system, a federation or confederation of interconnected systems that coexist: an Internet of Internets.

27.5   VIDEO ENTERTAINMENT AS THE AGENT OF CHANGE FOR TELEVISION

The third dimension of change is occurring within the TV system itself. Here, change will be rapid, with major consequences for culture and politics. The first generation of television was analog broadcast television, emerging just before and after World War II. It offered a limited number of channels and content options and was controlled by governments through ownership or tight regulation. Many millions of people watched the same few programs at the same time. This limited system was overcome in many countries as TV moved to the second generation – multi-channel TV distributed over cable, satellite, and now telephone, making available a much greater diversity of channels and programs. Now, as TV is migrating to online distribution over the Internet the question arises: what is next? One should not think merely in terms of yet another distribution mechanism for the same types of content. The change will be more profound.

Television has been around since the late 1930s as a consumer medium. In those 75 years, it moved from an analog black and white technology to color digital multicasting at a sharper resolution. Its bit rate per distribution channel has increased, if one is generous, by a technological compound annual growth rate (CAGR) of about 4 percent per year. In honor of the guiding spirit of the first decades of mass market TV, the leader of the US company RCA, which dominated TV technology for its first generation, this rate should be described as 'Sarnoff's Rate'. In contrast, 'Moore's Law' – referring to the doubling of performance every two years – describes technological change in the IT sector based on advances in the underlying semiconductors. This translates to about 40 percent a year, ten times as fast as TV technology.

But now TV is migrating to distribution over the Internet (Arendse et al., 2014; Cisco, 2014; Sherman et al., 2014). In the process it is moving away from the control of traditional TV organizations. This has been widely noted but the attention has been mostly on the widening of content options and providers. This is important, of course, but arguably even more fundamental in the long run is the breakdown of the system of (almost) uniform TV technology in favor of a system of multiple parallel types of TV. As the video system migrates onto the Internet and as TV sets become computer-like devices, different technologies can be offered. Competing providers of various technology modules, distribution systems, and content technology will emerge, and their rivalries will move TV from a system of technical uniformity to one much more resembling that of mobile devices, games, and apps.

This type of TV will include some of the following elements, in various combinations:

- 4K and 8K resolution, which sharpens the picture for large screens;
- 3-D quality;
- peer interactivity;
- person-to-computer interactivity (artificial intelligence);
- computer-enhanced reality;
- user-generated content;
- asynchronous viewing and individualization of content;
- branching plot lines and user participation;
- multi-platform distribution;
- distance-insensitive distribution.

Putting together these and other elements enables TV as a high-resolution, immersive, participatory, personalized, social, world-wide experience (see Carey, 2003; Mayer-Schönberger 2003; Werbach, 2003; Madden, 2009; Cesar and Geerts, 2011).

Some of the emerging television will continue to be linear, traditional, classic television of a 22-minute format – a half-hour show minus advertising and promos – surviving in the same way as newspapers, books, and magazines have remained alive. But they will decline in their economic and cultural role. The leading edge of creativity, both technologically and culturally, will be in those new media. The kind of television emerging will be partly a widening – more of everything. But more interesting is the deepening: more impulses, more information, more sensory impressions, and more richness. This continues a historic process of greater information intensity going back 450 years to Gutenberg.

27.6   THE CENTRAL PLAYERS IN THE INTERNET OF ENTERTAINMENT

We have now discussed the implications of the Internet of Entertainment on infrastructure, the Internet system, and TV. What will such a system look like? Who will be the main players in it? The emergence of centrifugalism in hardware, software, content, and interactivity leads to the emergence of new types of integrators. These integrators will be some form of what is today called 'clouds'. It is a continuation of concept that earlier was called 'time sharing', 'grid computing', 'utility computing', 'thin clients', 'terminal computing', and 'network computing'. The words change, the players rotate, but the basic idea is constant, that a user obtains computing resources such as storage, processing, databases, software, networks, and platforms from somewhere else.

On the consumer side, a cloud might start out as a content provider, such as Pandora or Spotify for music. It might then expand to provide storage services such as music 'lockers' of users' content, such as Apple iCloud, Google Music, or Amazon Cloud Player. Server farms are at the heart of clouds. In most cases, such server farms are offered by third parties to users, whether small or quite large, and to smaller clouds. Apple's 500 000 ft^2 iCloud and iTunes facility in North Carolina was constructed at a cost of $1 billion. Other cloud providers include the following (Statista, 2015):

- Amazon Web Services (AWS) is the largest cloud service provider by far and consequently owns the biggest server infrastructure. Launched in 2002, AWS provides online services for other websites or client-side applications. AWS powers thousands of companies, including Netflix, Instagram, Pinterest and NASA. Its estimated share of the 'infrastructure as a service' (IaaS) market is about 28 percent.
- Microsoft offers Windows Azure to enterprise customers and Skydrive to consumers (16%).
- IBM SmartCloud has a big capacity and growth rate (12%).
- Google owns the largest number of physical servers in its 40+ data centers. However, only a small fraction is offered to outside customers (4%).
- Oracle (Private Cloud) has about 3%.
- Rackspace (2.5%).
- Facebook has a growing capacity.
- Big telecommunications operators have acquired cloud providers, for example, Verizon with Terremark, Telefonica with Acens Technologies, and CenturyLink with Savvis.

These are clouds as infrastructure providers. Several of them also host second-tier media clouds that might be active in the media sphere, such as those of content-oriented companies without the technical orientation like Netflix or Hulu.

There are several reasons why an entertainment-based Internet system will lead to cloud-based video media (Noam, 2014):

1. *Technical standards:* For next-generation TV, interoperability is required of content types, users, devices, networks, of software operating systems, payment systems, and intellectual property rights (IPRs).

   For the different pieces in an advanced video service to interoperate there are several options. The first is a comprehensive standard. Realistically, however, full end-to-end, cross-device, cross-platform, cross-national standards are unlikely to emerge. There are too many companies, countries, stakeholders, technologies, and rivalries. Any such standard that might arise is likely to be out-of-date and inefficient, yet hard to change. A second approach is a vertical silo, in which a single firm provides all elements and controls the technology, and dictates them to others as end-to-end integrator firms like Apple do (Hazlett et al., 2011). This approach creates certainty and confidence, but it also easily leads to end-to-end control, even into the production side. The third approach is that of intermediary organizations that create interoperability. Clouds can do that. They bridge standards among different elements, and users only need to connect to a cloud provider.

2. *Convenience:* As everything electronic – even kitchen appliances – gets connected with everything else, things get complicated, and it is more effective to let the IT professionals do it from a distance. In such a scenario, consumer electronics move from consumer electronic hardware to consumer electronics as a cloud service.

3. *Legal and regulatory coordination:* As mentioned, each country has its own rules, and it is unrealistic to expect these rules to be the same worldwide. Attempts to 'harmonize' will only result in acrimony, delay, disappointment, and unstable compromises. More realistic is to expect that different countries will have diverse arrangements. But there is another possibility, the possibility of going through intermediaries who would tailor the material to comply with the various national laws before it goes to that country. This could be a cloud's function. These intermediaries could be large and sophisticated enough to be able to deal with the multiplicity of national rules. There are economies of scale and scope in compliance, for example because of the indivisibility of legal advice.

4. *Financial flows:* The various suppliers of special modules, whether they provide services, copyright licenses, apps, transmission, or storage require compensation from users or each other. Once the linear relation of a specific user consuming the product of a specific provider is replaced by a multiplicity of interacting users consuming and engaging with a diverse and changing menu of elements, financial flows need to be channeled through intermediaries. In other cases, some financing support will be extended by cloud providers to the producers of content, software, and applications, in the same way that Hollywood distributors pre-finance independent film production.

5. *Privacy and security:* From the perspective of content providers, a cloud arrangement helps protect copyrighted materials from piracy in comparison to physical media such as DVDs. A cloud provider can offer sophisticated security handled by expert security staff. It can monitor user behavior and based on such awareness provide security alerts.

6. *Marketing, branding, and quality control:* In a world of online abundance, the screening function of an intermediary is valuable.

To conclude, people have argued for a long time that the future of media will be one of domination by the traditional large, vertically integrated media conglomerates. But it may be more likely that the key media institutions of the future will be the cloud companies as the central integrators of the system. Some of them might be traditional media companies that have moved into technology. Others will be tech companies that have morphed into media. Google and Apple are the most obvious examples. A third category is hybrid 'tech-media' firms such as Netflix. And the fourth are the network platform providers as they move beyond pipes to apps and cloud services.

27.7 POLICY ISSUES FOR THE INTERNET OF ENTERTAINMENT

It is natural for each generation to believe that its issues and problems are brand new and thrust upon it. In reality, many of them are part of long-standing fundamental conflicts (for some of the literature, see Galperin and Bar, 2002; Wu, 2004; Liebowitz, 2006; Meisel, 2007; Noam, 2008; ACMA, 2011; Nuechterlein and Weiser, 2013; Whitt, 2013). It has been said that in literature there are only 20 plots. In ICT and media there are even fewer basic plot lines – about four:

- power (monopoly, competition, vertical integration, ownership);
- access (interconnection, compatibility, standardization, non-discrimination, affordability, universality, diversity);
- growth (innovation, infrastructure, development, industrial policy, trade); and
- protection (children, privacy, security, copyrights, reputation, national culture).

Applied to the Internet of Entertainment, this includes some of the following questions:

- How to assure the financial viability of infrastructure?
- Market power in the entertainment Internet?
- Does vertical integration impede competition?
- How to protect children, old people, and traditional morality?
- How to protect privacy and security?
- What is the impact on trade? What is the impact of globalization?
- How to assure the interoperability of clouds?

One should not expect many firms to be general cloud providers. The basic economics of this system exhibits strong economies of scale and scope. Fixed costs are high while marginal costs are low, and distribution costs are distance-insensitive. It also requires rapid technological innovation, and high investments and risks associated with it. And there are major network effects on the demand side. All this favors the emergence of a global oligopoly market structure. The important question then is how to keep such a cloud-based system competitive? The history of networks suggests that the strongest remedy to deal with market power by dominant players is through interoperability and interconnection. This would create a system not of parallel and separate clouds but of a 'cloud of clouds'.

The major question of a cloud-based media system is therefore the extent of interoperability among the various clouds. A mandated harmonization can easily stifle innovation, but if clouds are not interoperable, several things are likely to happen: market power over users who could not easily switch ('lock-in'); difficulty of the users of one cloud to freely interact with the users of other clouds; and market power by cloud operators over the providers of hardware, software, and content.

27.8   THE INTERNET OF ENTERTAINMENT AS A DRIVER FOR ACADEMIC RESEARCH

It was the philosopher of communication theory, Marshall McLuhan, who famously said that the medium is the message, meaning that the underlying media technology shapes the content. This also implies that the medium defines the research of the message. Change the media technology, and a new media system emerges for us to analyze and study.

As the underlying field of study has been changing at an accelerating rate, the research community has been falling behind. In factual knowledge, young students are often ahead of their professors. In teaching, universities are being challenged by new types of disintermediation, that of 'MOOC' (massive open online courses), which establish different models of instruction and different academic economics. In methodology, data used to be the scarce and slow resource. But now we are being overwhelmed by it. Accordingly, our research and data analysis needs to accelerate, too.

Here are some important questions for research on Internet-based TV, for various academic disciplines:

Industrial economics What is the market structure of online television? Will it be open and competitive, with everyone entering and providing content? Clouds will be central organizations, and there might therefore not be many of them, for reasons of scale and scope. If so, the media of the future will be more concentrated than those of the past. The conventional wisdom is that the new online media system is less concentrated than the old. But this is probably incorrect. The Internet industries were believed to be wide open and competitive and would open things up for the rest. But they exhibit strong concentration trends.

Another economic research question is how to assure the financial viability of the infrastructure. The financial balance between infrastructure, services, and users is a critical issue. The infrastructure is expensive and wants to be paid. Some of the media services are young and want to be left to grow. Users want to be served generously with free content and low-priced, flat-rate data service. Fundamental economics of competition push towards price deflation, but market power, and maybe regulation, pull in another direction. Developing countries want to see money from communications as they did in the days of traditional telecom.

These trends and the resulting market equilibria and media structure will therefore favor higher concentration. Current or foreseeable technology and entrepreneurship will not easily overcome that structure in a long-term sustained way.

Competition may also be affected by vertical integration. For example, if an ISP also owns a cloud service provider, that cloud might realistically have advantaged access to and by the ISPs' customers, whether 'net neutrality' rules exist or not. And with a strong customer base from a large ISP, it gains economies of scale and network effects. This also makes it attractive to the suppliers of content and of advertising. Conversely, the ownership of a successful cloud with access to content makes an ISP more valuable to end users, in comparison to an ISP without such vertical integration.

Already we are seeing some of these developments such as the creation and distribution of original content by the companies who will play a large part in the next generation of video, such as Amazon, Netflix, and Hulu.

Policy studies What are some of the implications for policy of such an Internet system? How does one keep that system open, competitive, and pluralistic? How does one ensure the interoperability of clouds, so a user or content provider is not locked into one cloud, but can operate across multiple clouds? These are questions of next-generation policy analysis that researchers have to tackle. Additional pertinent policy questions were presented in section 27.7 above.

Political sciences   For political science, what are research questions? How does the emerging system of online, cloud-based TV and the federated Internet affect democracy and political participation? Does it strengthen or weaken central authority, or localism? Does it strengthen political parties? Does it enable change?

Where will this take us? The optimistic idea is that people will not be passive recipients of news and analysis anymore but will engage in an interactive, collaborative community, a smart political crowd on a smart media cloud with citizen journalists making news into a conversation.

But the reality will likely disappoint. There will be some horizontal news collaboration by citizens. But the complexity of informational interaction, of visual images, of technology, all of them in the face of rising user expectations, is expensive and requires a combination of skills, organization, and capital. This actually raises the scale of news operations.

What about political participation? Of course, the Internet makes some political activity easier and cheaper. But it does so for everyone. Any effectiveness of early users will soon be matched by their rivals and simply lead to an expensive and mutually stalemating political arms race of investment in customization techniques and new-media marketing technologies.

On top of that, the low cost of online political participation exists primarily for the traditional narrowband Internet, which is largely text based. But the broadband Internet will first permit and soon require fancy video and multimedia messages. Politics will be customized to be most effective. Extensive databases and data mining techniques will be needed. None of this will be cheap. All of it is likely to favor private expert consultancies at the expense of political parties.

Will this cloud media system result in better policies? The idea that 'smart crowds' overcome the inefficiencies of governmental processes is unrealistic. Such hopes have accompanied almost every new generation of technology. This is a question truly waiting for detached research.

Similarly, there is a need to study the accelerating globalization of culture and the future of localism. For legal scholars, there are new questions on the nature of property in information, especially when it is interactive and created jointly.

For scholars of culture, there are hugely interesting questions to explore. What are the effects of 'enhanced reality', integrating virtual information into the real as we walk and drive, merging reality with heads-up unreality/virtuality?

One of the really interesting questions is what happens when the virtual media experience becomes stronger than real life. This is already happening with video games. It leads to disconnectedness from physical community, and it will accelerate.

Educational studies   The new online video environment will also be a major online platform for education. This is likely to be one of its most bit-intensive non-entertainment uses. It therefore also raises questions for researchers of education on the nature of the emerging educational system. How can research be supported when students out-migrate to online courses and credentialing that are priced at marginal cost of provision or less? How would quality controls function? What is the effectiveness of education provided to multi-tasking students on the go?

27.9   CONCLUSION

We now briefly summarize the analysis. The technological trends have enabled affordable online video content, and this is transforming the medium into an Internet of Entertainment. This change, in turn, creates major user demand that is a driver for telecom network infrastructure upgrade investments.

Taken together, these developments will lead to a rapid acceleration of innovation in video genres and technologies, and to content styles that will be a major impetus to cultural expression. The migration of TV to a distribution over the Internet has been widely noted. But the widening of content options and providers, as important as it is, is less fundamental in the long run than the breakdown of the system of fairly uniform TV technology in favor of a system of multiple parallel TVs. As the video system migrates onto the Internet and as TV sets become computer-like devices, different technologies can be offered to do what we used to call television. Competing providers of various technology modules, distribution systems, and content technology will emerge, and their rivalries will move TV from a system of technical uniformity to one of great diversity. Inevitably, this will have implications for new and different content types, styles, and genres.

Putting together the technical elements enables TV to become a high-resolution, immersive, participatory, personalized, social, and world-wide experience. Linear video will most likely continue to be around, in better quality. Even so, the new style of immersive content will be the frontier of technical and cultural creativity and will challenge established styles and industries. The emerging diversity of approaches, industries, companies, nations, and regulatory approaches will lead to a fragmentation of the Internet into a federated system. Similarly, the TV system will be fragmented. In this technological and organizational centrifugalism, bridging intermediaries will emerge, which we call 'media clouds'. These media clouds have major advantages that will make them the central institutions of the media system. There are also major economies of scale and scope leading to a concentrated market structure. Some of these trends, players, and issues will emerge first in highly developed online countries but the same dynamics will spread to most of the rest of the world.

This will lead to policy issues of how to maintain a media and Internet system that is competitive, diverse and open. The new environment creates a set of fairly predictable problems and conflicts. They are the fundamental trade-offs that each generation must renegotiate. We should do so in the present, even as we gaze forward to the new horizons.

REFERENCES

Arendse, B., A. Adeldeji and M. Mhlungu et al. (2014), 'Broadband as a platform for video delivery: What to expect from platforms and applications', in J. O'Neill, E. Noam and D. Gerbarg (eds), *Broadband as a Video Platform: Strategies for Africa*, New York: Springer International Publishing, pp. 81–93.

Atkinson, R.C. and I.E. Schultz (2009), *Broadband in America: Where it is and Where it is Going*, accessed 17 January 2016 at http://www.broadband.gov/docs/Broadband_in_America.pdf.

Australian Communications and Media Authority (ACMA) (2011), 'International approaches to audiovisual content regulation – A comparative analysis of the regulatory frameworks', Occasional Paper, accessed 1 January 2015 at http://www.acma.gov.au/webwr/_assets/main/lib310665/international_approaches_to_av_content_reg.pdf.

Benkler, Y. (2006), *The Wealth of Networks: How Social Production Transforms Markets and Freedom*, New Haven, CT: Yale University Press.

Broadband Commission (2013), *The State of Broadband 2013: Universalizing Broadband*, Geneva: International Telecommunication Union and United Nations Educational, Scientific and Cultural Organization, accessed 1 January 2015 at www.broadbandcommission.org/Documents/bb-annualreport2013.pdf.

Brown, I. (ed.) (2013), *Research Handbook on Governance of the Internet*, Cheltenham, UK and Northampton, MA, USA: Edward Elgar Publishing.

Carey, J. (2013), 'Peer-to-peer video file sharing: What can we learn from consumer behavior?', in E. Noam and L. Pupillo (eds), *Peer-to-Peer Video: The Economics, Policy, and Culture of Today's New Mass Media*, Berlin: Springer, pp. 129–48.

Cesar, P. and D. Geerts (2011), 'Past, present, and future of social TV: A categorization', paper at the IEEE Consumer Communications and Networking Conference (CCNC), Las Vegas, NV, 9–12 January 2011, accessed 1 January 2015 at http://ieeexplore.ieee.org/xpls/abs_all.jsp?arnumber=5766487&tag=1.

Cisco (2014), 'Cisco visual networking index: Forecast and methodology, 2013–2018', White Paper, accessed 1 January 2015 at http://www.cisco.com/c/en/us/solutions/collateral/service-provider/ip-ngn-ip-next-generation-network/white_paper_c11-481360.pdf.

claffy, kc and D.D. Clark (2013), 'Platform models for sustainable Internet regulation', paper at the 41st Research Conference on Communication, Information and Internet Policy, Arlington, VA, accessed 1 January 2015 at http://papers.ssrn.com/sol3/papers.cfm?abstract_id=2242600.

DeNardis, L. (2014), *The Global War for Internet Governance*, New Haven, CT: Yale University Press.

Dutton, W.H. (2014), *Politics and the Internet: Networked Institutions and Governance*, London: Routledge.

FCC (2010), *Connecting America: The National Broadband Plan*, Washington, DC: Federal Communications Commission, accessed 1 January 2015 at http://transition.fcc.gov/national-broadband-plan/national-broadband-plan.pdf.

Galperin, H. and F. Bar (2002), 'Regulation of interactive television in the United States and the European Union', *Federal Communications Law Journal*, **55** (1), Article 3, accessed 1 January 2015 at http://www.repository.law.indiana.edu/fclj/vol55/iss1/3.

Hazlett, T.W., D.J. Teece and L. Waverman (2011), 'Walled garden rivalry: The creation of mobile network ecosystems', *George Mason Law & Economics Research Paper No. 11–50*, accessed 1 January 2015 at http://ssrn.com/abstract=1963427.

LaRose, R., J.M. Bauer, K. DeMaagd, H.E. Chew, W. Ma and Y. Jung (2013), 'Public broadband investment priorities in the United States: An analysis of the Broadband Technology Opportunities Program', *Government Information Quarterly*, **31** (1), 53–64.

Liebowitz, S.J. (2006), 'File sharing: Creative destruction or just plain destruction?', *Journal of Law and Economics*, **49** (1), 1–28.

Madden, M. (2009), *The Audience for Online Video-sharing Sites Shoots Up*, Washington, DC: Pew Internet & American Life Project, accessed 1 January 2015 at http://www.pewinternet.org/files/old-media/Files/Reports/2009/The-Audience-for-Online-Video-Sharing-Sites-Shoots-Up.pdf.

Mayer-Schönberger, V. (2003), 'Crouching tiger, hidden dragon: Proxy battles over peer-to-peer movie sharing', in E. Noam and L. Pupillo (eds), *Peer-to-Peer Video: The Economics, Policy, and Culture of Today's New Mass Media*, Berlin: Springer, pp. 251–64.

Meisel, J. (2007), 'The emergence of the Internet to deliver video programming: Economic and regulatory issues', *Info*, **9** (1), 52–64.

Mueller, M. (2013), 'Internet addressing: Global governance of shared resource spaces', in I. Brown (ed.), *Research Handbook on Governance of the Internet*, Cheltenham, UK and Northampton, MA, USA: Edward Elgar Publishing, pp. 52–70.

Nielsen (2013), *A Look Across Media: The Cross-platform Report Q3 2013*, accessed 1 January 2015 at http://www.nielsen.com/us/en/reports/2013/a-look-across-media-the-cross-platform-report-q3-2013.html.

Noam, E. (2008), *TV or not TV: Three Screens, One Regulation?*, Report to the Canadian Radio-television and Telecommunications Commission (CRTC), 11 September 2008, accessed 1 January 2015 at http://www.crtc.gc.ca/eng/media/noam2008.htm#toc22.

Noam, E. (2011), 'Let them eat cellphones: Why mobile wireless is no solution for broadband', *Journal of Information Policy*, **1**, 470–85, accessed 1 January 2015 at http://jip.vmhost.psu.edu/ojs/index.php/jip/article/viewFile/64/43.

Noam, E. (2013), 'Towards the federated Internet', *Intermedia*, **41** (4), 10–13.

Noam, E. (2014), 'Cloud TV: Toward the next generation of network policy debates', *Telecommunications Policy*, **38** (8–9), 684–92.

Nuechterlein, J.E. and P.J. Weiser (2013), *Digital Crossroads: Telecommunications Law and Policy in the Internet Age*, Cambridge, MA: MIT Press.

OECD (2012), *The Internet Economy Outlook 2012*, Paris: Organisation for Economic Co-operation and Development.

O'Neill, J., E. Noam and D. Gerbarg (2014), *Strategies for Africa*, New York: Springer International Publishing. Sandvine (2013), *Global Internet Phenomena Report 2H 2013*, accessed 1 January 2015 at https://www.sandvine.com/downloads/general/global-internet-phenomena/2013/2h-2013-global-internet-phenomena-report.pdf.

Sherman, R., D. Waterman and Y. Jeon (2014), 'The future of online video: An economic perspective', Working Paper, accessed 1 January 2015 at http://www.indiana.edu/~telecom/people/faculty/waterman/Thefutureofonlinevidefinal6-11-14.pdf.

Statista, *Infrastructure-as-a-Service market share in first half of 2015*, by vendor, 2015 http://www.statista.com/statistics/478143/iaas-vendor-market-share-ranking-worldwide/

Van Eeten, M.J.G. and M. Mueller (2013), 'Where is the governance in Internet governance?', *New Media & Society*, **15** (5), 720–36.

Werbach, K. (2003), 'The implications of video peer-to-peer on network usage', in E. Noam and L. Pupillo, *Peer-to-Peer Video: The Economics, Policy, and Culture of Today's New Mass Media*, New York: Springer, pp. 95–128.

Whitt, R. (2013), 'A deference to protocol: Fashioning a three-dimensional public policy framework for the Internet age', *Cardozo Arts & Entertainment Law Journal*, **31**, 698–768, accessed 1 January 2015 at http://ssrn.com/abstract=2031186.

Wu, I. (2004), 'Canada, South Korea, Netherlands and Sweden: Regulatory implications of the convergence of telecommunications, broadcasting and Internet services', *Telecommunications Policy*, **28** (1), 79–96.

Wu, T. (2003), 'Network neutrality, broadband discrimination', *Journal on Telecommunications & High Technology Law*, **2** (1), 141–75.

Yoo, C. (2012), *The Dynamic Internet: How Technology, Users, and Business are Transforming the Network*, Washington, DC: AEI Press.

Index

Printed and bound by CPI Group (UK) Ltd, Croydon, CR0 4YY

27/10/2024

14580413-0003